WRECKED

Daily Devotions Penned by a Sinner

Tana Miller

Edited by Jackie Zagami

Publication Assistant: Gabriel Smith

Cover Design: Matt Lussier

Original Cover Art by

Nick Slye

DEDICATION

This book is dedicated to my husband Guy who loved me through my dysfunction and helped me to function, always believing God had a greater destiny for me than I could see. I will love you till my last breath.

I also dedicate this book to my two amazing children Angela Kristine and Jonathan Patrick. I am so thankful you have your own relationship with God, and you bring great joy to this mama's heart. My hope and prayer is that someday your children and your children's children can read the words of their grandma/great-grandma's book and know that there is a God in heaven.

Last but not least, much love to both sets of our parents. We love you more than words can say.

*"There is a God in heaven
who reveals mysteries."*
Daniel 2:28

*"So shall My word be that goes
forth from My mouth;
it shall not return void,
but it shall accomplish what I please,
and it shall prosper in the thing
for which I sent it."*
Isaiah 55:11

Thank You God for the journey of Your Word.
Like my girlfriend/mentor Beth Decker always says,
"Let's take an adventure!"
My year writing this book was just that,
An adventure!
I honor You today.

INTRODUCTION

Night after night young people would come into my home and say, "God Wrecked me tonight," meaning God had changed them from the inside out. Thus my title WRECKED. My prayer is, just as I saw these young lives changed, and as you read, you will be Wrecked by the grace, and power of a Mighty God.

I started writing this book in February of 2010, and when I put my pen down in January of 2011, I had taken a journey that would change my life forever. Truth be told, God's Word coupled with discipline, will change us from the inside out.

I would never be the same again after that adventure.

Due to a major health scare that changed the way I had to live or be put on daily insulin, WRECKED was put on the shelf. It was just four short months after I finished the book. This was physically life changing for me, and took the rest of my year to feel normal again.

Shortly after that, our family was launched into an unexpected place, as national television took over our normalcy with our daughter landing on American Idol. That journey from start to finish lasted over three years.

It would have been easy to give up on Wrecked through those years, but I believe in completing what we start. I have worked too hard, and God has done too much in me to lay it down.

I believe this is God's timing for you to read the words on these pages. Daily devotions will deposit His Word into your heart. Studying His Word and writing every day for 365 days was a joy. God spoke something new into my life on a daily basis, and I have to believe He will do the same for you. May God Wreck you in these pages.

Words from Tana's Family

Message from Jonathan

When I think of my mom, I think of three words: crazy, passionate and welcoming. She's crazy in a good way of course. She doesn't care what other people think of her. I have watched her in ministry my whole life, and she couldn't have done that without the passion God has given Her. She is one of the most passionate people I know. Her passion for people also helps her to be one of the most welcoming mothers I have ever seen. I remember growing up and living in the same house with some of my best friends. She took them in because of their family lives or because they had nowhere to go. To this day, we still have band practice, parties, free food, and showers at the house. The coolest thing about my Mom is that she has passed these three traits right down to me.

Love you mom, thanks for raising me in such an amazing way. Thanks for supporting my dreams and thanks for always being there through all my hard times. I'm glad your dream is now coming true through this book.

Message from Angela

When my mom was writing this book, I remember so vividly a late night when one of our favorite shows was on television. I called out to her and told her it was on, and asked if she could come watch it with me. She replied saying that she hadn't written her devotional for that day yet, and had no idea what she was going to write about. She then said that she had to spend the rest of the night working on it even though she was exhausted. It was that night that I learned what real discipline was. There is so much that I have learned from my mom just through her faith, character, and integrity. She's continuously a great example to me, and I can't wait to learn even more from her when I read this book.

I love you mom, and I am so excited to see what God will do through this book! As always, I'm proud of you!

Message from Guy

For 26 years I've been describing my wife as "godly, gifted and gorgeous." It's just as true today as when we got married in June 1989. Tana is a most amazing woman. Not only has she accomplished significant goals in her career, she also and more importantly, is an awesome wife and mother. Tana and I would both say that our best accomplishment is our two kids – Jonathan and Angela.

What's more impressive, is that Tana has succeeded in family and career despite a backdrop of pain, which the reader will begin to comprehend when they read this devotional. I have always admired that my wife never used her pain as an excuse to quit, but turned it into an opportunity to excel in life.

Obviously, Tana would rather that none of her pain would have ever happened. It has left a scar on her to this day. But in spite of it, she is a powerful woman of faith and a testimony to the life changing power of the grace of Jesus Christ. I hope the reader will also be inspired to overcome obstacles, no matter how severe they might be.

I love you baby, and I'm proud of you!

FOREWORD

Message from Ali Adamson

We were created for connection. Connection with one another and with God. It's these two passions that pour out onto the pages of WRECKED.

Tana has a passion for people and desires each one of us to live fully the lives we were created to live; that will only be discovered in a daily relationship with God. In WRECKED, Tana is powerfully vulnerable, sharing intimate stories from her past and her journey towards a full life.

WRECKED is Tana's heart on paper, which is why a daily devotional is so perfect. Tana is, at her core, a friend. She sees the potential in everyone she meets and desires to come along side and encourage them on towards their full potential. WRECKED is an invitation into this friendship. This poem reminds me of Tana and her heart for all the readers of WRECKED....

"Don't walk behind me; I may not lead. Don't walk in front of me; I may not follow. Just walk beside me and be my friend."

~Albert Camus

Message from Heath Adamson

I'm sitting on an airplane as I write this foreward.

Looking to my right, the storm clouds await their moment. To my left, a gentleman reads a newspaper. In front of me, an elderly couple each digest content in their own right. She is reading a magazine. He carries a Nook and an iPad. Across the aisle, the businessman surfs the Internet on his laptop. And I, well, I'm typing this on my phone. There is so much information at our disposal.

We are swimming in a sea of information. That same sea provides tributaries of which each person chooses to splash in. An iPad. A Nook. A Laptop. An immense amount of information carried to each one of us. And yet, our land is still parched, and our souls are still thirsty. A sea of information is apparent; we need an ocean of authenticity. Tana lifts her sail and beckons each one of us to climb aboard.

For the experienced traveler, the content Tana provides, serves as a reminder of what we easily forget, as well as a compass to where we should go. To the one who finds himself or herself in unchartered waters, and you wonder where in the world you are and equally where in the world you're going, take ease. Tana opens up her life in a way we can relate and understand. Open and honest tension within the human soul is difficult to find in a candy-coated world. Tana bears her soul, invites us in and reveals the mystery and beauty found in being one's self. Amidst all of life's distractions, and in that tension, we can then see Christ for who He says He is.

Insights from Scripture greet the reader each and everyday. Stories both humorous and heart breaking, remind us all that within the clutter of information this world has to offer, there is a divine Hand writing the next chapter.

As you read, it is my prayer that our friend can speak to your heart the way she has spoken to my wife and myself through this book. Amidst all of the wreckage, I hope that you also, will see how intricately God pulls the pieces together, even when some of them don't seem to fit quite the way they are supposed to.

Heath his wife, Ali, and two daughters, currently reside in Springfield, MO. Together they endeavor to leave a legacy for generations to come.

At the age of 17, Heath's life was dramatically transformed by an encounter with Jesus. Steeped in drug abuse and the occult, he came to believe in Christ for salvation.

Heath is serving as the national Assemblies of God youth leader, a ministry serving more than half a million students.

"Life is not wreckage

To be saved out of the world

But an Investment

To be used in the world."

L.B. Cowman

January

January 1st

A Simple, Sinful Soul

I am just like you. A person saved by grace. Maybe you don't know God, and someone just handed you this book. I dare you to read for the next 365 days. I promise if you do, you will be changed by the words of truth in it. I am a raw soul, a transparent soul. I hold position and leadership over hundreds of people at this moment in my life, but the truth is I live by grace every day of my life. I'm not afraid to tell you that I fail, we all fail. Walk with me this year as we read His word.

In 2010 I had someone come up to me and tell me that they had a vision of me. I always get a little weary when someone says that. I have been handed a lot of loony visions in my time. But I took a listen to what she had to say. Before I tell you what she said, I will say that this young lady had never heard my testimony, she did not know anything I had been through in my life. Physical, verbal, sexual and emotional abuse, hate, bitterness, greed and the list goes on. She did not know anything about me, and here she comes telling me she had a vision of me. My most shameful memory, which I'm sure I will share again later in the year, was one night at a party when I decided to drink and do drugs at the same time. Fully clothed, I decided to take a shower. You do very stupid things when you are high. I passed out in the shower, and the truth is I have no idea how long I was there. I woke to men and women coming in and out of the bathroom urinating. One after another, as I lay there in the shower, trying to come to. All these years the devil has used that memory to torment me. It's almost as if he says, "I urinate on you! You are nothing." I have proved him wrong, I want you all to know that in Christ you are everything! He died for you!

> "You are the light of the world."
> Matthew 5:14

The girl who had the vision of me told me I was laying on a shower floor with the water beating on me, but the water that was coming down on me was not real water, it was evil beasts. She said they were devilish with claws and fangs. They were beating on me like water. She then said that I stood up and began to sing songs to God. As I stood and sang, she said circling around my head was written music, like the notes and staff. As I kept pressing through in worship the evil beasts left. By the time she was done telling me the vision, I knew she had heard from God and I knew there was no way she could have known that was my most shameful memory of all time. God was speaking to her.
The truth is, if we press through our pain, trials, and storms with God's powerful word, we will stand! Even though the devil tries to tell you that you will do nothing in this life, God's word speaks the total opposite!

You are destined for greatness!

There is a purpose and plan for you just like there was a plan for me. He took me from the bottom of a dirty shower, with people coming in and out of the bathroom relieving themselves, to where I am today in total peace with purpose.

Where are you today? Are you feeling like there is no hope for you? Feeling like after the divorce, God has given up on you? Feeling like dirt after messing up again? Feeling a little hopeless?

If there is one thing I have learned about my Lord, it's that He reaches out to the wicked and sinful. The first time He proclaimed that Immanuel, God with us, was coming, was on a filthy dirty road to the public laundry and to a wicked man (Isaiah 7:14). Why didn't He choose a godly man? Why not a beautiful place to tell of the coming Savior of the world? Because, He came for the lost. He came for you and me.

> "For the Son of Man came to seek and to save what was lost."
> Luke 19:10

We were His purpose for coming.

I am a simple, sinful soul who longs to tell my stories of what God has done in my life. I will be transparent, real, and I will tell all in time.

You need to know that there is a reason you are holding this book in your hand today. This is a divine appointment at this time in your life.

The God who created the universe loves you with a personal love. I challenge you to call on Him and to seek Him. If you do this with a true heart and a faithful heart, you WILL find Him.

> "You will seek me and find me
> when you seek me with all your heart."
> Jeremiah 29:13

This was a promise given not only to the godly but to the ungodly. For those of you who already walk with God, you will be blessed as you walk with me this year and read God's word.

Dear God,
I pray for this reader. Change their lives this year. May they seek you with all their heart and find you. May we ever be changed by your word. I honor you today.

January 2nd

Breaking Faith

In Numbers chapter 20 a miracle happened, but God wanted to use a man to see it through. Some miracles come when we walk where God wants us to walk and do what He wants us to do. When we obey, and walk the path He wants us to walk, amazing things can happen. There is nothing like walking in the perfect will of God for your life.

At first we see a sad, depressing picture laid out in the beginning of the chapter. First of all, Miriam, the sister of Moses, whose legacy is spelled out through the beginning of the Bible, dies. She dies in a parched desert where there is no water.

"There Miriam died and was buried."
Numbers 20:1

This was an amazing lady who even as a child got Pharaoh's daughter to believe she needed a Hebrew woman to nurse baby Moses, her brother. So Miriam tells Pharaoh's daughter, she knows of one. Miriam goes and gets her mother to nurse Baby Moses in Pharaoh's palace. This was a brave amazing young lady who would turn into a mighty leader. A worshipper who played her tambourine as she crossed the red sea on dry land. A lady Moses loved, a sister to be remembered. In the beginning of Chapter 20 she is buried.

Just like you and I would lose a loved one, Moses lost someone dear to him, and I'm sure he was filled with grief. In the very next verse after his sister is buried, the community who is with him rises in opposition against him and his brother Aaron.

"Now there was no water for the community,
and the people gathered in opposition to Moses and Aaron.
They quarreled with Moses and said,
"If only we had died when our brothers fell dead
before the Lord! Why did you bring the
Lord's community into this desert,
that we and our livestock should die here?
Why did you bring us up out of Egypt to this terrible place?
It has no grain or figs, grapevines or pomegranates.
And there is no water to drink!"
Numbers 20:2-5

So Moses is grieving, and then his people rise up against him, but I love the next verse!

"Moses and Aaron went from the assembly to the entrance."
Numbers 20:6

Instead of totally freaking out on his people, Moses and Aaron go to the entrance of the tent of meeting and fall facedown before the Lord and His glory.

When your response to your situation is falling before the Lord and asking Him what to do, you cannot go wrong my friend. So God talks to Moses down on his face in prayer:

> "Take the staff, and you and your brother Aaron gather the assembly together. Speak to that rock before their eyes and it will pour out its water."
> Numbers 20:8

So Moses starts to move, to see water come from the rock, a miracle in the making. Moses obeyed the Lord but NOT all the way. Instead of speaking to the rock he struck the rock twice with his staff (Numbers 20:11). God was STILL faithful, and water poured from the rock, but Moses would pay the price for only obeying half way.

God disciplined Moses and Aaron by telling them that they would NOT bring this community of people into the land He was going to give them. He told them they would only see it from a distance (Deuteronomy 32:52). This is a very harsh discipline but God still gave the people water, this speaks volumes of His grace. Later in Deuteronomy when a little bit of this story is told again it says:

> "This is because both of you broke faith with me in the presence of the Israelites."
> Deuteronomy 32:51

When we hear from God, we must be sold out in obedience. Although we carry out what He says, we MUST make sure that it is done without any distractions. Some say Moses was so angry at the Israelites, that he lashed out in anger and struck the rock. But God told him to speak to the rock, and he would suffer for his actions in the end.

Breaking faith is when you obey, but you do it your way!
It's all about your response to your circumstance, how are you responding?
Friend, where are you today?
What is it that God has told you to do?
How has He told you to do it?
Then do it WITHOUT breaking faith.

Dear God,
Help us to obey in full with no distractions! I honor You today.

Sheba

"I did not believe these things until I came and saw with my own eyes."
1 Kings 10:7

The Queen of Sheba was filthy rich and powerful. She had heard of Solomon's fame and splendor. Many told her about everything Solomon had and the things he had done, but she was a woman who had to see it with her own eyes. Personally, I think anyone hearing of anything is wise to test it for themselves.

"She came to test him with hard questions."
1 Kings 10:1

Sheba brought a caravan of camels with her carrying spices, gold, precious stones and more, as gifts of offer Solomon, if her eyes saw that everyone was speaking the truth about this ruler.

"You have far exceeded the report I heard."
1 Kings 10:7

This story of Sheba and Solomon is found in the Old Testament, but there are traces of this story also in the New Testament.

"The Queen of the South will rise at the judgment
with this generation and condemn it;
for she came from the ends of the earth to listen
to Solomon's wisdom,
and now one greater than Solomon is here."
Matthew 12:42

In Luke 11:31 it says the same thing. Most believe the Queen of Sheba was the Queen of the South. This is the proclamation that a greater one than Solomon had now come.

This entire story of Sheba and Solomon reminds me of the three Kings that follow the star in the Bible and many of our Christmas stories we learned in Sunday school. The three kings hear of a ruler that has been born.

"Where is the one who has been born king of the Jews? We saw
A star in the east and have come to worship him."
Matthew 2:2

No matter what they saw and heard, just like Sheba they wanted to **"see it with their own eyes"** and test it.

"The star they had seen in the east went ahead of
them until it stopped over the place where the
child was. When they saw the star, they were overjoyed.
On coming to the house, they saw the child with his mother Mary,
and they bowed down and worshiped him.

Then they opened their treasures and
presented him with gifts of gold and of incense and myrrh."
Matthew 2:9-11

When they saw baby Jesus with their own eyes they presented Him with gifts. Just like when Sheba saw Solomon. My questions today for you my friends is have you seen Him with your own eyes? And what have you presented to Him?

Many may have told you the great things the Lord has done, but have you gone on a quest to find him for yourself? A journey like Sheba or the three Kings? They had only heard words but they were ready to see for themselves! Have you done this?

If you know Him already, you know He is ever faithful and loves with a love we cannot comprehend. Then what have you given Him? He is not looking for gifts of gold, myrrh and of material worth. He is looking for your heart in full surrender. He is looking for obedience.

I remember hearing about the Grand Canyon and the Taj Mahal in all their splendor, but until I stood and looked at them with my own eyes I did not fully understand.

I challenge you today friend, find Him and go on a quest like Sheba.

Dear God,
As this reader walks with you this year, may they find you and experience your amazing splendor. I honor you today.

January 4th

PICK UP YOUR SWORD

Have you ever felt pulled in a million different directions? The instant I woke this morning, I thought of all the important things I had to do today: Get a money order, fax important documents, get them notarized, clean my house, and get printer cartridges and stamps. Oh, and I forgot to mention to take care of me by going to the gym! It was very overwhelming when my mind started racing, so I made myself sit and take time to be with the Lord. I never want to be so busy that I forget about time with God! This year, I desire to hunger for His word. Sometimes we are so busy with life, work, and kids that we feel we can't pray. I want to encourage you today in those times to pick up YOUR SWORD! Your Bible is the word of God! Not only is it a beautiful bestseller that tells amazing stories, but the Bible says:

"In the beginning was the Word, and the
Word was with God, and the Word was God."
John 1:1

You are reading the words of the Lord when you read the Bible! I want to hunger for it this year more than ever before! That is my prayer. When I'm feeling pulled in a million different directions, I still want to take time to read the word of God!

"Take the helmet of salvation and the
SWORD OF THE SPIRIT, which is THE WORD OF GOD!"
Ephesians 6:17

Our Bible is our sword! And in those times of depression and being anxious, in those times when the devil tries to lie to us and lead us back to our vomit that we once lived in...PICK UP YOUR SWORD! FIGHT! Never give up! With His Word on our side we have already won the battle. Be encouraged today and now put this book down and read a chapter in your Bible, let it soak into your heart!

Dear God,
Forgive me for not hearing your voice and reading your word. Forgive me for being too busy to pray. Give me a hunger for your Word like never before this year! I thank you today for all you have done for me Lord. I thank you for never leaving me even when I don't pray and read your word. You are the most faithful friend I have! Give me such a desire to get to know you like John 10:27 talks about, that I would hear your voice so crystal clear! I honor You today.

Lose No Time

There is a woman in the Bible named Abigail. This lady inspires me so much! She was married off to a man named Nabal, most likely due to his great wealth. How many of you know money does NOT always buy us happiness? The Bible says she was intelligent and beautiful but Nabal was surly and mean (1 Samuel 25:3)! Abigail was an abused woman, a disrespected woman, and I'm sure in many ways a sad and lonely lady. Read the story for yourself! Abigail hears that David and his men (about 400) are coming to kill Nabal and all the people living under him due to his selfish ways. This was her easy way out!!!!!!! She could have taken off right then and there and been out of her situation! But NO!

"Abigail lost no time!"
1 Samuel 25:18

She gets together food! Ha! This is so great! Verse 18 -19 says she gathers bread, wine, sheep, grain, raisins figs and loads them onto donkeys! What a way to change a man's mind! Food! It just makes me laugh!

How many of you have ever made food as a peace offering...so funny. Due to Abigail's intelligence, I'm sure she had much more of a plan than food! She takes off right away from her household and meets David and his army. Imagine this, seeing a lady and donkeys standing up against 400 men with swords (vs. 13)! I wish someone would paint this picture for me because it's just an amazing thing to picture! What a lady of courage. She knew, like Esther, her life could end right then and there. She was doing the unthinkable: trying to save her home, family, friends, livestock and abusive husband from death. Truth be told she was a lady who walked with God. Even David recognized this in verse 32!

"She... bowed down with her face to the ground!"
1 Samuel 25:23

She begged David for her household to be saved; kind of sounds like what we should be doing for our unsaved family and friends. Pleading, not caring about all our makeup and the things we have, but getting right down on our face! Due to one ladies courage, one lady taking a risk and loosing NO time, Nabal's entire household was saved that night. What a great example to us.

"...if you had not come quickly to meet me,
not one male belonging to Nabal
would have been left alive by daybreak."
1 Samuel 25:34

"Go home in peace.
I have heard your words and granted your request."
1 Samuel 25:35

What was Nabal doing during all this? He was home having a party, and the Bible says he was not in his right mind!

"He was in high spirits and very drunk."
1 Samuel 25:36

So here is Abigail out saving his hide and he is having a party. Can you imagine? What is your Nabal situation today? You need to get on your face and give it to God; you need to lose no time, and with wisdom and intelligence move!

Dear God,

Help my situation; don't let bitterness and anger overwhelm me. Help me to take a risk and move forward. Help me to forgive. Help me to love even the unlovable. Help me to do the right thing. Help me to do Your perfect will in all areas of my life even when it hurts, even when there could be another way out, an easier way out. Help me to fall on my face and give you everything-- my very life. Thank you for loving me even when I fail. I honor you today.

January 6th

Self Control

I love Galatians 5:22-23. Read it today if you can. It speaks of the fact that if we have the Holy Spirit in our everyday life we will be changed. The fruit of God's Spirit living in us should show love, joy, peace, patience, kindness, goodness, faithfulness, gentleness and self-control. Do you see these things in your life today? Think about each one and say, "Am I at peace," "Am I kind to others," "Do I have self –control?" Hmmmm, sure makes you think.

God has taught me a great lesson in the past two months. I landed in the emergency room one night; I knew I was in trouble. My son's two best friends had gotten into a jet ski accident. The first things we were told on the phone were that one might be paralyzed and that one was med flighted to Boston and unconscious. My son and husband took off for Boston right away. I found myself a total mess. My daughter and I began to pray. I also was worried for my son who had never experienced anything bad ever happening to any of his close friends. God is faithful and heard our prayers. James, who they said could be paralyzed, walked out of the hospital just days later! Yes, he hurt his back very badly but he was walking! And Geritt, who was in very bad shape, took longer to leave the hospital but both boys were walking and alive! The event sent my heart into an irregular heartbeat that made regular life hard at times. Every time I went somewhere it felt like my heart was beating out of my chest. Every time I sat to watch a movie I could hardly breathe! The constant pounding in my chest was just horrible. It was very hard to think of anything else. I was angry at myself for getting so stressed and worried about something that it actually affected me physically. That had never happened to me before.

One day, shortly after, I drove myself to the emergency room. I knew that day something was very wrong. I had set my heart into an irregular heart beat that for some reason was not going back to what it used to be. I was sent into Boston with premature atrial and ventricular contractions. I was given two options: a very strong Beta Blocker drug or six days a week at the gym doing exercise! NOOOOOOOOOOOOOOOOO! NOT MY WORST NIGHTMARE! Exercise! Ha!

Actually, I refused to go on meds until I tried the natural way. So, that week I went to the gym and got a membership. I had not done this as part of my lifestyle for years! But, I needed to be self controlled and DO IT! Doctor's orders. Yes, I believe God can heal, but I also believe that God gives us people with wisdom, and sometimes He is trying to teach us a big lesson through trial.

Well, I did not like this lesson, but God was really doing a work in me. I began to make working out a normal part of my everyday life. My irregular heart beat is almost 90 percent gone! Every now and then I feel it, but I have to say I was even amazed at how quickly I could feel change! It was like I took a magic pill or something! This only made me want to be more self controlled and keep going. It's taught me so much in the last couple months.

It's the same way with our walk with God. When we have self control and take the time to have our meetings with Him, He meets us and we see changes in our heart and life. We begin to see more of the Fruit of His Spirit living in us.

"Guard what has been entrusted into your care."
1 Timothy 6:20

A lot of times we overlook the fact that our body has been entrusted into our care!

Listen to this:

"Do you not know that your body
is a temple of the Holy Spirit, who is in you,
whom you have received from God?
You are not your own; you were bought at a price.
Therefore honor God with your body!"
1 Corinthians 6:19-20

I know you just love hearing this coming off the holidays! Cookies, cakes, pies, french onion dip, and the list goes on! But truth be told, I did what the doctor ordered, and it worked! I feel great and have made working out a part of my daily life. It was not easy, and on some days I pouted all the way to the gym, but I make myself do it (self control)! Wouldn't it be great if we never let dust collect on our Bibles? If we soaked in the Word of God everyday? It's time to make God part of your everyday life. It's time to have self control in every area of your life! Trust me friend, you will see changes!

Dear God,
Thank you for the hard lessons you put me through. You know I hate every minute of them, but I thank you that you teach me every time. Thank you for once again proving that if I'm faithful you will also be faithful. I honor you today and I thank you Holy Spirit for dwelling within me even when I fail. Thank you today Lord for sending your Son. I want to see myself through your eyes and not my own today. Help me to be more self controlled in every area of my life and to draw near to you through this New Year. I honor You today.

Miracles in Your Ditches

It seems like the Lord tells us to do strange things sometimes in our walk with Him. I remember years ago at Bible College being in a prayer room one day and I felt the Lord tell me to take a mini-poster off the wall off. The exact words I felt Him say to me were, "Take it off the wall...it's yours." Very strange...almost like stealing! I remember thinking, "why in the world would God tell me to do something like that?" So I walked out of the prayer room. All the way up to my dorm room I felt a tug like I was walking away from something He wanted me to do. So I turned around and headed back! I went up to that mini-poster and started peeling it off the wall. There was brown tape all around it like it was there for years and years. I was asking God if I should go to India that day in the prayer room and when I flipped that poster and saw the side that had been against the wall for years, there was the exact missionary's face I was supposed to go work with! Just amazing. I was only 19 years old at the time.

There is a prophet named Elisha in the Bible in 2 Kings Chapter 3. In this chapter we read a story of something strange God told him to do but in the end a miracle came. The King of Israel, the King of Judah and the King of Edom were planning an attack; they had set out through the Desert of Edom. The Bible says after 7 days their army had no more water for themselves or for their animals. They sought out a prophet that they may, "Inquire of the Lord through him?" (vs. 11) An officer told them of Elisha son of Shaphat! They went to Elisha and told of their need. I love what happens next. Elisha says, "Bring me a harpist" (vs. 15) He wanted to get into the very presence of God through music and worship!

"While the harpist was playing, the hand of the Lord came upon Elisha and he said, "This is what the Lord says: Make this valley full of ditches. For this is what the Lord says: You will see neither wind nor rain, yet this valley will be filled with water, and you, your cattle and your other animals will drink. This is an easy thing in the eyes of the Lord!"

So the Lord speaks to Elisha to dig ditches...can you imagine? Such a weird request! If you read the Old Testament you see many times when God told Elisha and Elijah to do some strange things. But God's miracles always seem to come. It's so important that we get ourselves in the presence of God to hear His voice like John 10:27 talks about. If you read the end of 2 Kings Chapter 4 you see that the very next morning there it was..."water flowing from Edom and the land was filled with water" (vs. 20) The ditches kept the water there and safe.

Why did I share that story and my story? Because sometimes instead of believing that our ditch or trial can be a miracle we walk away, like I was headed for my dorm room! After all I was only 19; I had no money to go to India! I love this story because **the ditch became what held the very miracle they were in need of!** What miracle is getting ready to fill your ditch today? It's flowing in your direction my friend you just need to wait for it! There are miracles in your ditches!

Dear God,
So many times I just want to give up. It's so much easier to leave than to stay and work hard. It's so much easier to walk away than to seek your face. God I pray you would help me to long for a harpist to come, so I can begin to worship again. I pray that no matter what you tell me to do no matter how strange, that I will do it. That I would not be distracted from the worry of what others might think or say. I honor you today.

January 8th

Lonely Places

Growing up in a very large Italian family it was hard ever to be lonely! We were together on everyone's birthdays, anniversaries, holidays and even pets' birthday's (just kidding)! But it just seemed we were always together... For those of you who come from big families you know there is usually a lot of noise, and the smell of food fills the air most the time as the courses keep coming! It never failed at Grandma's house...First the artichokes, then the Italian chicken soup, all the meats and pastas, and the mounds of desserts! It just never stopped. Even at midnight the squid and periwinkles got put into the pot! I can remember all of us 11 grand kids partied till we dropped which most the time was on the living room floor of grandma's house! The older and bigger we got, the harder it got to find room, but those were some of the most fun times of my life in the Zinnanti family. Grandma made everything fun.

Going through day-to-day life, I found myself very lonely at times. I was my high school class vice president, very involved and had lots of friends, yet no one knew what was in my head and heart. There was a darkness that lingered within me. I was living the scripture Proverbs 14:13 which says, "Even in laughter the heart may ache." I almost always had a fake smile, but inside I was a mess. I made a decision two weeks before my sixteenth birthday, at the age of 15, that it would be easier to die than to live.

During my suicide attempt that day in my mother's kitchen I had an encounter with God. It was the first time ever! I heard a voice say to me three times, "There's more!" I heard it again, "There's more!" "There's more!" I had heard many voices in my home but this was different, this was not demonic, this I knew was the voice of a living God who I did not know yet.

I remember stopping what I was doing and running into the woods where I stayed for three hours. I remember yelling at God like the scene in Forest Gump where Lieutenant Dan loses his legs and then shakes his fist at the sky and has it out with God during the storm. Standing there, I yelled, "Oh yea?! Well if there's more, you better tell me what it is because I'm done here!" I had it out with God in the woods that day.

Two years later, my brother asked God to come into his life, and a year later I would come to know the one who gave me hope! For those of you who are lonely today, I want you to know Christ can fill that void and give you a new purpose and hope for your life. Do you know He wants to use your pain for His purpose?

Jesus knew what it was like to be lonely.

"But Jesus often withdrew to lonely places and prayed."
Luke 5:16

Yes He was the Christ, He had no sin, and He had His friends, but most the time when He went somewhere, it was as if a celebrity walked into the mall or something. Can you imagine if you went to the mall today and all of a sudden you see someone there that is on TV every day? I know what most teens would do! They would get their cell phones out and start taking pictures, and I'm sure within minutes a large crowd would form.

"News about Him spread all the more,
so that crowds of people came to hear Him and to be healed..."
Luke 5: 15

I can imagine after a while with crowds around Him all the time, He must have wanted to get away! But those away times were lonely. Sometimes in our lonely places we think God does not understand but friend, I'm here to tell you today, He understands so very much more than you know. During your lonely times I challenge you to call out to Him in your own way. Talk to Him like you would talk to me. Ask Him to fill your voids and give you hope. Read the word of God and He will speak to you through it.

"Stand firm, let nothing move you.
Always give yourselves fully to the work of the Lord,
because you know that your labor in the Lord is not in vain."
1 Corinthians 15:58

My goal today is to tell you there is hope in the lonely places.

Dear God,
First, I thank you for all you have done in my life. I also thank you for the fact that you still are growing me and making me more like you every day. I pray today that instead of letting 'things' fill my lonely places, I would call on you! God, I cry out to you today, I beg you to meet me. I ask you to take my pain and give me a purpose. I ask you to give me a hope that I have never had before. Remind me Lord that you know how I feel. Give me a drive to grow even stronger in you so I can impact the world around me. I honor you today.

"Don't waste the pain, let it drive thee.
Don't stop the tears let them cleanse thee, don't waste the pain."
~Jill Briscoe

Beware of Silver Platters

"For I know the plans I have for you," declares the Lord, "Plans to prosper you and not harm you, plans to give you hope and a future."
Jeremiah 29:11

I love how this scripture starts: "I know the plans I have for you." Did you know that God has a plan for your life? Are you in it? I don't know about you, but I want to be in the perfect will of God for my life.

I remember when my husband and I were very young; I was a pastor's wife with two small children at home. My husband was a part time pastor at the time, a painter on the side to make ends meet, and a seminary student. Financially, those were hard times. I can remember my car had a foot-long hole in the floor of the passenger's side so you could actually watch the ground pass by as the car moved! I used to throw a rubber mat over it and say to whoever got in the car, "Be careful that you don't fall through the hole!" Ha! That was a season in our life we will never forget, and when we look back on them now we can't help but laugh.

At the time I had been praying for a stay at home job to help make ends meet. One Sunday, this new lady who I had never met before came up to me and we started talking. Within our ten minute conversation I found out that she had two small children and was looking for someone to watch her kids while she took a new job. My heart jumped. I just knew this must be God! I told her how I prayed and asked the Lord for a job. I said yes to her right away. If you have not figured it out by now friend, don't do that! This particular occasion is what I like to call a "silver platter." If you are praying for something and then you see it in front of you, go away and get alone with God to *make sure* it's His perfect will before you take it!

"In all your ways acknowledge Him, and he will direct your paths."
Proverbs 3:6

Silver platters will come your way. The devil knows how to make them look just like God! So there it was in front of me, my perfect job on a silver platter! Instead of getting away with God and asking Him if this job was His will for my life, I just took it.

A few weeks went by and it was the night before the woman would drop her kids off to me at 7am. I woke in the middle of the night to a thick presence of God in our bedroom. I mean so thick I could not move. I asked the Lord, "What is it, what are you trying to tell me?" As crystal clear as day I heard the voice of the Lord say, "Guard your sheep." That's all I heard.

WHAT?! I had no idea what the Lord was trying to say to me. I began to pray through it, and begged Him to explain Himself. I was troubled because I was starting to feel as if He did NOT want me to take this job that was only a couple hours away. Up until this point I had been claiming to everyone, "Look at the job God gave me!" Look at my silver platter! Ha! We are so silly when we run way ahead of God then claim it was Him!

Anyway, I was upset and woke up my husband. He laid there for a few minutes then got up and walked out of the room. I figured he went to the bathroom or something. But, as I waited for him, I was getting frustrated! Where did he go? Didn't he care how troubled I was? Then all of a sudden he walked into the room like a storm and said, "Tana, God does NOT want you taking this job!" Wow. He felt the Lord in our house that night, and he got up to pray, and knew that my silver platter was not real silver at all. It was a fake. I blew it.

Long story short, I called her early the next morning and I did not tell her the Lord said, "Guard your sheep." I told her I took the job without praying, and the Lord woke me in the middle of the night to tell me I had walked out of His will. I thought this lady would leave the church, get her gun and head my way! Her first words were, "What are you doing right now?" She said she wanted to come over...yikes! I was scared! So as I was waiting for her, I was peeking out the front window. She finally arrived, and opened the back door of her car to get her shot gun! Ha, kidding! She actually pulled out Dunkin' Donuts® coffee and snacks! Now I was really confused! She walks through my door, puts her stuff down and starts crying so hard! It was very strange.

When she finally got her composure, she explained to me that she had jumped ahead of God, and that she knew she was NOT supposed to take that job! So, by jumping ahead of God, I actually put someone else out of the will of God. Be ever so careful where you walk. Make sure you are always in the perfect will of God for your life. Other people's lives depend on it.

To this day I have no idea what, "Guard your sheep" meant? But I do know she was going through a messy divorce, and I do know God was protecting my children from something. Friend, beware of things that look just like God. Beware of silver platters as you walk His way.

Dear God,
Help me to hear your voice so clear; it's so easy to walk ahead of you. I want to be in your perfect will for my life. I know it is there that I am safe. Thank you for the many times you have protected me and my family. Thank you that you actually care enough to watch over us. Thank you today for all the lessons throughout the years that you have taught me and are still teaching me. I honor you today.

Holly Point

I'm a nursing assistant as well as an ordained minister. I do EKG's, draw blood, and now work at the hospital on-call. I went back to school many years ago just to make money on the side when my kids got a little older. Through my years of nursing, I have come to see that nursing is an extension of God's hand. At least that's what it's supposed to be. Many times I have taken a shift only to run into a divine appointment with a soul longing to know more about God. I love these opportunities where I get to share all God has done in my life.

There is one story that will always stick out in my mind when I think of divine appointments while nursing. His name was John. I was working that year at a nursing home which was some of the hardest work I have ever done. I worked with people over the age of 70 most the time, and I never knew what floor or wing I would be on. I would just come in and fill someone's shift. One day I went in and ended up on a wing named Holly Point. Holly Point was for those patients who had money. They were single rooms and very private, and many of the patients put on Holly Point were dying, and their families wanted them to die well cared for. This was the case with John.

For three days straight, God put me with John. It would be the last three days of his life. John had advanced cancer. He could no longer walk, and I had to lift him with a Hoyer lift every time he had to use the rest room. It was very sad.

Because I was a minister, I had been given permission by the head nurse to share the gospel only when people wanted to hear it. As John and I talked and we got to know one another, he would ask me some serious questions that most of the world would only think about when they have days to live. The first day we talked a lot. The second day he was less attentive, and by the third day he could no longer talk and had turned very jaundice. He became so weak by the third day I had to feed him and give him total care.

In just a short time I learned to love John. Even though he could not talk, I kept talking. He had already prayed with me, and he felt like he was ready to go be with his maker. I knew when I left the nursing home that day I would not see him again due to the way he was breathing. My shift was almost over, so I gathered my things and went into John's room right before I left. I kissed him on the forehead and said goodbye. That day he had not said one word to me, and to my totally surprise as I turned to leave, all of a sudden he grabbed my sleeve. I turned around in shock. It took everything within him to lift his arm and when I looked at his face with tears in his eyes he whispered so soft: "Thank you." There was much space between the two words, like he could hardly get it out. I just could not believe what I was hearing. John thanked me that day because I gave him the Hope of Christ. That would be the last time I ever saw John.

The Word of God says:

"You are the salt of the earth."
Matthew 5:13

When I think of salt, I think of an awesome steak and fries and how after putting salt on it I love it so much more. Salt has also been used as a preservative. So, if we are to be like salt on this earth, we should be striving to make things better wherever we go and trying to preserve souls by telling them about the Hope of Christ. I'm not sure about you, but those are some awesome goals for me for a new year. Look for divine appointments in your life today. Remember when you are grumpy that there are souls all around you who need peace and joy in their life. I thank God for leading me to Holly Point that week.

Dear God,
I pray that we would be forever mindful of the souls all around us on a daily basis. Wherever we are, I pray that we would not forget there are many who don't know you. I pray you would help me to be more like you who has compassion on the multitudes, that I would take time out for someone in need. "Make me more like you" is my cry today, Lord. I honor you today.

Stopped at the Border

A few years ago, God started speaking to my husband and me, telling us that we would be leaving the church family we had poured ourselves into for over seven years. We could feel those winds of change, and it hurt. When change comes it's always hard. How will it hit our children? Will people think we don't like them? Where will we go? We knew God was speaking, but we did not know where we were going. We began to pray hard for direction.

I love Isaiah's heart here:

> "Then I heard the voice of the Lord saying, 'whom shall I send?'
> And 'who will go for us? And I said, 'Here am I. Send me!'"
> Isaiah 6:8

I did not add that exclamation point at the end of what he said. If you look yourself, it's there. He meant what he said! He would go anywhere and do anything the Master wanted.

God knows that my husband and I live our life for Him and the call He has placed on our lives. Yes, I am a sinner, but God loves and uses sinners! This is NOT my home. In this life we have like 80 to 90 years and then we are gone to be in our eternal home, and for some, much less time.

We have so many distractions in this life. Today I want you to think about your eternal home. It took only six days for God to create all we have here on earth! On the seventh day, He rested (Genesis 2:2). Think about all the bug and animal shows you have watched on television. The ways their skin changes color, the way they protect themselves, the way their bodies work, it's just amazing. It only took six days for God to create all that! Think of our universe and how it all works: Only six days. How about our anatomy with our own human bodies: 6 days! The word of God says:

> "Do not let your hearts be troubled. Trust in God; trust also in me.
> In my Father's house are many rooms; if it were not so,
> I would have told you.
> I am going there to prepare a place for you.
> And if I go and prepare a place for you,
> I will come back and take you to be with me
> that you also may be where I am."
> John 14:1-3

If it took six days for Him to create all we have now just think of this place He is preparing! He's been gone for years preparing! Our little human minds cannot even comprehend what awaits us! But most of all today, imagine if you had someone you love coming to stay in a room at your home. I know how I would prepare! I would get my finest sheets out, I would clean like crazy, make awesome Italian food, and more than any of that there would be an excitement in my heart waiting for them to arrive. No matter what you think of yourself today, God is excited for you to arrive. He waits with expectation in His heart. He waits with longing. He loves you. Are you ready for your eternal home?

I love to read about Paul and his missionary journeys! Paul and his companions walked where they were led by the Holy Spirit. Listen to this:

> "When they came to the border of Mysia, they tried to enter Bithynia,
> But the Spirit of Jesus would not allow them to.
> So they passed by Mysia and went down to Troas."
> Acts 16:7-10

I want to be led in that way by God. God stopped them at the border! It was during that night that God gave Paul a dream of where to go next. Wow… just imagine. So close with God that we know exactly where we are to go and what we are to do. Do you realize today this is exactly where Jesus wants you? He wants to be your friend. Friends tell each other what they want. God has mighty plans to use you on this earth so I hope you are listening.

Do you realize today that other souls depend on your life? There is nothing like knowing 100 percent that you are in the perfect will of God for your life. When Guy and I left our last church he was the Senior Pastor and the Sectional Presbyter. God led us to a church where my husband became the Senior Associate. He walked away from being Senior Pastor and leader of the entire section to Senior Associate. When we left, someone walked up to me and said, "Why are you guys taking a step down?" My answer to this person was, "There is no step down when you are in the perfect will of God for your life."

Are you where *God* wants you today? Forget what everyone else says to you! What does God want? God stopped Paul at the border, what borders are you at today? Are you in the perfect will of God for your life right now?

Dear God,
Help us to know today that this is not our home. Help us to walk in your perfect will for our lives. To know time is short and still so many don't know you. Help us not to be distracted by everything this world has to offer. Help us to hear from you very clearly as to where you want us and what you want us to do. You are worthy of our very lives God. I honor you today.

Who Cut in on You?

Who are the biggest influences in your life today? Think about it for a moment. Who do you aspire to be like? Who do you look up to? What are their morals like? If we are striving to be like Christ we need to keep moving forward. I'm a dreamer, always have been. I'm a district director for the Southern New England Ministry Network (SNEMN) Assemblies of God (AG) women's department which consists of three states. Never thought I would be doing this! I think it's very healthy to dream your big dreams. Think about your dreams today. Are they on a shelf somewhere? Do they need to be dusted off and picked up again?

"You were running a good race.
Who cut in on you and kept you from obeying the truth?
That kind of persuasion does not come from the one who calls you.
A little yeast works through the whole batch of dough."
Galatians 5: 7-9

Was there some sort of circumstance or person that stopped you in your tracks? Were you moving forward and then your life was turned upside down by something and now you find yourself not able to pray or feel the touch of God in your life? Everything, my friend, depends on your response to your situation or the people in your life...everything. You pretty much have two responses you can choose from:

1. Shut yourself off from the world, move into your darkness and withdraw.
2. Kick the devil—who is lying to you—in the butt and remove yourself from bad influences in your life and move forward!

"Who cut in on you," that scripture says. Who cut in on you? I understand what it's like to be in a dark situation. I have been a minister and pastors wife for over 26 years, and I still get into these ruts of living in stagnant waters! When we are in stagnant waters the green muck grows all around us! The Lilly pads keep growing and the slimy frogs keep croaking lies in our ears. This is NOT where Jesus wants us to stay. An old song I loved says, "It's time to get UP! Stand upon your Bible 'cause He's pouring out that latter rain!" MOVE! MOVE! GET UP! Do what you have to do to keep moving forward no matter what it is...no matter who you have to cut off in your life. Do it today! Yes, we need to love people but if someone is hurting your walk with God do something about it! Dont sit stagnant! If that person is your spouse, please seek the counsel of your pastor.

It was just about two years ago that I went through a dark time and could not understand what God was doing. I was trying so hard to move forward but felt all alone. Things were not happening the way that I thought they should be happening! When you go through these times its *imperative* that you read the word of God!

> "Faith comes by hearing and hearing by the word of God."
> Romans 10:17

When you are lacking in the faith area, you must read His word; sometimes it's the only thing that will get you through. During this time I did not want to read, but when I did it changed me. Here is what I read:

> "Consider what God has done: Who can straighten what He has made crooked? When times are good, be happy; but when times are bad, consider: God has made the one as well as the other."
> Ecclesiastes 7:13-14

What? In all my years of reading the word, I NEVER came across this scripture. God makes crooked times? Why? Because sometimes we need to be bent in order for Him to build character in our lives. If I never went through a bad time, I would not be the lady, mom, or minister that I am today. Now I will say, if someone has hurt you in a bad way you need to know that God is not controlling them like a puppet! God created each person to have their own free will, so if someone hurt you please know that was not God's fault! That person themselves hurt you! God's heart breaks when those things happen. But, if he controlled every person we would all be a bunch of robots! Who wants that? Life is life, and there is sin in this world, so we will get hurt. But, please remember today that everything depends on your response to your situation, my friend! Your soul depends on it; other souls depend on it.

Who cut in on you, and what are you going to do about it today?

Dear God,
Help my focus to stay on you. When I get distracted by circumstance and people, I pray you help me to dig into your word where I know I will be changed! Help me to press forward. God let me see through your eyes and not my own today. Let me see the amazing things I am going to do through you. Lead me in every area of my life and when those hard times come, I pray my response will be pleasing to you. I honor you today.

Locked in the Closet

"Where was God when I was locked in the closet?" This was a question I was asked many years ago, and I must say I was not quite ready for that question. This young lady had been sent to me and had been sexually abused for many years starting at a very young age. Her mom that adopted her did not want her teen son going out and sexually molesting others so she adopted a little girl named Jade so he could molest her. I know it's unthinkable, but it's true. Jade (not her real name) had multiple personalities— a mental disorder where someone flip-flops to other personalities. I believe sometimes it can be demonic, but other times its not. I believe it can be a God-given escape from the Hells and tortures a child goes through, sort of like escaping to another playful, peaceful world instead of your own, a true mental disorder. In any case, God gave me a love for Jade.

There were times where people at church had to come get me because Jade, a grown woman, was hopping around the church parking lot like a kangaroo. This was the most interesting friendship I had ever had, and my heart just went out to this young girl. It didn't matter how she acted, Jesus still died for her soul. I had a God given love for her.

As we sat on the steps one day, she told me how when her mom got mad she would smash her face into the bathroom mirror then put that same bleeding face in the toilet and rub it in feces. After a beating she would then be locked in the closet for days on end with no food and water. How do you answer a question like, "Where was God when I was locked in the closet?" So that day I said, "Jesus was with you in the closet Jade, He never left your side. And, His heart was breaking watching what was going on in your home."

Please know today that bad things will happen in this world due to sin. God NEVER intended for sin to enter the world. But it started with Adam and Eve in the garden. God wanted us to have a choice. *He wanted us to love Him because we wanted to, not because we had to!*

What have you been through today? I have a memory from age two that I will not share, but it's so bad that I did not remember it until I was married and had children. I remembered it in a flash back, the one and only flash back I have ever had in my life. It was like a moving picture in front of my eyes. The only thing I can think of is that God knew that was the time I could handle that memory. Why would God allow bad things to happen to little girls or little boys? It doesn't seem fair, does it? Like I have said before, He did not make a bunch of robots. Sin is sin, and people hurt other people. They have evil intentions. God's intentions were never evil. If God stopped every person ready to hurt another person, we would have a perfect world again...kind of like the garden. Humans let their flesh consume them and therefore they sin.

"There is not a righteous man on earth
who does what is right and never sins."
Ecclesiastes 7:20

"For all have sinned and fall short of the glory of God."
Romans 3:23

The name of this book is Wrecked: Daily Devotions Penned by a Sinner. I named it that because it does not matter if I have been a Christian for over 30 years, if I'm a pastors wife, If I'm an ordained minister, or if I'm a leader of women! I will still sin because everyone sins! Every day I go to God and ask forgiveness, everyday. I am a sinner saved by His grace. And guess what? You are too.

It's time to give the devil a heart attack as my friend Greg Hubbard would say! Take all the Hells you have gone through in life and start to use them for God's purposes! There are so many in this world that need to hear today, "I know how you feel!" Those addicted to drugs and alcohol, those who have had an abortion, those in a wheel chair, those who have seen the Hells of war, those who have lost a child, those who have lived through natural disaster, and the list goes on! No one can minister to them better than someone who has been through it! Take your pain, and know God wants to use it. Stop whining and move forward! It's so easy to put your party hat on, toot your own horn, and have your own pity party every day! So easy! But how about letting God use your pain for His purpose today!

Bad things happen. Bad things will keep happening. Such is life, Pick yourself up and move forward. I only have half my life left then I will be gone. I want to try to make a mark on my world today. How about you?

"Praise be to the God and Father of our Lord Jesus Christ, the Father of compassion and the God of all comfort, who comforts us in all our troubles, so that we can comfort those in any trouble with the comfort we ourselves have received from God.
For just as the sufferings of Christ flow over into our lives, so also through Christ our comfort overflows."
2 Corinthians 1:3-5

The sufferings of Jesus flow over into our life so that we can be forgiven. We can go to Him and ask for forgiveness. He died for you sin. How do your sufferings overflow? This scripture says, "So also through Christ our comfort overflows." Have you received comfort from Him? How is it overflowing in your life to others? Maybe it's time to stop being selfish, to do what God intended. "Where was God when I was locked in the closet?" Right there with you, and His heart was breaking.

Dear God,
I know I don't always understand why bad things happen, but I pray you use me like a tool. Use me and my life to bring comfort to others. Thank you for the times I have come and you have comforted me. Now, let the comfort I have received from you overflow into the lives of others. Help me to dig into your word for strength. I honor you today.

He Waits

I love the story of Samuel being mentored by Eli. The word says he was only a boy (1 Samuel 3:1) when he first heard the voice of the Lord. Three times he heard the voice of the Lord call him one night while lying down in the temple. He thought it was Eli, and each time he ran to Eli, woke him, and said, "Here I am; you called me." Eli would say, "I did not call you; go back and lie down." It took the three times for Eli to then realize that the Lord Himself was calling Samuel. Read this story for yourself this morning in 1 Samuel 3.

"Then Eli realized that the Lord was calling the boy. So Eli told Samuel, 'Go and lie down, and if He calls you say, 'Speak, Lord, for your servant is listening'.' So Samuel went and lay down in his place."
1 Samuel 3:9

Then the Lord came again and called Samuel. This time, Samuel was ready! Right away he said:

"Speak, for your servant is listening."
1 Samuel 3:10

Now remember, the Word says here he was only a boy (1 Samuel 3:1). What we see here is a boy taking the wisdom of someone quite a bit older than him (1 Samuel 2:22) The Word says Eli was very old. But Samuel does not even hesitate. He does exactly what Eli tells him to. When I picture this in my head I almost picture my own son when he was small. He would get so excited about things. So I picture Samuel running back to his spot with such an excitement and expectation! He just can't wait till the Lord calls again!

In 1 Samuel 3:10 the Lord calls and that's when Samuel says, "Speak, for your servant is listening." It's so amazing to me as I sit and let this entire story sink in today. Don't you wish your kids took exactly what you said and went and did it right away with such expectation? Ha! That was the first thing that came to my mind! But I love this story because it is one spot in the Bible, and there are many, where it proves that God speaks to children. We can learn so very much from this chapter.

First, who are your mentors? When they share wisdom with you, do you let it go in one ear and out the other, or do you actually apply it to your life? Last year God used mentors and friends to show me I was not the greatest team player. I like to do things myself so I can assure they get done with excellence and the way I want! That entire experience changed my life. I did not take what they said with a grain of salt! I quickly realized they were right, and God is now taking this Lone Ranger and making her into a much better team player. But it hurt, and it was humbling. Most of the time change will hurt in some form or another. But it's good for you! The wisdom we get from mentors will only make us a better person and much better leader. So start to apply things to your life even when it hurts!

Second, Samuel waits with expectation for the Lord to call again! Oh, if we were all waiting with such expectation. He was a boy, so I can just picture him laying there hardly able to breathe. As I read this today, I could only think about the way I wait on God. Do I wait with expectation in my heart for him to speak? Do I have an excitement, or am I just ready for the coffee to be done brewing so I can wake up! He was listening in the silence and waiting. This is the place where God wants us this morning. Listening and waiting, expecting.

The master of the universe and the God who gave the seas their boundaries is longing to speak with us today. Are you listening, waiting, and expecting today? I think we will hear much more if we are in this place of total surrender. Take time for Him today. He waits.

Dear God,
Thank you for speaking to children. Thank you for this example in your word of just a boy ready to hear from you. Bring me to that place of listening, waiting, and expecting. Let me hear what you want today in my life. Let me see that picture of who you are again today Lord. I honor you today.

January 15th

Just One

My heart is heavy this morning. A major earthquake hit Haiti and the pictures are just very moving to the point of tears. A mothers crying for a child, the filth the people are living in, a stray dog, or those who made it when countless dead bodies lay all over the ground. The pictures brought me to tears. But, there is one group of pictures that stood out and spoke to me this morning: A group of pictures of men and woman digging through the rubble in hopes of finding just one.

The pictures caught my heart. First I noticed they were so dirty. When you and I decide to go play in the snow, or go out in the mud and rain just for fun we can look forward to coming home to a hot shower. These people who are digging through the rubble are loaded with filth and they have no hot shower to go home to. They are down on their knees, some on their faces, in hope to hear one cry, one noise that will lead them in the right direction. They are getting dirty looking for countless souls, with not one care for themselves.

I noticed how there is such an urgency in their eyes. I'm sure most are looking for a child, husband, sister, wife, or brother, but most have an expression on their face of longing and urgency. Right now NOTHING matters to them except finding souls. Nothing. There are no distractions because they are all gone and leveled. I have been to some of the worst slums in the world in India, and I know that no matter how poor a people can be there are always distractions in their homes. But every distraction they have ever had is gone. So their focus today is on every lost soul that may still have a breath; every family member or friend that may still be out there in the countless piles of rubble.

It hurts to dig like that for hours and hours with expectation in your heart. After looking at the pictures this morning, I'm sure their knees get bloody and their hands get torn, but they continue hard work in order to find souls.

When they find a person in the rubble through the small hole they have made, they are filthy. Most have a chalk film all over them, and they are blinded by the light of day, and they are weak, and hurting. I'm sure you all know where I'm going by now.

Every single day of our lives, hundreds of souls walk by us, in schools, workplaces, parks, stores, on the street. Why don't we work as hard till it hurts to touch their lives with the hope of Christ? Why don't we get dirty doing it? Why don't we do it with urgency? Sometimes when Jesus moves you to another church or place it hurts. Sometimes when we are out all day doing evangelism we get tired and dirty. But nothing seemed to compare to the pictures I looked at this morning. The urgency in their eyes is an urgency I long to have for every day souls. People who lack hope, people who are hurting and need to hear I have been through some Hell myself! People who just need someone to listen.

"How, then, can they call on the one they have not believed in?
And how can they believe in the one of whom they have not heard?
And how can they hear without someone preaching to them?
And how can they preach unless they are sent?
As it is written, '**How beautiful are the feet of those who bring good news!**' "
Romans 10:14

I want to make a mark on the world for Christ while I'm still alive. I want someone to weep at my grave stone someday because I made an impact on their life. Just like I wept at Mark Buntain's grave, a famous missionary. I want to give my life for the cause of Christ. We are His. What about you today? As you go about your busy life this morning, getting ready for work, pulling teens out of bed, brewing your yummy pot of java, think about just one person and how you can work for that soul.

Dear God,
Make me a hard worker. Give me a passion that never stops. Help me to use wisdom and make me patient. May a day not pass that I don't think of the souls all around me. May I always be looking for opportunities to share your love and hope with people. Give me "beautiful feet" Lord. I honor you today.

January 16th

Hide in the Kerith Ravine

Elijah, who was a prophet said to Ahab, the very ungodly King of Israel:

"As the Lord, the God of Israel, lives whom I serve, there will be neither dew nor rain in the next few years except at my word."
1 Kings 17:1

I know I need water every day. I don't drink soda or anything else but my coffee in the morning, and water with a little lemon is all I need to get my motor running all day. I cannot even comprehend life without pure, awesome water. There are so many today without it.

So God gives Elijah, this word to speak, and I can imagine that the thought, "How am I going to drink?" went through his head. I know he trusted God, I know he heard from God but he was human and normal. He had needs too. So he did what he always did, and he went to God in prayer. This is what the Lord said to Elijah:

"Leave here, turn eastward and hide in the Kerith Ravine, east of the Jordan. You will drink from the brook, and I have ordered the ravens to feed you there."
1 Kings 17:2-4

First let me say it was always so amazing to me how God speaks so crystal clear to him and the next step always seems to come so quickly. Anyone else feeling my pain here? Ha! My answers just don't seem to come as quick. But the important thing for us to focus in on is they do come...in His time! His time is NOT always our time. It may not want to be what you want to hear but the answer will come.

So let's look at this word: "Leave here, turn eastward." God is bringing change again! "Go!" That is always a hard word. Sometimes it hurts. But in Elijah's case he knew he had to listen to God or he would die. Then the Lord tells him, "I have ordered the ravens to feed you there." Blah! Not sure about you but even though the Lord provided for him, I would have a hard time with that one. I carry my Purell® where ever I go! Ha. We are so totally spoiled. If God told me I was going to eat from a raven's mouth I'm not sure how I would handle it. I know for sure I would order everything WELL DONE. Something tells me I would NOT get what I want. But the point here is God was providing again, in His way, and Elijah was thankful.

Just a side note here: so cool to think that God has charge over the animals. He orders the ravens to bring Elijah food. In the story of Jonah, God orders the massive fish to swallow him. In Daniel, God keeps the lions from killing Daniel right in their own den. I just could not help but go here because it's just so amazing to me how we fear things when we really don't have to. God is in control no matter what's going on in our lives.

Ok, back to Elijah. The word says:

> "So he did what the lord had told him.
> He went to the Kerith Ravine, east of the Jordan and stayed there."
> 1 Kings 17:5

And the word says, "Sometime later the brook dried up" (1 Kings 17:7) I'm not sure how long "sometime later" is, but I'm sure a while had past, and there is NO account of anyone else being there at all except for Elijah and the ravens. If people knew a drought was coming, the first thing they would do is move where there is water. It's almost like the Kerith Ravine was some awesome little spot in the middle of nowhere; A cool little secret spot. And he went, and God led. When that "sometime later" came, it was time to move on. If Elijah would not have gone to the Kerith Ravine in obedience, there would not be the next couple of miracle stories in the word: The miracle of the widow's food, and the miracle of Elijah raising her son from the dead. You can read on yourself.

Do you realize today that every step you take is so important? Where you go leads you to the next big step and it will impact all those around you, everywhere. Souls actually depend on it. NO PRESSURE! But this is the truth.

The Kerith Ravine was a holding spot for Elijah; A hidden little safe place that God put him in. Are you in a holding spot today? You may not be thrilled with it, but God has you there for a reason. In your life it could be a sickness, a temporary job location, or a church. Maybe you love it because it supplies all your needs for the moment, or maybe you hate it. But it's your Kerith Ravine at the moment. You need to remember it's a safe place. Think on these things today and know that the Kerith Ravine was not the end for Elijah. There was so much more ahead of him.

Dear God,
Lead us. Meet us no matter where we are today. Be with us in our Kerith Ravine. Thank you for meeting every need that we have. You know us better than we know ourselves. May we never walk away from your perfect will for our lives. We honor you today.

January 17th

Go to the Ant

I remember one day many years ago, the kids were in school and I wanted to get a job for extra money to help my family pay the bills. I needed a mother's hours, and they just seemed not to be found. I began my search online and in the newspaper.

If there is one thing I believe in life, it's that God does not want us just sitting on our tails doing nothing! He doesn't want us just waiting for someone to knock on the door and say, "Here is the open door you have been waiting for!" I believe as we keep moving and working hard, God will divinely let us happen upon exactly what He wants. So I had been praying, reading, searching. It just seemed there was nothing out there until one day in the paper I saw a job at a hospital kitchen that said in big bold letters, "MOTHER'S HOURS!"

I have always been a dreamer and for years I had thought of going into the medical field. My mom was a nurse and blood and guts never seemed to bother me so I had always thought, "How great would that be!?" So when I saw the ad, the first thing I thought was, well at least I would be in the hospital, not a nurse, but feeding the nurses. Not quite my hope, but near it anyway! I was already a licensed minister at the time, but our church could not use me in any area for extra money to help with bills. I called and got the interview.

On the day of the interview, I went into the hospital to meet Tony, a big Italian guy who was over six feet tall. Right away we hit it off due to the fact that we are both Italian and seemed to have the same personality. The job seemed perfect. I could arrange my schedule around my kids' schedules! Perfect!

Somehow in my conversation with Tony I told him of my desire to someday go back to school to work in the medical field. A few days went by, and one day while I was cleaning the house the phone rang. It was Tony. He told me how every year this nursing home takes eight students and trains them to be a certified nursing assistant (CNA). He asked if I was interested. I told him, "Yes!" But, in my mind all I could think was, "Ching-Ching!" We were paying a mortgage, things were tight, and we did not have the extra money for me to go back to school. But, I went in to talk to the head nurse anyway to find out more about it.

My meeting with her was awesome from start to finish. She was kind, and not the least bit prideful. She shared with me about the class and the time frame to train us to be CNAs. She told me the starting wage, which was more than I had ever made. She went on and on and on. Sitting there, all I could think was, "I need to tell this lady that we have no money for this!" So finally I got my nerve up and let it out! I will never forget her words, "Oh, you don't have to pay for any of this, it's free!" The schooling, the books, the outfits, every single thing involved with this schooling was free and there was no catch to it, they just wanted you to start working at their nursing home. You did not even have to commit to a year!

I went through the schooling, and ended up staying there for four years. On top of that I fell in love with the patients. In gaining favor for very hard work, they allowed me to pray for patients only if they wanted it. I then started a nursing home ministry that I ran for years and it still exists today over 10 years later. That schooling led to more schooling, and every place I worked after that I learned more. In time I drew blood, did EKG's, helped deliver babies and the list goes on.

All of this happened because I did not sit around and wait for God's open door, I just worked hard. Searching, looking, praying. Jesus allowed me to happen upon it, but it took work.

> "Go to the ant, you sluggard; consider its ways and be wise! It has no commander, no overseer or ruler, yet it stores its provisions in summer and gathers its food at harvest. How long will you lie there, you sluggard? When will you get up from your sleep? A little sleep, a little slumber, a little folding of the hands to rest, and poverty will come on you like a bandit and scarcity like an armed man."
> Proverbs 6:6-11

The Bible looks at the hard work of the ant. It is an amazing creature. It seems to never stop! Always moving, always seeking out a path for victory!

I believe in hard work, and when you work hard, God honors it. I do believe in rest, but God worked hard six days and rested on one during creation. He was and is a hard worker. Your path that you are looking for will come to you with prayer, listening to God, and hard work! Don't sit around being lazy waiting for open doors! Go to the ant!

Dear God,
Never let me get lazy. Every bit of time we have is so precious. Help me to make it count. Help me make a mark on this world for you. Thank you for your creatures and how we can learn from them. Help me to be a hard worker. Help me to draw close to you through your Word and prayer. You are so very faithful. I honor you today.

January 18th

Salt, Light, and Sid

About six years ago, I was driving home from work at the nursing home and all of a sudden, an entire herd of deer ran across the highway. It was a very scary moment in my life. I stopped inches away from hitting a baby; it was frozen just looking at my headlights. Cars were spinning out and everything. Thank God no one hit one, and none of us hit each other! One car stopped along the side of the highway. It was an elderly couple, and they looked very shook up. I could not pass them by, so I parked behind them to make sure they were alright. I told them I was a minister, and what church we were at. Then I asked them if I could pray for them. After the prayer, he told me he was a minister too, and he thanked me for the prayer. I pulled away from the couple never to think of them again, or so I thought.

About two years later, one of our church members gave my husband some piano lessons from an amazing piano player who used to travel with a famous band. They were quite expensive lessons, so we were very thankful. He was an awesome guy--very friendly and energetic. He would come in and out of the office to give my husband Guy lessons, and every time he would stop and we would talk a bit. His name was Sid, and he got along extremely well with Guy. My husband learned so much from these lessons that we decided after the free ones were done, we would continue paying for them.

One day, Sid came into the office and stood in front of me with tears in his eyes. It was a very strange moment. Uncomfortable silence is what you could call it I guess. When I asked him what was wrong he said, "Nothing." Then he said, "About two years ago you stopped along the highway and prayed with my parents, my father means the world to me and I want to thank you!" It took me a minute to let that all sink in but then I thought, "NO WAY!" Sid was a Pastor's Kid (PK) who had walked away from the Lord. His dad was praying for him. I guess he went home and told his parents he was giving lessons to a pastor on Cape Cod and they said, "His wife stopped about two years ago and prayed for us along the highway." Can you even begin to believe this story? I have to say, I was amazed. It gave Sid an instant respect for Guy and I. By the time we left that church about five years later, Sid was playing the piano for ministry time at every service. He gave his life back to the Lord, and God was using him.

You know what finally sunk into my mind through all that? God has everything all planned out way ahead of time. He does NOT need our help. Two years before we ever met Sid, God was moving and planning and there was no way for us to ever know what He was even doing. God already knew Sid would walk through our church doors to give Guy lessons. Just amazing.

There are things going on in your everyday life right now that you don't even think twice about, that God will use in your future. It's so important to "walk your walk" like Jesus did while on earth– caring for others, stopping if you see someone in need. You just never know how God is going to use those things in your life.

I know what it's like to work hard and be busy. It's not easy to stop and smell the roses all the time. It's easy to see someone shaken up and know you want to stop, but also know that you need to get dinner on the table. But, I do know when Jesus saw a need, He stopped. The Bible says,

> "You are the salt of the earth."
> Matthew 5:13

I don't know about you, but when someone puts an awesome steak in front of me, I cannot wait to reach for the salt. It just seems to make the steak and fries taste so much better. Are you making things better around you today? Does it seem where ever you go you are spreading a little salt? Or are you leaving a sour taste? Think about it. Salt was and is still used as a preservative. Salt is considered to be an antibacterial. Bacteria makes things such as bacon, ham, or pickled vegetables spoil, but salt will protect and preserve these kinds of foods. Is God using you as a preservative today? It's all about your character in your everyday life, friend, and how you respond to everyday situations as you fly through your day. Will you stop on the road to help someone knowing dinner needs to get on the table?

> "You are the light of the world. A city on a hill cannot be hidden. Neither do people light a lamp and put it under a bowl. Instead they put it on its stand, and it gives light to everyone in the house. In the same way, let your light shine before men, that they may see your good deeds and praise your Father in Heaven."
> Matthew 5:14-16

Do people know you stand for God? My son is in a hardcore Christian rock band. Not really my kind of music, but they stand for God. They shine His light and everyone knows it. They were asked to play at a worship festival called Soulfest last summer, and God has opened doors for these kids. A group of kids from my son's public high school just asked one of the staff if they could write about my son and his band, Exiting the Fall (ETF), in the local paper after he received "Best Musician" for his senior class superlatives. I love this one quote from the paper that says, "With the support of their family, friends and God, Exiting the Fall has been able to reach new heights." hey know that ETF stands for God! Do people know you stand for God today? Do they see your light on its stand, or are you hiding it under a bowl? Maybe you don't know Him yet. I hope you find God through this book.

Remember Sid's story today and know that God is already working things out for you *years* ahead of time. There is no need to worry. Just go about your daily day being salt and light.

Dear God,
Help me to take the example of Jesus on earth and live it, even when I'm busy and seem to be loaded with things to do. Help me shine your light through practical things; a simple prayer, making a meal, or stopping to see if someone is okay. Help me to walk like you walked. Help me to think of others and not get self consumed. I honor you today.

January 19th

Stand For Something

I became a Christian my senior year of High School– a very hard time to have God totally change your life. Some of my friends in high school had been through almost everything with me, always supported me, always there. As soon as I started carrying around my Bible and sharing what God had done in my life, it was pretty much over. Not too many wanted to hang out with me, and I know they thought I was crazy. Before I had the Lord in my life, I ran to drugs and alcohol to ease the pain, which made it very easy to fit in, but then I started running to His hope, knowing that He actually had a plan and purpose for my life.

It seemed when I finally stood for something, I lost everything, when in reality, when I stood for something, I gained everything.

Just months after high school graduation, I landed at an Assemblies of God Bible College. God was renewing my mind from the drugs and changing my heart. I went there because my brother, my one and only sibling, was there. (By the way, Happy Birthday Lou! Today is his Birthday!) I did not even know how to pray yet, I just went there because I knew I needed to get out of the city I lived in. It was there that I learned how to pray and get to know God's voice. There at the University of Valley Forge in Phoenixville, PA.

Sitting in one of my classes during the first semester of Bible College, over 30 years ago, I learned about three men named Shadrach, Meshach, and Abednego. I remember the teacher kind of passing their story by and saying, "But, you all know that story." I did not know it and desired to, so I raised my hand and told him I did not know what he was talking about and would like to know the story. Big mistake. Every head in the room turned to look at me as if I was crazy! After all, how could someone come to Bible College and not have heard about these three guys who stood for God, a simple Bible story that most people hear in Sunday school class. Truth be told, that was the first time I had ever heard their names in my entire life. I think now I have read their story hundreds of times, and every time I seem to get something new from it.

Shadrach, Meshach, and Abednego were to be killed if they did not bow down to King Nebuchadnezzar's gods or the image of gold he set up (Daniel 3:14). Their very lives were on the line, somewhat like Esther when walking into the king's court knowing it was against the law (Esther 4 and 5). Her very words were, "And if I perish, I perish." (Esther 4:16). Shadrach, Meshach, and Abednego stood for God, as did Esther, and nothing was going to keep them from standing for what they believed in. Not even death. Here are the words of these three men:

"If we are thrown into the blazing furnace, the God we serve is able to save us from it, and He will rescue us from your hand, O king. But EVEN IF HE DOES NOT, we want you to know, O king, that we will not serve your gods or worship the image of gold you have set up."
Daniel 3:17-18

I love this scripture. All three were making a stand. They had faith that God could save them but they did not know for sure what would happen. God's ways are not always our ways. They risked their own lives making a stand. When they said the words "but even if He does not," they were saying "not our will, but His will be done." Read the story today in the book of Daniel and see what happened to them!

Many years have passed since my first days at Bible College, and today I know what I stand for. I went out this morning and voted. I have a voice, and so do you. This is something God has given to all of us. I stand for God and His Word. I am NOT ASHAMED to say so. God has raised me up into leadership not to sit back and be quiet, but to stand for something. And so I stand.

What are you standing for today? Do you have enough backbone to stand for what you believe in? My hope is that you stand for God. The great thing about standing for God is that He stands with you and never leaves your side. Stand for something today.

Dear God,
I thank you that I know what I believe in today. Give me a backbone, Lord that is backed up by your holy Word. Help me to love all that do not believe as I believe. Jesus, you were the perfect example of that, and I thank you today for that example that I can read about every day. Help me, Lord when I'm weak. Help me to stand for something so that souls might be touched by your hope. I honor you today.

The Place of Troas

"When they came to the border of Mysia, they tried to enter Bithynia, but the Spirit of Jesus would not allow them to. So they passed by Mysia and went down to Troas. During the night, Paul had a vision of a man of Macedonia standing and begging him, "Come over to Macedonia and help us." After Paul had seen the vision, we got ready at once to leave for Macedonia, concluding that God had called us to preach the gospel to them."

Acts 16:7-10

Troas was a place where Paul and his companions, including Timothy and Silas, stayed for only hours. They went to Troas to rest and to wait on the next direction from the Lord. During that same night, God directed Paul in a dream. The Bible says in Acts 16:10, "We got ready AT ONCE to leave." They were not there long at all. Resting, knowing God would lead, and waiting with anticipation. The place of Troas was a holding spot, a place of seeking, and waiting on God. Knowing the next step was coming but not knowing where it was yet. It was a place where they had to press into God. Within hours, God gave Paul a vision and told him to go to Macedonia. From Troas, they put out to sea and sailed towards Macedonia.

When Guy and I were dating, I made it very clear that I would not marry him if he wanted children. I was quite selfish at the time and did not want to have to stop my life to raise kids. I also did not think I would be a good parent. Truth be told, I was afraid of failing as a parent. We got married on June 3, 1989. Two years later, I was at church in a worship service. I was singing the song they were leading when all of a sudden, as clear as day, I heard the Lord say, "You will have a son and you are to name him Jonathan." Right in the middle of service! Why do we question God sometimes when we hear His voice? I knew it was Him, but the thought still crossed my mind, "Was that God or me?" It's easier to think it was you, because then you can just dismiss it if you want! I questioned God, but then in my heart I heard it again. I did not want to tell Guy right away because I wanted to still make sure it was God. So crazy how we do these things! I went home and said to the Lord that night, "God, if that was really you, (even though I already knew!) have Guy come to me and tell me it's time to start a family! Oh brother....not quite sure how God puts up with me sometimes! I wrote what I heard the Lord say on a piece of paper, folded it three times, put it in an envelope, and dated it June 1991. On the outside of the envelope I wrote "Time Capsule." Then I put in my bottom drawer, and sat in the place of Troas.

I'm telling you this because sometimes at the place of Troas we are ridiculous! We wait when we don't even have to wait, because God has already spoken!

We just don't want to hear it. Anyway, that same week, Guy was up in the attic, and I heard him called my name. I could hear our song playing up there. We had an awesome walk- in attic that Guy had made into his make shift space. He made World War II models and dioramas up there. Sounds fun, huh? So I went up, and among the battles of Iwo Jima, Stalingrad, and The Battle of the Bulge, we danced. I'm sure it would make a great movie! In our song there is a line that says, "Come with me my sweet and let us go make a family." Anyone want to name that tune?

During that line, Guy asked me if I wanted to start a family. I was in total shock. I said, "Hold that thought!" I ran downstairs grabbed my envelope marked "Time Capsule" and handed it to him. It was just three days before that I questioned God and put his direction to us on a piece of paper and shoved it in my drawer! A couple months later, I was pregnant with my son Jonathan Patrick.

There are times we NEED to sit in the place of Troas, and there are times we DO NOT! What is God speaking to you today? Are you waiting at Troas and wasting time when you don't even have to? The more you waste that time, the more souls could be at stake. Maybe you need to be there a lot longer than Paul, maybe for weeks, months, or years. Maybe God has you in a holding spot until you hear from Him how he wants you to take the next step in your life. I'm not quite sure where you are today, but in the place of Troas, seek Him and know the answer is coming.

Dear God,
I pray that every time I hear from you I will act and not question your voice. That I will "leave at once" like Paul did. In this place of Troas, I wait. I want and need your direction, your comfort, your love. Help me to seek you with all my heart and know the answer is coming in your perfect time. You are always faithful when we pray. I honor you today.

January 21st

Eunice

I spent my college years at Valley Forge University in Phoenixville, PA. Back then it was called Valley Forge Christian College. There was this girl I met there from Korea, her name was Eunice. I have never met anyone quite like Eunice. She prayed more than anyone else I had ever met! My dorm room was the last room on our hall, right next to the door, so every time someone went through the door in the middle of the night, I knew it. I heard every time that door opened and closed.

Every morning at about 5am I was awoken by that door! It began to bug me, so one day I got up to see who in the world was leaving the dorm at 5am! There she was, Eunice, still in slippers and with her comforter wrapped around her, walking across the field to the Memorial Chapel. Morning after morning, every day like clockwork at 5am I was woken by the slamming door, and almost every day I got out of bed to see her trekking across the field, even in snow and rain, to the Chapel to pray. I began to keep my eye out for when Eunice would come back. But, she never did. Until one day, I saw her coming into the dorm at about 9am. Could it be that Eunice was over there praying from 5am to 9am every morning? Four hours? I began to watch, and sure enough she was over there day after day for hours. She would come in with puffy eyes and her hair all plopped up on top of her head with a big smile. Not sure about you, but If I'm up at 5am I usually don't look so happy. Ha.

It's not like I did not pray, I spent at least an hour and a half each day back then in God's presence, but Eunice challenged me! And I like a challenge. She intrigued me! Did she have her own Starbucks® one-cup coffee pot in her dorm room waiting for her, is that why she always had that happy face? I'm sure NOT. It was so much more.

During my own prayer times, God began to speak to me about how He was going to use my music. I wrote songs and began to pray about recording an album. In prayer one night, I felt God's direction to call my tape (Yes, there was no such things as a CD back then!!!!) "Acknowledge Him." So "Acknowledge Him" it was. I began to pray and wait. It would cost quite a bit to process the tapes with shrink wrap and all, and I began to pray for the money. Much time went by and I got discouraged. I knew God wanted something and it was not happening in my time frame! Hate when that happens! So I decided to do something wild and crazy! That morning at 5am when Eunice left, I followed her! We hardly knew each other, but I wanted to get to know this girl whose passion was prayer.

I tell you this story because the part that I am about to tell you changed my life. Eunice walked in first; she could have given a rip if I was there behind her. She did not even turn to see who I was. She entered that chapel like nothing I ever saw. God was already there waiting for Eunice. They were very good friends and it showed. Seeing her in prayer touched my life in such a way that I went up to the altar, knelt, and began to weep, and pretty hard. In seconds she was over me with her hand on my head, and her exact words without knowing who I was, or where I came from, were "Acknowledge Him, acknowledge Him; the money will come, the money will come."

She said it twice, "Acknowledge Him, acknowledge Him; the money will come, the money will come." She said it very loud, and when she was done she walked about the room like I was not there. I could not believe it. I have to say in life I have met few like Eunice. Her example changed my life. Just like seeing my own brother's life change in front of my own eyes, it was what finally made me realize there was a God in Heaven. And I wanted Him. I've come a long way since those days. I wish I could say I pray like Eunice did— four hours a day. I can't. But, God knows my heart, and He knows that my goal is to waste no time. I do my best not to. It's hard.

There is a scripture in Proverbs that says,

"Trust in the Lord with all your heart and lean not on your own understanding; in all your ways Acknowledge Him, and He will make your paths straight."
Proverbs 3:5-6

This was the scripture I put on the very front of my tape, and the money did come. In one month, I had all I needed as I continued to pray. God was once again letting me see that He had everything under control. There was no need to worry. When He speaks, He means what He says, and in His time it will be done.

Have you ever met anyone like Eunice? I pray that today, you and I both will long to acknowledge Him in our ways and learn how to pray like Eunice prayed.

I don't know where she is today, but if you are reading this Eunice, thank you for your example.

Dear God,
Thank you for giving us certain people in our lives that just by seeing the way they live, we are changed. I pray I would be like that. That I will draw close to you and stay humble, that I will find you in the wee hours when it's still dark, that I will lose sleep to find out what it is that you want in my life. You are all I need today. I honor you.

January 22nd

A Child of Grace

Tonight I sat and read many letters from young ladies who live at the Rhode Island Teen Challenge. Their lives have been changed by the power of God at a district women's retreat they attended last week. The job I work for gives donations at Christmas and they were writing to thank me and our ladies of Southern New England for the donations. Here are some quotes from their letters:

"I have never been showed much love in my lifetime, and this Christmas I now know what it feels like to be loved by my Father in Heaven and people like you."
-Heather

"I am so blessed to have a sister in Christ to show me that God loves all his children, even me, even when I have felt I didn't deserve it."
-April

Letter after letter, I sat and read until I started crying. I am the Southern New England Ministry Network Women's Director. I am an ordained minister, but as I sat and read these letters, once again it reminded me who I really am: a child of grace. Without the grace of God, I would not be here today, my friend.

Yes, I am all these things, but let's go back and I will be transparent with you. When I was a teen, I did not know what to do with my pain. Therefore, I drank alcohol and did drugs to try and ease it a bit. I went to this house party one time and mixed both. Then, I went swimming. NOT safe at all! I decided after all that swimming I needed a shower. You do very stupid things when your brain is fried! Somewhere in that time frame, I passed out from too much in my system. I woke on the shower floor with the water beating on me. I was confused and had no idea how long I had been there. As I lay there, I realized there was someone in the bathroom on the other side of the shower curtain. I began to hear them urinating. I was scared as the water kept beating on me. As soon as they left, someone else came in, and I just lay there, as person after person came into the bathroom to relieve themselves. I was so afraid I did not move. I think this is one of the most shameful memories I have. Satan had me right where he wanted me. I know I already told part of this story but it's ok.

In the quotes I shared with you earlier, April said sometimes she did not feel like she deserved God's love. At that moment on the shower floor I felt like trash, like they were urinating on me. It was one of the lowest moments of my life.

But, Jesus had so much more for me! I just could not see it yet. I was blinded to any type of hope out there for me. Now He has me in a place where we have a budget for our Department and we can bless people. To sit and read these letters brought me back to the basics; the place where it all started! The place I came from, and the place I am at now. It's so very awesome to be reminded of that sometimes. God has done such miracles in my life. I would not even want you to know half the memories stored in my memory bank. Some memories are fearful, and some shameful, but those memories make me.

One of the scriptures that one of the young ladies wrote down was:

"Blessed are those whose ways are blameless, who walk according to the law of the Lord. Blessed are they who keep His statues and seek Him; with their hands."
Psalms 119:1-3

Some of these girls have been through it just like me, and to know this scripture is meaning so much to one of them....well, it blessed my heart.

We will NEVER be perfect; we WILL fail even when we walk with God. Our memories are simply to be used for God's glory. There is someone out there that needs to know they are NOT alone.

So today, simply be reminded of the basics. You are a child of grace.

Dear God,
Thank you, thank you, thank you for where you have brought me from to where I am now. I don't even have the words to express to you enough how I feel. Your grace is all I need. Thank you for sending your son for my sin. I need to be reminded now and then of my shame. Forgive me Lord. I honor you.

Who is Your Mentor?

I had a dear friend named Karen who once preached one of the most amazing messages I ever heard called The Peninnah Problem. Karen is gone now, but that message still rings on in my heart. Peninnah was Elkanah's wife in 1 Samuel 1:2. The other wife of Elkanah was Hannah. The Bible says Elkanah provided for Peninnah and all her sons and daughters (1 Samuel 1:4) but that he loved Hannah (1 Samuel 1:5). Hannah could not get pregnant, and it was eating her away inside. She wanted to give her husband a son. And Peninnah was the kind of lady who kept throwing it in Hannah's face that she could not have any children. I'm not quite sure how people can be so mean like that. 1 Samuel 1: 6 says that Peninnah, "Kept provoking her in order to irritate her!" She was very blunt about it. So Hannah went to prayer and asked her God for a divine miracle. He is still the God of miracles today.

The Bible says that when she was praying to God, a man named Eli walked by and thought she was drunk with wine or beer due to her passion in prayer (1 Samuel 1:15). Her response to him was, "I was pouring out my soul to the Lord." Oh to pray with such passion is my desire!

In 1 Samuel 1:19 the word says, "The Lord remembered her." He heard her prayer of passion, and a short time after she was pregnant with a son. "She named him Samuel, saying, 'Because I asked the Lord for him'." (1 Samuel 1:20)

Not even one chapter later we see the man Eli, who questioned Hannah's prayer, mentoring Samuel. 1 Samuel 2:11 says, "But the boy ministered before the Lord under Eli."

Yesterday I had a team meeting with my sectional leaders. My question to them was, "Who is your mentor?" To my surprise, there were some in the room that did not have mentors. Driving home, I found myself so very thankful for the women of God that are in my life as mentors.

Beth Decker, Peggy Musgrove, Esther Cory, Jacquie Schmidt, Meredith Giles, Nancy O'Brien, Jane Wise, Beth Grant, Kerry Clarensau, Dawn Crabtree, Jen Lange, Lena Hendrickson, Kris Zinnanti, Tracy Morrisey, and my dear Burt who died many years back. Every single one of these ladies poured into me at different times in my life. Without them I would not be who I am today. I needed their wisdom. So many times through them I realize how wrong I am. I need them and God knows it.

I did not sit back and wait for mentors to come my way. I sought them out. It takes much humility to seek out a mentor! But you must seek one out. I was hungry for wisdom from ladies that could help me through the trials of life, love, ministry, and children. I was a sponge that soaked in every word.

I am almost 50 (2016) and a very independent lady. I'm Italian, I have a backbone, and I like to run things! I am a born lone ranger, and a learned team player! God has humbled me through the years in many ways, and let me know that I need other people to pour into me. This was not easy, but I hungered to soak in wisdom from the pillars around me. I would call them and ask if we could have coffee. I would ask them to go places with me. For those who were far away, I would call and speak with them over the phone to gain wisdom or I e mailed. I always sought them out and gained nuggets that I still use today. Yes, I have my awesome husband who I love with all my heart and share everything with, but there is nothing like another lady to give you a gal's perspective. I still call some of these ladies to this day and spend time with them.

If you are a man reading this and you do not have a mentor or accountability friend in your life, you need one too. The Bible gives so many examples of this: Moses and Joshua, Naomi and Ruth, Jonathan and David, Paul and Barnabas, Timothy and Paul, and the list goes on and on, and on, and on.

The thing I love about mentoring as it is mentioned in the Bible is that they were not sitting in meetings all day. Young men or ladies were just side by side with their mentor in everyday life. Whoever was being mentored was just simply following around the mentor in their daily work and life. I think we make mentoring so hard sometimes when it's not. In the scriptures, they befriended someone. Spent time with them, and soaked everything in. Doors of opportunity would open to the ones being mentored due to their humility of wanting to learn and soaking it all in. This is what it's all about.

There are many young ladies I have mentored in the past ten years: Katie Foster, Jody Panarello, Krista Tarnowski, Amanda Porcelli, Ashley Rivera and my wonderful Molly Hurtado. Molly came to me as a student one day when I spoke at Northpoint Bible College. Her first words to me were, "I want you to be my mentor." I have many who tell me that, but I never hear from them again. Molly bugged me until I understood that this young lady was serious! I noticed her among the hundreds of young girls who get in touch with me due to her passion for bugging me! Ha! She sought me out, and kept calling until I realized God wanted me to pour into her. For two years at college Molly followed me around, setting up for events, going out to eat, coming to my team meetings, and the list goes on. By the time Molly graduated, she was credentialed and speaking in my District Retreat Workshops. She is an amazing young lady who today is the Executive Director at The ABC Women's Center in Middletown CT. She is empowering other women in crises situations.

Is your heart humble today? Are you a lone ranger who needs to be humbled and become a team player? Who is your mentor today?

Dear God,
I thank you for the countless people who have poured into my life and made me who I am today. But mostly I thank you for my mentors. The ones who have taken extra time to listen, let me cry on their shoulder, and who have brought me to humility. Bless my mentors today. Thank you for putting them in my life exactly at the right time. I pray for those who have no mentor today. Give them the passion and humility to seek one out. I honor you today.

Bad Seed

"Jesus told them another parable: 'The kingdom of Heaven is like a man
who sowed good seed in his field. But while everyone was sleeping, his
enemy came and sowed weeds among the wheat, and went away. When
the wheat sprouted and formed heads, then the weeds also appeared.
The owner's servants came to him and said, 'Sir, didn't you sow good
seed in your field? Where then did the weeds come from?' 'An enemy
did this,' he replied'."
Matthew 13:24-28

The thing I always think about when I read this parable is that no one even knew
the enemy had come until much time passed. The enemy came when they were
all sleeping. He sowed weeds among the wheat. He sowed when the ground
was flat and nothing had come up yet. It took time for the weeds and wheat to
grow to the point that the wheat sprouted. And that entire time, NOT one
person knew the enemy had come. To me, that is a dangerous place to be.

Are you sleeping today? Sometimes we do not see the enemy's seeds. They are
subtle. The enemy knows just how to make them look like everything else
around us. Sometimes we are not on guard like Jochebed, the mother of Moses!
The Bible says in Exodus 2:2,"She hid him for three months." She was hiding
baby Moses because of Pharaoh's order to throw all newborn baby boys into
the Nile (Exodus 1:22) I have no idea how a mother could hide a newborn for
three months, but I do know this: That woman must have always been looking
out the window, always watching, always praying, always on guard. Way too
many times we let our guard down and that is when the enemy can be ever so
subtle. He will wait till we are asleep. Most the time when this happens, we are
wide awake and just distracted by everyday life. Be ever so careful and on
guard or weeds will grow up all around and entangle you.

Sometimes I feel bad for the youth of today. There are so many distractions;
things that we never even thought of as a kid. My youth was spent outside
jumping into piles of dirt, taking walks with friends, riding my bike. We were
never distracted by the indoors because there was no X-Box, no cell phones or
texting. I didn't know anyone who even had a computer until I went to college.
Today, there are just so many distractions. We can be wide awake and so
distracted by everyday life that the enemy can come in and sow without us even
knowing. It is so very important to be on guard, to put on our armor!

"Finally, be strong in the Lord and in His mighty power, put on the full
armor of God so that you can take your stand against the devil's
schemes. For our struggle is not against flesh and blood, but against the
rulers, against the authorities, against the powers of this dark world and
against the spiritual forces of evil in Heavenly realms. Therefore put on

the full armor of God, so that when the day of evil comes, you may be able to stand your ground."
Ephesians 6:10-13

You can take the time to read about the armor of God in Ephesians if you want to. One piece of the armor is the "sword of the Spirit, which is the word of God." (Ephesians 6:17) His very word, The Bible, is our sword. When Jesus himself was tempted, He always talked back to the enemy using the word of God. "It is written," is what He would say! The Word is powerful, and we use it for combat.

I want to encourage your heart today. Do NOT be so distracted that the enemy can slip by and start to plant his seeds of discouragement, hopelessness, anger, unforgiveness, and hate. You must pick up your sword! You must begin to say to the enemy, "It is written!" But, how can you say that if you are not even reading the Word. Be on guard and grow.

Dear God,
Help me to be ever so careful of the distractions that come my way. God, I know you gave me things to enjoy life, and I thank you so much for that. Sometimes it seems that things can distract me so much that I don't even notice the evil one planting seeds. If that happens, I can't grow. God help me to recognize the enemy and fight. Help me to always remember to put on my armor. I honor you today.

Let Your Comfort Overflow

Isn't it amazing how God speaks to us, and then later in life the things He has spoken become second nature to us? They seem to spill out of us and on to others, and sometimes we don't even realize we are doing it. After the death of Moses, God started to use Joshua as the leader. Joshua, the legendary warrior! In Joshua chapter 1:5 it says,

> "As I was with Moses, so I will be with you;
> I will never leave you nor forsake you. Be strong and courageous!"
> Joshua 1:5

God was speaking strength and victory into Joshua's life. Then time passed. As you know, with time there comes trial. That's just life. Joshua walked with God during this time, but God was still teaching him lessons!

Between Joshua 1 and Joshua 10, so much happens. A prostitute helps prepare the way for Joshua's spies (Joshua 2:1-24); Joshua crosses the Jordan River on dry land, and throughout the entire event, God is speaking to him about how He will exalt him in the eyes of all Israel (Joshua 3:7); the Jordan was at flood stage (Joshua 3:15), but God was faithful and they passed through; God tells Joshua to choose 12 men from among the people, one from each tribe (Joshua 4:1-2); Joshua has an encounter with an angel, who says, "As commander of the army of the Lord I have now come;" (Joshua 5:14) he gets up early to get his tasks done (Joshua 6:12, Joshua 7:16); the walls of Jericho fall down (Joshua 6:20); Joshua is in prayer and the Lord says, "Stand up! What are you doing down on your face? Israel has sinned!" (Joshua 7:10); he faces defeat, but God keeps telling him, "Do not be afraid; do not be discouraged;"(Joshua 8:1) he learns to wait in holy ambush (Joshua 8:9); the army takes Ai (Joshua 8:28); Joshua sees the miracles of God in battle (Joshua10:10); and the list goes on!

After Joshua had been through trial, victory, and discouragement, we see him talking to his army commanders in Joshua 24.

> "Joshua said to them, 'Do not be afraid;
> do not be discouraged, be strong and courageous.'"
> Joshua 24:25

Sounds pretty familiar, huh? Sounds like Joshua was letting the comfort he had received from God overflow into the lives of others.

Years ago, when my children were small and not in school, I would take them to the park across the street from where we lived, and I would sit on the bench and let them release their energy for a couple of hours. I was going through a time where God was teaching me deep forgiveness from the inside out. I did not enjoy it. I was molested as a child, and still had hate and bitterness in my heart.

God was growing me and dealing with me. So, I brought my Bible to the park bench one day, and as I sat in the hot sun beaming down on me, God's word healed my heart. Here is what I read:

> "Praise be to God, the God of all comfort, who comforts us in all our troubles, so that we can comfort those in any trouble with the comfort we ourselves have received from God. For just as the sufferings of Christ flow over into our lives, so also through Christ our comfort overflows."
> 2 Corinthians 1:3-5

I sat in the hot sun that day and let God's comfort pour into my life. And I realized that the comfort I was receiving right then and there would now be used for God's purpose. The scripture you just read says, "Just as the sufferings of Christ flow over into our lives." In other words, His suffering flows into our life because now we can have forgiveness for our sin. In the same way, we must "let our comfort overflow." It's like a domino effect, if we will let God use us.

I cannot even count the number of times in my life from that day forward that God has used my testimony for His glory. From ladies' small groups in America, one-on-ones over coffee, hundreds of ladies in the red light districts of Kolkata, India, to thousands of people at conferences across the globe, God has used my voice to bring hope and healing to people who have been through pain. When Joshua spoke to his army commanders, he was doing the same. He had "been through it" and was letting the things he had learned from God overflow into the lives of his workers. By the way, if you have forgotten today, you are His voice, His hands, and His feet. He wants to use all you have been through, and like Joshua it will overflow into the lives of others.

Dear God,
Let the comfort I have received from you overflow into the lives of others. Help my bitterness and hate die. Help me hear your voice of comfort once again and realize that you long to use my pain for your purpose. Thank you for the countless examples in your word of people who let all they have been through grow them. I honor you today, Lord.

Teenager Trails

It's crazy how I can clean the house from top to bottom (just like spring cleaning), and within 24 hours you would never even know I cleaned! I spent the entire day yesterday getting my home spic-and-span; vacuumed every floor, mopped every floor, washed sheets, put away piles of laundry that have been building up in the laundry room, washed bathroom rugs, and the list goes on. Things that don't get done on a normal cleaning day got done yesterday. You know what it's like. After you are all finished, you sit back, take a deep breath, and feel like your life is now in order. Then you wake up! Ha. I live with two teenagers who I love with all my heart, but you know what it's like if you have teenagers, there seems to be trails left behind from where they have been.

I woke this morning all ready to face my day. My goal for this New Year is to meet with God first thing in the morning. To dig into His word, and then when I'm done share it with you. But, as I walked down the stairs there they were... trails...the trails of teenagers. Shoes everywhere, nail polish, back packs, and more piles of clothes! After all that work yesterday, I found myself distracted from my path into my office to spend time with God. I felt like Martha from the Bible in Luke 10:40!

> "Lord, don't you care that my sister has left me
> to do all the work by myself?"
> Luke 10:40

That same feeling of aggravation came over me as I looked around the living room and kitchen. Now I must say, I am very blessed to have a husband who works many hours but comes home and cooks dinner (he actually enjoys it!). He does laundry, and so on. But yesterday I did it all myself, and I kind of wanted it to last at least 48 hours. So before I could make it to my office, I found myself putting shoes where they belonged, wiping down tables, bringing things that belonged to my daughter to her room, and before I knew it I was not headed to my office anymore. Then when I finally made it in my office chair with my cup of java, I had wasted over 20 minutes. I went right to the story of Martha and Mary in the book of Luke!

The encouraging thing about this story is that even though Martha was not sitting at the feet of Jesus and listening like Mary, the Word says, "A woman named Martha opened her home to him." (Luke 10:38). Martha always seems to get the bum rap in this story. Even though she was distracted by all the work she had to do, she still opened her home to Jesus! Her heart was right in letting Him in and wanting to serve Him. But as she labored and served she got ticked at her sister for not helping at all! This was Jesus and His disciples; they were dirty, hungry, and thirsty. There was much work to be done. I have to admit, I would have wanted to be the hostess with the mostest too. And I know I would have been aggravated with my sister, just like Martha. My distraction this morning kept me from my office where I meet with God. Why do we do that like Martha? When Martha confronted Jesus and said, "Tell her to help me!" His words were:

> "Martha, Martha, you are worried about many things,
> but only one thing is needed.
> Mary has chosen what is better."
> Luke 10:41-42

I think if He said that to me I would have thrown down my cleaning supplies and sat there to sock it to 'em! After all, I know they would have been hungry and thirsty! Well, they would have had to wait! I would have let them feel their hunger!

This morning I also focused on when Jesus said, "Mary has chosen what is better. Jesus, as you know, was the most awesome example, but I wonder if any of the disciples were grumbling. They heard him talk all the time. I wonder if they were thinking, "Why doesn't Mary GET UP and help her sister? After all, we are hungry!" Or after Jesus said that, maybe they thought in their minds, "Man, why did He just say that? Now we will have to wait even longer for our drink!" I wonder what was going on in their minds as this all played out. Maybe they actually were just focused on His words?

I guess we will never know while we are still on this earth, but Jesus said it was better to sit at his feet and listen. Better not to be distracted. It takes great self-control and discipline for me to make it into my office to meet with Him in the morning. But truth be told, there are times I will fail. There are times when I will be distracted by the silly things that I think are so important... like teenager trails. So a bottle of nail polish sits on the coffee table one hour longer! What is the big deal, really? God is growing me. Don't let your service/ministry to God become a distraction! You can be ministering seven days a week and not hear from Him. Be careful, my friend. What distracts you today? What is keeping you from sitting at the Master's feet and hearing His amazing words? Teenager trails? I need to grow.

Dear God,
I pray nothing will distract me from all the words you long to speak to me. I pray I will long like Mary to put everything else aside and sit at your feet. And like Martha I will always welcome you in. Father I desire to hear all you have for me. Speak to me like never before. And even though I want to serve you, let not my service become a distraction. I honor you today.

I wrote this devotion over 5 years ago and I just had to write this now that my kids are grown and on their own. I miss their trails. Cherish the trails while you can.

January 27th

I Was Not Alone

I remember being in that "in between" time before I knew God. My boyfriend had asked me to go to a party where I knew there would be drugs and booze. My brother had become a Christian, and so I was starting to think about God and that there must be more to my life than just parties, sex, drugs and all the things that were filling my voids of pain. I'm sorry if some of you are uncomfortable reading this, but for thousands this is regular life. It was a weird time for me to be in. I was pulling away from the life I had lived and leaning toward this new peace that my brother was sharing with me. So anyway, I went to this party with my boyfriend, and I knew that night that I was not going to drink or do drugs. The party was in someone's basement, and there were so many people there. The basement was so filled with smoke, you could barely see across the room. I didn't mind that because I smoked about a pack and a half a day when they were 75 cents a pack! But, for the first time going to a party with my friends I did not drink or do drugs. I stayed in my right mind. I was only about 16, and I will never forget this night.

I sat on the floor and just watched as everyone got high and drunk. I remember thinking, "Do I act that stupid when I'm drinking and doing drugs?" For the first time ever I saw myself and I did not like what I was seeing. I sat there puffing on my cigarette with tears in my eyes. I knew a change was coming and I needed it to come soon! I was sitting there in silent pain and longing for something more! I was trying so hard to hold back the tears that were knocking at my tear duct doors! It was that night and that moment that I realized I needed the peace my brother had more than anything.

My brother and I grew up in a home where yelling was just normal. So my brother would yell at me to get off the phone or to do things around the house. But what made me want what he had was the change I saw in him. When he first became a Christian, I laughed! I said to myself, "Just another weird phase Lou is going through!" But this one stuck. For almost a year I saw major changes in his character. This love seemed to spill out onto me, and it was very strange and not what I was used to. My brother is now a pastor at an Assembly of God church in Boston and he holds more leadership in his section. That may mean nothing to you, but for me it is the grace of God. God is the one that hand-plucked us.

Even sitting in that smoke filled room with all those high people. God's call was knocking at my heart's door. He was calling me into His peace. He was calling me. ME, the one sitting there chain smoking. I could feel it. I could hear His call. I will never forget it. For those of you who do not know God and someone has given you this book, please know today it does not matter what you have been through, what you have done, or what someone has done to you.

"There is a God in Heaven."
Daniel 2:28

I am living proof today that in my darkness, wanting to kill myself, and chain smoking that night, there was a God longing for me to come to Him in the state I was in. He had a purpose for my life. I was just blinded to it until that night. He is knocking at your heart's door and I plead with you to run to Him! Seek out Christians who actually live what they preach. Plug into a church that preaches the Word of God.

"Faith comes from hearing and hearing by the Word of God."
Romans 10:17

This scripture in Romans promises that if you read the Word or hear the Word, your faith will be increased. Plug in somewhere if you want to get to know God. It takes us moving toward Him for a relationship to happen. I thank God for that night; in my darkness He moved toward me and I heard His call. What an amazing God that could love me the way I was. He loves you right where you are today. I beg you to turn to Him. You will NOT be disappointed my friend. If you already know Him I ask today that you remember where you came from. Remember His amazing grace and never forget it. He was with me in that smoke filled room that night; I was not alone.

Dear God,
I thank you for being with me at all times, even before I knew you. I thank you for watching out for me and protecting me from so much danger. I thank you for coming near to me even as I did the sinful things I did. You are an amazing God of grace and I owe everything to you. I thank you for using my life story now to touch the lives of others. I honor you today.

Life is Life

I was a teenager when I first noticed there were lumps in my breast. My mother was a nurse in Delmar, NY and I went right to her with my problem. Sure enough, I had three large tumors that were not noticeable from the outside but you could feel them. I went to a surgeon and at the age of 16, had to have full blown breast surgery on both sides. This was the prime of my life and I was scared. I wish I had my hope in Christ back then. I had major breast surgery before my junior year of high school. Back then they did not do small biopsies. They took it all at once. I was told as a teenager I would never be able to breast feed. And if I did there would be possible problems. Not sure what kept me going that year, but I was the vice president of my junior class, and very plugged in to most everyone and everything.

Through the years there has been problem after problem in that area; surgery after surgery, biopsy after biopsy. Not one time was it cancer. Thank God. Just tumors. I had two children and breast fed for three months-- with problems, but I did it. Every single time I prayed that God would heal me so I would not have to go through waiting for results again or surgery. But back then I was never healed.

Many years ago, we moved to Cape Cod and there were bad symptoms again. The center on the Cape said due to my long history, I should enter a program at the Dana-Farber Cancer Institute in Boston called Risk and Prevention. There is a large committee that sits with your case. Normally, only those who have had a cancer cell get accepted to the program. One month after sending my application in and my doctor recommending me, I got a letter saying I was in! Now I would be seen by the best of the best. I was in great care. I was told at the center on the Cape that things were very bad but when I got to Dana-Farber they said, "No big deal, we see this all the time." I was in the best care and God had opened the door for me. I still go there till this day.

11 years ago, I was told by my doctor at Dana-Farber that I had two more tumors. They are the kind of tumors that do not shrink. I was told to come back in six months for more pictures, because they wanted to keep watch over them. I will never forget the call. I was in the middle of shopping when my doctor called and told me that the two tumors that I had were totally gone. Her exact words were, "I have no way to explain this to you, because there is no way this could happen, but they are gone." So in the middle of the store I was in, I took ten minutes and told her I believed that God can still heal and that I had hundreds of people praying for me. God waited until I was with one of the best breast surgeons in all of Boston before I was healed. Why? Maybe so she could

hear about God? Who knows. Only God can know these things. Oh, how great it would be if there was never a trial in life. But she saw a firsthand miracle.

Have you ever read the book of Job in the Bible? If you have been through hard things in life, you need to read this book in the Old Testament. If there is one major thing I have learned from this book, it's that nothing happens to you unless it has already passed through the hands of Christ. Do you know that satan cannot touch you unless he asks permission from God? When you read the first chapter of the book of Job you will see an example of satan roaming through the earth looking for someone to hurt, then he comes to see God along with the angels (Job 1: 6-7).Here is what the Bible says:

> The Lord Himself said to satan, "Have you considered my servant Job? There is no one on earth like him; he is blameless and upright, a man who fears God and shuns evil."
> Job 1:8

WHAT?! At first this did not make any sense to me. The enemy got permission to hurt him, but not kill him.

Now it's important to remember there are three things that will hurt you in life: You, the enemy, and others. You and others are NOT God's fault. God does not make people hurt other people. He gave humans their own free will. His heart is broken when He sees this.

Why do bad things happen to good people? Possibly because God has more faith in us then we have in ourselves? I have learned that if none of the bad things in life ever happened to me, some tests God allowed, I would not be the witness that I am today. Job kept his faith but at times was weary. In the end God blessed him with much more than he had, but he still had pain from the past. There is a reason God gives us our memory bank. Sometimes our memory bank has real life scars attached.

At the end of Job we see he had grown children again, so much time had passed. In Job 42:11 it says:

> "All his brothers and sisters and
> everyone who had known him before
> came and ate with him in his house.
> They comforted and consoled him
> over all the trouble the Lord
> had brought upon him."
> Job 42:11

So much time passes and he has more than he did before, but yet they are comforting him. His life would still would never be the same. The kids he loved before, that were killed, could never be replaced by new ones. Life is hard. Life is life.

Doesn't seem fair sometimes does it? I always turn to Job 1:8 when I'm discouraged, and remember He must have faith in me and want me to learn something through my trial. Ecclesiastes tells us there is a time and season for everything,

> "...a time to weep and a time to laugh,
> a time to mourn and a time to dance."
> Ecclesiastes 3:4

Sometimes He chooses to heal, and sometimes He lets us walk through it. Hard times will always be. But it is so much better when you are walking with God.

Dear God,
Help me through this trial. Help me to remember Job 1:8 and that you must have more faith in me than I have in myself right now. I need your strength, help, and power to encourage my heart once again. Only with you by my side can I make it. I honor you today.

God's Perfect Bit

Taming the tongue takes self control, which is one piece of evidence that God's spirit is living within you.

> "But the fruit of the Spirit is love, joy,
> peace, patience, kindness, goodness,
> faithfulness, gentleness and self-control."
> Galatians 5:22

In James 3: 1-12 it shows how very dangerous our tongue can be if not used wisely. This whole chapter is wonderful and full of wisdom. It compares the taming of the tongue to a horse's bit and a ship's very small rudder.

> "When we put bits into the mouths of horses to make them obey us, we can turn the whole animal. Or take ships as an example. Although they are so large and are driven by strong winds, they are steered by a very small rudder wherever the pilot wants to go. Likewise the tongue is a small part of the body, but it makes great boasts. Consider what a great forest is set on fire by a small spark."
> James 3:3-5

When I was a 12-year-old girl I would go horse back riding; Bud's Bill was his name. I was not an English rider but a Western rider. I remember the first time I lost control of my horse. We were all in the barn and going in a circle from one end of the barn to another. We were bareback. Somehow Bud's got spooked and started running. He ran right out the barn door. I dug my heels into him but he was going wild. Then I pulled on his bit, his front legs went high into the air and I grabbed onto his neck for dear life! It was then that two workers grabbed his rein and I was safe. I will never forget the fear of that moment; if he would have kept running I would have been in trouble.

There is something amazing about a bit and how it controls a horse. A bit creates unity between the rider's wishes and the horse's performance. Somewhat like our walk with God. He is the rider, and how are we performing? Does He have to pull on the bit?

A bit is a straight or curved metal bar that goes in the horse's mouth. It presses on the tongue and applies pressure to the bars in the horse's mouth so it pretty much hurts! That's why the horse is obedient when the bit is pulled. Our bits get pulled through hard times. We call them trials. These times hurt, but they pull us back to God in one form or another.

The cool thing about bits is that you need the perfect one! Every horse's bit is a different size. It's imperative to get the right size and shape bit. If a bit is too thin for a horse, it puts too much pressure on the area and can actually hurt the horse permanently.

Here is where I want you to really listen; God knows the exact size of bit you need to get you back to where you belong with Him. It will be a perfect size for you. It will be exactly what you need. Always remember that when going through your trial.

Riders who know what they are doing only need to use their seat and legs to guide the horse. The bit is only used when needed. God gives us many chances to do the right thing by using His seat and legs to guide us, but hopefully when the bit is used we get the picture! I know that the many times I have been through hardship it was in those times that I grew the most.

James 3:6 says our tongue can be a fire, "a world of evil among the parts of the body. It corrupts the whole person." That is, if you let it.

"With the tongue we praise our Lord and Father, and with it we curse men, who have been made in God's likeness. Out of the same mouth come praise and cursing."
James 3:9-10

All that to say, are you taming your tongue? Are you helping or hurting with your words? Are you quick to be angry? So much so that you are not hearing what people are trying to say to you, but you are only hearing what you want to hear?

Are you hearing what God wants you to hear? God has an amazing way of teaching and drawing us closer. It's God's perfect bit; perfect placement, perfect shape, and perfect size. It gets us right where we need to be. Are you applying wisdom from mentors and leadership to your life? Or are you too proud for that?

"But the wisdom that comes from Heaven is first of all pure; then peace-loving, considerate, submissive, full of mercy and good fruit, impartial and sincere. Peacemakers who sow in peace raise a harvest of righteousness."
James 3:17

I have learned to love God's perfect bit. There are many times I need it.

Dear God,
Help me to learn to control my tongue. Help me to think before I speak. Help me to use wisdom with every word that comes out of my mouth. When leadership or mentors give me wisdom, help me to apply it so it may be life changing for me. Help me to be humble. I honor you today.

January 30th

Practice Your Casting

My husband and I rented homes for 12 years before we purchased our first home. My kids were young when we bought it. We were senior pastors at a church in Falmouth, MA on Cape Cod. The first time my mother walked into the house we were going to buy, her words were, "Your going to buy this?" Ha. I looked past the hole in the floor without the tile, the peeling wall paper, the mud all over the lawn where there should be grass, the mold in the bathroom and so on. I saw something much more-- potential--not to mention very, very hard work.

The house was an old 1900s farm house. Set back in the woods on half an acre. It was very private and to us, a little piece of Heaven. To make things better it was right across the street from the Cape Cod Canal. This is the body of water that runs from the Borne Bridge to the Sagamore Bridge— the only two ways to get onto the Cape. My husband was in his glory. He is a fisherman. Whenever I could not find him I did not even have to think, I knew exactly where he was.

We had a fruit tree in the yard and a beautiful giant buck that would come to visit it almost every day when the weather was right. One time we had guests over for a clam steam and right in the middle of dinner our amazing buck walked right into the yard, looked at all of us, and froze there for like five minutes before running out of the yard. Talk about dining entertainment! It was the most amazing thing that has ever happened at any dinner party I ever had. I loved it there. Sometimes the field mice would drive me crazy when the snow would fly but our cats usually took good care of them.

Within 90 days our home jumped $100,000 due to all the work we did. We gutted the bathroom, put down the tile; friends helped pull the wallpaper down, my husband grew a thick layer of beautiful grass. There was a nasty barn on the land that we painted white, added shutters and made it look happy to the eye. Planted flowers, painted, knocked down walls; we worked very hard for those nine months and it paid off.

Nothing compared to that walk across the street to the Cape Cod Canal. Nothing. Sometimes Guy and I would take our coffee and just sit there in the morning, always bringing his pole of course. We had an agreement with the neighbors; they let us walk across their land where their mansion was to get to the water. There were good people all around. We were on the Sagamore side of the canal so we had a perfect view of the bridge, it was just amazing. One time while fishing with his dad, my husband saw a giant shark come up out of the water and go back down with a big splash. They yelled and screamed for my mother in-law and me, but we were too late. When we ran to them their hearts were pounding and they were so excited. I told my husband after that day, "I DON'T want you wading out in that water anymore!" Ha. Sometimes the sharks and whales would somehow get into the canal at high tide.

I will never forget the day that my line got caught; I had to wait 20 minutes before Guy could come to where I was to unhook me from the seaweed. When my line finally came in there was a beautiful three-pound lobster that would not let go of my hook! I took that puppy, put it in my bucket, and told Guy I was done fishing for the day! We had lobster a couple hours later! It was an amazing life there across the street from the water. I met God there in a powerful way.

The water of the canal is not still. It's always moving. It's a quick tide. My husband knew the tide chart like the back of his hand. He knew exactly where and when to get the fish. We saved a lot of money on food when we lived there. The sea bass were giant. I learned how to cast in quick water. I have to say I stink at it, but I never stopped trying. My husband would cast his line out and, I'm not kidding, it went at least half way across the canal! He was an amazing caster. I would cast, and my line would not even make it a quarter of the way across! Sometimes it would plop 12 feet in front of me. So I would try and try again in the quick moving water to get my line out. You did not have much time when you did make it out. The water would carry your line so quick you needed to get it just right. My poor husband would rescue my line time and time again. I know he must have taken a deep breath every time I said, "Oh, I want to come too!" Most the time I brought my coffee and watched him do his art. I would watch and pray, I loved that almost just as much as I loved fishing.

The Word of God says:

> "Cast all your cares on Him for He cares for you."
> 1 Peter 5:7(NKJV)

God wants to take your stress and anxiety off of you. He told us to cast our cares on Him. The problem is that most of us go to God or an altar at church, stay for a few minutes, get up and instead of leaving our cares and anxiety's with Him we pick it back up and take it with us. If there was one thing I learned living near the canal, it's that you need to practice your casting! It's the same with God. We need to keep casting and casting and casting over and over again until we finally leave it there with Him! The problem is it's much easier to take it with us than to sit and give it to God. It takes work to actually let go of it.

I found through time as we lived at that farm house my casting got better and better the more I did it. Your casting of your cares on Him will get better and better the more you do it. Then one day you will realize it's gone. You will walk away with a perfect peace from God. It's time to practice your casting. I've learned it's an art.

Dear God,

Thank you for lessons we learn in everyday life. Thank you for beauty where you can speak to us just by what we see. Sometimes in life you take my breath away. I thank you for that. Most of all I thank you for the lessons I have learned through the years in life– the easy ones and the very hard ones. I honor you today.

The Table

I sat at my dear friend's funeral, my heat broken that we did not have more time together. She had lived her years so happy. Bert was a pastor's wife; we met at a pastor's wife retreat one year, three months after her husband, Jack, died. No one there would talk about Jack, but because I did not know him one night at the retreat I asked her about him. She loved to talk about Jack, the love of her life. That night we sat for about three hours into the night as she told me story after story of their life and ministry together. Bert and I had a connection I guess you could say. That night turned into a friendship that turned into her mentoring me. She was a picture of class. I wanted to be her when I grew up

I would go to Bert's house and everything was perfect right down to dog food in a crystal bowl! I would sit for hours at her beautiful dining room table as she would share the joys and hardships of ministry life. I soaked it all in. Hundreds of missionaries, guest speakers, people she mentored, and friends sat around that table just like me. Even some famous people. Her table was always perfect, always a place of meeting, and connecting. I know she loved our friendship and she would always say, "Jack would have loved you, Tana."

Her daughter called me two weeks before she died to tell me that she wanted to talk to me. I took the ride to her home and had my last visit with her in her hospice bed. It was so hard for me to see my mentor and friend in such pain. We had a wonderful visit. Her very last words to me were, "Jack would have loved you, Tana." Then she closed her eyes and went back to sleep. Someday I will see them again and we will sit at that big table in Heaven together!

Soon after Bert died, her daughter called me and asked if I wanted her dining set. I took the table. There were so many memories around that table that I could not help it. I already had a table, but hers also matched my hutch and had great value to me in my heart. For years now my family has sat around Bert's table.

It was 2004 when I was asked to fly to Tampa, FL to do a women's retreat called "Healed, Restored and Ready" for my dear friend Deanna Shrodes. I was told I would land, and a couple would pick me up. I was told they were older and used to live in southern New England where I live. I looked for them and we found one another. We made conversation and small talk on the long ride to the retreat center but then Judy asked me if I knew Bert and Jack! I could not believe it! She knew my Bert! We started swapping stories! Then I said, "Yes, and her dining table is in my dining room right now." Silence. I had never heard silence so loud. Then all of a sudden this lady who I hardly knew starts crying. I just sat there thinking, "Yikes, what did I say?"

She turned around and told me that years ago her and her husband had a new dining room table and God told them to give it to a ministry couple. After praying about it they gave their dining room table to Bert and Jack. I think we were all in some sort of shock! Could it be that their dining table made it into my dining room and now they were picking me up at an airport hundreds of miles away from my home? I know it's the craziest thing ever, but it's a true story. Judy told me that she has pictures of her kids as babies around my dining room table.

I call these things divine appointments. There is just no other way to explain how something like that can happen. We were just supposed to meet, that's all. God had a plan, on His time frame. But it did confirm in my heart that I was supposed to be there that weekend to speak! All that to say, there is an appointed time for everything, friend, everything. God knew right there at that moment a twilight zone feeling would come over all three of us souls on our way to a retreat. It was one of the most amazing moments of my life. God always seems to have a way of letting you know you are walking in the right direction. Don't forget that today.

> "There is a time for everything,
> and a season for every activity under Heaven"
> Ecclesiastes 3:1

His promise says this:

> "In all your ways acknowledge him, and he will direct your paths."
> Proverbs 3:6

I have found this to be so true in life. Do you trust that He has your life in full control today? When you don't, I pray you never forget this faith story. The song Bert wanted sung at her funeral was an old hymn called "Come to the Table." She loved her table. Although it has digs in it and color stains that were not put on right by her. I love my table. And Judy and Mel loved their table. But the Lord told them to give it away years ago so it would go to my mentor, then sit in my house. God is in control my friend.

Dear God,
How amazing are you, O Lord? I continue to see your hand on my life and my family's life. You have given me so many faith stories. God, I pray for this reader right now. Increase their faith to know you have everything under control right at this very moment. You prepare and you plan years in advance. I honor you today, Lord.

February

February 1st

My Son's Life

"Be **self-controlled** and **alert**. Your enemy the devil prowls around like a roaring lion looking for someone to devour. **Resist him, standing firm in the faith!**"
1 Peter 5:8-9

Self control means don't eat the entire pack of cookies! Know when to stop with the chips! When you take your clothes off do not put them on the floor...hang them! Make that time every day to read the Word of God and pray.

Alert means don't get too over tired! Make sure you use your time wisely. Get your rest! Keep yourself sober. Here is where I will probably not make any friends: Years ago on watchtowers, like we would see in The Lord of the Rings movies, they would NEVER EVER put anyone who had been drinking on watch. Whoever the watchman was had to be totally sober! He had to be the one listening for the hoof beats of oncoming danger from the enemy! It's the same with our spiritual life. You get tipsy my friend, and the evil one can have a foot in the door. Be alert! And not distracted in any way.

Now let's look at the end of that scripture in 1 Peter: **Resist him** (the evil one). When temptation comes your way, do you fall into it or do you turn away and like Joseph run?

"**Resist the devil**, and he will flee from you.
Come near to God and he will come near to you."
James 4:7-8

Our promise from God is that if we walk away from temptation or evil, the evil one will have to flee! I have experienced this first hand and it works.

1 Peter also says, "Stand firm in the faith." For those of you who do not believe there is a spiritual battle going on in our world today, you are so very wrong.

I woke one night and got up to pray, it was about 2am. I felt like my son's life was in danger. The first thing I did was go to his room and make sure he was okay and safe. He was there sleeping away and looked very happy. I could not understand this feeling I had. Now I know it was the Holy Spirit's prompting. I went up to pray and read the Word. I knew I had to stand firm in the faith and begin to pray that God would protect him. I prayed against temptation in his teenage life, I prayed against the devil hurting him physically in any way. I prayed against everything I could think of. I felt as if I was in a battle.

And just a side note here, I'm glad I don't drink anymore. If I did, I wonder if I might have had a hangover and not been able to hear from the Lord on this.

That's just a thought for those who are still struggling with drinking. God gives parents to be watchmen over their children's lives.

Anyway, the feeling was very strong that I was in a battle for my own son. I did not understand it, and when I was done I went back to bed. I woke the next morning with the same feeling. I just kept praying. This experience actually changed the way I pray for my kids to this day.

Less than one week later my son and daughter were invited to their friend's pool party. My son had a three-hour band practice before hand, so he ended up going to the pool party a little late. By the time he got there the kids were inside watching a movie together. They were all finished swimming. Jon was hot and sweaty due to drumming for three hours so he desired to get into the water. It was 9:00 at night. My son asked one of his friends to go out in the back yard with him. My son opened the sliding door, started running, and took a head first dive into the middle of the pool. Jonathan did not know that they had pulled the pool cover across the pool. It was dark and he could not see it.

In his own words: "I knew there was something wrong. I was in trouble. The cover sucked in around me, pulling me down. I began to pray. Somehow I was able to turn myself so my head was out of the water, but I could not move because of the pool cover. Tom reached out his hand and pulled me to the side of the pool." Well, as a mother hearing this from my shook-up kid when he got home, I was a mess! I had not told Jon that just a week before I was feeling like the enemy was going to try and hurt him. I could not believe what I was hearing.

This is the wonderful thing about walking with God. He will guard us and keep us safe. He will speak to us and guide us in every step and He will warn us of danger.

I believe with all my heart that God spoke to me to begin to pray against the devil's scheme toward my son that month.

What if I had not been a sober person? What if I was not walking with God? What if I was not standing firm and alert? As a parent, we have a responsibility to be watchmen over our kids. There will be times God wants to speak to you about them and their walk in life. Are you listening today? It's not up to the priest or minister to warn you. This is your walk with God. Are you resisting the enemy and pressing into God yourself?

Yes that scripture in James 4:7-8 says if we resist the devil will flee, but it also says:

> "Come near to God and He will come near to you."

Maybe it's time today to get a little closer to the one who made you. To hear His voice like John 10:27 talks about. In my case it meant my son's life.

Dear God,
Help me to always be on guard. Help me to always be alert and ready for everything the enemy might try to hurl at me and my family. Help me to know how to fight back with your Word and through prayer. You are a mighty God who directs and protects. I honor you today.

February 2nd

Thirsty?

The Bible says in Ecclesiastes that when:

"Desire no longer is stirred, then man goes
to his eternal home and mourners go about the streets."
Ecclesiastes 12:5

For some reason this scripture hits me hard today. If it says that desire is no longer stirred on our death bed then that must mean while we are living there must be desire being stirred! The sad thing is, there are countless people living with no desire. With no visions, hopes, or dreams, they are like stagnant waters. I have been around some stagnant water, and if there is one thing I remember about stagnant water, it actually smells bad. It stinks. Are you stagnant today? Is there any desire being stirred in your mind, heart, and life? If anything, there should be a desire to get to know God. Sitting in my office this morning and listening to one of my favorite worship singers online and reading scriptures like:

"Therefore, stand in awe of God."
Ecclesiastes 5:7

I think, "How can anyone get stagnant?" I have been through hard times just as much as the next guy. But it will not stop my desire to get to know the God who created the universe, who made the human body to function, and who has every hair on my head counted.

"Indeed, the very hairs of your head are all numbered.
Don't be afraid; you are worth more than many sparrows."
Luke 12:6-7

I have to hear from Him, I have to know Him, I have to feel His presence. If someone put a glass of clear, clean, fresh water in front of you, and a glass of stagnant water in front of you, which one would you drink? God desires for us to live in moving, fresh water and to have dreams and desires that seem out of our reach. This is when we live by faith. What are you doing today to get yourself moving? Are you truly thirsty?

I know when I jump into a fresh, cold body of water it does a number of things to me. If I feel unclean due to sweat, then when I get out, I feel clean. If I feel tired and I'm dragging, when I get out I feel alive and it wakes me up! I say to you all today: JUMP IN! Get thirsty! God is longing, waiting, and desiring to speak to your heart today. He promises to guide you and to lead you. Why would we not want to know what the Almighty God wants? Why would we not want to sit with Him? You can! He's there. He has not left you due to your sin. He is there just waiting for you to turn back to Him. Don't miss this opportunity. Call out to Him and talk to Him just like you would talk to a friend. He knows you better than you know yourself.

This morning in my kitchen there was a lady bug. It's February! When you look out my kitchen window there is snow on the ground. If I let that little lady bug outside, it would die in just an hour. But there is some sort of drive in this little bug that is making it actually stay alive today. The truth is it's thirsty. It's looking for water. Clean, clear, fresh water. I did not see one other bug anywhere. During this last summer I had like 20 ladybugs in my kitchen! Today, it's the only one left, all alone. It was so close to the kitchen faucet. It's so thirsty that it's still alive.

"I thirst for God, the living God."
Psalm 42:2

Are you thirsty today?

Dear God,
Make us thirsty. Make us so thirsty that we have a will to live even in the hardest circumstances; when we feel so alone. You are there. Make us thirsty! Wake us up and wash us clean. Help us NOT to put other things before you, Lord. I honor you today.

Grandpa LeFevre

On my mother's side of the family all four grandchildren are Christians. We all love the Lord and try to serve Him the best we can. We had a grandfather who was one of the most incredible examples of marital love I have ever witnessed. My grandmother got Alzheimer's disease at a young age, and I can remember the horrors grandpa lived with. One time, Grandma left the water on in the bathtub and forgot about it. The entire house flooded. She would ask us kids the same questions over and over. It got to the point that Grandma had to go into the nursing home. My mother was the head nurse on the wing with my grandmother. It was so hard. There were times when my mom would walk into her room with my grandfather and my grandmother would think her own daughter was having an affair with her husband. It was heart breaking, as many of you already know. It's a heartbreaking disease.

This did not stop my grandfather; he loved her with a love that was just amazing. Every single day he made his way to that nursing home. I remember as a young adult going to visit and the sights and smells were so hard. But he loved her, in sickness and in health. Grandpa loved her right through her passing. He was just amazing.

The day before my wedding, June 3, 1989, my mother got a phone call from the doctor who had just seen my grandfather. We were all at our house in New York waiting for my husband's family for our wedding rehearsal and rehearsal dinner. I was so excited, the decorations were up, and this was the happiest time of my life. All of a sudden, my mother got off the phone, ran to the bathroom, slammed the door, and started to vomit. The doctor had told my mom that her dad had two weeks to live. The mood changed in an instant. It was so hard to be happy and celebrate knowing that Grandpa, who we all loved, had two weeks to live. I was going on a two-week honeymoon! Grandpa ended up living four weeks, and then he died.

He was a wonderful man. I will never forget his love for my grandmother through the loss of her mind. It takes a very special person to be able to do that. For years he went to visit her, and he never ever had a date with anyone else. It was only Grandma for him.

Many years after his death, I took a trip to Arizona. My mom told me before I went that she wanted me to "hook up" with my grandfather's sister, who I had never met before. So I called her and we made plans to meet in Arizona. After all, we had a common interest: my grandpa. The day arrived and we finally met. As we were talking, I noticed that every single time I mentioned my grandmother she would freeze up, get unpleasant, and stop talking. It was very strange. Because I did not know her, and I'm a pretty bold person anyway, I asked her, "Why is it that every time I mention my grandmother you get angry?" These where her exact words to me: "Your grandfather had a call on his life to be a minister. When he met Virginia (my grandmother) he walked away from the call God had on his life."

I sat in total shock.

My brother and I are both ordained ministers. My cousins Jeff and Eric, who are brothers, are both also involved in ministry. All four of us are. I always wondered how we all came to know the Lord when there was not one other person on the face of the earth praying for us. We all became followers of God at young ages. I always wondered why, until she told me that my grandpa had the call of God on his life. This is something I never even knew about.

Right at that moment I knew that he walked away from the call of God due to a deep love he had for my grandmother. But at the same time he began to pray for his four grandchildren. What I would give to know what he prayed! Possibly for the call of God to hit all four of his grandkids? I don't know. All four of us are active in ministry. We eat, sleep, and live for God. We all have the call of God on our lives. I know today with all my heart that it's because of Grandpa LeFevre. God heard his prayers, God sent people even after he died to minister to my brother and I and my two cousins.

Friend I want you to know today, God is hearing your prayers. It may be after you are dead and gone that the answer may come, like in my grandpa's case, but God still hears your prayers. Never stop praying. Never! I wish he had time to see all four of us serving the Lord. I wish he had time to see his seven great-grandchildren serving the Lord. I wish I could thank him for his prayers.

"The prayer of a righteous man is powerful and effective."
James 5:16

"God has surely listened and heard my voice in prayer."
Psalm 66:19

It would be great if we saw answers to our prayers right away, wouldn't it? But this is not always the way God works. I'm living proof.

Dear God,
I thank you that you hear our prayers. I thank you for someone praying for me. I pray you help me to draw nearer to you every day of my life. To never give up hope on anyone or anything. But that I will just keep praying. I honor you today.

Stop Whining!

"As he went along, he saw a man blind from birth. His disciples asked him, 'Rabbi, who sinned this man or his parents that he was born blind?' 'Neither this man nor his parents sinned,' said Jesus, 'but this happened so that the work of God might be displayed in his life.'
John 9:17

Hmmmm, this is a very interesting scripture, isn't it? Why are people born with disabilities? Why do I suffer with sugar issues day after day? Sometimes I wake and only my husband knows how hard it is for me to just get moving in the morning. Not one person out there would ever know what I go through, only Guy. My poor husband, when I get needy I go to him! I never complain to others or use my physical issues as an excuse! As long as these two legs keep moving I'm moving forward!

This man was born blind and somehow his disciples automatically think he has done something wrong, some sort of sin or short coming. But NOT SO! Jesus makes a giant statement here: "This happened so that the work of God might be displayed in his life."

When I see people who live without a limb, or who are blind, or who suffer day after day with cancer and still have a smile, I am just so inspired by their will to go on and on. Many of you may remember Joni Eareckson Tada, a woman who loves God and was paralyzed from the waste down in a diving accident.. Joni reached more people in that wheel chair for the glory of God than she ever reached while she was walking. She would paint with her mouth and her paintings became world-famous.

Or how about Bethany Hamilton? This beautiful teenager had her arm bitten off by a shark and still surfs the water with a smile on her face. There is just something about someone who can still live a happy life and be content with a disability or disease. 4 years ago my insulin delay took me by surprise and I am bound and determined to move forward through my daily diet and checking my sugar. If God chooses to heal me, great! But if he does not, I will move forward anyway!

One thing I love about this scripture in John 9 is that Jesus tests this blind man's obedience. He puts mud on his eyes and tells him to go wash in a specific pool.

"'Wash in the Pool of Siloam.'" So the man went and washed, and came home seeing."
John 9:7

I wonder if the man would have been healed if he had gone to another pool to wash. Why didn't Jesus have pity on him and just wipe the mud away himself, and then the man would see right then and there? Because I believe Jesus knows that even people with disabilities and diseases can have a back bone if they want to! They can have just as much drive and passion about something as anyone else! It is that person that has to make the choice!

That blind man could have said, "But why? Lord you know I can't make it to the Pool alone! Can't you walk with me and help me!" But he did NOT! The Bible says:

"So the man went!"
John 9:7

He got moving without whining! Because of his obedience, drive, and passion he was healed!

How about you today? Are you whining?

You know how aggravating it can be when the child you love with all your heart is whining and whining! Think about God's ears.

Whatever you are going through today, it's time to stop whining and start moving! God wants to use you to change the world, and the sooner you realize that the sooner lives can be changed.

I live with symptoms, and unless God heals me, I will always live with frustrating symptoms. I will not whine. I will move forward.

That is a choice.
That is YOUR choice!

Dear God,
Help me not to whine. Help me to know that no matter what hurts, no matter my disability or disease that you want to use me in a powerful way. You long to use my life as a testimony of your grace. Even if I cannot move, I can change the world through prayer. God help me to have a passion for all you have for me. I honor you today.

February 5th

Let Him

I remember as a young adult in high school my very favorite classes to go to were my art classes: sewing, painting, wood shop, and pottery. Anything I could make with my hands I was excited about. I loved pottery more than anything. I was horrible on the wheel, but I loved to prepare the clay. Four at a time we would go into the back room and slap the clay. Slapping the clay was a process that the clay went through before the potter could mold it. If the air bubbles were not slapped out of the clay, then the pot would not form correctly and it could explode while in the kiln. We had to split our piece of clay in two, lift it up, and slap the two pieces together; the air bubbles and junk would hit the slapping wall in front of us. It was just a mess in that room. I remember how dirty and chalky I was after pottery class. I remember our shoes would be a mess when we left the slapping room.

But it was fun. I loved it. Just slap, slap, slap. There was just something about it that made me happy. I was perfecting the clay. I loved the feel of it; the fun of being back there with friends and the mess. I guess all teens love messes! And co-ed situations! Ha.

I wish it was that fun when the Lord tries to perfect us. But it's not. It does not bring great joy to my heart when I go through a trial. Most the time it hurts. I call it pruning. We all prune our plants, trees, and bushes because we know if we do they will come up better and grow bigger than ever before. But when it happens to us, we hate every minute.

Truth be told, He cannot mold us into the beautiful masterpiece He desires unless He prepares us first.

"O Lord, you are our Father.
We are the clay, you are the potter; we are all the work of your hand."
Isaiah 6:48

Preparation takes time. In the Book of Jeremiah, we see Jeremiah watching the potter work on his wheel. The pot he was shaping was marred.

"So I went down to the potter's house, and I saw him working at the wheel. But the pot he was shaping from the clay was marred in his hands; so the potter formed it into another pot shaping it as seemed best to him."
Jeremiah 18:3-4

When looking up the word marred in the dictionary it says "damaged, imperfect, disfigured." I think at one point or another we are all damaged, imperfect, and disfigured! Anyway it was marred.

"So the potter formed **IT** into another pot."
Jeremiah 18:4

I love this. The potter did NOT throw it out and grab a new piece of clay just because it was damaged, disfigured and imperfect! He took **it**, crushed **it** back into a ball, and started forming **it** again! When I used to work the wheel I did this time and time again! I stunk at the wheel. Almost everything I did was disfigured! Usually I ended up throwing the piece of clay out because I had crushed it and formed it so many times that the air bubbles got back into it and it could not be used. God is the Master Potter. He will only crush and reform when needed.

Friend, we are the clay today. The question is: are you willing to let him slap the junk out of you? I don't mean that in an abusive way. I'm talking about the Lord's pruning in our lives. Sometimes it can hurt. But He will NEVER throw us away. He is gentle and loving. He will continue to reform us and make us:

"As seems best to Him."
Jeremiah 18:4

Best to Him is not always best to us. But His promise is:

"I will bind up the injured and strengthen the weak."
Ezekiel 34:16

Sometimes the only way He can do this is by reforming us. If our sides are too weak and our clay is worn, He will crush us and make our clay walls stronger.

Let Him.
In the end we are beautiful.

Dear God,
Crush me; get all the imperfections out of me, please. I am weak, Lord. Make me strong today. Do what you have to do. Through it help me to stay joyful, strong, and help me to keep my praise on. I honor you today, Lord.

February 6th

Dry Bones
"A cheerful heart is good medicine,
but a crushed spirit dries up the bones."
Proverbs 17:22

This is such a picture of life.

We go through good and bad times. When I think about my own life, I know there have been times when I have had a very cheerful heart, but there have been other times when my spirit was crushed and I had a hard time moving forward. Some of those crushing times happen when we are so young, and we do not even realize that we are crushed yet.

Osteoporosis is a disease that people can get when their bones dry up and get brittle. The very interesting thing about it is when looking at symptoms of the disease, you see that most people don't even know they have it until their bones start to fracture on their own.

Do you realize you can walk around almost fractured and not even know it? This was me.

I remember at about age 13 standing at the bus stop with the girls from my street, Kaine Drive. We were all standing around smoking together before school. All of a sudden, two of the girls started joking about a man on our street who had taken them into his home molested them. I could not believe what I was hearing. Then another couple of girls shared the same thing about the same man. I finally got enough courage to share with all four of them that he had done the same to me. But unfortunately he had gotten me alone without anyone else in the room. It went on for some time as he and his wife babysat me and took care of me sometimes. All five of us stood there in shock as we realize this man was a serious pedophile as well as a college professor. Somehow finding out they had been through some pain by the same man brought me a weird sort of comfort. I had been molested by him starting at age five. For years I felt all alone, and for the first time ever I realized I was not alone. Standing at the bus stop that morning was the first time I ever told anyone except my family about what happened. Unless they had brought it up, I never would have opened my mouth.

I was walking around almost fractured and I did not even know it. That morning changed my life. It dug deep and it was not good for my emotional health. I was crushed in spirit and my bones were drying up, and I did not know how to get out of that situation. Not one person ever told me of the hope of Christ until five years later. Those 5 years were some of the hardest of my life.

94

Do you realize today how many people around you are crushed in spirit? Do you even care? The book of Proverbs says,

> "Even in laughter the heart may ache."
> Proverbs 14:13

There are countless souls walking around the earth crushed in spirit, some never even talking about it; countless fractures waiting to happen.

My sister-in-law, as a young teenage girl, told me a story one day of when she was driving down the road and she saw a girl walking. God clearly spoke to her and told her to turn the car around and tell this girl about the hope God can give. She was obedient to what the Lord told her to do. As she spoke to this girl walking on the side of the road the girl shared with her that she was on her way to commit suicide. What if my sister-in-law had never stopped?

There are countless souls walking around the earth crushed in spirit, some never even talking about it; countless fractures waiting to happen.

I was one, some of you were one. What are you going to do about it when you see someone crushed in spirit? They need the hope of Christ.

For Osteoporosis you can take supplements. Calcium and Vitamin D are used to help bone loss. They cannot increase bone density but they can help to prevent additional bone density loss.

Just like us. No person can help us to gain back what we have already lost. We will carry around memories forever. But there are things that we can do to heal our crushed spirit.

The first part of that Proverbs 17:22 says,

> "A cheerful heart is good medicine"
> Proverbs 17:22

The medicine prescribed for a crushed spirit is a cheerful heart. But how do you get a cheerful heart? First, it is good to know you are not alone. I remember feeling relieved when I found out someone else had common ground. Seek out a support group that will encourage your journey.

> "The joy of the Lord is your strength."
> Nehemiah 8:10

Joy? How do you gain the joy? By reading the Word of God! I have said it before.

> "Faith comes by hearing and hearing by the Word of God."
> Romans 10:17

You will increase your faith and joy when you hear the Word of God. Make yourself go to church. Or, how about sitting and actually picking up your Bible? Or letting your Bible App read to you on your iphone!

Today friend, I don't want you to have a crushed spirit. You might be a fracture waiting to happen.

A pencil cannot stand alone, but group it together with 20 other pencils and put a rubber band around it and it will stand on its own.

You need people; you need the Word of God. You need a cheerful heart— its good medicine.

Dear God,
Help our dry bones. Help us move forward to gain a cheerful heart. I honor you today.

Life Preaching

"How, then, can they call on the one they have not believed in? And how can they believe in the one of whom they have not heard? And how can they hear without someone preaching to them? And how can they preach unless they are sent?"

Romans 10:14-15

When most of us think of a preacher we think of a man or woman behind a pulpit in a church somewhere or maybe a person walking on the mission field. But do you realize we are all preachers? Those of us who live for God, we all have the call to share His hope and light to the world.

I have preached for over 30 years this year. I've preached to small groups of three or four, and I've preached to thousands. I have preached to people in America and in the red light districts of India. If there is one thing I have learned in this walk with God, preaching DOES NOT always mean you are behind a pulpit and have a three-point sermon.

Preaching is your life and the way you live it.

I once worked long shifts at a long term care hospital with older people that I loved. It was physically the hardest work I ever did in my life. It required a lot of physical labor. One day in particular, I came on my shift and faced one of the hardest things I had ever done. But through it, God once again grew me.

The instant I came on to the shift I knew there was something very wrong. There was a horrible stench in the air. It was one of the worst smells I have ever experienced, and in the hospital I had experienced many bad smells. The nurses were all standing in the middle of the hallway in a huddle, which was something we never saw. I walked up to the group and they were all fighting about who was going to go in and help a man who had gotten sick. His bed needed changing and he needed cleaning, with him in it. He could not use his legs so he was bed ridden.

So while all these nurses were fighting about who was going to go in and clean this poor old man, he sat in his room in his own mess. Not sure about you, but there is something wrong with that picture! After listening, I walked up to the group and told them I would do it. I could not handle the thought of this poor man in his room waiting for them!

When I walked in he was crying. He was totally embarrassed. All he kept saying was that he rang the bell over and over and no one came. I believed him because I had seen it done many times before. I assured him all was well and that we were going to take care of everything. The entire 50 minutes that I spent in that room I was holding back the gags. I did not let him know that. It was the worst. The entire bedding had to be changed, he was a mess but the bed under the sheets also needed to be cleaned. I went through about 20 pairs of gloves in that hour. We talked almost the entire time. I told him it was not his fault, and after a while I think I eased his embarrassment. I never shared a scripture with him, although I did tell him God cared about him. I did not preach a three-pointer, nor did I tell any Bible stories, but I know when I left that room that man felt the love of God through action. I had preached a sermon.

I'm going to be honest, of all the nasty things I have ever done in my life that was the very worst. I cannot even begin to express how horrible the smell was. I'm sorry, I don't mean to gross you out but it was very bad. During the uncomfortable silence I prayed. I asked God to help me make it through. I was doing it because I knew Jesus himself would have done it. Jesus would not have let that man sit like that. He would have helped him.

Anyway, like I said, it took about 50 minutes. When I was done, he thanked me like crazy. And had tears in his eyes.

That day at work was not like normal. The instant I came out of that room I had gained instant respect among my co-workers. Everyone wanted to know, "How was it?" I felt like saying, "How do you think it was? Take a whiff!" It was horrible! They let me take an extra break, they let me do pretty much what I wanted that shift. But the truth is, they saw Jesus that day. They all knew I was a minister already, but I did not have to pull out my Bible and bash it over their head. I just had to help a poor old man who was in tears and embarrassed. They had heard a great sermon. That's how very simple it is.

People can hear someone preaching to them just through action and love sometimes. Think about that. Are you preaching with your life today?

Jesus preached everywhere he went even when he was not speaking.

Dear God,
Help us to preach with our hands and feet as well as with our mouth. Let us do the things you would do no matter how hard they are. You are such an amazing example for us to follow. Thank you for the opportunities that arise almost every day of our lives. Please help us to share your love through how we live. I honor you today.

February 8th

Panda Express

I'm sitting at the Boston airport getting ready for another journey to India. We love India. I'm sitting in front of a Chinese food restaurant called Panda Express. As I sit here, I feel excited, very emotional, and just in wonder of the divine appointments that will come our way even on our journey to the land that we love. The next two weeks I will be writing on our journey, and from India.

As I sit in front of the Panda Express and wait for my awesome husband to come back with my coffee, I cannot help but think of Paul and his missionary journeys. There must have always been this sense of anticipation and excitement; never knowing exactly who or what he may encounter, or when.

"And now compelled by the Spirit, I am going to Jerusalem, not knowing what will happen to me there. I only know that in every city the Holy Spirit warns me that prison and hardships are facing me. However, I consider my life worth nothing to me, if only I may finish the race and complete the task the Lord Jesus has given me-the task of testifying to the gospel of God's grace."
Acts 20:22-24

Whenever you go to another country there are always risks, but just like Paul our hope and trust must be in Christ. Just getting on any plane going anywhere is a risk, not to mention the car ride to the airport! Our lives are in the hands of God just like Paul's life was!

On a journey like this I always pray for divine appointments that Jesus would put me near and around people that may need to hear of His hope. I take every journey very seriously and that's not just when I leave the country, that's even when I go get food for my family, go shopping, or go to the gym, that's everyday life. How about you today? Do you realize that divine appointments are all around you? This life is a grand adventure full of the unexpected. I love it.

I love how Paul starts by saying, "And now compelled by the Spirit." (Acts 20:22) This was a God-given desire he had to fully surrender to the plans God had for him. To say, "I consider my life worth nothing to me, if only I may finish the race and complete the task the Lord has given me!" (Acts 20:24) Wow, what a heart. I know that scripture challenges me and I'm sure it does you too. Our lives are His. Being fully surrendered to God and doing what He says. My husband and I have lived it for over 26 years together. Where He leads, we follow. Even on unexpected journeys. Paul knew what unexpected journeys were all about. Any time he landed in prison you still saw his faith.

"Be wise in the way you act toward outsiders;
make the most of every opportunity."
Colossians 4:5

On our journeys the people we come across should not be viewed as inconveniences, they should be viewed as opportunities. It seems as we go about our daily life in getting to the places we go, we hardly view others as opportunities. We MUST change the way we are. If we are living our life as His, we MUST remember He may have that unexpected person He wants us to talk to. Do you even care? It might mean their soul. Think about that. I'm so glad that someone cared enough to think about my soul many years ago.

So as I sit here passing this next hour in front of the Panda Express, and watch all these people walk by me at the airport, I'm so ready for this journey. Bring it on Lord!

Can you say that today? If not, ask God to help your attitude and to see the opportunities!

Dear God,
Bring it on! We are ready for all you have for us. The people, the places, the opportunities! We love you today. God, take any fear and insecurities we have and melt them away. Make us bold through the power of your Holy Spirit. I honor you today Lord.

Countless People

There is just something about being in a plane over the Atlantic, looking out of the window and seeing the clouds below you. Then landing in India and seeing hundreds of homes, cars, and fields. There are countless people. They are everywhere. You kind of get a bird's eye view of Christ looking down on the multitudes when you are up in the sky.

Now here at the London airport during a layover, I see a Jewish man with an awesome black hat and a long beard. I wish I had that hat! I see an Indian husband and wife with colorful orange and green clothing. There are sights, smells, and sounds that I'm not used to. There are so many people and so little time.

> "When He saw the crowds, He had compassion on them, because they were like a sheep without a shepherd. Then He said to His disciples, 'The harvest is plentiful but the workers are few. Ask the Lord of the harvest, therefore, to send out workers into His harvest field.'"
> Matthew 9:36-38

In just four hours we will be in India. I have to say 14 hours on a plane is not fun, unless you have the money to be in first class. We are tired, cramped, most of us have headaches from our lack of sleep, but as I sit here on the plane and look around me tears come to my eyes. Could it be that the same compassion that Jesus had when He looked at the crowds is bringing this burning to my heart?

There is a world represented in this plane: People from all over, accents that I have never heard before. Jesus said that the masses of people he was looking at were like a sheep without a shepherd. If there is one thing I know it's that when a sheep does not have a shepherd, that sheep is in danger. There is no guard over him to protect and warn him. There is no one to guide him in the right direction. The sheep wanders chasing after things.

Jesus says to his disciples that they need to pray for more workers. That is one thing I have felt in the past 24 hours as countless people pass me by. There are hundreds of people in the Hub airport of Frankfurt, Germany. All I can think of is, "Lord there is so many, how in the world are we to reach them all?"

When was the last time you prayed: "Lord, send forth workers to work for you? There are not enough of us to reach all these countless people!" My heart aches as I see people that I have never seen before and I will probably never see again just pass me by and I sit here with the hope and peace of God.

I remember my very first trip to India in 1985. I was only 19 years old on my journey alone because I felt God leading me there. For my long flight there was a Krishna man sitting next to me. I remember that night as everyone slept, he took out his beads, rolled them in his hands, and chanted for three straight hours. Although I do not believe what he believes I admired his dedication and commitment to prayer. It challenged me. If only those of us who know the living God would get a hold of prayer like that! Can you imagine if all of us would pray not caring who was around or what they thought? Praying to a mighty God that He would send forth workers! I'm telling you, lives would be changed. His prayers opened a door for me to speak with him about the hope and love of Christ. He was going to meet his wife for the first time in an arranged marriage. He wore a white outfit, kind of like hospital scrubs. A little pouch hung from his neck to his waist containing his prayer beads. I could tell he lived a very simple life.

I will never forget that man that night on the plane. His chanting and prayers for three hours changed my life forever.

Friend, there are countless souls out there right now. What are you going to do about it? Jesus wants you praying and working.

"Whoever finds his life will lose it,
and whoever loses his life for my sake will find it."
Matthew 10:39

Dear God,
Break my heart for countless souls. May I weep due to the lack of workers and the loads of work that is yet to be done. Make me bold yet gentle like you. Help me Lord to have your heart of love for those who do not know you, who wander today like lost sheep. I honor you today Lord.

Nancy O'Brien

I'm reminded today of the grace of God in my life. It took almost a year of my brother Lou asking me to come to his church before I actually went! We were in high school and he had started a Bible club. He was always carrying around his Bible and the entire school knew. Yes, my brother was the Jesus freak of Guilderland High. One day, due to my unhappiness I went with him to church. Not to mention I wanted to get him off my back! I had on short shorts, a tank top, and flip flops. I remember when I walked in I felt a little strange because most people were more dressed up. Not one person looked at me in a bad way. Not one person wondered or cared about what I had on. Truth be told, if I had gotten one negative look I would have been out that door so fast! But these people loved on me from the second they met me.

I did not realize that Alcove Church already knew me. My brother had that entire church praying for me. They were waiting for the day that Lou's totally messed up sister would walk through that door! Ha! I don't think they cared much what I had on. I know now they were rejoicing.

There was this one lady named Nancy O'Brien. She caught my eye from across the room due to her flower child nature. Her blond hair was long and hung straight down, and she had on a skirt of many tie die colors and every time the music was more upbeat she started dancing. I was intrigued by her. My boyfriend at the time was a Grateful Dead follower so I felt at home with Nancy. My boyfriend and I were always in tie die and on drugs. This lady was different. From the instant I met her she embraced me. I think she saw herself in me. From the day I met her she poured into my life. We did music together, we hung out for hours together at their home just talking. Sitting and talking, something my family only did on a rare dinner at the table sometimes. But this talking was different. It was talk about a God who cared for us. Nancy and her husband Bruce would tell us stories of before they knew God. They became my spiritual mentors.

As time went on, their daughter Kris became my very best friend and married my brother. Those days at the O'Brien home were some of the best I ever had. They were the early days in my walk with God.

"When a woman who had lived a sinful life in that town learned that Jesus was eating at the Pharisee's house, she brought an alabaster jar of perfume, and she began to wet his feet with her tears. Then she wiped them with her hair, kissed them and poured perfume on them. When the Pharisee who had invited Him saw this, he said to himself, 'If

this man were a prophet, he would know who is touching him and what kind of woman she is, that she is a sinner.'"
Luke 7:37-39

Figures, huh? Someone has to gossip about a woman who has lived a sinful life. Why do we do that? Why don't we embrace all people like Jesus himself did? The Word of God tells us to love all those who sin! This holy man did not like the fact that a sinful lady was blessing Jesus. I cannot even begin to tell you how that irks me. (Is "irks" even a word?) Anyway... this story in the Bible, every time I read it I'm reminded of the first time I walked into Alcove Church. As far as I know, no one was talking bad of me. Oh I'm sure there was a couple, I'm just glad I didn't know about it.

This scripture reminds me of Nancy, my friend who stood by my side as a spiritual mentor. She took my brother and I in as her own, to show us what the love of God was all about. The grace of God is an amazing thing my friend and I hope and pray you reach out to Him in your own way. That's all He asks of you today.

You will never be rejected by God. Never. No matter who may talk bad of you, shun you, irk you! It does not matter. Jesus is always there waiting for you. He was waiting for me and so was Nancy O'Brien. I thank God for His people and their love.

Dear God,
You are amazing and your grace is amazing. Thank you for never giving up on us. For never hurting us, for always being there when the world shuns us. I honor you today Lord.

February 11th

A Legion of Beggars

While we are here in India, we have devotionals at night with our group of about 23 people. After devotions last night we were talking about the services we will have this week. In India when people become Christians and ask Jesus into their lives, many times demons will manifest themselves and that person will be delivered. I told the team that my husband and I have a gift in this area. We feel God uses us with people who are possessed by demons. He has given us a love for these people and helps us know how to pray so they are delivered.

Maybe you have never seen this nor believe it happens but I am here to tell you today I have seen grown people picked up and thrown against walls, with not one person touching them. There is a devil who hates you and me, and he will try anything with someone who does not know the hope of Christ. If they live in sin it is an open door for the evil one. Many who are possessed and let the enemy in will cut themselves. We see this in Mark 5:5 where the man with a legion of demons cuts himself. They are living in an oppressed world and they need God's love and hope. I guess Jesus has given Guy and I love and compassion for them.

We must know that God has already won the victory! Even the devils know this. In Luke 8:30-31 it says:

"Jesus asked him, 'What is your name?' 'Legion,' he replied, because many demons had gone into him. And they begged him repeatedly not to order them to go into the Abyss."
Luke 8:30-31

This scripture cracks me up! As scary as the evil one may seem my friend he is scared of God Almighty so much so that he knows God has already won the battle. The devils are begging God to not order them into the Abyss (Hell). It says here, "They begged him repeatedly!" They were scared! If there was any sort of fight here, where the devil had any power at all, they would not be a legion of little beggars!!!! We see clearly here they are begging like little kids. They have no power over Christ, they only want to seem as though they do.

"The weapons we fight with are not the weapons of the world.
On the contrary, they have divine power to demolish strongholds."
2 Corinthians 10:4

Having demons may be a serious stronghold in your life if you are not living for God. Through God and His Word which is living and active, we have divine power to cast out demons!

In Luke chapter 8, Jesus did not wait for the demon possessed man to get saved and then deliver him. Jesus commanded the demons to come out.

"For Jesus had commanded the evil spirit to come out of the man. Many times it seized him, and though he was chained hand and foot and kept under guard, he had broken his chains and had been driven out into a solitary place."
Luke 8:29

"When they came to Jesus, they found the man from whom the demons had gone out, sitting at Jesus' feet, dressed and in his right mind; and they were afraid. Those who had seen it told the people how the demon possessed man had been cured."
Luke 8:35-36

If you have the Holy Spirit in you there is no need to fear! Jesus is stronger and greater than any legion of demons, no matter how they try to scare you!

Think of what Jesus did when He walked this earth. He healed, he raised dead people, he cast out demons, so many things yet his Word says:

"Greater things will you do in My name."
John 14:12

When He said this he was talking to those filled with the Spirit of God. Is that you today?

Are you living in fear or are you ready today to know your place? Your place is victory! Do NOT fear a legion of beggars!

Dear God,
You are so powerful, use us Lord to help set people free that they might come to know your freedom and power. They will know the hope of you. Thank you for all you did for us while you walked this earth, and thank you for your power through your name and word.

Come Walk with Me

Yesterday at a church in India we were able to meet the little girl we sponsor. We send money to her each month so she can go to school. Her mom was there. Her mother is Muslim, but is so happy her daughter— who lives in an impoverished area of Delhi— is getting educated.

We could not speak to each other unless an interpreter was there, but her words were all over her face.

Today, we went into that exact slum to a ministry they have called the Home of Hope. Hundreds of ladies from the slums came for a women's retreat that we held for them. It was so amazing. We had to walk 10 minutes into the slum in order to even get to the building. I was able to speak for one hour, and I gave my testimony of what God has done in my life. I also preached the story of Abigail in the Bible and how she did the right thing in the circumstance that she lived in.

As I was preaching, there she was— the mother of my sponsor child, sitting on the floor with the other ladies in the third row. When our eyes locked, her smile was so big. I could not believe she was there. Usually Muslim men will not let their wives go to things like that when they know they are Christianity-based, but due to the blessings we have given their family, I think his heart was touched enough to let her come. The joy of the Lord filled me as I saw her smile.

I wish so bad I could take you all for that 10 minute walk to the Home of Hope I would give anything to let every person in the world experience it. The slum of Delhi is so big; it just keeps going on and on and on. The poorest of the poor live there. The sights and smells are amazing, and the bulls and cows that walk around everywhere are considered holy.

> "As for me, I am poor and needy,
> yet the Lord is thinking of me right now."
> Psalm 40:17

Most people in America would respond to this scripture by asking God why He would allow such a place. While we pick out beautiful floors for our homes, these people have dirt and mud for their floor. One lady brought her baby to the retreat, whose hand and arm had been badly burned. I have never seen a burn so bad in all my life. She had the babies hand and arm wrapped in a dirty rag, which I'm sure was all she had. How could God allow this place to be?

The minister of Home of Hope and his wife have erected the ministry in the slum of Delhi, and it has become a beacon of light for all the slums to see, right there among them on their turf. Because they have never lived any different, they do not know how very poor they are. But, they have the joy of the Lord. The smiles of hundreds of women tell a more inspiring story than has ever been written. Most are abused, beaten, and wondering where their daily bread will come from. Yet, joy, so much joy. Some lifted up their hands during the songs we sang in praise to God. Some experienced his presence for the very first time.

You may not think God cares, but I saw first hand today that God cares enough to send a humble man and woman to care enough about these people that they gave their very lives for them. I wish I could take you all for that ten minute walk. I wish. Here is what the ladies who live for God in the slums of Delhi believe:

"I give my burdens to Him and He takes care of me."
Psalm 55:22

"When I trust in Him, I will never be disappointed."
Psalm 22:5

"He is everything I need."
Psalm 23:1

Hundreds of ladies today, trusting God for the food they eat. They were all given a bag with things to take care of themselves with, such as a washcloth, soap, hand sanitizer, hair bands, and the list goes on. You should have seen the smiles when they saw the little Ziploc® bag they would get on their way out the door. I don't know about you, but I have tons of wash cloths and many bars of soap in the pantry. They truly know that the joy of the Lord is their strength.

When we were packing up to leave today and heading back out to the bus for our 10 minute walk back through the slums, I saw her! Our sponsor child! Her mom had gone home and told her we were there. She ran all the way to the Home of Hope in hopes of finding us. We embraced. I then had to say goodbye to her. She turned to leave and there was this beautiful 10 year old girl now walking in bare feet, back to her home in the slums. I could not hold back my tears. I wanted to grab her and bring her home with me.

Today, take time to think of those who do not have what we have. Do you even care? Hundreds are right under our noses in America. We go about our day sometimes and don't even think about them. I wish I could take you for that 10 minute walk.

Dear God,
Thank you for what you have given me. Help me not to take it for granted like I do most the time. Let me see all I have and thank you for it. Thank you for giving me three meals a day, a pantry full of daily needs, and the walk I walked today. I honor you Lord.

Safeguards Are Godly

Well, I'm stuck home this morning in an Indian hotel. My husband gets to go to an awesome church and preach. I wish I was with him. The food is very, very hot and I'm having a bit of tummy trouble. I was given some medication for it but it's not easy. Our bodies are funny things.

"Do you not know that your body is a temple of the Holy Spirit, who is in you, whom you have received from God? You are not your own you were bought at a price. Therefore honor God with your body."
1 Corinthians 6:19-20

I'm not sure how you can honor God with your body when you are feeling so crummy! Ha! But, God knows when we need rest and I take this as a sign that I need rest.

When you ask Christ into your life the Holy Spirit dwells within you. Imagine for a moment if you went to church one day and there was cow manure all over the pews and rug, piano and tables. Just imagine how you would feel. So nasty I'm sure! This is how the Holy Spirit feels when we sin, when there is sin in our lives! It's hard to keep yourself pure, but we need to do our best to live a holy life.

For those of you who think you have it all together, that you are sin-free, remember this scripture:

"So, if you think you are standing firm, be careful that you don't fall. No temptation has seized you except what is common to man. And God is faithful; he will not let you be tempted beyond what you can bear. But when you are tempted, he will also provide a way out so that you can stand up under it."
1 Corinthians 10: 12-13

Not one of us is sin free! We can never get cocky and think we are above sin. We are sure to fall if we think that way. We need to stay humble and always know sin is lurking around the corner.

We need safe guards! Our family had safeguards on pretty much everything when the kids were here. Our computers were covered with an internet filtering program called Covenant Eyes® (www.covenanteyes.com). My husband's, my kids' and my computer had this awesome program where Guy and I got a report once a week to show us exactly what sites were hit, and if any were bad. We had a parental control DVD player called ClearPlay (www.clearplay.com) that took any movie and took out anything bad that we don't want to watch. There are 35 settings. We got sick of watching a movie with our kids when they were young and telling them to turn their heads, and the movies were PG-13! This unit can take an R-rated movie and if you want, you can make it G rated. (Check into it— well worth the investment.) Some may think we are very strict but we didn't want our kids falling into sin like we did. We are not blind, and we know that they will sin, but while they are under our roof why not protect them?

Do you have safeguards? Are you tempted by things that you can safeguard yourself from? Then why not? It's something to think about anyway. To me it's well worth it.

So here I am in this hotel not feeling the greatest, thinking about the grace of God and my kids at home. Thinking about how grateful I am that they were safeguarded at a young age. Thinking about my stupid body and how sick I felt last night. But, it has me in a place of thought.

> "We are hard pressed on every side, but not crushed; perplexed, but not in despair; persecuted, but not abandoned; struck down but not destroyed. "
> 2 Corinthians 4: 8-9

He is a faithful God who keeps us even when our bodies are weak physically and spiritually. Don't forget part of that scripture that says:

> "And God is faithful; He will not let you be tempted beyond what you can bear. But when you are tempted, He will also provide a way out so that you can stand up under it."
> 1 Corinthians 10:13

God will always provide a way out for you my friend, will you take it? Or will you fall? I desire to stand firm in my faith. I'm not perfect, and I'm sure there are times I will fall into sin. Be it a sinful thought, or who knows what, but I will do my very best to safeguard myself and my family. I think that's godly.

Dear God,
I pray today that every person reading this would desire to serve you in such a way that they would guard their lives from sin. Safeguards are godly. Help us Lord to stay pure and live for you. To stay humble and never think we are above falling into sin. I honor you today Lord.

World's Greatest Valentine

"For God so loved the world that he gave his one and only Son, that whoever believes in him shall not perish but have eternal life."
John 3:16

This scripture is world famous. We see it on TV, at football games, on billboards, on morning shows, and more places. Sometimes due to everyone having a sign with this scripture on it, it's not taken seriously. God gave His son Jesus. Jesus left His thrown in Heaven to come to earth and be born of a young girl. He lived His life worthy of His purpose then He died a gruesome death. His body was beat so bad and cut so bad you could hardly recognize Him.

Now friend, that is love.

I'm not sure if I could ever give my son. I love him so much. You think about if you could give one of your children for everyone else. He gave us a gift. He gave us the most beautiful valentine.

I remember when my son Jonathan was an infant. Rocking him to sleep, the love I felt for him. Then he grew into a handsome boy. I remember one night at dinner when Jon asked his dad, "Dad, Jesus is in our heart right?" Dad said, "Yes." Then Jon said, "Doesn't the food hit him in the head on the way down?" We sat there and laughed so hard. I'm sure there were many times when Mary laughed at the little boy Jesus as He grew into a man. He was her joy. Now my son has a full beard and eats anything and everything without questions!

Some of you get depressed on Valentine's Day. No one is giving you candy and flowers. There are no surprises, or special gifts. Maybe you have only been hurt by men or women in your life. I'm here to remind you today that someone has given you a valentine, and you need to focus on that today.

A Savior bleeding on a cross, a man who could have called ten thousand angels to take Him down but His love for you kept him there, that is your Valentine. He knew when He made it through, that His blood would cleanse us from all of our sin. That is a deeper love than you could ever know.

That is a beautiful valentine.

You need to see yourself today through the eyes of Christ and not your own. Some of you have little self esteem and you could hardly think a God in Heaven could give his life for you.

See through the eyes of Christ today and know that God so loved you that He gave His son.

"When I was a child, I talked like a child; I thought like a child, I reasoned like a child. When I became a man I put childish ways behind me. **Now we see but a poor reflection as in a mirror; then we shall see face to face.** Now I know in part; then I shall know fully, even as I am fully known."

1 Corinthians 13:11-12

It's time to buck up and open your valentine. It's time to see a beautiful reflection. To know your worth is so very much. You cannot even comprehend how great a love He has for you.

It is the world's greatest valentine.

Dear God,
Thank you for such a deep love, that you would send your son to die for my sin. Take away any depression I may have today due to my circumstance. Let me see a beautiful reflection of myself. Let me see my worth today and all you have done. I honor you today.

A Simple Prayer

Over a thousand children came today for a children's outreach we held in New Delhi, India. It killed me to see the children behind the gate that could not make it in because they were not sponsored. The ones who made it in experienced things that some there have never seen. They will never forget today, neither will I.

When the service was over we had prayer time. It took some serious time for us to pray for that amount of children. As I was praying for the children, I was reminded of a simple prayer that a woman prayed over my brother one time. We were very young and our mother had brought us to a church service. All I remember is people were getting healed and running around happy. Other than that I don't remember much. But a woman placed her hand on my brother and simply said, "Lord, someday use this boy for your service." That's all she said.

As child after child came through the line today, I placed my hands on their filthy shirts and said, "Lord someday use this child for your service." I prayed more for them than that, but I made sure to pray that prayer. As I prayed over each child tears welled up in my eyes as I thought of my own brother and how God had changed his life due to a simple prayer. Today my brother is a pastor in Boston and the leader of the other pastors around him. Somehow I know, years ago, that God heard that simple prayer that woman prayed over my brother. We don't think those quick prayers mean much sometimes, but they do.

Lives were changed today; thousands of little lives. Not one kid left until we prayed over them. Hannah's prayer in 1 Samuel 1:10-12 was hardly a simple prayer, yet it had a simple purpose: She desired a son. Her words were:

> "O Lord Almighty, if you will only look upon your servant's misery and remember me, and not forget your servant but give her a son, then I will give him to the Lord for all the days of his life."
> 1 Samuel 1:11

This is what we did today: We gave these kids to the Lord for all the days of their life. We claimed their little souls, and that they would come to know the Lord's hope and peace.

I took a walk through the slum of Delhi today. I have walked through slums before, but this was the worst thing I have ever seen in all my years of life. I can't even put it into words, yet these kids showed up today joyful and ready for all God had for them. We are not the first to pray for these children. The pastor and his wife here have given their very lives to serve the people in the Delhi slums. This is why the children keep coming. And this is why Muslim mothers keep dropping them off. I had three Muslim mothers come up to me and ask if it was okay for me to pray for them even though they were Muslims. I gladly prayed for them and hugged each one. I asked God to show His great love to them.

Why do we make prayer so hard sometimes? In many ways for some it has become ritualistic. The lighting of candles, incense burning, and more. Prayer is simple when spoken from the heart to God.

A simple prayer spoken in faith, with a simple purpose:

> "Lord, someday use this boy for your service."

How simple can it get? But that boy has now touched thousands of souls in his lifetime. And now his four children will do the same! Nina, Dominic, Andrew and Mason walk with God! Auntie Tana prays so.

Dear God,
I thank you that you want us to just express how we feel. You can handle it because you already know. Help me Lord to know that even simple prayers are powerful and can change the world. Thank you for your amazing grace and how you love your children.

Adventures with Bengali Bob

It's easy to say you trust God, you won't fear, and nothing will shake you. Well today we got into a taxi in New Delhi with our friend Bob McGurty, and the taxi driver got totally lost. What should have been a 30 minute trip turned into two hours. When we left in the taxi it was light, and when we arrived at the right destination it was dark.

I have to say I have not laughed that hard in a long while. The driver stopped 13 (or was that 14?) times for directions. It was dark, and it's stressful enough driving in India in the light, let alone driving in the dark. At one point I actually found myself afraid. We were headed down a dirt road and there was a temple on our right, and nothing in front of us but darkness. Bob and my husband were both in the car but I actually yelled at the taxi driver to turn around and head back to the main road. I wondered where that fear came from. It's so strange how fear can well up inside when you least expect it.

I remember as a little girl being so afraid of the dark I had to have a night light. I also remember one night in the home I grew up in, having to pee so badly and wetting the bed due to my awesome fear of the darkness. I would rather have peed the bed than get up in the pitch black and find my way to the light switch.

There was just something about that dirt road that the taxi driver was driving on... heading into darkness. It was crazy and it scared me. Horrible thoughts passed through my mind. I had shared a message only a few hours before of how God is our hope, how He is there through the hard times, and how He will not leave us, yet when I was heading into a dark place I was afraid. The past can really creep up on you if you let it. I had two big guys to protect me, not to mention the driver, but there I was being a wimp. So crazy.

"I tell you friends, do not be afraid of those who kill the body and after that can do no more. But I will show you whom you should fear; Fear Him who, after the killing of the body, has power to throw you into Hell. Yes I tell you, fear Him. Are not five sparrows sold for two pennies? Yet not one of them is forgotten by God. Indeed, the very hairs of your head are all numbered. Don't be afraid, you are worth more than many sparrows."
Luke 12:4-7

Even if someone killed me, I'm God's. I would be present with the Lord in an instant. Truth be told, I just hate pain, so I get scared. I guess I'm normal. Ha. There is scripture after scripture in the Word about trusting God and not being afraid. Seek them out and meditate on them.

"May the God of hope fill you with all joy and peace as you trust in Him, so that you may overflow with hope by the power of the Holy Spirit."
Romans 15:13

There is nothing to fear. I have to remember that more often.

Driving down that dirt path in the darkness was not the first time I've been afraid, and I'm sure it will not be the last, but our hope and trust needs to be in God. Do you have fear that you need to surrender to Him? The important thing is not to live in it, but to overcome it through prayer and God's word.

I may have been afraid, but I will never forget that Bengali Bob adventure!

Dear God,
Thank you for loving me even when I fear. I'm not sure why I do that. Help me to have my hope, faith and trust in you totally. Help me to overcome. You are all I need, and I do not have to be afraid anymore! I honor you today.

Beautiful Angela

It was 1994, and I was home on bed rest with my second baby, my beautiful Angela. For anyone reading that has been on bed rest, you know it's a hard time, especially when you have other small children at home. I had Jonathan, who at the time was not quite two years old. It's easy for the doctor to say you have to stay in bed and not move; he does not live your life. I did the best I could to stay down, and my mother and mother in law helped me out. Guy was working two part time jobs and getting his Master's degree all at the same time, so as you can imagine me being down was not an easy task.

During this time I also could not go to church or anywhere else for that matter. One night a man came to our church and spoke, he was a missionary to Bangladesh. I remember Guy coming home from church that night and sharing with me how God spoke to him at the prayer time and told him that He wanted him to go help for one month and teach at the Bible College there. I could not believe what I was hearing. For six years I had prayed that God would give my husband a deep burden for the people I love in India. These people God told my husband to go to were the same people group. My heart was filled with joy and I remember I cried almost all night. I knew that he would fall in love with the people just like I had.

A week before Guy was to fly to Bangladesh I started not feeling well. Our beautiful Angela was 3 months old at the time, Jon had turned two, and Guy was headed to the land I love. How good could it get? Then my "not feeling good" turned into pain. More pain than I had ever experienced before. I knew something was very wrong. I called the doctor, and he said , "Give yourself some time. You just had baby." So I relaxed and tried to make myself think it was all from child birth. Finally all of a sudden, like a balloon popping, I felt better. As a matter of a fact, I felt great in an instant. It was the strangest thing until 60 seconds later my body went into total shock. I was shaking from head to toe. I could not stop my teeth from chattering. I was freezing. We called the doctor who told me my body had gone into shock and I had to get to the hospital as soon as I could. My appendix had ruptured and poison was all throughout my body.

I was rushed into emergency surgery. I came out of that surgery looking 20 lbs heavier due to all the fluid they pumped in me. I had a giant drainage tube coming out of my tummy with something that looked like a hand grenade on it. Every hour on the hour for weeks I had to empty the poison draining from inside of me into the toilet. It was horrible. It was also one week before my husband was to go to a place that I had prayed that God would put on his heart for years.

I can remember him leaning over me in my bed after surgery saying, "Tana, I'm not going. I can't leave you like this." With everything I had in me I told him he was going and that I felt this was just a distraction. I knew I had plenty of people to help me. My heart longed for him to be there and to fall in love with the people God gave me such a heart for.

All that's to say, Guy went on the trip, and is still taking trips there to this day because God did give my husband a great love for the people of India and Bangladesh. He is faithful.

Distractions will come your way. Some are just distractions, and some are fire balls hurled your way by the evil one. I also believe during this time that God was testing our obedience. I want to encourage you today that no matter what God has spoken to you, do NOT sway from it. No matter if someone you love is down or if finances are not coming through. Don't sway from it!

Most of you have heard the story of Noah and the ark. What a strange task that God gave to Noah. To build a giant ark when there was no rain. It took great faith for him to move forward and to take all the distractions that came his way in stride. But he did it!

<blockquote>
"Noah did everything just as God commanded him."
Genesis 6:22
</blockquote>

When Guy left, God took great care of me and my two babies by sending awesome people to help. And we were just fine. God will take care of you if you walk in perfect obedience.

Just thought I would let you know my beautiful Angela turned out pretty awesome. This devotion was written on her 16th Birthday she is now 21(2015).

Dear God,
Help us to walk where you want us to walk. Help us not to waste time. Help us to dodge all the distractions that will come our way in life and to walk in your perfect will and way. You are amazing and I thank you for your faithfulness. Bless our children Lord. I honor you today.

February 18th

Is Your Ax Dull?

For the past eight years I have been working in the health care system. One great thing about health care is that you will never be out of a job. I work my health care job on call. Throughout the years, depending on where I worked, I would learn new skills.

My first health care job lasted three years at a nursing home where most of the patients were losing their minds. It was the hardest labor I have ever done, and the messiest. But I fell in love with the people there so much that I started a nursing home ministry, developed a team, and loved on those people. When I left the area, the team continued to run the ministry, and still continue to minister there today. The hardest thing about working with the elderly was that I knew they would die soon. They were people I loved. It was hard.

After my work at the nursing home, I worked in a maternity ward for three years. Whatever job I took it seemed I learned more and more. With the elderly I learned so very much, but with the little babies it was a new ball game. I learned how to set up sterile tables for operations, assist with birth, care for the afterbirth and placenta that by law had to be saved for seven days (very messy). I assisted with and did set up for circumcisions, assisted in C-sections, helped the new mothers, and my most favorite was having the babies in the middle of the night. I would rock them, hold them close and pray over them. Sometimes it would get crazy in the middle of the night and I would have my hands full but I loved every minute of working in the maternity ward.

After three years there my family and I moved farther north and I started to seek out a job. Maternity was not open, so I went where the door opened to surgical holding. I would get the patients ready for the anesthesiologist and doctor before they went into surgery. The unit is very sterile and clean so that part of it I enjoyed. In this unit I was required to go back for more training to learn phlebotomy (blood draw), and I needed to be EKG certified. It seems along the way I have learned so much. I love to learn.

I was so excited doing my first 50 sticks with a needle. It came very natural to me and I was told I was good at it. When you put your hand to the plow and work hard, God will honor your effort. Just before we came on this trip to India I was offered to be trained as a lab associate. I'm not sure if I can do it yet, but training is something I welcome and I hope to learn more as I get older.

I hope you welcome learning. We can always be learning, always be growing. I never want to be stagnant. It's only stagnant water that smells bad. Muck grows all around. I never want that in my life. I want to learn as much as I can for as long as I have my mind.

I came across a scripture this week that I loved, it made me think and hope again for more training in many different areas of my life.

"If the ax is dull and its edge unsharpened
more strength is needed, but skill will bring success."
Ecclesiastes 10:10

There is nothing wrong with skill, its how our mind grows. Some shy away due to not having finances, being afraid of something new, or thinking they are too old to go back to school. We disable ourselves. I'm here to tell you today if it's the Lord's will, He will open the door. Every single thing I have done in the medical field including the training has been free. I have never paid one cent. And everywhere I go I keep growing and learning. I just walked in at the right time.

Where are your hopes and dreams today? Do you need your ax sharpened? When an ax is sharpened it brings heat, sparks and sharpness. The old is grinded away and a new fresh shine appears. Maybe it's time for you to sharpen yourself. What are you interested in? What does God want you to do? These are all things God is not just going to lay on your lap; you need to put forth some effort.

Dear God,
I pray we will never get dull. That we will always want to grow and be sharp for you, no matter where we are working and no matter what we are doing. I desire to learn more. Help us to never lose our dreams and to never sit in stagnant waters. I honor you today Lord.

February 19th

Dysfunction into Function

Tonight was our first night home from India. My husband and I had made a commitment to be on a panel of married couples for our church youth group. We had volunteers to be questioned about marriage by the youth. They are doing a series on love. We were the oldest married couple. It was kind of a crazy day due to jet lag and a 10-hour time change. I was falling asleep by the end of the night. When I was answering the last question half way through my answer I said to myself, "Hmmm what was the question?" Ha. We wanted to keep the commitment because in 2010 when this was written the youth pastor (Clark) lived at our house to be with our kids while we were gone. Anyway… it was crazy but fun.

It's amazing how when you are very tired you can say profound things. The question that was asked to us was, "What is real love?" We were the last couple to answer. When I took the microphone I said, "Real love is when someone takes your dysfunction and makes you function." This is what my husband did for me after all.

Coming into marriage I was so messed up. When you are molested as a child, intimacy is something you fear rather than enjoy, something that is hurtful rather than joyful. The first two year of marriage I was so messed up. If not for Guy and his patience, I'm not sure what would have happened. Not to mention he is a man of God and knew Jesus had put us together for a greater purpose. Now after 26 years we have a very healthy intimate relationship, not to mention fun! God has just brought us so far.

Guy really did take all my dysfunction (and trust me, there was much!) and made me function. I know God was the one who gave him the wisdom and understanding to deal with me. I'm so very thankful for real love. Truth be told, there are many who don't know the Lord that have real love. There are many living in healthy relationships that don't have the Lord's hope yet. But there is something about being able to pray with your spouse and getting into the presence of God together.

True love is someone who cares enough about you to help you function, even if it means they will have to sacrifice for a while. That's when you know you are loved, deeply loved. I thank God my husband loves me like that. I thank God he has been with me in sickness and health and through all the trials we have been through in the past 26 years. I could not imagine life without him.

"Two are better than one, because they have a good return for their work: If one falls down, his friend can help him up. But pity the man who falls and has no one to help him up! Also, if two lie down together,

121

they will keep warm. But how can one keep warm alone? Though one may be overpowered, two can defend themselves. A cord of three strands is not quickly broken."
Ecclesiastes 4:9-12

Read that scripture one more time. Notice how it's talking about two people but at the end it says, "A cord of three strands is not quickly broken" in verse 12. In this scripture the third strand is Christ. When a couple loves God and Christ is the head, it's amazing how very strong your marriage can be. This is what I have had for 21 years this year, not to mention the keeping warm part! I'm always freezing and Guy is always hot! In more ways than one! Haha. Ok, back on track here! Don't mess around with someone that can't love your dysfunction. When you truly love, you love all, including the messes. In this lifetime not many get to experience that kind of love and I'm thankful that I have.

Dear God,
I thank you for someone loving me enough to take all my dysfunction and helping me to function. You are an awesome God. You ministered to so many like this when you walked this earth. I thank you for never giving up on me and seeing a functional young lady that I could not see. I honor you today.

February 20th

Fields and Butterflies

Years ago when I was 19, I went on a mission trip and lived in Calcutta, India for four months. I lived below the flat of the Buntain's and a couple named The Shaw's took care of me. Calcutta is now spelled differently, but for the sake of the time frame of this event I will spell it the old Calcutta way. Our church at the time had a sponsor child named Mark Khazanchi. He was 10 years old.

When I arrived in Calcutta I had my passport, luggage, and Mark Khazanchi's picture, ready to find him. A man with a Jeep picked us up from the airport. The trip to the YMCA where we were going to live was never ending. Traffic was crazy, smoke filled the air, and when we passed the town dump we all had to cover our faces because the smell was worse than ever. It was easy to forget the picture of a little boy in my hand with everything I saw around me. When I finally remembered, I put the picture in front of our driver just enough that he could see it out of the corner of his eye. Right away he stopped the Jeep and pulled over. I wondered what I had done to make him upset. He sat there, turned around, and with tears in his eyes he stared at me. I'm sure you can imagine I was a little scared not knowing what I had done.

A few minutes went by and he told me that Mark Khazanchi was his son. He then told me if not for our support his son would not be able to go to the Mission of Mercy School. I could not believe out of all the drivers that could have picked us up, my sponsor child's father picked us up. To me it was a strong confirmation that I was to be there the next four months. While I was there I got to know Mark and his father. Mark was an eager boy ready to learn. He wrote this poem for me while I was there:

The Town Child, By Mark Khazanchi, 1985
I live in a town on a street
It is crowded with traffic and feet;
There are buses and motors and trams,
I wish there were meadows and lambs.

The houses all wait in a row,
There is smoke everywhere I go.
I don't like the noise that I hear
I wish there were woods very near.

There is only one thing that I love,
And that is the sky far above.
There is plenty of room in the blue
For castles, clouds, and me too.

I was so impressed with Mark's poem that I sent it in to *The Cry of Calcutta*, a publication that the Calcutta church used to put out. In Volume 9, March 1986, Number 3 they printed Mark's poem with a picture of us both. I still have it to this day, 29 years later.

As I mentioned before, on this most recent trip to New Delhi, I was once again able to meet another one of my sponsor children (who is also 10 years old and a beautiful, eager to learn young lady) and her mother who came to our woman's retreat.

The night before that women's conference I woke around 3am. I began to pray that God would use me when I spoke, that He would anoint me to preach His gospel. Then a very unexpected word came to me. As I was sitting in silence this is what the Lord said: There will be a woman there whose desire in life is to see green fields and butterflies.

This was one of the weirdest things I have ever heard the Lord say to me. I thought to myself, this is her heart's desire? How strange. Then my mind raced back to Mark's poem from 1985. He wished for meadows, lambs, and woods to be near. I guess when we have all that we never have it as a heart's desire to see it. Oh, how we take so much for granted.

I'm not sure where Mark is today, but I do know that one of the ladies at our conference wished for green fields and butterflies. Today as you go about your day, make sure all the things you see with your eye you do not take for granted. Soak in the fields, creatures, birds and butterflies. Thank God that you are not picking the black soot out of your nose every night like our missionaries are in India. Who knows maybe someday someone will give Mark this book and he will read this?

The butterfly is a symbol of new life. They are beautiful and no two are alike. You are unique and there is no person like you. God desires to use you and your unique gifts. Soak in your blessings today.

> "Therefore, if anyone is in Christ, he is
> a new creation; the old has gone, the new has come!"
> 2 Corinthians 5:17

Today do not take for granted the beauty in your life and fields and butterflies.

Dear God,
Let us remember *The Town Child* today and all the things we have. Help us not to forget the missionaries and people who give their time and live in places where their very lives are given for your sake. Help us to soak in the beauty around us and not take it all for granted. I honor you today.

February 21st

Lingering Things

"When you pass through the waters, I will be with you; and when you pass through the rivers, they will not sweep over you. When you walk through the fire, you will not be burned; the flames will not set you ablaze."
Isaiah 43:2

Today we forgot about a pot simmering on the stove and left the house. Came home to the fire alarms on and smoke in the house. A horrible smell filled the air on all three levels. You could tell that the pot had been in flames on the inside and on the outside. It was a total miracle that the counter or wall did not catch fire. God is so good.

I told my family it was a divine miracle and someone held back the danger. When I washed the kitchen there was a film of soot on the counter, cabinets, and floor. It was just horrible. This is the first time in 26 years that we have had a close call with fire. Our poor dog was a mess when we got home. Arwen is a black lab and a smart cookie so I know she knew danger was near. Poor baby.

It's amazing how when the danger is all gone, it can still linger.

Remember that today. The fire and danger is all gone but the smell of it lingers and the soot Is still around I'm sure!

When you make it through the fires of temptation in your life and you take a deep sigh and say, "Whew, I made it through without falling!" Be ever so careful my friend because the danger is still lingering. You may not see the fire but it still lingers.

The thing about being so close to fire is you have to work hard to get rid of the smell. Tomorrow I will wash down all the floors and walls with nice scented stuff. This has to be done to get rid of the lingering smell. It's hard work to get rid of the things that linger.

What is lingering in your life? Are you living with it or are you working hard to get rid of the things that will hurt you? Sometimes they are common sense things, if you are an alcoholic then don't walk into a bar. But it's the subtle things that you need to worry about more! What books are on your bookshelf? What DVD's are you watching? Everything you put into yourself makes up you. You know yourself well, is it healthy for you?

Are you working hard to get rid of the lingering things that are a danger to you?

I hope you can answer yes to that question. Sometimes it's even a person or people who are a very bad influence on your life. It takes hard work and hard steps to get rid of bad smells.

Trust me; there is a very bad smell in this house. The stuff that was in that pot was burnt to a crisp. The smell lingers. Tomorrow I have a lot of hard work ahead of me to try to pinpoint where I need to scrub most.

You need to do the same today. Pinpoint what needs the most scrubbing. And work hard to get it done. God is faithful and if you have fallen, He will forgive. But it's best to clean house and get rid of things that you know will make you fall.

Scrub lingering things.

Dear God,
Thank you for our close call today to remind me about things that linger. Help me to clean up my own life and to get rid of the things that bring me down. I thank you for your faithfulness and protection in my life. I know there are many times you protected me that I don't even know about, even when I did not deserve it. I honor you today.

One Hundred and Twenty Thousand

It's amazing when you flee from what you know God wants you to do, how very miserable you become. A perfect example of that is the story of Jonah. But have you ever been there yourself? I know I have. It seems the Lord bothers me until I turn and do the right thing.

Jonah was so miserable that he wanted to die. The Lord had sent a great storm, and the boat Jonah was on was in danger.

> "He went aboard and sailed for Tarshish to flee from the Lord. Then the Lord sent a great wind on the sea, and such a violent storm arose that the ship threatened to break up."
> Jonah 1:3-4

Jonah himself knew this all was going on due to him running from God. So he finally gives up.

> "'Pick me up and throw me into the sea,' he replied, 'and it will become calm. I know that it is my fault that this great storm has come upon you.'"
> Jonah 1:12

Well, the men ignored him at first and tried to row back to land but it got worse and worse so they finally threw him in the water.

I think with all my heart that Jonah thought that he was going to die. He never knew a fish would come and swallow him. There was no way he could have known that he would be one of the greatest children's Bible stories ever. He thought that when they threw him in, that was it. He would sink and die; even if the water got calm they never would let him back on the boat he would just die. This is how low he had gotten due to running from God. He wanted to die.

Then again in the very last chapter Jonah gets angry with God and once again we see him talking about death.

> "Now, O Lord, take away my life,
> for it is better for me to die than to live."
> Jonah 4:3

> "But God said to Jonah, 'Do you have a
> right to be angry about the vine?'
> 'I do,' he said. 'I am angry enough to die'."
> Jonah 4:9

I do believe running from God and His perfect will for your life can make you so miserable that you just want to die. We need to give our life in full.

Full surrender to God means being able to say, "I'm yours 100%. If you want to move me, move me. If you want me to stay put than I will. I will marry who you want me to. I will be directed by you and will obey." I know some of you reading may not understand this and think it's weird but I have lived my life like this ever since I gave my heart to Christ.

My husband and I only want God's perfect will. That's it. Anywhere else and we will be miserable.

There was a purpose for God wanting Jonah to go to Nineveh. Here it is:

> "Nineveh has more than a hundred and twenty thousand people who cannot tell their right hand from their left, and many cattle as well. Should I not be concerned about that great city?"
> Jonah 4:11

The purpose God had for Jonah was to touch souls. God's compassion was for those one hundred and twenty thousand people.

So I ask you today, Is there a city he wants you to touch? Is there a people group you are running from? Are you miserable because you know you have walked away? Trust me, sex, food, drugs, drinking, and more will NOT satisfy you but only for a very short season. Then you will be miserable again. It's only in the perfect will of God for your life that you have perfect peace.

There are souls out there that God wants you to impact. If you walk away it will not only affect your life but many souls.

Dear God,
Help me always walk in your way. Always. When we hear you say to turn, help us to turn. I know it will not always be easy saying goodbye to those we love and starting over, proving ourselves once again, but God may I always jump at your word and move! I honor you today.

My Husband's Glasses

This morning Guy forgot his reading glasses. We talked on the phone and he said he wanted to meet me half way to his workplace to get his glasses. I asked him where he wanted to meet and he said Laser Quest, where my son worked as a young man. It's this giant laser tag place that is very noisy and busy most the time. Anyway....on my way there I thought to myself, "We would never be meeting in this place unless our son worked here." It got me thinking.

Sometimes I think way too deep. It made me think of the fact that we have no idea how our choices and decisions affect the lives of others. My son chose to work there and therefore my husband and I met there so I could give him his glasses. I know if Jon did not work there we would have met somewhere else. This is kind of a stupid example but it's kind of the same with the things we go through in life.

In my short life I have been through a lot. Sexual abuse, five breast surgeries, hernia surgeries, countless small tumors removed, an appendix rupture, and the list goes on. But through every single thing after it was over, there was always someone that came to me and said they were going through the exact same thing. I was able to give them wisdom, help them, pray for them, and comfort them.

The things we go through affect the lives of others, whether they were painful to us or not. No matter what we go through we can use our pain for His purpose.

If you have Christ in your life do you know that Satan cannot touch you unless he asks God's permission? If you don't believe me check out the first chapter of the book of Job. In this scripture in Luke here is Jesus talking:

"Simon, Simon, Satan has asked to sift you as wheat. But I have prayed for you Simon that your faith may not fail. And when you have turned back, strengthen your brothers."
Luke 22:31-32

In the book of Job, the Lord was the one who actually said to Satan:

"Have you considered my servant Job? There is no one on earth like him; he is blameless and upright, a man who fears God and shuns evil."
Job 1:8

God has way more faith in us than we do in ourselves. He knows that when we go through trials it builds character. It's very easy to get angry at God for allowing you to go through things. But you must remember there are some things he NEVER intended you to go through. But then again, there are some things he did intend you to go through. God will allow you to go through trials in your life to test you.

> "Consider it pure joy, my brothers, whenever you face trials of many kinds, because you know that the testing of your faith develops perseverance. Perseverance must finish its work so that you may be mature and complete, not lacking anything."
> James 1: 2-4

"Yipeeeeee. I'm going through a trial!" If you're like me that is NOT how you respond. Pure joy? Consider it pure joy? I don't think so. Most the time we ask God, "Why?"

I love how James 1:4 says if we persevere through the trial we will be mature and complete, not lacking anything! Read that again and let it sink in. Our trials grow us. Make us more mature. More complete to help others.

If you look back at Luke 22:32 in the beginning of this devotion it says, "But I have prayed for you, Simon, that your faith may not fail. And when you have turned back, strengthen your brothers."

God prays that we don't give up faith, that we make it through the trial. I know how I have clung to peoples' prayers for me at times. I feel them. Imagine the Maker of the Universe prays for you. Luke 22:32 ends with the fact that when you have turned back, strengthen other people! I wonder if the Lord put the words "when you have turned back" due to Him knowing that we get angry and walk away sometimes. But in this scripture we see the entire reason for trial, "Strengthen your brothers." How can we help to strengthen someone if we don't know what they are going through, if we don't know exactly how they feel? It all makes sense!

Remember today that every choice you make, every trial you make it through, every hard thing you are facing right now, God is praying for you that your faith will NOT fail. You will be stronger and more mature and complete to help others.

So I gave my husband back his glasses this morning outside of Laser Quest and all this went through my mind. Like I said, sometimes I think too much. Ha.

Dear God,
You are amazing. Even though I hate it when I go through a trial, I thank you for them. You have made me a great witness due to the things you have helped me through in my lifetime. Your grace and peace are more than I could ever ask for. I pray for this reader, Lord that they would not lose faith and trust in you. Meet all their needs. I honor you today.

A Mother Knows

I remember when my son Jon was about four years old, he awoke from a nap and I happened to see that he was up. I walked in and sat on his bed. He seemed at such peace just laying there. He pointed to the corner of the room up to the window sill and said, "Look at the angels mommy." I turned and looked thinking he drew a picture or something. I saw nothing and said, "Jon what are you talking about?" He said, "The boy and the girl angel." After talking with him a bit more he told me they were there in the bedroom with him. He was not the least bit scared he was at perfect peace.

A mother knows when her kid is playing and when they are telling the truth. I know my Jonathan had a visitation that day with two angels. There is no doubt in my mind he saw them.

I have never seen angles, I have seen and experienced the demonic but never have I seen beautiful angels. I have had friends who said they have seen angels. I can imagine it's an experience that would change your life forever.

I have to say, we should not seek after seeing angels but we should seek after God, and if He so desires, He will open our eyes to see such things.

Some angels look just like you and me.

> "Do not forget to entertain strangers, for by so doing some people have entertained angels without knowing it."
> Hebrews 13:2

Can you imagine? There are angels walking around the earth that look like you and me. It's almost like a testing. Will we reach out to them, help them, smile at them, and take the time to go the extra mile for them? Or are we too busy, too in a rush? Remember this scripture throughout your week. You just never know who you have entertained in your path. It's so very cool to think about it. Truth be told, this is how we should treat everyone.

Most of us know the Christmas story. No, not the one with the leg lamp! Ha. The one about a beautiful young girl named Mary in whom God found favor. She was highly favored by God, and she was a virgin. The Word of God says:

> "God sent the angel Gabriel to Nazareth, a town in Galilee, to a virgin pledged to be married to a man named Joseph."
> Luke 1:26-27

This scripture shows us that God sends angels out on tasks.

> "Are not all angels ministering spirits sent to serve those who will inherit salvation?"
> Hebrews 1:14

This is pretty intense when you really sit and meditate on it all. Most know the children's story of Daniel and the Lion's den. At the first light of dawn when the King went to see if Daniel was still alive, Daniel yells to him:

> "My God sent his angel and he shut the mouths of the lions. They have not hurt me., because I was found innocent in his sight."
> Daniel 6:22

We could go on and on of the many people in the Bible that had encounters with angels. We need to keep in mind today that angels are just as real today as they were in the Bible. God is still sending angels to minister to us. Sometimes we do not even see how God sends them to protect us. He is so very faithful.

Seek God today and think of how very much he cares for you. He cares enough that you have unknowingly entertained angels.

Dear God,
Help me to be kind, to notice everyone around me like Jesus did when He walked the earth. Help me never to be too busy, too distracted or too prideful. Let me have compassion like you Lord. I honor you today.

Through the Eyes of Christ

"But who are you, O man, to talk back to God? Shall what is formed say to him who formed it, 'Why did you make me like this?' Does not the potter have the right to make out of the same lump of clay some pottery for noble purposes and some for common use?"
Romans 9:16-21

Are you happy with yourself? What do you see when you look in the mirror? I have this awesome picture that some of you may have seen before. It's a picture of a little kitty looking in a mirror and his reflection is a mighty lion.

It's so important that we see ourselves through the eyes of Christ and not our own sometimes. Oftentimes so many people's self esteem is being beaten down, but we are all precious in His sight. We may not feel that way sometimes but this is such an awesome scripture. Who are we to question God and His ways?

If you are not happy with yourself today, think about why. If you are upset because you are overweight, is that God's fault? No. He does not make us eat the entire sleeve of cookies or bag of chips. Oh man, now I'm getting hungry! Many things we blame God for are NOT His fault at all, but it's so much easier to blame God than to face the simple truth that we put ourselves in that position.

Look at the second part of that scripture; it talks about the potter having the right to make common use things and things for noble purposes out of the same lump of clay. I just think that's an intense scripture. Pretty much, God rules. He can do as He pleases. But the thing to remember is that the noble and common are made from the same stuff. He loves both the same. Some who stay humble He will lift up. In grace He will have favor on them. He did this with Joseph over his brothers. He picked young Mary to carry Jesus. It's just something He does.

You can sit and get angry about it if you want but that will not get you anywhere. Is it time for you to change in your life?

Maybe it's not even physical, maybe it's spiritual for you. When was the last time you picked up your Bible? Is it just collecting dust on a table somewhere? When was the last time you talked to God at all? When was the last time you told Him your heart's desires or goals, praised Him for the beauty you saw today, sat in His peace? Maybe you need change.

I think change starts with attitude. How is your attitude toward your situation right now? Is it stinky, or positive and optimistic? We need to have faith when things don't look so hot.

Let's think of pottery for a moment. I have some very expensive things that I only pull out of my hutch about twice a year. I would call that noble pottery. Then I have pottery that I use every single day. That is the stuff that is most important to me, because without it I could not live everyday normal life.

So just because something is for common use does not mean it is not important. To me my common use pottery is most important. Yes, I love my noble pottery. When I dress my dining table for a holiday I love to look at it and embellish it, but my common pottery is what I depend on almost every day.

I hope you understand where I'm going here. Just because God may raise someone up as a leader over you or to a position does not mean they are any more important that you.

Think on these things today. I turn to some of the representatives that work under my leadership sometimes for prayer or for wisdom. There is nothing wrong with that. Some are older and wiser than me! God may have picked me as their leader, but I need them and they are very important in their role.

I hope you know today how very important you are. You need to see yourself through the eyes of Christ. He loved you so much that He sent His only son to die for you.

Dear God,
Help us to see your great love and how very amazing you are today. Thank you for loving us all the same no matter where you place us. Help us to get rid of anger and bitterness to make room for peace. I honor you today.

February 26th

Plugged In

Last night was a very crazy night here in Southern New England. The wind was blowing so hard you could hear things flying around outside. At about ten o'clock at night I was sitting in front of the television watching HGTV. I was watching some guy redo a couple's house. My brain was so fried from a long day and not feeling well, so I sat there kind of numb, just watching TV. My husband was upstairs, my son was downstairs on the computer, and my daughter was playing her electric piano in her room (2010). Then all of a sudden it happened. The electricity went!

I sat there in pitch black, heard my son making ghost noises in the basement, my daughter laughing, and my husband's footsteps coming down the steps. I got the candles and lit up the living room. Within minutes we were all together in the living room under blankets talking and laughing.

Every summer we vacation in Maine in a cabin on a lake with no electricity. To me it's the highlight of the summer. Sitting around the fire all day by the lake reading and soaking in nature with NO distractions, just us and God, playing board games! Yes, board games do still exist! Sometimes we don't even get cell phone service. It's awesome, for a few days anyway!

Last night felt like Maine to me. I began singing camp songs and my son in a silly voice joined along. To me it was fun! There is something great about the power going out.

We woke this morning to no electric. I got up at 5:30am and headed out for ice so our food does not go bad. You don't realize how habit-forming some things are until they are gone! Everywhere I walked in the house I was flipping on light switches that would not work. Ha. Just habit I guess. I thought to myself, "I wonder if they sell battery operated power strips!" All I could focus on was that I could not plug my coffee pot in! We are so spoiled here in America. I just went to India and had not one cup in 18 days! I survived!

Not having power got me thinking: When the power is on, and everything is plugged in, our world lights up. We have light, access to pretty much anywhere in the world with Internet, the ability to cook, and make creations, and the list goes on. Life happens smoothly when we are plugged into our power source. I love black outs for a day or two but truth be told we need to be plugged in for our life to move forward as it has to. We work, and the kids go to school. We need our natural power sources.

It's the same way with our walk with God. If we are not plugged in we will eventually get discouraged and sometimes depressed. If you have ever withdrawn from people or places you know this to be true. My friend is in recovery and told me the other day that it's been hard staying home alone. When she is out helping people, working, or just being with others there is a sense of purpose in her life. In other words, when she is plugged in there is purpose.

Many people plug into the wrong things to fill their voids. I did that for many years until someone told me about God and the peace He gives. The great thing about God is it would not matter one bit if you were stranded on an island with no electric for the rest of your life, you could still plug into His peace, power, and awesome presence. He is a power source that will never go out.

I just want to encourage you today that if you have tried plugging into everything and you are still unhappy, if you are lacking peace and purpose in your life, try plugging into an awesome Bible- believing church and God himself. He is always there waiting for you to talk to Him. He will never leave you. Plug in, and the great thing is there is NO electric bill!

"Who shall separate us from the love of Christ? Shall trouble or hardship or persecution or famine or nakedness or danger of sword? As it is written: 'For your sake we face death all day long; we are considered as sheep to be slaughtered.' No, in all these things we are more than conquerors through Him who loved us. For I am convinced that neither death nor life, neither angels nor demons, neither the present nor the future, nor any powers, neither height nor death, nor anything else in all creation, will be able to separate us from the love of God that is in Christ Jesus."
Romans 8:35-39

Dear God,
Help us to stay plugged into you even when we are going through trial. If someone is reading this right now and they don't know you I pray you draw them to you today Lord. Help them to plug into all you have for them and their life. I honor you today.

A Plank in My Eye

Shortly after becoming a Christian I traveled with a group called Christian Music Ministries (CMM). I wanted to live for God, but someone had to teach me what was right and wrong according to God's word. We had a fall and spring tour where we would travel all over New England, and even farther west to visit churches and hold concerts. I was growing, and desired to know more about God. The group consisted of about 60 of us all together, I think. We were taught how to lead others to God through the book of Romans. After concerts were over we would meet with people in the middle aisles and bring them to the back aisles to pray with them, if they desired. I can't tell you the many people I prayed for through CMM.

One night the director of CMM was reading this scripture:

"Why do you look at the speck of sawdust in your brother's eye and pay no attention to the plank in your own eye? How can you say to your brother, 'Brother, let me take the speck out of your eye,' when you yourself fail to see the plank in your own eye? You hypocrite, first take the plank out of your eye, and then you will see clearly to remove the speck from your brothers eye."
Luke 6: 41:42

As I stood in the middle aisle waiting for people to respond to his message, this scripture he was reading starting bothering me. I stood there waiting for others to respond while all along God was doing something in me. All I could think of was that I was the worst hypocrite of all. Here I was leading people to the Lord, leading them through the book of Romans but I myself was not giving my all to God. I had a serious plank in my own eye!

I remember turning to two of my friends and saying, "I have a plank in my eye!" I had not surrendered everything to Him. I was still living in very ungodly ways and was not the greatest example to others. I know none of us are perfect, but I was totally going against the Word of God in a few areas of my life.

That night instead of waiting for others, I ended up walking into the back room with my two friends. They talked with me for a while and prayed for me. I fully surrendered my life to Christ that night due to Luke 6:41:42. Isn't it just amazing how God's Word can change us?

Read that scripture again right now. When you think of a speck and compare it to a plank there is a world of difference. Do you see the sin in everyone around you today and fail to see the sin in your own life?

I will never forget that night as long as I live because it was life changing due to the word of God.

The Word says:

> "Do not judge, and you will not be judged. Do not condemn, and you will not be condemned. Forgive, and it will be forgiven."
> Luke 6:37

Somehow leading all those people to the Lord and praying for all of them I failed to see I was in worse shape than them. How could that ever happen? Well, mostly pride. I'm so glad God knows how to take care of the planks in our life.

Dear God,

You are so faithful. Help me to keep myself pure and to see the sin in my own life before I ever even think about the sin in others lives. I honor you today.

I Stand Amazed

Today I just cannot escape the grace of God. When I think of where I have been and where I am now I stand amazed at His hand of grace on my life. As I spoke at a great church this morning I shared all God has done to bring me where I am today. I shared His Word and how God wants to use each one of us for His purposes. I love prayer time where people come and weep when they realize the hand of a living God is on their life and that He actually wants to use all they have been through for His grand purpose.

You cannot even begin to know right now how God wants to use you! You may not believe it or you may have had your self esteem beaten down but it does not matter my friend, God still wants to use you for His glory.

It does not matter what you have done to others or to yourself, it does not matter what Hellish things have been done to you, it does not matter if someone told you all your life you were a mistake, it does not matter at all! God STILL wants to use you. One of my mentors Dawn Crabtree used to say that we all have our own tool box. In my tool box are tools that you don't have and in your tool box there are tools that I don't have. We have been through life's experiences and each time we made it through, we gained a new tool. Your tools can touch a select group of people with all you have been through. The question today is: Are you using them?

I believe God does not want the things you have been through to sit on a shelf. He wants to use them! Will you let Him? Will you get past your shame and become transparent enough to touch and change the lives of others? Souls are out there waiting for just one person to tell them, "I know how you feel, I have been through that."

It takes a great humbling getting past shame, guilt, and bitterness. It's time to lay that all down today. Lay it down before the master of the universe, He is there waiting.

It's hard to believe the one who created all things would look down and care for me and you. After all, isn't He kind of busy? But His love is never ending. The Word of God, speaking of love says:

> ## "It keeps no record of wrongs."
> ### 1 Corinthians 13:4

He loves you today. He doesn't sit up there saying, "She did this!" Check! "He did that!" Check! "Can you believe he fell there again?" Check! "Can you believe she did that again?" Check! He sits up there and thinks, "Wont you come to me, all who are weary? I want to give you rest. I'm here and I'm waiting! I will never leave you or forsake you." I'm sure His thoughts go on and on. He prays for us, He loves us.

I stand amazed today. Anytime I share what the Lord has brought me through I stand amazed.

He is more than amazing. In my darkest hours, His peace kept me.

I remember God leading me to India that one time when I was 19 years old, and when we finally opened the door to our room at the Calcutta Y, I was in shock that I would have to live in that room for the next four months. On my bed were little black hopping bugs. The Walls did not go up to the ceiling; you could stand on your bed and look over to the next room. You could hear the chants of Muslims and you could hear the giant rats in the courtyard at night. I remember my second day there weeping on my bed telling God I could not stay there. During my pleading with Him I felt as if a hot blanket fell on me. It's hard to explain the experience but that's what it felt like. I heard Him say, "My Grace will keep you here. You're staying." I did stay, and that summer changed my life forever. We were blessed a week later to be moved into another place to live. Felicia Shaw took us there it was 1985.

All that's to say, His grace is amazing. I believe that night in my room at the YMCA in Calcutta, the grace of God fell upon me. I hope you know He loves you today and that with Him you can get through anything!

"Fear not, for I have redeemed you;
I have summoned you by name; you are mine."
Isaiah 43:1

I stand amazed today.

Dear God,
How great is your love. Thanks. With everything you do, you think of me. It's just amazing and very hard to comprehend such a deep love like that. I come to you with a thankful heart today in praise. You are so awesome and I stand totally amazed by you and your grace. I honor you today.

March

March 1st

Nellie
"Now Faith is the substance of things hoped for,
the evidence of things not seen."
Hebrews 11:1

I love to read about Helen "Nellie" Herron Taft. She was born in 1861 and was America's First Lady from 1909 to 1913. She was the First Lady when the Titanic sunk and Oreo cookies appeared on store shelves! Very important times!

At 17 years old Nellie had a dream of someday living in the White House. Although her motives may not have been the best ever, I admire this lady just for basing her decisions in life on her goals or dreams. Years later she would walk into the White House as the First Lady and drive everyone crazy with her micro-managing. Her nickname was Nervous Nellie by the staff.

But at age 17, she began telling people that the White House would someday be her home. That's just amazing.

Although, even today, there are a lot of dreams that are not pleasing to God, I still admire someone who actually knows what they want and is so passionate about it that they someday fulfill what they have always desired. That just does something to me emotionally.

I believe God wants us to hope. It takes great faith to hope for something. It may seem so out of reach due to not having the money for it or being old and not having the energy, but if we have faith, it won't matter if we are poor or old, God can do the impossible!

"Against all hope, Abraham in hope believed
and so became the father of many nations."
Romans 4:18

I love this scripture. When every single thing is coming against you, and you believe you can never accomplish your goal, you have to go to God because it's just not true. He is a loving father who desires to fulfill your heart's desires.

"Delight yourself in the Lord and
He will give you the desires of your heart."
Psalm 37:4

For years I have been telling people some of my hopes and dreams, and I still have so many that have not been accomplished yet. For some to be accomplished, I would need a great deal of money. For some, I would need a great deal of energy. For some, I would need the grace of God. Truth be told, I will hang onto my dreams and my hopes until the day I die.

Many years ago I was sitting with my friend and mentor Peggy Musgrove. At the time she was the National Women's Director for the Assembly of God denomination. She was at our church speaking and afterwards, I took her out to lunch. During that visit I looked this amazing lady in the eye and said, "Someday I will be the District Women's Director for Southern New England." I remember she patted me on the hand and said, "You dream your big dreams, Tana!" She never laughed or made fun of me but she told me to dream my dreams and I did. In 2006, after nine years of hard work as a Sectional Women's Representative, I was chosen to lead the ladies of Southern New England District. This year 2015 marks 10 years as District Women's Director. Wish I had the energy I had 10 years ago! Ha!

My hopes and dreams were not prideful. I did not desire to lead due to position. I desired to lead because I had a burning passion for woman to know that God wants to use them for His glory, and that He wants to use all the pains that they have been through for His purposes! I wanted to help set a fire under the amazing ladies of this District so they could then turn around and touch the lives of others. Not all position is prideful. God can actually use position for His glory. Don't fear it, just stay humble and in prayer to hear His voice like John 10:27 talks about.

Maybe every desire that Nellie had was not for the greatest reason but she hoped and never lost the passion for what she was hoping for.

I admire Nellie for that.

Dear God,
Keep us in prayer as we lead. It's only by your grace. Never let us lose site of the countless souls that need encouragement and hope. Help us to believe the impossible because you can do anything. I honor you today.

March 2nd

The Pied Piper

I was watching the news tonight and it was one bad thing after another. A 16 year old girl was raped by her bus driver. A father was hurting and killed his baby. Then a man breaks into a home and is hurting a mother. When the father tries to help, he is murdered. What's going on? Is this world going totally mad or what?

"In which you used to live when you followed the ways of this world and of the ruler of the kingdom of the air, the spirit who is now at work in those who are disobedient. All of us also lived among them at one time, gratifying the cravings of our sinful nature and following its desires and thoughts."
Ephesians 2:2

I know there are many who read these devotions that do not have a relationship with God. I still tell you that He is alive and will totally change your life if you let Him. At the same time there is an evil one that the Bible clearly says tells us lies. His lies will bring discouragement, hopelessness, pride and everything that will lead to pain. I believe when men and woman act out in anger and murder, or lust consumes them in such a way that they must hurt a young child, it's much more than that person's flesh. I believe evil is involved.

"Be self-controlled and alert. Your enemy the devil prowls around like a roaring lion looking for someone to devour."
1 Peter 5:8

As Christians he cannot harm our soul, Jesus' blood on the cross and resurrection already won the victory over the devil. We stand on God's word. Are you ready to fight the devil and his schemes?

I hesitate to share this story, but I believe it's very relevant to what I want to say. For those of you who read this devotional faithfully you have read that we just went to India on a trip where we did ministry in the slums. The couple we worked for lives among evil spirits. The evil was thick. You could feel it. Every single day I pray for this couple who risk their very lives there.

One day, our team of 22 was walking through the slum. We walked kind of in twos in a line to one side of the road. Every day we were taking turns riding rickshaws. That day was my day to ride in the rickshaw with two other ladies. So we were buzzing along when all of a sudden I saw this man. The instant we saw him we knew he had demons. He was old and energetic; he had a flat cricket bat in his hand. He was swinging it back and forth and then he saw our team. In an instant the man went to the head of our line of people and began marching in front of them moving his cricket bat back and forth. Almost like he was mocking us and leading the team through the slum himself. Like a Pied

Piper. Words cannot explain how I felt as I watched this. You saw in an instant that the spirit inside of him recognized the spirit in all of us. He had a sick mocking smile on his face as he marched in front of our team. Now remember, I'm buzzing by in a rickshaw with my friends. As soon as we passed by him he looked right at us and licked the air with the most perverted look on his face and horrible actions. I have seen that look in his eyes before and it was a legion of demons in this man.

You may be reading this thinking I'm crazy right about now but friend I wish so bad I could make you see there is evil that wants to harm you. BUT at the same time there is a God that wants to protect you and comfort you. God has already won the victory over evil!

When I saw this on the street, it reminded me of a story in Acts 16 where Paul one day goes out to pray when a slave girl who had a spirit followed Paul and the rest of the men with him shouting:

> "These men are servants of the Most High God,
> who are telling you the way to be saved."
> Acts 16:16-18

The bible continues and says that she kept this up for many days. She was mocking them. Paul got so sick of it that he finally speaks to the spirit and says, "In the name of Jesus Christ I command you to come out of her!" She was healed in an instant, and the evil spirit came out of her. I wish I could say I spoke to that man on the street and that he was healed, but I can't.

When I saw that man it broke my heart. He was consumed with evil just like the nightly news tonight was filled with flesh and evil.

All this is not to depress you today, it is to encourage you to get to know God. If you don't know Him, speak to Him today. You don't have to talk a special way or be something that you're not. Just be you. He knows you better than you know yourself anyway. He made you whether you believe that or not.

It only takes you reaching out to Him, because He is already there.

Dear God
Please forgive me of my sins. I ask you to come into my life today and help me to live for you. I give you everything. I fully surrender to you today. I want to learn to hear your voice. Help me to read your Word. I honor you.

Fake Armor?

I can tell this story now and laugh, but it was not quite as funny many years ago. For those of you who have been in ministry for a long period of time you know that there are many things that happen upon you in the middle of a church service that are totally unexpected. We have had almost everything happen: People disrupting the prayer time, people standing on pews and doing weird things. Truth be told, we want all people to walk into our churches. Jesus died for all. That includes even those that are mentally ill.

It was a normal service and we were in the middle of the worship time. The band was playing and people were beginning to enter into the presence of God. Some were sitting, some kneeling, and some raising their hands. I was looking around at the sheer splendor of the moment and just soaking everything in. All of a sudden, from the corner of my eye, I saw a woman who came in dressed in the The Full Armor of God children's costume. This inspirational company makes a kids costume constructed of hard plastic to go along with the scripture about God's Armor in the book of Ephesians.

"Finally be strong in the Lord and in His mighty power. Put on the full armor of God so that you can take your stand against the devil's schemes. For our struggle is not against flesh and blood, but against the rulers, against the authorities, against the powers of this dark world and against the spiritual forces of evil in the Heavenly realms. Therefore **put on the full armor of God,** so that when the day of evil comes, you may be able to stand your ground, and after you have done everything, to stand. Stand firm then, with the **belt of truth** buckled around your waist, with the **breastplate of righteousness** in place, and with your **feet fitted** with the readiness that comes from the gospel of peace. In addition to all this, take up the **shield of faith**, with which you can extinguish all the flaming arrows of the evil one. Take the **helmet of salvation** and the **sword of the Spirit**, which is the word of God."
Ephesians 6:10-17

The child's costume had the belt, hard plastic breastplate, shield, helmet, sword and two things that went over your feet to cover your shoes! All were child sized!

And here she came, the helmet hardly fitting her head. Dressed in the full child's costume— The Armor of God! I kept my eye on her. She walked to the very front of the church, when she got to where the very first pew was, and she knelt down on one knee and lifted the sword as if she was giving honor to someone. I'm sure in her heart she was giving honor to God but I hope you understand where I'm coming from. This was a very odd sight to see in the middle of a Sunday morning service.

Not too long after this lady entered in her armor costume, our wonderful ushers nicely brought her back out to the lobby where she was asked to take the armor off. She willingly took off her hard plastic fake armor and came back into service, sitting in the back.

Now almost 22 years later I can't help but laugh when I think about it; that sight of her walking down the aisle with her child's costume, hardly fitting. Some people are ill but some just need a little extra attention. I got to know this dear lady, and years later she passed on. She really was very sweet and loved God very much.

It's nice for kids to have the armor of God costume. It's a great way to teach them the scripture in the Bible, and how very powerful it is to pray on the armor of God. I encourage you to go to that chapter in the Bible and read it in its entirety.

But, I think sometimes we put on fake armor. We try to make people think we have it all together, our prayer life is perfect, and we are digging in the Word, but truth be told, we are all talk and NO action! Pride is what initiates this.

> "Let him that thinks he stands take heed lest he fall."
> 1 Corinthians 10:12

This is dangerous ground to be on.

The armor of God is a serious thing that the Bible says we should pray on; it is a defense against the devil's schemes! So I ask you today: Have you prayed on the Armor of God before in your life time? bOr are you wearing fake armor? Think about it. Take the time to pray.

Dear God,
All masks are off today. See me for who I truly am. I know you see right past my smile into my aching heart at times. Forgive me for trying to be something or someone that I'm not. Help me to be honest with myself, others and you. I honor you today.

Glimmer of Hope

Jack Lengyel: A football coach with a dream.

He took over the Marshall College football team after a horrible plane crash that killed the entire team. This story rocked the entire area. If you watch the movie that was made about it you will cry and be inspired to take on the world. You can put Marshall College into your computer search and read newspapers about it.

Jack Lengyel was an amazing man. Walking into something dead and bringing health to it. I often tell my husband Guy that he has a gift at bringing health to things; after all, he brought health to me after many years of marriage! Bringing health and stability to something is a blessing and a gift. It takes hope, patience, and time. Jack walked into a mess and brought hope. He even made history and believed in the impossible, something that was never done before. He had the NCAA agree to allow Marshall College freshmen eligible to play in 1971. This was a big deal back then!

There is something he said that is quoted in almost everything you read on him:

> "The moral of this story isn't about winning and losing,
> but **THAT YOU DO PLAY THE GAME.**" ~Jack Lengyel

He said this early on during his arrival to Marshall, when the team was on a losing streak. He wanted to keep the hope alive, and if just playing the game and keeping things going was how it was done then he was going to do it! The people that were left were still dealing with grief. This was an amazing man to have a hope like this. He was not looking for the glory of winning, he was looking for a glimmer of hope in just keeping things going.

Read this scripture and see how it reflects the same:

> "One day as Jesus was standing by the lake of Gennesaret, with the people crowding around him and listening to the word of God, he saw at water's edge two boats, left there by the fishermen, who were washing their nets. He got into one of the boats, the one belonging to Simon, and asked him to put out a little from shore. Then he sat down and taught the people from the boat. When he had finished speaking, he said to Simon, 'Put out into deep water, and let down the nets for a catch.' Simon answered, 'Master, we've worked hard all night and haven't caught anything. But because you say so, I will let down the nets.' When they had done so, they caught such a large number of fish that their nets began to break. So they signaled their partners in the other boat to come and help them, and they came and filled both boats so full that they began to sink."
> Luke 5:1-7

First of all, I live with a fisherman. I know that when he has it in his mind the fish are NOT biting, that's it! He is done for the day. He goes home, uses the outdoor hose to hose off everything from boots, net, tackle box and anything that has muck on it. He is ready for a cup of coffee and to put his feet up somewhere.

I can just picture this story. It says the fishermen are cleaning their nets already; their job is done (Luke 5:2). Then after fishing all night and not catching one thing, Jesus tells them to put their nice clean nets back into the water. Can you imagine? It was a dead thing. They knew they would NOT catch a thing. But they did it anyway! Someone, and I stress the word ONE, gave them a little glimmer of hope. A miracle happened that night because of Jesus.

Who are you giving hope to? Are you an optimist or do you go around and see the negative in almost everything? Do you think before you speak? It only takes ONE person to give a glimmer of hope. That one little glimmer of hope can change a life forever. Your words can change a life forever. Your silence, with you hanging in there with someone, can change their life forever.
It also will change you.

Dear God,
Make me a person of hope; someone that can see past the darkness and past dead things. Help me to hang onto your Word that says with you, all things are possible. I honor you today.

<u>Until Sunset</u>

"Choose some of our men and go out to fight the Amalekites. Tomorrow I will stand on top of the hill with the staff of God in my hands. Moses, Aaron and Hur went to the top of the hill. As long as Moses held up his hands, the Israelites were winning, but whenever he lowered his hands, the Amalekites were winning. When Moses' hands grew tired, they took a stone and put it under him and he sat on it. Aaron and Hur held his hands up one on one side, one on the other so that his hands remained steady till sunset. So Joshua overcame the Amalekite army with the sword."
Exodus 17:9-13

This is the most amazing story and it encourages my heart. When Moses Gets tired and weary against the Amalekites Aaron and Hur actually sit him down and hold up his hands and I'm sure his arms. It's such a total picture of teamwork, friendship, caring, victory and the list goes on. Tonight I spoke to over 100 young people. It's amazing when you share your story and God's word with people, how God can move. But it was so awesome I sat on the front pew of the church and just loved to watch, as young people were praying and crying with other young people. God was moving and it reminded me of Aaron and Hur. As people who follow God we are to be a support for one another. We cannot do it alone. We need our brothers and sisters to hold up our arms when we feel we can't make it. How many times does someone have to tell you that before you will actually receive help, encouragement and love?

Not receiving help can sometimes be an act of pride. But that's why we are all here, to be a help and encouragement to one another. This picture of Aaron and Hur is one of the most amazing examples of this in the Word. When you are truly living and walking with God you will except help from others. We need each other! We need to go the extra mile for one another like Aaron and Hur did for Moses. You can only hope and pray for amazing people like that in your life. The Word says these guys held his hands up "till sunset." (vs. 12) Just amazing. Who has tried to help you? Why don't you receive what they have to offer? Stop fighting. God may just want to use them in your life. Tonight I saw people helping people in front of my eyes and it was great. In return God will use you to do the same.

Dear God,
Use us to help one another till sunset if need be. Let us be someone that our friend can cry on. God I thank you for people who care in my life. I thank you for saving my soul and giving me brothers and sisters who care, not sure what I would do without them. I honor you today.

March 6th

Take Your Transparency Off of the Shelf

Sometimes there are pivotal moments in your life where you realize all the things that happened to you happened for a reason. Some of the youth that hang out with my kids say it this way: "God wrecked me tonight!" I'm not used to all this new youth language, but I will say that this week, God wrecked me. That's a good expression. It means that God did something amazing in you. Thus, the title of this Book.

If you have been reading this devotional every day, you know that I just spoke to 100 young people. For some reason, I am a lot more transparent with teenagers than I am with adults. Being transparent is a very vulnerable place to be. Here is how the dictionary defines the word vulnerable:

> "Capable of, or susceptible to, being wounded or hurt."

When you are transparent you open yourself up to judgment. But sometimes transparency is the very thing that can touch a life forever. I have been judged before, but I am at the point where I don't care anymore what people think of my past. God has changed my life forever, and it's time to be transparent and let people see that God can use a life that satan tried to snuff out.

When I spoke to the youth group this week, I gave my testimony and shared some stories of things that happened when I was in high school; just amazing stories about the things God was doing in my life at that time. I was very open with the youth group and I was very transparent. God used my transparency.

I have been getting letters from teenagers and young adults ever since I spoke this week. They have touched my heart in a very special way. But there was one kid that will never really understand what he did to me. It wrecked me in a good way. He wrote a great letter to me on facebook, and because he did not use a picture of himself as his profile picture, and I did not know him by his real name, I clicked on his picture to see if there were more pictures of him so I could know who had written me this letter. When I did, I saw that he had written the message to me 18 hours prior to me seeing it, based on his facebook status. His status, which is kind of like a title at the top of any facebook page, said, "Tana Miller is my hero." I cannot even begin to tell you what happened to me when I saw that. I began to weep and cry harder than I have in a long time. I just sat at my desk and kept crying.

It's times like these that my life seems to pass by me in a flash and I realize that everything that has happened to me in this lifetime has happened for moments like this. For those of you who know me, you know I try to stay humble. I want God getting all the glory. Yes, I'm excited most the time and have a ton of energy! I make mistakes and God is still growing me, but when I saw a young person put that as their status, it wrecked me big time!

This young person saw Jesus in me this week for one reason, I was transparent. I told all; even things that were shameful. I held nothing back. I wanted these kids to see what I'm doing now and how very far God can bring us even if we have a shameful past.

I have often said, if one person can weep at my grave and say, "This lady changed my life," everything will be worth it. So when I read this kid's profile status today, I can't tell you how much it broke me.

Please don't judge my words, I know God is the one who changes lives, not me, but I tell you today, God wants to use your pain for purpose.

Some of you have had the stories of your life on a shelf. Some of those stories are shameful and painful for you. If you were to tell your story, it would make you very vulnerable. None of us want people to judge us. But I tell you today, your transparency can change lives. It is worth the risk if it changes lives.

Jesus was a servant.

> "Just as the Son of Man did not come to be served,
> but to serve, and to give his life as a ransom for many."
> Matthew 20:28

You and I are here to serve.

> "You are not your own, you were bought at a price."
> 1 Corinthians 16:19-20

I want to remind you today that you are not your own. Jesus Christ died for you, and you were bought at a price: His death on a cross.

He deserves for us to take our transparency off the shelf. It took time in my healing to use these stories for His glory, but I encourage you to know today that God desires for you to be transparent no matter how hard it may be for you.

Take your transparency off the shelf, dust it all off, and in time use those stories!

Dear God,
I thank you that someone saw all you have done in my life. I thank you that you finally brought me to a place where I can no longer fear peoples' judgments about my past. I pray for the reader, that you will help them to realize you have given them their story for a reason, not to sit on a shelf. I honor you today.

March 7th

A Drop in a Bucket

This morning I feel spring in the air. There is a magazine on my desk with all spring-like bed covers and many pastel colors. Out the window the sun looks brighter and the air is warmer. New England's winters are so hard sometimes. They can get you down and keep you moving at a slower pace. But the thing I love about the Lord is that even in the midst of a hard New England winter here in Massachusetts, there is still joy and strength when I meet with Him in the morning.

Reading His word seems to make me come alive. I'm sure my cup of java helps, but I am encouraged and uplifted when I read of His might and power. For some it may be just a story, but for me it's life. I have lived it. He has proven Himself time and time again. Or He has "shown up," so to speak! His Word is alive and active. It is the best-selling book in all of the world, and I think that is because people are looking for some kind of hope. If only they would make the words on the pages part of their daily life. He will never hurt us, leave us, or forsake us. We are safe within these pages.

My husband and I visited a place in Calcutta (Kolkata), India where they make idols. Much incredible craftsmanship goes into each one; hundreds of long hours in the hot India sun. It was one of the most amazing things I have ever seen. But, it's a dead idol. Not living; made of metal, clay, hay, or stone, but not alive. There are many God's and idols, but I thank God that my Father is alive and meets with me, guides me, and will forever be with me.

"To whom, then, will you compare God? What image will you compare him to? As for an idol, a craftsman casts it, and a goldsmith overlays it with gold and fashions silver chains for it. A man too poor to present such an offering selects wood that will not rot. He looks for a skilled craftsman to set up an idol that will not topple. Do you not know? Have you not heard? Has it not been told you from the beginning? Have you not understood since the earth was founded? He sits enthroned above the circle of the earth, and its people are like grasshoppers. He stretches out the Heavens like a canopy, and spreads them out like a tent to live in. He brings princes to naught and reduces the rulers of this world to nothing."
Isaiah 40:18-23

"'To whom will you compare me? Or who is my equal?'
says the Holy One."
Isaiah 40:25

I did not come to this conclusion just because I read it in a book. My first encounter with God was at only 16 years of age and from that point on, over the last 33 years, God has proven to me that He is faithful. Maybe the Bible is just a pretty book on your coffee table to you, but I hunger to read it and soak it all in. I promise you today that if you are seeking, need a fresh start, or need hope and a change, and you open the pages of this book, it will change you. I discipline myself to open the pages and read because I believe I need to be changed on a daily basis. This is how He grows us and builds in us a strong character.

I love to just sit and read about his might and power. Like the Bible said, we are like little grasshoppers to him. All of us billions of people are like grasshoppers. This is how big He is. Read these scriptures today, and look them up and meditate on them again. I don't think we could ever get it in our hearts and minds how very mighty He is.

> "Who has held the dust of the earth in a basket, or weighed the mountains on the scales and the hills in a balance?"
> Isaiah 40:12

> "Surely the nations are like a drop in a bucket."
> Isaiah 40:15

Today as you go about your day, remember just how big He is. His bigness is not just measured in size alone, but in the great love He has for you. So much love that His son was tortured for your soul.

Dear God,
When I think of your awesome power I feel safe and sure that all is under control. I may not understand all I go through, but I am sure of the fact that you will never leave my side, and I thank you for that. You come like the wind and breathe on me. I honor you today.

God Stepped In

In 1 Kings 19 we see Elijah fleeing from the wicked Queen Jezebel. She had installed 850 prophets of Baal and ordered the slaughter of any prophets of God who opposed her. Ahab was her husband and he was very swayed by her. Alone he was very conscientious, but his weakness was Jezebel. She had amazing influence on him and it led him to be a very wicked king of Israel. So in 1 Kings 19 we see Elijah running away from death.

> "Elijah was afraid and ran for his life."
> 1 Kings 19:3

Even though God had displayed his power so strong on Mount Carmel, Elijah was running. This is how bad Queen Jezebel's reputation was. Elijah was very afraid. We see that Elijah went a day's journey into the desert alone. And not only was he afraid, but he was ready to end everything. This is a man who knew the voice of God, who verses later in 1 Kings (verse 13), could determine God's voice among other forces. He knew God, and here we see him ready to die. He actually ditched his servant in Judah before he went alone into the desert, and I believe it's because he thought this would be the end of his life.

> "He came to a broom tree, sat down under it and prayed that he might die. 'I have had enough, Lord,' he said. 'Take my life.'"
> 1 Kings 19:4

I can imagine he was feeling very overwhelmed, but he had seen God's power in so many ways. When I read this, it's hard to believe that he just wanted it all to end. If this can happen to the prophet Elijah, it can happen to anyone. This is a man who had seen miracles, and now he was asking God to take his life. Once again we see God's mighty hand in this story. Elijah had experienced God's provision and miracles just chapters before in the Kerith Ravine by the brook, and he was about to see once again that God loved him. The Word says that he fell asleep under that broom tree.

> "All at once an angel touched him and said, 'Get up and eat.' He looked around and there by his head was a cake of bread baked over hot coals, and a jar of water. He ate and drank and then lay down again. The angel of the Lord came back a second time and touched him and said, 'Get up and eat, for the journey is too much for you.' So he got up and ate and drank. Strengthened by that food, he traveled forty days and forty nights until he reached Horeb, the Mountain of God. There he went into a cave and spent the night."
> 1 Kings 19:5-9

This is just so cool. Remember a time when you were very weak. Maybe it was a sickness, the flu, or a time when you fasted to draw close to God? When we are weak, the last thing we can do is think about getting up and preparing something. So God sends an angel, and this angel actually makes a fire while Elijah is asleep. Not sure about you, but that is something very cool to think about. It says that the cake of bread was over hot coals; Elijah was so weak, there is no way he could have made that fire. There was also a jar of water. It's just so amazing when you think about it. The angel woke him two times to eat and drink, to take care of him. We read that that food and drink strengthened him. This is how very much God still had a purpose for him and loved him. God still had some plans; there was still work to do!

It's just amazing that God loves us in such a way that when we are ready to give up, He is right there to encourage us once again and to even send people and angels to help us. Elijah was still going to be used to mentor Elisha. I'm sure while Elijah was lying under that tree wanting to die he never thought he still would be used in such a powerful way. I'm so glad God does not give up on us.

It would not be until 2 Kings, chapter 2 that Elijah gets taken away to Heaven in a whirlwind by a chariot of fire and horses. The anointing that was on him was now on Elisha. The hopelessness under that broom tree made him want to die but due to God alone sending an angel to strengthen him, and due to God still having a plan for him, we see the man Elisha being used in such powerful ways that even prophets knew that he was being used. When Elijah was taken away, Elisha was upset and picked up Elijah's cloak that had fallen when he was taken to Heaven. Elisha took Elijah's cloak and struck the water. I think he did this out of anger and this is what happened:

"He took the cloak that had fallen from him and struck the water with it. 'Where now is the Lord, the God of Elijah?' he asked. When he struck the water, it divided to the right and to the left, and he crossed over. The company of the prophets from Jericho, who were watching, said, 'The spirit of Elijah is resting on Elisha.' And they went to meet him and bowed to the ground before him."
2 Kings 2:14-15

I know that if God had not stepped in, Elijah would have died and Elisha would have never been used. This is the great love He has for you today. He has a plan and purpose for your life. There is no way Elijah could have seen just how great that purpose was sitting in his depression and fear under that tree. But he did what the angel told him to do. And God stepped in. Let God step in on your life.

Dear God,
When we are blinded with fear, anxiety, and depression I ask that you come to us, and like you took care of your prophet, take care of us. Thank you for a love that sees past our sin and failure. It's the most amazing love I have ever experienced. I honor you today.

The Necklace

Sometimes when I write I take the risk of readers not believing the stories that I'm telling. I promise you everything I share is true and not made up.

When I became a new follower of God my senior year of high school I was just beginning to learn how to pray. There was only one kid in the school that I knew loved the Lord. I asked him if he would like to pray after school for our school mates. He lived nearby so I asked if he wanted to come to my house. We made a list of names, and every single week we would pray for our friends one by one.

> "Again, I tell you that if two of you on earth agree about anything you ask for, it will be done for you by my Father in Heaven. For where two or three come together in my name, there am I with them."
> Matthew 18: 19-20

I had read this scripture and wanted to put it into practice. During that year I cannot tell you the amazing things that were going on with our classmates at Guilderland High School in NY. God was moving in amazing ways. One of my friends Nancy prayed and asked God to come into her life in the school parking lot. She ended up going to a Bible College after graduation and still loves the Lord today.

One friend called me one day and said, "Tana, I know you carry your Bible around. Can you tell me about that?" She asked the Lord into her life and still lives for Him today. Her two daughters are now worship leaders and living for God. I just can't even tell you the fruit that came from my prayer days with my friend; there are so many more stories.

There were times when we were praying together when we had our own struggles going on, and we would pray for each other. I was so upset one day because I had lost my gold necklace. In school that day, I told my friend that we had to pray! I had to find this necklace that had sentimental meaning to me. When we got to my house, I opened the door and we began to walk up the stairs to the living room where we prayed every week. There on the top step stretched out like someone had it in two hands and just draped it across the top step was my necklace! When my brother and I left that morning there was NOTHING on the steps and my parents were already gone for work. I was the first one in the door and not one person had been there since. But, there it was. A joy came over us because we had just witnessed a miracle. Prayer that day was amazing, as you can imagine.

I want you to think for a moment about if that had happened to you. How would you have felt? It made me think that God cared about the little things in my life, even my necklace. The things that we don't think the God of the universe would be bothered with, He actually cares about. That's because He cares about us and our emotions, feelings, and desires. He loves us that much.

Such an excitement came over me when I picked up that gold chain. I knew somehow, supernaturally, it was placed there. It was also another victory in that house for me. I had seen many demonic things go on there, so to me this was the Lord putting His stamp on the fact that I was protected and watched over in that house at 9 Kaine Drive!

I know this is a strange story to tell, but I wanted you to hear it because there are things that mean the world to you, and when little things happen to us, sometimes we don't think God would care about them so we don't ask. But I tell you, He does care! Pray!

You need to go to Him even with the little things. The day we prayed for my necklace I did not have an expectation in my heart that anything like that would happen! I was totally in awe and blown away when I saw it spread out on the top stair. I was in shock! It filled me with joy that He would care that much.

What are you missing today? What do you desire that you don't think He would care about? Seeing an old friend? Reconciliation? Find something you misplaced?

That He would lead you to the right job? The list goes on.

Truth be told, He cares about all that because He cares about you! He wants to grant your heart's desires. He cares about the little things that you don't think He would want to be bothered with.

I'm not sure how that necklace got there that day, but I know it was because we prayed.

Dear God,
Help us to not lose sight of the fact that you care about the little things in our lives; the tiny things that we are hurt over. It's such an amazing thought to think that you desire to meet every need in our life, that you take the time to care, and that you answer our prayers. I honor you today.

<u>Crossing Your Red Sea</u>

It's so easy to turn to a Bible story, like the parting of the Red Sea in Exodus, and believe it for someone else. It's another thing to believe it for yourself. Today think about some of the impossible situations you are in.

When looking at the story of the parting of the Red Sea there were so many impossibilities. First, no Israelite army could stand against the mighty Egyptians! Everyone knew that! The Israelites came to a place in Exodus, chapter 14 where they were caught between the Egyptian army and the Red Sea. How could they get across the sea? Their situation looked hopeless. But I love Moses' words to the Israelites:

"Do NOT be afraid. Stand firm and you WILL see the deliverance the Lord will bring you today. The Egyptians you see today you will never see again. The Lord will fight for you; you need only to BE STILL."
Exodus 14:13-14

Wow, not sure about you, but if I was between the sea and the Egyptian army, I'm not quite sure I could stand still. Oh, how I long as a leader to be that sure of the fact that God *will* come through for His people! Too many times we have our eyes on the things we fear or the hopelessness of the situation, and forget that miracles can happen! God is the one fighting for us. We are not alone. We are to be STILL and watch Him work.

As soon as Moses said that to his people, God spoke to him and said:

"Why are you crying out to me? Tell the Israelites to MOVE ON. Raise your staff and stretch out your hand over the sea to divide the water so that the Israelites can go through the sea on dry ground."
Exodus 14:15-16

This just makes me laugh! It's like the Lord is saying, "Hello, Moses! Don't you see the army that is about to kill you!? You must move forward!" I love the fact that the Lord said, "Why are you crying out to me?" and His next words were "MOVE ON!"

Too many times we sit and pray when the answer is right ahead of us, even when it looks impossible! Sometimes, it's time to move and act rather than sit on our butts and wait for God to come through. We somehow think He will knock on our door and give us that new job, or an envelope of money to meet our needs! It's time to pray as we are **on the MOVE**! Get up, seek out, and move forward. Do something new! Sometimes change is what we need to continue to move forward.

Just imagine the reaction of the Israelite army when they saw the waters part. I can imagine that was one of the most amazing things they had ever seen. And the Bible says they were marching on dry ground as then crossed. We focus most of our attention on the walls of water on each side of them, but it was a total miracle that the land they were walking on was dry! It should have been mud and hard to walk on, but it was dry. Can you imagine? Many years ago, a children's movie was made about this. I loved watching this part in the movie because it also showed giant whales and sharks swimming around, as if the Israelites were looking into a giant fish tank! Until that movie, I had never even thought about the animals. It was all such a miracle.

What are you standing between today? It looks as if you cannot move to the left or to the right. You think your situation is seemingly hopeless. Maybe the Lord is trying to say to you, "Why are you crying out to me? MOVE ON!"

This does not mean that He does not want you to pray, but maybe you need to pray on the MOVE! Get up. Go for it! Move toward that impossible dream! Walking through the Red Sea was totally impossible, but through God, it became possible.

What is your Red Sea today? Cross it!

Dear God,
Help us to dream the impossible and to not look at the negative or hopelessness in our situation. Help us to get up, move on, and believe You *will* come through for us just like you did this miracle for Moses. You are still the same God that was with Moses! I thank you for that. Help me to have a faith that will part seas today. I honor you Lord.

Back Stage

Have you ever been involved in a high school musical? If not, you don't know what you are missing. It really is a team effort, and it seems that back stage is wild and crazy at times. People are rushing around, grabbing the next costume. I was in *Hello, Dolly!* years ago at Guilderland High in NY and loved every minute!

Now the years have passed and my daughter is in her high school musical at Beverly High. Opening night is tonight (2010). Last night I was there to see the dress rehearsal, and back stage a flood of memories came to me as I saw the kids running around getting in their costumes. I saw three girls in a corner going through tap steps, and two young kids practicing their waltz. It all seems so crazy that time has flown so fast; that I am now handing out programs at my daughter's musical. It's times like these that I think about the grace of God.

Please don't judge me as I share with you another memory from my high school years, only to show you once again the mighty grace of a living God.

In *Hello, Dolly!* I was a dancer and a singer. This tall boy had to actually pick me up and throw me up and around his neck. I can't even tell you how scared I was. The funniest thing is that I'm not a dancer! In order for you to sing in the musical, you had to also try out for dancing. I remember during the auditions for the musical, all the girls waiting in the hallway to audition had their leg warmers and dance outfits on, and there I was in my sweat pants. I could not remember the steps if you paid me!

The time came for our entire group to go out in front of the judges to audition. I knew I did not know the dance at all, but I was brave! After all, in order to sing I had to audition for dance as well. When we got out on stage there were at least 25 people watching. Many were my friends and peers. The music started, I was not a dancer, and it did not come natural! I could hardly remember the steps. All I remember is when everyone was leaping one way, I was leaping the other! I am totally not exaggerating! They were to the left and I was to the right. I could see people watching and laughing, and I saw my friend talking to our amazing director with smiles on both of their faces, and he pointed at me. It was very humiliating, but I had a big smile, and half way through the audition I was laughing my head off as I was leaping all over the stage in the wrong direction. It's very funny as I think about it now.

The funny thing is even though I stunk, they casted me to do the hardest dance move— being picked up and put over a kid's head. The director was smart, and wanted to stretch us in ways we did not want to be stretched. Very smart.

As I stood back stage at my daughter's dress rehearsal last night, I remembered one night from my own musical. I had just finished with my last scene: A parade that marches out to the front of the stage. After the final scene, I would go take that costume off and be done until we came out at the end for the applause. When the entire group of people from the parade was rushing backstage, myself included, somehow I got pushed and my nose hit the clothes rack. It hurt so bad I was crying. The mothers who were helping with the show said I had to go to the emergency room to see if my nose was broken. They got my mother and brother who were sitting in the audience, took me to the hospital for an x-ray.

I had never been for an x-ray. I was alone in the room with the technician when she asked, "Any chance you could be pregnant?" I was in total shock that she asked that. I was scared, and fear ran through me thinking about my mom sitting right outside with my brother, who loved Jesus and had been bugging me at the time about needing God! I knew in my heart there was a chance that I could be pregnant.

I told the technician that there was a chance and asked her to PLEASE NOT tell my mother or brother! The technician said that she could no longer do the x-ray due to the chance that I could be pregnant, but that she would not tell my mom. I will continue this story, but let me pause and tell you that I was not pregnant. I only knew there was always that chance. At the time, I was only 15 years old and on the pill. This is a very shameful memory, but this is what I did:

I walked out into the waiting room and totally lied. I told my mother and brother that the technician was a Christian and she prayed with me. I told them that after she prayed with me I felt better so I did not need an x-ray. My mom sat there with a bit of a confused look on her face, and I'm sure my brother was thinking that God was answering his prayers. When I think of this today I cannot even believe it. It's so crazy. I lied right to my mother and brother. I was so lost back then. The funniest thing is they believed it. I'm sure my brother gave it as a testimony to the group of people that was praying for me. I never did tell them I was sorry for that. I'm sorry, Mom and Lou.

I thank God that he takes my shame and reminds me that I'm a new creation, just like a butterfly is trapped in its darkness and finally set free to fly. Well, that was me.

Three years later I started to follow God. But now after all these years, sometimes I will see and hear things that remind me of my past and the mighty grace of God.

This is what happened to me last night back stage at my daughter's rehearsal, as I had that memory:

"Forget the former things; do not dwell on the past. See, I am doing a new thing! Now it springs up; do you not perceive it? I am making a way in the desert and streams in the wasteland."
Isaiah 43:18-19

"Therefore, if anyone is in Christ, he is a new creation; the old has gone, the new has come!"

Dear God,
Today I think of your mighty hand of grace and what I have become. I can hardly believe how I was one time in my life. I'm so glad you loved me through it all. I honor you today.

March 12th

The Muffin Lady

The other day I heard a man talking about Native Americans. He said that they never judge a man by looking at him. They walk around behind him and see what he is looking at, and what he has gone through before ever judging him. I pondered a while on that. It reminded me of the saying, "Don't judge a man until you've walked two moons in his moccasins."

Just imagine meeting someone that smelled like smoke, looked like they could have been high, had a cuss mouth and had barely any clothes on. As a person who loves God, how would you respond to them?? I would love them anyway. My husband and I lead some ministries at church that require us to love every week. And I don't mind doing this every week, because that used to be me.

What if people wrote me off as soon as they saw me walk into Alcove church that day back in 1984? I have heard awesome people of God make prejudice comments about others. When this has happened in the past I was in shock. As followers of God there is NO place for this. God sent His son to die for everyone, even the bum on the street. His love goes way beyond our comfort zone! Truth be told, it does not matter if you are uncomfortable, you are to love everyone. This does not mean we have to like their sin, but we have to love them with the unconditional love of God. Sometimes it's a very hard pill to swallow if you have been hurt by them.

When Jesus died for everyone he was like that Native American walking behind a man, the only big difference is that He already knew what we would go through. He knew we would sin. That's why He died, and that's a lot of love.

"Do not think of yourself more highly than you ought, but rather think of yourself with sober judgment, in accordance with the measure of faith God has given you."
Romans 12:3

As Christians we tend to categorize sin: this is worse than that, or that is worse than this. In God's eyes, sin is sin. Our sin is just as bad as the next guy and until we realize that, we will never truly understand humility, forgiveness, love, or the heart of God.

We are to love with the amazing love of God. If you have never been loved this may be a very hard task. But we need to strive to let God heal us and learn how to love with His love.

Years ago I was asked to speak at a Valentine Banquet at a church. When I was done speaking a line formed of about 20 ladies that wanted to speak to me. I had so much fun talking to them in my beautiful new red dress that I had purchased just for the occasion. One woman caught my eye; her clothes were dirty, she had hardly any teeth, and the closer she got to me in the line, the stronger her smell got. She smelled very bad.

To top it all off she was eating a muffin and talking to the lady next to her. As she spoke, pieces of the muffin were hitting the other lady! After I spoke to each lady in the line I gave them a big hug; then came the muffin lady. She spoke to me for about six minutes; pieces of her muffin were flying from her mouth and hitting my new red dress. My first thought was that I could not hug her because then the little muffin bits would smush into my dress. As you can tell I was very preoccupied by the muffin bits. Anyway, I knew in my heart that I had to hug her. After all I had hugged everyone else. So when the time came I gave her a big hug because I knew that's what the Lord would have done. It's so funny when I think about it now. That was the end of the red dress.

I know if I stood behind that lady and could see everything in life that she had been through I would have not looked at her the way I did that night. I would know what caused all those wrinkles all over her face, I would know why her teeth were gone, and I would see where she came from and what she has done. I would even know why she is not cared for properly.

This is like our Lord. He sees all, knows everything, and even sees where we are going before we go there. He has more faith in us than we do in ourselves.

"Do not judge, or you too will be judged. For in the same way you judge others, you will be judged, and with the measure you use, it will be measured to you."
Matthew 7:1-2

She taught me a great lesson that night. I don't know her name but I will never forget the Muffin Lady

Dear God,
Help us to not judge others. Let us know they have been through so much that we cannot see. If we would only take the time to get to know people before we form our opinions of them. Forgive us Lord. I honor you today.

The Silhouette

A couple days ago I shared with you how getting involved with my daughters musical had been like a step back in time for me– Just so many memories.

Every night that the musical is playing, I walk to the back of the lobby and look at the art display. Usually the art is by students and they sell it to make money for musical funds. But some artist who I do not know, donated an entire lot of art to the school. For the past three nights I have walked in the back of the lobby and looked at the art. I have always loved looking at people's art. You kind of see how the artists look at things by looking at their art. Anyway, this art is kind of dated, the mats are colors from like the 70s and some of the frames are old. Even the style of the art is old. I have yet to see anything that I wanted to purchase.

It's not like I don't like old things. I actually love old things. One room in my house is dedicated to old black and white pictures of my great grandparents and my grandparents. I have a basket in the room of old kitchen tools such as a rolling pin, an antique egg slicer, and more. I just have always loved looking back at history and old things. But for the past three nights, not one painting or any print had caught my eye, until last night.

I have always loved that old art where someone sits behind a screen and the person doing the art draws or paints a silhouette of his or her face. Silhouettes have always intrigued me, I'm not sure why. There is something about seeing someone from the side and how they usually only make them black and white. I've always wanted one of myself, but I don't even know where I would go to get that done in a professional manner.

So last night I was checking out the art in the lobby again I did not see anything but out of the corner of my eye I saw a clearance table! It was a bunch of random art, not framed. As I got closer, I saw there were three 8x10 pieces of art that were framed. They were silhouettes! I grabbed the first one and looked it over, the frames of the three silhouettes were modern and beautiful, and every single thing on this table was five dollars! Now that's my kind of price range! The back of the silhouettes said:

"Mary R. Smalley posed silhouette
Framed by Kenneth C. Smalley
8 Bosworth Street, Beverly, MA 01915
$35.00"

They really are professionally framed and you can tell! They are just beautiful.

So I'm looking at the first one of a boy, then the second one, another boy. When I picked up the third silhouette I stood there in shock. I just don't know how to say it or relay it to you, it was me. I stood there holding that 8x10 silhouette and it was me as a 13-year-old girl. Chills went up my spine. It looks exactly like me.

I'm not sure if you have ever seen silhouette art, but most of them have hair that is all clumped together. This silhouette is different. The hair is long, which you do not see much of, and the hair is also messy. It had my upturned nose and it looked exactly like my lips and chin. I felt like I was looking at an old picture of myself!

I stood there holding it for a few minutes. It was a very weird moment. I wish I knew who this picture was of. I brought it to the man and handed him my five dollars. I knew the people I was with would wonder why I was buying a silhouette of someone else, but in my mind it was the Lord's gift to me. It's going right in my black and white room! It's perfect. There were times in antique shops that I almost purchased one of these but this one was my profile! And only five bucks! Can't beat that!

That Silhouette reminded me that God loved me! No matter how many people may think I'm going a tad overboard with this, I felt this was His gift to me that night. I have always wanted one, and the last three days have been a reminder of how far He has brought me by His grace. This was like the period at the end of the sentence. It's an amazing thing to know the Father loves you.

> "Oh Lord, you have searched me and you know me."
> Psalm 139:1

> "You knit me together in my mother's womb. I praise you because I am fearfully and wonderfully made."
> Psalm 139:13-14

He knows the curves of your face today. He knows how many hairs are upon your head.

> "How precious to me are your thoughts, O God! How vast is the sum of them! Were I to count them, they would outnumber the grains of sand."
> Psalm 139:17-18

He made your Silhouette and He thinks of you today.

Dear God,
Thank you that you care about the little things. Your reminders of love are amazing at times. Thank you that when I was still unformed, your word says your eyes saw me. You knew back then what would be today. I honor you Lord.

Walk the Plank

As young kids that lived on Kaine Drive in Albany, we called ourselves the Kaine Drive Crusaders. Our family was one of the first to purchase a house in a growing development. Duplexes and houses were going up all over. Every new family that moved in with kids became part of the crusader pack. Back then we played with good old mud and dirt and we loved the woods. But there was one thing we really loved! When new houses were being built, we would go to those houses after the construction crew left and play in them.

The thing I loved about growing up in the 70s and early 80s is that we totally used our imagination! There were no cell phones, Internet, X-box or anything like that. No distractions from the good outdoors and nature. These new houses that we were not supposed to be in were perfect for the imagination. They were great castles and we were princes and princesses. They were stages and we were rock stars! Sewer pipes became caves and army holes. What a blast we had.

The best memory I have was the day we played Walk the Plank. There was this two-by-four sticking out the side of one of the new houses for some reason. Below the two-by-four was a 10-foot drop to a dirt pile. We were so excited when we saw it and the same thing was going through all of our minds. The two-by-four would become a pirate ship plank! The plank led into a big empty unfinished room which would become where we all hung out and manned the deck. We had such a blast that day. I remember the rush as it was my turn to walk the plank. Going out onto the very end of the two-by-four and then knowing I would have to jump 10 feet into a dirt pile. This is one of the best and most fun memories I have from Kaine Drive. Jumping that far was a leap of faith for me. I remember standing at the very end and actually being scared. But after I had done it I felt like I conquered the world! I was now equal with the boys! Firecracker, Firecracker, boom, boom, boom! You have to be almost 50 to remember that one!

Standing on the edge of the plank my imagination ran wild. There were giant fish and things that would hurt me down there. I kept my eye on the dirt pile. I knew once I reached it I would be safe.

Peter saw Jesus walking on the water. At first he and the disciples thought he was a ghost. The Bible says they:

"Cried out in fear."
Matthew 14: 26

This actually made me laugh out loud when I first read it. Can you imagine? They spent all that time with Him and they thought he was a ghost? That's laughable to me. It's also a very funny thought to think of all the disciples screaming in fear of Him. Just picturing them all on the boat terrified, it just makes me laugh.

"But Jesus immediately said to them:
'Take courage! It is I. Don't be afraid.'"
Matthew 14:27

I admire Peter so much. He is the only one recorded to have actually talked back and stepped out in faith.

"'Lord, if it's you,' Peter replied,
'tell me to come to you on the water.'"
Matthew 14:28

You can see by the way he worded this that he was still very unsure, but he spoke anyway! Then he actually:

"Got down out of the boat, walked on the water
and came toward Jesus."
Matthew 14:29

The Bible says as soon as he took his eyes off Jesus and put them on the water, fear came over him and he began to sink.

"Immediately Jesus reached out his hand and caught him.
'You of little faith,' he said, 'why did you doubt?'"
Matthew 14:31

Well, I can tell you why Peter doubted—because he took his eyes off the very thing that made him safe! In this case, Jesus. In my case, a nice soft dirt pile.

When we take our eyes off what is safe and look all around at the distractions or temptations, we will fall and most of the time get hurt or drown. But when we keep our eyes on the very thing that is safe for us we will not be distracted by anything else! I am just so happy we have a God of second chances who will always extend that hand to us even when we fail.

No fear today, walk the plank!

Dear God,
I thank you that you are the God of a second chance. You always reach your hand of compassion out to us time and time again. Thank you for sending your son. Help me to keep my eyes on you and not my circumstance. I honor you today Lord.

March 15th

Do Hard Things

Today in New England it is cold and raining! It's been raining for about 48 hours straight. I have at least two friends whose basements are flooded! I feel so bad for them! On a day like today I love to just stay in and clean and get my house in order, but work was calling this morning and I had to get some of it done. I work from home and love my job with all my heart. When I was done working on the major project I had to finish today, my first thought was, "I MUST clean the basement and do laundry." I started heading downstairs when all of a sudden I realized I had not cracked open my Bible today or done my devotional.

How quick we forget to dig into His word when we see all the work for our jobs and home that needs to be done! I stopped at the stairs and realized that Jesus knows, and I thank God He is always there to love us anyway!

Writing this devotional has been totally awesome. It is keeping me in the Word every single day, but as you can imagine sometimes I sit to do it and am distracted by all the things I need to get done. This is today. I just sat down and said, "It's time to get into the Word!" Making a commitment is not an easy thing. It means sacrifice and self control. It means giving up many things that you want and need to do sometimes. But we need to learn to do hard things. It grows us.

It's like taking a carrot and peeling it. God strips away at us. The carrot is not ready to eat until it's cleaned and peeled. Same with us, we are not ready to be used by Him until He cleans us and strips away the things that can hold us back from being as effective as we can be. It's called the building of our character. I thank God that He is still growing me after over 31 years of walking with Him.

There are so many scriptures about working hard and doing hard things. Let's look at a couple:

"He who works his land will have abundant food,
but he who chases fantasies lacks judgment."
Proverbs 12:11

"All hard work brings a profit, but mere talk leads only to poverty."
Proverbs 14:23

For years I talked about writing a devotional and just never did it. Now I'm doing it! And the Bible says:

"So shall My Word be that goes forth from my mouth; it shall NOT return void, but it shall accomplish what I please, and it shall prosper in the thing for which I sent it."
Isaiah 55:11

Sometimes profit does not always mean money. I profit every day from writing these devotions when I have people tell me how much they are touched by what was written. I can't tell you how much it means to me to know God has used me in a way like that. This is how He wants to use you, but it takes doing some hard things. It takes Sacrifice!

I remember when my son took his first job at the age of 16. He worked at a tea shop in Mashpee, MA. Jon was a dishwasher. He had the job only two weeks when his boss approached me one day when I came to pick him up. She told me that he was one of the hardest workers she had ever had. After two weeks she was giving him a one dollar raise! She told me not to tell anyone and she laughed. She then said something that made me feel very proud; she told me that when his job was done, and he was waiting for the next load of dishes to come in, he would go around and ask others what he could do for them! He would ask the sandwich makers if he could help make sandwiches and he would ask those who clean if he could help.

She told me most the dishwashers just stand there and take a break, but he would do this! As you can imagine I was very proud that Jon was working so hard at the age of 16 that someone recognized it. He is a great kid.

All that's to say, how do you work when no one is watching? Do you slack off? Do you relax when you know there are things you could be doing?

My husband and I have always been very hard workers. Our four parents were very hard workers. I think my children get their work ethic from us. They see what we do every day. I'm very proud of that.

My son is now 23, but when he was 18 he got a letter and cookies from his workplace. The letter said:

> "Thank you for always showing up for shifts
> with a friendly smile and a hard working attitude!
> -Laser Quest Danvers Management Team"

As a person who loves God, do you show up to work with a smile on your face and a hard working attitude? This is what I want to be known for! Sometimes as a Christian you don't even have to share verbally about God's love; people can see it in your hard work and attitude! I hope this is you today. Hard work is not easy, and maybe it's time in your life to do hard things.

Dear God,
Make me a hard worker. Help me to never be a slacker! I want to share your love through my attitude and by going the extra mile. Help me to do hard things! I honor you today.

March 16th

Love Yourself

Before I get started on today's devotion, let me just say Happy Birthday to me! Ha! Yes, today is the day of my birth. Today I am 49 years old and feeling it. Things are not all where they used to be and sometimes my body cannot keep up with my passion, but thank God it still moves! Haha! I want to do something for me today. Most likely I will go get my gray hairs covered later, which is long overdue! But it's the kind of day where I want to spoil myself. Do you know there is NOTHING wrong with taking care of yourself and spoiling yourself a bit? As a matter of a fact, neither is loving yourself. Do you love yourself? I know that's kind of a weird question, but think about it today.

Trust me, if I had money to mess with, all those things that are making me look my age might just be fixed within a month! But instead of thinking of the outward things, let's think of the inward. Do you love yourself? Do you realize it's something God wants you to do?

Some of us have been so hurt that our self-esteem has been beaten down and beaten down. Therefore, the last thing we can do is love ourselves. When you look in the mirror you hate yourself. Shame and anger have built up throughout the years and it's blinding you to the fact that God never intended for that to happen. We are to love ourselves. Take the time to read through these scriptures for a moment. Then we will talk.

"Do not see revenge or bear a grudge against one of your people,
but **love your neighbor as yourself**, I am the Lord."
Leviticus 19:18

"Honor your father and mother,
and **love your neighbor as yourself**."
Matthew 19:19

"**Love your neighbor as yourself**."
Matthew 23:39

"The second is this: '**Love your neighbor as yourself**.'
There is no commandment greater than these."
Mark 12:31

"Love the Lord your God with all your heart and with all your soul and
with all your strength and with all your mind and,
Love your neighbor as yourself."
Luke 10:27

"The entire law is summed up in a single command:
"**Love your neighbor as yourself**."
Galatians 5:14

> "If you really keep the royal law found in Scripture, '**Love your neighbor as yourself**,' you are doing right."
> James 2:8

There we have seven pieces of scripture that tell us to love our neighbors as ourselves. How can we do that if we do not love ourselves? It says in James 2:8 that if we love our neighbors as ourselves we "are doing right." It says in Galatians 5:14 that the entire law "is summed up in a single command!" In other words, it's a command for us to love our neighbors as ourselves. How can you do that if you don't love yourself? So it must be a command for us to learn to love ourselves.

Here is how I learned to love myself: I started to see myself through the eyes of Christ and not my own. When you see yourself through your own eyes, sometimes you can only remember the shame and horrible things you have done in the past. I have been very transparent with you all on other pages of this book of things I have done, and they are shameful. If you see yourself through the eyes of God you see the fact that He sent His one and only son to die for your soul. That must mean **you are worth quite a lot**. See yourself through His eyes today and **see your worth.**

> "Whatever other commandment there may be, are summed up in this one rule: '**Love your neighbor as yourself**.' Love **does no harm to its neighbor**. Therefore **love is the fulfillment of the law.**"
> Romans 13: 9

In this scripture we see that real love will not harm. So stop harming yourself with horrible thoughts that the enemy plants there. Stop hurting yourself. If you are cutting, or self mutilating, stop it! Move forward and see your worth through God's eyes! This scripture says again that love is the fulfillment of the law! God desires that you love yourself today. Until you do that you can NOT be the person He wants you to be, you cannot love your neighbor with the love that comes from Christ, and you cannot be healed of all He wants you to be healed of.

His desire today is to use you in a powerful way. He longs to use the hurts you have been through for His glory. There is someone out there that needs to know that someone else can relate with them. Climb above your guilt and shame and start to love yourself. That's the only way you will ever love your neighbor the way God intended.

So today I'm not only going to love myself, I'm going to spoil myself. Happy birthday to me!

It was NOT always this way. I had plenty of birthdays filled with self-hate and shame.

Not today!

Learn to Love yourself.

Dear God,
Thank you for helping me to love myself and see my worth through your eyes. The fact that you would give your one and only son for me is amazing. I can't even imagine it. Help me to see past my shame and realize you long to use me to touch my neighbors and all those around me. I honor you today Lord.

Tigerlilly

When our family lived on Cape Cod, we owned two cats that were sisters, and one black lab. We owned half an acre of land that was surrounded by woods. There were 20 acres of conservation land behind our home to me, it was awesome. Totally private. A five-man hot tub was on the back deck and almost every night my husband and I would soak and recap the day. I sure miss that house. One night while we were in the hot tub, a giant raccoon walked right across the deck. There was so much wild life there. We saw it all the time. Now I live on a busy street and think back to our Cape Cod house and the quiet we had there all the time.

Our three animals have always been part of the family. Arwen, our awesome black lab, we have had for about 11 years, and Fluffy is a small black cat. Arwen and Fluffy do not get along; they pretty much hate each other under the same roof. Tigerlilly, our other cat, is another story! We've had Fluffy and Tigerlilly since they were kittens. They were so cute and grew up together, but you could tell as the years went on that Tigerlilly was the leader and ruled the house! She was double-pawed on all four feet and three times the size of Fluffy. She was the boss. Our cats were house cats, we did not let them outside due to ticks and wild animals, but you could tell Tigerlilly had a wild heart. She wanted the outdoors. A few times she escaped and got out, and I would find her on the front deck punching around a mole or a mouse! So nasty. I would always check her for ticks and put her back where she belonged.

It got to the point where we had to be very careful. Whenever the door would open we had to make sure she was not around! Then we moved to our awesome house with the hot tub. We had this screened in front porch and Tigerlilly would hang out there quite a bit and watch the birds! She had boundaries that she did not like. Her confinement drove her crazy. She was born to be wild!

She started digging at the screen, and I would spank her and fix it but time and time again she would do it until she got out. One night I woke to a very strange noise. I turned on the back porch light to see her playing with a coyote! Running in circles with it! As soon as the coyote saw the light it took off and I called Tigerlilly inside the house. She was out there running with danger and she did not even realize it!

Do you know there have been boundaries set up for you for a reason? It may be your job, it may be school or the home you live in, but most are set up for protection and order. Tigerlilly did not like boundaries!

She dug through the screen one day and we did not see her for almost three days. I was sure something got her, but then three days later in the middle of the night she was at my daughter's loft window, which was on the roof, meowing! I'm sure there must have been something on the ground scaring her to the roof! She was always walking on the edge, always stepping over her boundaries that we had set up for her! She was a very bad cat and got spanked all the time! Ha!

Even in creation the Lord set up boundaries!

> "He gave the sea its boundary so the waters
> would not overstep His command."
> Proverbs 8:29

Imagine if there were no boundaries for the sea. What a mess! No boundaries at work. What disorder! No boundaries for our teens....well we won't go there! The world would be chaos without boundaries!

Well, the time finally came for Tigerlilly to find out that crossing her boundary was more than just dangerous, it would take her life. Even after getting disciplined and spanked she would always return to her sin! Ripping apart my screen! Haha! But after she would come home we would love her and check to make sure she was ok.

God does the same with us! We return to our sin and cross boundaries, but he is always there to love us even when we fail. The problem is, when we cross over boundaries that are safe for us we put ourselves in harm's way! We put ourselves in danger.

One night Tigerlilly left, and she never came home again. We waited for that third day when she would show up on the roof, but it never came. We cried and missed her so much. I missed her giant paws and the way she would protect my daughter at night. But that was it; something got her and killed her.

Are you crossing your boundaries today? Maybe it's time for you to get back where you belong: to a safe place!

Don't end up like Tigerlilly.

Dear God,
Help me to know that boundaries are set up to protect me. Even if I don't like them I pray that you help me to obey my leadership and do what I'm told at work. Help me not to cross over into areas of danger. I honor you today.

Love Follows Me
"The Lord is my shepherd; I shall not be in want."
Psalm 23:1

I don't think a day goes by that I don't want something– from my cravings of chocolate to something new. All I have to do is remember my walks in the slum of Delhi with Pastor Koshy and Joicy and I soon forget all I need. The truth is I need nothing but the grace of God in my life.

Shepherds protect and take care of their sheep. This is what He does for us.

"He makes me lie down in green pastures;
he leads me beside quiet waters."
Psalm 23:2

When was the last time you took a walk with God? Just wandered out in nature and soaked in all He has created? When was the last time you laid in a green pasture or put your feet in the water and just listened to the quiet sounds of bugs buzzing by, or a fish jumping. Some of us might say not since we were kids! Take time to get alone with Him in all He has created today. For us New Englanders, spring is coming!

"He restores my soul. He guides me
in paths of righteousness for His name's sake."
Psalm 23:3

He restores us, no matter what we have been through. His restoration will come if you let it. He will also guide us if we listen, but if you don't listen, you will miss out of the best things He has for you.

"Even though I walk through the valley of the shadow of death, I will
fear no evil, for you are with me; your rod and your staff, they
comfort me."
Psalm 23:4

I remember a time when I was going into emergency surgery because my appendix had ruptured and the poison had sent my body into shock. I thought for sure I was dying. I was very calm and every single person that was coming at me with needles and medical stuff was getting an earful. I was preaching the gospel, on what I thought was my death bed. I needed to tell just one more person about the love of God. I did not fear. I knew if I died I would be with Him. Are you ready for that today?

"You prepare a table before me in the presence of my enemies.
You anoint my head with oil; my cup overflows."
Psalm 23:5

When I prepare a table for guests it's usually beautiful. There is a name card at every place setting and a gift at every plate for every lady. I have learned classiness from my mentors. I prepare my table this way to make the people sitting at it feel very special. I'm sure the Lord's classiness is way better than my classiness! It says He prepares a table for us in front of our enemies. This is such an amazing scripture. It shows how thankful He is for us. It's hard to think that way sometimes. Scripture says, "He anoints our heads with oil and our cups will overflow." In other words, we will never want or need. He will always supply. What are you afraid of? There is nothing to fear at all!

"Surely goodness and love will follow me all the days of my life, and I will dwell in the house of the Lord forever."
Psalm 23:6

Boy do I thank God for His goodness and love. What a cool way David put it: "goodness and love will follow me". His love and goodness will follow ME! We cannot escape from Him. Is He bothering you with His love today? This is such a good thing. Let Him in. Don't push Him away. And then the awesome promise: forever and ever we will dwell in the house of the Lord.

When I woke from the emergency surgery and someone finally handed me a mirror, I did not recognize myself. They put so much fluid into me that it put about 20lbs on my face. I'm totally not exaggerating, ask my husband! I could not believe it when I looked at myself, but my first thought was, "I'm alive." I laughed for a moment thinking of my last words to all the medical staff. I wish I was a fly on the wall and could have seen myself!

But what I remember most was there was no fear, even in the end. I was in so much pain and shock that I knew it was over. Yet, I had such a peace. All I cared about were the others around me. I told my husband what to tell my kids when they got older. It was crazy. But it was NOT time yet. God had other plans.

What are you going through today? His love is following you. Don't fight it.

Dear God,
Thank you that your goodness and love follows us. I am living proof of that today. Whoever is reading today I pray they turn to you 100%, that they would stop fighting your awesome love, and that they embrace all you have for them. I honor you today.

Teamwork to Make a Dream Work!

It takes teamwork to make a dream work! 1 Corinthians 3:7-9 talks about planting.

"It's not important who does the planting, or who does the watering. What's important is that God makes the seed grow. The one who plants and the one who waters work together with the same purpose. And both will be rewarded for their own hard work. For we are both God's workers. And you are God's field. You are God's building."
1 Corinthians 3:7-9

It takes one to work the soil, one to plant, and one to water. It's God who makes things grow as we work together.

Teamwork enables us to become more effective in building the kingdom of God than would individual efforts alone. A perfect example: Think of yourself planting a garden alone. Now, think of yourself and three friends planting a garden. Yes, you can do it alone, but it will take longer and you will have to work harder. When you add your three friends it will get done faster and you can encourage each other along the way. A team effort is always better.

But for many control freaks, well, God will have to change your heart like He changed my heart and attitude. You think you are the only one who can do it because then it will be done perfectly! Stop micro-managing everything! Have faith in the other workers that God has given to you. They will only grow when you give them a shot, not to mention you will grow by learning to let go and trust those whom God has given to you.

Did you know that on a warm day, about half of the bees in a beehive stay inside beating their wings while the other half go out to gather pollen and nectar? Because of the beating wings, the temperature inside the hive is about 10 degrees cooler than outside the hive. The bees rotate during the day. Without this teamwork, there is no honey. There are also bees that guard the door to the hive. Just amazing teamwork!

I hate geese, always have. I'm scared of them. In the past when I have approached them on the ground they hiss and run at me. Not to mention there's nasty poop everywhere! But we can learn a lot about teamwork from geese.

Have you ever wondered why they fly in a V? Those geese in front rotate their leadership. When the lead goose gets tired, it changes places with one in the back while the back one flies to the front and leads. By flying as they do, the members of the flock create an upward air current for one another. Each flap that a goose makes with its wings creates lift for the bird right behind it. This is why the lead goose gets tired— no one is in front of them creating lift. The flock gets 71% higher in the air than if each goose were to fly on its own. Do you see the teamwork here? It only gets better.

When a goose gets hurt or sick, two other geese will also fall out of the V formation and stay with it until it's able to fly again. Imagine if all people did this with their friends and family! What a better place the world would be.

Just amazing.

Your "I can do it myself" attitude robs others of the opportunity to participate, grow, and learn.

God says in Ephesians 4:11:

"It was He who gave some to be apostles, some to be prophets, some to be evangelists, and some to be pastors and teachers, to prepare God's people for works of service, so that the body of Christ may be built up until we all reach unity in the faith and in the knowledge of the Son of God and become mature, attaining to the whole measure of the fullness of Christ."
Ephesians 4:11

God has gifted all of us in so many ways! You can go to 1 Corinthians 12:7-11 and read about the different gifts He gives His people. What is the purpose of all this?

"So that the body of Christ may be built up until we all reach unity in the faith and knowledge of the Son of God."
Ephesians 4:12-13

I hate to inform you, but it's NOT all about you! You can do GREAT things with your gifts alone, but couple them with the gifts of others and you can do AMAZING things. Just like the geese, you will create lift for one another to help one another. This is what it's all about.

What are some of your dreams today? Get your team together! It takes teamwork to make the dream work.

Dear God,
Help me to know I cannot do it alone. Break my pride and soften my heart. Help me to enable others to use the gifts God has given to them, and to be excited about them along side of me as we move together! I honor you today.

He's a Joy to Love

I remember when I was a kid, my mom had to have dinner on the table when dad got home or he would get upset. Sometimes if the house was not in order he would also get upset. When I first got married, I had lived with that for so long that it was under my skin. I always made sure that when I got home, which was usually before Guy, all was clean and done! And dinner was on at the proper time.

One day, I came home from work and Guy's car was there. A streak of fear came over me. I knew there were dishes in the sink and things were NOT cleaned up. My walk from the car to the apartment we lived in was horrible. I was so scared. Guy and I were in ministry as youth pastors and I had no reason to feel this way at all, but we were newly married and I never wanted him upset with me.

I walked into the house, and when I did I saw lines in the carpet. He had vacuumed the floors. Then I looked to the right and the dishes were done! I thought he was going to be so mad! I walked into the spare room where he was working and I said, "I'm so sorry things were not done." His words were, "So what! I can clean to you know!" Guy grew up in a home with two other brothers. They did all the chores and he was used to it. I can't tell you the relief I felt. This was not what I was used to.

Now we have been married for over 26 years and I let him do whatever he wants! Haha! He cooks a lot, he cleans, and he does a ton around the house. I love it. I remember at Bible College the boys there used to throw around this scripture:

> "Wives, submit to your husbands as to the Lord, for the husband is the head of the wife as Christ is the head of the church, His body, of which He is the Savior. Now as the church submits to Christ, so also wives should submit to their husbands in everything."
> Ephesians 5:22-24

A lot of times the boys there left out the last part of the chapter! Let's take a slow, hard look at it:

> "Husbands, love your wives, just as Christ loved the church and gave himself up for her to make her holy."
> Ephesians 5:25-26

It says here that husbands should love their wives like Christ loved. God sent His son to die for us. It was the ultimate sacrifice. He gave the most precious thing He had to us to save us. This is how it says a husband should love his wife: giving everything; total sacrifice of the best things he has for his wife; striving to lead her to holiness. If you are married today and you are a man, are you doing these things? How about you single men? You need to get it in your blood that this is how the Word says you are to treat your wife.

> "Cleansing her by the washing with water through the Word, and to present her to himself as a radiant church, without stain or wrinkle or any other blemish, but holy and blameless."
> Ephesians 5:26-27

What this is saying is that husbands are supposed to be the spiritual leader of the home. They are to get the Word into their wives and their children. Once again, he is to lead his wife to holiness.

Are you somehow encouraging your wife with the word today? Are you praying with her and for her? When she is hurting are you there to encourage her? Or are you way too distracted by other, selfish things? You single men who know the Lord, remember this. When you get married, you have the responsibility of being the spiritual leader in your home.

> "Husbands ought to love their wives as their own bodies."
> Ephesians 5:28

I go to the gym almost every day and the way people look at themselves in the mirror totally cracks me up. Some people really love their bodies. I would say 80% of the people admiring themselves in the mirror at the gym are the guys. It's kind of funny actually. Even if you don't love your body you still feed it and clothe it, which means you care for it.

Men are to love their wife like they admire and take care of themselves. They are to be the godly leader of their home. They are to love them as Christ loved the church and gave Himself for it. I don't know about you ladies, but if you had that kind of guy I don't think you would have any problem submitting!

I thank God for my husband. In over 26 years of marriage he has never raised his voice once to me. We have never screamed one time at one another. Yes we are normal and we bug each other sometimes, but both of us are self-controlled when it comes to losing control. But truth be told, my husband lives these scriptures. And because of it, I love submitting to him. I obey him because of his love for me. He always puts my desires and dreams equal to his. He is a joy to love. So if you get anything from this, it works both ways, a godly man loves like Christ and a godly woman has no problem submitting to that.

Dear God,
Help us once again to love like you love. To give like you give. I pray for the singles and married people reading, bless them in their marriages or future marriages. Help them to live out their marriage through your word. I honor you today.

March 21st

Fear NOT

For years and years my husband and I have labored in ministry together. Most all of our ministry has been so very fulfilling. There is nothing that beats being in the very center of God's will for your life. But as you can imagine, there have also been hardships. How can there not be when our churches are filled with hurting people?

The enemy knows just what to do to try to bring us to our very lowest point. He knows what chords to strike to bring worry and fear. He is on the prowl, ready to torment anyone who is on the move for God!

When my husband and I took our very first senior pastor positions at a church on Cape Cod, we were so filled with joy. We knew that was exactly where Jesus wanted us for that season in our lives. We moved into a little house in Falmouth on a quiet street. The church people moved us in and brought food and flowers. I felt so welcome and loved by our new church family. We were not there one week when my family came to see the new place we would call home. They spent the day with us then they piled into their cars to leave. My kids, who were small at the time, were sitting at the kitchen table while I said my goodbyes. I was so filled with joy about this new chapter in our lives!

No sooner did my family pull out of the driveway when the phone rang, and by this time I was sitting with my kids. The male voice on the other end of the phone said, "Is this Tana Miller?" I said, "Yes." Then he said something that I cannot repeat. I said very firmly, "Excuse me!?" Then he said it one more time. I cannot even tell you the fear that ran through me. He knew my name. My kids asked me what was wrong. My first thought was to go around and lock every window and door, so that's exactly what I did. Then I called my husband to come home. The phone call came at the exact time that my family pulled away so the enemy was putting thoughts in my head that someone was watching the house.

When you have had a past like I have had, the enemy uses things like this to torment us and make us think on the past and the things that are behind us! We cannot give in to it! At the same time, we must use wisdom and take the appropriate steps to be safe where you are in that moment. That is not a lack of faith. That is being smart and using wisdom.

After my husband came home we called the police and gave a report just in case it ever happened again. I was shaken up and cried on my husband's shoulder. I'm human! But the worry and fear of someone watching me after that day led me to not feel safe in my new home.

The word of the Lord says:

"For God has not given us a spirit of fear,
but of power and of love and of a sound mind."
2 Timothy 1:7

The devil will try to bring fear and worry into your life but we MUST stand on God's word! I began to tape pieces of scripture up on my kitchen cabinets and quote them to get over the fear of that phone call. This was not the first time in our ministry that something like that had happened, and we have made it through before.

Here is what I believe: satan was trying to steal my joy. From that day forward I never got a phone call like that again on Cape Cod! Satan used whoever called my home to put worry and fear into my life. This is exactly what he does, and when this happens we MUST focus on the Word of God!

"May the God of hope fill you with all joy and peace as you trust in Him, so that you may overflow with hope by the power of the Holy Spirit."
Romans 15:13

"Do not be afraid of those who kill the body but cannot kill the soul."
Matthew 10:28

"Be strong and courageous. Do not be afraid or terrified because of them, for the Lord your God goes with you; He will never leave you nor forsake you."
Deuteronomy 31:6

If you have worry and fear right now due to certain circumstances, I challenge you to dig into the Word of God tonight. If you have to tape scriptures up all over your house, do it. Get God's word into your heart and mind. I even had scriptures taped to the steering wheel of my car! You do what you must do to get God's word into your mind.

I said earlier that the man that called my house knew my name, but I tell you right now there is a God in Heaven that KNOWS YOUR NAME! He has already won the victory! Stand on the Word today!

Dear God,
You are amazing. I'm sure there will be more times in my life when I worry and fear, but when those times come I pray you will help me to soak my mind with the Bible and your promises. I thank you for the fact that you will always be there, and that you will never leave me. I honor you today.

March 22nd

Set Apart

When I was pregnant with my firstborn, I had a rare condition where I had way too much amniotic fluid. When I tell you my tummy was unnatural, I'm not exaggerating at all! I looked very out of order! My face, arms, and legs were so small and skinny, and my tummy was giant.

I remember walking into a store one time with my mother-in-law and this guy working there did a triple take. While kind of laughing, he said, "Wow, are you having triplets?" Hahaha!

I could sit on the couch and put my dinner plate right on my stomach. It was like I had my own portable tray-table or something. I laugh now, but it was NOT funny at the time. It was very painful and very dangerous for my baby. Sleeping at night was a chore. At times I could not even breathe.

One night I was home alone and Guy was at work. The phone rang, so I walked to the kitchen to pick it up! Yes, it was a phone attached to the wall with a cord, remember those? Haha. It was my doctor. He had no tact, and he just came out with these words: "Your baby will be born with Down Syndrome." I had some tests done that are normal for all mothers, and I guess somehow the tests showed that something was wrong. Well, it did not matter at all if there was something wrong, Guy and I knew we were having the baby, but as you can imagine that is hard news for anyone.

I began to weep. He had no words of comfort for me, just said I'm sorry and goodbye. I called my husband and cried and cried. We began to pray.

It's easy in times like these to think that in an instant your world will be changed, but we began to pray for a healthy baby. My labor was a nightmare. There is a special way of breaking the water when you have this condition. If it breaks all at once it's a danger due to the force of so much water on the baby. So they planned on a special water-breaking just for us! Ha.

We went to the hospital that morning very excited. The doctor got out all the special tools. He placed a towel under me then pin-pricked my amniotic sack. The water was supposed to trickle out in very tiny amounts, but from the get-go nothing went right. The instant he put the tiny little needle in there, there was an explosion! The water came out so hard and fast it was going out into the hallway. Nurses were running, grabbing anything they could to stop it from going into the hall. Guy and I watched my tummy getting smaller and smaller and smaller. I'm not kidding, my stomach shrunk almost a foot! Then it stopped on what was my baby. What a relief it was; I could breathe!

The rest of the story is very long, so let me give it to you quickly. It was about 20 hours of labor and two hours of pushing. When he crowned they told me I had a choice. Due to his size, he would not fit. They said could break his collar bone and get him out, or do a C-section. I was not about to let them break my little baby's bone so I had a C-section with my first child. Jonathan Patrick Miller came out not crying, the cord was wrapped around his neck. His first cry made my heart leap. He was nine pounds, 11 ounces. My big, baby boy. After one night with him I knew he was totally healthy. He would look at me while eating. It was one of the best moments of our lives.

In this world there are so many choices. For me, abortion is not an option.

"You knit me together in my mother's womb. I praise you because I am fearfully and wonderfully made; your works are wonderful."
Psalm 139 13-14

"Your eyes saw my unformed body. All the days ordained for me were written in your book before one of them came to be."
Psalm 139:16

But can you imagine all the people in the world who are being told what I was told about the baby growing inside me and they are aborting their babies? When I think about it, I want to cry. Those tests CAN be wrong! And God still does miracles! When you get the doctor's report friend, and you are over your initial reaction, please always remember God's report! His will be done. And we WILL be able to keep walking! Even if my child was born that day not 100% healthy, Guy and I would have loved that child more than anything! God has a plan for every child.

God's word says in many places that God has a plan for us as early as in our mother's womb. Who are we to change what He has ordained? But remember, His mercy is great and if you have had an abortion, God's forgiveness and love are right there for you today. Turn to Him, cry out to Him, and He will meet you.

When God called Jeremiah, this is what He said:

"Before I formed you in the womb I knew you, before you were born I set you apart; I appointed you as a prophet to the nations."
Jeremiah 1:5

I'm not quite sure how much clearer it has to get. He has set you apart and has a plan for your life. Some of the most beautiful people I know have disabilities.

Dear God,
I thank you that my mother did not abort me. I thank you for my life and how you are using all I have been through for your glory. I pray you give readers hope, hope to keep their baby, hope to know you are in control no matter what the doctors say. All will be well, you are our peace. I honor you today.

186

March 23rd

Pot Holes

This morning is one of those days where you just want to stay in bed! It's rainy and cold again! You just want to pretend you are on vacation and put the covers up to your head. Well, that's me anyway. But life is life, and needless to say we all had to get up this morning in the Miller home.

While driving my daughter to school this morning (2010), I was swerving around way too many pot holes! I could not believe how many and how big they were! One time I hit one and the thought came over me, "If an older lady hit that she would have lost control!" It almost made me lose control of the car! When you hit a pot hole you can get hurt!

We had a very hard winter here (again) and the salt from the plows kill the pavement. It breaks up the road like it's nothing! Crumbles it right up! So now we are left with many holes that can hurt. We as people are so much like pot holes!

We go through very hard times and each one seems to break us up. Crack us. A pot hole is not a healthy thing to have on the road, and when we are filled with holes it's just not healthy.

When I hit a pot hole I can get hurt. When people come your way, can they get hurt? Are you that unhealthy? Does anger and lack of self-control consume you? Do you make people almost lose control when they are with you? Are you being a good example or a bad one?

> "My grace is sufficient for you, for my power is made perfect in weakness. Therefore I will boast all the more gladly about my weaknesses, so that Christ's power may rest on me. That is why, for Christ's sake, I delight in weaknesses, in insults, in hardships, in persecutions, in difficulties. For when I am weak, then I am strong."
> 2 Corinthians 12:9-10

Do you delight in your weaknesses like this scripture says? Or are you a bomb ready to explode when people are near you? This word says that weakness, hardship, persecutions, and difficulties make us stronger! His power is made perfect in our weakness! It grows us and builds character.

Spring is right around the corner and very soon here in New England we will see the filler trucks. They go around after the first thaw and fill all the pot holes. The holes need to be filled with something in order to make them healthy and safe to drive on again!

What are you filling yourself with? Are you hanging out with someone who is filling you with ungodly things and making you unhealthier, or are you filling yourself with the Word of God and thinking on things that will lead you closer to Him?

"Finally, brothers, whatever is true, whatever is noble, whatever is right, whatever is pure, whatever is lovely, whatever is admirable—if anything is excellent or praiseworthy--think about such things. Whatever you have learned or received or heard from me, or seen in me, put into practice. And the God of peace will be with you."
Philippians 4:8-9

Is this scripture a picture of you or are you a broken-up, falling apart pot hole? Maybe you are doing great, but people keep hurting you. Take heart in David's example:

"David was greatly distressed because the men were talking of stoning him; each one was bitter in spirit because of his sons and daughters. But David found strength in the Lord his God."
1 Samuel 30:6

We need to let the Lord fill us up and make us healthy and safe again.

"Those that wait on the Lord will renew their strength. They will soar on wings like eagles; they will run and not grow weary, they will walk and not be faint."
Isaiah 40:31

We are more like pot holes than you think.

Dear God,
Fill us up! Give us a heart today that is ready to receive all you have for us. Help us to have enough self-control to think on things of you. Help us to not hurt others when they come our way, but to encourage them. Help us to find the time to wait on you. I honor you today.

Kay

When you work as a nurse in a nursing home, you learn to love your residents. There were so many ladies and gents that I fell in love with. There were some that were very hard for me to handle, but in a nutshell I was very happy working there, and a few of the residents I loved like family. One of those people was Kay.

I worked at one of the cleanest, highest paying nursing homes on Cape Cod. Couples could even live together if they wanted to. It was just a wonderful place to work. Not a scent of urine in the air! We worked hard to keep the place spotless and to give the best care possible to the patients.

I did almost everything, from bathing patients who had lost their minds, to feeding them, to wheel chair aerobics, to bingo! I loved bringing joy and laughter to them, so many were so lonely. When I had down-time I would walk the halls and just look for someone to talk to and share time with. I loved hearing their stories of how their families made it through the wars and how they purchased things for pennies way back when. The most amazing stories come out of nursing homes, if someone would just take the time to listen.

There were so many awesome ladies and gents there. One was even a CIA agent all of her life. There was Harry, who was about 6 foot 5 inches. I would push him down the hall in his wheel chair and we would both sing songs at the top of our lungs together. Ha. There was Sonia, who made things with her yarn and needles. You name it! Blankets, doilies, placemats, hats, and just about everything! Then there was Kay.

There was something about Kay. We bonded. She was as sharp as a tack in the brain, and Italian, so right away we hit it off. One day I was walking the halls, looking for someone to talk to. Kay was in her room and very distraught. I asked her what was wrong, and she said she lost her necklace. She told me it was a solid gold chain holding a Saint Anthony pendant. Many residents were devout Catholics. They prayed to saints. I do not pray to saints, I pray to God, but I did not tell Kay this. I felt bad for her. I could tell this necklace meant something really special to her, so I began to hunt for it.

My first thought was that it had been stolen. Unfortunately, many things get taken by crooked workers. But, we searched for almost 45 minutes. I kept praying, "Lord, help me find Kay's necklace." NOT one time did I say, "Well Kay, you know you are NOT supposed to pray to the saints! You only have to pray to God!" Sometimes you just need to love and be there for a person rather than preach at them! Sometimes you just NEED to be quiet and feel their hurt. And love like Jesus did.

So I decided to put gloves on and go through the trash. I could not believe it, there it was! We had found it. She was filled with joy, and she could not thank me enough. I had earned instant respect at that moment from Kay. She was sharp as a tack but had accidentally thrown it away! I have to laugh here because I found the ricotta cheese in the spice closet the other day! I had to throw the entire thing out! And, I'm pretty sharp. Just thought I would throw that in for a laugh!

Anyway, I took this instant respect I had just earned from Kay and used it! I said, "Hey Kay, do you know I come in and do a church service during the week?" She said she did not know that, and that she would start to come. She was a woman who stuck to her word. She started coming faithfully to our services at the nursing home, all because I took the time to care and find her Saint Anthony necklace. I did not condemn her for praying to saints, I loved and helped her.

For the four years that I led the services there, Kay's face was always in the back of the room with a smile. She would always ask for special prayer, and then one day she gave her life to the Lord by praying a simple prayer. She wanted to know that she would go to Heaven when she died. Kay would sing the songs in the service and mean them with her entire heart, even with Saint Anthony around her neck.

The point I'm trying to make today is, as Christians, we need to use wisdom. We don't always have to beat our belief over people's heads. Sometimes, we just have to look for those opportunities that will change a life forever. Most of those opportunities will come, without us having to say a word, with just helping and being there for a person. Once that person knows you are sincere then they will want to know what you have to say to them.

It's gentle. It's not harsh. I have met so many judgmental Christians. They instantly loose people within the first five minutes of the conversation because of their insensitivity.

"But the fruit of the spirit is love, joy, peace, patience, kindness, goodness, faithfulness, GENTLENESS, and self-control."
Galatians 5:22-23

I heard someone say that gentleness is power, or strength, under control. The power and force of water can be brought under control by the turning of a water wheel. It's kind of like that. You need wisdom to know how much force you must have at every opportunity. So many people blow it. If I would have slammed Kay that first day and told her not to pray to Saint Anthony she would have dismissed me and avoided me. But I loved her and helped her, and through those next four years, Kay and I had many conversations about not praying to the saints, but praying directly to God. She wore her pendant because it was passed down from family, but in the end Kay was praying to God. Because of gentleness. Gentleness is truly a powerful thing under control.

God is gentle:

"He does not treat us as our sins deserve or repay us according to our iniquities. For as high as the Heavens are above the earth, so great is His love for those who fear Him; as far as the east is from the west, so far has He removed our sin from us."
Psalm 103:10-11

Jesus does not come with judgment, He comes with gentleness to restore our relationships with God.

"For God DID NOT send His Son into the world to condemn the world, but to save the world through Him."
John 3:17

I hope you can apply this to your life today. Are you a harsh, judgmental person? You need to have the compassion and love of Christ. Pray that God would change you. We are not here to condemn, we are here to love. Through our love, Kay's all over the world will come to God.

Dear God,
Break me. Change me. Help me to not judge, but to focus on the fact that you do not judge me, you love me through it all. I honor you today, Lord.

March 25th

The Valley of Baca

Last night my son and I were watching TV together. It was a documentary called *The Elephant Man*. I've never seen anything like it in my life. It's this family that lives in China and one of their children, the oldest boy, suffers from facial tumors. I mean, you would not even believe what he looks like. It was all real and they even did interviews with him. He does not look human. I'm not sure why they call him he Elephant Man. He does not look like an elephant.

As I watched this story, I just could not begin to believe there was a person alive on earth suffering like this. Yet the things that he said were humble, and you can tell he is very thankful for his family. It was so sad. I'm not sure why I like to watch things like this, but I do. I like real things! The news, amazing stories, history makers, and such. Love it!

But this gripped my heart. You could almost feel his pain. When I see things like this, I think about all the things I complain about. Stupid things! Even my physical issues are NOTHING compared to this poor man. Yet his choice is to live. That touched my heart more than anything. His brother and sister have left their dreams and desires for their own lives to help their mom and dad take care of him. It was just an amazing story.

Think about this past week and all the things you have complained about. If you have the time to look up on YouTube "The Elephant Man, China", do it so you can see for yourself. His name is Huang. Our strength comes from the Lord. I have no idea what Huang believes, but if he does not have God, he is an amazing man.

"Blessed are those whose strength is in you, who have **set their hearts on pilgrimage.** As they **pass through the Valley of Baca**, they make it a place of springs; the autumn rains also cover it with pools. **They go from strength to strength.**"
Psalm 84:5-7

The first part of this scripture talks about our strength being in Christ. Truth be told we cannot do it alone; sometimes it's just too hard! We need Him. I looked up the word "pilgrimage" and it said two things: "A journey to a sacred place", and "The course of life on earth". So it's saying blessed will be those who have their hearts set on Heaven, or those who push forward and set their heart on their journey here on earth.

We all want to go to Heaven, but many times we focus on that rather than on the fact that God also wants us to set our heart on our journey here. He has great things planned for you!

There is nothing wrong with being excited about our journey here.

Reading on in this scripture it says, "They pass through the Valley of Baca, they make it a place of springs". The Hebrew meaning for the word "Baca" is "weeping", "tears", or even "misery". So we have set our hearts on pilgrimage and our journey is bringing us through weeping and misery. Hmmm, sounds pretty spot-on to me. If you have been reading faithfully then you know my story, and you know what I have been through, but to me it's NOTHING compared to this man, Huang. Yet he chooses to live. But this is life.

The thing I love about this scripture is that it says nothing about *staying* in the Valley of Baca! The exact words are, "They pass through the Valley of Baca!" WE DON'T STAY THERE. We are just passing through! Thank the Lord!

The verse ends with: "They go from strength to strength." It takes trial for God to build a stronger character in us.

Are you in the Valley of Baca today, like Huang still is?

Remember, you won't be there forever and in the end you will be stronger.

Dear God,
During this time please keep me strong. Do not let me forget that you will never leave me. Let me feel you near my side, and help to make me stronger through the Valley. I need you Lord, like my body needs water. You give me strength. I honor you today.

March 26th

Hard Seasons

When all you have left is faith because there is nothing left to hang onto, it can be a scary place to be. You are unsure of your future, unsure of your circumstance, and you wonder how God is going to work it all out.

We were being teased here in New England with very warm weather this week, then all of a sudden we wake up today, and it's freezing and snowing! Sometimes we New Englanders get so sick of the cold weather. But there is no place like New England!

There is nothing like seeing the seasons change; nothing. My favorite season is fall. I love to take long drives and look at the colors, stop at a farm stand and get some fresh veggies, and maybe even pick a pumpkin off the farmers hay bales. Words cannot describe how much I love that.

It seems as though at the end of the year, you wonder where the year went. It all happens so fast. I have often wondered why winter is the longest season. Usually, from the end of October to about May 1st, I'm freezing. Why couldn't God have made summer the longest season?

Winter can be depressing. Sometimes it's so cold you want to stay in bed! You try to save on cost, so your heat is down, and man it gets hard. But I find ways to press on in the cold, hard winter. I put layers and layers on. Yes, it's very attractive. Haha. I get my little space heater out.

It all reminds me of life. I think God made winter the longest season because it's the hardest. He loves to bless us and see us happy. He longs to fulfill the desires we all have in our hearts, but he builds our character in hard times.

Have you had a hard day today? When you go through hard times, whether physical, work-related, financial, or whatever, it's very important to remember that it's a season, and even the winter season lasts only six months or less. Then things change.

During hard seasons, I always try to dwell on the fact that the season will be over soon. New growth is coming, comfort from the sun, or Son, is coming.

"Come unto me you who are weary, and I will give you rest."
Matthew 11:28-30

"And my God will meet all your needs
according to his glorious riches in Christ Jesus."
Philippians 4:19

His promises will not fail. When we are weary, He gives rest. When we have a need, He has all we need today. Take the time to read this scripture slowly. Your season will be over soon and God's perfect will be done.

> "There is a time for everything,
> and a season for every activity under Heaven:
> a time to be born and a time to die,
> a time to plant and a time to uproot,
> a time to kill and a time to heal,
> a time to tear down and a time to build,
> a time to weep and a time to laugh,
> a time to mourn and a time to dance,
> a time to scatter stones and a time to gather them,
> a time to embrace and a time to refrain,
> a time to search and a time to give up,
> a time to keep and a time to throw away,
> a time to tear and a time to mend,
> a time to be silent and a time to speak,
> a time to love and a time to hate,
> a time for war and a time for peace.
> What does the worker gain from his toil?
> I have seen the burden God has laid on men.
> He has made everything beautiful in its time."
> Ecclesiastes 3:1-11

I think in these scriptures, if you really think about it, you can see just about anything and everything you have ever been through.

But He makes everything beautiful in its time.

Don't give up today!

Dear God,
Be with the reader right now. As they read your Holy Word may they know you have never left them, you are right there with them now. You are there to comfort and give joy. I honor you today.

March 27th

Don't Get Burned!

Is there any such thing as being too close to temptation? You better believe it! The problem is, many Christians think they can handle it. They start hanging with old crowds or doing things of the past which only lead's to doing old things. Things that will once again make them fall. When God changes us, He changes us. Many times we don't heed the warnings and get a little too close.

Years ago, Guy and I took a trip up north. We just wanted to drive and see how beautiful the fall colors were. We drove about two hours and stopped at little shops. On the way home we went to a farm stand. Usually when you go to farm stands alongside the road there is no one there, but this time the farmer was there. I was quite excited about the corn-on-the-cob and Guy was looking at the hot peppers. The farmer walked over to him and said, "You better be careful, the fumes of those peppers are flammable." My thought was, "Yea right! Give me a break! There is no veggie that has flammable fumes when you cook it!"

Well, we got home that night, and it was so many years ago that I don't even remember what we were eating, but I know I put my corn in the pot. Guy wanted me to sauté the peppers so he could put them on top of whatever was cooking. I cut them up and was still thinking how silly the farmer was for saying the fumes were flammable. I put butter in the pan and threw in the peppers. Not even one minute later it felt as if someone put fire in my nose. I was screaming and crying. Guy came running in the kitchen. My nostrils were burnt. Are you laughing yet?

Trust me, it was NOT funny while it was going on, but now I laugh my head off when I think of this night. Guy and I still talk about it. My nostrils were totally burnt. Kind of like when you burn your tongue, but the pain was intense. The rest of the night I had cold rags shoved up my nose. After about an hour we were laughing, but boy it hurt. For the next week it hurt.
I guess I should have listened to the farmers warning.

This is how it is when we get way too close to things that can make us fall and lead us down unhealthy paths! The farmer warned me that the peppers were flammable and I laughed. How many times do we laugh when people say, "Be careful"? But the truth is, we do need to use wisdom and be careful. God will also warn us. Will we listen, or will we brush those promptings of the Holy Spirit away? Will we line up our actions with the Word of God?

"For we do not have a high priest who is unable to sympathize with our weaknesses, but we have one who has been tempted in every way, just as we are - yet was without sin."
Hebrews 4:15

He knows what it's like to be tempted. He has been there. Temptation is NOT fun, but there is always a way out! That's how much love He has for you, that even when you get too close He is still there for you.

"And God is faithful; He will NOT let you be tempted beyond what you can bear. But when you are tempted, He will also provide a way out so that you can stand up under it."
1 Corinthians 10:12-13

We are human; sometimes we get too close to being burnt once again! We will learn from our mistakes because we are not perfect like Jesus was. This scripture is a promise that we can be like Him and withstand temptation. He will always provide a way out! There is always a door in the right direction. Will you take it today? Will you make wise decisions or will you get a little too close?

Also recognize the enemy. Most the time our flesh wants to be too close to sin, but many times it's the enemy tempting us as well.

"Resist the devil, and he will flee from you."
James 4:7

A few ways to resist the devil are to not be so close to temptation, to listen to the wisdom of others, and to obey the Father.

Don't get burnt!

Dear God,
Help us to heed warnings, from friends and from you. When we feel that feeling inside saying something is wrong, help us to not ignore the Holy Spirit. Thank you for your forgiveness when we fall. I honor you Lord.

Take Refuge

I have only been in real danger a few times in my life. Times when I actually knew I could be in big trouble and could die. One of those times was years ago, driving down the road with my boyfriend, who was doing drugs and trying to hide if from me. He was seriously angry with me and told me that he was going to kill me. He was driving way over the speed limit and I was getting ready to jump out of the car. I knew he meant it, and I knew I was in danger.

There are plenty of other stories I could tell. Some you have already heard. It's one thing when your life is in danger, but when your loved one is in danger, well, that is a different story! I can handle the thought of myself in danger, but not my husband nor my children.

One time in India, my daughter and my husband were very much in danger. Their car was surrounded by protesters. Some friends of ours were with them, and they told my daughter, who was only 14 at the time, to get under the seats. About 150 people surrounded the car and they were very angry. Thank God Beth and Dale knew the language. It saved them from being taken out of the car.

My son and I had stayed behind at our friend's apartment because he did not feel so well. I called Guy just to see how things were. I could tell the instant someone answered that something was wrong. They told me what was going on and Jon and I began to pray. I have never felt so sick in my gut. I was weeping and all I could think of was my daughter, husband, and my two friends in such danger. There was nothing I could do about it. I did not even know where they were! It was the most horrible feeling I have ever had in my entire life. After a couple hours they made it home and I cannot tell you the weight that was taken off me. They were home and they were safe!

I cannot even begin to believe how the Father must have felt when His only son knelt on the Mount of Olives and said to Him:

> "Father, if you are willing, take this cup from me;
> yet not my will, but yours be done."
> Luke 22:42

Pretty much Jesus was asking if he really had to go through with what He was about to go through.

He was in danger of crucifixion, which was one of the most painful deaths. When I think of that night I was away from my daughter and husband and I knew they were in danger, it kills me inside to think of God the Father knowing His only son would have to die. The ache in my heart that night was more than I would want anyone to ever feel. I'm sure the Father's ache was something I will never be able to comprehend.

Unless Jesus died, He never would have rose and conquered death and Hell forever. He had to die. That, my friend, is true love. Danger to His physical body brought life to our souls.

I have said it before in these devotionals that even if our physical body is in danger, nothing can take our soul if we are living in a relationship with Christ. Nothing. So even if we are in danger, there is no need to worry. But come on, we are human. We worry.

Time after time in the Gospel we see God come through for people in danger. I have written about many: Abigail, Queen Esther, Daniel, Shadrach, Meshach and Abednego, Jonah, and the list goes on and on.

"The prudent see danger and take refuge."
Proverbs 27:12

Another word you can use for "prudent" is "wise". Jesus did the wisest thing. He took refuge in the Father. This is exactly what we need to do when we are in danger or someone we know is in danger. We need to go to the Father and take refuge in Him. He is our refuge.

"And the peace of God, which transcends all understanding,
will guard your hearts and your minds in Christ Jesus."
Philippians 4:7

Take refuge.

Dear God,
Help us to run to you when we or someone we love is in danger. Give us your peace that will pass our understanding while in the fire. You are all we need today, and we take refuge in you. I honor you today Lord.

Last Prayers

"They are not of the world, even as I am not of it. Sanctify them by the truth; your word is truth. As you sent me into the world, I have sent them into the world. For them I sanctify myself, that they too may be truly sanctified."
John 17:16-19

In this scripture, Jesus is praying for His disciples. Right afterwards He prays this prayer:

"My prayer is not for them alone. I pray also for those who will believe in me through their message."
John 17:16-19

That, my friend, would be you and me. We are still reading the message for the disciples! You can hear His heart as He cares for all our souls. He prayed these prayers right before He was arrested and betrayed by Judas. He already knew all that was to come when He knelt and prayed.

"Jesus, knowing all that was going to happen to him, went out and asked them, "Who is it you want?"
John 18:4

He offered himself, betrayed and rejected in the end, and only caring about our sanctification, and our souls. He gave himself so that we might have life. We now have salvation through His death on the cross and His resurrection. He knew it was the Lord's will for Him to walk the road to the cross and die. I have never known a deeper love.

"Jesus commanded peter, 'Put your sword away! Shall I not drink the cup the Father has given me?'"
John 18:11

These are His very last words in prayer before He was betrayed:

"I have made you known to them, and will continue to make you known in order that the love you have for me may be in them and that I myself may be in them."
John 17:26

His last words to His Father were about you and me. If that does not do something to you today than I'm not quite sure what will convince you of your worth. The Bible says in John 17:17, "His word is truth!" He is truth. This is not just something I believe because I read it in a pretty book this is something I know because I have lived it for over 31 years. His word is true and just. It's embedded within me and I trust in it. His promises are for you today.

This may have happened thousands of years ago, but God forgiving your sins is as real today as it was when Jesus died on the cross.

I remember kneeling at an altar for the first time. I was filled with shame. I knew no one could love someone like me. I remember the peace and freedom I felt when He met me there. This is exactly what He has for you today. You don't have to go to a church and light a candle. You have to cry out to Him exactly where you are, and how you are at this moment, and He will meet you. His words of love for you and me, in the book of John, are still His heartbeat today. Just confess your sins to Him right where you are. The Bible is truth. If you have one, read it. If you can't understand it, go get a Bible that is easier to read. There are so many ways now to get His words into our hearts. As you go day after day not picking up your Bible, He is still there loving you and waiting for you to talk to Him. I love to listen to my Bible App read to me in the morning.

"Father, forgive them, for they do not know what they are doing."
Luke 23:34

His last prayers were for you.

Dear God,
I'm not sure what I would have prayed knowing I was about to die a painful death. All I can say is thank you. You gave everything for me. Help me now to give everything to you. I honor you today.

Kaleidoscope of Opportunity

I can almost promise that every single one of you reading this has had some form of a kaleidoscope at some point in your lifetime. It's the most amazing children's toy ever. These days you can get cheaper ones or very expensive collectors' versions. But do you know who David Brewster is?

Sir David Brewster was born in 1781 and lived until 1868. He was a Scottish scientist. He was known as a child prodigy, kind of like my nephew Dominic. The kid is amazing! He talks about the wars on my husband's level and he is going into the ninth grade (2010)! He just received a $120,000 scholarship to go to a private high school in Boston! Sorry, had to brag! Anyway, back to Mr. Brewster.

Here are some of the things David Brewster accomplished: He made his first telescope at age ten. At nineteen he was awarded an honorary Master of Arts degree, as well as a license to minister the gospel! He did not like being in the pulpit. He couldn't take people looking at him, so he used his ministry gifts in other areas. At twenty-six years of age he was awarded a Doctor of Letters degree, which is amazing for someone that age! The man wrote over 2,000 scientific papers. He was knighted by William IV, which in those days instantaneously gave you a very high social status. It sounds like the Lord's favor was on this guy! He was the one who invented a lens that made the light from a light bulb reflect into darkness. In other words: the flash light. He made the light go from just lighting up a room with a bulb to being able to pierce through darkness. Man, you would think his name would be tagged onto that one! The man's face was on cigar boxes!

I think David Brewster would be shocked to know that his most enduring legacy, or what he is known for today, is his invention of the kaleidoscope! The kaleidoscope was like universal mania! Ha! A toy both the rich and poor could enjoy. Still today, if you go into any kids' store you will find them. All kids get at least one at some point in their young life here in America. I remember my first kaleidoscope! You just want to look into the light and turn the end for hours.

I know one thing, this guy did not have too much idol time! He was always thinking, and always moving forward with ideas and vision! He lived the scripture that says:

> "Making the most of every opportunity, because the days are evil."
> Ephesians 5:16

Brewster made the most of every opportunity, even if that opportunity means a toy that would bring happiness to many children.

A cool thing about kaleidoscopes is they are ALL different. Some are very tiny and some are giant. Some cost cents and some cost thousands of dollars. Kind of like us. We are ALL different.

If you look at the tail end of a kaleidoscope it looks like a mess. But when you put your eye to it and point it to the light, then the beads, stars, and sequence become a mesh of beauty. We are so much like this little toy. When we are pointed to the light we become so much more beautiful than we already are.

David Brewster knew what his gifts were. He knew he was not gifted to be in a pulpit, but he walked, lived, and breathed his gifts in other areas. That is ministry, too.

> "Therefore do not be foolish, but understand what the Lord's will is."
> Ephesians 5:17

He looked for opportunities to make people more knowledgeable, to make people live better lives, and to make them happy. These things are just as important as being in the pulpit when they are done with godly intention.

Opportunities can be used in bad ways, too.

> "From then on Judas watched for
> an opportunity to hand him (Jesus) over."
> Matthew 26:16

Have you made the most of your opportunities? Are your goals and the things you are working toward done with godly intention or selfish intention? Are they to help people grow? Are they done in a way that points people toward the light? Or are they done so your face can be on a cigar box?

Your life is a kaleidoscope of opportunities today. Don't blow it.

Dear God,
May we be filled with godly intention. Help us to make the most of every door that may open for us. Help us to stay humble and hungry for you. I honor you today.

<u>Doors of Faith</u>

"Now then, my sons, listen to me, blessed are those who keep my ways. Listen to my instruction and be wise; do not ignore it. Blessed is the man who listens to me, watching daily at my doors, waiting at my doorway. For whoever finds me finds life and receives favor from the Lord."
Proverbs 8:32-35

I want to wait at God's door! I want to know all He has for me in this life. I'm sure you feel the same. If you are reading today and you do not know Him or have just started your relationship with Him, you need to open that door!

"I stand at the door and knock. If anyone hears my voice and opens the door, I will come in and eat with him, and he with me."
Revelation 3:20

For all of my life, as far back as I can remember, my dad has had a picture on his dresser of Jesus knocking on a door. If you look close, there is NO doorknob. The doorknob is on our side. We are the ones who open the door. It's sad to think of so many who have this famous picture in their home but have never opened the door between the Father and themselves. He is not a dead God; He still speaks to us today.

We need to know He is waiting for us to open the door. The entire reason He created us was to have fellowship with us. He longs for that, and I hope you long for that. Why would we not want to hear from the one who made the universe? Open the door to Him today, so you can be in communication with Him.

"Call to me and I will answer you and tell you great and unsearchable things you do not know."
Jeremiah 33:3

Here is another promise from God:

"Knock and the door will be open unto you."
Matthew 7:7

So our main scripture talks about **watching and waiting** by the door. We must first open the door to Him in our hearts, but then wait on Him to hear what He wants us to hear. When I looked at what Webster's Dictionary had to say about the word "watching," it said:

To look or observe attentively or carefully; to be closely observant and stay alert; to look and wait expectantly or in anticipation; a period of close observation often in order to discover something

And according to the same dictionary, to "wait" is to:

Remain or rest in expectation, or to remain, or be in readiness.

When you think about what Webster says and apply it to waiting on God the Father, it brings the watching and waiting to life! He wants us to always be ready for the next thing He has for us. How will we know if we are not watching and waiting? We need to be able to listen! This takes discipline!

<blockquote>
"Now then my sons, listen to me."
Proverbs 8:32
</blockquote>

<blockquote>
"Listen to my instruction and be wise; do not ignore it."
Proverbs 8:33
</blockquote>

It's so amazing to me that when we open the door to God and wait, He begins to open doors for us. Paul talks about this:

<blockquote>
"On arriving there, they gathered the church together and reported all that God had done through them and how He had opened the door of faith to the Gentiles."
Acts 14:27-28
</blockquote>

These are the doors of faith. Watch and wait on Him today!

Dear God,
Give us the discipline and desire to open the door and wait on you, to have a deep longing to hear from you. Help us to not let a day go by unless we have met with you, Lord. Begin to open doors of faith in our lives. I honor you today.

April

April 1st

Afterbirth

For years I have worked in the maternity ward as a CNA. I was trained in afterbirth legal care. I would assist with the births and then when baby was cozy in the arms of mom and everyone was happy, I would clean up the floor and take the bloody afterbirth cart into the biohazard room. You have to be very careful because it's quite a mess. I would sometimes triple-glove up! You also must be very careful of needles that are always in the mess of afterbirth. Everything has its place so you take it off the cart slowly and put it where it belongs, blood and all.

After every birth, for legal reasons, the placenta must be saved in the freezer for seven days. I would have to put the placenta in a biohazard bag, label it, and put it in the freezer. After you care for the placenta, tools, and needles, you have to dispose of the cover that goes over the cart. This is the biggest mess of all. You have to have a very strong tummy for this line of work which is something I am very blessed with. When everything is in its place, it's time to clean the cart and floor, and then sterilize everything. Now the cart is ready to be stocked again and put back in the room for a new birth.

Why did I just tell you all that?

When something new is birthed there will ALWAYS be some sort of mess to deal with. The birth of a new baby brings joy and happiness more than words can say. The birth of a new ministry or new leader brings the same kind of joy. Just like there is messy afterbirth with a baby, there is always someone who will not be happy with the arrival of new leadership, or someone who does not like change at all, so they find any way they can to make a mess.

When my husband and I took our first senior pastorate we had some people leave because they did not like the change. Change is hard. It leaves you out of your comfort zone. You have to prove yourself all over again! Truth be told, change is hard work. And some would rather run than work hard. By the time we left our awesome church, seven and a half years later, it was better than when we came! God blessed us with an amazing core group of people that were working hard. But, we had gone through the afterbirth stage and made it through! Afterbirth is messy sometimes, but you have to keep your hands in it to take care of it!

I cannot even begin to tell you how many birthing carts I have made sterile throughout the years, but each one sits in fresh, clean rooms ready for new birth.

"If you confess with your mouth 'Jesus is Lord,' and believe in your heart that God raised Him from the dead, you will be saved."
Romans 10:9

"It is with your mouth that you confess and are saved."
Romans 10:10

"For God so loved the world that He gave His one and only Son, that whoever believes in Him shall not perish but have eternal life."
John 3:16

When we come to Christ in full surrender for the first time it is also new birth. Most of us who have done it remember the exact day because our new birth made such a change in our lives. The afterbirth stage when we come to the Lord is hard. It's very easy to give our heart to the Lord on Sunday, but then Monday through Friday you have to live it.

I remember my first year. The first year after giving my life to the Lord was one of the hardest ever, but I kept my hands in the afterbirth! I did NOT give up. Did I fail? YES! But, I kept moving forward in the grace of God. That moving forward, in time, gave me a beautiful sterilized new birth cart. Now I can turn around and help bring others to new birth in the Lord. But I was not always at that place in the beginning.

Has the Lord led you into a new place of ministry? Are you feeling overwhelmed in the afterbirth stage? Have you thought of coming to the Lord for hope and peace for the first time in your life?

If so, this devotion is for you.
It will not be easy.
It will be hard and sometimes messy.
Move forward and do NOT fear!

"For the Lord your God is the one who goes with you to fight for you against your enemies to give you victory."
Deuteronomy 20:4

Dear God,
I thank you for always bringing me and my family through the messy times. We made it, and I thank you. You have proven yourself faithful time and time again. I honor you today.

Determination to Die For

We have all seen the determination of the ant. We see them carry things way too big for themselves. I have seen them carry grasshoppers and other bugs that were five times the size of them, but as a group they carried it with ease.

I have only had two problems with ant infestations in my lifetime. One time, our family moved into a house that we rented in the winter. We loved it, painted the rooms, and made it our place. Then the spring came! All I can say is nightmare! The home was totally infested with those little sugar ants.

If you left one tiny crumb anywhere there was thousands of ants! One time there was a piece of Honeycomb cereal in the sink and when I got home from work there were thousands of ants! The thickness of the pile was about half an inch and the width of the pile of ants was about half a foot. A line of them went from the sink, up the wall, and through a tiny crack. I knew not one person would believe what I was seeing so I took video of it to show the landlord! After some time we found out that they were nesting in the walls. They tried to poison them out, but it did not work. The landlord let us out of our lease. We had to move.

The only other ant issue we have ever had was while we were living in India. The ants there were so tiny and you could see through them. They were very hard to deal with. When I would wash the dishes and set them to drain, I would come back a little while later and there would be hundreds of ants all over the new clean dishes. Nasty! We had to put our sugar in the middle of a bowl with water in it, so that when they tried to go for the sugar they would drown. They would actually die trying to reach the sugar!

I will say they are very determined!

Some of you have lost that kind of determination today, determination you are willing to die for. Many of you think you will never get any kind of determination back in your life. You have fallen into depression due to pain, lack of self-control, or your self-esteem has been beaten down time and time again. You need to know it's a lie from the enemy. You can get your determination back!

> "Not that I have already obtained all this, or have already been made perfect, but I press on to take hold of that for which Christ Jesus took hold of me."
> Philippians 3:12

You were made for a purpose— God's purpose. We must press on so that purpose can be fulfilled in our lifetime. Don't give up!

"Forgetting what is behind and straining toward what is ahead, I press
toward the goal to win the prize for which God has called me
Heavenward in Christ Jesus."
Philippians 3:13-14

We must stay determined like Jesus was determined. Do you think it was easy for Him to cry out in the garden and know what He would go through, but yet keep His mind focused on doing the will of the Father? No.

The hardest thing ever is to know what you will have to go through but to keep your mind focused on the purpose, the goal, the will of the Father in your life. Jesus Christ was the most amazing example we will ever have of that. Stay determined today, and focus!

God can give you a determination you are willing to die for just like the ants.

It's called passion. Jesus had passion. If you keep this, if you fight your flesh and the evil one, you can change the world.

Dear God,
Help us to stay determined, and to have passion and vision. To fight against the evil one and our flesh in whatever circumstance we are in! Thank you for the example of Jesus. I honor you today.

April 3rd

Treasure

I know it's hard for some of you to imagine, but you are God's treasure. When I was a little girl, my father had what he called The Ditty Box. It was full of his ditties— silly little things like tiny bobble heads, chains, jacks, and more. Small treasures that, whenever dad said, "Let's go look and see what's in The Ditty Box," my brother and I jumped. We were always excited to see his small treasures.

When my kids were small we got them shoe boxes and let them decorate them. We called them treasure boxes. In my son's treasure box there were all kinds of little things: Old broken matchbox cars, a broken silver chain, a ripped baseball card, and more. One day, while looking through Jon's treasure box, I realized that every single thing in it was broken and tattered in some way. There was nothing perfect. Yet he loved everything in his treasure box more than any other toys he had.

I'm sure you can already tell what I'm going to say. We are God's treasure. We are not perfect; we are broken, tattered, and torn. Yet He loves us more than anything else He has created. Yes, it's amazing to think of His death on the cross and all He gave for us, but what about His resurrection! He rose for us! When He rose, everlasting victory took place! He put us in a special place just like a treasure box. A place where we are safe, a place where we are admired. He loves you today.

What are your treasures?

"Do not store up for yourselves treasures on earth, where moth and rust destroy, and where thieves break in and steal. But store up for yourselves treasures in Heaven, where moth and rust do not destroy, and where thieves do not break in and steal. For where your treasure is, there your heart will be also."
Matthew 6:19-21

I remember my dream and treasure that I was fighting for in high school was to be a famous singer. I sang with a band from our street, and before we did a live concert in front of about 700 kids at school, I downed an entire bottle of booze all by myself. I went wild on stage and sang some Pat Benatar and Cher's "Half Breed!" Ha. My entire treasure was selfish. My goals, dreams, and treasures all pointed toward me.

We are Christ's treasure, and there is nothing selfish about it.

"Ill gotten treasures are of no value,
but righteousness delivers from death."
Proverbs 10:2

I remember one time while I was looking through Jon's treasure box with him, I accidentally dropped a little car he had, and it was as if I crushed him or something! It hurt him that I hurt his treasure. This is how our Father's heart hurts when His children focus in on the wrong kind of treasures.

Every example God has ever given us has nothing to do with selfishness.

You are His treasure. If you weren't, He would not have died for you. He knew you would be broken, He knew you would be tattered. But He put you in His treasure box.

Dear God,
Thank you that you handpicked each one of us. That you love us enough to consider us your treasure! I honor you today.

Raggedy Ann

When I was a young girl I would write poetry. In some ways it was an escape for me to vent my feelings. I hid a lot of my bitterness and anger from my best friends. Ever since I was a girl, I've always saved and filed almost everything. I have files and files. Every card anyone has ever given me that tell me what an impact I have had on their life, every poem I've ever written, every accomplishment in print, they all have their own file.

I was reading the poetry from when I was in junior high the other day, and I came across this tiny poem I wrote. I must have been about 13 or 14 years old. It's called "A True Friend."

A True Friend

As I glare to the corner of my room,
There sits an old friend.
Her big sad eyes,
Eyes that helped me see the light many times.
Her old torn dress,
Worn from many tears.
All the times I threw her around like she was nothing;
She can still sit there and smile.
Maybe that's what a true friend is,
But she's just my Raggedy Ann.

Today (2010) my beautiful daughter did the special music on Easter Sunday in our church for the three Sunday morning services. What an amazing gift. She captures the masses. I'm not just being an emotional mom, I mean it. She has a gift like no other. She has an anointing like no other. I watched from the back as our church family was blessed by her. When she was done I watched as she would go back to her friends and sit. She has true friends that she "tells all" to, cries with, and they all encourage each other in the Lord.

She has the most amazing friends; she tells them everything. When I think of myself at that age and then I see her, I'm so happy and blessed. She is a solid girl. She does not need Raggedy Ann; she has friends that love God. She has nothing to hide from them. Angela has Christ and He is the best friend of all. She has so much more than I ever had at her age.

"And if the Spirit of Him who raised Jesus from the dead is living in you, He who raised Christ from the dead will also give life to your mortal bodies through His Spirit, who lives in you."
Romans 8:11

"To them God has chosen to make known among the gentiles the glorious riches of this mystery, which is Christ in you, the hope of glory."
Colossians 1: 27

This is the difference between my daughter and me at her age; Christ in us. I did not know the Lord personally until I was 18 years old. She grew up on the church pew. But it's not just about knowing God, it's about having a relationship with Him. This is what Angela has.

Yes, she is a normal teen who has ten thousand stuffed animals, but she does not need to use a rag doll to cry on because she goes to her Lord, and she has friends who will encourage her.

Is God in you today? Is He your hope? Do you go to Him with the things you are feeling inside? Let Him resurrect you today.

I wish someone would have shared the hope of Christ with me as a child, about the fact that I could have had a real relationship with Him. God bless all you kids and church workers!

Instead, I had Raggedy Ann.

Let Him give you life today.
Communicate with Him.

Dear God,
I thank you that my children know you. I thank you that they have real friends that really care about them. I thank God that they speak with you and that their hope is in you. This is all I could ever hope for in this lifetime. I honor you today.

April 5th

You, His Resting Place

"'Heaven is my throne, and the earth is my footstool.
Where is the house you will build for me?
Where will my resting place be?
Has not my hand made all these things,
and so they came into being?' declares the Lord.
'This is the one I esteem: He who is humble and contrite in spirit,
and trembles at my word.'"
Isaiah 66:2

There is so much to digest in this scripture I hardly know where to begin. First, the Lord says, "Heaven is my throne, and the earth is my footstool." I guess what I get from this more than anything is the bigness of God. He is bigger than we can even begin to comprehend. He is omnipresent, everywhere at one time. How can a big God like this not have everything under control? Friend, all is well. Everything is under control, even if it does not seem that way around you.

You would think that a big God like this, who sits on the Heavens as His throne, would esteem those who have rank, power, or position, but this is NOT the case with our Lord. He says, "This is the one I esteem: he who is humble and contrite in spirit, and trembles at my word."

He who is humble. Think about your life for a moment. Are you humble? Or the more you move up the ladder, do you let pride creep in?

He who is contrite in spirit. Contrite means repentant, sincere remorse, or a desire for atonement. Are you sorry for your sin today? Does it even bother you? Do you desire to live for God and be forgiven? I wonder if you are contrite in spirit today.

He who trembles at my word. There is so much disrespect for the word of God. Where has the reverence gone? This book is not just a coffee table book. It's an active book. Have you trembled at His Word lately?

As I meditated on all those questions today I found that God, through the years, has humbled me. There was a time I was not humble. He has gifted me in many areas and as a teen I let all that go to my head, and pride and power became my master. Through the years, as God stripped away the pride, He humbled me. I thank God for that. I know now I'm nothing without Him. I need Him like the air I breathe. Needing Him daily is being contrite in spirit.

The area I fall very short in is trembling at His Word. I desire it very much. I can't wait to read it, but do I tremble at it?

215

I remember one night while I was at Bible college, I was coming off of a seven day fast. I woke in the middle of the night to the most amazing presence of God in my room. I mean I could hardly move. My entire body was trembling. I asked Him what He wanted. I heard nothing. But I felt Him thick. I got up and began to read the word of God and pray. I think of this when I think of trembling at His word; that there would be such a reverence for it, to know it is holy.

Through all this remember today: He is a big God.

Every single thing is under control.

If you are prideful, you need to be humble. If you are not contrite in spirit, you need to ask Him to forgive you and fully surrender. If you do not tremble at His Word, you need to realize it is Holy and active.

> "For the word of God is living and active. Sharper than any double-edged sword, it penetrates even to dividing soul and spirit, joints and marrow; it judges the thoughts and attitudes of the heart."
> Hebrews 4:12

He wants you to be His resting place today.

Dear God,
All I can say is let us see your bigness today! Open our hearts and forgive us for seeing you as small. You can do anything, and you have everything under control. I honor you today.

The Article

I'm not just a minister, I'm a pastor's wife. Every year our district has what they call Pastor's Wife Retreat. We younger ministry wives learn from the older ones; so many of them pour into my life. I met two of my mentors at those retreats.

In 1995 I had written an article for our Denominations weekly magazine, *The Pentecostal Evangel*. The article was called "Bitter Free." Because the nature of it was so private I did not use my name. I had the *The Pentecostal Evangel* put "anonymous." The article told the story of how I forgave someone that hurt me sexually. That pain almost took my life. But God brought me to a place of forgiveness. A place I needed to be.

At one Pastor's Wife Retreat we were matched up with someone to be our prayer partners for the year. When I saw who I was matched with I was excited. She was about 30 years my senior, but so very classy. She had awesome hair, classy clothes, and spiked three-inch heals! I did not know her at all and that night we talked for the very first time. Her name is Dawn Crabtree. As we sat and talked, I learned that she ran a few women's Bible studies, choirs, worked in the church office, and more! I was amazed by this lady. She was older than me, but had a drive for ministry that I longed to have. I could feel her passion for ladies and ministry; I knew we would be lifelong friends.

We sat for about half an hour and talked. Nearing the end of our talk she pulled out an article that she had cut out of a magazine. She told me about this article that she had read not too long ago that touched her heart, and that she was using it to minister to her ladies. The article was called Bitter Free." She had clipped it from the *Pentecostal Evangel*. I sat there in shock at first, as I realized this was NOT a coincidence that we were matched up. It took a minute before I could even tell her I wrote it. What are the chances of that? It is just amazing some of the things God does sometimes. As long as I live, I will never forget that moment. It proved to me once again that God was in complete control of my life.

Friend you never can really know how God is using you, even when you do not see it with your own eyes. As I came to know my friend and mentor through the years, I learned that she walked a road to be free from bitterness as well. "Bitter Free" was more than just words on a page to her, she lived it firsthand. This is why when she read it, she cut it out and kept it. She spoke a message one time called " ABCs of Forgiveness." She had walked the walk so she could talk the talk.

When you think about your life today are you bitter at anyone? Or are you bitter free?

I can tell you right now that I can lay my head on my pillow tonight and I am not bitter at anyone. It took years for me to get to this place. But God is the one who does the work in our hearts. And God did it for Dawn, too.

> "Get rid of all bitterness, rage and anger, brawling and slander, along with every form of malice. Be kind to each other, just as in Christ God forgave you."
> Ephesians 4:31-32

But what about someone who has hurt you? Raped you? Beat you? Why should we forgive them?

I know you are NOT going to want to hear this, just like I did not want to hear it the first time Jesus spoke it to my heart, but if that person you are bitter at was the only one on the face of the earth, no matter what they had done Christ still would have sent His son to die for their soul.

When God spoke that to me, it changed me forever. I saw things in a different light. His love is unconditional. Sometimes unconditional love is hard for our small human minds to even begin to comprehend. Yet He longs for us to love like He does. It's very hard to say the least!

I will NEVER forget when Dawn pulled out that article and that it would start a lifelong friendship. I will NEVER forget all He has done in my life and the times He has proven Himself to me. I will NEVER forget the times I forgave the ones who hurt me.

I am bitter free.

Dear God,
Help this reader to know that your love has never left them, not ever! I pray the anger and bitterness that is stored up will be given to you tonight. Set them free. It's only hurting them. I honor you today.

<u>Eagles' Wings</u>

Have you ever wondered how you made it through a particular time in your life? Maybe it was a sickness, a recovery, a financial difficulty, or a dry time in your walk. I have been through times like these. Times when I felt I could not even break through to hear the voice of my Lord. It's in those times that He can renew us and we will soar. I know at times we don't feel like we are soaring because what we are going through is hard work just to make it through. But we are soaring.

Right before Moses was given the Ten Commandments the Lord spoke a word to him to tell the people of Israel.

> "You yourselves have seen what I did to Egypt, and how I carried you on eagles' wings and brought you to myself. "
> Exodus 19:4

A few chapters before this scripture in chapter 13, we see them crossing the Red Sea. They saw a divine miracle of God. Even though God parted the waters it was still very hard for them to cross, and I'm sure by the time they got to the other side they were totally exhausted. With an army behind them there was also some who had fear in their hearts. Time and time again, even after seeing miracles, the community of Israelites was grumbling against Moses and Aaron because they didn't have food or water. Even when God did miracles and supplied water like in Chapter 17, they still grumbled.

I know myself, and I consider a hard time as a time when I remember grumbling in one sort or another. It's very easy to grumble during a hard time. But I have to admit, if I saw the Red Sea part, I'm not sure I could get that one out of my head! Sometimes I wonder how they could have grumbled so much, seeing one divine miracle after another.

In Exodus 19:4 God said He carried the Israelites on eagles' wings. I'm sure the walk they were walking did not feel like they were soaring on eagles' wings, but they were living out His divine plan and purpose, therefore they soared. So even when you don't feel like you are soaring, sometimes you are.

I've had dreams before that I'm flying. I see myself sitting on an eagle and it is amazing; the wind in my hair, the sights, the sounds. It's the most amazing experience. Yes, the Israelites saw many sights, but I see hardly any evidence in the scripture of them feeling like they are soaring through with ease.
Truth be told, it was NOT easy, but yet God says:

> "I carried you on eagles' wings and brought you to myself."

Do you see what I'm trying to get at here friend? God carries us through things sometimes that will bring us closer to Him. The walk is not easy but He has not left our side.

"Those who hope in the Lord will renew their strength. They will soar on wings like eagles; they will run and not grow weary, they will walk and not be faint."
Isaiah 40:31

He knows we get weary and faint. He knows we lose our strength and get lonely at times. If we put our hope in the Lord this is His promise today: We will soar on wings like eagles; He will get us through the hard time. Even if we grumble!

Dear God,
Thank you for the times I did not even know I was soaring that you carried me through. You are forever faithful. How could I ever thank you for all you have done for me today. I honor you today.

April 8th

Pop the Bubble

If you had any bit of Sunday school in your lifetime you know the story of Zacchaeus the tax collector. The song goes:

Zacchaeus was a wee little man, and a wee little man was he.
He climbed up in a sycamore tree, for the Lord he wanted to see.
And as the Savior passed him by, He looked up in the tree,
And He said, "Zacchaeus, you come down from there;
for I'm going to your house today, for I'm going to your house today."
Zacchaeus came down from that tree as happy as he could be,
he gave his money to the poor, and said, "What a better man I'll be."

Well, I did not remember all those words. I had to look them up! Tax collectors were known as sinners for the lies they told and taking people's money.

This story of Zacchaeus is so awesome. First, I find it amazing that this short man would actually climb a tree to see Jesus walk by! How many grown men would do that even if they were short or tall? Not many! You can find this entire story in Luke 19:1-10.

"He wanted to see who Jesus was, but being a short man he could not, because of the crowd. So he ran ahead and climbed a sycamore fig tree to see Him, since Jesus was coming that way. When Jesus reached the spot, He looked up and said to him, 'Zacchaeus, come down immediately. I must stay at your house today.' So he came down at once and welcomed Him gladly."
Luke 19:3-6

As the story goes on you see people muttering and involved in gossip. They wondered how Jesus could be the guest of a sinner. They were talking about how horrible it was that Jesus was fellowshipping with them and loving them as who they were. I love the words of Jesus:

"For the Son of man came to seek and to save what was lost."
Luke 19:10

If you get a chance to read those verses in full today, read them. It's another story about the grace of God. But what about this man named Levi the tax collector? It is almost the same type of story, but why, as a kid, did we hear all about Zacchaeus and not Levi? You will know in a moment.

Levi's story is in Luke 5:27-32 and Luke 2:13-17. Jesus sees this tax collector sitting at a tax collector's booth. Jesus says to him:

"Follow me."
Mark 13:14 & Luke 5:27

Right away, just like Zacchaeus, he welcomes the fact that Jesus wants to spend time with him.

So much so that it says:

> "Levi held a great banquet for Jesus at his house."
> Luke 5:29

So here is Levi, the sinner and tax collector holding a banquet for Jesus while the Pharisees are muttering and involved in their gossip (Mark 2:16), talking about Jesus. I'm not sure about you, but there is something very wrong with this picture! No wonder Jesus wanted to spend time with sinners!

Truth be told today, Jesus makes a major statement when the Pharisees gossip and ask the Disciples why Jesus is doing this. The Bible says:

> "On hearing this, Jesus said to them, 'It is not the healthy who need a doctor, but the sick. I have not come to call the righteous, but sinners'."
> Mark 2:17

Not that he does not love the righteous, He does! But when there are righteous so filled with pride, and the sinners are the ones putting on a party for Jesus, well, give me a break. How could the Pharisees point the finger when they themselves are gossiping? It's so crazy.

This is a perfect example of our Savior, loving the unloved. Loving those souls that people snub their noses at. I want to be like Jesus today. Do you?

Levi's name was changed to Matthew and he was one of the twelve disciples.

God loves sinners today. I'm a sinner by the way! When was the last time you had dinner with a person that does not know God? Are you so into your little Christian bubble that you have no friends that are sinners? Maybe it's time to seek some out.

Maybe it's time to love like Jesus loved.

Dear God,
Forgive us when we are like the Pharisees! Humble us. We are all sinners. I honor you today.

Bread of Life or Barbie

What are your motives and intentions? Are they to draw attention to yourself, or to draw attention to the Father in all things?

I remember years ago in one of our churches there was a lady who always sat in the front pew. She always wore very tight clothes and had a body like Barbie. I thank God for every person that walks into church. God knows how I walked into church the first year I followed God, I actually did not have a lot of clothes on! Ha! I thanked God she was there and that God was doing so much in her life. She did NOT need to do anything to gain attention. You could not help but notice her when she walked in.

One day she got excited during service and decided to jump up on the first pew in her spiked three-inch heels. She took the scarf off from around her neck and began to swing it around. While doing that, she was making a whooping noise. The ushers came and ushered her down. For those of us around her it was a tad laughable and uncomfortable.

Why do we do things like that? I say "we" because we ALL have done things for attention, maybe not quite to that extreme. It's all about the intentions of our heart. Her intention and my intention are just the same if we are trying to draw attention to ourselves and not God. No matter if what I do is not so extreme. It's not so much the act and what is done as it is the matter of the heart. Pride creeps in and that can be very dangerous.

Pride crept into the heart of Judas. The intentions of his heart changed. He let greed get the better of him. He wanted more attention. When Jesus was anointed at Bethany by Mary, Judas was the one who muttered:

> "'Why wasn't this perfume sold and the money given to the poor? It was worth a year's wages.' He did not say this because he cared about the poor, but because he was a thief; and as keeper of the money bag, he used to help himself to what was put into it."
> John 12:5-6

Some say it was possible that Judas became frustrated over Jesus' unwillingness to be crowned king and lead a rebellion against the Romans. It was all about pride and power to Judas. If Jesus was crowned and he was one of his disciples, well, then the light would be on Judas, too. It was all about him and the attention that was being drawn to him. This is not a good place to be. This all left Judas so open to letting Satan take control. You must be so very careful my friend. It's not about us, it's all about Him.

The Book of Luke and John both say that Satan entered into Judas.

"Then satan entered Judas, called Iscariot, one of the twelve. And Judas went to the chief priest and the officers of the temple guard and discussed with them how he might betray Jesus. They were delighted and agreed to give him money."
Luke 22:3-5

"As soon as Judas took the bread, Satan entered into him. 'What you are about to do, do quickly,' Jesus told him, but no one at the meal understood why Jesus said this to him. Since Judas had charge of the money, some thought Jesus was telling him to buy what was needed for the Feast, or to give something to the poor."
John 13:27-28

This all started with one thought in Judas' mind about being better than Jesus. The truth is that Jesus already knew the intent of his heart. This scripture is proof that He knew the intent of their hearts. He had just done a powerful teaching and not all of the Disciples liked what He said or how He said it.

"'The words I have spoken to you are spirit and they are life. Yet there are some of you who do not believe.' For Jesus had known from the beginning which of them did not believe and who would betray Him."
John 6:63-64

So even before Jesus spoke this word, He knew the intent of their hearts. Don't you think God knows your hearts intent today? He is still God. Do you want to draw attention to yourself or to Him? Think about that today and be ever so careful not to let the enemy creep in.

Dear God,
Keep our hearts and minds pure before you. Let the intentions of our hearts want to draw people to you. May our hearts beat for souls. I honor you today.

Shake It Off

Here is a newsflash for you today: Just because Christians call themselves Christians does not mean that they will not hurt you. I sat with a friend tonight who shared with me about being hurt in the ministry. For any of you who have been in ministry for 30+ years, you know at one season in your life you will get hurt. As a matter of a fact, you don't even have to be in ministry for 10 years to know that one. It may not be a direct act from someone. It may be you pouring and pouring into someone's life, countless hours helping, and meeting, all so they would turn their back on God and go right back where they started. Ministry can hurt.

Jesus shared that in His hometown. He had the hardest time in ministry.

> "Jesus said to them, 'Only in his hometown, among his relatives and in his own house is a prophet without honor.' He could not do any miracles there, except lay His hands on a few sick people and heal them. And He was amazed at their lack of faith."
> Mark 6:4-6

You know what it's like being rejected by family who do not understand a God who has changed you. God must have done something in your heart, or you would not be doing daily devotions in this book. Don't you think Jesus, as He walked the earth into His own hometown, was hurt? He did feel emotion. He was hurt even by people who called themselves holy as well as His own disciples and friends. If Jesus Himself can be hurt in ministry, don't you think we can be hurt? But we need to shake it off.

In the book of Mark when Jesus was sending out the Twelve two by two, He gave them instructions:

> "If any place will not welcome you or listen to you, shake the dust off your feet when you leave."
> Mark 6:11

It's so easy to be hurt when even Christians do not welcome you, or random people will not listen to what you have to say about God's hope. I love what Jesus said here. He pretty much said to shake off the dust and MOVE ON. Sometimes there is just nothing you can do. You are pure in your own heart but someone is not going to forgive you. There is nothing you can do to make them forgive you. As long as your heart is pure before God that is all that matters. You have done all you can do. You can just hope in time they will lay down their anger.

I remember in the early years of ministry every little thing shook me. If someone spoke meanly to me, it would bother me for weeks. If someone said I did something wrong in the church office, I just could not shake it.

As young kids in our 20s, my husband and I were ready to change the world. We were in full-time ministry and loving it. Then we got hurt by a church leader. We did not know how to shake it off! It's not easy to shake something off when you know that the person who hurt you is damaged, and has damaged so many you love. We needed our district leadership to step in and teach us how to shake it off. Never forget that we need our elders and leaders to help us through hard times. We need their wisdom to help us through. If you don't have a mentor, you need to seek one out!

Please remember that when you "shake the dust off" as Jesus said, this does not mean you stop praying and loving people. To shake something off is action. It's moving forward. It's through this shaking off that God builds the deepest character in our hearts. He changes us. He makes us better and more effective in ministry.

I had a sweet young lady call me the other night crying. I love her so much. My exact words to her were, "You need to shake this one off." We cannot let the enemy steal our joy. It's so easy sometimes. The enemy loves building walls up between people that love God, and everyone for that matter. Sometimes the best thing is to shake it off and move on.

Where are you today? Has someone hurt you badly? Do you feel as though you're bitter or angry, you're hurt, and you just cannot get past it?

I'm sorry. I have been there, and I know it's a very hard, hurtful place to be.

But like Jesus said:

"Shake the dust off your feet when you leave."
Mark 6:11

He's growing you.

Dear God,
Help us when people hurt us. It's not easy. Help us to stop making mountains out of mole hills! You are forever faithful and I honor you today.

April 11th

Huldah

There was a woman in the Bible who knew what it meant to live a righteous life, and to count the cost. Her name is Huldah. She was an incredible woman that God raised up; A prophetess in the reign of King Josiah. She was married to Shallum, the keeper of the royal wardrobe. She could be found sitting in the central part of the city ready to receive and counsel any who wished to inquire of Jehovah. It was almost as if she was sitting there just waiting for divine appointments. Very cool.

King Josiah became king at eight years old after the death of his father. He was king for 31 years. In the eighth year of his reign at age 16, he began to seek God. In the twelfth year of his reign at age 20, he began to speak against sin and clean house.

> "Under his direction altars of the Baals were torn down; he cut to pieces the incense altars that were above them, and smashed the Asherah poles, the idols and the images. These he broke to pieces and scattered over the graves of those who had sacrificed to them."
> 2 Chronicles 34:4

In the eighteenth year of his reign at age 26, he decides to repair and restore the temple. So he gets his faithful workers to do it, and they put up new beams and tear down walls. In the middle of it all Hilkiah the priest finds a scroll! A book of the law, a part of the Bible itself (2 Chronicles 34:14) Can you imagine? It reminds me of the movie National Treasure or something! Just an amazing find. Most scholars believe that the book of the law was part of Deuteronomy.

Immediately, King Josiah sends some of his best men to Jerusalem with the book to find the prophetess Huldah to prove its authenticity. He knew Huldah heard from God.

> "Go and inquire of the Lord for me and for the people
> and for all Judah about what is written in this book."
> 2 Kings 22:13

Can you imagine being known in all the land for hearing from God? Man, I would love to be known for that.

Not only does Huldah prove its authenticity, but she begins to prophesy about the future. That prophecy creates a domino effect in King Josiah's life and he ends up removing all idols from the territory belonging to the Israelites. But unfortunately that does not remove some idols from some of their hearts. Though many Hebrews were given over to idolatry, there was a king that knew it was time for righteous living.

The lamp of righteousness was burning so strong in the heart of one woman that it was pouring over into the life of a king.

Huldah was known for her prophetic insight and her righteousness. This was an amazing lady. She was known far and wide in the kingdom of Judah. If that was not the case, King Josiah would never have sent five of his best personal men to her with the book. Never.

Only a deeply devout woman, an intellectual woman, and a respected woman, would have been sought out by a king and a priest to give her opinion as to whether or not this scroll was indeed the word of the Lord. It turned out to be one of the most important scrolls in the history of Israel.

Huldah was used to bless the nation of Israel.

> "Righteousness exalts a nation."
> Proverbs 14:34

I believe God used her because of her righteousness. The king even grew in righteousness. It's sad to know that as soon as King Josiah died, Judah went back to its godless ways again. So sad.

Huldah's name may only be in two chapters of the entire Bible, but she inspires me to live righteously; to seek God with all my heart and to hear what He has to say to me. I believe when we draw close to Him, He grants wisdom and favor. This is what He did in her life.

How about you today? Do you have idols in your life? Idols can be anything you put before God.

Are you doing your best to live in righteousness?

Living a righteous life DOES NOT mean you will not sin. You will always sin; this is why Jesus was sent in the first place.

It only means that God is first.

Dear God,
Help us to live righteous lives, to put you first in everything. I honor you today.

Buck's Reminder

The first house we owned on Cape Cod was across the street from the Cape Cod Canal and set back in the woods on a half-acre of land. The house was almost 100 years old and needed lots and lots of TLC. It was an old farm house, so there were little mice that loved to come in to get warm in the winter. The cats loved that house!

The wild life at our first home was amazing. One time, a giant turkey decided to hang around all alone for a couple of days. I mean this thing was so big I was scared of it. He just would not leave. I had to run to my car because I was scared he would peck me! It was so strange to see one all alone and content like that. We were always seeing fox and coyotes. One time there was even a very strange but beautiful tagged bird that stayed in our yard for almost 24 hours. We are a family that loves wildlife, so it was all very welcome.

But nothing beat our buck. On the land behind the house was a pear tree, and every year we had a giant buck that would come and eat the pears. Many deer would come, and fawns too, but there was NOTHING like our buck.

The back room of the house was brand new. The former owner had built it before we moved in. All around the room were big windows on all sides so you could see all around you. I loved it. And no one could see us because we were surrounded by woods. So awesome. This room was amazing to entertain in. It was so beautiful when it snowed, or in the fall when we could see the season all around us as we hosted a dinner party. One side of this big room was where the television and sitting area was, and the other side was our dining room. The girls could sit and drink coffee while the boys watched the game, and everyone was happy!

One night when we were hosting a dinner party, I remember there was snow on the ground and the outside just looked so beautiful. The sun would sparkle off the snow and it just added to the grand splendor of the room. The table was packed with family and friends. All of a sudden, in the middle of eating, all of the stories we had been telling became a reality for our friends! Up and over the hill stood our buck. Everyone just sat in awe. The buck came closer to the house and just stood there for about 20 minutes. The entire Lussier family and Miller family froze in awe.

He stood there as if he was posing for a picture. The sun was going down and I cannot even begin to tell you the majesty of it all. It really was majestic. As we just sat there it took our breath away. We no longer wanted to eat, it was so amazing. Well, maybe I'm doing that Italian over-exaggerating thing when I say that! But it really left you in total awe. How many times in your life do you get to sit at a dinner party and have live entertainment right outside the window like that? It was just amazing.

Whenever I think of that moment I think of the majesty of God. I know our buck was amazing but I know someday when we get to Heaven we will be in total awe. More awe than I can ever begin to imagine. The buck is my reminder.

"Thousands of thousands of angels in joyful assembly."
Hebrews 12:22

"The great street of the city was of pure gold, like transparent glass. I did not see a temple in the city, because the Lord God Almighty and the lamb are its temple. The city does not need the sun or the moon to shine on it, for the glory of God gives it light."
Revelation 21:21-23

I'm not sure about you today, but as I sit and read scripture after scripture on Heaven, I know the majesty of God, and the place He has prepared for you will be much more amazing than the feeling I had looking at our buck that day!

Are you ready for that? Ask Jesus to forgive you of your sins right now. There is NOTHING you have done that His love will not forgive. You need Him. He longs to be part of your life today.

My buck came for pears. My Lord will come for souls.

Dear God,
I pray for the reader right now. Father, I pray that as they call out to you that you take their breath away! Just blow their mind with your love as you begin to lead them. I honor you today.

April 13th

Dusty Bible?

Today I assisted for C-sections at the hospital. No matter how many times I see birth, no matter what kind of birth it is, I am always in total awe. I'm in awe of the doctors' wisdom in every situation; I'm in awe of the charge nurses, but most of all I'm in awe when I see that beautiful baby come out! No matter where it comes out! Hahaha.

Today there was a big, eight pound, 11 ounces, baby that came out of the tummy, and man was he a big chubby boy. He was so angry at the doctors when they pulled him out. He had a hearty voice and was beautifully healthy. Birth and life are just the most amazing things.

Ok, I don't want to gross anyone out, but in a C-section, it's just amazing how they have the uterus outside of the body as they repair it, and then just tuck it back in the body and sew everything back up as good as new! It just amazes me every time. The speed and pace in the C-section operating room is just beyond what you can imagine. You need to be ready for anything at anytime, and it needs to be done quickly!

As a CNA I need to know where everything is stored. If the doctor needs a special tool due to how the labor is going, I MUST know where it's located and run and get it. It's to the health of the baby and mother that I do it with speed, and that I know what I'm doing!

As I worked today in this fast paced environment, it made me think of the fact that we as people of God need to know what we are doing! We need to have a good knowledge of where everything is in the Word! Truth be told, we will NEVER know or remember every single thing, but just like my job at the hospital we MUST have a great awareness of where everything is. How well do you know your Bible today?

The word of God is VITAL to our growth and health. Just like the tools I need to run and get are VITAL to the health of baby and mother. How much time do you spend reading the Word each day? I have to tell you, I wrote this devotional in one year. I started writing in January of 2010, and every day as I dug through the word of God I learned something new. I have a better awareness of where certain stories are, and I flip much quicker to things. It's the same when I work in the maternity ward. The more I rummage through stock cabinets and look through the clean utility room, the more I know where things are so when the doctor wants me to run and get something I know exactly where it is.

Your growth depends on it. The growth of others depends on your knowledge of the Word.

In the Great Commission Jesus told His disciples:

> "Therefore go and make disciples of all nations, baptizing them in the name of the Father and of the Son and of the Holy Spirit, and teaching them to obey everything I have commanded you."
> Matthew 28:19-20

It's interesting, even though Jesus' heart beat was souls, he did not say, "Go lead everyone to salvation." He said, "Go and make DISCIPLES," and, "Teaching them to obey everything I commanded."

How can you make disciples if you don't know your Bible? How can you teach them what He commanded if you are not reading and knowing where things are in the first place? Since I have been digging and studying every day since January, I am much more aware and I can move quicker through my Bible.

Today is your day to become passionate about reading the word of God.

> "For the word of God is living and active. Sharper than any double-edged sword, it penetrates even to dividing soul and spirit, joints and marrow; it judges to thoughts and attitudes of the heart."
> Hebrews 4:12

Do you have a dusty Bible?

Dear God,
Help us! Give us a deep hunger for your word today. Let us sacrifice "things" like TV, games, or whatever in order to grow in your word. We honor you today.

April 14th

Press through the Mess

I have a dear friend who just went to the emergency room a little while ago. The doctors are saying she has a brain tumor and might need surgery tomorrow. Why do things like this happen to amazing people? And to those who give their lives for the work of God? We could drive ourselves crazy trying to answer that question. I will say that the word of God says:

> "Trust in the Lord with all your heart and
> lean not on your own understanding."
> Proverbs 3:5

God's ways are NOT our ways. I know and have shared countless times in this devotional that it was through the darkest times in my life that God grew my character more than any other time.

I noticed something pretty cool this afternoon. I had our beautiful black lab Arwen outside, and new, spring life was pushing through the ground everywhere.

Have you ever seen an iris? I have to be honest and say I do not like irises. They are not my favorite flower! If you look at one and touch it, it's very frail. If you are not careful you can easily rip its odd shaped petals. Even though it's a weak and frail flower, somehow it manages to push its way up out of the hard, winter frozen dirt! It pushes past the stones, and what I noticed today is it was even pushing itself through the mess of the last bush that was rotted there. To me it's just amazing how something so gentle and frail can have enough strength to push through such a hard mess.

I looked all around my yard and it was happening everywhere! It's so much easier to say that we must push through a hard time than it is to actually push through, but we must! When those who are weak and frail get so discouraged that they have lost hope, we need to help hold up their arms and help them through. We need to pray, to encourage them with words of hope through God's word.

Maybe the weak and frail person is you today. You just don't know how to push through your hard mess. Please don't give up. I know it's easy for me to say because I'm not having to walk in your shoes, but please don't! Try to hang on to the word of God. Read these scriptures slowly if you can:

> "Set your mind on things above, not on earthly things."
> Colossians 3:2

> "Everything is possible for him who believes."
> Mark 9:23

"Be strong and of good courage; do not be afraid, nor be dismayed,
for the Lord your God is with you wherever you go."
Joshua 1:9

"In the world you will have tribulation;
but be of good cheer, I have overcome the world."
John 16:33

"I consider that our present sufferings are not worth comparing with the
glory that will be revealed in us."
Romans 8:18

"I can do everything through Him who gives me strength."
Philippians 4:13

"Being confident of this, that He who began a good work in you will
carry it on to completion until the day of Christ Jesus."
Philippians 1:6

I could just go on and on writing scriptures of hope. You are the one who needs
to apply these words to your heart. There is no way I can make you do that. My
job is to give you the word of God.

God has a great plan for your life, but sometimes it's just easier to stay covered
in the dirt.

Press through the mess!

Dear God,
Please help my friends. God, I don't see what they are going through today, but
it may be horrific. If it's physical, depression, abuse, or addiction I pray you give
them hope. God, as they take time to read these scriptures, touch and bless
their hearts to press through. Help them to see their purpose through your eyes
and not their own. I honor you today.

April 15th

Learned Extravert

Are you the kind of person who would rather be by yourself all the time and never have to deal with people? I think at one point in our lives we have all been in a place where we want to run away from responsibilities or the norm for a while. But then some just want to stay there.

Did you know that that is NOT a place where God wants you? We need each other.

When I first met my husband it took a ton of work to get him to talk. He was very quiet and an extreme introvert. He would always think before anything would come out of his mouth. It's a quality that he still has and that I admire very much. Now for those of you who have read these devotionals, you know I love to talk! And I have learned through the years to try and think before I talk, but I still mess up. I'm Italian. I'm very much an extreme extrovert, and I thrive when I'm around masses of people. Confession: I like the center of attention.

Through the years my husband has become a learned extravert. This takes work and discipline. This takes knowing that God did not intend for you to be alone and a hermit all the time. He has taken God's word and applied it to his life. He calls Starbucks his "other office." Once or twice a week he meets a group of men there for java and to talk about anything and everything.

Think about you. When was the last time you spent time with someone and just talked to them about your life and their life? When was the last time you let someone cry on your shoulder? When was the last time you asked someone out for coffee? You know the Bible actually speaks about us sharpening one another.

> "As iron sharpens iron, so one man sharpens another."
> Proverbs 27:17

As an introvert, you might not always seek out the opportunities that God might have for you. It's more comfy to stay home and not be around people. I believe today that God wants to stretch some of you out of your comfort zone. It's not like you have to be like the extraverts you know today, just that God would bring you to a place of knowing that you might have something very special to offer someone and they might actually have something very special to offer you, too. When we spend time together, especially when we know the Lord and talk about His word, we can sharpen one another. Who would not want that today?

After 30 years of discipline and pulling himself out of his comfort zone, my husband is an amazing learned extrovert. This has also made him a better pastor. He guards his quiet time (which we ALL need by the way), but there is a good balance of alone time and people time. How can we sharpen each other if we are always alone? It just can't happen.

Also, when we are with others we are accountable. It's very easy to fall or do what does not please the Lord when we have no one to be accountable to. Be on guard!

Think about this today. Who are you accountable to?

> "A man that hath friends must show himself friendly."
> Proverbs 18:24

Are you friendly today?

> "Greater love has no man than this:
> that he lay down his life for his friends."
> John 15:13

Do you have friends that you want to lay down your life for today?

I think today God might want to change some hearts. Trust me; I'm NOT perfect at all.

Please know we all need each other today!

Maybe God wants to make you a learned extrovert, and pull you out of your comfort zone a little so you can help sharpen another. Or be sharpened by another.

Dear God,
Help us to never get comfortable the way we are. God, I always want to be growing and changing for the better. Help us, Lord. I honor you today.

April 16th

Peace Be Still

Today my firstborn turns 18 (2010). Happy Birthday Jon! I have been very emotional this morning. I'm not sure if I'm just being a mom, or if it's the new hormone therapy I'm on. Hahaha. It's so crazy to think of how fast the years went by. The memories that flood me are the highlights of my son Jon's life.

I remember when he told me he saw two angels in his room at four years old, the day he got baptized in the Holy Spirit at age six, times I have seen him worship with hands lifted to God, and the day he wanted to get baptized in water. Through the years, this walk he grew up with became part of his life. Along the way, growing up on the church pew, he met God. His character is like no other youth I know, and I'm not just saying that because I'm his mom. You pretty much could ask anyone that knows him. It's real, and he walks with God. I'm not saying the kid is perfect, but there is just something special about him.

Since the time he was little, God's amazing favor has been on Jonathan. God would speak to him in dreams. I remember two times when Guy and I were praying for direction, and Jon woke and said God gave him a dream. The dreams were very detailed and confirmed the exact things we were praying about. Jon's band has had the favor of God on it. The Lord has swung open doors that I never even thought would open. For example, Soulfest, which is a music festival on the East Coast with thousands of kids. It's just amazing.

Today, Jonathan left a little while ago to get his first tattoo. He has wanted one for a very long time, but we always told him he had to be 18. I could not wait to hear what he was getting because to me, a tattoo is something you put much thought into. I was amazed when I heard what he was doing and I realized once again that he has been through things in life that brought him to this choice. Times he failed, and then confessed, times when he had walked through hard times, but made it through knowing God still loved him no matter what.

His choice was a ship on a raging sea. It's a design of waves that look like they will engulf the boat at any minute. It says, "Peace Be Still."

"That day when evening came, He said to His disciples, 'Let us go over to the other side.' Leaving the crowd behind, they took Him along, just as He was, in the boat. There were also other boats with Him. A furious squall came up, and the waves broke over the boat, so that it was nearly swamped. Jesus was in the stern, sleeping on a cushion. The Disciples woke Him and said to Him, 'Teacher, don't you care if we drown?' He got up, rebuked the wind and said to the waves, 'Peace be still!' Then the wind died down and it was completely calm. He said to His disciples, 'Why are you so afraid? Do you still have no faith?' They

were terrified and asked each other, 'Who is this? Even the wind and the waves obey Him!'"
Mark 4:35 39

To me the fact that Jonathan picked this picture and scripture for his tattoo says a lot about what is inside of him.

Do you know today that no matter what storm you are in, God can calm it?

Maybe you don't even believe in God, and like me you pretty much have tried everything else to try to ease your pain in life. Why not give God a chance? I know firsthand that He is the only thing that can give you perfect peace and a hope that will keep you.

My son knows this, too. So I say to you today friend, call on God today and "Peace be still."

Dear God,
Thank you for the calm. Thank you that you can just command and it will be done. Forgive us for our lack of faith in life. I honor you today.

Fight On Your Own

I remember as a little girl growing up in a home that was filled with the spiritual realm. It was alive and active all around me. Most of it was evil. I know MANY of you reading this can relate and have experienced this yourself. Things would happen in my home. I remember nights that my bed would shake on its own. I remember two separate times when I heard audible voices downstairs, one of those times my mother was with me and heard it too. I remember one time my friend saw a lady floating over the dining room table. And the list goes on, but truth be told, it's not worth talking about! The devil tries to put fear in us, but Jesus Christ has already won the victory over the devil, death, and darkness.

> "For God has not given us a spirit of fear,
> but of power and of love and of a sound mind."
> 2 Timothy 1:7

Fear like that is NOT from God. You would think that after you become a Christian and surrender your life to Christ that these things would not happen anymore, but the evil one is all about torment. He will try to put fear in your heart even in a home that is dedicated to God.

A while back, my daughter shared with me a time that she was home alone one night. Angela has grown up on the church pew. We are not perfect, but try to have a godly home where the Lord has reign. She said one night when she was alone in our house, she was overcome with fear. She said she could only stay in the spare room; any other part of the house scared her. She got her daily devotional book and opened it to that day's date and read 2 Timothy 1:7 about God NOT putting fear into our hearts. This word helped her fight the evil she felt. What a wonderful feeling to know she did not have to call me, but had it out with the devil on her own. To me that says a ton about her character and relationship with God.

It does not matter if you have dedicated your home to the Lord or not, the evil one will try to torment us until the day we die. We must fight. We are in spiritual warfare almost every day.

Anytime the devil tried to tempt Jesus, what did he say first? He said, "IT IS WRITTEN!" He came back at the devil with the Word! Do you feel like you know your Bible enough to fight the evil one who puts roots of fear in your heart? If not, what will you do about it? It's time to start memorizing scripture, so when those times come you can have it fresh in your head. If you have a hard time remembering things, maybe highlight the scriptures in your Bible. I've made an entire page in the back of my Bible that I wrote hand picked scriptures on. If there is a person manifesting demons near me, a fear I'm dealing with, or any kind of thing the evil one is trying to hurl at me, I turn to that page and begin to read. I begin to speak directly to the devil and remind him of his place.

"The weapons we fight with are not the weapons of the world. On the contrary, they have divine power to demolish strongholds."
2 Corinthians 10:4

There is a stronghold called fear, and if you let it, it can haunt you. I cannot tell you the many times I have quoted the Scriptures out loud to the evil one when he would try to put fear in my heart. In Ephesians 6:10, it talks about the spiritual armor of God. I have written about this in this devotional before, but the one piece I would like to remind you of today is:

"The sword of the spirit, which is the word of God."
Ephesians 6:17

Jesus used the Word.

If you read this chapter, every piece of armor is to protect, but the sword is the only piece that is used to pierce the enemy. The sword symbolizes the word of God. Do you know the Word enough to fight with it? Fear is NOT from God and you need to begin to collect scriptures that you can read out loud when you are being tempted or tormented.

"Praise be to the Lord my rock, who trains my hands for war, my fingers for battle. He is my loving God and my fortress, my stronghold and my deliverer, my shield, in whom I take refuge."
Psalm 144:1-2

"The Lord will rescue me from every evil attack and will bring me safely to His Heavenly kingdom. To Him be glory forever and ever. Amen."
2 Timothy 4:18

"Resist the devil, and he will flee from you. Come near to God and He will come near to you."
James 4:7

"The one who is in you is greater than the one who is in the world."
1 John 4:4

"No weapon forged against you will prevail."
Isaiah 54:17

My daughter did not need me that night she was home alone.
Learn to fight on your own.

Dear God,
Help us to know your word more and more every day. Help us to fight on our own without fear. The evil one is already defeated and has no hold on us. I honor you today.

April 18th

<u>One Hope</u>

Do you realize you are called today? If you don't know the Lord, He is calling you. The entire reason He made Adam and Eve in the first place was to have fellowship. He longs to have fellowship with us. Just like you love to spend time with your friends, I love to spend time with the living God. I hope you do too. If you know the Lord, you are also called today. We are all called. He has a specific plan for our lives and wants to use each and every one of us for a purpose. Have you sought out what that purpose is in your life? Have you asked Him?
Have you taken any classes in your church or anywhere else that will show you where your gifts are? Where you should be plugged in?

"Just as you were called to one hope when you were called."
Ephesians 4:4

He is our hope today, our peace and shelter from the storm, the lighthouse we run to for safety. If I did not have the hope of Christ, I'm not quite sure where I would be today. I fail, I'm human, but He still calls me. You may not think He calls you because you think you have done things that are too bad for Him to listen. I say to your heart today, His grace and mercy are like none other you have ever met. He has an unconditional love that surpasses anything. I love Him and I thank Him.

"I urge you to live a life worthy of the calling you have received."
Ephesians 4:1

Paul said those words while he was in prison, and then he stressed keeping peace and bearing each others' pain together. Your "calling" does not have to mean full-time ministry like some people. Your calling means knowing the One Hope and telling others about Him. You may work as a lawyer, teacher, cleaner, bagger, model, nurse, secretary, carpenter, and the list goes on and on. But we are all ministers! We all can live our life worthy of the call. We all can share the one hope, Jesus Christ, wherever we are.

Sometimes sharing this one hope means being there when a co-worker, who does not know God, is crying about something, or just giving someone a hug. It can mean making Christmas cookies for a neighbor who you don't know or making a meal for a family who has been through a hard time. Why do we make sharing the love and hope of Christ so hard? He loved, so we love, it's as simple as that.

Think about yourself today. Are you sharing this hope? Do you take the time to love, care, or be gentle in situations? Or do you just not care?

I walked around for years in darkness. What I would not have given for just one person to tell me about the hope of the Lord. How He could fill up the voids I had, instead of me filling them with booze and drugs. So many years went by without one person sharing that hope with me. I must have been around God followers in the malls, stores, out in public, but yet not one shared that hope with me.

"Hope deferred makes the heart sick,
but a longing fulfilled is a tree of life."
Proverbs 13:12

You have what most are seeking. If you know it, share it.
Do no fear. Give them one hope.

Dear God,
I thank you for all you did when I heard your call. I pray those who are reading will know they are called by you and that you have a mighty plan for them no matter what they have been through or what they have done. Bring them to the rest you provide today. Give them your hope. I honor you today.

You Are Not a Mistake

Has there ever been a time in your life when someone said something that hurt you? Something that was said out of anger or without thinking? I know that it hurts, and I also know there have been times in my life when I have done it myself and have had to tell people that I am sorry.

> "Reckless words pierce like a sword,
> but the tongue of the wise brings healing."
> Proverbs 12:18

There has been about four times in my life where I can recall someone telling me I was a mistake. It may not seem like a lot of times, but every time it cut like a knife, beat down my self esteem, and the list goes on. I'm sure this must have happened to one of you who are reading. It's not easy, but I want you to know today that no matter what has been said to you in your lifetime, you are NOT a mistake!

The person that said I was a mistake did not know the Lord and said it out of anger most the time. God has totally changed this person's life and they are no longer the same!

Through the years I have preached messages called "You Are Not a Mistake." One year I spoke at a big event that I put on every year and I shared this message. It's amazing to me how you touch people's lives and never know about it until years later.

My daughter and I were out shopping one day about an hour from our home. On the main strip we were on, we saw a God centered book and gift store. Where we lived on Cape Cod, we did not have stores like that so we decided to stop. We walked in the store to a nice smell and beautiful gifts everywhere. Half way through the store we came to where the register was. I stood in total awe with tears in my eyes when I saw what was on the wall. There behind the register smack dab in the middle of the wall was a giant picture of the hand of God holding what looked like a brand new baby. The quote under the picture was "You are not a mistake!" I could not believe it! It sent chills up my spine.

When the store owner came out I asked her about the picture, and after speaking for just a minute she said, "You are Tana Miller!" She had been at that big event and heard my message a few years ago. She said she had her friend paint this picture because God had touched her heart with my message. The picture was on sale for $350, and you could order the picture in all sizes for many prices. All because I preached a message called "You are not a mistake."

It was just the most amazing thing that we stopped at that store that day and ended up seeing a picture that I never knew existed and was created due to a story in my life about reckless words. Tell me friend, what are the chances of that? That's what I call a divine appointment.

I want to encourage you when people hurt you with words. Don't get bitter, use your stories; they will touch lives that you never thought could be touched. People like to know they are not alone. Just make sure you use wisdom in your words as you share your hurtful stories. Let people know how you made it through.

"The tongue of the wise brings healing."
Proverbs 12:18

I hope to bring healing to people's lives through every story I tell.

Now I leave you with a scripture that I hope you read over a few times slowly to let it sink in.

"A man's wisdom gives him patience;
it is to his glory to overlook an offense."
Proverbs 19-11

Dear God,
When people hurt us with reckless words and offend us, help us to use wisdom. I pray every single person reading knows they are not a mistake! I honor you today Lord.

Pinky Hold

Do you wonder sometimes how you will make it through? I just had friends, who I call family, go through such a hard time. This young man Ezra found out he needed a very serious operation. Things did not go as planned and just days after his operation he went back in again for another surgery. Any of you who have been through a situation like that know that you cling to God in prayer every second for your loved one. Thank God Ezra is well today and we pray it will stay that way!

Do you remember as kids how we used to grab onto cars or trucks on our skateboards or bikes? It did not matter if you had a great hold of the vehicle with your hand or a pinkie hold! No matter how you held on, that truck or car would pull you where you needed to go. On our street we even would grab onto the back of motorcycles! Even if you had to go up a hill, that tiny hold you had would make all the difference in the world. If you were tired, weary, or just could not get to your destination on your own strength, you held on! Those were the days!

Friend, hang on! If you are going through a very hard time like Ezra and his family just went through, don't stop reaching out to God, even if you only have a pinky hold. Sometimes instead of reaching out to God, we are too weak and we will depend on others for prayer. **Please know that's an ok place to be!** Do you think He loves you any less just because you are discouraged, worn out, or need help from others? NO! He knew we needed help, that's why He sent His Son!

"So do not fear, for I am with you; do not be dismayed, for I am your God. I will strengthen you and help you; I will uphold you with my righteous right hand."
Isaiah 41:10

"Do not be anxious about anything, but in everything, by prayer and petition, with thanksgiving, present your requests to God. And the peace of God, which transcends all understanding, will guard your hearts and your minds in Christ Jesus."
Philippians 4:6-7

I'm not sure what you are dealing with right now at this moment as you read, or what your day has been like, but I spoke with Ezra's dad tonight and he said during Ezra's second surgery he had an amazing peace. Friend, a peace like that only comes from God. Many friends and family were praying and a mother's heart was broken, but she had a pinky hold.

When we hang on to God, He glides us through in peace.

Keep your pinky hold a little tighter!

Dear God,
Help us never to let go and to realize that it's ok for others to help us. I thank you for the many times you have helped me glide. I love you and I honor you today.

The Things Promised

Take the time if you can to once again read Hebrews 11, what some call "The Faith Hall of Fame." Let's look at a couple of these scriptures:

"By faith Moses, when he had grown up, refused to be known as the son of Pharaoh's daughter. He chose to be mistreated along with the people of God rather than to enjoy the pleasures of sin for a short time. He regarded disgrace for the sake of Christ as of greater value than the treasures of Egypt, because he was looking ahead to his reward."
Hebrews 11:26

Here's what this chapter says about Abraham:

"For he was looking forward to the city with foundations, whose architect and builder is God."
Hebrews 11:10

Noah, Enoch, Abel, Rahab, Moses, Joseph, and others were still living by faith when they died. I want to be known for living by faith until I died!

"All these people were still living by faith when they died. They did not receive the things promised; they only saw them and welcomed them from a distance. And they admitted that they were aliens and strangers on Earth."
Hebrews 11:13

The part that captures me in this verse is, "They did not receive the things promised." Some were living full speed ahead with the hope of their promises. They were living by faith, thus ended up in this chapter.

"Now faith is being sure of what we hope for and certain of what we do not see."
Hebrews 11:1

At the end of chapter 11 we again read:

"These were all commended for their faith, yet none of them received what had been promised. God had planned something better for us so that only together with us, would they be made perfect."
Hebrews 11:39-40

I want you to take a minute and think of what God has promised you. Do you even know? What are your passions? Dreams? There is a great big plan out there for you. Are you praying about it? These people were promised some awesome things, but we see two scriptures here that say they lived by faith when they died and when they died they still had not seen their promise in complete fulfillment. As a matter of a fact listen to this:

"Some faced jeers and flogging, while still others were chained and put in prison. They were stoned; they were sawed in two; they were put to

death by the sword. They went about in sheepskins and goatskins, destitute, persecuted, and mistreated--**the world was not worthy of them.** They wandered in deserts and mountains, and in caves and holes in the ground."
Hebrews 11:36-38

So we read these verses about what some went through, and thrown in the middle of this scripture is this little verse that says:

"The world was not worthy of them."
Hebrews 11:38

Wow. They lived their life faithfully, yet were persecuted for the Gospel's sake, and the world was not worthy of them! The fact that the Bible says those words in 11:38 says to me, God was pleased.

Will you be happy if you do not see your promise for another 40 years, or will you grumble? Do you know God has perfect timing? His timing is NOT ours MOST the time.

The things He has promised you may not even come to complete fulfillment before you die. Can you be happy knowing that God is in full control?

"God had planned something better."
Hebrews 11:40

If we die before our promise has come to pass, we won't care about all that anymore, we will be with Him.

The things promised keep our faith alive.

Dear God,
Please be with this reader right now. Let them feel your presence in a powerful way. Keep their faith alive and keep them passionate about you and the promises you have given to them. If they don't know you, I pray you speak to them right now as they sit in the quiet. I honor you today.

April 22nd

Onlookers and God

In the Miller home today there is an excitement in the air! The Launch, our Southern New England District Youth Convention, starts tomorrow morning with the Fine Arts Festival. The kids are all excited. My kids are very involved along with tons of kids from our youth group and all across Southern New England! My daughter Angela will be singing Friday night and my son's band, Exiting the Fall, will be opening the day on Saturday with three rocking songs! I love all these kids.

There is just something about an event with thousands of young people on fire for God! Worship is over the top. Now rest assured they are full of sugar from their long bus rides from three different states and they are hyper like all teens are, but get these kids into the presence of God and watch out!

The thing I love about the youth convention is that kids come expecting! I have overheard our own youth group in the past week talking to kids about the convention and they are always saying things like, "You have to come, and you can't miss it! It's amazing!" The kids know after years and years of camps and conventions that God's power comes down and lives are changed forever!

I love when young people come expecting! It's a powerful thing!

At the day of Pentecost in Acts, the people who loved God came expecting. Thousands of onlookers came to Christ from seeing God's power come down on Christians! Some onlookers said:

> "They have had too much wine."
> Acts 2:13

Onlookers were seeing divine miracles and the tongues that the people who followed God were speaking were their own native tongues from other lands. They were in shock and did not understand. Therefore they thought they were drunk, when the truth is that God's power came down. I'm not sure why they thought they were drunk, it's not like people speak other languages when they have had a few! I think they just did not want to admit the fact that they were seeing a miracle!

> "About three thousand were added to their number that day."
> Acts 2:41

Can you imagine? They came to Christ because they saw the power of God come down on others, then they heard Peter and the Apostles give them a little direction on how to get nearer to God (Acts 2:38-39), and next thing you know they are all coming to know God. Three thousand of them!

"In the last days, God says, I will pour out my Spirit on all people. Your sons and daughters will prophesy, your young men will see visions, your old men will dream dreams. Even on my servants, both men and women, I will pour out my Spirit in those days, and they will prophesy. I will show wonders in the Heaven above and signs on the earth below."
Acts 2:17-19

This scripture is youth convention! God's spirit moves among these young people and I stand in total awe. I have not missed it in years, due to the fact that I love to see God's spirit poured out on young crowds like this! And on my kids.

When the onlookers thought the Christians were drunk, Peter says:
"These men are not drunk, as you suppose.
It's only nine in the morning!"
Acts 2:15

And he went on to say that God's spirit had poured out on them!

The reason I came to God was not because of a church service. It was seeing my brother Lou totally change in a year's time! I saw what the power of God did to a young man's character. As an onlooker I had many doubts, but could not deny the fact that God's power had done something to someone.

Are you an onlooker today? Or do you know the power of God? If you have never been to a place where God is doing miracles and moving among people I feel bad and I hope and pray you can experience it. There is nothing like it. Jesus loves onlookers. As a matter of a fact, even though you may not know Him, He knows you and died for you.

So thousands of kids in Southern New England are getting ready for The Launch, including onlookers! The boys are packing their sour candy, Monster drinks, and guitars, while the girls are packing their makeup, stuffed animals, and cameras. As they pack they are getting excited and they are coming expecting.

God's spirit IS going to pour down.

Do you know God today, or are you an onlooker? I sure wish you knew God's power and could experience it. Call out to Him today!

I was an onlooker that now knows God.

Dear God,
I pray for anyone reading today that does not know you. I pray they will see your love and power, and that they will know you are God. I honor you today.

Jamie

A few weeks ago, this kid at our church came up to me after service with tears in his eyes. He said that he wanted me to know that he reads my devotions every day, and that they have really helped him. This blessed my heart to know that a young kid was reading every day.

Jamie was brought to church by his friend Trevor, just one kid inviting another to church. God changed Jamie's life forever. That was just four months ago. From the get-go you can tell that Jamie McNeil has a call on his life.

Today (2010) we walked the halls of the Southern New England Fine Arts Festival. Jamie, only four months young in his relationship with God, entered a short sermon category contest at the festival. In my mind I knew he would get up there, but I pictured him being shy and glued to his notes. The minute Jamie got up to preach, the spirit of the living God took over. I have never seen a young person preach with such an anointing. Now, I have a niece Nina that can preach, but I'm telling you I have never seen anything like this. The anointing of God came over this kid in his actions, words, gestures, and it was amazing. The passion for preaching the word of God was all over him. For those of you from the East Coast, it was as if Jamie got up there and Greg Hubbard took over! Ha! Greg is an evangelist and he is who Jamie was preaching like. It blew my mind.

When God called Jeremiah, the Lord said:

> "Before I formed you in the womb I knew you, before you were born I set you part; I appointed you as a prophet to the nations."
> Jeremiah 1:5

Jeremiah's response:

> "Ah, sovereign Lord, I do not know how to speak; I am only a child."
> Jeremiah 1:6

But here is what God had to say to that:

> "But the Lord said to me, 'Do NOT say, 'I am only a child.'' You must go to everyone I send you to and say whatever I command you. Do NOT be afraid of them, for I am with you and will rescue you, declares the Lord.' Then the Lord reached out His hand and touched my mouth and said to me, 'Now, I have put my words in your mouth. See, today I appoint you over nations and kingdoms to uproot and tear down, to destroy and overthrow, to build and to plant.'"
> Jeremiah 1:7-10

I love how the Lord says in this scripture, "Do NOT say, 'I am only a child.'"

Hundreds of kids entered the Fine Arts Festival, preaching, leading worship, performing vocal solos, guitar solos, and drum solos, submitting art and photography and the list goes on and on and on. The talent of the young people in this place was totally amazing. I just cannot tell you how I was blessed.

Seeing Jamie, only four months walking with God, and hundreds of other young kids being used by God today, reminded me of Jeremiah's words! God wants to use young people!

You are never too young to be used under the power and anointing of God! And you are never too young in your walk with God to be used under the power and anointing!

If you are reading and you are young today, please know God still wants to speak things to your heart! He wants to show you exactly what it is you should be doing. For those of you who are my age, well, we may move a tad slower but He desires to use us just the same.

Young and old alike, the call of God does not change!

I went up to Jamie after he spoke, patted him on the back, and said, "This, my friend, is what you were born to do." Not one person in that room could doubt the fact that God's hand was all over Him.

Do you know what you were born to do? What is your passion, young person? Please know today that God wants to use you just like Jamie!

It does not matter how old or young you are! God is saying:

"'You must go to everyone I send you to and say whatever I command you. Do NOT be afraid of them, for I am with you and will rescue you,'" declares the Lord. Then the Lord reached out His hand and touched my mouth and said to me, 'Now, I have put my words in your mouth.'"
Jeremiah 1:7-9

This is what I experienced today through Jamie.

And it's not just for him, it's for you too.

Dear God,
Please let every young reader know that you long to use them. Even if they are young in the Lord like Jamie. Father, pour out your spirit on this generation. I honor you today.

April 24th

God of All Comfort
"In a flash, in the twinkling of an eye."
1 Corinthians 15:52

Tonight I got some horrible news that a friend of mine died in a tragic accident. One minute someone can be there, and the next gone. I read a quote the other day on facebook that someone had put as their status and that didn't say who the quote was from. It said:

"Everyone will die, but not everyone will live."

This is so true. All of us will die someday, but after that death not all of us will live. Only those who knew the Lord will be with Him, "In a flash, in the twinkling of an eye." The chapter goes on to say:

"We will be changed."
1 Corinthians 15:52b

Eternal life after death is beautiful; it is nothing to be afraid of. But I have to say, when it happens before you expect it, it hurts and it's hard.

"My sheep listen to my voice; I know them, and they follow me. I give them eternal life, and they shall never perish; no one can snatch them out of my hand."
John 10:27

If you know the Father personally and are striving to live for Him in all you do, you are going to Heaven when you die. Heaven is a free gift from God according to John 3:16. It is not earned or deserved. It is grace.

It may give us peace to know they are with God, but it still gives us a hole in our hearts to know they are no longer with us here on Earth. It hurts.

I ask you today friend, do you know God? Personally? When was the last time you talked to Him? When was the last time you asked Him what He wanted for your life, and read the book that He said would give you faith?

Are you ready to go to Heaven if you were to die tonight? Will you live after death?

These are questions that many in this world do not think of until they lose someone, or are diagnosed with a horrible illness.
I'm here today to tell you it's easy to know whether you will have life after death. Just say to Him tonight, "God, I need you. Help me to live for you. Come into my life today." Just talk to Him and tell Him what is in your heart.

I don't want any single one of you to not know how easy it is to know God. He is a friend. He will not hurt you. Turn to Him today.

If you are hurting from loss, please know He is the God of all comfort.

"Praise be to the God and Father of our Lord Jesus Christ, the Father of compassion and the God of all comfort. Who comforts us in all our troubles."
2 Corinthians 1:3-4

I want you to know He is there for you. Don't be afraid to talk to Him today. He is the God of all comfort.

Dear God,
Touch the hearts of people who have lost loved ones all over our world. Comfort their hearts. Surround them with your love. I honor you today.

God's Grace and Naboth's Vineyard

Ahab, king of Samaria, wanted to purchase and use Naboth's Vineyard.

> "Let me have your vineyard to use for a vegetable garden, since it is close to my palace. In exchange I will give you a better vineyard or, if you prefer, I will pay you whatever it is worth."
> 1 Kings 21:1-2

First let me say, I wish someone would come up to me and say that about my house that has been on the market for over two years and has not sold (2010)!

Naboth's reply:

> "The Lord forbid that I should give you the inheritance of my fathers."
> 1 kings 21: 3

So Ahab goes home and is angry!

> "He lay in his bed sulking and refused to eat."
> 1 kings 21:4

This just cracks me up. The king is lying around whining like a little baby. What an amazing picture. So his evil wife Jezebel comes in and pretty much tells him he is a wimp. She tells him to take what he wants! This was her way about almost everything. After her advice, she does not even give him the chance to do it, she does it herself! So she writes letters pretending to be King Ahab, and even puts his seal on them. She sends them to the elders and nobles who lived in Naboth's city near his vineyard. The letters told them to take Naboth out and stone him to death. They said that he had cursed both God and the King. So the elders and nobles did exactly what she said, thinking it was a command from the King.

> "They took him outside the city and stoned him to death."
> 1 Kings 21:13

As soon as Jezebel tells Ahab he is dead, Ahab goes down to take possession of the vineyard of Naboth. Meanwhile, God is speaking to Elijah the Tishbite, giving him a word for Ahab. God even told Elijah exactly where the King was at that moment. He goes and confronts King Ahab and gives him a word from the Lord:

> "You have sold yourself to do evil in the eyes of the Lord.
> I am going to bring disaster on you."
> 1 Kings 21:20

This totally freaks out King Ahab!

> "When Ahab heard these words, he tore his clothes, put on sackcloth and fasted. He lay in sackcloth and went about meekly."
> 1 Kings 20:27

So here he is afraid, knowing that what he had allowed to happen was evil. Then we see an amazing thing happen. God speaks again:

> "Have you noticed how Ahab has humbled himself before me? Because he has humbled himself, I will not bring this disaster in his day, but I will bring it on his house in the days of his son."
> 1 Kings 21:29

What?

Here is what I want you to think about today my friend. If God Himself can see the humility of an evil man's heart and forgive him, how much more will He forgive those who strive to keep their hearts pure before Him?

His grace and compassions are not like ours. His grace goes beyond our understanding. It reaches to the darkest pits. He is the God of a second chance.

That is the grace of God.

Dear God,
I'm not sure how you can forgive me sometimes, but I'm sure glad you do. I thank you for your grace. I thank you that you change me daily. I honor you today.

April 26th

Stronger Through the Burning
"You are the light of the world."
Matthew 5:14

Every summer we rent out a cabin on a lake in Maine. It's beautiful. We only have electricity for one hour a day when the generator is on. We ruff it, but it's breath-taking there. Words cannot describe it. There is just something about getting away from the "real world." No TV, no distractions from the internet, no phones ringing off the hook, not even light.

It's amazing when you live without light. You never know how you depend on it until it is gone. We never knew this until we went to the little cabin in Maine for the first time. When the black darkness came, it was about 9:00pm. Yes, we could light candles and put on the gas lanterns, but it was nothing like electricity. It seemed we were all in bed and asleep by 10:00pm because we got sick of trying to see our card game or whatever else we were trying to do.

In the cabin we have gas lights and oil lanterns on the wall that must be lit with a match. I love it because it reminds me of Little House on the Prairie. I imagine my husband getting out his fiddle and dancing around the room like Pa! Haha! Now that would be a site.

My two kids take turns with the lighter to light everything up around dinner time.

When you light a fire or a candle, there is always a burning before everything lights up. This is what I want to talk to you about today.

Are you going through a trial?

"Dear friends, do not be surprised at the painful trial you are suffering, as though something strange were happening to you. But rejoice that you participate in the sufferings of Christ, so that you may be overjoyed when his glory is revealed."
1 Peter 4:12-13

I have said it before, we must go through trial to build our character and make us stronger. We go through trial to grow us. This teaches us how to live on faith and prayer. When we have been through the burning process, then we can emit light.

When my kids go around lighting all the wicks of the oil lanterns, it seems they snuff out two or three times before burning steadily. The truth is, sometimes we DO NOT burn so well! The good burning must happen before the lantern is lit to the fullest. And when we finally get that flame, it seems the entire room can light up. If you turn the knob to raise the wick so that more of it will burn, the room gets bright. If you turn the knob to put the wick down into the oil so less of it will burn, the light is hardly seen. The more of the wick that's burning, the more light that shines.

How do you burn today? I wonder if you have ever been asked that before. When you go through trial, do you live in the joy of the Lord or do you curse God? In any trial there can be joy when you have Christ. And His joy becomes our strength.

"For the joy of the Lord is your strength."
Nehemiah 8:10

If you have never experienced this, I pray you will. Cry out to God. He only wants to make you stronger through the burning.

When you finally make it through, you will light up a part of your world and people will see like they never have before.

God will use your burning so others around you to see much clearer.
You are the light of the world.

Dear God,
Help us to have joy in our trials. Some may be grieving today. Some turn to other things to fill their voids and ease their pain, but I pray you speak to them today. May their burning light others' paths and make them stronger. I honor you today.

Record Book of Wrongs?

"It keeps no record of wrongs."
1 Corinthians 13:5

The Bible says that true love keeps no record of wrongs. How many of you lay your head down at night with lists of who you are angry with? How many of you save letters from five years ago of people you don't get along with? Steps eight and nine in Celebrate Recovery, a Bible based, 12-step program that my husband and I lead, says this:

"Evaluate all of my relationships. Offer forgiveness to those who have hurt me and make amends for harm I've done to others, except when to do so would harm them or others."

There was a person in my life that hurt me for 10 years. One month before they died I extended a hand of forgiveness and led this person to Jesus Christ over the telephone. We prayed a prayer together. I thought that was the end of my ministry to them, until I was told by my sister-in-law that her grandmother felt God leading her to that same person that same week. Her 90-year-old grandmother (Grandma BJ) went over to this person's house and right up until the day that this person died she ministered right to their heart.

Are you willing to forgive those who hurt you? I am so thankful that God forgives me on a daily basis! Where would we be without that?

"If you, O Lord, kept a record of sins, O Lord, who could stand?
But with you there is forgiveness."
Psalm 130:3-4

What an amazing scripture this is. God keeps NO record book of wrongs for those that walk with Him. Why do you?

"For as high as the Heavens are above the earth, so great is His love for those who fear Him; as far as the East is from the West, so far has He removed our transgressions from us."
Psalm 103:11-12

I'm not quite sure why we do the stupid things we do sometimes. Why do we keep record books of wrongs? He said, she said. This is NOT the love of God. Can you just imagine if that's the way He treated us? I hope and pray tonight as you lay your head on your pillow that you have no record books of people who have hurt you anywhere.

"A man's wisdom gives him patience;
it is to his glory to overlook an offense."
Proverbs 19:11

This scripture is NOT easy to live, but it's called self-control which is a fruit of God's spirit in you. You can read about that in Galatians 5:22.

Read this slowly and listen carefully to what it has to say:

"For if you forgive men when they sin against you, your Heavenly Father will also forgive you. But if you do not forgive men their sins, your Father will not forgive your sins."
Matthew 6:14-15

Although God is forgiving, He is also a just God and hates sin. For those who walk with Him, He demands that you be obedient, and forgive and love with His love, which keeps no record of wrongs.

For many years, even as a pastor's wife, I hated. When someone hurts you for a very long time, it's hard to let go of that pain and forgive. But I did it and you can do it. It does NOT happen overnight and we are NOT perfect, but you need to start down that path the best you can.

Do you have a record book of wrongs tonight?

Dear God,
Forgive us. Forgive me. Help us, God, to keep no record of wrongs. Teach us to learn to love with your love. I honor you today.

April 28th

Boarder Babies

At work today we had what the maternity department calls a boarder baby. A boarder baby is a baby who will be in the nursery for days because mom is in the ICU or other similar reasons. I can't even begin to tell you how adorable this baby was. I look forward to seeing her tomorrow. She is so beautiful. I know she is a mix of something due to her darker skin and beautiful slanted eyes. She is just perfect.

One thing we have to do with boarder babies is give them extra love and physical contact. They are not hearing mom's voice, and for some reason dad is not always around, sometimes because he's tending to his wife. So they need a lot of love. This is the perfect job for me! So toward the end of my shift today, I was rocking her and holding her tight. It made me think of when I first became a Christian. I was a baby in the Lord, felt kinda lost, a boarder baby.

My mom and dad at the time did not know the Lord, so my church family became what I was to this boarder baby today. My church family became my spiritual family. This is the great thing about coming to God and getting plugged into a church: If not one person in your family knows God, you still have an entire church family that will love you and pray for you. Now, I understand many of you have been hurt by churches and church people. I'm very sorry. I too have been hurt by people in ministry, but most of the time your church can become a big support to you and what you are going through. Not everyone will hurt you, so don't check everyone off the list!

"I will not leave you as orphans; I will come to you."
John 14:18

I thank God for Alcove Full Gospel Church, the church that took me in at age 18. I was a serious boarder baby. I was so messed up, sleeping with my boyfriend, doing drugs, drinking my pain away, and the list goes on. It took some special people to love me. And they did just that.

I did not know how much I needed them at the time. Their love for me changed my life.

"And let us consider how to stimulate one another to love and good deeds, not forsaking our own assembling together, as is the habit of some, but encouraging one another, and all the more, as you see the day drawing near."
Hebrews 10:24-25

Just as the boarder baby at work today needed special attention and love, so does every new believer that walks into a church. I hope the church is ready. I thank God that our church has Celebrate Recovery, Foundation Growth class, small groups for all kinds of situations, and on and on. We are ready. I'm so glad that the church I walked into was ready for me.

There are countless boarder babies in thousands of churches all over America. Friend, if your family is dysfunctional or if you don't have a family please know that there is the family of God.

I know this because they took me in, and without having my church family there for me in the beginning, taking care of me spiritually, I would not have made it. They gave me the word of God more than anything and loved me unconditionally.

Are you a boarder baby today? Do you feel all alone? Do you feel like you want to seek God, but don't know how can you do it when not one around you is feeling the same? The truth is that all you have to do is go to God alone. He is right there with you. Talk to Him. He is the best listener. But you also need to know that it's very important to plug into a church family that is there for support, love, and prayer. Also, you need to grow in the Lord. I know I needed my church family and their ministries for that. I'm just not sure where I would be today without them loving on me.

So as I rocked that beautiful boarder baby today my life passed before my eyes, and I just wanted to hold her closer and rock her longer. If you find a church that really cares about you, they will want to love you like that. And as you grow in God you will learn to let them.

Dear God,
Lead everyone reading to a place where they can grow and be loved with your love. Let them know they can reach out to you right now where they are. Make yourself so real to them. I honor you today.

Don't Write Them Off

Why is it that as soon as some Christians see something they are not used to or they cannot relate with, they write someone off? They choose not to be near "those" kinds of people. I was with a friend not too long ago who wanted some family members to plug into a ministry. As soon as I suggested Celebrate Recovery, my friend's comment was, "No, I don't want them near those kinds of people." Let me remind you all today that I was one of THOSE kinds of people, and Jesus takes broken and hurting people and makes them into something beautiful.

As soon as some so called Christians see a tattoo, or a kid with multi-colored hair they instantly think, "They must be a heathen and they need God!" Well, how do you know that person does not love God with all their heart? Stop pointing your fingers in judgment. Stop it! Seeing from a distance and judging by sight is dangerous. And I would not want to be in your shoes. Jesus took the time to get to know souls. How about you? Or do you write them off?

My husband always says:

> "Remember, for every finger you are pointing in judgment,
> there are three fingers pointing back at you!"

Go ahead, make a pointing finger right now. See the three fingers pointing back at you? Be ever so careful my friend. Jesus hung out with pagans. He loved them and spent time with them. I was a pagan, and am glad that Christians spent time with me and did not write me off. I did everything wrong, but they still cared and never made me feel like they did not want to be with me. The truth is, they really did want to be with me because they had the heart of Christ.

How do people who don't know the Lord feel when they are around you? Are you sharing your opinion about what you don't like about them before you love them with God's love?

> "As surely as I live, declares the sovereign Lord, I take no pleasure in the death of the wicked, but rather that they turn from their ways and live. Turn!"
> Ezekiel 33:11

Do you think they will want to turn from evil ways if you are judging and condemning them? In Bible college years ago, we learned about friendship evangelism, which is spending time with those that don't know the Lord and loving them in truth. There is nothing fake about it, just loving them right where they are. I'm not talking about compromising what you believe or falling into sin. I'm talking loving people like Jesus did. Why do some Christians make this so hard?

Just love people, just the way they are!

My name is Tana Miller. I smoked a pack and a half of cigarettes a day for four years of my life. I did drugs and drank alcohol to take away the intense pain I felt from sexual abuse. I tried to kill myself at age 16. I let a lot of flesh hang out. And I had a serious cuss mouth. I'm so glad Christians did NOT write me off. They loved me.

God handpicked me. He had a plan for my life, and still has a plan for my life even though I have tattoos and my nose pierced. He knows my heart and desires to use me to touch countless ladies in America and overseas who are in pain and need a Christian who won't point a finger at them. These women who need someone to love them just the way they are. This is my desire.

In order to see a Savior they need to see a servant in you.

"Abstain from sinful desires, which war against your soul. Live such good lives among the pagans that, though they accuse you of doing wrong, they may see your good deeds and glorify God on the day He visits us."
1 Peter 2: 11-12

"The Lord is not slow in keeping His promise as some understand slowness. He is patient with you, not wanting anyone to perish, but everyone to come to repentance."
2 Peter 3:9

Did you notice that scripture said EVERONE?
Don't write them off.
"Them" was me.

Dear God,
Thank you for your mercy. I thank you for Christians who loved me just the way I was. Who took the time to teach me about your word. I thank you that you long to use me today and until the day I take my last breath. I honor you today.

April 30th

Tangible Letters and Your Story

I sat down tonight for almost an hour and read some of the letters in my files. I have tons of files with cards and hand-written letters that have been sent to me. It's always great to keep tangible things like this in a file. That way if you are ever discouraged or feel like you are not making a dent in the world, all you have to do is pull out your letter file.

I actually pulled my letter file out tonight because I have not looked at it for quite a while. What a blessing, reading all the way back to 1997 in some cases. It brought back so many memories. Some of the names I do not even remember. I tried to recall some of the things that were talked about in some of the cards and I just can't remember them all.

There were letters from Teen Challenge gals, letters from my mentors, encouraging words, and congratulations for when I was ordained. There were words from young ladies in places I have spoken, ladies who wrote because they had a word for me from the Lord, and the list goes on. But tonight there was one letter that stuck out. It was written in November 1997.

"Bless you for helping me open a room which had been shut for 42 years. My heart can now truly begin to mend."

I remember this lady. She was older. I don't even know if she is still alive. Can you imagine not sharing what pain you have had in your heart with anyone for 42 years? I know when I was a kid, if someone got molested or hurt by another it was swept under the rug and not one person talked about it. The night that she came to church I shared my life story. Then shortly after, I got this amazing letter from her. At the bottom of the letter is this:

"Hear my cry, O God; listen to my prayer.
From the ends of the earth I call to you,
I call as my heart grows faint;
Lead me to the rock that is higher than I.
For you have been my refuge,
a strong tower against the foe.
I long to dwell in your tent forever and
take refuge in the shelter of your wings.
For you have heard my vows, O God;
You have given me the heritage of those who fear your name."
Psalm 61:1-5

So here she was, a beautiful precious senior saint of God living with secrets for 42 years. And her scripture told me that she was able to stay sane by making God her refuge and shelter, a strong tower against the devil's darts for her soul. Just amazing. I did nothing but tell my story.

Let me remind you today that you also have a story. Almost all the letters and cards I read tonight were in response to my testimony. My story can touch some, but your story can touch those that I cannot touch. Are you hiding it or telling it? God gives us our memory banks for a reason. It's not to be hidden, but to be shared. Do not be ashamed. It will touch souls.

Do you know that you are a letter, and a testimony of God's grace?

"You yourselves are our letter, written on our hearts, known and read by everybody. You show that you are a letter from Christ, the result of our ministry, written not with ink but with the spirit of the living God, not on tablets of stone but on tablets of human hearts."
2 Corinthians 3: 3

We are like my letter file. We are loaded with a lifetime of stories, praise, sadness, and joy. Letters are meant to be read. They are meant to have result.

Save your tangible letters. Tell your story. See results.

"Our comfort overflows."
2 Corinthians 1:5

Dear God,
I pray for the person reading. God, let them know they have a story to tell. No matter what they have been through in life, let them see results as they begin to share it. I honor you today.

May

May 1st

Maggie

I found out the other day that my co-worker, Maggie, who has been leading me around the maternity ward to help me get to know the unit, loves God. I could tell there was something different about her. Over a year ago we trained together in the phlebotomy unit, so when I walked into the maternity ward we remembered each other. Even when we were being trained in drawing blood and doing our required 50 sticks I could see a joy in her, and I had that feeling that she knew the Lord. Now God has brought us back together a year later for a reason.

The other day we had a room full of babies and only two were fussy. We were sitting together all alone in this room, rocking babies and talking about everything God has done in our lives. All I could do was sit there and think, "I can't believe I'm getting paid for this!" The hearing screens were done, the Bilirubin blood test and heel test were all done, and everyone was clean and wrapped up like little glow worms, with their tiny hand-knit hats on. And there Maggie and I sat; rocking and talking about what Jesus had done in our lives with tiny babies in our arms. What a feeling.

There is just something about being around someone who genuinely loves the Lord. It's almost as if I could see the joy of the Lord in her, in her actions, and how she responded to others. As I sat and rocked with Maggie and the two babies, she told me her story. Divorced and a single mom, she shared how if not for the Lord, she did not know how she would have made it through. As I sat and listened, I once again was so encouraged of the amazing things our Lord can do for a hurting soul. I know it so well because that's what He did in my own life.

If there is one thing I have learned through the years, it's that somehow in the darkest moments His joy breaks through and it becomes our strength.

"Do not grieve, for the joy of the Lord is your strength."
Nehemiah 8:10

If not for His joy breaking through and becoming our strength, I'm not sure how we would live sometimes.

I went to a women's night two nights ago at church, and four ladies shared their stories. One lost her teenage son and had to identify his body, and one was widowed two times before the age of 33. God follower or not, life is life and we have to live it. God never promised perfection in this world, as a matter of a fact He said we would encounter hard times. But He promised His strength. This strength is what I recognized in Maggie.

"Rejoice in the Lord always. I will say it again: Rejoice! Let your gentleness be evident to all. The Lord is near."
Philippians 4:4-5

I saw God's characteristics in Maggie. I saw His gentleness. And this is why I wondered about her. Well, I wonder no more. She loves the Lord and He has helped her through.

Let me ask you today my friend, is your gentleness evident to all? When people are around you, do they wonder? Do they wonder what is different about you, or do you blend in too well? When God's spirit is living within us, people will know. When you are a true Christian, there are fruits in your life that they will see. According to Galatians 5:22, these fruits are: love, joy, peace, patience, kindness, goodness, faithfulness, gentleness and self-control. Are people seeing those things in you? If God's spirit is in you they will wonder what is up with you! Too many Christians have no fruit.

I'm so glad Jesus put Maggie in my life, a woman who made it through the storms of life; a woman who I wondered about because of the fruit of God's spirit in her character (Name change out of respect).

Do they wonder about you?

Dear God,
I pray people wonder about me due to the change in my character. I pray for this reader. Change us Lord. Let us gain your love, joy, peace, patience, kindness, goodness, faithfulness, gentleness and self-control. Help us to disconnect from things that drag us down. I honor you today.

May 2ⁿᵈ

Nothing is Too Small

For years I led worship and prayer time for children's church. I would get them all pumped up with awesome music and hand movements. After we sang like three or four songs, then we would have a time where the leaders would kneel down and the children would come and get in lines. One by one they would give prayer requests to us. Nothing was too small for Jesus to answer. Some would ask for prayer for their dog's eye infection, cuts on the finger, mommy's car that doesn't work, their X-box that was broken, and so on. They came to that altar ready to pray. Their precious hearts were sincere. Jesus loves little children.

> "Then little children were brought to Jesus for Him to place His hands on them and pray for them. But the Disciples rebuked those who brought them. Jesus said, 'Let the little children come to me, and do not hinder them, for the kingdom of Heaven belongs to such as these.' When He had placed His hands on them, he went on from there."
> Matthew 19:13-15

It's so awesome how Jesus stood up to the Disciples and pretty much said, "Be quiet! They can come to me!" This once again showed the Master's humility. I'm sure they learned a ton by hanging out with Jesus. Also, we see the same sort of story here:

> "People were bringing little children to Jesus to have Him touch them, but the Disciples rebuked them. When Jesus saw this, He was indignant. He said to them, 'Let the little children come to me, and do not hinder them, for the kingdom of God belongs to such as these. I tell you the truth; anyone who will not receive the kingdom of God like a little child will never enter it.' And He took the children in His arms, put His hands on them and blessed them."
> Mark 10:13-16

It says Jesus became indignant, which means "to express strong displeasure at something considered unjust, offensive, and insulting." He desired to bless the children. This scripture also says anyone who will not receive God's kingdom like a little child will not enter Heaven. I guess this must mean that Jesus cares about the little things, because at children's prayer time they came to me with little things; things that were no big deal, but to them were a very big deal, things that you would chuckle at, because their requests were so very cute. Does Jesus want us to come to Him so simply? Yes.

He wants us to come and speak from the heart, with everything your feeling, not hiding anything, because He already knows your thoughts anyway. Simply, like a child. Why do we make it so hard?

The class I taught this morning was called "Understanding Who You Are in Christ." Many of us lack self-worth because our self-esteem has been beaten down through the years by abuse, lies, and dysfunction. But His word says different!

We are Friends of God (John 15:14), we are heirs of God (Romans 8:17), a chosen race, a royal priesthood (1 Peter 2:9), tablets for Him to write His love letter on (2 Corinthians 3: 2-3), and so much more. But one of the scriptures in my lesson this morning said:

> "The Spirit Himself bears witness with our spirit
> that we are children of God."
> Romans 8:16

So we are children of God. Yes, we have grown, we have walked through some serious fires, but does this mean we can come to God like little children? Friend, nothing is too small.

There is a story in 2 Kings that proves this. A company of prophets went to the Jordan River to build a place for them to live. Elisha was with them.

> "They went to the Jordan and began to cut down trees. As one of them was cutting down a tree, the iron ax head fell into the water. 'Oh, my Lord,' he cried out, 'it was borrowed!' The man of God asked, 'Where did it fall?' When he showed him the place, Elisha cut a stick and threw it there, and made the iron float. 'Lift it out,' he said. Then the man reached out his hand and took it."
> 2 Kings 6:4-7

In case you have not noticed, this was a divine miracle. God had been using Elisha to do miracles. But it was just an ax head that he borrowed; a stupid ax head. But to him, it was not stupid.

Why do we get scared to come to God with the little things? What is it that you have not given Him because you think it's too small today? Nothing is too small.

Dear God,
Help us to remember that you love us like you loved the little children. You want everything we have to offer. Thank you, Father. I honor you today.

May 3rd

Polished Arrows

Tonight as I was getting dinner ready and using the can opener to open a can, I thought to myself, "How many times in my life time have I opened a can of olives?" Probably hundreds and hundreds of times in my life. Somehow that got me thinking of how I have been driving for over 49 years, and how I can type very fast without looking at the keyboard, thanks to typing class in high school. I know you are wondering where I'm going with this!

Sometimes things become second nature. I can type so much faster than I can write with a pen, so even as I type this devotion, it's just second nature. Picking out a recipe that I have been throwing together for years becomes second nature, and driving is the same. There are things that have become part of our daily life that we don't really give a second thought to. It's just something we do, so it becomes very repetitious.

Repetition can be good and bad. When I'm repetitious about going to the gym and working out, that's a good thing. But when I sin and have committed that sin before, that's something that has to be changed in my life. Doing my hair, well, that's another story! I hate it more than anything, but I do it because if I don't it looks like a rat's nest!

What kinds of things are second nature in your life today? When it comes to repetition, are they good or bad? Are they healthy or not healthy for you?

When things get repetitious we tend to not think too much when we're doing them. For instance, when I went to the gym today I walked two miles and watched The Price is Right. Truth be told, I did not think too much about the walking at all, my mind was elsewhere.

While making dinner tonight there were five teens in the house going up and down the stairs, moving my son's drum set. So while I was getting our taco dinner ready, I was not really thinking about making it at all.

I want you to think about your Bible reading. Do you read your Bible at all?

Is it second nature?

If it is, has it become so repetitious that you are not really putting the thought into it that you should be? Are you picking up your pile of daily devotional books and just doing the same old routine? Or are you cutting out all the distractions and really making an effort to let apply what you are reading to your heart and life?

"In the shadow of His hand he hid me;

he made me into a polished arrow."
Isaiah 49:2

My husband and I go shooting with his 22, and I'm a pretty good shot. I would much rather shoot a rifle, though! When I was in junior high I got into archery. It's not as easy as some may think, and if you are not careful you can scrape and burn your inner arm very badly. Technique and practice mean everything with this sport.

In archery, your arrows are one of the most important things. If you go online you will see that the choices are countless. You can even put weights inside the middle of the arrows. But there is one thing that does not change: Your arrow must be ready! It must be sharp and polished to be as effective as it can be. You will not nail the target at your best with a dull or unready arrow.

The word of God is vital in polishing us. It increases our faith and helps us grow in the Lord. If you do not understand your Bible when you read it, it's time to get one that you understand and that makes sense to you.

"Faith comes from hearing the message, and the
message is heard through the word of God."
Romans 10:17

"All scripture is given by inspiration of God, and is profitable for doctrine, for reproof, for correction, for instruction in righteousness: that the man of God may be perfect, thoroughly furnished unto all good works."
2 Timothy 3:16-17

"Study to show thyself approved unto God, a workman that needs not to be ashamed, rightly dividing the word of truth."
2 Timothy 2:15

Trust me, God knows we are NOT perfect! We will fail, but we must focus when we read our Bible.

We need it like we need air.
Are you ready to hit the target today?
Are you a polished arrow?
If not, get to work.

Dear God,
Make me into all you want me to be, Lord. Help me to have discipline to focus and set that time aside to dig into your word and polish my soul. I honor you today.

Remember

"My feet have closely followed His steps;
I have kept to His way without turning aside.
I have not departed from the commands of His lips;
I have treasured the words of His mouth more than my daily bread."
Job 23:11-12

Don't you wish you could say these words right now and know it's the truth?

Have your feet closely followed his steps? Have you been obedient in all things this week? Have you sinned at all? Have you treasured the words of His mouth more than your daily bread? In other words, have you have made every effort this past week to put prayer and reading the Bible before anything else? I know we strive for these things, but truth be told, most of the time we fail.

Job said these words while going through a very hard time, yet I know they are true. The Lord was the one in Job 1:8 to say that there was no one like Job, that he was blameless and upright. That He feared God and shunned evil. Can you imagine the Lord being able to say that about you?

I know this week I have failed and gone to Jesus. Oh, how I long for the Lord to say these things about me.

Job put his trust in God while in a dry and lonely time, a time when Job could not even feel God near. During a time when he was angry, he remembers the things he had done to stay close to the Lord. Before remembering all the good in the scripture given above, this is what Job said:

"Even today my complaint is bitter. His hand is heavy in spite of my groaning. If only I knew where to find Him; if only I could go to His dwelling! I would state my case before Him and fill my mouth with arguments."
Job 23:2-4

I love this scripture because it shows that Job was a normal human being. He sounds Italian! Ha! He sounds like he just wants to give the Lord a piece of his mind. How many times have we been there my friend? God put Job through a trying time because he was blameless. Sometimes we desperately need these times of testing!

"But He knows the way that I take; when He has tested me,
I will come forth as gold."
Job 23:10

I can remember being at Bible college and getting very sick. I had to leave college for the semester. I was so upset. I packed my things and got ready to fly back to New York from Pennsylvania. Before I left my dorm room crying, I reached into my little scripture box and pulled out a scripture. Job 23:10 was the scripture I pulled out. I knew it was a testing time for me and I hated every minute.

I love what Job did through the testing time: He remembered! He remembered the positive! He remembered how he had walked with the Lord and put Him first, how he had desired the word of God, and how he had not departed from the commands of God's lips.

How many times have we gone through a hard time and all we can do is get angry and whine about what we are going through? We need to do what Job did in chapter 23. We need to remember the good and how we are going to get back to the place we once were. As my awesome husband would say, "We need to keep our praise on!" This is NOT an easy thing to do, but what a great example Job gave of this in chapter 23.

Maybe your health is not bad, maybe you feel dry and you have walked away from God.

> "Remember the height from which you have fallen!
> Repent and do the things you did at first."
> Revelation 2:5

Even in Revelation it says that if you are in a hard place to remember where you were!

Next time you are angry at God, next time you are in bed and cannot get up, please think about the great things the Lord has brought you through. Think about where you were and how you will get back there!

Remember!

Dear God,
I pray for the reader. Whatever they are going through, help them to remember, Lord. Help them to remember good times and healthy times, and give them the strength to get back to the place they once were. I honor you today.

Post-It® of Grace

I don't know about you, but I need to write almost everything down. Some of you may have the gift of being able to remember everything. I wish that was my gift! I am new to the maternity ward at this hospital, and NOTHING is the same as the Maternity Ward I used to work at for three years! So when my awesome c-worker Maggie teaches me, I write every single thing down! Even with my work in ministry my desk is always loaded with Post-its®! Phone numbers, people to call, scriptures I come across for my devotionals. They are everywhere! Post-its® and notes have become part of my everyday life. I guess when I was younger I could remember a lot more. Those were the days!

In Genesis is the account of Noah, starting at chapter 6, and in it God gave Himself a Post-it®! He was angry about the sin in the world.

"God saw how corrupt the earth had become, for all the people on earth had corrupted their ways. So God said to Noah, 'I am going to put an end to all people, for the earth is filled with violence because of them. I am surely going to destroy both them and earth. Go make yourself an ark of cypress wood.'"
Genesis 6:12-14

God is a God of mercy, but He is also a just God. He never intended sin to enter this world. So He makes a covenant between Him and all of life on earth. He put up a Post-It®!

"And God said, 'This is the sign of the covenant I am making between me and you and every living creature with you, a covenant for all generations to come: I have set my rainbow in the clouds, and it will be the sign of the covenant between me and the earth. Whenever I bring clouds over the earth and the rainbow appears in the clouds, I will remember my covenant between me and you and all living creatures of every kind. Never again will the waters become a flood to destroy all life. Whenever the rainbow appears in the clouds, I will see it and remember the everlasting covenant between God and all living creatures of every kind on earth.'"
Genesis 9:12-16

As you know, rainbows can take your breath away. I have not even seen too many in my lifetime. It seems the weather has to be just right. But when you see it, you stop everything, even your car, to get out and admire how amazing it is. One time when I was 12 years old, I saw the most amazing double rainbow that took my breath away. The rainbow is God's Post-It® of grace.

"Whenever I bring clouds over the Earth and the rainbow appears in the clouds, I will remember my covenant between me and you and all living creatures of every kind."
Genesis 14-15

His covenant and promise was never to flood the Earth again to wipe out everyone due to sin. Instead, He sent His very own Son to die for our sin.

Imagine if you could look down on Earth right now and see everyone's secret sin: Kids being molested, people beating other people, some people getting so high and then getting behind the wheel of a car. Not everyone has lived these things first hand like me and many others of you, so just imagine you could see it all for a moment: Young girls and boys being sex trafficked across the nations, some starting at age 10. Wouldn't you want to end all that? And God intended the garden to be sinless. But He gave man free will to choose. We failed. We still fail.

His Post-It® means the world to me when I see it.
It's a Post-It® of grace.

Dear God,
I pray we will take the time to think on your Grace today. I thank you for the amazing rainbow: A covenant in your word that is still right in front of our eyes today. I honor you today.

May 6th

Come to Your Senses

"Do not let your heart envy sinners, but always be zealous for the fear of the Lord. There is surely a future hope for you, and your hope will not be cut off."

Proverbs 23 17-18

Our hope in Christ is not cut off. There is always hope.

Even if you have walked away, turned your back on Him, or have done horrible things, God's grace is always there waiting for you to turn to Him. Even though this is hard for some of you to hear, the most horrible, evil people on death row can experience the grace of a mighty God. They only need to call out to God and ask forgiveness. Yes, some are murderers, molesters, rapists, but the hand of God is waiting. I know that someone who hurt me for years is now with God in Heaven because that person turned to Him before death. I was the one who prayed with this person. It was the hardest thing I ever did in my life. God walked me through deep forgiveness.

Forgiveness does not mean you have to trust someone. It does not mean you have to hang out with them. It does not mean you have to let them around your kids. It simply means you have forgiven.

Your bitterness is not hurting the one who hurt you. Your bitterness is hurting you. Let it go.

"There was a man who had two sons. The younger one said to his father, 'Father, give me my share of the estate.' So he divided his property between them. Not long after that, the younger son got together all he had, set off for a distant country and there squandered his wealth in wild living. After he had spent everything, there was a severe famine in the whole country, and he began to be in need. So he went and hired himself out to a citizen of that country, who sent him to his fields to feed pigs. He longed to fill his stomach with the pods that the pigs were eating, but no one gave him anything. When he came to his senses, he said, 'How many of my father's hired men have food to spare, and here I am starving to death! I will set out and go back to my father and say to him: Father, I have sinned against Heaven and against you. I am no longer worthy to be called your son; make me like one of your hired men.' So he got up and went to his father."

Luke 15:11-20

So here we have a son who has taken his share of his wealth, his father's hard earned money. He wastes it all on wild living. I'm sure sinning had a lot to do with it. Finally the Bible says:

"He came to his senses."

At one point he desired the pig's food because he had nothing. His thoughts went to his dad's hired men who were eating better than he was. It's like a light came on and reality hit.

He realized how stupid he had been. So he goes back where he came from.

"While he was still a long way off, his father saw him and was filled with compassion for him; he ran to his son, threw his arms around him and kissed him. The son said to him, 'Father, I have sinned against Heaven and against you. I am no longer worthy to be called your son.' But the father said to his servants, 'Quick! Bring the best robe and put it on him. Put a ring on his finger and sandals on his feet. Bring the fattened calf and kill it. Let's have a feast and celebrate. For this son of mine was dead and is alive again; he was lost and is found.' So they began to celebrate."
Luke 15: 20:24

This is what our Father does. He waits.

When we do stupid sinful things and then come back to Him in full surrender, He throws His arms around us! He says, "Bring the best robe, put a ring on and get the feast ready for the celebration!"

"There is surely a future hope for you,
and your hope will not be cut off."
Proverbs 23 17-18

He will never cut us off.
Come to your senses.

Dear God,
Help us to come back to you in full surrender. I honor you today.

What is Your Task?

"And now, compelled by the Spirit, I am going to Jerusalem, not knowing what will happen to me there. I only know that in every city the Holy Spirit warns me that prison and hardships are facing me. However, I consider my life worth nothing to me, if only I may finish the race and complete the task the Lord Jesus has given me--the task of testifying to the gospel of God's grace."
Acts 20:22-24

I love to read about the journeys of Paul. You just never know what he will happen upon as he goes about his way. He never knew what would take place at each place he went to. Many times he landed in prison and had divine encounters with angels. Many times he would head one way and the Lord would tell him to turn and go another way. He was a pilgrim on a journey after the will of God. The Holy Spirit acted as his guide, warning him of danger and hardships to come. But yet he says,

"I consider my life worth nothing to me,
if only I may finish the race and complete the task."
Acts 20:24

It takes amazing faith to walk not knowing what is to come. Knowing your very life could be on the line. Priscilla and Aquila were dear friends of Paul, and I'm sure if Paul lived his own will, he would be happy just being near his friends. Priscilla and Aquila as a couple sponsored churches in their home (Romans 16:3-5); they had the same heart for souls as Paul. Anytime Paul was in their area he lived with them and worked alongside them for countless hours. Yet as he is leaving his friends behind again in Ephesus, he say:,

"I will come back if it is God's will."
Acts 18:21

I'm sure everything within him wanted to stay. But his task was his passion; the task of testifying to the gospel of God's grace. He wanted to make a mark on the world and nothing could stop him.

"For I have not hesitated to proclaim to you the whole will of God."
Acts 20:27

"In everything I did, I showed you that by this kind of hard work we must help the weak, remembering the words the Lord Jesus Himself said: 'It is more blessed to give than to receive.'"
Acts 20:35

Even thought he longed for souls to be changed, it was hard.

Sometimes doing the perfect will of God for your life is the most painful thing you will ever do. He will ask you to leave those you have poured and poured into, and your heart will break. But friend, there is nothing like being in the perfect will of God.

At the end of Acts 20, Paul says farewell to the Ephesian elders. Just try to feel what Paul might be feeling as you read this scripture:

"When he had said this, he knelt down with all of them and prayed. They all wept as they embraced him and kissed him. What grieved them most was his statement that they would never see his face again. Then they accompanied him to the ship."
Acts 20: 36-38

Following Christ in faith will hurt sometimes. This is the ministry of the gospel of grace. But the joy you get from being in the perfect will of God for your life will overshadow any pain.

Are you in the perfect will of God for your life, or are you running from it?

What is your task?

"Forgetting what is behind and straining toward what is ahead, I press on toward the goal to win the prize for which God has called me Heavenward in Christ Jesus."
Philippians 3:13-14

Dear God,
Show us our Task. Give us strength to strive for it and joy to endure it. I honor you today.

Epitaph

Death is not something you want to think about every day. When a good friend has died, or when you come across a horrible car crash like my parents just did, it gets your mind thinking of life after death. And for the record here, there is life after death. You will not come back to this earth as something else; you will go to your eternal home, either Heaven or Hell. Hell will not be a party place. If you read the book of Revelation and other books of the Bible, you will get a glimpse of Hell.

"Then they will go away to eternal punishment,
but the righteous to eternal life."
Matthew 25:46

"The angels will come and separate the wicked from the righteous and throw them into the fiery furnace, where there will be weeping and gnashing of teeth."
Matthew 13:49-50

"Where their worm does not die and the fire is not quenched."
Mark 9:48

"They will be punished with everlasting destruction and shut out from the presence of the Lord and from the majesty of His power."
2 Thessalonians 1:9

Not sure about you today, but I do not want to think about anyone I care about going to Hell. Heaven is a free gift; it is not earned or deserved. He hands it to you, the question is: Will you open it? Stop making it so hard on yourself. Jesus takes us just as we are.

Have you ever thought about your epitaph? An epitaph is what is written on your gravestone. Here are some examples of frequently used epitaphs:

**May the journey on your next adventure be as joy-filled
as your time with us. See you soon!**
***

**To the world you may have just been somebody,
but to all of us you were the world.
Thank you for the time you spent here!**
***

**I can only hope we shall see each other again
in that place where there is only love and no shadows fall.
You have touched my very being...I shall remember you.**
***

**Life is not measured
by the number of breaths we take,**

**but by the moments
that take our breath away.**

I know it may seem a little morbid to you, but think about your epitaph today. What would you want written on your gravestone?

Have you touched other lives along the way? Has your life made some sort of mark in your part of the world? I do not say this in pride, I say it with all humility; I know I have touched lives along the way. If you cannot say that maybe you need to start thinking about life and death and what this life really means to you. Why are you alive? Do you realize God has a purpose for you on this earth? There is even purpose in all the pain you have gone through. He wants to use your pain for His purposes.

I want my epitaph to catch people's eye as they walk by my gravestone. I want my epitaph to get them thinking about their own eternal life, this way God can still use me when I'm not on earth anymore. I have thought about it and I want it to say something like:

IM NOT HERE!
I MADE MY MARK IN MY PART OF THE WORLD FOR CHRIST,
AND NOW I'M WITH HIM.
HOW ABOUT YOU?

JOHN 10:27

God wants to use you friend to make a mark on this world. If your self-esteem has been beaten down then I know it's hard for you to even think this way, but I tell you today, there is someone out there that needs to hear your story! It will touch their life.

"Do not conform any longer to the pattern of this world, but be transformed by the renewing of your mind. Then you will be able to test and approve what God's will is--His good, pleasing and perfect will."
Romans 12:2

He has a mighty plan for your life today! His will brings perfect peace.
Think about your eternal soul today. What will your Epitaph say?

Dear God,
I thank you for life, but I cannot wait until the day I'm walking in Heaven with you. You have been forever faithful on this earth. Touch the life of the reader today, God. I honor you.

May 9th

Generations

"With my mouth, I will make your faithfulness
Known through all generations."
Psalm 89:1

As a mother, the biggest joy I could ever have in my life is to see my kids serving God. They grew up on the church pew. All they have ever known is family, God, and people. There comes a time in their life where they have to make a choice if they want this Christianity to be their own.

I am so very thankful today that my son and my daughter have chosen to serve God. This does not mean they are perfect by any means! Note: Neither is mom! But they have their own time with God and they desire to follow His will for their lives.

My brother and I became God followers in our teen years. We were the first generation to give God our lives. I'm so thankful that all six of our kids (my brothers combined) love and serve God. There is no greater joy! It brings much peace to a mother's heart when your kids are out and about with their friends, to know they have a relationship with God.

My desire is to pour out as much as I can while I still have breath into the generations around me; old and young. I love on the older generation at church and I try to reach out to the youth when I can. I guess if there was a scripture that said it all for me it would be this one:

"Since my youth, O God, you have taught me, and to this day I declare your marvelous deeds. Even when I am old and gray, do not forsake me, O God, till I declare your power to the next generation, your might to all who are to come."
Psalm 71:17-18

This week there is a two-day gathering of pastors from three different states. The District Youth Director has asked a few kids to minister to the adults. Two of those five kids are my daughter Angela, who will sing and play the piano, and my niece Nina who will preach. Both of these girls are very powerful at what they do and I know I will cry like a baby while each is ministering to hundreds of adults. But there is just something so amazing when you think of my life as a teen and then see their life as teens. God is so very faithful.

"Great is the Lord and most worthy of praise; His greatness no one can fathom. One generation will commend your works to another; they will tell of your mighty acts. They will speak of the glorious splendor of your majesty, and I will meditate on your wonderful works. They will tell of the power of your awesome works, and I will proclaim your great deeds.

They will celebrate your abundant goodness and joyfully sing of your righteousness."
Psalm 145:3-7

This scripture is exactly what is happening as Nina and Angela get up in front of adults and use the gifts God has given to them. It is embedded in them because the Word of God has been with them since a young age, and they make the choice to serve God on their own. It brings tears to my eyes just thinking about it.

My sister-in-law Kris has three more boys. One of her boys, Dominic, is going into high school and just got a four-year scholarship for $30,000 a year to go the best high school in the city of Boston. The one JFK went to. Yes, I did say $30,000 a year, for four years! Dominic is filled with the joy of the Lord and has a brilliant mind.

I can't wait to see what Jesus is going to do through the other two boys, Andrew and Mason. They both have such unique personalities and gifts. I only wish I was closer in distance to my other side of the family and their kids!

As you can tell I'm just a very proud mom and aunt. I thank God that the generations after my brother and I are serving God. He is forever faithful.

I encourage you today; maybe your kids are not serving God. Never stop praying. Their salvation and health are only a prayer away.

For those of you who cannot have kids, I ask you to love the kids who do not experience healthy love. There are thousands of them in this world today.

For those of you who are young and do not yet have children, begin to pray now for your children and their children. Your prayers will change generations.

For those that are old and your time for raising kids is over, take a deep breath and meditate on the word of God today, and be that prayer support that your family needs. You are honored.

Dear God,
I pray for the reader right now. Bless them this day and encourage their hearts to pass on your love, hope, and power that they may see it in the next generation. I honor you today.

It's Not about You

"When I felt secure, I said, 'I will never be shaken.' O Lord, when you favored me, you made my mountain stand firm; but when you hid your face, I was dismayed."
Psalm 29:6-7

I love this scripture. It's so true! When we feel secure, when doors have opened for us and all is well with no trials, when our job is secure, our marriage is going great, our kids are doing well in school and in their social lives, we can say to the Lord, "I will never be shaken." But the instant it seems like things have been mixed up a bit, and trials come, someone comes into work that you butt heads with, someone who mocks what you believe, or you are having a hard time paying the bills, all of a sudden we wonder where God went and why? We are dismayed! The truth is He is still there. He is always there.

Friend, it's not about you.

It's not about if we are going through a horrible time, trying time, or a great and happy time.

It's not about us.

It's all about the fact that no matter what kind of time we are going through, He has NOT moved.

Sometimes it seems when we are going through dark times that God has hid His face. This is what the Psalmist was feeling, but God is right there when you call out to Him my friend. He is always reachable. He is a prayer, scream, and tear away. He has not left you. Many will forsake you in this life, but He will not. He is a safe place.

"Never will I leave you; never will I forsake you."
Hebrews 13: 5

Are you tired today? Are you worried?

Many of you have to get up today and do the week all over again. Some are doing the 7am to 3pm, some doing the 9am to 5pm, some are staying home with the kids, and some are in the same office, at the same desk, and go to the same meetings all over again. As long as things stay the same we can handle it. At the hospital, they have told the staff that there will be some serious layoffs next week. I'm blessed and do not have to worry about it because I'm a per-diem worker. I'm not an extra cost; I do not get benefits from them. They are trying to help the budget. These are the testing times.

If you are tired of how it's all consumed your mind today you need to be still for a few moments and think on Him. Quiet your heart and mind. Think on His promises that all your needs will be met.

> "And my God will meet all your needs according to
> His glorious riches in Christ Jesus."
> Philippians 4:19

Do you really believe that today?

Time and time again He has proven Himself to the Miller family. Anytime we have had a need that went beyond our reach, He always came through. Always! He has always been faithful, reachable, and a firm foundation.

How are you today?
It's not about you, remember.
Do you need to be still?

Dear God,
I pray for this reader. Help them to find the time today to be still and alone with you. Speak a new word to them, Father. Calm them. I honor you today.

<u>Baggage</u>

What kind of baggage are you carrying around? Sometimes we don't think we have any and then one day we realize it's there.

I cleaned out my purse this afternoon. You never realize how bad it is until you go to clean it. It looks beautiful from the outside, but inside, well, I kept the garbage pail right next to me during the cleaning. Old, receipts I didn't need, candy wrappers, loose change, and things that needed to be put back in their place, it all seems to store up on the bottom of my purse!

Then there are the backpacks of my teenagers! I don't go in them, but every now and then if they are in the kitchen, near the garbage, I clean out the side pockets! So nasty! Old food bags from sandwiches and sometimes even nasty food left in them, crumbs galore, ad I'm not sure what else! Usually I take it all and just chuck it because I hate looking at it! It's just amazing how it piles up everywhere! We never even realize it until we go to clean it out!

This is how we walk around. On the outside, like my kids' backpacks and my awesome purses, we look great! We do not even realize the baggage that is piling up sometimes! It's the baggage of unforgiveness, sin, and shame. Maybe today it's time to get the garbage and clean things up a bit!

> "Therefore, since we are surrounded by such a great cloud of witnesses, let us throw off everything that hinders and the sin that so easily entangles, and let us run with perseverance the race marked out for us."
> Hebrews 12:1

I do know one thing: After cleaning my purse out this afternoon, it was much lighter! Why do we burden ourselves so? Why do we put on extra baggage all the time? It is so not worth it. Throw it off! It can weigh us down. Or we can get lost in it!

In 1 Samuel 9:20-21, Samuel tells Saul that he is chosen to be king. In Chapter 10 we see Saul talking to his uncle and he does not tell his uncle that Samuel told him he would be king! The truth is, Saul did NOT want to be chosen! With that in mind, read this:

> "Finally Saul son of Kish was chosen. But when they looked for him, he was not to be found. So they inquired further of the Lord, 'Has the man come here yet?' And the Lord said, 'Yes, he has hidden himself among the **baggage**.' They ran and brought him out, and as he stood among the people he was a head taller than any of the others.

Samuel said to all the people, 'Do you see the man the Lord has chosen?

There is no one like him among all the people.'"
1 Samuel 10:21-23

The Lord had chosen Saul and there he was hiding among the baggage, kind of like Jonah running from the perfect will of God.

I ask you today my dear readers, Are you bogged down by baggage? Are you hiding from what God wants for you today? It's time to clean things up, make your load lighter, and walk the path that the Lord has for you today. Ask the Lord to forgive you for running away from the mess!

Get rid of your baggage.

Dear God,
Help us to not hide! Help us to run to your perfect will for our lives. Help us to clean things up! I honor you today.

May 12th

Dirty Sneakers and Tangible Love

"How beautiful on the mountains are the feet of those who bring good news, who proclaim peace, who bring good tidings, who proclaim salvation."
Isaiah 52:7

I met the most amazing lady in the entire world this year. Her name is Joicy Baby and she lives in New Delhi, India. Every single time I read Isaiah 52:7 I will think of her.

One day she took us for a walk through the slums. She had on light brown sneakers, and I had on white sneakers. By the time we got back, our sneakers had walked through manure galore, food, human waste, and every foul thing you can imagine. I would not even walk into my hotel room with them because of the germs that were on them.

As we walked through that slum, everyone knew Joicy. She is like the Mother Theresa of the New Delhi slums. No fear! Though you could see evil in the eyes of some, and lust in the eyes of most, there was no fear at all in Joicy. You could tell she had walked those paths hundreds of times. I personally felt lost. I felt like I was in a maze and going in circles. I was distracted by some fear in me and the sights, sounds, and smells. Joicy was in front of me and all I could do was keep my eyes on her feet. Her sneakers were getting very dirty with mud and muck. But as I watched her sneakers get dirty, all I thought of was, "How beautiful on the mountains are the feet of those who bring good news…"

People of all religions there, who don't know Joicy's God, love her because her love is tangible. The needs of the people don't depend on if they know her God. If Joicy feels led to help a Muslim family, she will. The people there love her and her husband because to them, the two of them are a safe place. They see God's love through their lives.

I think this is an amazing picture. Sometimes we have to get dirty to be beautiful. To get down in to the muck and mire to meet tangible needs so people can see who Jesus really is.

Our church goes to a place once a month called Lifebridge. We feed the homeless.

Most pastors I know go to the bedside of those that are sick and in the hospital and pray for them before surgery. This is hands on tangible love.

My husband and I do a ministry called Celebrate Recovery for anyone addicted to anything. We spill our life into them because we know how hard addictions are because we have been there.
This is tangible love.

I remember when my sister in law lived in the ghettos of Philadelphia. When I went to visit I was offered drugs right outside the church door. She would walk with no fear, by herself, into the projects and do Bible Studies with the ladies who had given their lives to Christ. She would tell me how the smell of urine and sights of abuse would not stop her. This is tangible Love.

What kind of Tangible love are you living today?
Where are you walking to make a change?
If you see a need do you care?

Are your sneakers dirty?

Dear God,
Help us to put the needs of others over our own needs. If that means we must get dirty to be tangible so be it! Break us and make us. I honor you today.

Candle Snuffer?

"Though the fig tree does not bud and there are no grapes on the vines,
though the olive crop fails and the fields produce no food,
though there are no sheep in the pen and no cattle in the stalls,
yet I will rejoice in the Lord, I will be joyful in God my Savior."
Habakkuk 3:17-18

Back in the day the crop was everything. The crop would mean food to eat and money to gain. When the crop failed, it would mean great devastation for some. Some had to sell things off just to eat. When reading this scripture today, can you honestly say that if all you have was all of a sudden gone, you would still rejoice and be joyful? Episodes of *Little House on the Prairie* come to mind. I can hear the emotional music building in the background when the crop failed and Charles brings his fiddle to the town store to try and sell it for money. Hard times are not fun times. But most of us have been there.

It's not easy staying joyful through hard times, let alone rejoice through them, yet here is what the word of God says:

"Be joyful always; pray continually; give thanks in all circumstances, for this is God's will for you in Christ Jesus. Do not put out the Spirit's fire."
1 Thessalonians 5:16-19

We can put out the Spirit's fire? Like a candle snuffer? Be ever so careful my friend. You must surround yourself with encouraging people. Hopefully you have a church body to pray and encourage you. If you do not, I encourage you to please seek one out.

To pray, be joyful, and give thanks in everything is God's perfect will for our lives. We must strive for it. This takes discipline and self control. When you are in a hard situation, most of the time you just want to crawl into bed and stay there for a couple of days! In those times, even if you stay in bed you MUST soak your mind in the word of God. Nehemiah 8:10 says:

"For the joy of the Lord is your strength."

We must strive for His joy because it will become the means to help us through. Please notice it says the joy OF THE LORD. This is not some kind of joy we try to make up! His joy imparts to us! He can fill us with a supernatural joy. Just like the Word says:

"And the peace of God, which transcends all understanding, will guard your hearts and your minds in Christ Jesus."
Philippians 4:7

To "transcend" means "to rise above!" Sometimes, a peace will come over you and you will not even know where it came from. This is God's peace. You cannot understand it in the middle of your storm, but there it is. Just like His joy. You need to begin to pray for this joy if you are having a hard time. He will be very faithful to your prayers. He can give you a supernatural joy and peace in the middle of your trial. This is His will for you.

I can remember when I was 19 years old, going through one of the biggest trials of my life. I began to cry out to God in the middle of the night when all of a sudden I felt as if someone put a warm blanket around me. I sat there on the bed for a minute trying to figure out what had just happened, and the Lord let me feel His amazing grace. I had a visitation from Him at that moment that I will never forget. His joy came from Heaven that night into my darkness. Within an hour I was asleep, and the next morning I was ready to face the day.

Can you say today that you will rejoice and be joyful no matter what may come? Please know He is near, just a prayer away.
Or are you a candle snuffer, snuffing out all He has for you?

Dear God,
Help us to long for your word in times like these. Help us to pray always for your joy and peace through our storm. Help us to not be too proud to lean on our brothers and sisters! I honor you today.

May 14th

<u>Memories</u>

Today we took a ride to Cape Cod, the place where our family lived for seven and a half years; where my kids grew up. First, we went to our home that was just sold. I unlocked the realtor lock box and my kids went running inside. There is always a strange smell to things that sit dormant. We have not done a stitch of work to this house since we put it on the market.

When we got to my son's room there was Silly String still on the ceiling that he and his buddies put up there many years ago. We were all laughing about memories in that room. Then Jon saw a tube of toothpaste above the bathroom mirror where he used to keep his toiletries, and grabbed it. Teens totally crack me up. God only knows how long it has been there!

Then we hit my daughter's room. The curtains I made her were still hanging, and one of her sun catchers was still on the wall. There is a spiral stair case in her room and all the little notes she wrote on it were still there. Behind the door were all the marks we had made through the years of how tall the kids had grown. As I began to walk through the house I thought of joyful times and hard times. I thought of the many things God spoke to me in that house. I thought of the many things I accomplished in my home office. The memories just kept coming, but best of all was when I walked out to the back deck and looked out to the 20 acres of conservation. All I could hear was quiet; it was wonderful. These kinds of things are very emotional to me. God gives us our memory banks for a reason.

After stopping at the house, we went to the church we pastored for all those years, about half a mile from the house. To the kids, we were coming home. I remember that feeling when I was a kid! It was so exciting. My kids ran into the church and just went from room to room saying Hello. At one point my son said, "Mom, as I walked through the building there was not one part of that building I did not have a memory in." That place will always be special to us. There is something about being home.

Home can have good and bad memories. Sometimes you just want to write them off, and sometimes you want to think on them for days because they make you so happy. What was your home like? Everyone has their own story. When you go to a place with so many memories, it's amazing how the sights, smells, and people trigger those memories.

Jesus went home in the Bible. Here is what it says:

"Jesus left there and went to His hometown, accompanied by His disciples. When the Sabbath came, He began to teach in the synagogue, and many who heard Him were amazed. 'Where did this man get these things?' they asked. 'What's this wisdom that has been given Him that He even does miracles! Isn't this the carpenter? Isn't this Mary's son and the brother of James, Joseph, Judas and Simon? Aren't his sisters here with us?' And they took offense at Him. Jesus said to them, 'Only in his hometown, among his relatives and in his own house is a prophet without honor.' He could not do any miracles there, except lay His hands on a few sick people and heal them. And He was amazed at their lack of faith."

Mark 6:1-6

So when Jesus first went to what He called home, people were in awe of Him, wondering how He could come up with such wisdom. But just minutes later they were talking about Him and soon after their attitude and feelings went sour.

Does this remind you of anywhere?
Your home, perhaps?
I'm sorry.

Regardless of our feelings of home, there is a reason for our memories. God wants to use your memories. In time when He has done deep healing and you are ready, there are stories that you will tell. They are your stories that no one else can share. Maybe they are happy memories and someone needs to hear them. No matter what they are, they are for you to tell someday.

The response from people to your life's stories is not your problem; Jesus was the one who said:

"Therefore go and make disciples of all nations."

Matthew 28:19

Every single time I teach my class for new believers or people who want to build a firmer foundation in their walk with God, I use personal stories along with His word. I use stories of my life that are memories from the past. God can use your memories and stories to pour into new believers so they know they are NOT alone.

Think about your memories today.
Think about home.
What are you not sharing that God might want you to share someday?
He always has perfect timing.

Dear God,
Thank you for the memories we have. Good and bad. Help us to be brave enough to realize that there is someone that needs to hear what is inside of us. I pray for this reader Lord, and in time I pray you use them to pour into someone's life. I honor you today.

May 15th

Why Worry?

"And the Lord commanded the fish,
and it vomited Jonah onto dry land."
Jonah 2:10

"You will drink from the brook, and I have
ordered the ravens to feed you there."
1 Kings 17:3

Why do we worry?

Many times in the word of God we see God commanding. Not just leading men and woman of God, but even the birds of the air and creatures of the earth!

Here we see Jonah running from God, and God commands this giant fish to swallow him. I think the Lord was giving him some alone time to think about what he had done! After his time was up, the Lord had the fish vomit Jonah! It's so funny when you think about it. "Hey fish, time to vomit Jonah onto the land now!" And Elijah, in a hiding place the Lord led him to, was fed by ravens! These birds brought bread and meat in the morning and night!

Why is it that we think about these Bible stories and seem to think of them as nice things in the past, but not relevant to today? God still commands the creatures. He still commands the birds. He is still God.

"Jesus Christ is the same yesterday and today and forever."
Hebrews 13:8

If I was stranded on an island somewhere I would begin to pray for the miracles of God to take place. I would not just want the ravens to bring meat and bread, but I think I might ask for some lobster or clams, too! Ha. God still does miracles my friend. The same God of the Word is the God we serve today. There is NO need to worry about anything in your life!

"He gave the sea its boundary so the
waters would not overstep His command."
Proverbs 8:29

"For He spoke, and it came to be; He commanded, and it stood firm."
Psalm 33:9

Why do we fight Him? His ways are NOT our ways. They are better. You may not be able to see that now but you will.

I'm sure Noah wondered how in the world he would obey God's command to gather two of every single creature. Imagine if God spoke that to you. But then we read Genesis 6:20:

Two of every kind of bird, of every kind of animal and of every kind of creature that moves along the ground will come to you to be kept alive."
Genesis 6:20

Once again, God commanded. Two of every animal, creature, and bird made their way to him at God's command.

Many years back I saw Noah at The Sight and Sound Theatre in Brandson, Missouri. For those of you who have not been there I highly encourage you. It was one of the most amazing shows I have ever been to. At one point the curtain opens to the entire inside of the ark, and most of the animals are real. I had never seen anything like it. Hundreds of them. But I remember sitting there thinking, how did Noah do it? How did he gather them all? Then I read Genesis 6:20.

Sometimes when God commands us we fear we cannot accomplish what He wants. Never forget that He still commands today.

He is God of all things around you. He knows who your boss is; he even knows how many hairs are on your boss's head! He knows you don't have the money to purchase food this week. He knows you are cold. He knows you're sick of being single! He knows.

"And even the very hairs of your head are all numbered. So don't be afraid; you are worth more than many sparrows."
Matthew 10:30

Be at peace today my friend.
Why worry?

Dear God,
Help us to get it into our heads that you are the same God today as you have always been, and that everything is under control. I honor you today.

May 16th

He Never Cringes

Many years ago, when I first became a mom, I was a bit overwhelmed. I never had any younger siblings or cousins. I truthfully did not know that babies do not sleep through the night. No one ever told me. What a surprise it was when I got home and found out that they actually wake up and scream to be fed at night! I did not even know this in the hospital because I always gave my son back to the staff at night to get a good night's sleep. By the time my daughter came along I was ready.

> "Like newborn babies, crave pure spiritual milk, so that by it you may grow up in your salvation, now that you have tasted that the Lord is good."
> 1 Peter 2:2

We were going over this scripture in my foundations class today, and I was encouraging those who have given their lives to God to grow in Him. Read His word and pray! New Christians should desire God's word, or what this scripture calls "spiritual milk," like real newborns crave mother's milk.

Do we? Do you?

The other night I worked the graveyard shift in the maternity ward for the first time in about three years. I used to do it all the time, but have not in a while. We were totally loaded that night, and every single room was booked. We actually had some moms on the labor floor because there were no more rooms left on the postpartum floor. Needless to say, the nursery was full! There were three, and sometimes four of us to about 13 babies. Not all the babies in the unit were with us, some were with their moms. It was so funny you had to laugh at times! All the babies would be quiet and then all together like five would start to scream. Sometimes you would smell a pungent order and follow your nose, but most the time they were hungry. We can only lift one at once, so some would have to scream until we could get to them.

Think for a moment about a baby who desires to eat. That baby will scream until he or she is fulfilled. Do you desire the word of God like that?

There is a big difference between our response and God's response to our children. I remember those nights when I was so very tired. Jonathan or Angela would start to cry and I would cringe inside. I would think, oh man, I have to get up! NO! It's freezing out there, or I'm so tired. But I would get up and care for my babies. God cares for His children as well, but He never cringes! His first response to our cry for Him is love. The minute He sees we desire His word or presence or anything from Him, His heart is full. Always waiting, always desiring for us to come to Him.

Do you crave His word? I'm a very visual learner. I need to see things to get them into my heart and mind, so I would print out scripture and put it everywhere when I was a younger Christian. There would be index cards taped to my dash in the car and on the kitchen cabinets.

Everyone is different. We remember five percent of what we hear, 15 percent of what we read, 35 percent of what we study, and 100 percent of what we memorize. How do you need to get God's word into your heart today?

One of the ladies in my class today said that she would get scripture CDs, something I've never had. They are scriptures that are sung on a music CD. She said she would be able to memorize scripture that way. Hey, as far as I'm concerned friend, whatever it takes! How do you learn? Be creative, think outside of the box. Do what it takes for you to desire more of the word of God!

We should desire the Word like newborn babies desire to be fed.

I thank God that He responds to our cravings in love! And truth be told, we come to Him as we are. Full of sin and shame at times.

He never cringes!

Dear God,
Your mercy is overwhelming at times. Thank you. I honor you today.

May 17th

Super Size It

Tonight was my night to do the Panera Donation Pick-Up for our Ministry we run tomorrow. For those of you who run any kind of group ministries, Panera Bread® donates food left over at the end of the night, and you get amazing stuff. We use the pastries for the coffee hour, and we get tons of breads and bagels for our group to bag and take home with them. It is a great blessing, and if we did not go get it the entire lot would be put in the garbage. Such a waste. After working in the slums of New Delhi, that is a hard thought for me to handle. What I picked up tonight could feed a big family there for an entire week.

My son came with me tonight to help and I'm not sure why but they are always so nice to us when we pick it up. They give us free coffee and drinks. Maybe they are happy that it will not get dumped in the garbage. Maybe they are happy knowing it will bless our ministry, or they just don't want to carry everything into the back lot to the dumpster! I'm not sure what it is, but they are always happy to see us and they bless us every time.

"Give and it will be given to you. A good measure, pressed down, shaken together and running over, will be poured into your lap. For with the measure you use, it will be measured to you."
Luke 6:38

I thought of this scripture tonight as I filled my free cup of coffee. I thought about the last time I gave. I'm thankful that I can say that just this afternoon my husband and I made our check to the child that we sponsor in India. We love to give to missions. There have been times when our tithe or missions-giving is due, and we give even when we don't have it. God has always met our needs and we have never been in want for food or anything. I have seen this promise in scripture fulfilled. I have seen the pouring of His blessings. He is ever faithful.

It does not matter if your gift is big or small. Whoever gets it will be blessed.

In Luke 9, Jesus feeds five thousand people with five loaves of bread and two fish. You can read the story in Luke 9:10-17. They prayed over the small amount of food and God did a miracle: There became so much food that the disciples picked up twelve basketfuls of leftovers!

I have a modern day story of a miracle like that. I love to have people over, and I love to give food to people. If they are sick or just moved into a new home, my giving is food. And it's such a blessing to them. One night I had made lasagna, the size I usually make for my family of four.

Usually when I make lasagna, there are only a couple pieces left over. Well, this one night a few years back, we were getting ready to sit down to eat dinner when there came a knock on our door. We had a surprise visit from another family from our church. Mom, dad, and four kids! Right away my mouth said, "Please stay for dinner!" I was not even thinking. It was in my heart to share and give. But as I walked into my kitchen to put more plates on the dinner table, a streak of fear came over me. What did I just do? I invited these close friends of ours to stay and did not have enough food prepared. You would not have seen it on the outside, but I was totally freaking out on the inside. I began to pray that Jesus would do a miracle, pretty much because I did not know what else to do. There was corn on the cob in a pot on the stove and the lasagna on the table with garlic bread. Yummy smells filled the air.

We all sat down to eat and before the prayer was said I made a joke about praying that God would multiply our food! We all kind of laughed, but in my heart I was worried. I don't know how to explain what happened that night, except for a modern day loaves and fishes. All ten of us ate lasagna until we were full. There was still one piece of lasagna left in the pan and no one could eat it because we were all full. I'm telling you it was a miracle. I believe with all my heart that God did a miracle that night. He multiplied our food. Laugh if you want, but I know how my boys eat.

We gave that night. We gave all we had to offer. Your offering is not what matters. It's the offer that counts. Even if your offering is small, God can Super Size it!

Have you offered anything as of late? Dinner to a sick neighbor? Cookies at Christmas? Money to the poor? What do you have to give?

If you give you will be blessed, I promise you that. We are so very blessed by Panera® every Tuesday night. And even if you think what you have to give is small, I promise God will use it for His glory.

He will Super Size it.

Dear God,
Give us great faith to believe that the miracles of yesterday are still available today! I pray for the reader right now, that you increase their faith by giving what they have to others. I honor you today.

May 18th

A Constant

"For I was hungry and you gave me something to eat, I was thirsty and you gave me something to drink, I was a stranger and you invited me in, I needed clothes and you clothed me, I was sick and you looked after me, I was in prison and you came to visit me."
Matthew 25:35-36

"I tell you the truth, whatever you did for one of the least of these brothers of mine, you did for me."
Matthew 25:40

It was God himself that spoke these two verses in the book of Matthew. Read them again before you read on. You might be wondering, "When did I give the Lord something to eat? When did I give Him a drink or some clothes? When did I visit the Lord when He was sick? I didn't think the Lord got sick!" Then we read the next verse and the Lord himself says that when you do things for others you are actually doing them for Him. You are accomplishing His mission!

Think about your past year of life. Have you invited anyone over to eat? Have you brought anyone out for a muffin or coffee? Has there been a stranger in your home at all? How about within the last ten years? When was the last time you gave a bag of clothes to The Salvation Army or a family in need? When did you bring some homemade soup to a friend who may be sick? When have you ever walked into a prison to visit? Ever?

The Lord Himself says that if we do these things we are doing them unto Him. The truth is that when we do these simple, practical things it can change the lives of people forever.

I remember before I knew the Lord, every single Sunday morning my brother Lou would come into my room and ask me if I wanted to go to church! No matter how hung over I was I knew it was coming. I tried to pretend I was sound asleep most the time. He would open my door, "Tana….Tana….Don't you think you should go with me this morning?" I would roll over and say, "NO!" But he did not give up, no matter how many times I rejected him. No matter how many times I gave him the finger.

He was a constant in my life; something that I did not want to admit that I needed.

Are you a constant in anyone's life? Something they know will be there even when rejected and hurt?

In reference to the verses above, do you faithfully visit or write anyone in prison? Do you faithfully have a friend you minister to? Do you faithfully do anything? Please remember that when you do, you do it as unto the Lord. He is honored. And souls are changed.

There was a four-year period in my life where I was a constant to someone and got nothing for it in return except God's joy. I led a nursing home ministry. I faithfully went with my team and we sang songs, and I would preach a message from the Word. Most were dementia patients or had Alzheimer's, but mixed in were a chosen few who were as sharp as a tack. You never knew what was going to happen.

During a service once, one of the dementia patients started to wheel himself out the door. When I asked him where he was going he said, "New Hampshire!" But all of us as a team were a constant. We were with the least of these. And through those four years many came to the Lord in their own way, with what they had left. God was honored and souls are in Heaven because we were faithful.

Sometimes your reward here on earth will not seem too great. You will be hurt and rejected.

But Your Father in Heaven sees. He does not forget. Your reward will be in Heaven.

> "Blessed are you when people insult you, persecute you and falsely say all kinds of evil against you because of me. Rejoice and be glad, because great is your reward in Heaven."
> Matthew 5:11-12

Be a constant.

Dear God,
Please help us not to give up on those around us. Help us to be a constant in the lives of others like you are a constant in our lives. You will never leave us or forsake us. I honor you today.

May 19th

Barbies in the Bathtub

"Train a child in the way he should go,
and when he is old he will not turn from it."
Proverbs 22:6

It's amazing how quick time has passed. My son is going off to college in the fall and in two more years my 16-year-old will be gone too (written in 2010). I cannot even imagine life in the fall without my son. I even keep talking about things that are going on in the fall and my kids keep reminding me that Jon will not be here! It hits me hard every time. I guess I have to start thinking about hot pots, a dorm fridge and all the fun stuff we had when we were in college. He will be going to Northpoint Bible College because he feels that's where God is leading him right now. As a mom, I'm so very happy that my kids hear from God on their own.

I have a very funny memory of Angela in the bathtub at age six. As a matter of a fact I videotaped the entire ordeal! Now when we watch it we laugh so hard, but it speaks volumes to us!

It's only in this video that you can see how if a child is raised in the things of God, they may not understand everything but they will begin to mimic what they see. This can be very dangerous in some ways, but I thank God that Angela and Jon do not just mimic anymore, but have chosen to walk with God on their own. They realized what they learned in the Sunday school books was reality and they now have their own personal relationship with God.

The video of her at age six starts with all the naked Barbie and Kelly dolls lined up for church. Are you laughing yet? I think there were a couple puppies at church, too. They are all lined up sitting along the tub. You can hear Ang preaching to them. Many Barbies give a loud, "Amen!" Then Angela puts her mouth down in the water, comes back up, and spits water in the air. That is a very funny part in the video; wish you all could see it. Then one by one she takes the Barbies and Kellys and puts their hard plastic arms up in the air. Angela shouts loudly (and I mean LOUD),"Praise Him!" You can hear me in the background laughing so hard and trying to keep my composure while videotaping. It's just so funny.

Years ago in church we used to sing this song, part of it went:

"Under my feet, under my feet, Satan is under my feet."

When we sang the song in church, the worship leader would jump in the air when he sang the word "feet." It was like we were stomping on the devil's head.

Well all of a sudden in my cherished video, revival hits the bathtub! Angela starts to sing the song as loud as she can: "Under my feet! Under my feet! Satan is under my feet!" The naked Barbie's are all getting up and pouncing on the devil's head. They are all jumping, and then one Barbie does a split in the air and starts spinning around, jumping up and down on one foot. By this time I can hardly see what I'm videotaping because of the tears in my eyes. I'm laughing so hard the tears are rolling down my face. Of all the videos I have of my kids, this one is the best, and I'm sure someday we will have a blast showing it at her wedding or something!

It's amazing how our kids mimic what they see. If you see kids that grow up with parents that hit, you usually see them hitting. If they grow up with parents that have a cuss mouth, they will be cussing, and the list goes on.

I want you to think about how you grew up today. Did you mimic things that were handed to you? If they are unhealthy things, do you still do them?

Are you a parent who is doing unhealthy things that your kids are going to learn to mimic? There comes a point and time in a child's life where they move from mimic to reality. In those moments, they have choices to make. Are you helping your kids to make the right choices? Or are you training them in unhealthy ways? It is never too late to change your ways.

I have found that when I am wrong the best thing to do is to tell my kids, "I'm sorry, I was wrong." Don't let pride keep you from admitting you are wrong. When we share our faults with our kids they actually can learn from it.

I am so very thankful for my kids and how they have chosen to love the Lord due to a firm foundation.

And I am thankful for the Barbies in the bathtub.

Dear God,
Thank you for giving us kids. Help us to be that example they need from day one, or to get them around those that will have a godly influence on them at an early age. I honor you today.

Hurled Hailstones

"Joshua said to them, 'Do not be afraid; do not be discouraged.
Be strong and courageous.'"
Joshua 10:25

Joshua had seen the hand of the Lord in a powerful way. The Lord gave the Amorites over to Israel. In this scripture we see Joshua with much faith speaking to the army commanders and kings. He was repeating something that the Lord had spoken to him just about 18 verses before this verse.

"The Lord said to Joshua, 'Do not be afraid of them; I have given them into your hand. Not one of them will be able to withstand you'."
Joshua 10:8

Let's check out the miracles God did for Joshua between verse 8 and verse 25.

"The Lord threw them into confusion."
Verse 10

"The Lord hurled large hailstones down on them from the sky, and more of them died from the hailstones than were killed by the swords of the Israelites."
Verse 11

"The sun stopped in the middle of the sky and delayed going down about a full day. There has never been a day like it before or since, a day when the Lord listened to a man. Surely the Lord was fighting for Israel!"
Verses 13-14

I'm not sure about you, but if I saw these things happening in front of my eyes I think I would be encouraging God's people to not be afraid or discouraged as well! But I wonder, if Joshua had not seen miracles in front of his eyes, how he would have responded?

Sometimes the Lord promises things, and we don't see those promises for many years. Have you been there before? I prayed for some people for six years before I ever saw my prayers answered. That is not an easy place to be.

It seems that when we see the miraculous hand of God move, it boosts our faith! It increases our expectation in the fact that He controls everything; even the weather and us. It gives us a picture of His power and might so we can say we are strong and courageous!

But what about the times we suffer? What about pain in our bodies or a mother who has lost her teenage son? What about the times we cannot see the miraculous hand of God moving? Do you find yourself encouraging others during those times? Most of the time, the answer is no.

Will you give yourself a break today? You need to realize you are not perfect. Sometimes in life we go on emotional roller coasters. Sometimes we simply cannot understand why God is working in a certain way. To us it just does not make sense. We are not seeing the sun stop.

But we also need to know that it's in those times that He is working behind the scenes. We just cannot see it. There is a reason for it all.

I had a hard day physically today. I don't talk much about it, but I want you to be encouraged through my hard time today. I want you to know we can be strong and courageous even when we do not see hurled hailstones! I'm not seeing any today friend, but I know He is with me. I feel His presence and He has not left me. His word is all I need to make it through days like these. When you wonder why some are healed and some are not, when you wonder how you will pay that bill that has been sitting on your table for weeks, just remember there is a much bigger picture.

During these times I encourage you to read the stories of the miracles of God. They will increase your faith and expectation for God to move in your own life. Don't just pray for others, begin to pray for your own needs. Sometimes it seems so much easier to pray for others rather than ourselves. But pray anyway! He hears.

And in time He will give us our own version of hurled hailstones.

Dear God,
Remind us of your power and the fact that you are in control. Nothing can touch us unless it has already passed through your hand. I honor you today.

May 21st

Dragon Fish

Tonight is a very weird night. My husband is half a world away in Africa and my kids are hours away at a high school prom. I cannot even tell you the last time I was home alone for over 24 hours. I'm not even kidding you. I put my feet up a few hours ago all by myself and watched a good movie. I can't tell you the last time I did that by myself either! It made me realize I'm way too busy. I need some me-time.

It's strange when you're alone with a free day. For me, I usually don't have free days so today, after I dropped off the kids, I hardly knew what to do with myself but clean! I chose to pamper myself instead. You need to know there is nothing wrong with that. You need that sometimes. It's healthy. But there are also dangers of being alone when you know no one is around. Be on guard because the evil one will tempt you.

Having spare time makes you do things you would not normally do. For me, I'm fascinated by the deep dark ocean. I explored the ocean online about an hour ago. I love to look at the creatures God has created; it just amazes me how creative He is. I came across a fish today that got me very excited: the dragon fish.

I love the movie *Finding Nemo*, which I'm sure most of you have seen. That's the movie I chose to watch tonight. There is a part in the movie where Nemo and Dory drop a pair of goggles way down into the deep darkness of the ocean. They see a beautiful light in front of them, so they follow it. In minutes, they see what the light is attached to, and it's a horrid looking fanged fish. I did not know until tonight that the fish in the movie is called a dragon fish. To be exact, *Grammatostomias flagellibarba* is its formal name.

It's a ferocious fish that lives like 5,000 feet under the sea in the darkness. It's small, only about six inches long. It has a long barbell attached to its chin, with a light producing organ called a photophore. The photophore was the light that Nemo and Dory saw in the distance. It was this fish's organ! So funny. The fish is smart. It lures it's prey by the beautiful light, then as soon as it is taken in, the fish grabs it with its big fangs.

It sounded too familiar to me as I sat and read about it. This is exactly what the devil does.He makes the things he tempts us with look so beautiful and great, but the bite in the end is stinging and painful.

"He is dragged away and enticed. Then, after desire has conceived, it gives birth to sin; and sin, when it is full-grown gives birth to death."
James 1:14

We are tempted by our own evil desires and we are tempted by the evil one who puts thoughts in our minds to make us fall. He lies directly into our ears. I know you all know exactly what I'm talking about. But you need to know that temptation is NOT sin. Look at the scripture above. The scripture says, "after desire has conceived." This means after you act on that temptation, then it becomes sin. The evil one knows how to make things look like they come right from God sometimes, that's why it's so important to pray before you make important choices in your life. Satan lights up his little photophore and tries to lure us in. Some are dragged away, but this is why it's so important to know you can call out to God in time of need.

"No temptation has seized you except what is common to man. And God
is faithful; He will not let you be tempted beyond what you can bear.
But when you are tempted, He will also provide a way out so that you
can stand up under it."
1 Corinthians 10:12-13

"Let us then approach the throne of grace with confidence, so that we
may receive mercy and find grace to help us in our time of need."
Hebrews 4: 15

"Watch and pray so that you will not fall into temptation. The spirit is
willing, but the body is weak."
Matthew 26:41

I wonder how many minutes it took for God to create the dragon fish? I know, I think of the weirdest things sometimes. Even though it's ferocious, it is a very amazing fish. It's very smart.

Be on guard, friend.

Dear God,
You continue to amaze me with the things you make, including us. I thank you that you already won the battle for us on the cross. I honor you today.

Digging Cisterns

"My people have committed two sins: They have forsaken me, the spring of living water, they have dug their own cisterns, broken cisterns that cannot hold water."
Jeremiah 2:13

It's so much easier for us to plan out our own steps. Our lives are busy, when can we make the time to ask Him to guide and lead us like Proverbs 3:5- 6 talks about? After all, some of us work 9 to 5, come home, cook, and with the little time left try to relax only to get up and do it all over again.

So instead of sitting at His feet we plan, we schedule, we dig. When we do it ourselves it's a reflection of who we are. That's why so many cisterns are broken, because we are broken.

It's so crazy that we do this when springs of living water are at our fingertips. He is always there and has given us something so much better than a cistern. He has given us living water – a constant flow of it. If you don't know what I mean by that let me put it into simple words: Constant hope, constant peace through every storm, constant guidance. It's all there for you just waiting for you to dip in.

But we have forsaken Him.

"Yet I hold this against you: You have forsaken your first love. Remember the height from which you have fallen! Repent and do the things you did at first."
Revelation 2:4-5

We have done our own thing.

"The steps of a good man are ordered by the Lord, and He delights in his way."
Psalm 37:23

We need to get back to where we once were with Him.

I want you to think of the time when you walked the closest with The Lord. Maybe it was when you first became a Christian? Maybe through a trial? If it's right now, I hope you thank the Lord for that! But if it seems many moons away you need to get back to where you once were with Him.

He never moved. You did.
You are wasting time digging and digging when you don't have to.

Think about when you bundle up, go outside, and shovel the snow-covered driveway. The energy and strength it takes, not to mention the PAIN that goes into that! The digging and digging into the wet hard snow. This is exactly what it's like when we dig our own cisterns! The energy and strength it takes to plan our own steps, not to mention the pain when we realize we have walked away from everything He intended.

Stop digging.
Start seeking.

Dear God,
Help us to get back to seeking you with all of our hearts. I honor you today.

A Tour Back In Time

I love to remember how far I have come! When I was a kid, even as young as 12 years old, thoughts of killing myself had already entered my mind. I came across this poem I wrote in junior high, and I'm not sharing this to depress you, but so you can see how very far the Lord has brought me in this life. It brings great joy to my heart to take a tour back in time and remember. To see the miracle He has done.

Little Dark World

My feet keep taking me places, places that are so far from my mind. I cannot see or hear. It's like living in a world of danger. I can't express the way I feel to others. I don't know what it means to laugh or to love. You don't know what it's like to be able to smell things all around you and only see darkness. It's so frightening. I don't know what to believe in. I don't know how to control my emotions. I don't know who loves me, or who thinks I'm some kind of weird creature that walks on two feet. I don't know a lot of things, but I do know that I'm alive. I do know that I have to keep walking in my little dark world.

Tana Miller, age 13

Are you depressed yet? Can you believe the absolute darkness in this little poem? I can hardly believe it myself. Some of the poems I wrote as a young girl are just so dark. The hopelessness that comes to mind when I read them is amazing to me. I have an entire file of poems like this that I wrote between the ages of 13 and 18. I'm so filled with the joy of the Lord now that I cannot believe it's the same person when I look in the mirror. I'm so glad that the hope and peace of Christ came into my life.

I needed Him and He knew it. He reached out to me and He is reaching out to you right now. When was the last time you looked back? Opened a box in the attic to remember? Remembered the past no matter how joyful or sad? This is not our home. Our home will be with the Lord in Heaven someday. Life can hurt. But in life He gives peace.

> "Make every effort to be found spotless, blameless and at peace with Him. Bear in mind that our Lord's patience means salvation."
> 1 Peter 14-15

No matter what we went through or what we are going through right now, His patience means salvation. He is more patient than anyone I have ever met on the face of this earth of ours. I know that when I fail time and time again, He is right there loving me.

I love to look back because it fills me with joy knowing that my teens now have the joy of God. They do not live like the poem I wrote. This is exactly what God can do through a generation if we let Him.

We will NEVER be perfectly spotless and blameless. We will always fail. There will be times when the past will creep up on us, but those are the times to reflect on the joy and strength we have now. If needed, surround yourself with friends and people to encourage your heart.

> "As iron sharpens iron, so one man sharpens another."
> Proverbs 27:17

Truth is, we need one another. We need His word. There was an old song years ago that I loved called "Look How Far You've Come." When was the last time you did that?

> "Therefore, if anyone is in Christ, he is a new creation;
> the old has gone the new has come!"
> 2 Corinthians 5:17

When was the last time you took a tour back in time?

Dear God,
Although it's wonderful to know we are new in you, it's so good for us to remember how far we have come. I thank you today for the reader and the amazing things you are doing in their heart right now, at this moment. I honor you today.

<u>Who Am I?</u>

Tonight I got the greatest picture of my husband e-mailed to me. He is in Africa right now with a team, and God is moving in a powerful way. In the picture, he is surrounded by little African children who are laughing their heads off and love being near him. He must be a very strange sight to them with his bald white head, but the picture made my entire night. It put a big smile on my face to know God is using him in a powerful way to touch lives there in Africa.

There have only been a couple of times in my life when I've gotten the feeling of what it would be like to be a single parent. The first time was two summers ago when my husband had moved to a new town for work and I could not move for two months, and the second time is now, for the next two weeks while he is gone. It gives me so very much respect for single parents. It's not easy and can be lonely. But this picture tonight will help me through the next two weeks! I printed it and it's looking me in the face even as I write.

King David prayed a prayer that I read today that made me very thankful. With Guy away it makes me think of how very much I have. I'm not talking about riches, a home, cars and all those kinds of things, I'm talking about what matters most. King David said:

> "Who am I, O Lord God, and what is my family,
> that you have brought me this far?
> 1 Chronicles 17:16b

This is my heartbeat tonight.

The king "sat before the Lord" in 1 Chronicles 17:16a. This in and of itself shows us a picture of King David. It shows a rare trait in someone who has power. It's called humility, something that pleases God. It showed humility that David would take the time to thank the one who exalted him to the place he was.

King David goes on to say:

> "Let the promise you have made concerning your servant and his house
> be established forever. Do as you promised, so that it will be
> established and that your name will be great forever."
> 1 Chronicles 17:23-24

Pretty much what King David is saying is, do the things you promised in my life, so you will get the glory for it!

When Guy and I were in high school and we gave our lives to God, our friends knew we had totally changed. There was no denying what the Lord had done. Before that, Guy played *Dungeons & Dragons* for 40 hours a week, and most of you know the story of how messed up I was. Both of us, when first giving our hearts to the Lord, had promises spoken over us; words from the Lord of how He desired to use us.

Here in these scriptures the King is saying: do what you promised in my life Lord, so you will get all glory. This is my desire tonight! Just seeing that picture of Guy with the kids in Africa reminded me of something God spoke to me about Guy when we were first married. One night in prayer the Lord said, "Your husband will minister to the nations." Already in our married life he has touched so many people from so many places. And he did not have to go overseas for that. They are all in our churches. If you have not noticed, the nations have come to us. Looking at the faces on all the African kids tonight, God is getting all the glory!

Tonight I just have a thankful heart.

What are some promises God has given you? Have any come to pass? If so, have you humbly gone to the Lord like King David and said: Who am I?

Dear God,
Humble us, no matter what position you put us in. We are nothing without you Lord. May you get the glory in everything we do. I honor you today.

May 25th

<u>The Cause of Christ</u>

Isn't it amazing that people who try to bring peace seem to be rejected and some even killed? Jesus himself, who is peace, was chosen over a murderer to be crucified.

Mohandas Karamchand Gandhi was sitting in first class on a train in South Africa when they threw him off because he was Indian. This started his non-violent protest and campaign that led to rights for ALL Indians in South Africa. Not to mention national attention. In India he was considered a hero. They invited him to come. He fought for India's Independence from the British Empire. Britain finally granted India's independence, but then when the Muslims and Hindus went at it he said he would not eat until there was peace. Can you imagine? A group of people, who we would call admirers, came to see him one night, and a man named Nathuram Godse was with the group. Godse killed Gandhi that night, January 30, 1948. Gandhi was 78 when he died.

Martin Luther King Jr. a Baptist preacher in Alabama fought for civil rights. He was arrested over 20 times, assaulted four times, and his home was bombed. At age 35, he was the youngest Nobel Peace Prize winner. He gave his prize of $54,123 to help with the Civil Rights Movement. He fought against injustice! At the age of 39, he was on the balcony of the Lorraine Motel when James Earl Ray murdered him. There are so many more people I could tell about who wanted to fight for peace and human rights.

The world will hate you.

I remember becoming a Christian in high school. I lost almost every friend I had. Some were friends that I had spent almost every weekend with for two straight years prior. But now because the peace of God came into my life and because I carried my Bible, they no longer wanted to be seen with me. Did it hurt? Yes. But I had something I never had before: Perfect peace.

"If the world hates you, keep in mind that it hated me first. If you belonged to the world, it would love you as its own. As it is, you do not belong to the world, but I have chosen you out of the world. That is why the world hates you."
John 15:18-19

Months after walking with the Lord, I was in study hall one day and one of my best friends who had rejected me had tears in her eyes. Her exact words were, "I know I need what you have, but I can't do what you have done." What had I done? I had made a stand for peace. Not for world peace, but for Tana Zinnanti Miller peace. I had finally found the hope and peace I was looking for. God had changed my life. I was made fun of and rejected, but I was not ashamed. Today

I'm still friends with a lot of people who rejected me back then, but they know now it was not a phase I was going through. They know I still live it, and I'm willing to die for it.

Here is one thing I know. When all hell breaks loose around you, He is your peace. When everyone you know turns and rejects you:

> "For the sake of His great name the Lord will not reject His people, because the Lord was pleased to make you His own."
> 1 Samuel 12:22

I am willing to walk where He wants me to walk today; I am willing to pay the price for people's words and torment. Today was just one of those days for me, and during my storm He covered me with His peace. I am willing to die for that— to let people in this world know they do not have to walk it alone. They do not have to live hopeless and hurting. Even when there is no one else around to hold your hand, He is there.

Do you have a cause today? Are you willing to die for your cause like the two men I talked about? Do you have a passion so embedded in your heart that you will move forward no matter what?

He gives me peace, and I want others to experience it.
I have found my cause— the cause of Christ.

Dear God,
I thank you that you surround us with your perfect peace in the midst of anything. You are worthy of all praise today. I pray that the reader would learn to know you are right there for them, right now. I honor you Lord.

Humble Pie

Do you need to eat a piece of pie today? Humble pie?

I may hold positions at the hospital and for my church district, but without God by my side I am nothing but a child saved by grace. I would NOT want to do any of it without Him!

Jesus was the perfect example of humility.

He knew He was getting ready to leave this world and go to the Father in John 13:1, but yet he decides to love on His disciples. I have walked the slums of India and I can imagine the streets where they walked were just as dirty. I would imagine their shoes were open, exposing the foot in many areas. The slums of Delhi have manure, puddles of muck, compost piles of food, ash, and the list goes on, all laying in the streets. I'm sure they walked the same kind of roads in many places to get where they were going. Their feet were one of the dirtiest parts of their bodies.

> "He poured water into a basin and began to wash His disciples' feet, drying them with the towel that was wrapped around Him. He came to Simon Peter, who said to Him, 'Lord, are you going to wash my feet?' Jesus replied, 'You do not realize now what I am doing, but later you will understand.' 'No,' said Peter, 'You shall never wash my feet.' Jesus answered, 'Unless I wash you, you have no part with me.' 'Then Lord,' Simon Peter replied, 'not just my feet but my hands and my head as well!'"
> John 13:5-9

I want you to really picture this for a minute. This is right before Jesus was betrayed. Up to this point, the Disciples have walked with Him and seen many miracles. He makes the lame to walk, turns water into wine, and feeds the five thousand with only five barley loaves and two small fish. He heals the blind, raises Lazarus from the dead and the list goes on and on. But yet now He kneels to wash the manure, muck, and mire off their feet. This must have totally freaked them out! I know it would have bothered me to see the Master do that. He was a servant example, one I can only pray to be like. This was true love and humility.

He did not say, "I am the king, bow down!" Or "Fill the basin with hot water; it's time for you to wash my feet." He wanted to leave a mark on the world so He became lowly.

Friend, if there is one thing I have learned in life it's this: If you want to leave a mark on the world you must become lowly and humble. In this chapter, Jesus says:

"I tell you the truth; no servant is greater than his master,
Nor is a messenger greater than the one who sent him. Now that you
know these things, you will be blessed if you do them."
John 13:16-17

We are the body of Christ. God will grant blessings and favor to those who are humble, that's just the way He works.

Jesus is pretty much telling them, "You better watch yourself and eat some humble pie and realize who you really are: A child of grace."

"Now that I, your Lord and Teacher, have washed your feet, you also
should wash one another's feet. I have set you an example that you
should do as I have done for you."
John 13:14-15

Let me ask you today: When was the last time you washed someone's feet? Who is "someone" anyway? A neighbor? Family member? Coworker? Maybe the washing of their feet is simply going the extra mile for them, even if they are the one who is supposed to be getting YOUR coffee in the morning!

God help us.
Do you need to eat a piece of pie today? Humble pie?

Dear God,
Forgive us for thinking we are all that! We are to be that example, like you were such a great example to us. Help us honor and serve those who work for us. I honor you today.

319

<u>Somewhere Out There</u>

Last night I was driving in my car when I came across the most amazing moon. The clouds were moving fast and the moon and the clouds together just made for the most beautiful sky. All I could do was think to myself, "My husband is in Africa and he is seeing the same moon." Very cool thought. As I kept driving, a very old song came to mind by James Ingram and Linda Ronstadt, called "Somewhere Out There." Some of the lyrics are:

> "And even though I know how very far apart we are,
> it helps to think we might be wishing on the same bright star,
> and when the night wind starts to sing its lonesome lullaby,
> it helps to think we're sleeping underneath the same big sky."

Yes, it was like a scene from a movie. I started to sing the song at the top of my lungs in the car with the moon in the distance. Pitiful I know. That's what happens when you live with someone for 21 years and all of a sudden they are not around, and not reachable. Anyway, tonight I just cannot get that picture of the moon out of my head. It was so amazing. I wish my daughter, with her awesome picture-taking abilities, was with me. I would have pulled over and let her get a few shots.

I know you have all been there: Seeing the moon light up the sky. It could be pitch black and then the moon pokes through the clouds and the entire sky lights up. There is just something about moonlight; it brings comfort, romance, and a feeling that you're safe. God created the moon for purpose:

"And God said, 'Let there be lights in the expanse of the sky to separate the day from the night, and let them serve as signs to mark seasons and days and years, and let them be lights in the expanse of the sky to give light on the earth.' And it was so. God made two great lights-the greater light to govern the day and the lesser light to govern the night. He also made the stars. God set them in the expanse of the sky to give light on the earth, to govern the day and the night, and to separate light from darkness. And God saw that it was good."
Genesis 1:14-18

He brought order to what we call night and day. He gave us a nightlight by creating the moon. Like I said, moonlight brings comfort, romance, and a sense of security, but it also brings an amazing awe.

Yesterday I did think of my husband looking at that moon, because to me, the moon is romantic and I'm missing him so. Its one thing when your spouse is across the country, but when they are across the world, it's a very different feeling. By the time I got to where I was going, I once again was in awe of the wonder of God. It was such a breathtaking sight. And it lit up the sky. We take for granted the nature and sights around us every day.

When was the last time you looked at the night sky? Take the time when the weather is nice to check out the night sky again. He set the moon and the stars in the sky to give you order and light. He did that for you. I want you to know that God is not just somewhere out there. He is right by you, even now. He is the only one who is omnipresent, meaning He can be present everywhere at the same time. He sees you right now where you are, and He is not far away.

"Where can I go from your Spirit? Where can I flee from your presence? If I go up to the Heavens, you are there; if I make my bed in the depths, you are there. If I rise on the wings of the dawn, if I settle on the far side of the sea, even there your hand will guide me; your right hand will hold me fast."
Psalm 139:7:10

He is not somewhere out there today.
He is right there in your room.
Talk to Him.

Dear God,
Thank you for caring for us enough, to bring order to the day and night, for giving us such an amazing nightlight. I pray for the reader now, let them know you are there and help them to not fear. Let them call on you. I honor you today.

Q & A's

I was sitting and reading Proverbs chapter 27 and it took a while. It was so deep that I had to stop and think after every verse. I wanted to apply it to my own life. So today, I'm going to share with you some of the scripture in this chapter and let you do the same – apply it to your life.

When was the last time you talked about yourself and all the great things you are doing? Do you do that a lot? Think about it.

> "Let another praise you, and not your own mouth;
> someone else, and not your own lips."
> Proverbs 27:2

Do you provoke people to anger? Do you do it because you are unhappy yourself? Do you provoke because of your anger against certain people? Think about it.

> "Stone is heavy and sand a burden,
> but provocation by a fool is heavier than both."
> Proverbs 27:3

In case you didn't notice, it calls a provoker a fool.

When people around you do ungodly things, do you shine your light? Are you bold enough to stand for what you believe in, yet wise enough not to turn people away with stupid words? Do you say them in love?

> "Better is open rebuke than hidden love."
> Proverbs 27:5

Do you listen to counsel from friends or mentors? Does it bring joy to your heart when they give you wisdom about a bad choice you are making? I need my mentors! I'm not sure what I would do without them.

> "Perfume and incense bring joy to the heart and the pleasantness of
> one's friend springs from his earnest counsel."
> Proverbs 27:9

Ladies, if you are married, do you annoy your husband? Do you argue with him about every little thing? Are you very needy? Do you give more than you get? Do you quarrel because you have to win the argument? To make a marriage work you must give more than you get, even if you don't like it!

> "A quarrelsome wife is like a constant dripping on a rainy day."
> Proverbs 27:15

When someone sharpens something (e.g. a pencil, a stick getting ready for marshmallows, a dull knife), they scrape a piece of it away. When was the last time you were sharpened? Did you receive what was being said to you?

> "As iron sharpens iron, so one man sharpens another."
> Proverbs 27:17

When people give you praise, does it go to your head? Do you get way too big for your britches? Or do you humbly receive it?

> "Man is tested by the praise he receives."
> Proverbs 27: 21

If you are in ministry, do you know your church people? Do you spend any time with them? Do you know what your teens are doing on the Internet or what movies they are watching?

> "Be sure you know the condition of your flocks;
> give careful attention to your herds."
> Proverbs 27:23

Proverbs 27 is amazing. Go ahead, read the entire thing today and soak it in.

Dear God,
When we read the Word, I pray we will let it change us. We need to be changed on a daily basis. At least, I do. I honor you today.

May 29th

<u>Mayday, Mayday, Mayday!</u>

Tonight at the local mall, a band was playing that my kids like, called Mayday Parade. I actually like a couple of their songs, too. I did not go. Getting away from the crowd of teens that is usually in my own home was very nice today. Anyway, for some weird reason, when they left I could not get the word "mayday" out of my head. All I knew was that it was a cry for help, so I took a look at where the word came from.

As most of you know, the word "mayday" is a distress call! The word "mayday" originated in 1923 by a man named Frederick Stanley Mockford. Frederick, a senior radio officer at a London airport, was told he had to make up a word that authorities could recognize as a word that meant something happening was very serious if it was said. "Mayday" comes from the French word "venez m'aider," meaning, "Come help us."

Something I did not know was that the law says that when someone gives a Mayday over the radio, it must be said three times: "Mayday, mayday, mayday!" Saying it three times distinguishes it from a regular message about a Mayday somewhere else. So the rule is, it must be said three times.

Mayday is a HELP call. Did you know today that God gave you a helper? It's interesting to me that "mayday" is said three times because we have the **Father, Son** and **Holy Spirit.** All three are there for HELP, peace, hope, saving, shelter, and so much more.

I remember one time, I was on the road and the kids were in the back seat in car seats. It was lightly raining on Cape Cod and I was on my way back home from church. I was on the on-ramp to a main road, and when I turned to go onto the highway, my entire car hydroplaned so bad that I did an entire 360 right in the middle of the highway. I had not one bit of control of the car. I remember shutting my eyes and screaming, "Jesus, Jesus, Jesus!" No lie, I really did. I did not even know if there were any cars on the highway, I just started screaming because it seems when I lose all control, He is my helper. When we finally came to a stop, I could not believe that all I saw were cars in my rear view mirror coming my way. No cars at all were on the highway when I spun. It was an amazing miracle that we did not flip over and that we did not hit anything. I will never forget that moment. In all my life I have never felt what I felt in that car that afternoon ever again. My Mayday was Jesus.

"But when the Helper comes, whom I shall send to you from the Father, the Spirit of truth who proceeds from the Father, He will testify of Me." John 15:26

"Nevertheless I tell you the truth. It is to your advantage that I go away; for if I do not go away, the Helper will not come to you; but if I depart, I will send Him to you."
John 16:7

"And I will pray to the Father, and He will give you another Helper, that He may abide with you forever, even the Spirit of truth, whom the world cannot receive, because it neither sees Him nor knows Him; but you know Him, for He dwells with you and will be in you. I will not leave you orphans; I will come to you."
John 14:16-18

Notice Jesus said, "And He will give you another helper." God and His son Jesus were already helping, if you had not noticed. The Father sent the Holy Spirit to us. But the Holy Spirit has always been part of the trinity. Even at creation, the first chapter of the Bible says:

"Now the earth was formless and empty, darkness was over the surface of the deep and the Spirit of God was hovering over the waters."
Genesis 1:2

The Holy Spirit was there from the beginning. We are blessed that just like God sent His son, He sent the Holy Spirit as a helper to us, to dwell with us and in us. If you have a cry for Mayday in your life, please know today that you can cry out to the Father, Son, and Holy Spirit.

"Mayday, mayday, mayday!"

Dear God,
Forever faithful you are. I thank you for coming up with an intentional plan. First you sent your son because we were a mess, then the Holy Spirit. Thank you. I honor you today.

Freedom Is Never Free

Our Pastor said something this morning that I will never forget. He said, "Freedom is never free." He read the bios and showed the pictures of about 20 different people who had died while fighting for our freedom. He asked war veterans to come to the front of the church so we could pray over them. We take for granted those who have served for our country. They pretty much pay for our freedom. Sometimes it does not seem fair that we sit comfortable at home while they are out serving. Sometimes days go by and we don't even think about them. Our freedom in this beautiful country comes with a cost. It was not free to the motherss, wives, sisters, and brothers who have cried at the graves of their loved ones who died fighting for it.

I just want to pause for a moment and thank all of you who have served for my freedom. I thank you.

Today was the day of my son's graduation party, and I guess it has not hit me that in the fall he will no longer live under my roof (2010). Words cannot express how much I will miss what he brings to this house on a daily basis, but I know God has wonderful plans for Jon. Jon is free. He grew up in the presence of God. He did not know the trials of a dysfunctional home, abuse, or having a lot of pain in his life. His happiness came with a cost.

When my husband and I became Christians in our teens we went through much trial. We were rejected for making a choice. It cost something to now live for God and do what He had called us to do. Jon now lives in freedom because his mom and dad fully surrendered all to God. We have a home where God dwells and peace is a constant. I thank the Lord for that in our lives. We may not have lots of money and the best of everything, but our needs are met and God is ever faithful.

I thank God for my American freedom and the peace in my home today. You will see me up at 5:00am on the Fourth of July to get my kids to the Chatham parade on Cape Cod -- the best Fourth of July parade ever! I am patriotic through and through. I'm the one wearing the giant flag hats and red, white, and blue beads around my neck. I love it and soak it all in. When the Veterans walk by I get tears in my eyes. I honor them.

"God is not unjust; He will not forget your work and the love you have shown Him as you have helped His people and continue to help them."
Hebrews 6:10

He sees all you have done today, whether it was fighting for our freedom here in America, or fighting for everlasting souls. Our freedom in Christ came with a serious cost. Jesus Christ died on the cross and paid the penalty for our sin.

Some of you labor in prayer for those you love; you pay the price of staying up for long hours and tarrying in prayer. Some of you go out of your way to help a soul in need; making dinners for the sick and traveling long miles to be at someone's bedside when they are in the hospital or sick at home. There is always a cost to make someone else happy, encouraged, or free.

Through the last almost 25 years of ministry, I cannot tell you the number of people I have prayed for to have God come into their life. Hundreds. I have had some come up to me that I have not seen in years and say, "Do you remember when you prayed with me?" Some I do not remember. But my freedom came with a cost, and it's not about us praying with people, it's all about the price that was paid for our freedom that is now causing a domino effect into the lives of others. It's all about Him and what He did to make us free. He is a humble God that would come, and in love, do something like that. But at the same time He is a warrior and He is just.

"The Lord is a warrior; the Lord is his name."
Exodus 15:3

"Who is this king of glory? The Lord strong and mighty,
the Lord mighty in battle."
Psalm 24:8

Our God is not a wimp. He is mighty. He came and gave and died for our freedom. Only great people die for a cause.

Today we have words printed on our money that say, "In God we trust." That same money with those same words is passed from hand to hand as men pay for young baby girls who are being trafficked right under our noses in our own American cities. God help us. What price will you pay for the people around you? What price will you pay for your own family members?

Freedom is never free.

Dear God,
Wipe away our tears God, freedom can hurt. Mothers have wept. I honor you today.

The Happy Troll

"The Lord is my light and my salvation – whom shall I fear?
The Lord is the stronghold of my life – of whom shall I be afraid?
When evil men advance against me to devour my flesh,
when my enemies and my foes attack me,
they will stumble and fall.
Though an army besiege me,
my heart will not fear;
Though war break out against me,
even then will I be confident."
Psalm 27:1-3

When I read this scripture, a scene from *Saving Private Ryan* enters my head. The sniper in the movie always quotes scripture before he shoots, and he is the best shot ever. It seems in the most stressful times of the movie he is always quoting scripture. He stood on the Word to take his fear away. He was an actor, but I wonder what he is like in real life stressful situations.

How about you? I have been in fearful situations where I knew that someone was going to hurt me. I have been afraid. I have been hurt in life and so have most of you. Most the time my heart did fear, until I learned that God helps me to be confident no matter what the circumstance.

I want to be very transparent today and tell a story that I have never told. A few years ago, my dear friend was sick in the hospital, so my daughter and I chose to go to the toy store and get her something fun and cute to make her smile. We walked the aisles searching for the perfect little friend to keep her company. The only stuffed animals that interested me were Care Bears, so I carried one around for two aisles until I saw something that brought back so many memories.

Remember the little, fat, naked trolls with long hair? Sometimes they have purple hair or orange hair. Back in the 70s every kid had a few. We would braid their hair and brush it forever. They would be lined up on the shelves in our rooms. Since my friend and I are almost from the same time era, I chose to get her a smiling, happy troll. I know her, and she knows me, so I knew that this would make her happy. Angela and I picked out the perfect one. She loved it.

Why is it that sometimes our own brothers and sisters in Christ tend to wage war against us? I never expected what would happen next.
About two months after my friend was home and doing well, we were in the middle of Sunday morning service and communion was about to be served. While my husband was praying, a lady came up behind me and told me that she could not take communion until she told me that she had something against

me, and then she walked away. In case you don't know, you don't do that to someone. If you have something against someone, you tell them what it is. You don't say you have had something against them, and then walk away.

There was no way I was now taking communion after that. I went to get her in the line. I told her we needed to talk. She began to tell me how evil it was that I bought a troll and gave it to my friend. She told me the history of trolls and everything about them, to be honest friend, I did not care. I just cared about my dear friend and what would make her smile. It was a rubber, little, fat guy with an awesome smile and awesome purple hair. A child's toy that I got for $6.99!

I guess she had kept this anger in her for two months. When you have anger against someone or if they have hurt you, please do not wait two months! All that time, I had no idea I had hurt or offended someone by getting a happy troll. Her anger was only hurting her.

Don't do that to yourself.

"Get rid of all bitterness, rage and anger."
Ephesians 4:31

In other words, don't carry it around for months. Even after we talked things were never the same. All that over an adorable happy troll. I can honestly say I cannot tell you the last time I have laid my head down on a pillow at night angry at someone. I refuse to do that. If I'm angry or upset I go to them and talk to them.

After this happened she would not let it go. She actually left the church, and in her leaving letter she mentioned the fact that I bought a troll for my friend. Jesus knew my heart, and my heart was pure before Him.

To you today I say, when it seems like someone is "out to get you," whether it's someone who knows the Lord or not, hold your confidence. If you know your heart is pure, let them judge. There is nothing you can do about it. Like my husband always says, "When people point a finger of judgment at you, there are three fingers pointing right back at them."

"Though war break out against me, even then will I be confident."
Psalm 27:3

Dear God,
May we never, ever lay our heads on a pillow at night with anger in our hearts. I honor you today.

June

Anxious?

"Do not be anxious about anything,
but in everything by prayer and petition, with
thanksgiving, present your requests to God."
Philippians 4:6

Since today I'm very anxious, I thought I would write about it. I did this to myself. It's because I have way too many "irons in the fire," or as some say, "I'm spinning too many plates."

I'm writing this devotional which takes about an hour and a half every day, I'm working these two jobs and tonight I'm doing a graveyard shift at the hospital. Before that, I'm also teaching at our ministry tonight because my husband does not get back from Africa until tomorrow morning, I just finished the lesson a little while ago. I have to get my daughter and her friend at 2:30pm, run errands, and be at the church by 5:30pm. Somewhere in there, I have to sleep to get ready for the graveyard shift, shower, and pick up the dinner for our ministry tonight.

A few minutes ago I felt overwhelmed and my heart filled with anxiety. I thought, "How am I going to do this?" The most important thing to me today is finding some time for sleep, but it looks like there is not too much time for that. I was feeling stressed. When I don't get sleep before I do an 11:00pm to 7:00am shift, I really start to lose it at about 5:00am.

Tonight I'm even speaking at church on being anxious in some areas, and here I am feeling overwhelmed and anxious. I don't think I would be feeling this way if I did not have to stay up all night, but I will not call in, I will work and do the best I can.

The truth is, life is life and we will be anxious at times. I had to stop, take a deep breath and say, "Lord, I know I cannot do this without your help. I need your strength today." I don't know about you friend, but I cannot make it today without the strength of my God. He promises in His word that He will strengthen us. Let's look at a couple scriptures today! Trust me, I need to hear them.

"But those who hope in the Lord will renew their strength. They will soar on wings like eagles; they will run and not grow weary, they will walk and not be faint."
Isaiah 40:31

"God is our refuge and strength, an ever-present help in trouble."
Psalm 46:1

There is a story in 1 Samuel about David that helps us to see that our strength is in the Lord.

> "When David and his men came to Ziklag, they found it destroyed by fire and their wives and sons and daughters taken captive. So David and his men wept aloud until they had no strength left to weep. David's two wives had been captured --Ahinoam of Jezreel and Abigail, the widow of Nabal of Carmel."
> 1 Samuel 30:3-5

Let's stop right here for a minute and just imagine this. He comes to the place where his wives are supposed to be, and they are gone! And their sons and daughters have been taken captive. They have no clue what is being done to them. For those of you who know the story of how David and Abigail came together, well, it's a beautiful love story featuring a very strong, beautiful lady. It's in 1 Samuel 25, read it sometime. And here she and his other wife are gone. As you see, it says they wept aloud. I'm sure those tears were mixed with anger and much anxiety over not knowing what to do next! You know how you feel when you have cried really hard? Well this is how they were all feeling, mixed with anger. The scripture goes on:

> "David was greatly distressed because the men were talking of stoning him; each one was bitter in spirit because of his sons and daughters."
> 1 Samuel 30:6a

So David finds out his wives, sons, and daughters are all taken captive and now his own men are mad at him and talking of stoning him! It says he was greatly distressed, or we could say "very anxious!" But I love in this scripture how he responds:

> "But David found strength in the Lord his God."
> 1 Samuel 30:6b

Today with the pressure and stress I'm feeling, I needed to stop, breathe, and think on God's promises and how I can do nothing in my own strength. My strength comes from God.

Do you need to stop and take a breath today? Soak your mind in God's Word. Trust me I know firsthand today, it helps!

Anxious? What are you going to do about it?

Dear God,
We need you. I pray for the reader. When the pressures of everyday life are felt and they call on you, make yourself so very real to them God. I honor you today.

June 2nd

<u>Coming Home</u>

Today my husband came home after being in Africa for two weeks. I have to admit that I hated being away from him so long. But I cannot tell you the anticipation in the air at the Miller home just waiting around for him to arrive. I'm sure it was the same for all the families of the team that went to Africa with Guy. They were delayed in New York City, so that made us sad!

When Guy pulled in the drive way, I opened the window so our dog Arwen, a black lab, could see her master. She has not been herself since Guy went away. She totally freaked out when she saw his truck. After he parked the car, we all ran out of the house, including Arwen, and attacked him. I could tell he was very tired. My son and daughter grabbed the cases and brought them upstairs. The house was totally filled with joy.

Guy began to open little sacks of things. In one, an entire loot of jewelry. African necklaces, bracelets and wrist bands, all home made. He pulled out beautiful fabric place mats, and all kinds of things. African masks hand carved and painted, it was so fun. He even pulled out some snack bars that the kids ate right away.

Through all of the gift-giving, Guy told us so many stories about adventures he had taken with Greg Hubbard, a long time friend. We laughed and laughed as he told us that he and Greg got lost on on moonlite horse ride. Here they are in the middle of Africa, in the dark, and they along with the guide have no idea where they are. All of a sudden, the guide says, "We must run!" Meaning, make your horse run! Guy said he almost fell off the horse three times he was laughing and crying so hard! We were laughing as he told the story.

After Guy went to bed and all was settled down, I got to thinking of my heavenly home. First I thanked God for bringing my husband back to me safe and healthy. Then I began to think of the anticipation that our Lord must feel as he waits for that day we will all be with Him.

"But our citizenship is in Heaven. And we eagerly await a Savior from there, the Lord Jesus Christ, who, by the power that enables Him to bring everything under His control, will transform our lowly bodies so that they will be like His glorious body."
Philippians 3:20-21

Well I tell ya, I can't wait for that glorious body! Hahahahaha! Nothing will hurt anymore! To think that the same anticipation and excitement that our family felt today is the same that our Lord feels about us just amazes me. He loves you that much. You may think today that no one cares for you. You can't even get a social security number or a green card fast enough, but guess what? Your citizenship is in Heaven friend! And He waits for us and has good gifts for us.

Think about this for a moment: He created this earth in six days. On the seventh day He rested. He made this amazing world, the universe, every single insect, all of our anatomy, the oceans below with all its creatures, and the list goes on. In just six days.

"Do not let your hearts be troubled. Trust in God, trust also in me. In my Father's house are many rooms; if it were not so, I would have told you. I am going there to prepare a place for you. And if I go and prepare a place for you, I will come back and take you to be with me that you also may be where I am."
John 14:1-3

This statement was said by Jesus to the Disciples thousands of years ago. He said he is going to prepare a place for us. If our world looks and is the way it is in six days, just imagine friend what Heaven will be like if He has been creating it for thousands of years.

It reminds me of that show on TV where they make a special effort to renovate a kids room. Every single thing in the room has things that that kid loves in it. This is the way I imagine it. Our Father knows us better than we know ourselves! It will be amazing.

If you have never had joy in your home I pray you come to know the Lord. You will be part of an amazing family. I thank God I came to know Him at the age of 18.

I look forward to my coming home.

Dear God,
I pray for the reader today. May they come to know you in a very powerful way today. I pray that you reach them right where they are right now in their relationship with you. I honor you today.

June 3rd

<u>Ready for Marriage?</u>

The year is 2010 and today is my 21st wedding anniversary. Let's talk about love, marriage, and who you may marry for a few minutes. I have to say that I love my husband now more than ever. We have broken down every weird wall of non-communication through the years. I don't think there is one thing he does not know about me. Communication is the key in a healthy marriage. Respect and not doing the things you know will bug or hurt your spouse is another key. Avoid them, steer clear of them. I can be totally myself with my husband without any word of judgment against me. Even when I'm wrong, he loves me anyway. He will never put me down or embarrass me in front of anyone. I love him for that.

Many could say having God as the center of your marriage is a great thing as well, and I totally agree with this, but I have met many very healthy, happily married couples that do not know the Lord. Believe it or not there are many happy non-Christian couples who are living this scripture and they probably don't even realize it.

"Love is patient, love is kind. It does not envy,
it does not boast, it is not proud. It is not rude,
it is not self-seeking, it is not easily angered, it keeps no record of
wrongs. Love does not delight in evil but rejoices with the truth. It
always protects, always trusts, always hopes, always perseveres. Love
never fails."
1 Corinthians 13:4-8

I have seen hundreds of couples get divorced through the years. Almost all of those couples were Christians who were not willing to bend to letting God change them. Not their spouse, them. Guy and I are NOT the same couple we were when we got married; there were some rocky times early on in our marriage due to tons of baggage from our former lives.

Coming into marriage with baggage is not always smart unless you have gotten some help for it. To know the person you will marry actually got help is a very positive thing for you to see in their character! This means when you are willing to help and give wisdom as a spouse someday, they might actually receive it. They might actually apply it to their life, if you are living it.

Intimacy to me was a fearful thing, something that most the time had only hurt me. Sexual abuse and so much more will do that to you. If not for Guy living this scripture and being patient and someone who perseveres, we just might have ended in divorce. I'm not afraid to admit that now because we have such a wonderful marriage. But I needed to be willing to let God change me inside and it took years. He built my self-esteem and built me in the word of God. I will always love him for that.

For those of you not married yet, read that scripture over and over. Read it with your love, and just a note here, if they are not willing to sit and read it with you, you may want to think twice. Does the person that you are engaged to or dating seem to be patient? Are they kind, even when upset? Do they envy others? Are they prideful? Are they rude or self seeking in any way? Are you? News flash: Marriage is about giving, not getting!

How's their anger level? Any record books laying around of all the horrible things you have done? It's so sad that I see record books of wrongs almost every day on people's facebook profiles; they have nothing to do with love. Love keeps no record of wrongs.

Do they tell you the truth? Do they want to protect you from evil? Do you trust them? How is their hope level? Think twice friend before you marry someone who is very jealous all the time and tends to blow up at little things. If that is you, you need help. Trust me, when Guy and I first got married, most of the answers to my own questions were negative. I was not the least bit patient, I was selfish, and had a giant record book of wrongs that I loved to carry around with me. Thank God I am not the same person!

The secret is to be willing to let God change you.

My record book with chapters and chapters of many different people is gone for good. There is always hope, always; as long as there are two people willing to change to make each other better.

Last year, Guy and I renewed our vows in India. We wrote our own vows and our friend Bob McGurty led us in them. One sentence I said was, "Guy took my dysfunction and made me function." He only could do that because he is living 1 Corinthians 13:4-8. I am living it now too.

It is better to hurt someone now then to enter into marriage because you are afraid to hurt them. If you have any doubts at all you need to get out. I'm not trying to depress you; I'm speaking the truth in love. Our God is big enough to let you know. He is big enough to speak to you like it talks about in John 10:27. As his people we are supposed to be listening anyway.
God confirmed in many ways, way back when, that I was to marry Guy and I am so glad I did.

God knew I needed him.
Read 1 Corinthians 13:4-8 again later.

Dear God,
Be with everyone reading today as they continue to read 1 Corinthians 13:4-8. Touch their hearts and change them like you changed me. I honor you today.

June 4th

Eye Service

I have this memory from when I was 12. These were the days when I was a bean pole, not a lick of fat on my body, and tall and strange-looking. My teeth were weird and my hair was always nasty and greasy. Yes, these were the days back in 1979, when 12- and 13-year-old girls pulled their hair back in pony tails and did not care what they looked like. Now, they all have cell phones and pay $60 for their highlights! It's crazy how times have changed.

I remember going to a Bible book and gift store with my best friend Pam White and her mom Helen. My mom had brought me to some church meetings and I was wishing my mom was with me. We were walking around the store and I was looking for things that cost pennies because I only had a handful of change in my pocket. I remember it was a small gift shop, and there were so many cool things to look at. I came to a white magnetic pole that had rubber magnets on it. The magnets had quotes on them. One said, "John 3:16," one said, "God said it, I believe it, that settles it." But then I saw one that I knew my mother would love. It said, "Give us this day our daily bread." I had to have this magnet. I can't remember the price of it. I'm sure it was under $2.00 but I did not have it with me.

Next thing you know, I take it off the pole and sneak it into my pant pocket. Helen purchased her things, and I walked out of that store with the magnet! This was the first and last time I ever stole anything in my life. I know if I just told Helen I wanted it for my mom she would have gotten it for me. She was one of my mom's best friends. So funny how quick we make bad choices. I was such a messed up kid that I did not even feel bad about it. Not one bit! All I could think of was the joy I would see on my mom's face when she saw it. I did not often see joy in her face back then.

I was doing something to make someone else happy, NOT counting the cost! I was putting myself in a sinful situation and a compromising situation to make someone else smile.

And step by step it got worse and worse and worse.

Most of you know my story and just about 3 or 4 years after I ripped off this $2.00 magnet, I tried to kill myself in my mother's kitchen. It did not happen overnight, it was one bad choice after another just trying to make other people happy. I was trying to ease my pain by getting attention from others in any way that I could.

I was a people pleaser.

The only problem: I was miserable.

Who are you trying to make happy today? Whose attention are you trying to get? Have you put yourself in a sinful, compromising situation to try to gain their attention or to gain attention for yourself? Are you miserable?

> "Not with eye service, as men-pleasers, but as
> bondservants of Christ, doing the will of God from the heart."
> Ephesians 6:6

Since that day I have never stolen another thing, but for years after that I would try to be a people pleaser, doing anything and everything I could to make people happy. When I would finally achieve my goals and see people happy, I would leave them and go be miserable alone.

When we are people pleasers we will make quick, rash choices!

Friend, it's time to work on you instead of everyone else. It's time to "do the will of God from the heart" and stop gaining your self esteem by making everyone laugh. It's time to put a smile on your own face and not everyone else's'. It's time to stop with all the eye service.

> "Be self-controlled and alert. Your enemy the devil prowls around like a
> roaring lion looking for someone to devour. Resist him, standing firm in
> the faith, because you know that your brothers throughout the world
> are undergoing the same kind of sufferings. And the God of all grace,
> who called you to His eternal glory in Christ, after you have suffered a
> little while, will Himself restore you and make you strong, firm and
> steadfast. To Him be the power forever and ever. Amen."
> 1 Peter 5:8-9

Dear God,
Help us to be filled up with your word and presence. Help us to have a strong desire to please you more than any man or woman. I honor you today.

A Gift or Rage?

There was once a young girl who had been captured in a raid and taken to a foreign country to be made into a slave girl. You would think she would be angry and bitter at her new master. You would think hate would fill her heart. But here we see a hint of grace:

"Now bands of raiders from Aram had gone out and had taken captive a young girl from Israel, and she served Naaman's wife. She said to her mistress, 'If only my master would see the prophet who is in Samaria! He would cure him of his leprosy'."
2 Kings 5:2-3

Naaman, her new master, was commander of the army of the king of Aram. His master thought he was a great man and he highly regarded him. Naaman was a valiant soldier but he had leprosy.

The surprise is that this young servant girl is not thinking, "Let this man rot in his leprosy." He took her from everything she had ever known, from her family, friends, and life. Yet we see grace here, and a love beyond understanding that can only come from God.

"Naaman went to his master and told him what the girl from Israel had said. 'By all means, go,' the King of Aram replied."
2 Kings 5:4-5

So some time goes by, and picking it up at verse 10, Naaman is at the door of the Prophet Elisha's house. Elisha does not see him there.

"Elisha sent a messenger to say to him, 'Go, wash yourself seven times in the Jordan, and your flesh will be restored and you will be cleansed'."
2 Kings 5:10

Here is where it gets funny to me. This is such an amazing picture of pride. If you see yourself here, please beware.

"Naaman went away angry and said, 'I thought that he would surely come out to me and stand and call on the name of the Lord his God, wave his hand over the spot and cure me of my leprosy'."
2 Kings 5:11

He is a commander of an army, you would think he would be used to some orders, but yet he has a hard time with one of the most important orders he will ever get. If that was me I would be running for the Jordan as quick as I could! I would look ridiculous! I would be running so fast and crazy! But here we see him pouting. Grown men pouting; not a pretty sight! As a matter of a fact he went beyond pouting and was intensely angry.

> "So he turned and went off in a rage."
> 2 Kings 5:12

I just cannot even imagine it. Here is a servant girl who should be mad at him, but instead gives him a lead that there is a prophet that can heal him. Then he goes to Elisha and is upset at the way he delivers the message. Then he wonders why Elisha does not choose better water for him to dip into!

> "Are not Abana and Pharpar, the rivers of Damascus,
> better than any of the waters of Israel?"
> 2 Kings 5:12

The man was prideful. Yet even in his pride God heals him. In time he goes to the Jordan and dips himself seven times.

> "His flesh was restored and became clean like that of a young boy."
> 2 Kings 5:14

Do you see yourself in Naaman? Please grow up! Stop thinking you deserve something better than all those around you. The servant girl got the picture, the bigger picture. God requires obedience and humility even from master commanders with piles of gold! God's hand of grace gave Naaman a great gift that day of healing despite his pride. This is the same God that loves you today friend. You may be just like this man, but He loves you and wants to give good gifts to you.

Will you walk away from Him in a rage? Or will you open the gift?

Dear God,
Once again this is such a great picture of your grace. Help us to open all the gifts you have for us. I honor you today.

June 6th

Church Hoppers

Tonight was Pastor Appreciation Night at our church. Each pastor, all five of them, had a basket assigned to them where people from the church could drop off gifts, cards, and cash. It's so fun reading people's thoughts about the things you have done to help them, when you did not even know they felt that way. We have a giant bag of cards. I'm so tired now I can't even think to read them all or go through things. I read a few, and the words just mean so much to me, and I think my husband will drink Starbucks coffee for free for the next two months!

So now after such a special night of food, fellowship, and fun, I'm sitting in my office and I'm listening to my daughter in the next room singing and playing worship music, and I hear my husband and another pastor downstairs clapping and yelling at the TV. I just feel so blessed tonight to have people love me, and to have a church family. And I must be totally hormonal because I have tears once again.

We just had a couple who is involved with our recovery ministry leave for six months. Right before they left we gave them a $50 gift card to Cheesecake Factory as a group. We thought they could get a nice dinner out together before they take off. This couple has shared their testimony with our group many times and they do not come from a back ground with a lot of love and affection. They got up in front of everyone, and the husband cried real tears and shared how he realizes how thankful he is for his church family. He knows they all will be praying for them and that they really care, something he said he has never had before until he came to our church. When you don't come from that, it means everything.

I want to highly encourage you today to not be a "church hopper." Plug in somewhere! Don't hop from church to church in hopes of finding the perfect church, because guess what? You will not find it! No church is perfect! Pastors are men and women who are just normal people with a call on their life. Here's a reality check for you: They fail! They are not perfect. Your eyes need to stay focused on God and not on man. But the word of God says nothing about being a church hopper. It says everything about being committed to a body of believers.

"Not forsaking our own assembling together, as is the habit of some, but encouraging one another, and all the more, as you see the day drawing near."
Hebrews 10:25

Assembling together as a body of believers is not an optional thing. If you are living the Word and wanting to be faithful, it says to "not forsake our own assembling together." In other words, go to church. Get involved. The entire purpose of the church can be found in Ephesians 4:12:

> "For the equipping of the saints for the work of service,
> to the building up of the body of Christ."
> Ephesians 4:12

The church is there to help you live your faith. The church is there to not only build you up, but to equip you, so in return you can build others up someday with your own story and the Word.

Tell me this, how can you be equipped or equip others if you are hopping from church to church? How can someone really invest in you if you are there one Sunday and gone the next? In your own friendships, in the past have you ever gotten close to someone who was there one day and gone the next? Sorry, it just does not work that way. You need to plug in. If you think you are so great that every church needs you and you need to hop every week to bless every church, than you seriously need to eat some humble pie! I'm sorry, just trying to speak the truth in love here.

> "Speaking the truth in love, we are to grow up
> in all aspects into Him, who is the head."
> Ephesians 4:15

Tonight once again I was reminded of how blessed I am to have my church family. If you are already plugged in, are you giving and not just getting? I'm not talking about your money; I'm talking about giving of yourself to help the ministry of the church. If you don't know it already, the ministry of the church is PEOPLE! People are the church. What are you doing to encourage the body? Sometimes it may seem so simple, like filling mugs with candy to hand to new visitors, but you have no idea the impact you just made on that one visitor. How do you know that that is not the first gift they ever got from anyone in their life? There is no ministry more important than another. It's so important to find your place. As a matter of a fact, it's God's will for you to find your place.

Stop hopping.

Dear God,
You desire us to be part of the body, but you also desire us to stick around enough to be able to minister. People will not trust until we gain their trust. I pray for the reader that they would stop hopping and plug in; that they would seek you for wisdom and direction. I honor you today.

He lifted Me, He Set Me, He Gave Me

When was the last time God put a new song in your mouth? What do I mean by that? Is your praise in stagnant waters? Do you rejoice on a daily basis? As of late I just can't help it. I'm just so proud of the things my kids are doing and I find myself crying and happy all the time. Someday my kids will be out of this house and with families of their own. What about then? What about when they are not around me every single day? Will I still be rejoicing on a daily basis?

I believe if you keep your mind fixed on all He has done even in your own life, and you live the Word on a daily basis, you cannot help but to rejoice and thank and praise Him.

"I waited patiently for the Lord: He turned to me and heard my cry. He lifted me out of the slimy pit, out of the mud and mire; He set my feet on a rock and gave me a firm place to stand. He put a new song in my mouth, a hymn of praise to our God. Many will see and fear and put their trust in the Lord."
Psalm 40:1-3

In 2007 when I walked the aisle to become ordained as a Minister, my brother prayed over me and gave me this scripture. If anyone knew the slimy pit I was living in before I came to the Lord, it was him. He knew that my entire life was stuck in the mire! When I was eighteen, right before salvation, I was on the pill, smoking, drinking, and drugging to escape my bitterness and fears. The songs in my head were not songs of praise they were songs of self pity. One of my favorite songs at the time was "Treat Me Right" by Pat Benatar, an anthem I sang for many years. Trust me; it was not praise coming from these lips.

After much prayer from many people, I actually went to church one day with my brother. There I gave my life to the Lord, and things did NOT change overnight. Just because you become a Christian does not mean your pain goes away. It just means now you have the Lord walking through it with you. I walked through most my pain with the Lord for almost 15 years as a pastor's wife before I was truly free of it. He was faithful, and when I failed, He loved me through it.

If you don't know what that feels like I can only pray you walk with Him someday. It's amazing.

He lifted me, He set me, He gave me.

"He lifted me out of the slimy pit, out of the mud and mire; he set my feet on a rock and gave me a firm place to stand."
Verse 2

As of late, things have been awesome, but there have been times in this walk that are stormy and dark. When you can't find praise in your mouth, think of where you came from. Think of when you went from point A to point B in your walk with God. Meditate on when you were stuck in the mire and ask yourself, "How am I different now?" Trust me friend, when you do this there will be a new song inside your soul, and even if you don't have the strength to sing it out loud, He hears it.

The place you have been given is a firm place to stand even when your trial has you in bed crying. Your firm place waits for you to get up again. You don't lose it just because you are depressed.

When you don't know what song of praise to sing, remember your past and start to sing, "He lifted me, He set me, He gave me."

Our past can sometimes bring us back to praise.

Dear God,
You are so very faithful. You have been patient with me, and I pray you prove yourself to this reader. Let them feel you walking through the trial with them. I honor you today.

June 8th

We Must Run!

My husband told the funniest story tonight. I was totally falling off of my chair laughing so hard. He just got back from Africa and he went with a good friend of his, Greg Hubbard. Greg and his awesome wife have been friends of ours for years. We have been through some interesting ministry together that's for sure. But this story of the two of them tops it all for me.

Writing this devotional has been a wild ride. God seems to confirm even my titles some nights. A few weeks back while Guy was away in Africa, I wrote one on Moonlight The very next day when I got up, Guy wrote from Africa saying he took a moonlit horse ride. Just amazing how God is confirming every aspect of this devotional you are reading.

So I'm thinking of this beautiful romantic moonlight ride, and wait until you hear this. The mission's team is all on horseback following a guide. There was one guide in the front and one in the back. Greg does not like the way his saddle feels, so he asks if he can stop for a second to fix it. Guy stopped with them. So the guide in the back of the line, my husband, and Greg are all stopped on their horses. They are totally engulfed in getting it fixed for Greg. When they finally are ready to ride again, all three realize the entire team is gone! They don't see them, they don't hear them, and they are nowhere to be found. The team just kept riding and pretty much left them there.

So the guide said to follow him, and my husband said they were going at a slow pace. This was not some safe park all fenced in, this was the wild! So all three are riding horseback in the wild of Africa in the pitch black with just the moonlight to light their way! My husband said that all of a sudden the guide turned around and looked at Greg and Guy and said, "We must run!" Guy said a streak of fear almost came over him! If your guide is saying that, well, that's not too good! So Greg, Guy and the guide start to run on their horses. This is the funny part: Guy and Greg don't ride and for any of you that know Greg, he is like 6 foot 5, and I'm sure he was killing the horse! Haha! Guy said that after a while they had to tell the guide that it was also killing them! Ha!

Before they went on the moonlight horse ride, one of the guides gave them rules. One of the rules was DO NOT RIDE IN THE TALL GRASS! This was mostly due to lions and big snakes. So where is the guide running with Greg and Guy now? In the tall grass! Guy said he was laughing so hard and hurting so hard at the same time that he almost fell off the horse three times. I'm sure Greg had the same experience. Finally it came down to them screaming, "Where are you?" in hopes of finding the team.

In the end, they caught up with the team and were safe. I'm sure Greg will be sharing that story somewhere, and I can't wait to hear his version! You have to know both of them to really appreciate this story.

The more I thought about the story tonight, the more I thought about Joseph in the Bible. Guy and Greg were in a dangerous situation. At any moment one of those horses could have been pounced on by wild animals in the dark. It's kind of funny thinking of Greg and Guy for dinner. And they ran right through the dangerous tall grass to get out.

Joseph was a faithful man.

> "Potiphar put him in charge of his household,
> and he entrusted to his care everything he owned."
> Genesis 39:4

God had granted Joseph favor time and time again. The Word says:

> "Joseph was well-built and handsome, and after a while his master's
> wife took notice of Joseph and said, 'Come to bed with me!'"
> Genesis 39:6-7

So truth be told, Potiphar's wife was out of control and totally hot for Joseph. This poor guy! The Word says in verse 10, that day after day she asked him to go to bed! Can you imagine the temptation he felt? I'm sure Potiphar would not marry an unattractive lady.

> "How then could I do such a wicked thing and sin against God?"
> Genesis 39:9

> "He refused to go to bed with her or even be with her."
> Genesis 39:10

Joseph was in a dangerous situation. One day, she grabbed him by the cloak, and once again begged for him to sleep with her. The Word says:

> "He left his cloak in her hand and RAN out of the house!"
> Genesis 39:12

When you are in a dangerous, tempting situation, sometimes you need to run! Go! Even if you have to run right through the tall grass, more danger, and more temptation to get out!

As brothers and sisters in the Lord, sometimes we need to look at one another and say, "We must run!"

Sometimes it takes the run to stay pure in your walk with God.

Dear God,
Help us to always run from tempting situations, to keep our hearts pure. I honor you today.

Calgon Moments

Have you ever felt overwhelmed? There was a commercial many years ago about a product called Calgon. In the commercial, there was usually a stressed mom doing laundry with one kid in the kitchen making a mess, and the door bell ringing and the phone ringing at the same time. The phone had a cord attached to the wall, remember that kind anyone? Haha! Now Calgon has many products, but then it was a bath bead that you put in your bath water for ultimate relaxation and ultra moisturizing! Their slogan was, "Calgon, take me away!" In other words, in your most stressful high pressure moments, get in the bath and chill out! Treat yourself, get away!

You need to know that is healthy and okay! You can take time for you! You know how much you can handle. Sometimes it feels like you have so many plates to juggle that you are spinning! You're a mom or dad, you're a leader, a taxi driver, a counselor, a friend, and the list goes on. If you are a very hard worker, you want to do things with excellence and leave no stone unturned. When you are spinning so many plates, you need to make time for you.

When Jesus walked the earth, He did things with excellence. He always thought before He spoke. One great example of this is John 8:4-8:

"'Teacher, this woman was caught in the act of adultery. In the law, Moses commanded us to stone such women. Now what do you say?'" They were using this question as a trap, in order to have a basis for accusing him. But Jesus bent down and started to write on the ground with his finger. When they kept on questioning him, he straightened up and said to them, 'If any one of you is without sin, let him be the first to throw a stone at her.' Again he stooped down and wrote on the ground.'"
John 8:4-8

So we see He thinks before He speaks, and people were always asking Him questions. I believe when He bent down to write, He was thinking about what He would say instead of just saying it. Very wise.

He is going around healing and teaching people. He is mentoring 12 men and pouring himself into them. He was even dealing with their farts, burps, and humanness. He made time for those people that not one other person stopped for. Jesus was spinning many plates to say the least. And there is a scripture that shows us He had His Calgon moments!

Jesus is walking along one day when a man with leprosy falls on his face and begged Him to heal him.

"Jesus reached out his hand and touched the man. 'I am willing,' he said. 'Be clean!' And immediately the leprosy left him. Then Jesus ordered him, 'Don't tell anyone, but go, show yourself to the priest and offer the sacrifices that Moses commanded for your cleansing, as a testimony to them.'"
Luke 5:13-14

I want to stop here a moment to highlight the fact that Jesus said, "Don't tell anyone!" He knew when word got out that the crowds would be like modern day paparazzi.

The word of God says that the man with leprosy did not keep quiet, or perhaps those around who saw the miracle happen spread the word. Needless to say, the word got out that Jesus healed him.

"Yet the news about him spread all the more, so that crowds of people came to hear him and to be healed of their sicknesses. But Jesus often withdrew to lonely places and prayed."
Luke 5:15-16

You see! Jesus withdrew to be alone for his Calgon moments! Maybe He was not in a hot bath, but instead a cold cave, yet he was not being crushed in a crowd with everyone touching Him. He could breathe for a few minutes alone.

I want you to remember that most of these Calgon moments for Jesus were lonely. Many of your Calgon moments are lonely. He knows how you feel.

It's ok for your Calgon moment to be lonely because He wants to meet you there.

When you are having that alone time that is stress free and quiet, please never fail to remember Jesus in a cave somewhere having His moment as well. He is the one that can fill you during those times of relaxation and pampering.

Jesus made sure He took these times! It's says, "He prayed."
What a perfect example for us.
The place of prayer is the best place for us to take our Calgon moments.

Dear God,
When it seems life is pressing in all around us, help us to run to the place of prayer. I honor you today.

June 10th

Optical Migraine

I had a crazy experience today. I was sitting in my office chair, when all of a sudden I saw something to the right of me. You are all going to think I have totally lost it when you hear this.

I saw what seemed to be a rainbow made out of triangles as high up as I could see, and going as far down as I could see. Almost like a half circle. It seemed that it was made of zigzags and it was a range of colors. It was always moving, almost like sparkles. I thought it was something in my eye at first, so I kept opening and closing my eyes.

Ten minutes later when I realized it was still there, I began to worry. It got bigger and brighter and seemed to take up the entire space of my vision. I began to wonder if it was physical or spiritual.

I closed my eyes and there it was. In the darkness of my closed eyes it was as clear as day, moving, sparkling. I have to admit, it was beautiful. I said to the Lord, "Father if this is physical, heal me, but if this is spiritual let me see what you want me to see now." I waited and saw no vision or anything. After a while I opened my eyes and tried to get on with life and what I was doing, but as you can imagine it was hard with this moving thing to the right of me.

About 20 minutes into it, I went upstairs to paint my face. My brother always said, "If the house needs painting, paint it! Haha! So I'm putting make up on, and this rainbow is still big and moving, when all of a sudden it moves upward. I mean like the entire thing went up as far as I could see. It stayed above me for like five minutes, then went away as quick as it came. The entire time that I had this experience I kept thinking, "Is this you, Lord? Are you on your way?" I mean it looked as if the gates of Heaven were going to open to the right of me.

When all was said and done, I did the right thing and called the eye doctor. Before I even finished what I was saying, he said, "Did it look like a moving kaleidoscope of color?" I said, "Yes!" He told me it was an optical migraine. There is no pain with these until after it's over, and it only lasts up to an hour. I only got a tiny little pressure behind my eye and took some Advil. It has something to do with the brain's blood circulation being disturbed. He said it was no big deal unless it happens all the time, but I did schedule an eye exam anyway because I have not had one in years. My vision is 20/20.

All that to say, this afternoon when it was going on, I could not help feeling that the Lord was coming back or something. I mean it; I thought something supernatural was going on. It just made me think about how just like today, it's all going to happen right in the middle of whatever we are doing in our daily life.

There I was in the middle of work and it hit! No warning, no clue anything was coming. And it was breathtaking. I know that sounds weird, but I was in awe of it.

"For as lightning that comes from the East is visible
even in the West, so will be the coming of the Son of Man."
Matthew 24:27

"No one knows about that day or hour, not even the angels in Heaven, nor the Son, but only the Father. As it was in the days of Noah, so it will be at the coming of the Son of Man. For in the days before the flood, people were eating and drinking, marrying and giving in marriage, up to the day Noah entered the ark; and they knew nothing about what would happen until the flood came and took them all away. That is how it will be at the coming of the Son of Man. Two men will be in the field; one will be taken and the other left. Two women will be grinding with a hand mill; one will be taken and the other left. Therefore keep watch, because you do not know on what day your Lord will come."
Matthew 24:36-42

That scripture really speaks for itself. Are you ready? If Jesus came back today, will you go with Him? He is coming and He will come when we do not expect it. I thought He came today in the middle of my optical migraine.

I can't wait. After today, I know it's going to be an amazing experience. We all will see beauty, and it will come so quick that we will not even think about anything else except what is happening around us. We will see Him.

Dear God,
Help us to be so ready for your return. Help us to repent and always keep watch like your word says. I honor you today.

June 11th

Trevor's Cupie

Have you ever been just amazed at how quick the years pass by? I went to youth group at our church tonight and saw a teen girl of whom I have very old video footage. When she was three, she was potty training. I asked her in the video, "What do you get when you do poo-poo on the potty?" Her response: "Chocolate!" The video is so cute. When Coral Sunshine Moretti walked by me tonight, all I could think of was that video and how quick the years have passed! It's like one day, you blink your eyes and you are older and more things in your body hurt! Haha.

There was this small kid that my son befriended quite a few years back. He would come down to Cape Cod and stay with us. He always had a smile and was pretty hyper most the time. He knew how to make me laugh. One time, he stayed with us for about a week. During that week he took this plastic cup we had in the house and with a permanent black marker wrote on it in kids scribble, "Trevor's Cupie!" His name is Trevor Panarello, but he took ownership of Trevor's Cupie. We still laugh about it today. When this kid got a hold of sugar candy, his motor would start. You had to watch Trevor because you just never would know what could happen. One time at church during a man hunt game in our brand new sanctuary, a very nice-sized hole appeared in the new freshly painted wall. Guess who?

Tonight I sat back and watched an anointed young man lead worship, a young man moved by God's spirit who led the youth into the very presence of God. It was Trevor Panarello. Yes, the original owner of Trevor's Cupie! You blink, and in a matter of years what once was is no more. Although you still need to seriously watch Trevor when he has had too much sugar! Haha!

The movie *Passion of the Christ* made me think of how Mary was with Jesus right from the time of His birth through His death on the cross. I'm sure Jesus did not get chocolate when He pooed on the potty, but guess what, He still had to be potty trained. Just because He was God does not mean He automatically knew how to use the potty chair! His mom was there and taught Him. The movie shows Jesus as a young carpenter. Mary saw all these stages of His life. I'm sure there was never a "Jesus Cupie", but I can assure you that when He was small, the king of the universe got hyper like all children. Then one day, she catches Him teaching in the temple. She knew from day one that He was fully God, but I'm sure this was a reminder again that she was going to lose Him to the Father's perfect plan.

I don't know about you, but in my mid 40s I just feel like half my life is over and everything is just moving so quickly (2010)! Sometimes it makes me sad because

I know I have to give my own kids over to the perfect will of God for their lives, and my empty nest is right around the corner.

This is a breaking in every parent, a time of full surrender.
It's not easy to let go, but it's God's will to let go.

> "For this is what the Sovereign Lord says: I myself will search for my sheep and look after them. As a shepherd looks after his scattered flock when he is with them, so will I look after my sheep. I will rescue them from all the places where they were scattered on a day of clouds and darkness."
> Ezekiel 34:11-12

The shepherd knows his sheep. He knows how many there are and he knows the different characteristics that make up each one so he can call them by name. When one is lost, he will leave the others to go search for that one. He guards them from the evils that lurk. He can take care of them better than we can.

This is what brings me comfort.

Don't be afraid to let go. If you don't have children, remember He knows you by name and all those you care for. He sees the time flying by and He knows your concerns and cares better than you know them. He made all those you care for. He is God. Rest in Him today.

As I saw Trevor up there tonight, my mind flashed back to that kid's scribble on that big white plastic cup that said "Trevor's Cupie." God sure is faithful.

If you get a chance tonight, read Ecclesiastes 3. It's in the Old Testament.

> "He has made everything beautiful in its time."
> Ecclesiastes 3:11

Rest. Even on the days of clouds and darkness, He is there for those you love.

Dear God,
Help us to trust in you and give everything to you even those things we love the most. We trust you with them tonight Lord. We give them over to your perfect will. I honor you today.

Healthy You

Outside our home here in New England there is a peach tree. This poor tree! We have tried so hard to help it. For some weird reason it leans to one side. So much so that my husband had to bungee cord it to the fence. The lean in it is out of control. When the fruit grows, it only weighs down the tree more to one side. It's pretty pitiful and it really should be cut down. The peaches are not healthy. They grow to a point and then start to look very strange. Most are already falling off and they are only a forth of the size they should be on the ground. You would not catch me eating the fruit from this unhealthy tree if you paid me!

One day when my mother in law came to visit, she pruned the tree thinking it would somehow bounce back. She is an amazing green thumb whereas I kill pretty much everything. I have never had a plant.

There are three plants in this house: Two in my husband's office, and one in the kitchen. I have nothing to do with them because I kill all plants. Not intentionally, I'm just horrible at keeping them alive. When we lived on Cape Cod, my window boxes contained fake flowers! So for me to even think I could help this poor peach tree is a joke.

There was a time in my life when I was very unhealthy, even after I became a Christian. I was selfish and prideful. As I grew in my pride, God found ways to break me. During those days, I had friends, but no fruit for God's Kingdom. Not sure about you, but I would much rather advance God's kingdom than anything else.

I remember a time my friends took me to see Rez Band, a Christian rock group. (Are any of you laughing yet? I'm totally dating myself.) Anyway, they were very down to earth and personal with us after the concert, and sat around talking to us about how God could change our lives. I remember I sat there and said, "Amen!" over and over and over. As if I was some sort of leader in the room. Pride, pride, it was all pride. Horrible. People like that will not bear good fruit. They will be turning people away, not attracting them at all.

Do you realize the best way to preach the Bible is the way you live your life? If you are unhealthy, well, let's let God's word say it:

> **"No good tree bears bad fruit, nor does a bad tree bear good fruit."**
> **Luke 6:43**

I just love this scripture. If you are healthy, and trying to do your best for the Lord in all humility, this word promises that you will NOT bear bad fruit. That is a promise. God knows you will make mistakes, but remember He also knows the true motives of your heart.

He knows that all unhealthy trees bear bad fruit, just like my peach tree. By fruit I mean, whose life are you touching for God's kingdom?

Is there a soul somewhere that can say that you have made a dent in their world?

Think about that question. If not, could it be that you are unhealthy in some area and therefore people do not desire what you have? Many times we have talked about the fact that if you have God's spirit living within you, there will be evidence of that! People will see it.

> "But the fruit of the Spirit is love, joy, peace, patience, kindness, goodness, faithfulness, gentleness and self-control."
> Galatians 5:22

I can promise you that if people see these things in your life on a daily basis, they will want what you have. There is not a ton of genuine peace rolling around the world these days. And if they see you living out these things, they will know they can trust you to be there for them.

> "For out of the overflow of his heart his mouth speaks."
> Luke 6:45

What are you talking about on a daily basis? If it's all about you and the things you are doing, how quick do you think God's kingdom will advance? You may not even realize it, but you are actually turning people away by doing that. People, even those that don't know the Lord, have a hard time with a prideful soul.

It's time to get healthy. It's time for change. If you do not change, God will find ways to change you.

The peaches are now on the ground outside rotting. I don't want that to be what my fruit ends up looking like. How about you?

Focus in on a healthy you.

Dear God,
As we read about the things that should be evident in our lives, may we be willing to change to be more like you. We cry out for change. We cry out for forgiveness. I honor you today.

June 13th

The Ultimate Diploma

My son graduated from high school today and we are so very proud. The year is 2010, and I'm excited to see what the Lord is going to do in his life. It was a long day. The day started with teaching my discipleship class, then church. I had to rush out of church to get Jon to the school an hour early, and then I had to sit and wait for it to start. Then the crowds poured in. It was a long graduation, but so awesome. The highlight for me was when I saw my son walk across the stage. Very proud. We came home, I made food for a small army, and then we took pictures on the lawn. It was a very happy day. Jon got his diploma.

I have a high school diploma and a college diploma. Each time I graduated, I was filled with excitement and wonder of what the Lord was going to do with my life. I'm just blessed and honored that He desires to use me and that He gives me His grace day after day! I worked hard for my diploma, yet there is another kind of diploma I look forward to.

There may be some of you reading that have never heard what I am about to share, so I hope you know it's directly from God's word. There are books in Heaven, and one book is called The Lamb's Book of Life. Simply put, if your name is in the book you are going to Heaven, but if your name is not in the book you are going to hell. Many have asked, "How could a loving God send anyone to hell?" Well, that loving God time and time again gave you chances to know His word and surrender your life to Him, but you were the one who chose not to! So is He sending you to hell, or are you sending yourself to hell? As a matter of a fact, if you are reading now, here is another chance for you to receive His love and gift to you. He will never give up on you, but you are the one who chooses.

"And I saw the dead, great and small, standing before the throne, and the books were opened. Another book was opened, which is the book of life. The dead were judged according to what they had done as recorded in the books."
Revelation 20:12

"If anyone's name was not found written in the book of life, he was thrown into the lake of fire."
Revelation 20:15

Living for God and serving Him is NOT a wimpy thing. It takes hard work and self control. It takes not caring what people think of you or what you believe. It means losing friends who think you are crazy, but gaining a church family. It's hard work. In a sense, having your name in The Book of Life is like getting the ultimate diploma!

You work hard, sacrifice, lose friends, gain more than you had, resist temptation, seek His face, lean on Him when you are down, gain more joy than you have ever had, all to one day have your name called like my son's name was called today. Someday your full name might be called. I know my name, Tana Angela Miller, will be called. I know most my family's names will be called. How about you? Are you unsure of your name being in the book?

Give your life to Him today. Why do people make it so hard? Seek out a church that stands on God's word to grow in your faith. If you care about your friends, family, and children, this will be the most important thing in your life. If you think what I'm writing is crazy, then I feel sorry for you because that means that you don't know God and that your name is not in the book. It breaks my heart. Turn to Him today friend, He waits.

Living for Him means you have to overcome many things in this life, but here is what God's words says:

"He who overcomes will, like them, be dressed in white. I will never blot out his name from the book of life, but will acknowledge his name before my Father and his angels."
Revelation 3:5

I hope and pray you take this to heart today. Think about it. I hope you never forget it. It's like the ultimate diploma

Dear God,
I pray for this reader. Make yourself so real to them right now. May they feel you right there with them. Speak peace to their soul. Draw them to you, Father. I honor you today.

June 14th

Collections

Have you ever had a collection? For years I have had one collection after another. It started when I was a girl. I collected rocks. My Uncle worked with gems, so he gave me my first rock collection. Each gem or rock was placed in its own little bag and hand labeled with what was inside. I remember I had them all lined up on my dresser, one after another. I loved looking at them, pulling them out of the bags and then putting them back.

My next collection was music boxes. I had any kind of music box you can think of.

When I became a teen, I collected dolls. I'm so glad they are gone now. Old dolls freak me out!

As I got older I collected those little high heeled shoes. I had shoe everything! Every place you looked in my bedroom there were mini high heels. I even had the giant black display high heel. After that it was Coca-Cola everything. I'm not sure why I loved collections so much, but I must say almost every collection got out of control. This is the first time ever in my life I do not have a collection. They are all in storage. I got sick of them.

My front room is all missions-themed. Every bit of décor in that room is all from our trips to India and Africa. I guess as far as any collections around my house right now, that is the extent of it. When the kids were younger and I was home with them, I was way more into my collections, but as they grew and my time was freed up to work, the collection bug bit less and less. My time was taken up with work and other things.

What are you collecting?

I know you have "things" you collect. For some, it may be tea cups or old cars. For others, spoons, license plates, matchbooks, or magnets from other states. But for a moment I want to talk about the things we collect within us, in our hearts.

For many years of my life I had a giant collection of bitter thoughts and memories. I never got rid of my collection of bitterness until 1996 when I gave it to God. For many years I had a collection of fear that lived within me. It was out of control. I collected hate, and rage. I also had a giant collection of addiction. My addictions started with nicotine and led to water bongs, acid trips, and more. Sometimes our collections are very unhealthy and we need to get rid of them.

I got sick of my giant Coca-cola collection, so when we sold our first house, the lady buying it said she loved it and I left it there! Sometimes you just need to leave the things you are collecting inside of you behind! You need to have strength enough with the help of the Father to get up and walk away from them and never look back. If you need help along the way, your church family and friends will hopefully be there for you. But I can promise you, God is there and will help you through everything.

I said before that when my kids were home, I collected a lot. When they got older, I got jobs to fill my time up and now I don't collect so much. This is how it is with the things inside. If we have idol time we can feed our bitterness with thoughts of anger toward others, but if we keep ourselves busy, we have less time to think on those things.

Here is what I suggest: If you have an unhealthy collection inside your heart and you are filled with idol time, take steps that will help you focus your thoughts on things that will rid you of adding to your collection! Some suggestions would be reading a great book, reading the word of God, reading this devotion! Haha. Be accountable to a friend who has a common interest with you, and perhaps your kids. It's so important to come up with ways to guard your heart of unhealthy collections.

"Above all else, guard your heart, for it is the wellspring of life."
Proverbs 4:23

If I were to pick up all my boxed collections in storage, it would weigh me down. Thank God they are boxed up and put away.

I'm thankful that the collections inside me are put away too. I have given them to my Lord and He gets rid of them permanently!

Stop unhealthy collections.

Dear God,
I am not the same, and I pray for this reader that you change them like you changed me. I don't want to store junk anymore. I honor you today

Deepest Lessons, Darkest Hours

"Why would God allow me to go through all this?" Have you ever asked this question? As humans we want answers, and we want them NOW! Hardship is not easy to go through, but it is part of life.

If you have children, you have disciplined them. Whether they are teens or younger, it's never easy to take something that's important to them away from them in order to have them refocus on what is truly important in life. A few years back, we told our son Jon that for an entire semester of school he had to step down from his band, Exiting the Fall, until his grades came up. It was the hardest thing we ever had to do. He was so upset, and I'm sure the band was not that happy either. But what happened? His grades came back up, and he just graduated from high school not too long ago! Even though it hurt Jon, and us to go through this discipline, it all worked out well in the end.

So back to the question, "Why do we go through hardship?"

> "Endure hardship as discipline; God is treating
> you as sons. For what son is not disciplined by his father?"
> Hebrews 12:7

We need to take the hardships we go through as discipline from the Father. Don't you just love that? NOT! But this is how we must take it as it hurls at us.

> "If you are not disciplined (and everyone undergoes discipline), then
> you are illegitimate children and not true sons."
> Hebrews 12:8

There you have it! That is an intense Word right there! We will be disciplined, and the Father calls that hardship. I hate hardship. But I have to admit that I have learned my deepest lessons in my darkest hours.

My son's band has done very well; they have played SoulFest, which is a giant Christian music festival on the East Coast. Out west they call their giant festival Creation. The band plays all around the local area, so after I told Jon at age 16 that we were pulling him out of the band for a semester, I went in my room and cried because I knew that just killed him. Don't you think the Father feels when we are hurt through that kind of discipline or hardship?

If I have cried and been upset after seeing my kids hurt by the discipline we give them, don't you think the Father in Heaven feels it ten times more? Well, I'm letting you know today, He does.

He hurts when we hurt. Even though He knows we will grow and He will build awesome character in us for going through it, it still hurts Him like it hurt me on my knees crying after pulling my son out of his band. But it's the best thing for us.

> "Our fathers disciplined us for a little while as they thought best; but God disciplines us for our good, that we may share in His holiness. No discipline seems pleasant at the time, but painful. Later on, however, it produces a harvest of righteousness and peace for those who have been trained by it."
> Hebrews 12:10, 11

Today I wait for that harvest. And most the time, the waiting room is painful. Count it all joy, friend. You will learn your deepest lessons in your darkest hours.

Dear God,
Help us all with the hardships that seem to be hurled our way daily. Life can be so hard, but you are ever faithful. I honor you today.

Last Words

If you knew you were not going to be here tomorrow, what would your last words be to those you love? I know to my kids I would say, "Never settle for second best in your life, spouse, and everything you do. Know exactly what it is that God wants, and do it with all your heart." To my husband I would say, "Thanks for taking my dysfunction and making me function!" Then I would give him a French kiss! Haha.

I guess it depends on who you are saying goodbye to. We have left three churches in our 21 years of ministry, and our goodbyes were tearful and hard. It's always hard when you pour into a place and then have to leave. Are you in a time of change right now? It's not easy.

The writer of the book of Hebrews had some amazing last words, or you could call them exhortations. It seems when you say goodbye, you want to highlight things that are of importance. And I just love the things that are highlighted, so let's look at some of them!

The writer starts by telling those he's leaving to keep on loving each other. Then right from that the writer says:

> "Do not forget to entertain strangers, for by so doing,
> some people have entertained angels without knowing it."
> Hebrews 13:2

I love this scripture, and the writer felt it important enough to highlight the fact that angels are among us. I hope you know that today. I don't think I have ever seen one, but this scripture pretty much says we will not know them. They must blend in with everyone at the mall or where ever we are. I bet we all have seen them and don't know it.

Then the writer says, remember those in prison just like if you were their fellow prisoners! I love this. When was the last time you thought of men and ladies in prison? Maybe we should start! God wants to touch their hearts right where they are, too! It says, remember those who are mistreated. Countless billions are mistreated every single day in our world right under our noses. When was the last time you even gave a thought to them?

> "Marriage should be honored by all, and the marriage bed kept pure, for
> God will judge the adulterer and all the sexually immoral."
> Hebrews 13:4

The marriage bed is kept pure by being faithful to your spouse. Here is a thought: I bet you've never read in a daily devotional that God is the one who created the orgasm! God created sex, one of the best things going! It brings much joy to a couple, and God is the one who created it! He is a very creative God in case you have not noticed. The problem is, there are way too many couples who don't communicate with one another in every area of their relationships, including sex. That's why they take off and mess up. Communication is the key. It's very important!

"Keep your lives free from the love of money and be content with what you have, because God has said, never will I leave you; or forsake you."
Hebrews 13:5

So many times while reading the Word I have come across the scripture that says He will never leave us, but it's very cool to me that it's mentioned in the same verse as money! Don't let money rule you.

"Remember your leaders, who spoke the word of God to you. Consider the outcome of their way of life and imitate their faith."
Hebrews 13:7

I love this. In other words, cherish your mentors in the Lord. Imitate them, and in return spill out. We need them!

Hebrews 13 tells us to obey our leaders and submit to their authority, and it also says we should share. To share is simple, but important enough for the writer to encourage. This may be simple, but powerful at the same time. It says that when you share, God is pleased. When was the last time you shared?

Take time today to apply these last words from the writer of Hebrews to your life. Very wise last words.

Dear God,
You are so awesome, creative, and simple. I love that about you. Change us Lord. I honor you today.

When You Fast

Thick juicy cheese burgers and chocolate shakes, tacos and refried beans, watching the game on television with yummy chips, dips, and snacks. We all love food. America is one of the most obese places on this earth, so this proves we love to eat! Fasting has never been my favorite thing to do, but the Bible does not say, "If you fast." It says, "When you fast."

"When you fast, do not look somber as the hypocrites do, for they disfigure their faces to show men they are fasting. I tell you the truth, they have received their reward in full. But when you fast, put oil on your head and wash your face, so that it will not be obvious to men that you are fasting, but only to your Father, who is unseen; and your Father, who sees what is done in secret, will reward you."
Matthew 6:16-18

Fasting is the giving up of food to draw nearer to God. This could be giving up a lunch time, or any time in order to read the Word and pray. I also believe when a pressing need arises, God looks for those that will, "Stand in the gap" for the need and fast and pray. Ezekiel 22:30 talks about how God looked for a man who would stand in the gap on behalf of the land. Fasting goes hand in hand with prayer and the word of God. We see this in Luke 2:36-37, 1 Samuel 1:6-8, Nehemiah 1:4, and so many more places in the God's word.

"So I turned to the Lord God and pleaded with Him in prayer and petition, in fasting, and in sackcloth and ashes."
Daniel 9:3

The longest I have ever fasted was seven days with just water. I had reasons for my fasting. I wanted to Draw near to God and hear His perfect will for my life. He did amazing things in those seven days. Make sure if you are doing a long fast that you wean yourself off food and wean yourself back onto food. I got myself very sick after this fast by eating like crazy as soon as it was over. Don't be foolish, and know what you are doing. There are awesome books you can read to help you.

God will honor your fast.

I want to speak with those of you that say, "What about me? How am I to fast on all this medication and chemotherapy? You do not know my situation!" You are right, I don't know your situation, but God does! A few years back I was diagnosed with Lyme disease. For two straight years I suffered, hardly able to walk. Only those very close to me knew what I was going through. I had a Monday through Friday pill pack that required me to take about 10 pills and supplements in a day. During those two years of meds to kill the parasites inside of my body, I could not fast food. I got so sick if I took the medication three times a day with no food in my tummy. I learned through that, that God sees the heart. He knows more than anyone that it's the thought that counts. I learned to be very creative. We serve a very creative God, so why can't we be creative? I fasted the things I loved most. For you it might be painting, reading, watching a great movie, or something else. I sacrificed those things in my life and fasted from them to draw nearer to God. In other words, I would not sit in front of the television at night, instead I would go and read the Word and pray. God honors that. I hope you know that you can fast from so much more than just food. 1 Corinthians 7:3-5 even talks about fasting from sex! God knows your situation and He honors us giving up anything to draw closer to Him.

Have you ever fasted? Do you have a list of needs that you would love to see God meet? Whenever I take the time to fast, God moves in powerful ways.

Fasting should be part of our daily life. Just like reading the Word and praying. I challenge you today to try a fast and draw near to the one who loves you.

Dear God,
Help us to lay aside all we love to draw nearer to you. Someday we will wish we did this a lot more than we do now. I honor you today.

June 18th

Masks Off!

Every year our youth group hosts a formal event to honor the recent high school graduates where they come up with a theme. Tonight is my son's night, and the theme is Masquerade. I found my daughter the most amazing mask from Italy at a garage sale last Saturday. She put about $25 into it and now it looks just amazing. Right now there are three teen girls here getting ready, and from what I can hear, two are on their way over to get their hair done. The boys have not arrived yet, but they need to get ready too. Teens just crack me up. These girls have been getting ready for the last hour and a half, and the event does not start for about two more hours. They even got fake eyelashes to enhance the extra, mega makeup over their eyes.

My husband and I are going tonight because they will honor our son Jon. We went out today and got some things so we can look just as amazing as the teens! Haha. I remember getting ready for a formal as a teen and the excitement that was in the air. I felt like that today, walking around the mall with my husband and picking out things together. So fun! We will not be wearing masks tonight, but from what I hear many are wearing all kinds of masks.

There is a scripture in the word of God that reminds me of masks. It says:

> "Even in laughter the heart may ache."
> Proverbs 14:13

There are so many people in our world wearing masks, the kind we cannot see. They wear their smiles, laugh, act like everything is under control, but deep down inside they just want to die.

Not everyone is like Job in the Bible, and come right out and say what they feel! Some hide it deep inside. Is that you today? Are you wearing a smile while the entire world thinks you are fine and dandy? Dandy: Now there's a word for you! You need to take your invisible mask off today.

You may not be the kind of person who likes people to see you cry, but I will tell you today, there is power in a tear. Tears show humility. Tears take what's inside, and they turn you inside out so the mask has to come off! There is just so much power in a tear. Do you know God records your tears?

> "You number my wanderings;
> put my tears into your bottle;
> are they not in your book?"
> Psalm 56:8

Tears mean so much, He counts them. Most the time when masks come off, tears come along with the action. You need to know today that's ok. It's time to take your mask off.

Tonight at this youth formal there will be tons of kids walking around with masks on. The sad thing is when they sit down to eat and take their masks off; some will still be wearing invisible masks. If this breaks my heart as much as it does, imagine how much it breaks the heart of God.

Be ever so aware of those around you. First impressions mean nothing. It's only when you get to know someone that you see if they have a mask on. Be careful of your words around others. Even if they have a smile, they may be clinging to the last knot on their rope of life.

I challenge you today: Masks off!

Dear God,
Humble us. Break us. Help the fake to crumble. Masks off, Lord. Thank you for counting my tears. I honor you today.

June 19th

Prolonged Promises

Have you ever been promised something by the Lord? God promises many things, but His time frame is not our time frame. I can remember God's promise to me that certain people I was praying for would come to know Him in a personal way. I did not see some of those prayers answered until over ten years later. His time is not our time.

In Genesis 13:14-17, the Lord promises Abraham that He will give him the land.

"Lift up your eyes from where you are and look north and south, east and west. All the land that you see I will give to you and your offspring forever."
Genesis 13:14-15

"Go walk through the length and breadth of the land
for I am giving it to you."
Genesis 13:17

It almost sounds like it's going to happen right away, but about 680 years pass by and in Deuteronomy 34 we see the Lord speaking to Moses.

"The Lord said to him, 'This is the land I promised on oath to Abraham, Isaac and Jacob when I said, 'I will give it to your descendants.' I have let you see it with your eyes.'"
Deuteronomy 34:4

I did not write out the entire verse! So, the Lord is just letting Moses know that the same promise to Abraham is now his promise hundreds of years later, but he also would not see this promise lived out.

"I have let you see it with your eyes, but you will not cross over into it."
Deuteronomy 34:4

Moses died shortly after. Joshua was now the leader, and the Israelites listened to him and did what the Lord had commanded Moses. God speaks to Joshua in Joshua 1.

"I will give you every place where you
set your foot, as I promised Moses."
Joshua 1:3

"Be strong and courageous, because you will lead these people to inherit the land I swore to their forefathers to give them."
Joshua 1:6

As the new leader, he directed a military campaign to take control of the land God had promised. He took action. He takes the land.

God then puts him in a place where he can challenge the people. He tells them a little history.

"Long ago your forefathers, including Terah the father of Abraham and Nahor, lived beyond the River and worshiped other gods. But I took your father Abraham from the land beyond the River."
Joshua 24:2-3

He is giving the people a choice. Serve false gods like some forefathers, or serve the living God who fulfilled the promise!

"Throw away the gods your forefathers worshiped beyond the River and in Egypt, and serve the Lord. But if serving the Lord seems undesirable to you, then choose for yourselves this day whom you will serve."
Joshua 24:14-15

"As for me and my household, we will serve the Lord."
Joshua 24:15

God is actually using history and the respect that the people had for Abraham and the forefathers as a tool to now help the people make a serious choice of who they will serve. It's just amazing to me that what was promised hundreds of years before was then being used as a tool to draw men to Him.

Why does God do that? Why do so many promises take so long? Maybe because He knows the longer we wait and history passes, the more souls can be touched along the way and brought to a place of choice.

"Not one of all the Lord's good promises
to the house of Israel failed; everyone was fulfilled."
Joshua 21:45

While you sit in the waiting room for your promise, do not forget this story.

Dear God,
We wait. Help us Lord to submit to your timeframe. I honor you today.

June 20th

A Faithful Father

I know for some of you it's hard to imagine a faithful, heavenly Father when your own father has never been faithful. When he has done nothing but hurt you. For you today I write this devotion. You reject the love from your heavenly father because you cannot believe that He won't hurt you in some way. Some of you have been abandoned, abused, rejected, and all you have received is broken promises. I'm here today to tell you there is a God in Heaven who will never hurt you, reject you, leave you, or break His promises to you. He is a faithful father.

To trust in your heavenly Father takes great faith if you have been hurt. It's a risk for some, because they think somehow they will end up hurting again. I'm here to tell you today, take the step of faith. Trust Him. He will never hurt you. He will only be there for you in your darkest hour.

"Never will I leave you; never will I forsake you."
Hebrews 13:5

Some of you were abandoned by your dads. He left you. To forsake means to quit or leave entirely. Did your dad quit on you? Some of you have a dad that is there all the time, as a matter of a fact he is in the next room right now, but the sad thing is he is absent. He may be there in the flesh, but he has never been there for you. I want you to know your Father in Heaven is there in spirit and there for you. He will never abandon you, never. Even when you turn your back on Him and reject Him, He waits for you.

"I will not leave you as orphans; I will come to you."
John 14:18

"The one who calls you is faithful and he will do it."
1 Thessalonians 5:24

He calls you today, He is faithful and He will do what He has promised in your life no matter what anyone says to you.

"If we are faithless, He will remain faithful,
for He cannot disown himself.
2 Timothy 2:13

Disown in the dictionary means to deny the ownership of, or responsibility for someone. You see, your earthly father can do this. He can walk away; he can be *in absentia* right there in the next room. But your heavenly Father will NOT disown you. He will never walk away from His responsibility to you. Never. Take a step of faith today and believe it. Give Him a chance.

He will not hurt you, call on Him.
He will not abandon you, cling to Him.

He will only love you, trust in Him.

Dear God,
I pray for the readers who have a hard time with trust. Who think that reaching to you in faith is a risk. Prove yourself to them God. I honor you today.

Living Sermons

Do you know today the Lord wants to speak through you? It does not matter where you come from, what you have done, or what someone has done to you. God desires to use all people as His mouthpiece. I remember feeling the call of God as a young lady at Bible College. God confirmed my call into full time ministry while I was there. I knew He desired to use me to preach His word. As many years passed, I was licensed as a minister then ordained in 2007. But the truth is, it does NOT take a piece of paper for God to use you! Yes, it shows you are accountable to someone, which is so very important, but the truth is, long before I ever had my license to preach, God was using me. He wants a humble soul rather than a piece of paper. God desires to speak through you. Like David and his last words:

"The Spirit of the lord spoke through me; His word was on my tongue. The God of Israel spoke, the Rock of Israel said to me: 'When one rules over men in righteousness, when he rules in the fear of God, he is like the light of morning at sunrise on a cloudless morning, like the brightness after rain that brings the grass from the earth.'"
2 Samuel 23:2-4

We see in this scripture there were times God spoke directly to David himself and times God's word was on his tongue to speak to others. This is how it is when we walk with God. He desires us to make the most of every opportunity everywhere we walk. We are a living sermon.

Living sermons at home.
Living sermons at the grocery store.
Living sermons at the workplace.
Living sermons at the beach.
Living sermons at the mall.
Living sermons every single place your feet take you.

Yes, God desires we speak the Word, but are you also living it? Do you practice what you preach or are you like so many who are hypocrites? Stop it! Don't even speak the Word if you are not going to live it! And stop thinking you are not good enough to speak His holy word. Until the day you die you will fail him. You will always have to ask for forgiveness. God knew this and that's why He sent His Son to die for our sin. He needs us to be His light and voice on this earth. People need the hope of Christ. If not for that, I would not be alive today.

"How then, can they call on the one they have not believed in? And how can they believe in the one of whom they have not heard? And how can they hear without someone preaching to them? And how can they

preach unless they are sent? As it is written, 'How beautiful are the feet of those who bring good news!'"
Romans 10:14-15

Countless people all over the globe need to see a living sermon, someone who is not only living their life as a light to the nations, but also speaking and taking action to draw souls to God. How can they hear without a preacher! Are you preaching with your words? Are you preaching with your life? Would God be pleased?

"Preach the Word; be prepared in season and out of season!"
2 Timothy 4:2

When seasons change in the Miller home, I box up winter coats, mittens, and hats. I get out the flip flops, bathing suits, and tanning oil. I'm never prepared for winter in summer nor summer in winter. But this scripture says that in every season of our life, good or bad, year round, we need to be ready for ever opportunity God gives us to share His word. Even if that means His word will be the way you live your life.

You can only be ready in season and out of season if you are in the Word every day, soaking it into your life so that it changes you.

Be living sermons today.

Dear God,
Help us to speak your word and live your word. I honor you today!

June 22nd

<u>Keep Your Praise On</u>

Don't tell God how big your storm is; tell the storm how big your God is!

This is the saying my son just had tattooed on his arm. It's such a powerful word.

Since I was a 16-year-old girl it seems I have had one physical storm after another. They just never stopped, right through child birth and even until now, 18 years later. It's always something. But like I have shared in the past, it was in my darkest storms that I have learned my deepest lessons.

It seems the past few weeks have been quite stormy in my life. In the dictionary it says that a storm is a disturbance of the normal condition of the atmosphere. I totally agree. What is the atmosphere usually like around you in your everyday life and what is it like through your storms? Chances are they are so different. Storms are usually very violent and can really shake you. But instead of screaming at God about how angry you are or crying to Him about how you are going to make it through today, it's time to start speaking to the storm! As my husband put it in a text to me this afternoon, "Keep your praise on!"

When you keep your praise on you can be joyful through the storm and speak to it and say, "It does not matter what I'm going through because my God is a big God! He made the universe and there is NOTHING He cannot handle or take care of in my life!"

For chronic pain sufferers, for those who live with fear, for those of you who are in a wheel chair, for those with lost limbs, for those with cancer, for those who have had miscarriage after miscarriage, KEEP YOUR PRAISE ON. God is in control even in the darkest hour. Even in the middle of our storm.

Job kept his praise on when he said:

> "He knows the way that I take; when
> He has tested me, I will come forth as gold."
> Job 23:10

Daniel kept his praise on when he said:

> "My God sent His angel, and He shut the mouths of the lions. They have not hurt me, because I was found innocent in His sight."
> Daniel 6:22

Jesus even kept His praise on.

> "Jesus called out with a loud voice, 'Father, into your hands I commit my spirit.' When He had said this, He breathed His last."
> Luke 23:46

He knew even at His death that His Father was in total control. He was fully God and fully man. Just a few minutes before this we see the man coming out when He says:

"My God, my God, why have you forsaken me?"
Matthew 27:46

He feels forsaken, and in minutes He is speaking to His storm by claiming, "Into your hands I commit my spirit."

Do you see what I'm trying to say here friend? It's not like you will be perfect! But you need to keep your praise on and start speaking to your storms!

Today I did not want to speak to my storms. They made me tired just to think of them. I thank God for a husband who reminded me to keep my praise on today. Cherish the friends that encourage you! When was the last time you said thank you to them?

There is a song that Chris Tomlin sings called, "How Can I Keep From Singing Your Praise?" Part of the lyrics are:

"And though the storms may come I am holding on,
to the rock I cling. How can I keep from singing your praise?"

"I will sing of your love and justice; to you, O Lord, I will sing praise."
Psalm 101:1

Here is your friendly reminder today,
Keep your praise on!

Dear God,
Help us in pain, emotionally and physically. Help us to speak to the storms in our life and be fixed on the fact that you are a mighty God, way bigger than our storms. I honor you today.

June 23rd

Belteshazzar

There are two kinds of dreams: a normal random dream you have, and a dream you know comes directly from God. Most my normal dreams are of me flying or crazy things like that, but the instant I wake from a dream I know comes from God, I have to get up. A few years back I had a dream, and as soon as I woke my heart was pounding, and I knew I had to begin to pray. I asked the Lord what He was trying to tell me. I felt the Lord say to me that I was to call a particular person that had hurt me, and share with them about what happens when we die and how they can go to Heaven. I did not want to do it. I had forgiven this person, but never had I shared the gospel of salvation with them. I did not want to be obedient.

After sharing this with my husband, I knew I had to call. I made the call and spent about 25 minutes on the phone. In obedience to what the Lord told me to do, I brought the person through the book of Romans, sharing that Heaven is a free gift and that all sin and fall short. After about 10 minutes of sharing the Word, I asked if they wanted to pray with me a prayer to ask God into their lives. In just a minute we were praying together over the phone. After our prayer we hung up, and that was the last time I ever spoke to that person again.

About a week later one of my friends who lives near that person was in a store and felt the Lord say to her that she was to go to the exact person I called. That person was obedient and went. They prayed together and read God's word together. After hearing this I realized God was doing a great work in the person I called on the phone.

Less than four weeks later I got a call that that person God told me to call had died. I cannot tell you what went through my heart and mind. What if I had not been obedient? What if I had not made that call? How would I have lived with myself? I believe with all my heart that right now, because I was obedient and my friend was obedient, that that person is in Heaven with God. Walking with Him and talking with Him.

Daniel was a person in the Bible who was gifted at the interpretation of dreams. He was chosen by the King along with some others to serve in the king's palace. He was an Israelite. The Bible says he had no physical defect. He was handsome and he was a great learner.

"Well informed, quick to understand,
and qualified to serve in the king's palace."
Daniel 1:4

They were to be trained for three years and after that they could enter the king's service. When they arrived, the chief official gave them new names. Daniel's new name was Belteshazzar.

Not only did Daniel interpret dreams for the king, but he had dreams of his own and knew the meanings. There were times when the "wise men" could not interpret the king's dreams, but God would speak to Daniel.

> "No wise man, enchanter, magician or diviner can explain to the king the mystery he has asked about, but there is a God in Heaven who reveals mysteries. He has shown King Nebuchadnezzar what will happen in days to come."
> Daniel 2:27-28

Daniel took the time to wait on God and hear from God to direct him.

If you read the first six chapters of the book of Daniel you will see there were many times Daniel was disobedient to the king's laws, but obedient to the God of Heaven. God honored him for that. One day when he disobeyed a law, he was thrown into a den of hungry lions.

> "My God sent His angel and he shut the mouths of the lions. They have not hurt me, because I was found innocent in this sight."
> Daniel 6:22

There were many times God spoke to him to go to the king and he went in obedience. My question to you is this: Have you ever felt that urgency in your heart that you have to call someone? Did you ever have God drop a name in your heart to pray for someone or something? Did God ever wake you in the middle of the night to pray for a missionary? Did you ever feel like someone was in danger? What did you do? Did you pray for them? Call them? Whatever God told you to do, did you do it? Were you obedient? Did you ever feel like a dream was more than a dream, but instead of asking God what it was all about you went back to sleep?

I challenge you today friend, pay attention to your urgencies. Pay attention to dreams that wake you and bug you with an urgent feeling, and pray to God.

I know the person a few years back that I called is with God today because of it. Belteshazzar was obedient and we must be too.

Dear God,
Help us not to ignore urgent feelings and dreams you give to us. It may mean someone's everlasting soul. I honor you today.

June 24th

Glutton Free

It's interesting to me that Daniel's first temptation in the book of Daniel is food.

Did you ever stop to think of food as a temptation? Or as a sin? Do you realize it can become your god, or a sin, if it's eaten with a lack of self-control? The Word says anything that we put before God becomes an idol in our life (Exodus 20:3). The word of God speaks clearly about a glutton.

> "Their destiny is destruction, their god is their stomach,
> and their glory is in their shame."
> Philippians 3:19

Adam and Eve found this out in Genesis 3:1-3. The Word says not only was the serpent crafty, but it also says:

> "The woman saw that the fruit of the
> tree was good for food and pleasing to the eye."
> Genesis 3:6

It was not just about the fact that the serpent lied to her and told her she would gain wisdom; it was also a total lack of self-control. She was tempted by food. She went against what God had told her to do.

It's also interesting that Jesus himself was tempted by food in the wilderness.

> "The tempter came to him and said, 'If you are the son of God, tell
> these stones to become bread.' Jesus answered, 'It is written: 'Man
> does not live on bread alone, but on every word that comes from the
> mouth of God.''"
> Matthew 4:3-4

Jesus had been fasting, and the Bible says he was hungry. If Jesus himself can be tempted in this area, what makes you think you are exempt? We live on food but also on the word of God!

Daniel was not a vegetarian. Daniel 10:3 tells us this, but he did not want to eat the meat at the king's palace because some of the food was offered in sacrifice to idols or blessed in the name of gods. His name might have been changed when he got there by the leadership, but his convictions were not changed. I know today, even in America, this still happens. Even if you have never seen it, it's going on right under your nose. I have eaten in Chinese restaurants that have altars and so have you. I'm not telling you to not eat out and enjoy yourself, I'm just saying be careful. There are so many things in life we can put before God, and one of those is food. It can be the gym for some of you. It can be the television, X-box, facebook, reading novels, boyfriends and girlfriends.

Let me ask you this, have you spent time with God today? Reading the Word or in prayer? What are you doing right now? Have you done that for more than an hour or two? You can't spend time with the God who longs to show you amazing things? Or who longs to touch your family members and missionaries across the nations with your prayers to Him?

I have never been obese, but I know I would feel much better if I took off about ten pounds. I do know one thing; I have self control in this area. If my teens eat a sleeve of cookies in one shot, I have one. I have disciplined myself to not eat things even when I want to. I'm not perfect, and trust me there are plenty other areas God is working on in my life, but it's good to talk about this area because you don't hear about it much. When our appetite is winning and we have no control, it draws some into deep depression and moves them away from God, but when we have control we feel better about ourselves. That promotes a closer walk and relationship with God.

Try to be glutton- free today.

Dear God,
Help us. We need you in this area of our lives. Help us to get our everyday lives under control and realize its fruit of your spirit living within us. I honor you today.

June 25th

<u>The Real Jesus</u>

I don't know about you, but any movie I have ever seen about Jesus portrays Him as this man who is built with pretty nice size biceps, bigger than the average man. Usually in the movies He has a beautiful face with perfect cheekbones, eyes, and lips. And always in every single movie I have ever seen, He has beautiful long hair, kind of like one of those guys on the cover of a romance novel. Am I alone here? Don't you agree? It's like, just because He is God and does miracles and dies for us, he has to be beautiful. The word of God gives us a very different picture of the real Jesus.

"He had no beauty or majesty to attract us to him, nothing in his appearance that we should desire him. He was despised and rejected by men, a man of sorrows, and familiar with suffering. Like one from whom men hide their faces he was despised, and we esteemed him not. Surely he took up our infirmities and carried our sorrows, yet we considered him stricken by God, smitten by him, and afflicted. But He was pierced for our transgressions, he was crushed for our iniquities; the punishment that brought us peace was upon Him, and by his wounds we are healed."
Isaiah 53:2-5

So let's look at this Word. It's a harsh word about his appearance. No beauty, nothing in his appearance that someone would desire him. Think of your friends, usually there is at least one thing that is desiring of them, something that they are known for. Eyes, cheekbones, long legs anything! But the Word says nothing! In this scripture we also see that it says he had no majesty to attract us. The word majesty means supreme greatness or authority, so in other words it's saying that even though he was fully God, you would have never known it. And this to me says He had to be one of the humblest people that ever walked planet Earth.

He was familiar with suffering. Just like pastors see suffering around them all the time, He knew what this was like. Everywhere He went people suffered. But then He was pierced and knew suffering Himself. It's one thing to suffer, but He was also despised, so much so that men hid their faces from Him, and then killed Him. So He did not look like the cover of a romance novel, yet by the stripes He received on His back with a whip, we are healed.

If you search Google Images for Jesus you will see a handsome man. I bet if Jesus were walking the earth today we would not even know who He is. The sad thing is, He came, He died, and He rose, and people still do not know who He is.

It feels wrong to even say this, but the opposite of beauty is unattractive or ugly. Could it be the Savior of the world was ugly and had not one bit of beauty?

Friend this is NOT me speaking, this is Isaiah 53:2-5, just thought I would remind you in case you think I'm going to Hell right about now. This is what the word of God says! Do you think the Father had a bigger plan in this? The Father could have made Jesus the most amazing looking guy ever! He could have blown the romance guys out of the park! There was a reason for this; there is ALWAYS a reason why the Father does what He does.

Could it be the real Jesus was average or below average in appearance to prove a point? Like, you don't have to have one bit of beauty to change the world! Or that God desires to use every single person no matter what they look like.

Friend, I encourage you today, change the world. He longs to use you to touch the lives of people one soul at a time. If you don't know Him today, get to know the real Jesus.

Dear God,
Your ways are not our ways. Thank you for touching the lives of so many. I honor you today.

June 26th

Grumpy Christians

Today I was working at the hospital and it was time to leave. I was tired and could not wait to get home to eat. Not a speck to eat or a drop to drink for eight hours! It was crazy busy. I was waiting outside the elevator and an older man walked up, I would guess about 65 years of age. He had white hair and a white beard, and was wearing a suit and tie and nice shiny leather brown shoes. Very sharply dressed.

I said hello, and he did not even say hello to me, just looked at me with this grumpy look. I felt a bit uncomfortable being that we were getting into the same elevator. We get into the elevator and he was just so grumpy, almost rude, like who am I that I would say hi to him. As I stood there I happened to see a little pin on his shirt that said "Clergy!" Can you even believe that? Who in the world would want to be a Christian if a man like that shared the gospel with them?

Now the truth is I have no idea what he was going through, he could have heard people's painful stories all day, he could have been going to visit his very sick wife on the second floor for all I know! Now, I'm not happy every minute of my life, there are times when I'm down or don't feel like being social, but the truth is if I'm a Christian and someone says hi to me, I will say hi back. I would never in a million years wear a pin that says "Clergy" if I was not going to act like Jesus would. I don't even put the fish on my car because if I speed I don't want to give Christians a bad name! Not that I speed all the time!

I just have a very hard time with what happened today. I wonder if I had a pin on that said I was an ordained minister or clergy if he would have said hi back. Makes you wonder. Why are so many Christians miserable? The truth is God's joy is our strength! We need it. How do we attain it? By soaking your mind every single day in the word of God, and taking time to pray and meet with Him and spending time in praise and worship. I promise you friend, if you are reading His word, meeting with Him, and spending time in worship you will not be grumpy. And if you are, it's not God's will for your life. Now, the only other thing I thought was, maybe he could not hear me? Whatever the case may be, never be like that! He still could have smiled when I smiled at him.

I think when we act like that it gives not only Christians a bad name but God a bad name.

"Rejoice in the Lord always. Again I will say, rejoice!"
Philippians 4:4

"A cheerful heart is good medicine, but a crushed spirit
dries up the bones."
Proverbs 17:22

"Give thanks in all circumstances, for this
is God's will for you in Christ Jesus"
1 Thessalonians 5:18

Maybe it's just me, but if we are to give thanks in all things we actually might have a smile on our faces. I know that most of us have hard times in our lives. We have one right now with our home not selling; I also live with pain every day of my life. But I will choose to be joyful because when we have Christ and He is in control, we are not supposed to be grumpy Christians!

Dear God,
I pray for the reader, that they will take this to heart. I know times are hard, but let them get your word in them to such a point that they will bubble over with your joy! I honor you today.

June 27th

Even In My Sin

I am the kind of person that does not get angry very often. Only two things make me very angry. One is being late for anything. I hate to be late. I like to be at least 15 minutes early to almost everything that I don't have to run myself. If I'm late, it upsets me very much. The second thing is I hate waiting for people. If I'm running late and have to sit and wait for someone, I get so angry. If it's my family I show it, if it's someone else I don't show it, but I pretty much bubble inside. I hate to be late!

My kids are the best ever, they really are. I'm their biggest fan. So much so that I want to go on the road with them and never let them go! God is helping me to let go! It's very hard. But I don't like waiting for them. This morning I got upset because we were only five minutes early to church when I wanted to be at least fifteen minutes early. My poor kids, they see it more than anyone!

I'm usually angry in the car. I think that's one of the only places they ever see me angry is when we are driving somewhere and we are late. I hate even admitting I get angry, but I'm human and I know I get angry about stupid things sometimes. My kids have put up with me for years and I'm not afraid to admit to them when I'm wrong. Sometimes my lack of self control can turn into sin.

Today after church I felt bad that I had been angry on the ride to church, and it made me think about the character of our God. He knows what it means to wait. I'm not quite sure how He does it. The night I had so much to drink that I passed out in someone's bathtub, only to wake too many people coming in and out using the bathroom, He was there waiting for me in my sin. Just like the day I tried to kill myself in my mother's kitchen and I had a divine appointment with a mighty God. It's priceless to me that even in my sin, He was waiting for me.

The Word talks so much about us waiting on Him, but this devotion today is to remind you that He is waiting for you. Maybe you have not experienced His voice yet like John 10:27 talks about. Maybe you are angry and you don't know how to get rid of your anger. Even in your anger He waits for you. That's how much He loves you.

> "And therefore will the Lord wait, that he may be gracious unto you, and therefore will he be exalted, that he may have mercy upon you: for the LORD is a God of judgment: blessed are all they that wait for him. "
>
> Isaiah 30:18

This is such an amazing scripture! His longing is to be gracious to us. Yes, He is a just God, but His patience is like no other. Imagine if God were like me today in the car? What about all the times we were late at doing His will for our lives or late for doing something that He desired for us to do? Or even too late, where we missed the opportunity. Oh how I thank God for His mercy.

What if we waited on Him like He waits on us? That would be amazing.

I hope you see today that He longs so much for you to come to Him, that He is waiting for you, and He has no anger. Anytime that He waited for me, before I knew the Lord, I only felt love. A deeper love than I had ever known. I wish I could be more like that. But I fail.

I'm just thankful He waits for me.
Even in my sin.

Dear God,
Thank you. Help me to wait on you like you wait on me. I honor you today.

June 28th

Rain Down Righteousness

"You Heavens above, rain down righteousness;
let the clouds shower it down.
Let the earth open wide, let salvation spring up,
let righteousness grow with it;
I, the Lord, have created it.
Woe to him who quarrels with his Maker,
to him who is but a potsherd among the potsherds on the ground.
Does the clay say to the potter, 'What are you making?'"
Isaiah 45:8-9

Tonight my dysfunctional past crept up on me and got me all stressed out. I then cried for about an hour. When this happens, and it has not happened in a very long time, I feel like broken shiny glass all over the ground. Then Jesus rains down His righteousness and patches me back together again making me a beautiful mosaic piece of art. Reminding me of His love and that no one is there to hurt me anymore; reminding me that I am now a child of God.

I had to look up the word potsherd when I read this scripture. I love its meaning! Potsherds are fragments of broken pottery. That's what I felt like tonight. God once again was breaking me, because I questioned some things He was doing, and in a sense I quarreled with Him. This scripture indicates there is more than one person/potsherd smashed on the ground. There are many people of God quarreling, or questioning Him. It seems to me that in my hardest cry I feel closer to Him, I feel Him rain down righteousness on me and into my heart and life. It's a breaking of my will, my heart, my control, my pride, and my everything.

As I was doing a study of the word potsherd so I could understand this scripture, I found that potsherds were not just some cheap pottery like you see on the streets of Kolkata. In Kolkata, India you can purchase a cup of tea on the street. It comes in a tiny tea cup that is made of pottery. When you are done drinking the tea you just smash your tea cup on the street. There are broken tea cups all over the streets of Kolkata. When we went there in 2006, I wanted to bring some of these tiny tea cups home and I paid one cent for each cup. But my study of this word said that potsherds had great value, not like cheap Kolkata tea cups. The dictionary said they had the kind of value as if someone had been to an archaeological site and dug up a treasure. Potsherds were priceless.

This made this scripture come more alive to me tonight. When we quarrel with the Maker, and when we do not understand the things going on around us, we are broken, but still priceless. To Him we have the same value of a priceless archaeological find. You just cannot put a price tag on some things. That's what we are to Him even when we don't understand.

Take a minute and read that scripture one more time.

The main scripture at the top of the page was not written to those who did not know God. Isaiah 45 starts by saying:

> "This is what the Lord says to his anointed,
> to Cyrus, whose right hand I take hold of."
> Isaiah 45:1

Just a few verses down you read:

> "For the sake of Jacob my servant, of Israel my chosen, I summon you
> by name and bestow on you a title of honor."
> Isaiah 45:4

So when the Lord is speaking about the potsherds he is speaking to his anointed, those who hold His hand and to the chosen who He gives honor to and summons by name. Could it be the anointed and chosen are smashed potsherds quarreling with God?

Friend, we need to be smashed potsherds on the ground sometimes so He can then rain down righteousness.

Dear God,
Rain on me tonight. I honor you today.

June 29th

Hope

"We have this hope as an anchor for the soul, firm and secure.
It enters the inner sanctuary behind the curtain."
Hebrews 6:19

Sometimes hope is the only thing left to hang on to. My husband and I had our small group ministry today and it seems so many are going through such hard things. Just because you become a Christian does not mean all of a sudden everything is perfect and hunky dory! Needs are great in all our lives! We need hope!

First, I love this scripture because the writer of Hebrews compares hope to an anchor. When a captain drops his anchor, it secures his entire ship. This is what hope does for us; it secures us to know God is in control and we do NOT have to worry. It is firm and secure. It took me a while after becoming a Christian to realize that.

What is all this about entering the inner sanctuary behind the curtain?

Many times in the Old Testament it talks about the holy of holies, where the Ark of the Covenant was with the stone tablets (the Ten Commandments). In the Old Testament, no one but the high priest could enter to offer sacrifices to God. If others entered they would be struck dead. It was the holy of holies.

"The Lord said to Moses: 'Tell your brother Aaron
not to come whenever he chooses into the Most Holy Place
behind the curtain in front of the atonement cover on the ark,
or else he will die.'"
Leviticus 16:2

It was a holy place. All that to say that our main scripture at the top of the page says:

"It enters the inner sanctuary behind the curtain."

What does? Hope does! In other words friend, Hope has no boundaries! Hope enters everywhere and reaches out to anyone!

When the New Testament rolled around and Jesus died for our sin, the Word says:

"The curtain of the temple was torn in two from top to bottom."
Mark 15:38

Now anyone could go to Him, anytime.

Many people in this life will disappoint us. Why? Because they are human people who are

387

imperfect. Hello, that includes you and me!

"Hope does not disappoint us."
Romans 5:5

Just like He will never leave us, forsake us, or hurt us, Hope will never disappoint us. It actually is like a lifeline, or as they so greatly put it, an anchor.

"Blessed is the man who trusts in the lord,
and whose hope is the Lord. For he shall be like a tree
planted by the waters, which spreads out its roots by the river,
Aad will not fear when heat comes;
but its leaf will be green, and will not be anxious in the
year of drought, Nor will cease from
yielding fruit."
Jeremiah 17:7-8

As long as your roots stay in the river, meaning you stay in His word and in communication with Him and keep your hope in the Lord, I promise you today, you will make it! Don't give up!

Dear God,
Let us lean on the hope that has been around forever. I honor you today

June 30th

R-Rated Nation

Maybe I have to take a reality pill or something but the PG-13 movie my husband and I saw tonight was not appropriate for 13-year-olds! We talked about it in the car and then we realized that most 13-year-olds probably see all those things in their own home. I don't know, after I thought about it I remembered that I saw most of it in my own home before the age of 13. But if my kids were that young again I would NOT want them seeing it.

The movie dealt with this one rich kid who sits in front of video games most the day and gets served upon. Many times in the movie he texts his nanny to bring him everything he wants! Then his dad takes him to the country by a lake and he does not know what to do with himself. Man, when we were kids all we needed was a lake and some rocks to skip and we would be there for hours.

Just watching this movie tonight stirred up memories, but also made me realize once again how things have changed so much since I was a kid. When I was in high school there were no computers. I did not know anyone anywhere who had a computer in their home. People were lucky in the late 60s, early 70s if they had a black and white TV. I can remember the time when my Uncle Jimmy made my dad go out and purchase his first TV. They would sit in the back yard with an extension cord hooked up to the television that was sitting on a tray table and watch their sports, smoking cigars.

Back then, if you saw a girl get pregnant in the eighth grade you knew someone had abused or raped her. These day's girls get pregnant in the eighth grade by choice. There are even high school daycares so high school mom's can finish their education. Don't you think we quite possibly could be enabling them? All you have to do is go to the school nurse for condoms; it's as simple as that. What happened to innocence? What happened to purity? What happened to one nation under God?

We do NOT live in a PG-13 society anymore. PG-13 is for the birds these days. This is an R-rated nation. Walking through the mall tonight and looking at all the giant advertisements and what young kids have to look at all the time, its crazy! When we were kids we did not have to deal with all that in our face, around the clock! God help these kids to grow up knowing that they do not have to look like the men and ladies on every giant advertisement to be accepted, loved, and cherished by someone.

All the elementary school kids have easy access to porn. Unless mom and dad are monitoring their computer and cell phone activity like my husband and I did and do, these kids can do anything and see anything they want. If you are a parent you have responsibility.

> "Do not conform any longer to the pattern of this world,
> but be transformed by the renewing of your mind."
> Romans 12:2

> "Flee from sexual immorality. All other sins a man commits
> are outside his body, but he who sins
> sexually sins against his own body."
> 1 Corinthians 6:18

> "Your beauty should not come from outward adornment, such as
> braided hair and the wearing of gold jewelry and fine clothes.
> Instead, it should be that of your inner self, the unfading beauty of a
> gentle and quiet spirit, which is of great worth in God's sight."
> 1 Peter 3:3-4

Just because we live in an R-rated nation does not mean we need to live in an R-rated household! Watching that movie tonight made me realize that what I saw on the screen was no big deal to 13-year-olds. It broke my heart. It breaks God's heart.

Dear God,
Help the youth of today to keep their way pure in this R-rated nation. I pray you raise up moms and dads to guard their kids from things that can damage their emotions forever. I honor you today.

July

July 1st

Many Nails

I saw something today and I have not been able to get the picture of it out of my mind. My son was driving and we came to a stop. I looked to my right and there was an old telephone pole. I have never seen anything like it. There were hundreds and hundreds of old nails stuck in the telephone pole. Some nails were small, some large, some bent, some hammered all the way in. Some nails still had signs of the old poster or paper that it once held hanging from them by a thread. I sat there and stared at this pole. I'm really weird about these things! Hundreds of garage sales, events, and missing pets were part of that pole's history. That one pole has helped hundreds of people.

It made me think about us. When there is history in someone there will be signs of it. If someone pours and pours out into ministry, always taking care of others and never taking care of themselves, they will probably die an early death. Even as we normally grow there are signs of aging in our skin, body, hands, feet, and hair.

I remember visiting a Bible college once. Someone had told me there was this famous lady, who I will not name, living in the dorm. She actually was there to die. She was blind and could not get out of bed. The students spoke of her because even though she was blind, she was known for her prayer life. They said that she never stopped praying for missionaries and people. All the time they could hear her praying. I made my mind up that I wanted to see this lady who had become a part of history there, due to her walk with God. So, I knocked on her dorm room door and went in. I was a little scared; I think I was like 18 or 19 at the time. She looked horrible, like death. Her skin wrinkled and she was a bit jaundice. She could not see me, but she reached out her hand. She began to pray. I will never forget that day.

Seeing that pole today reminded me of this lady. Old, beat up, rusty, and wrinkled. Yet both the pole and this old lady had helped hundreds of people. Hundreds.

The truth is, when we pour out it will take some years off of us, but we need to take care of ourselves. When I die someday I do not want to be like a fresh clean new telephone pole. I want to look like that one I saw today. Filled with heritage and filled with signs of helping hundreds and hundreds of people. No one will ever be able to take the picture of that telephone pole out of my head. I will always remember it.

Just one nail on that pole represented probably at least fifty to one hundred people at an event. Sometimes that one seed that you sow will represent fifty to one hundred people. Do you see where I'm heading here?

If there is one thing I hate more than anything it is planting seeds. Gardening is NOT my thing! I killed every single house plant that I have ever had. Getting on your knees, digging in the dirt, row after row; it's time consuming, it's hard work, and you get dirty. Depending on where you are it can even be dangerous. Like on Cape Cod where ticks hang out on the grass. It's the same with planting seeds in souls.

Mark Buntain was the first missionary I ever worked with overseas. The man heard the call of God and went to Calcutta, India at a very young age on a boat with his young wife and baby. He stayed there his entire life and died an early death. I know living in Calcutta took a toll on his life. Any day that we had ever been there, we had to clean our noses out at night because of the soot in the air. He and many others, like my friends Dale and Beth, give their very lives for the call of Christ to plant that one seed. But that one seed turns into fifty and then one hundred.

In that great city which is now spelled Kolkata, there are now hundreds of ministries that represent thousands and thousands of souls. All because one man planted the seed; one nail in the telephone pole of life. And then another, and another, and another.

It's all worth it in the end.
It's souls.
It won't be easy.
It will be hard.

"No weapon forged against you will prevail."
Isaiah 54:17

Dear God,
Help us; it may take a toll on us. It may even kill us. But it will be worth it all in the end. I honor you today.

July 2nd

History

I love history and I love the show House Hunters on HGTV. Maybe that's why when I was a kid and my grandparents brought my cousin and I across the country, I loved it so. We stopped at every historical thing and saw many Presidents' homes. I love to see history come alive as you walk through a historical home or stand at the grave of someone who changed the world.

I have not yet experienced the history of the Bible by going to the holy land, but someday I hope to. Walking where Jesus walked would be just amazing and seeing where things happened in the word of God.

But I have to say, I am ever thankful that I saw this country when I was 12 years old. I only wish I could have given the same opportunity to my kids.

I remember a trip to Virginia where we visited Mount Vernon, home of George Washington, and Monticello, home of Thomas Jefferson. There I was with queer red sunglasses on and a bonnet (Yes, I said bonnet!). I had a white t-shirt on that said "Virginia is for Lovers"! When looking at the pictures today, I just laugh. But I can remember walking into the homes; the rules were to touch NOTHING! There were ropes up in front of every room. I loved everything about it: The smell when we walked in, the way the heel of my shoe made a rich sound as it hit the floor, the ceilings that were so low I could jump up and touch them. I would stand at the giant rope that guarded a room and just fantasize that I was back in time and that I was the one who had to make the bed or cook the food. My imagination ran wild. I loved every minute of it.

We saw the great corn palace, Old Faithful, the hot springs, California, the Grand Canyon, the graves of many presidents, Valley Forge National Park, and the list goes on and on. I was very blessed to see all that I saw on this trip and I thank God for it.

One thing I love and that took my breath away was Mount Rushmore in the Black Hills of South Dakota. I remember as a kid the thing that stood out the most was a picture I saw of a man standing inside the eye of one of the Presidents when the carving was going on. That's how big these heads are. It took 14 years and 400 people to carve all four presidents. I'm so honored and privileged to have seen that amazing work of art.

I went to Valley Forge Christian College in Pennsylvania. Going to Valley Forge National Park was almost an every weekend thing. I have awesome memories of that Park! Mostly, they consist of making out with my husband in the little forts that were built for the solders that served in the cold. Haha.

Truth be told, there is just something about walking where a great battle happened or where a person who changed the face of our country is buried. Smelling the same smell in a home where someone historical lived, and knowing they smelled that smell too. I know I'm a tad strange sometimes, but these things excited me. They were the people who fought for our independence. And I thank God for each and every single one. For every solder that froze at Valley Forge as I got to know my husband there!

When was the last time you took time to think about what others have done for you? Your life is the way it is due to the sacrifice of others. Your salvation is also yours due to the sacrifice of your heavenly Father. When was the last time you took the time to thank Him too?

Take the time to be thankful. I know we need God in America so much more than ever before, but if you go overseas you will start to be very thankful that you live in the land of the free and the home of the brave.

Take the time to be thankful today that we live in America and for His grace that saves our souls.

"Thanks be to God for His indescribable gift!"
2 Corinthians 9:15

Dear God,
I thank you that as a young girl you let me see history! I pray for the reader that they would not only thank those that gave us independence in this country but that they would thank you for giving us free will and grace. I honor you today.

A Torch

If there is one piece of history that I love more than anything it's the Statue of Liberty. I can't even ride over on the boat to Ellis Island without crying. Just the site of Lady Liberty makes me very emotional. Her symbolism for freedom and international friendship has made me fear for her life many times with all the terrorism that goes on. She stands as a light with her torch lifted high. That's what I want to be: a torch.

France gave the statue to the U.S. in recognition of the friendship France now has with America due to the American Revolution. The statue and its pedestal were a joint effort between America and France. The sculpture who made her face and brought her to life was Frederic Auguste Bartholdi. They did most the work in France, then boxed her up and brought Lady Liberty over on a ship. She was in 350 individual pieces and there was 214 crates full of her. I'm sure they were big crates! The boat arrived in the New York Harbor in June 1885. It took four months to assemble her on the pedestal America had made for her, and on October 28, 1886, there she stood. Her pedestal made by America and Lady Liberty given by France. Both countries had raised funds to make it happen. The tablet she holds says July 4, 1776 in honor of the Declaration of Independence, her torch represents liberty shining bright, the seven points on her crown represent the seven seas and continents, and I bet you did not even know there are broken chains at her feet that represent escape from oppression! I just love that! She stands there as a symbol of teamwork between two countries. Just amazing.

The part on Ellis Island I love the most is The New Colossus, a poem written by Emma Lazarus, chosen for The Statue of Liberty. Around this time of year in July you will always hear me breaking out in loud song singing it:

"Give me your tired, your poor,
Your huddled masses yearning to breathe free,
The wretched refuse of your teeming shore.
Send these, the homeless, tempest-tossed to me,
I lift my lamp beside the golden door!"

I learned the song in elementary school, and I remember even then it stirred me. Not sure why, but it never left me and I get very emotional any time I am at the statue.

William M. Evarts was the one who led the fundraising effort for the pedestal the Statue of Liberty stands on. He also spoke at the unveiling of her on October 28, 1886. At that unveiling he read The New Colossus in its entirety.

There were many ways he raised money, but one way was to solicit works of art, including poetry. One of the pieces he had donated was The New Colossus. It's now on a plaque mounted on the inner wall of the pedestal of the Statue of Liberty. To me it's like a vision statement for America.

Maybe the history of the Statue of Liberty means nothing to you, but I cannot help thinking of every single man and lady that has fought and died for our liberty and freedom around this time of year. I cannot help but think of countries that come together in peace. But most of all I cannot help but think of the fact that we are supposed to be a torch to the world. She holds her torch high.

I want to be a torch. I want The New Colossus to be my theme song! Give me the huddled masses yearning to breathe free, so I can point them to Christ. The world is ready for a Savior, are you ready to lift your torch and not be ashamed? Are you ready to be a light?

> "For you were once in darkness, but now you are light in the Lord.
> Live as children of light (for the fruit of the light
> consists in all goodness, righteousness and truth)
> and find out what pleases the Lord."
> Ephesians 5:8-10

> "You are the light of the world. A city on a hill cannot be hidden.
> Neither do people light a lamp and put it under a bowl.
> Instead they put it on its stand,
> and it gives light to everyone in the house.
> In the same way, let your light shine before men,
> that they may see your good deeds and praise your Father in Heaven."
> Matthew 5:14-16

I want to be a torch.

Dear God,
As Lady Liberty stands holding her torch let us hold up our torch. No matter how black the darkness is around us. Thank you for the men and woman that gave their lives for our freedom. Let us be willing to give our lives. I honor you today.

July 4th

"I Hope You Dance"

Tonight was the most amazing night. We went to see fireworks on the Harbor in Marblehead, MA. There were hundreds of people, but the most amazing jazz and blues band ever. It's amazing to me how people come together on a day like the fourth of July. Talking, laughing, and dancing. After the fireworks were over, hundreds stayed to watch the band. Just the most amazing talent. To me there is a freedom in dancing. I love to dance in church, I love to dance at weddings, and I love to dance in the middle of a park in Marblehead. Why is there such controversy in the Christian community about dancing?

We know the culture of the Jewish people was to dance. And the culture I come from is very into dancing. I have the most awesome memories of me and my Grandmother Gaetana dancing the polka at all the clambakes we went to way back when. From the time I can remember there was dancing in my life. Now I know as well as the next guy there is some inappropriate dancing, but I'm just talking about someone who loves God who wants to dance. I'm free and I dance.

When I dance, I don't care what anyone around me thinks. I think that's a place that God wants to bring us to. When I dance in church or somewhere else it's the same way. Tonight by the harbor on our own blanket I danced, the wind blowing, to amazing music. There is such a freedom in that. I'm sorry if you disagree with me and I'm not out to offend anyone, but when was the last time you danced because you are free?

Tonight as I was dancing I was looking at everything around me, fireworks still going off, as I looked up at the sky all I could think of was, "God you are amazing to create all this!" I just felt such a sense of freedom in me. I hope you know what that is like. It comes from Christ. He is amazing.

"David wearing a linen ephod, danced
before the lord with all his might."
2 Samuel 6:14

"Then Miriam the prophetess, Aaron's sister, took a tambourine in her hand, and all the women followed her, with tambourines and dancing."
Exodus 15:20

People of God, we should be free. There was a reason David and Miriam danced: There were great victories that had taken place.

Friend, I tell you today. If you know Christ and are in relationship with Him, a great victory has taken place in you!

I hope you dance.

Dear God,

Set us free from people's opinions. Set us free Father, to only think of you, may we dance before you with all our might. I honor you today.

July 5th

Second Set of Hands

I have this memory of when I was a young girl, of my mom bringing me to the doctor. I don't remember much about it, but I remember he had a big dark stained wood desk and it was a very formal office. I must have been about eight or so. My mother and I sat in his office, and he told me I needed a shot. I totally freaked out and I remember trying to get out of his office. I finally ran under his desk and it took like three people to get me out from under the desk. That's all I remember, but I was so scared. I guess most every kids hates shots.

Now, about 36 years later, I'm the one putting needles in peoples arms. It's so funny, no matter where I am when I shake someone's hand, I always seem to look at their veins and think to myself, "Hmmm, he has good veins." Or, "Wow, I see no veins. I would hate to have to stick her." I'm sure those of you who draw blood do the same thing. You become vein conscious and always seem to look at peoples arms.

We all go through different seasons in our life and I am not the same person I was 30 or 40 years ago. I don't fear the same things, and I don't rejoice over the same things as I did as a kid, teen, or young adult. It's just amazing to me how God brings us from point A to point B.

If you were to tell me I would be taking peoples blood even as a young adult, I would have laughed. If you would have told me when I was a young teenager that I was going to be an ordained minister someday I would have probably cussed at you and said, "What are you #@%#*@# crazy!" I am not the same!

You are not the same. The things that hurt you back then don't hurt you now. Your struggles are different than they were 10 years ago. You are in a new season. What has God done in your life to get you from point A to point B?

He can take something you are afraid of and make it into something of which you are the leader. He can make you bitter-free. He can help you quit smoking. All I know is everything is much easier, and there is so much more peace with Christ than without Christ.

Tomorrow, I'm working in the holding unit for pregnant moms. I have never worked there before so I went in today for a couple hours just so I'm not walking into it blindly. It helped, but I had brain overload. The nurse that was training me to put the labs into the computer said, "Really, you are just a second set of hands tomorrow." She said that because I probably will never work in that unit again. Then she said, "Some hands are better than no hands."

She was right. Who is your second set of hands right now? To get to point A to point B and be healthy, you need accountability. Tomorrow I will be there as a second set of hands, and even if I don't know exactly what to do I will be a great help to the nurse.

Who are you letting help you? Who is your second set of hands?

Do you even know you need a second set of hands? Yes, we have the Lord. I could quote tons of scripture about how He helps us, but you need real people as well to get from point A to point B and to be healthy. People keep you accountable. Maybe for you it's a spouse you are accountable to, a friend, or a relative?

Who knows what path you are on right now, and how you are going to accomplish your goals? Who encourages you? Who do you talk to about your temptations and struggles? If your answer is no one then you need to seek someone out. Ask God to help you find a mentor or someone that can pour into your life.

I know in my own life I could have never made it from point A to point B without help. Real flesh and bone people pouring into me and loving me even when I fail. I am the person I am today due to those second set of hands, and I thank God for each one.

If your response today is, "I'm good! I don't need anyone helping me," than I give you this scripture:

"So, if you think you are standing firm, be careful that you don't fall!"
1 Corinthians 10:12

In other words, if your response is, "I'm good," watch yourself friend! You do want to make it to point B. With a response like that, some don't make it.

"As iron sharpens iron, so one man sharpens another."
Proverbs 27:17

Who is sharpening you?

"Perfume and incense bring joy to the heart, and the pleasantness of one's friend springs from his earnest counsel."
Proverbs 27:9

A friend is more than just someone to hang out with, they are to give you wisdom, counsel, and hopefully if they are healthy, they are helping to sharpen you and make you a better person.

Who is your second set of hands?

Dear God,
I pray for this reader. If they do not have a second set of hands I pray that you help them to find one; a healthy one or two. Please lead and guide them Father. I honor you today.

July 6th

The Crush

I totally hate soda. My daily drink is water, ice, and fresh lemon juice in it. I could drink it all day and I love it. My husband likes any kind of seltzer water, so between the two of us we hardly ever have anything else in the house. We also have two teens that get sick of no drinks other than seltzer and regular water. A few weeks back my son said he loved Crush. He said there was orange and purple Crush, so I hunted and found it. Their friends were over and one of my kid's friend's said, "I love Crush!" I never even knew there was Crush! I know it's been around forever, but I'm not up on soda.

Tonight at church, my husband shared about a different kind of crush.

"Yet it was the Lord's will to crush him and cause him to suffer."
Isaiah 53: 10

This scripture is talking about the Father in Heaven sending His only son to die for our sin, to suffer, to be crushed. My husband then said, "How could anyone think that God is not for them when they know the Father crushed His only son for us?"

I know many of you are thinking, "Why would He do that?" To humanity it makes no sense. I think this is why the Word says:

"Trust in the Lord with all your heart
and lean not on your own understanding."
Proverbs 3:5

His ways are not our ways. Our ways are not His ways. It's in the crushing we grow most. There are some things in my life right now that I don't understand. But it's in the crushing that He builds my character.

There is another scripture I want to share with you today:

"I want to know Christ and the power of His resurrection and the fellowship of sharing in His sufferings, becoming like Him in His death, and so, somehow, to attain to the resurrection from the dead."
Philippians 3:10

To me, the fellowship of sharing in His sufferings means we will and can suffer in this life, but it also means there is greater purpose in the crush. So that we might attain resurrection!

Are you ready for the crush? What are you going to do when you fellowship and share in His sufferings? Get bitter? Hate? Or rejoice and know that all is under control?

Nothing can touch you unless it has already passed through the hand of Christ first. Nothing.

We must go through the crush in order to attain resurrection at times.

Please know today He loves you, He suffered for you, and He will NEVER leave you through the crush.

Dear God,
Help us when we share in your sufferings. Help us when we are crushed. We need your word on a daily basis. Give us a greater hunger for your word. I honor you today.

One of Those Days

Have you ever had one of those days that are just a bad day? Everything goes wrong, almost everything stresses you out? I am not ashamed to admit that today was one of the worst days I have had in years. It was seriously one of those days!

I have been working my second job at the hospital like crazy, and I had set aside today to do work on my full time ministry job. Last night I was online late at night, and all was well. So this morning was the only day I have to work from home at my computer. I go on and there's no internet. I hate computer problems! To make a very, very long story short, I spent about (and I'm NOT exaggerating) four hours on the phone with troubleshooting! Three times I got disconnected, and when I did, it took about another 30 minutes before I could speak to a real live person. Then I had to tell that person everything all over again! They wanted me using the only computer that actually plugged into the wall, all others are wireless. And that computer is the only one that sat in the heat without air conditioning. So for almost four hours I sat in the basement hot and on hold.

I realized today how very spoiled I am. I was so miserable that after about three hours I just wanted to cry. To top it all off, I could hardly understand the man and lady who were on the phone with me. They were not from this country and I had a hard time understanding them. I cannot even count the times I said, "I don't understand what you just said." It was horrible. It was one of those days.

It's over now! I'm online and running again. I had tons and tons of work emails and many fun emails to catch up on when I got back on. When I sat in the basement today all I could think was, "This is such wasted time!" I was so angry that all this time was being wasted. I could not even get up and clean or anything because I had to sit right there. If there is one thing I hate more than anything it's wasted time. My very favorite scripture in the Bible is:

> "Abigail lost no time."
> 1 Samuel 25:18

But truth be told, my incredible secretary and great friend, Judy Kelch, set me straight tonight! I called her at home to tell her why I did not answer any of her work emails today. As I shared with her about my day and told her it was such wasted time, her response was, "Tana, it was not wasted. You have no idea why God had you going through that! Maybe it was for the person on the other end of the phone." See why I love her so! I let it sink in.

Maybe God was keeping me from an accident? Maybe the kind words I gave to the lady that got my internet going were the only kind words she has heard in a year? Maybe God was making me thankful for what I have by making me sit in the heat? Maybe God wanted me still? Who knows? What Judy said to me tonight was a wakeup call. It once again took the focus off me and on to the bigger picture. We don't often think about the bigger picture do we?

Yes, it was one of those days, but one of those days that God was doing something. Remember, He is always working, moving, planning things years before we see divine appointments happen. That's the kind of God He is.

"And we know that in all things God works for the good of those who love Him, who have been called according to His purpose."
Romans 8:28

As I read this I laughed. We do know that in all things God works! I know this, yet I got myself so upset. Hey, I'm normal, human, and I'm not afraid to admit it. I'm so very thankful today for God's word that I can soak into my mind and heart. And I'm so very thankful for friends and mentors who help me see the bigger picture on one of those days.

Seek out friends and mentors, and soak your mind in His word today. We need it!

Dear God,
Forgive me. Thank you for using my friend tonight to sharpen me. I pray for the reader, God. If they are going through one of those days I pray you help them. Give them a hunger for your word. I honor you today.

The Bigness of God

The other day, I put a blanket out back and lay in the sun. I can't tell you the last time I did this, but it felt great. I don't do well in the backyard. The work and daily tasks are way too close. I'm much better somewhere else. I also get very restless. I flipped over and began to look at the green all around me. I saw all these tiny creatures way down deep in the grass. There was this tiny little bug hanging on for dear life to a blade! All I could think about when I was looking at this tiny bug was God. He looks down on us, and He sees billions of us at once. We are all so busy with our daily lives and yet He looks for one that will spend a little time with Him.

"God looks down from Heaven on the sons of men
To see if there are any who understand, any who seek God."
Psalm 53:2

He is such a big God. Proverbs 30:4 says that He has gathered the wind in the hollow of His hand, wrapped the waters in His cloak and established all the ends of the earth. This is the one who looks down on us; His greatness is beyond our comprehension.

He is also great because in humility He came. He met with those who no one else wanted to meet with. When men wanted to throw stones, He brought peace. I can remember so many times before I knew Him that I would sit and think, "There must be more to life than this." Even in my sin and darkness, His love reached out to me on a personal level. He cared about my desperate, unfair cries to Him when I was in trouble. That's how much He loved me. I wish someone would have told me years before I knew Him that He was looking down on me and waiting for me.

Jesus was walking on a Jericho street one day, and there was a large crowd all around Him.

He stopped under a sycamore fig tree, looked up, and called a very short man by his name.

"Zacchaeus, come down immediately. I must stay at your house today."
Luke 19:5

Zacchaeus climbed the tree because he wanted to see the one everyone was talking about.

When people heard what Jesus said to Zacchaeus they began to gossip.

"All the people saw this and began to mutter,
'He has gone to be the guest of a 'sinner.'"
Luke 19:7

I'm so glad that Jesus spent time with sinners. That He called them by name. I'm so thankful that the Lord called me by name in my sin and darkness. He reaches out to sinners.

What is seeking God all about? You could say that even though Zacchaeus did not know Jesus personally, he was seeking Him when he climbed a tree to get one glimpse of Him. This was a prominent man in the community; a tax collector and very wealthy. I'm sure he did not have jeans and a t-shirt on; yet uncaring of his clothes, he climbs. When looking up the word "seek", in many dictionaries they all said about the same thing: to go in search or quest of. Isn't that what Zacchaeus did? Wasn't he seeking God? I think there are many that don't know Him that are in search or quest of Him and that is why He reaches out to them.

This is where I see the bigness of God. The humility of God is the bigness of God.

> "He sits enthroned above the circle of the earth,
> and its people are like grasshoppers."
> Isaiah 40:22

Not sure where you are at today. Maybe you know Him on a personal level, maybe you don't. But I bet if you are reading this right now you are seeking. He sees that.

As I sat and looked at that bug on a blade, I saw the bigness of God.

Dear God,
You are amazing. Wow. You are so big that you would reach a hand to our level. I honor you today.

July 9th

From Pit to Promise

Do you feel like someone has thrown you into a pit today? Like there is no way out? No hope? Friend, there is always hope with Christ. We go from pit to promise.

Joseph and the prophet Jeremiah were both thrown into cisterns at two different times. In each case, the intention was to kill them. Both men had received promises from God, yet they sat wondering how long they would sit in a pit. I wonder what went through their minds the first few minutes. This was never God's intention for their lives, sitting in a pit. God did not move the hands of Joseph's brothers, or the officials that spoke with the King about killing Jeremiah.

Why do we always blame God for our pits? Most of them are never His intention. Yet He sits with us in them.

Joseph went looking for his brothers and found them near Dothan.

> "They saw him in the distance, and before he reached them, they plotted to kill him. 'Here comes that dreamer!' they said to each other. 'Come now, let's kill him and throw him into one of these cisterns and say that a ferocious animal devoured him.'"
> Genesis 37:18-20

This was not God's intention; it was Joseph's brother's intention. In the case of the prophet Jeremiah it was no different:

> "Then the officials said to the king,
> "This man should be put to death."
> Jeremiah 38:4

> "They have thrown him into a cistern where he will starve to death, when there is no longer any bread in the city."
> Jeremiah 38:9

Once again, it was the officials' and king's intention, not God's intention.

You should go to these scriptures and read both stories. You will see that God was with both Joseph and Jeremiah in those pits. After all, He had given them promises.

God spoke to Joseph in dreams about the great leader he would be and that even his own brothers would bow down to him (Genesis 37:5-8).

> "'Do you intend to reign over us? Will you actually rule us?' And they hated him all the more because of his dream and what he had said."
> Genesis 37:8

409

God spoke to Jeremiah many times about being appointed as a prophet to the nations (Jeremiah 1:5).

> "I appoint you over nations and kingdoms to uproot and tear down, to destroy and overthrow, to build and to plant."
> Jeremiah 1:10

I wonder if those promises came to their minds as they sat in the mud and dirt in a pit? God was with them in the pits. He knew that man could not stop His plan, no matter what kind of stupid things they did.

God smiled.

He knew that this distraction would only make Joseph and Jeremiah stronger for the tasks that lay ahead.

Hang in there friend, and go from pit to promise.

Dear God,
If someone is thinking, "What promise has God given me?" I pray they would read your word and all the amazing promises you have given to us. Give us patience to wait for them, and thank you for sitting with us. I honor you today.

July 10th

Seasons Change

Do you remember going back for a visit to your high school or elementary school after you had been gone for 10 or 20 years? Everything seemed so small. In your mind it was so big, but when you walked the halls and found your locker it was as if the guy from *Honey I Shrunk the Kids* was there somewhere. Maybe you are still in high school. Well, someday you might just experience this.

It seems as we grow in our young years the schools, houses, and places that we have been start to shrink. I can remember in 2006 going to my grandfather's funeral. A few of us cousins took a road trip about three miles down the road to Summit Avenue, to the house all of us 11 cousins hung out at when we were growing up. We knocked on the door and asked if we could walk around the back of the house. I was in total shock. What I remembered as this giant back yard and giant back porch was this tiny living space and tiny back yard. I stood there amazed and tried to picture our family once again in the back yard. Even the front porch and pillars seemed small. Then I realized: I grew up. We snapped a few shots of us in front of the house and left.

We rent the home we are living in right now because our home has not sold yet. Last weekend the kids who lived here two years ago and their parents, the owners, came for a visit. The kids were running through the house two years older saying, "Mommy, my room seems so small." It's just amazing to me as we grow up how things can seem so small.

As I got thinking about it, it's the same in our walk with God, and going from being a baby Christian to an adult Christian. Everything you have gone through just seems so small!

My husband and I have been through quite a few trials in our many years together, a large number of them being my physical well being. Everything from breast surgery to an emergency appendix surgery, getting Lyme disease when we moved to Cape Cod, and the list goes on. My husband is so amazing. It almost seemed like a few years would not go by unless I was having another surgery. For those of you who have sat and waited for test results for days, or who have swallowed the mix to empty yourself out, you know how stressful and hard it all can be. When you are going through it, sometimes you just want to curl up in your bed and go to sleep forever. You daydream about walking with Jesus with your new body! But the interesting thing is now that all that is in the past and we walked through it, it all seems so small. When it was happening it was life altering, but as time passed it became only a small memory.

This is our walk with God.

We will walk through the fire, or as my girlfriend Jody calls it, the "blazing" fire! But some years later that blazing fire will be a tiny spark near a coal somewhere. Only a memory of how God helped you through. It will seem so small.

They are only seasons. Seasons change.

Not sure what you are going through today. All could be amazing in your life, and we should thank and praise the Lord for those times. But if it's not **well with your soul** today, I want you to know that in time this season will seem small. You may not be able to even imagine that right at this moment. I promise you; someday you will look back and see your life-altering moments as small smoldering sparks.

> "The Lord will keep you from all harm. He will watch over your life; The Lord will watch over your coming and going both now and forevermore."
> Psalm 121:7-8

Dear God,
Help us all through good and bad seasons. I honor you today.

The Back Burner

Why do so many Christians put their God-given talent on the back burner? Do you realize whatever it is that you do well you can use for the Lord in one way or another? If you are gifted at carpentry, painting, working with animals, kids, and the list goes on. If you are plugged into a church somewhere you should think about what you're good at, and if they have a ministry for that, plug in. If they don't have a ministry in that area, think out of the box and talk to the leadership about starting one.

There is a church on the western side of our district where they have a man who is a gifted gardener. He got the church planting a giant vegetable garden on the church property. Now the entire church shares the fruit of their labors. They share what they grow and it's a great blessing to everyone. There are so many ways to minister. You can minister to those that don't know God, but you also can minister to those who already walk with Him by blessing them.

There is a couple that goes to our church that have the gift of hospitality; they also run the motorcycle ministry at our church. Every year when the teens go to Soulfest, this couple hosts the teens. It may not seem like much to you, but to the parents who want their kids safe for a week it is a great blessing. And it is a ministry. I think there are way too many Christians who also need to be ministered to and blessed and sometimes we put that on the back burner.

I myself need that. What would I do without it? We all need encouragement and blessing.

I went into nursing in 2003. Going back to school after two kids was not easy, but I knew in my heart I had a gift with people and not many people can handle blood and guts. My mom was a nurse and our home was ER-central. Everyone came knocking on our door from as far back as I can remember with gashes, cuts, broken arms, and much more. Nothing bothered me from day one.

I worked for the first two years at a nursing home. Most of the beautiful elderly had lost their mind. To help them and keep them clean was a ministry. Every time I did it I prayed, "Lord, if this is me someday, please send someone to take care of me like this." After two years of ministering there, I worked three years in maternity. Blood was part of everyday life there. I think it's a God given thing for those things not to bother you. To be in a room for a C-section and not have the cut bother you. If you are a surgeon it is a great talent that you can cut someone open like that because not many can do it. The next two years I worked in surgical holding and now I'm back in maternity. There are times in the middle of the night when I rock some who are hungry and I breathe a word of prayer, "God bless this child, and keep him or her safe." All the talents I have in the nursing area can be used for the glory of God.

If you work a job that is not in a full time ministry position, I want to encourage you today. God wants to use your talents and gifts.

We had a missionary get up at church today and share her passion for horses. She spoke so passionately for training them and being with them. Her husband wanted to be a missionary, so she sold everything that she had that involved her horse hobby, thinking her love and passion for horses would be put on the back burner now that she was going overseas. She knew God had spoken to her that they would be going and that it was His will. To her joy and surprise, when she got there someone begged her to care for their horses and now she works with kids over there who are learning to ride.

Don't you see? Whatever your passion and love is, whatever your talent and gifts are, God wants and desires to use them. You do not have to be a great preacher to be used powerfully for God. You can be anything, or do anything and have the same anointing. God can anoint you to be the best horse trainer there is. God can anoint you to give an 80-year-old woman a bath. God can use you as His hand of peace and comfort. He needs willing hands.

Be encouraged today, move forward with your talents and passions. They are there for a reason, no matter what they are. They are not there for the back burner!

> "For this reason I remind you to fan into flame the gift of God."
> 2 Timothy 1:6

Put your hands to the plow and get off the back burner! Keep fanning and moving forward with your talent and gifts until they ignite! God wants to use them!

Dear God,
Please let everyone know they can do something. No matter what it is, it can be used for you.
I honor you today.

They are Watching

Can you be so confident in your walk with God that you would want other people who know the Lord to be and act like you? I have to say that I would want people to surpass me, to go farther with God, to walk closer with God. Oh to be able to say like Paul:

"Follow my example, as I follow the example of Christ."
1 Corinthians 11:1

Follow my example? Follow my example? This week I have read the Word and prayed. I have walked with God. But follow my example in everything? I'm not sure if I would want to shout that from the mountain top! I get angry, frustrated, and sinful at times, we all do. Wow, to say "follow my example" is a very large and serious statement to me.

In the movie I was watching tonight, the opening quote was, "I don't want to be a product of my environment, I want my environment to be a product of me." I pondered that thought. Would I really want the environment to be a product of me? How about you? Would you want the environment to be a product of you? Well, maybe the God in me.

As I walk and talk in normal everyday life, even in Christian circles, I see back-biting, gossip, and abuse. Sometimes I wonder: Who are the Christians, and who is not? I have had so many people who do not walk with God nor care to tell me that this is why they do not desire to be a Christian: because they have been hurt. If more of us could say, "Follow my example as I follow the example of Christ." I think there would be a lot more happy people in this world.

Truth be told today, I desire to be able to say what Paul said. Do you? How can we work toward it? When I work in a non-Christian environment I desire to work hard, and to prove myself with excellence in the way I work. In some of the places I work there are ungodly things that go on, but I don't enter into them!

I went to lunch one day with a bunch of co-workers. I was very uncomfortable due to the conversation. I did not enter into it. Making fun of people is just not my thing. The Lord died for everyone and therefore everyone is worth something. So, one way to draw closer to Paul's statement is to not enter into sin. Do not enter into the things that go on around you that you know are NOT pleasing to God. They may be in your face on a daily basis! What are you doing? Entering in, or living for God?

The only way we will make a dent in our world or "our environment" for Christ, is to go against the flow. People will notice when you are not swearing or entering into gossip. They will notice when you are not short tempered and when you are going the extra mile for them.

I want to be able to say, "Follow my example!"

When will I ever get there? We all sin; we all fall short of God's glory and grace. But the truth is we have victory in Christ! He is the one, through us, that can change our environment or our little part of the world. Just like I was at that lunch table with my co-workers and I made a stand by not entering into conversation. It's time to make a stand today and go against the flow wherever you are. To make a stand no matter how small it may seem to you.

> "How can a young man keep his way pure? By living according to Your word. I seek you with all my heart; do not let me stray from your commands. I have hidden Your word in my heart that I might not sin against You."
> Psalm 119:9

They are watching.

Dear God,
As we follow you, help us to be able to say, follow my example. Grow us Lord. Make us more like you on a daily basis. I honor you today.

The Teacher

Jesus called himself the teacher.

"He replied, 'Go into the city to a certain man and tell him, 'The teacher says: My appointed time is near. I am going to celebrate the Passover with my disciples at your house.'''"
Matthew 26:18

Everywhere you looked in the Bible He was teaching in one way or another. Sometimes by the things He did, sometimes with the things He said. Everything He did had a purpose in its action.

"Every day He was teaching at the temple.
But the chief priests, the teachers of the law
and the leaders among the people were trying to kill Him.
Yet they could not find any way to do it,
because all the people hung on His words."
Luke 19:47-48

"The people came early in the morning to hear Him at the temple."
Luke 21:37-38

As Jesus lived His life on this earth, His passion to teach rubbed off on the disciples. The book of Acts is full of it. Barnabas and Saul met with the church in Antioch for an entire year and taught great numbers of people there. Peter, in word and action, was a teacher.

"They devoted themselves to the apostles
teaching and to the fellowship."
Acts 2:42

These examples of teaching were given to us for a reason. Even if we are not the most amazing teacher up in front of people, or speak with eloquent words or in parables like Jesus himself, our very life can be a teacher.

My husband is an amazing teacher, so gifted. If I ever have a question on doctrine or the Bible I go right to him. I am an okay teacher, but it is not my comfort zone. I enjoy preaching and evangelism much more. But I believe God has used my life in many ways to teach. The ones the Lord has given me to teach to the most are living right in this home: my two kids. I can say with all my heart the way my husband and I have lived our lives in front of our kids has taught them.

Yes, we have had times of Bible study and devotion as a family, but I think the way we have lived has been the best teacher of all.

The teacher has taught us, and change is the key. My husband and I are no longer the same so this rolls off of us onto our kids. We all need to grow up!

"Then we will no longer be infants, tossed back and forth by the waves, and blown here and there by every wind of teaching and by the cunning and craftiness of men in their deceitful scheming. Instead, speaking the truth in love, we will in all things grow up into Him who is the Head, that is, Christ."
Ephesians 4:14-15

2 Timothy 3:16 talks about how scripture can thoroughly equip us. It says it's useful for rebuking, correcting, training, and walking in righteousness. All these things are taught. He was the master teacher and that rolled onto those who walked with Him and right onto us. If we let it, this rollover effect can change generations to come.

"Since my youth, O God, you have taught me, and to this day I declare your marvelous deeds. Even when I am old and gray, do not forsake me, O God, till I declare your power to the next generation, your might to all who are to come."
Psalm 71:17-18

It's time for you to realize you are a teacher in one form or another. Like me, it may not be your most amazing gift, but who is watching you? Who are you teaching by your actions, and are they what you should be teaching? You are a teacher, so start growing up and teach godliness.
Godliness comes with change in you. God wants and desires to use you in this area. He desires to equip you.

Let Him. He changed me. I thank God for the teacher.

Dear God,
I thank you that I am not the same. Do the same today for this reader. Help them to know that you long to use them in order to teach. Be it through their life or through your word. I honor you today.

July 14th

<u>Former Things</u>

Most of us can remember our past. The first things that come to my mind are things that went on in my preteen and teen years. I think I started smoking at the age of 13. At first, I stole my mother's butts from the ashtray and then we all found ways to smoke. Back then a pack was fifty cents. Now it's up to almost ten dollars a pack to kill your lungs and shorten your life! I remember one summer that I was high all summer from the time I got up till the time I went to sleep. My friend and I put ourselves in some very potentially dangerous situations. When I count the number of times I got in a car with a drunken friend behind the wheel, or the number of times I drank until I passed out, due to memories of abuse and pain I'm so happy I'm still alive. I don't like to remember those former things.

What are former things anyway?

When looking on different dictionary sites, I found the common definition for "former" was "past, long past, or ancient." The memories I shared above are long past and I'm sure you all have long past memories of your own. Some we don't even want to share with anyone due to embarrassment, shame, or just not wanting anyone to judge us. Not too many of us have ancient memories, most of those are in our history books. But many of us also have past memories. Some are from only a few years ago.

> "Forget the former things; do not dwell on the past.
> See, I am doing a new thing! Now it springs up; do you not perceive it?
> I am making a way in the desert and streams in the wasteland."
> Isaiah 43:18

I guess today I wanted to encourage those who struggle with past former things – the things that only happened yesterday or 10 years ago. I talk to countless Christians who have been hurt in the ministry. The church is run by people, normal people, so therefore they are not perfect and some will fall or fail. It's the same with people in the church, we are NOT perfect. That's why it is imperative to keep our minds on Christ and NOT people.

It's crazy to me that when I read the words "former things," my mind automatically goes to bad things. I know there must be someone reading whose mind is going to the positive things first! Good for you! We tend to dwell on the negative. What's wrong with us?!

The truth is, I want to encourage those who have had hurt in ministry. This scripture tells us to forget the former things! Do NOT dwell on the past! We must let God help us to overcome. It's so easy to live in bitterness and to let it change you. Remember your bitterness is not hurting the one you are bitter at, it's hurting you. This word says He is doing a NEW THING! Thank God for new things! It's almost like the next verse is a question, "Don't you know this is happening to you?" or "Do you not perceive it?" I guess that must mean that some of us don't even know or don't even realize that God is doing a new thing. Now to me that is a scary thought! How can we not know God is doing a new thing? Maybe we are too busy being bitter to notice.

It says that God makes a way in the desert and brings streams to wasteland. Friend, only God can do that. In the early part of our years as young youth pastors we were very hurt in ministry and almost walked away from the call of God on our lives. For many years I was bitter and tried to overcome. It's a discipline and it takes much self control. It took years, but God has gotten the victory. Just three years ago the person that hurt us, after all these years, called us crying and said he was sorry. My response to him was, "We forgave you years ago!"

Years before God got victory in my heart He was trying to do a new thing. The problem was I did not perceive it. Or better said I did not want it. I wanted to hold on to the hate, anger, and rage. Many times God wants to do new things, but because we refuse to change, we miss the blessing. God desires to bring streams to your wasteland today! What are you hanging on to?

Forget the former things.

Dear God,
Help us to forget the pains of the past and know you want to use them for purpose in our future. I honor you today.

July 15th

The Perfect Portion

I have come to the conclusion (after spending two days with my friend and co-worker Judy, who just dropped mad weight) that I have to eat much healthier. For dinner last night we had chicken salad with grapes, nuts, avocado, and cottage cheese. It was so yummy. The problem is, when I ate an entire chicken salad sandwich, about a cup of cottage cheese, and half an avocado, I still wanted more! Truth be told, I could have eaten another sandwich, another cup of cottage cheese and another entire avocado! One key to my friend's more healthy living: portion control.

You know what it's like when you eat too much! There is this place to eat on Cape Cod called the Brazilian Grille. It's an all-you-can-eat-place; a must-go-hungry kind of place! There are these Brazilian guys dressed like cowboys with chaps and hats. They come out to you, put their giant sword on your table, and it's filled with meat. Right there in front of you they cut the meat off the bone. They just keep coming! Forget conversation at this place because the cowboys keep coming! Every three to five minutes they are asking, "Do you want lamb? Do you want prime rib? Do you want scallop in bacon? Do you want wings? Do you want...? Do you want...? Do you want...?" I have never left the Brazilian Grille hungry. As a matter of a fact, I usually feel sick when I leave because I eat too much!

You know what it's like when you eat too little! Last night is a perfect example. I told you that I could have kept on eating last night; the reason was that I had not eaten hardly anything all day. The day was busy and I just did not eat. That's not good because then you want to just keep going when it's time to eat! I remember thinking during the day, "Man, I could go for a nice steak right about now!" Not sure about you, but when I am hungry it's a giant distraction for me! Hard for me to work or think about things clearly when I'm hungry. I get grumpy.

Portion control when eating is everything. You also know what it's like to eat at home or out, and you feel just perfect after you ate! Not too full, not too empty. You had the perfect portion! Love that feeling!

Did you know that God is our portion?

> "You are my portion, O Lord; I have promised to obey your words."
> Psalm 119:57

You are the one who chooses the size of this portion.

Although there can never be too much of God in our lives, I remember a time that I fasted so long, and hid myself away with Him, that I became so spiritually-minded that I was no earthly good. There NEEDS to be a balance.

Then like we all have experienced, there have been those times of not reading our Bible or praying and it becomes a distraction in our lives because we need Him and His words to us.

I'm here to tell you today, God is our portion. That feeling you get after a perfect meal when you're not too full and not too empty, that is the right balance for when we walk with our Savior. We MUST have balance. We always need more of God, but without balance we lose wisdom.

Where are you today? Is He even your portion at all? Are you reading the word of God or is your Bible getting dusty? I cannot live without His word in my life. I cannot.

Let Him become the perfect portion in your life.

Dear God,
We so need your word and your presence. I honor you today.

July 16th

<u>Come to My Relief</u>

What has ever come to your relief? Sometimes after an amazing workout, a giant drink can come to our relief. When people are in dangerous situations, other people can come to their relief. I remember as a kid getting very sick and my mom putting the vaporizer by my bed with Vicks® and a washcloth on my head. She always came to my relief when I had no strength and was weak. She always brought comfort and hope for me to make it through my sickness.

Maybe some of you have never had relief. I don't know your situation. Maybe you are living in a hellish circumstance and there is no way out. Someone handed you this book. You hardly feel any kind of relief and if anything, you feel trapped. I've lived in hellish situations, but at least I had my mom. Maybe you don't even have that. I want you to know what the word of God says to you this day:

> "O Lord, hear my prayer,
> Listen to my cry for mercy;
> In your faithfulness and righteousness
> come to my relief."
> Psalm 143:1

You have a promise today my friend that His faithfulness and righteousness will come to your relief. Did anyone ever tell you that? Talk to Him right now like you would talk to me. Be honest and real. You cannot help your circumstance at the moment, but He can help your circumstance. He is faithful to answer if you call to Him.

> "Know therefore that the Lord your God is God;
> He is the faithful God, keeping His covenant of love
> to a thousand generations of those
> who love Him and keep His commands."
> Deuteronomy 7:9

He is faithful. Faithful can mean reliable and if you have never had reliable before, put your trust in Him today. He loves you. He is also righteous.

> "He restores my soul.
> He guides me in paths of righteousness for His name's sake."
> Psalm 23:3

So in both these scriptures we see Him as reliable. A reliable and faithful friend does not leave us when the going gets rough. He is the restorer and the guide. I thank God for His righteousness. In Ephesians 6 we read about the Armor of God. In verse 14 it talks about the breastplate of righteousness being in place. So, not only does He restore us, but He will protect us. Begin to ask Him to come into your life and make a change in your circumstance.

Even when we sin, He is always there with His faithfulness and righteousness to bring relief and wash us clean. There is no rest after a sinful act, until we go to God. To know He still longs to guide us, restore us, and protect us, and that he is reliable and will never leave us brings me peace and hope.

I thank God for His mercy. The mercy that Psalm 143:1 talks about, how would we live without it?

Come to my relief today God, I want all you have for me.

Dear God,
Through so many years you have been my relief. Make yourself ever-faithful to this reader. I honor you today.

<u>Caught in the Crossfire</u>

Those of you who have grown up in abusive homes or homes filled with anger know that many times as a child you get caught in the crossfire. The sad thing is, we are way too young to understand yelling, smashing, and harsh anger. But you are caught like a crab in a net.

This is the deck of cards you were dealt. It's not God's fault, it's called human will. God has nothing to do with it. Men sin, ladies sin, and thus is life.

I'm sure in one way or another all of us have been caught in the crossfire during a season in our lives. My husband and I have always made sure not to talk about church problems with our kids, or in front of our kids. Never! If you are in ministry and reading this, I have met way too many Pastors' kids that walk away from God due to hearing all the church junk that they do not need to be hearing. Their little ears should not deal with that crossfire at all! Nor should their ears have to hear your fighting. It confuses them, puts fear in their hearts, and it is a total lack of self control on your part.

> "Guard what has been entrusted to your care."
> 1 Timothy 6:20

Are you guarding your kids or children that are in your care?

I was watching a movie today where gangs were shooting at one another. The man holding the gun would aim for his target and then in defense the other person would get ready to shoot. Common people on the street who had nothing to do with their fight were getting shot. This is EXACTLY what happens when you fight in front of your kids, or get angry and spout off what you are angry about to others. Many more can get hurt than who we are aiming for. Crossfire is very dangerous.

What about Christians who hang out together? Someone starts talking about someone else, and they don't think before they talk. Just their conversation alone is shooting crossfire. And many times I have witnessed people getting hurt from it. Be ever so careful in conversation. Conversation can become crossfire. On many occasion I have been hurt by it.

> "Set a guard over my mouth, O Lord;
> keep watch over the door of my lips.
> Let not my heart be drawn to what is evil."
> Psalm 141:3-4

Did you notice something in this Psalm of David? David is praying that he will stay pure in his words. When was the last time you prayed for yourself and your lack of self control? Most of the time when we think about self control we think of ACTION! In other words we have to be disciplined and not do this or that! It's so much more than that! When was the last time you actually took the time to pray about your self control issues? To pray about all the bullets you shoot on a daily basis where people get hurt in the crossfire? When? We need to pray about our weaknesses. This is how God changes us.

"A gentle answer turns away wrath, but a harsh word stirs up anger."
Proverbs 15:1

"A hot tempered man stirs up dissension, but a
patient man calms a quarrel."
Proverbs 15:18

I hope you're not caught in the crossfire today. But more than that, I hope you're not shooting the bullets.

Dear God,
I pray for not only myself, but for the reader. I pray we would give you everything, even our words. Help us to live as not to hurt anyone else. It's a normal thing for those who have been hurt to want to hurt others. Break that in us, Lord. I honor you today.

Backwards Grace

Some of you may know the story of Paul and Silas being stripped, beaten and then severely flogged in Acts 16:22-26. After this happened they were thrown into prison. At midnight, Paul and Silas were praying and singing praise songs to God.

"Suddenly there was such a violent earthquake that the foundations of the prison were shaken. At once all the prison doors flew open, and everybody's chains came loose."
Acts 16:26

This is a famous story in the word of God, but let's look a little deeper and go backwards in Acts 16. The reason they were in prison was because Paul became troubled by a slave girl who had an evil spirit. She followed them for many days and was shouting things about them. Just like you and I would be, he was sick of it, and spoke to the spirit:

"'In the name of Jesus Christ I command you to come out of her!' At that moment the spirit left her. When the owners of the slave girl realized that their hope of making money was gone, they seized Paul and Silas and dragged them into the marketplace to face the authorities."
Acts 16:18

This story too, is a famous story in Paul's missionary journeys. Going backwards again in Acts16, starting at verse 11, this is where Paul meets Lydia. Lydia is one of my favorite ladies in the word of God. Paul and Silas heard about a prayer meeting that was going on, so they went.

"We sat down and began to speak to the women who had gathered there. One of those listening was a woman named Lydia, a dealer in purple cloth."
Acts 16:13-14

Lydia was baptized that day with all the members of her household. She started holding meetings in her home. She was the hostess with the mostess. So up until this point we see a miracle happen in prison, demons being cast out, and Paul and Silas touching countless lives along the way! So much so that churches are being started.

Going back even further in Acts 16 we see Paul and Silas being totally led by the Holy Spirit.

"When they came to the border of Mysia, they tried to enter Bithynia, but the Spirit of Jesus would not allow them to."
Acts 16:7

"Paul and his companions traveled throughout the region of

Phrygia and Galatia, having been kept by the
Holy Spirit from preaching the Word in the province of Asia."
Acts 16:6

So on top of everything that had already happened we see them hearing from God and being led by the Spirit.

I shared all this backwards history with you for a reason, and I hope it touches your heart today.

Right before Acts 16, Paul got into what the Bible calls a "sharp disagreement." So much so that he parted the company of a friend.

"Barnabas wanted to take John, also called Mark, with them, but
Paul did not think it wise to take him, because he had deserted them in
Pamphylia and had not continued with them in the work.
They had such a sharp disagreement that they parted company.
Barnabas took Mark and sailed for Cyprus, but Paul chose Silas and left."
Acts 15:37-40

We know that our flesh and the enemy are what build walls between us and our brothers and sisters in Christ. No place here does it say there is any reconciliation between Barnabas and Paul before they left for their journeys. This just touched my heart.

I hope you know today that no matter what state of unforgiveness you are in, no matter how angry you are, God still wants to use you. As we see here, He will still guide you, the enemy will not harm you, He will use you to touch souls, and He will still do miracles! Even in our failures and sin, He longs to use us to be a light for Him. I like looking at things backwards in the Bible; it paints a much bigger picture of the mercy and grace of God.

God wants to bring peace and healing in our relationships, but what a wonderful thing to know that even when we are not there yet, He still wants to use us.

Dear God,
Forgive us and heal our relationships. I honor you today.

428

<u>Mrs. Berry</u>

Not sure why my mind got thinking of Mrs. Berry tonight. I wish so bad I would have taken a picture of her and I together, all those years ago. The truth is she was my friend from when I was around the age of 10, and as a young girl I did not think to have a picture taken.

Mrs. Berry lived in my next-door neighbor's basement. They had converted it so she could move in. She was their mom and mother in law. She was getting old and they wanted to care for her. I don't even remember how my relationship with Mrs. Berry started, but I cherish the memories.

She was a very healthy thing in my life. She would show me pictures and tell me stories of when she was young. My guess is she was about 70 or over when I began to spend time with her. I'm sure her heart was filled with joy to be spending time with a child.

In time, permanent walls got put up, and this became Mrs. Berry's home for the rest of her life. We would do crafts together and she would make her way around the few rooms she had, to show me little tokens of her past. As a child this was so healthy for me, and I wish more children would spend time with the elderly. It helps kids not to be scared of seeing an older person and it brings joy to the elderly.

I remember the day my mom told me Mrs. Berry had died. I sat in my room and cried all day. I'm in my middle 40s now and I still cherish these memories of spending time with an older woman.

This would add to my passion years later of working at a nursing home and starting services there. Each Christmas, along with the teachers, we would bring the children from our school to sing songs through the nursing home. The joy that filled the halls! They just love when someone will take the time to care or give time. Many ladies were widows, some in their right mind and some not, but it did not matter when the children came.

Today I want you not to forget anyone over the age of 60. I know we don't hear this much, but we need to reach out to them and touch their lives like they touch ours. I hope today it makes you think of someone possibly in your own family who you have not spoken to in a very long time, or someone you know in a nursing home. When was the last time you went for a visit.
I know it's hard, and sometimes nursing homes are not in the best shape, but you will bring joy to someone's heart.

> "If anyone does not provide for his relatives, and especially for his immediate family, he has denied the faith and is worse than an unbeliever."
> 1 Timothy 5:8

I know in many cases this scripture is so hard to read. My next-door neighbors lived it by taking their mom into their home and caring for her until the day she died. It's even harder when you have relatives and immediate family who have hurt you.

> "Do not rebuke an older man harshly, but exhort him."
> 1 Timothy 5:1

I want to end with another story. My beautiful grandmother who I loved with all my heart died in a nursing home. I am her namesake. We had a close bond. Her mom and I would sit and talk English and Italian together as she rocked in my grandmother's chair. I have so many wonderful memories of my grandma: The smells in the air when you would enter her home, the many times she would slip me hundred dollar bills when her time was getting short.

Eventually, I began to see pictures of her not looking like the amazing lady I knew, and I made a choice that I was not going to see her. Biggest mistake I ever made. In my mind I had many reasons. I never saw her again until she died. I say that because I don't want you to live with regret. I do live with regret over this. No matter how I felt I should have gone, even if it was hard on my heart.

There are elderly all around us. My current next-door neighbor's name is Anna. I would guess she is about 80. The times that I do go there to visit she lights up! Just like Mrs. Berry used to light up when she saw me walk in the room.

Who can you bring joy to today? Don't forget the elderly.

Dear God,
Thank you for these beautiful people who many times are forgotten. Help us to find wonderful creative ways to reach out to them, and to teach our kids love toward them. I honor you today.

Crumbs

Yesterday my kids were told that their life was pretty much over until the house was clean! No computer, television, going out and doing things until the smell of Mr. Clean was in the air. My daughter started cleaning, and my son came home from work with two friends to help! Are you laughing? Sounds like an 18-year-old, huh? I did not pass it up because the basement, where he lives, was pretty bad! I could hear loud music, so I went to check on things in the basement. When I went down to make sure they were cleaning, Jon was in his room putting things away, Jamie was fluffing pillows on the sofas and Trevor told me he was "hardcore vacuuming!" I had never seen someone "hardcore vacuum" before, but it was pretty interesting. Haha! These kids just crack me up. Within a few hours the aroma of Mr. Clean filled the house once again.

And once again I felt whole. There is just something about a clean house.

Then last night all the teens came from the beach to my house. Matthew works at a local fast food joint, so he brought a ton of fast food for the kids, and they raided the kitchen, and then the basement, trailing the beach sand stuck on their shoes through the house. I'm trying to make this fun to read for you!I actually love having these kids here and would not give it up for the world, they are wonderful. I went to bed before all the teens left.

I woke up this morning, came downstairs to make my desperately needed java, and noticed that there were crumbs everywhere. I stepped on something with my bare foot and noticed it was all over the floor. Ah, my floor was now the beautiful beach. My kitchen table had evidence of chicken, salt, burgers, you name it! I walked down to the basement to see how many kids were actually in my home. You never really know till morning! These kids are wonderful and they do have boundaries when they sleep here. I trust them 100 percent.

I was up at 7:30am, came back up the stairs and just started laughing. I will miss all this in two years when my second goes to college! I love them all. As I was wiping down the kitchen table, it got me thinking. Those of you who read this everyday know I'm a very deep thinker. It made me think of our lives. No matter where we go or what we do every day, we leave crumbs. Crumbs are a fragment of something left behind.

What kind of crumbs are you leaving?

Fragments of something left behind can be good or bad. Encouragement to your co-workers is good, and my clean beautiful floors are good. Beach sand all over my newly clean floors is bad, you yelling at your family for an hour is bad. Do you see where I'm going here? Your character is leaving crumbs, where ever you go. How are you living? Here are some crumbs that you want to leave:

"For this very reason, make every effort
to add to your faith GOODNESS;
and to goodness, KNOWLEDGE;
and to knowledge, SELF-CONTROL;
and to self-control, PERSEVERANCE;
and to perseverance, GODLINESS;
and to godliness, BROTHERLY KINDNESS;
and to brotherly kindness, LOVE.

For if you possess these qualities in increasing measure, they will keep you from being ineffective and unproductive in your knowledge of our Lord Jesus Christ. But if anyone does not have them, he is nearsighted and blind, and has forgotten that he has been cleansed from his past sins."
2 Peter 1:5-9

We can clean up the bad crumbs in our life if we want to, just like I cleaned up all the crumbs around my house this morning.

Good crumbs, bad crumbs, you choose.

Dear God,
Help us to leave Godly fragments wherever we go. I honor you today.

July 21st

His Hassock

I was having fun today looking through old pictures. I was looking at pictures of my siblings and cousins as teens hanging out in my parent's house that they owned in Albany, New York. What killed me most was the furniture! A lazy-boy chair and couch with these big bright colorful flowers and orange couch covers on top of them. It was so funny! The curtains had those little pompom balls hanging off of them! The lamp shade was like an orange-red and all of us kids were crammed in the basement, not giving a rip what it looked like! We just wanted to all be together as our teenage hormones raced into early next spring! Besides, those were the colors back then. But I noticed something while I was looking through these pictures that I did not remember; this round dark green footstool. I stared at it for a while and tried to remember it but could not. These pictures were almost 26-years-old when I was 18! I can hardly remember what happened last year, let alone 26 years ago! Haha.

As I got to thinking about the footstool I started to wonder, out of all the pieces of furniture there are, why does the footstool have so many names? It's so strange! Footstool, footrest, ottoman, and hassock all mean the same thing. I looked it up and began to read about them. It was so interesting, even back in the 17th to 19th centuries there were so many names for them! The smallest ones they made back then were not more than 12 inches tall and were mostly used for children. These were called crickets. The ones 12 inches tall to 20 inches tall were called different names such as: misses stools, table stools, or stools to sett on. Maybe there are so many names today because back then they kept giving this strange piece of furniture new names all the time! Some things never change. I read that in 2008, *Country Home Magazine* made the footstool one of the top ten collectibles in the world!

I was trying to remember all the footstools my husband and I have had through the years. We had these two matching comfy chairs that both had their own ottoman. I wish I had them now! We had a big giant footstool that went with the couches down in our basement that I gave away last summer because it took up so much room. And all of us have had makeshift footstools as we put our pillows on the coffee table while watching a good movie! It's comfortable to put our feet up and get cozy.

"Heaven is my throne, and the earth is my footstool."
Acts 7:49

"This is what the Lord says:
Heaven is my throne, and the earth is my footstool.
Where is the house you will build for me?
Where will my resting place be? Has not my hand made all these things,

and so they all came into being, declares the Lord."
Isaiah 66:1-2

It's so cool to picture this! The Bible even says in a ton of places that He will make our enemies a footstool for our feet.

"Sit at my right hand until I make your enemies
a footstool for your feet."
Psalm 110:1

It's a comfortable place when you do not have to live in fear of your enemies anymore. God wins. It's a place of peace and rest, the evil one has already lost.

It made me think about creation. If the world is His footstool then His intention was to have it be very comfy. His intention in the garden was peace and not sin. But He gave man free will and we blew it. This is why He gave us His son, in place of our sin.

The thought that I want to leave in your head today is that He still says that the earth is His footstool. Just because we blew it doesn't mean he no longer wants to relax with His creation. I love my relationship with Him. I don't put on any masks. He knows EVERYTHING about me and I talk to Him and tell Him exactly what I'm thinking. When I'm mad, sad, filled with grief, happy, confused, and the list goes on, I tell Him. He loves me anyway. He already knows we are not perfect, yet He wants to put His feet up. He loves us that much.

I'm glad I saw that round, dark green hassock in my old family pictures today. It reminded me of my relationship with my heavenly Father.

He loves His hassock!

Dear God,
This is such a cool way to look at things. As we rest with our feet up, may we always think on that. I honor you today.

July 22nd

God Shelves

When you walk through the streets of India, you see, hear, and smell so many things. I will try to paint a picture for you: Never-ending horn honking and the sound of motor bikes if you are near the city; soot in the air; around every corner on the street, a fire brewing yummy Indian Tea; people cooking on every corner; fruit stands on every corner; beautiful clothes hanging everywhere of any color you can think of; People crowding in on you, asking you to come to their shop.

One thing will catch your eye wherever you go: the makeshift altars in the shops, streets, and homes along the streets. Many homes have a "god shelf" where all the pictures of gods are lined up. Along with them, a picture of what the world thinks Jesus looks like. Sometimes you think this is just overseas, but most of you know that there are places where we eat right here in America where altars are set up right in front of us.

Today my husband and I went to Salem, Massachusetts. We live right next door, but never go. So we made a point to check it out. As you know, Salem has a rich history. It's called Witch City. We walked for hours; there are so many shops and places to eat. We had a total blast. I saw a bag in one of the shops today with a $25 price tag on it. I bought the same exact bag in India for three dollars, so that kind of made me laugh. But everywhere you went, no matter what store you were in, there were all kinds of gods. Just like in India, the gods were mixed in with pictures of Jesus. The truth is, all of the pictures of Jesus that we see in America show this attractive guy with long hair that looks like he should be on the cover of a romance novel. The real Jesus in the word of God was not attractive.

> "He had no beauty or majesty to attract us to him,
> nothing in his appearance that we should desire him."
> Isaiah 53:2-3

But yet there are all these pictures of America's Jesus, mixed in with gods, all over Salem. Alongside of them were real crystal balls and all kinds of witch stuff. Most of it is there for for sale as souvenirs. I did not realize how many people come to Salem just to see these sights and its right next door to me.

> "You shall have no other gods before me."
> Exodus 20:3

It's so easy to walk through countries in our world, or stores like in Salem, and judge others.

But here is the truth friend, anything that we put before God can become another god in our lives. Anything.

We need to stop pointing fingers at others and look at ourselves!

What kind of things are you spending your time doing every single day of your life, as your Bible sits and collects dust? Hours upon hours of gaming, playing on facebook or the computer, reading books, painting, selling on eBay®, crafting, and the list can go on and on and on. I'm NOT saying these things are bad at all! I do many of them, but I'm just saying that if we have time for other things, then we have time to spend with God!

Taking two hours a day to get my daily devotions together has been a great sacrifice this year. I have had to give up things to dig into God's word every single day. I have had to meditate on my days, and think of lessons I have learned. It has been a discipline and it has taken self-control. At times I have felt like I am a carrot and God is peeling me, one peel at a time. He's taking the junk off and making me clean and ready for what is to come. Sometimes it's not a fun place to be, but it makes you see your own god shelves.

> "These men have set up idols in their hearts."
> Ezekiel 14:3

> "You have forsaken me and served other gods."
> Judges 10:13

> "Worship the Lord your God and serve Him only."
> Luke 4:8

Think about your life. Are you putting anything before God? What has accumulated on your god shelf? Maybe it's time to do some serious dusting.

Dear God,
Help us to always put you first, to never judge others until we look at our own lives. Help us to spend our time with you first! I honor you today.

Solitary Places

Solitary places. Hmmm, what's the first thing that comes to your mind? First thing in my mind is our little waterfront log cabin in Maine that we rent every year. We light a fire in the morning down by the lake with our coffee and stay there all day, reading and drinking coffee. All you can hear is the loons and our black lab, Arwen, jumping in and out of the water. The kids take off in the canoe to do some exploring and it's just the most amazing solitary place. Our family looks forward to it every single year.

But there are other kinds of solitary places.

> "Jesus often withdrew to lonely places and prayed."
> Luke 5:16

There is a solitary place of prayer. It can be a beautiful cushioned seat at your church, a comfy oversized chair in your home, the corner of your living room, or like Jesus, your solitary place of prayer can be a lonely cave somewhere. Most of the time in a solitary place, you are alone and it is not always easy. Being alone can be healthy or dangerous.

There is a story of Jesus healing a demon-possessed man in Luke 8. The man who was possessed by a legion of demons lived in the tombs. As soon as he saw Jesus, he cried out and fell at His feet. The demons screamed:

> "I beg you, don't torture me!"
> Luke 8:28

This man lived under the total control of the evil one. One thing I found quite interesting about the entire story is that many times this man had been seized, and chains were put on his hands and feet. The town knew he was not safe.

> "He had broken his chains and had been
> driven by the demon into solitary places."
> Luke 8:29

Read that again! This tormented man, "had been driven by the demon into solitary places."

The devil himself will bring you to solitary places. There are many evil things that can happen in a solitary place! Most men and women are NOT always accountable in their solitary places! My family makes every effort to be accountable in their solitary places. On every single cell phone, computer, and lap top we own, we have an accountability program, where even if someone went on something bad, and then deleted it, you would see all of that on the monthly report that gets sent to you! You must make sure you stay accountable in your solitary places, friends! And make sure your kids are accountable as well! All can fall into temptation and sin no matter who you are!

I remember as a child, the different places that I was molested in were solitary. As I got older, I knew that these places I was brought to, by two different men, were solitary man caves used for sin. My first memory of one of the solitary places was at the age of two; I did not have that memory until years later when I was married with children of my own. I could tell you in detail what both rooms in two different homes looked like. For ten years I was brought to solitary places away from anyone else so man could use me. When there is a mix of the devil, your own flesh, and a solitary place, you have a bad mix.

Solitary places can also be places of great victory in your life! When you go through a time of fasting and prayer, you are usually alone and God begins to speak into your life. When was the last time you went to that solitary place? After all, this is one of the reasons we were created, to have fellowship with Him!

"Very early in the morning, while it was still dark, Jesus got up, left the house and went off to a solitary place, where He prayed."
Mark 1:35-36

"When you pray, go into your room, close the door and pray to your Father, who is unseen. Then your Father, who sees what is done in secret, will reward you."
Matthew 6:6

What does your solitary place look like today? Would you want the world to see it? Is it a good or bad place? Is it a healthy or unhealthy place? What can you do to go from unhealthy to healthy? What is stopping you? God longs for us in solitary places.

Dear God,
Make our solitary place a healthy place that will change us for the good. I honor you today.

Babble Not

"And when you pray, do not keep on babbling like pagans,
for they think they will be heard because of their many words.
Do not be like them, for your Father knows what you need before you
ask Him."
Matthew 6:7-8

This scripture intrigued me. This verse is right before the famous prayer, the "Our Father." It's talking about hypocrites who pray standing in synagogues and on street corners to be seen by men (Matthew 6:5). One version of the Bible uses the words "vain repetitions" instead of babbling. The online dictionaries all call babbling pretty much the same thing: foolish or meaningless chatter.

It's so interesting to me that the scripture says, "And when you pray do not keep on babbling." In order for that to be written, I guess there must be many Christians who babble on, in vain repetitions or foolish and meaningless chatter! A believer who's main intention is to be heard by men. Wow. I wonder how many times I have done this in the past. I wonder how God hears our prayers. I have seen movies before portraying God hearing our prayers and sometimes, He hears everyone at once and then it will focus in on one person. I don't know how God hears our prayers but I know He hears them. If you study this chapter, the babbling is linked to pride of heart. God cannot honor that in us. I have been there and I was not balanced. Thank God I am not the same.

So if this is what he doesn't want, what is it that He does want? Sometimes fewer words are better. More is not always best.

"Be still, and know that I am God."
Psalm 46:10

How do we know He is God when we are still? It's in those still moments that we hear His voice. (John 10:27) We are quiet and not talking. We are trying to hear and working to calm our hearts. It's in this place of humility that we avoid babbling. It's in this place that He molds us into what He wants us to be. It's called full surrender.

The "Our Father" prayer that almost everyone has heard at least one time is a very simple prayer. It's a prayer of humility and a guide on how to pray. Let's take a look at it?

"This, then, is how you should pray:
Our Father in Heaven, hallowed by your name,
Your kingdom come,
Your will be done
On earth as it is in Heaven.

Give us this day our daily bread.
Forgive us our debts,
As we also have forgiven our debtors.
And lead us not into temptation,
But deliver us from the evil one."
Matthew 6:9-13

The prayer begins with praise and worship to God; honoring Him for who He is! When was the last time you started your prayer time with praise and worship? Try it soon!

Then we ask the Lord to meet our daily needs. Trust me; He knows our needs better than we do. We don't have to say much about that! We then ask Him to forgive us of our sins. I do this on a daily basis, and I hope you do too.

It talks about forgiveness. Have you forgiven? Examine yourself today. It's not easy, but your unforgiveness is only hurting you.

"Lead us not into temptation, but deliver us from the evil one." Straight and to the point! If you notice there is a ton of direction or "meat "in this scripture, and not a lot of meaningless chatter!

Truth be told, no matter how we pray, God is going to hear us. You need to know that He hears your heart first! He knows your intentions.

Babble not.

Dear God,
Teach us to pray in full surrender; humble, and ready to listen. I honor you today.

Bother Me

"Then Jesus told His disciples a parable to show them
that they should always pray and not give up.
He said: 'In a certain town there was a judge
who neither feared God
nor cared about men.
And there was a widow in that town
who kept coming to him with the plea,
'Grant me justice against my adversary.'
For some time he refused. But finally he said to himself,
'Even though I don't fear God or care about men,
yet because this widow keeps bothering me,
I will see that she gets justice, so that she won't eventually wear me
out with her coming!''
And the Lord said, 'Listen to what the unjust judge says.
And will not God bring about justice for His chosen ones,
who cry out to Him day and night?
Will He keep putting them off?
I tell you, He will see that they get justice, and quickly.'"
Luke 18:1-8

Jesus loved to tell parables, He shared this one to encourage His disciple's hearts to always pray and not give up! This parable reminds me of one of my favorite movies of all time, *The Shawshank Redemption*. In *The Shawshank Redemption*, Andy, a smart young man, earns his way to work in leadership. He decides he wants to expand and improve the prison library. Most everyone laughs at him, because it has never been done before. He had a dream. He makes a choice to write a letter a week to the state senate for funds. The movie shows how faithful he is at writing and checking to see if any mail has come for him. Finally after six years a shipment of new books comes for him with a check for funds to purchase more books. The letter states that they now consider the matter done and do not want to receive any more letters from him! The scene ends with Andy joking and saying, "Now I will send two letters a week."

I shared that because God does honor those who are faithful! Over and over the word of God confirms His faithfulness. This movie proves it to be true in other areas as well. Andy waited six years for his check from the state senate, but it came. It came because he faithfully wrote letters and drove them crazy. The scripture up above tells the story of how the widow kept bothering the judge asking him for help. She DID NOT give up. The judge finally says, "I will see that she gets justice, so that she won't eventually wear me out with her coming!" Too many times we give up in prayer. Too many times we think there is no more hope, or, "He is not hearing my prayers!" But the truth is, He hears every prayer and things happen in His time.

When was the last time you bothered God? When was the last time you went to Him so much that He had to take notice? When was the last time, like the judge said, that you wore Him out with your coming? Why does it seem all those times are when we are in great need with a sickness or urgency of some kind? Why can't we be urgent in our prayer for our families, friends, and needs? Being urgent in prayer is being faithful. When we are urgent we cannot wait another day! We must go to Him. Andy was faithful in writing his letters once a week, but I hope and pray you go to Him every day! Your urgency could save someone's life.

Body of Christ, we must take heed to this scripture, and pay attention to the message Jesus was trying to get across! If every single person who loved God acted on it, we could change the world through prayer. He longs for us to cry to Him day and night!

Pretty much the Lord was saying, "Bother me!"

Dear God,
Forgive us for our unfaithfulness. Help us to be urgent in our prayer life. I honor you today.

July 26th

Bug Spray and Band Aids

We know we are on vacation when we get to the little log cabin on the lake that we rent every year. We are in the middle of nowhere. It's so beautiful here that I cannot even begin to explain it. Right now the only sound I hear is the chimes blowing in the wind. In the early morning and around dinner time, the loons will kick in and I will know I am at my Heaven on earth. The gas lanterns are all ready for tonight and we are trying to get the coffee brewing now. I see God here in the amazing nature and creation all around. Down by the water if you look to the right, you see the beautiful mountains, something we do not have close to my house. I love to just sit and look at all these things that are eye candy to me. I see God everywhere. There is just something about a giant lake, mountains, the quiet, and a percolated cup of coffee in my hand.

Last night on the other hand, well, that was a tad different. My husband told us to put everything we wanted in the truck by the front door because we were leaving at 5am this morning. Packing and preparing is not always fun. We were all yelling across the house, "Hey, did you pack this?" and "Did you pack that?", figuring out what food to bring and not to bring. There is so much preparation when we come here because we rough it a bit and we need to make sure we have everything we need.

Think about the last time you went on a trip. Maybe you did not rough it, but you always made sure you had every single thing that you needed. You get out all the luggage, and if you're like me, you start to make lists and piles of things to pack. I know the girls will relate when I say you need to know what you will wear every single day. Here, I don't worry too much about that, because no one sees me but the cows and the loons! You have your hair care, face care, contact care, special foods, coffees, and the lists go on and on. Here the most important things are bug spray and band aids! Although, my laptop and books are next in line.

There is a place we are all going to someday, it's our eternal home. Have you stopped to think about it? The book of Revelations speaks clear on Heaven and hell. Many people joke about hell, that they will pass the beer around and it will be one giant party. Sorry, that is not what the word of God says. It will be a place of eternal punishment and sorrow.

"If anyone's name was not found written in the book of life,
he was thrown into the lake of fire."
Revelation 20:15

Not sure what you think, but that does not sound like my beautiful lake here in Maine. There are so many more scriptures on hell in the Word. You should check them out one day.

> "But man, despite his riches, does not endure; he is like the beasts that perish. This is the fate of those who trust in themselves."
> Psalm 49:12-13

Have you ever come upon a perishing beast? Its stench can be smelled a quarter mile away. But Heaven is a free gift; all you have to do is open it. It's a place of perfect happiness and eternal communion with God. Have you ever been perfectly happy? That is very hard to find on planet Earth, but Christ gives you a joy that is beyond our understanding, even in the darkest hour.

Reading in Revelation 4, here is a mini description of Heaven: The one who sat on the throne had the appearance of Jasper and Carnelian. A rainbow, resembling an emerald, encircled the throne. Surrounding the throne were 24 other thrones. On those thrones sat 24 elders. Before the throne was what looked like a sea of glass, clear as crystal. I could go on and on with so many more things that the book of Revelation says, but you will have to read it for yourself. The best part is this:

> "The twenty four elders fall down before Him who sits on the throne, and worship Him who lives forever and ever. They lay their crowns before the throne and say: 'You are worthy, our Lord and God, to receive glory and honor and power, for you created all things, and by your will they were created and have their being.'"
> Revelation 4:10-11

We will be with Him and that's all that matters!

In preparation to come here to Maine, I thought about preparation to meet my maker. He asks for nothing more than to open the gift He has freely given to you, and in full surrender, try to live every day by His word. I promise you, you will be forever changed and no matter what comes your way He will walk through it with you. There will be no face care, eye care, and hair care! I will have a new body, the Word says. I'm sure we ALL say "amen" to that one! I wonder if there is a wish list! Haha.

The most important thing in preparation for Heaven is not bug spray and band aids; it's a pure and humble heart ready to receive all He has for you. It's that simple. I promise you, my beautiful lake here in Maine with the awesome sound of loons, cannot even begin to compare to what He has for us. Have you made your choice? He lets us choose. Are you ready?

Dear God,
Examine our hearts. I pray every reader would choose you. I honor you today.

I Took a Walk with God

Sitting on the outside porch at our little cabin in Maine, you can look down and see the water, but you cannot see how amazing it is until you actually walk down there. There are about fifty little trees that block your sight from the water and amazing mountains. As I sat here today looking down there, trying to see my husband and dog swimming in the lake, it made me think of dreams that God has placed in my heart.

I know they are going to be amazing, I know how beautiful they will be, but I can't see the bigger picture yet. Trees or daily life can block my view, but they are only there to build character and amazing potential in me. The incredible thing is even with fifty trees in the way, I still see the lake sparkle and I can see its beauty. It's amazing, and nothing is impossible with God.

In my devotions here, reading the word of God and another book, it has helped me see that I am living for the goals and dreams of tomorrow. Somehow I have made myself think that tomorrow's dreams are much more important and fulfilling than today's walk through daily life. I find myself working and always striving for tomorrow's dreams, but what about being fulfilled and content with today? Making myself believe that somehow tomorrow will be bigger and better can totally distract me from today! Until this trip, I never even knew I was like this. I love how God can blow you away and grow you, even twenty five years into your walk with Him.

I took a walk with God today, and thought about all that I read.

I let it sink in and it changed me. This is what it's all about friend.

Today is just as important as your big dreams and goals. As I walk down to the majestic lake, I stop along the way to look at the flowers and beauty. Somehow I seem to miss all that when my eye is on the sparkling lake. When my mind is constantly is looking to what's ahead. Don't miss out on your daily walk; there are so many doors of opportunity where God wants to use you. If you are so distracted by what lies ahead in your life, you will miss out on opportunities, and souls may not be touched along the way by your life!

I don't want you to give up on your dreams and goals. For you, maybe it's being a nurse or owning your own store. Maybe it's teaching a class or winning the giant pumpkin prize at the fair.

Our dreams have been placed there by God and He wants to grant our hearts desires. Whatever your dream in life is, just make sure you don't miss out on the daily walk along the way. I have realized here that there are things I have missed out on because my mind was on where the next stop is in this life! I need to live to the fullest where I am! I need to focus on the fifty trees that block my sight from the lake, or the beauty and things I will learn on the path to it. They will only grow me, change me, and make me ready when I reach my dreams. There is NOTHING wrong with dreaming! There are so many dreamers in the word of God!

There is a movie that I love with all my heart: *Yentl*. There is a scene in the movie where the man looks at the lady and says, "What more do you want?" Her response is, "More!" I find myself like this. I'm only in my mid-forties and I have already seen so many of my dreams come to pass, but I find myself wanting more! This is not a bad thing, as long as your motives are not for self but for the purpose of Christ, and as long as on the walk to your dream you are not distracted by the dream itself, that you don't live for today.

Maybe like me, you need to take a walk with God today and think on these things. Don't miss out because your eye is on the dream.

"Be wise in the way you act toward outsiders;
make the most of every opportunity."
Colossians 4:5

"Trust in the Lord and do good;
dwell in the land and enjoy safe pasture.
Delight yourself in the Lord and
He will give you the desires of your heart."
Psalm 37:3-4

You cannot enjoy that safe pasture if you are not living life to the fullest today. Take a deep breath and live! Today is just as important as tomorrow. And today will grow you!

Dear God,
Thank you for changing me once again. I pray for this reader, that you speak to their heart and meet their needs. I honor you today.

What Do You Have To Give?

Do you remember as a kid doing the Spirograph craft? Back then we would take the plastic pieces and pin them into the board with straight pins. Then we would take little round discs and put them into the plastic piece. With our colored pens we would move the round plastic disc around the bigger plastic piece making a beautiful design. Round and round and round we moved the little disc until we saw a beautiful picture on our paper.

And thus, the seasons of our life.

Sometimes we feel like we are going round and round and round. Not moving anywhere, but what we miss sometimes is that beautiful picture God is creating.

In the Miller home we have had good and bad financial seasons. There was a point years ago, when my children were in strollers and I stood in food pantry lines for our food. I remember during that time someone had given us a second car. Now it was not the greatest, it had a hole in the floor that we put a plastic mat over. But I had asked the Lord for a second car many times so I would be able to take the kids places. My husband had gone to prayer that night at church, when he came home he told me that God had spoken to him to give the second car to a family in our church. I was upset, but knew he had heard from God. So we gave it away. I began to pray again. Within one week a dear friend of ours whose husband had passed away, walked up to my husband and handed him the keys to her husband's Volvo. I'm talking heated butt seats! God had honored my husband's giving. God gave us a car beyond our imagination. He will always meet your needs, but when you give, He will give back overflowing.

Then there were seasons in our life when God had blessed us in an amazing way financially. We purchased a home on Cape Cod, a fixer-upper. We fixed it up, and within nine months the house jumped one hundred grand in value. We sold the home and walked away with a check for more than my husband and I make combined in one year. We put that money down on a dream home, one half mile from the church where we were pastoring. We were feeling very blessed, and whenever we could we were blessing others: Making meals, giving money, gifts, time. If someone was in need we tried to help in whatever way we could.

I want you to take note that even when we did not have money, when we were struggling for our daily bread, we still gave. We gave what we had to give even if it was not much. There is a measure of giving that every human soul has.

Some time has passed and God told us it was time to move, to leave our beautiful home that I thought we would be in for many years. We walked where He told us to walk and now that home still has not sold. We were put back on the Spirograph board and our major time of financial blessing is gone. But we still give. We give our tithes to God and we give what we can, when we can.

> "Do not withhold good from those who deserve it,
> when it is in our power to act. Do not
> say to your neighbor, 'Come back tomorrow'
> when you have it with you."
> Proverbs 3:27-28

We may not have a ton of money to our names, but we will be a family that gives as long as we live. I hope and pray you live by this scripture. I wish more people did. God wants to use you to bless others that are in need.

What do you have to give today?

Dear God,
No matter what season this reader is in may we be givers. Give us giving hearts. I honor you today.

July 29th

Extra Vitamin D

Earlier this morning I was trying to write and I could not think about what I wanted to write about. I read the Bible and prayed, but nothing. I decided to wait until later and now I know why. What a day. Quite possibly the worst day I have had in quite a while. I hate days like that, don't you?

I had my agenda for the day: Go to the doctor, bring my son to work, go get my check, go to the bank, get a 70th birthday card for my mom, and the list went on. Somewhere in there was going to be the gym and some down time. Well my agenda was stopped in a flash! Sometimes God puts us in a place we do NOT want to be! He has his reasons, not sure of all of them right now, but He has His reasons.

I went to the doctor at about 1:30pm with many other things on my mind. I think my brain is in its comfort zone when I'm triple-tasking. It's just the way I tick. I'm not hyper, but I am high strung! Haha. So I came out from my appointment ready to roll on to the next task, and turned the key to a totally dead car. I mean, it just clicked! Click-click-click! No turnover at all. I called my husband to tell him I was calling AAA. Little did I know that he was home, and that his truck was doing something funky too! Even if I had needed him to rescue me, he probably would not have been able to! Sigh, when it rains it pours! For some reason it always rains and pours during vacation for the Miller family! Imagine that!

I was thanking the Lord that it was only my battery! It's only four years old, but it was totally fried! They did a starter check and checked almost everything else and all was well! AAA put a new battery in, and I was ready to roll again! Now, let's talk about the waiting room!

I came out of my appointment at 2:20p.m. AAA did not arrive until 4:30p.m.! For those of you who have triple-tasking on the brain most the time, you know that I did not do well in that situation. To top everything off, it was 92 degrees and I was in the hot sun. I could not go into the building because it was way too far away from the car and I did not want to miss AAA if they showed up.

Little did I know it would take two hours for them to arrive. So I leaned on my car for two hours, asking God why I was getting this extra vitamin D! All I could think about was my tasks.

Sometimes when we run with many tasks, Jesus says, "Halt!" I never understood the quote, "Stop and smell the roses," because they always made me sneeze! So there I stood, waiting with many tasks. He was trying to show me something. After looking at the clouds for two hours I think I got it. It was no major word from God, no life changing moment, just a simple, "Rest, I'm in total control."

I remember a moment like this, years ago. My daughter was six years old. She was quite ill and they made us bring her to Children's Hospital in Boston. After nine months of hard testing they found out that her gall bladder was not working! She needed major surgery to have it taken out. We were very upset. I remember one time, when I left her at the hospital and went outside waiting for when they needed me again, I sat on a bench in front of Children's Hospital in tears. I remember seeing mom after mom bring in their sick children. Some had tumors on their heads, others had tubes coming out of everywhere, and some had cancer. Jesus had me on that bench, for that one hour, for a reason. I then really started crying, and they were not tears of sorrow, they were tears of joy! God had put me in the waiting room to show me instead of feeling sorry for what we were going through I needed to rejoice! No, it's not fun thinking about that fact that your child is going in for major surgery, but Angela did not have tumors or cancer or any of the other things that I saw that day sitting on that bench.

Getting extra Vitamin D is NEVER fun if it's not a planned thing, but God has His reasons for everything. Who knows, the AAA guy said my battery was so corroded on the inside, maybe on my next long trip I would have been stranded somewhere? Maybe He was keeping me from a bad situation? Who knows, but I do know everything happens for a reason. He halted me today.
Not always fun, but much needed, even if I didn't know I needed it. Even if I didn't want it!

> "Rejoice in our sufferings, because we know that suffering produces perseverance; perseverance, character; and character, hope."
> Romans 5:3-4

So can we equal the waiting room or extra Vitamin D time to sufferings? When you tick like me, the answer is yes! Even if my nose is burnt tonight, I know something was produced in me today like perseverance, character, and hope. You can get bitter or better.

How about you? Need some extra vitamin D?

Dear God,
My nose hurts. I honor you today.

July 30th

<u>OCD Always Hope</u>

Do you live with someone who is not well? Perhaps they have obsessive-compulsive disorder (OCD), filled with anxiety and involved with hoarding. Perhaps they have so much hate due to past hurt that they take it out on you, or verbally abuse you. Maybe you do not live with them, but they are a close friend or family member. Every time you spend time with them it hurts your heart because you want so badly to help, but do not know how. Maybe this person is you. Maybe it feels you are caught in a trap and cannot get out.

First I want to say no matter what you or your friends are going through, God loves you. So much so that He sent His only son to die for your sin and my sin. I hope you see today, this is how much you are worth, that the God that created the universe sent His son to die for you just the way you are right now. Did He intend for things to get obsessive-compulsive? No. Did He intend for anger and bitterness to take over? No. But He loves you. Do you hear me? He loves you.

He loves us in our anger, He loves us in our lack of control, and He loves us in all things. Thank God, thank God, thank God! That's all I can say.

> "But God demonstrates His own love for us in this:
> While we were still sinners, Christ died for us."
> Romans 5:8

I thank Him for His great love today.

As of late, my heart hurts. I love many who are hoarding, who are not well mentally, and who live in obsessive-compulsive situations. Some are very near and dear to me. Many times I tried to help by going and trying to make a dent in cleaning and helping, but that does not get rid of the compulsions that are down deep inside of someone.

Many years ago I had a friend, we will call her Lori. On the outside I would guess she came from a clean home, or was taken care of by someone. One night she called me very suicidal, instead of calling 911 and having them do a well check, I grabbed a friend and headed to her place, I had never been there before. When we arrived, the door was locked and there was no answer. Because I was already there and concerned for her safety, I had the land lord open the door to do a well check with us. Lori was not there. When he opened the door I was in total shock. You could not see the floor. There was rotting food everywhere. It was not just a hoarding situation; it was a board of health situation. Worse than anything I had ever seen on television or in my lifetime. I would have never known. It broke my heart. She was out with a friend and was drunk, and that is why she called me suicidal that night. She was not in her right mind. She was out of control. But God still had a deep love for her.

In the past month I sat with someone I love. How it hurt for me to realize once again that this person was not mentally well, hoarding in an organized way, and out of control. I just want to help so badly, but the truth friend is sometimes we cannot. All we can do is pray. God does hear our prayers and I have seen people with OCD completely be totally changed! It takes hard work and dedication, but it can be done. God DOES hear our prayers for our friends and family who need it. God even hears your prayers if I'm talking about you. Cry out to God, and ask Him to direct you to someone who can help you, then begin your search for that resource! When we are out of control we need help. God is there, but we need accountability and council, we cannot live without it. It is nothing to be ashamed of. This is the path to wellness. God desires wellness and health in your mind and in the minds of your friends and family today.

It will take time.

If you have a friend or family member today like this, you need to love them. Give them a listening ear, a hug, a prayer, and resources. They need to make the calls and ask for help, but you can provide phone numbers and resources. You can even sit with them while they are on the phone and hold their hand.

We need to love all, because He loves all.

At some point in our lives we are all out of control. God is the one who brings order to that. God is the one who brings hope to that.

> "Against all hope, Abraham in hope believed
> and so became the father of many nations."
> Romans 4:18

> "Be strong and take heart all you who hope in the Lord."
> Psalm 31:24

With the right resource for help, and God by your side, your life and the lives of anyone can be changed forever! I have seen it with my own eyes friend.

There is always hope.

Dear God,
Thank you for taking my dysfunction and making me function as a healthy person. I honor you today.

Men Among the Myrtles

"Then the man standing among the myrtle trees explained, 'They are the ones the Lord has sent to go throughout the earth.' And they reported to the angel of the Lord, who was standing among the myrtle trees."
Zachariah 1:10-11

"During the night I had a vision and there before me was a man riding a red horse! He was standing among the myrtle trees."
Zechariah 1:8

Before reading about Zechariah's vision today I had never even heard of a myrtle tree. It intrigued me. I began to do some studying. One thing I found out is that myrtle trees naturally look like they have been pruned. They are beautiful in shape and pretty much look perfect.

In Isaiah 55:13 the Lord uses the myrtle tree as a sign of hope.

"So this is my word that goes out from my mouth:
It will not return to me empty, but will accomplish what I desire
and achieve the purpose for which I sent it. You will go out
in joy and be led forth in peace; the mountains and hills will burst into
song before you, and all the trees of the field will clap their hands.
Instead of the thorn bush will grow the pine tree, and
instead of briers the myrtle will grow."
Isaiah 55:11-13

The myrtle tree is used here to represent something positive, instead of briers. If you get caught in briers, you will be cut up and hurt. "But instead of briers, the Myrtle will grow," is what the Word says. That's why I find it so cool that in Zechariah's vision, Jesus Christ on the red horse, and the Angel of the Lord is standing among the myrtles; a tree that won't hurt you, a tree of hope and safety.

In Zechariah we see an amazing picture, the Angel of the Lord is standing among the myrtle trees and we see angels reporting to Him.

"They are the ones the Lord has sent to go throughout the earth."
Zechariah 1:10

The Lord is the sender, and the Angel of the Lord receives the reports from the angels, an amazing picture. Then right after the angels report, we see the Angel of the Lord goes right to God. In Zechariah 1:12 we see this. It reminds me of Job 1.

"One day the angels came to present themselves before the Lord, and satan also came with them."
Job 1:6

I won't speak about Job chapter one, but we see that angels and the evil one must report to God. The evil one, satan, brings pain and hurt, and the angels bring acts of kindness, messages from God, and they minister and serve us as the Lord speaks to them. We don't even know it half the time.

"An angel of the Lord appeared to Him in a dream and said, 'Joseph son of David, do not be afraid to take Mary home as your wife, because what is conceived in her is from the Holy Spirit.'"
Matthew 1:20

"Are not all angels ministering spirits sent
to serve those who will inherit salvation?"
Hebrews 1:14

God is in total control and even the Angel of the Lord in Zechariah began to pray for the people that the angels told him about.

"How long will you withhold mercy from Jerusalem
and from the towns of Judah?"
Zechariah 1:12

God himself prays for us! Read Romans 8:26.

God is the one who sent the angels out to "check on things!" You are in very good hands, my friend. Very good hands.

As I sat tonight and let this all soak in, all I could think about was the fact that God even placed Zechariah's vision in the perfect place; a place that represents hope, the opposite of pain and hurt. He always sets everything in its perfect time frame and spot.

Are you worried today? Are you trusting in Him? There is no need to fear today. No need.

Dear God,
You have reminded me once again you are in total control of everything. I honor you today.

August

August 1st

Town Herald?

On our vacation this year we just sat by the fire most the day. It was Heaven. We made the tiny walk back to the log cabin for bathroom breaks, cups of java, and to stretch our legs, but I just wanted to go back to my spot right on the lake. Every time we go to Maine I buy sparklers. My kids are getting a little old for them, but I'm the one who really wants them! We cannot purchase them where we live in Southern New England, but they are on every shelf in Maine. This year I got four big twelve-packs. I did not realize it until that night that I did not get normal sparklers. The first one I lit was more like a bottle rocket. They were colored: green, red and gold. Very cool. Anyway, we got to the point that night where we were throwing entire boxes into the fire and watching the big explosion of colored flames.

When it's pitch black by a lake and you are hearing the night sounds, you want the fire high so you can kind of see around you. At least I do, because I would not want a wild animal sneaking up behind me. Anything we threw in the fire was pretty much totally destroyed; even soda cans would melt right in front of us. The fire would hurt anything that came in contact with it. I had to get a very long stick for my marshmallow because I could not get near enough without getting burnt. My son was becoming a pyromaniac, and at that point I knew it was time to retire inside with my oil lamp!

> "Without wood a fire goes out;
> Without gossip a quarrel dies down."
> Proverbs 26:20

This scripture compares gossip with the wood you put on your fire. The more gossip, the hotter and more dangerous things can get. And just like the things I threw in the fire, gossip will burn and hurt people along the way.

Years ago in ministry, when I was what I now call "a people pleaser," I had an experience that taught me a great lesson. A young dating couple in our church was fighting, and being the peace maker that I am, I thought I could help with the drama. I entered into gossip with her as she shared her side of the story and I entered into gossip with him as he shared his side. In the end, they both made up and then told everyone how horrible I was for being on both sides. All that to say my heart meant well, but because I entered into the gossip, I got burnt. Gossip can only sting in the end, and it bites like a snake. The more you enter into it the more it will destroy.

This scripture reminds us that without gossip a quarrel dies down. I don't care who you are, even if you have been in ministry all your life, there has been a point where you have entered into some form of gossip. Sometimes, even when people tell you things and say, "Just pray for them," it can be a form of gossip. The truth is they just wanted to be the first to share the new news!

We would do good to live by this scripture:

> "Keep your tongue from evil and your lips from speaking lies,
> Turn from evil and do good; seek peace and pursue it."
> Psalm 34:13-14

I want you to examine yourself today. Have you entered into gossip without even thinking about it? Maybe you actually desire it. Maybe it pumps your adrenalin and you love it. Friend, I'm here to tell you, it will bite you in the end. There is nothing positive that can come from gossip.

Listen to what the word of God says in Ephesians:

> "Do not let any unwholesome talk come out of your mouths, but only what is helpful for building others up according to their needs, that it may benefit those who listen."
> Ephesians 2:29

There are so many ways we can help people and approach situations without gossip. If you do not know it by now, gossip is not healthy. We need to strive to think before we speak! If you really want to say something, maybe you should stop and ask to yourself, "Will that benefit this situation I am in right now?" before you open your mouth. Learn not to add any more wood to the fire!

Are you the town herald? Time to stop.

Dear God,
I thank you that we learn from our mistakes. I honor you today.

457

Shield and Buckler

When you go to Bible College as a Missions major, you hear hundreds of missionary stories. Many of them increased my faith and helped me on my many journeys to India, a country that the Lord laid on my heart when I was just a little girl. Some were almost too hard to believe. Some I thought of as I walked the streets of Kolkata praying God would keep me safe. One story was told in college of this missionary who was held at gun point. He began to pray. When the shots were fired, they hit an invisible wall about a foot in front of him and the bullets dropped to the ground. The man holding the gun ran away because he could not believe what had just happened. The Lord had been a shield to the praying missionary. I have never seen anything like this before. Nor have I had this experience myself. But the Word promises He is our shield and buckler. A buckler is a round shield that you put your arm through as a means of defense and protection.

In 1 Samuel 17 is the story of David and Goliath. If you went to Sunday school growing up, you have heard the story, but if you are like I was, you may not know it.

"A champion named Goliath, who was from Gath, came out of the Philistine camp. He was over nine feet tall. He had a bronze helmet on his head and wore a coat of scale armor of bronze weighing five thousand shekels; on his legs he wore bronze greaves, and a bronze javelin was slung on his back. His spear shaft was like a weaver's rod, and its iron point weighed six hundred shekels. His shield bearer went ahead of him."
1 Samuel 17:4-7

Every day this giant would shout at the ranks of Israel for them to choose a man and have that man fight him.

"If he is able to fight and kill me, we will become your subjects; but if I overcome him and kill him, you will become our subjects and serve us."
1 Samuel 17:9

For forty days the Philistine giant Goliath shouted the same thing. Grown men ran in fear. Then the boy David desired to stand against him.

"You are only a boy, and he has been a fighting man from his youth."
1 Samuel 17:33

Saul did not want David to fight the giant. After David told him he would anyway, Saul dressed him in his armor, wanting to protect him. David did not like the feel of it because he had killed bears and lions with no armor on, and he desired to kill the giant the same way. Long story short, without any armor and just a slingshot and stones, David hit the giant in the forehead and killed him. These are his words standing against the nine foot man:

"You come against me with sword and spear and javelin,
But I come against you in the name of the Lord Almighty, the God of the
armies of Israel, whom you have defied. This day the Lord will hand you
over to me."
1 Samuel 17:45-46

There are times in our life when we may happen upon a dangerous situation.
These are the times we must have faith like David the boy, or faith like the
missionary who had an invisible wall that protected him, due to his prayers.

"Take up shield and buckler; arise and come to my aid."
Psalm 35:2

"He is my shield"
Psalm 18:2

"He is a shield for all who take refuge in him."
2 Samuel 22:31

One time I took my daughter, who at the time was thirteen, into the red light
districts of India. We went in for Bible studies with the girls who were trapped in
the districts. We knew the risk, bringing a young beautiful white girl in, but I also
knew that if she came with me it would change her life forever. It did.

Sometimes we need to step in faith when danger is at the door, and know that
He is our shield and buckler!

If you are a missionary today overseas, or someone right here in America, He
will fight for you! Do not be afraid with God on your side. Even if someone is
bigger, stronger and has more armor on! Even if your attack is in the spiritual
realm. What are you afraid of today? Take refuge in Him.

Dear God,
We are safe in your arms and you do the impossible for us. I honor you today.

August 3rd

Blink and It's Gone

Today is my mom's birthday. I lived with my mom and dad for eighteen years, then my sister-in-law and I got an apartment together for a summer, and shortly after that we left for college. Any summer we came home, I lived at home. I was always excited to get back to my roots, my things, and my mom. My mom has been through a lot. Her mom and dad are gone, and her brother died at a young age as an alcoholic. Be the time she reached her 50s everyone in her family was already gone.

How do you count the memories? I have many of them and so do you. Some good, and some bad. I remember on the day before my wedding we were waiting for family and friends to come to the rehearsal. I knew they would be there within the hour and I was so excited. This was the happiest time of my life. The phone rang and it was my mom's father's doctor. He told my mom my grandfather had two weeks to live. I was going on a two week honeymoon. At first I did not know what happened, but I saw my mom get upset on the phone and then she ran to the bathroom and started to vomit. I think it was all way too much at once. But that night she held the rehearsal dinner at our home and wore her smile as best as she could.

When I think of all the memories, and the memories I have with my own kids, and the fact that my son is off to college in just three weeks, it just does not seem possible. Where does the time go? I love the movie *The Passion of the Christ*. I love the way it shows the relationship between Mary and Jesus. There is one point in the movie where Jesus makes his mom a table, and they joke about it and throw water at one another. Another time, she is playing with him as a child. The truth is, no matter what we have been through in this lifetime we all have some memories we want to remember. I'm sure after Jesus died and rose again; Mary's mind went back to the laughter and wished she could start all over again!

Life can be a crazy thing. You blink and it's gone.

Mary, the mother of Jesus, had natural emotion when she found Jesus as a boy teaching in the temple. She knew He was the son of God yet he was also her boy. He had gone missing for three days. I know myself, and if my son or daughter went missing, I would flip! I would be so worried, I would search until I would find!

"When his parents saw him, they were astonished. His mother said to him, 'Son, why have you treated us like this? Your father and I have been anxiously searching for you.'"
Luke 2:48

460

There was shock, anger and happiness all mixed into Luke 2:48, and rightly so. I would have been happy, but you better believe my kids would get a lecture, as I got lectures.

I remember the Easter that my parents handed my brother and I Easter baskets and lectured us on drugs. By that time, my brother and I had already done laced drugs. We were messed up before we came to know the Lord. We all walk through things we regret.

I'm not saying all this to depress you today I'm telling you all this because life is Life. And it goes by quickly. Very quickly. My mom turned 70 today (2010). Where did the time go? The carefree days when she was in the back yard playing with the dog and we were on the swings?

I want you all to know today that it's okay to live. It's okay to hurt and to feel emotions like Mary felt when finding her son, because life is life. There will be times when you are anxious, mad, upset, happy, expecting, and the list goes on. Emotions are normal and natural, but we MUST keep them under control.

"David was greatly distressed because the men were talking of stoning him; each one was bitter in spirit because of his sons and daughters. But David found strength in the Lord his God."
1 Samuel 30:6

Life is life and things can get stressful, but like David we need to find our strength in God. Run to Him today no matter what you are living. You will turn around tomorrow, blink, and it's gone.

Dear God,
I pray the reader would know that their emotions are natural and normal. Help us to keep them under control, and help us to find our strength in you and your word. I honor you today.

August 4th

Oak and Ink

Many of you love the books Jane Austen wrote, as well as the amazing movies that have been birthed because to her writings. She would never know how her countless hours sitting at her desk could snowball into Hollywood. It's almost as if she lived out what she wished for her life in her writing. Her books consist of *Sense and Sensibility, Pride and Prejudice, Mansfield Park, Emma, Persuasion,* and *Northanger Abbey*. She was an amazing writer that could paint an amazing picture in your head.

She died when she was only 41 years old. I'm 44 right now so to me that is a very young age to die. To accomplish all she did at such young years is amazing to me. Then I think that in the 1800s they did not have all the distractions that we have now. Young people did not have phones, TVs, X-box, and the list goes on. They had ink and pens and played outside.

In 1802, Jane agreed to marry Harris Bigg-Wither. She changed her mind overnight and broke the engagement. She never married. For some reason she did not do well in that area. That's why I think she was so successful at putting romance on paper, and boy can she bring it in a very appropriate way.

I picture her sitting at an old oak desk with an inkwell. Dreaming about her life like a normal young lady. Dreaming of the man who will sweep her off her feet and painting pictures of him with her pen. I picture long lonely nights when she would write and get her pages wet from tears. She was was a Christian Anglican, of the Church of England. Her father was a rector in several parishes and her brother, Henry (considered her favorite of her brothers) later in his life became an Anglican clergyman. I'm sure she had head knowledge of God, but I'm not sure about heart knowledge? Regardless, I'm sure there were nights when she wrote that she would question God about the things that were NOT happening in her life, that WERE happening in her books!

Pride and Prejudice, my favorite movie of all time (NOT the five-hour version, the Kiera Knightly version), was published as a book in 1813. The new Hollywood movie came out in 2005. Imagine this for a moment. The heart of a young lady writing in 1813, sometimes in tears, and it continues on 192 years later as people are still making movies from images in her mind and heart! I have a book at home called *Women Who Changed the World* and Jane Austen is in it. At her young age she established novels as a form of entertainment. To be that young and to accomplish an amazing task like that, I don't know about you, but it makes me want to be a history maker. One Hundred and ninety-two years after *Pride and Prejudice* first published, it is one of the most popular books of all time. And she will never even know it.

I want you to know today that no matter how old you are God can still use you in amazing ways. I use Jane Austen as an example of planting seeds. I don't know if she knew God on a personal level, but she planted seeds with her pen. You see, sometimes just in our everyday life, like Jane, we go about our business never even knowing that God can use what we are doing to change and touch hearts 192 years later.

You will NEVER know 192 years from now what has been accomplished through you. Jane never in a million years would have known that Hollywood would embrace her writings years later. She would never know that a movie would even be made about her own life. She would never know that the tears and seeds she planted with her pen would linger in the hearts of people like me, who like to sit and watch a great movie or read a good book. She died before there was such a thing as a television. But her life and the things she did snowballed, and she would never know it.

Do you see what I'm trying to get across here? I'm sure Jane, sitting at that desk, was only having fun and doing something that made her happy. Even after people started to notice how good she was, she was having fun and just living. Never did she ever think this could happen. As you have fun and do things that make you happy, as you work hard in this life, you are planting seeds. You have no idea the impact they will have years from now. This excites me.

You may be home thinking you have not accomplished much in life, but you cannot see the bigger picture. My dear friend, there is a much bigger picture.

> "But as for you, be strong and do not give up,
> For your work will be rewarded."
> 2 Chronicles 15:7

Do not give up.

Dear God,
As we live help us to strive for excellence. We never know years from now, the souls you will touch through us. I honor you today.

August 5th

__Are You Kidding Me?__

Okay, so let me tell you about my week. Less than a week ago I wrote a devotional called "Extra Vitamin C." The devotion was about my car and my husband's car breaking down on the same day. A week later, one is fixed and the other is not. The home that we own on Cape Cod has finally sold, and we are losing $70,000 that we had originally put down. The difference from what we paid for it to what it is selling for now is a little over $200,000. New England home prices are crazy!

My dear Uncle Anthony went to be home with the Lord two days ago, and I worry about my family. To top all this off, I come home tonight and my main computer has a serious virus. It was perfectly fine this afternoon! Everything I need for my upcoming meetings Sunday to Wednesday is on the computer, so I guess I have to call the Geek Squad tomorrow to come help me. The last time I called them it was about $400! Why do things like this happen when we are seeking God, loving God, and trying to do our best for Him? And why do they happen in large groups all at once!?

Right away we tend to think, "What did I do wrong? Why would all this happen at once?" My emotions run wild, which I'm sure yours would too. Anger, sadness, confusion, fear, and the list goes on. These are the times we need to heed to the scripture:

"Be still, and know that I am God."
Psalm 46:10

Tonight, before I turned my computer on to find the horrible virus, my husband and I watched *Schindler's List*. I left the movie ready to write. My heartbeat was souls. I had tears in my eyes because of the last scene in the movie where the Jewish people give Schindler the ring that has a quote from the Talmud saying, "Whoever saves one life saves the world entire." Schindler breaks down and cries, saying over and over again, "Just one more, I could have saved one more!" Then he looks at his car and gold pin and says, "If I sold these I could have saved one more person!" Very moving scene. There were 1,100 people there that last day as Schindler said goodbye. He gave every bit of money he ever had to save these people. The movie ends with the real people who Schindler saved from death putting stones on his grave.

When I think of souls like Schindler did at the end of the movie, it puts my week into perspective. I don't understand it all, and when it happens to you, you don't either, but there are reasons far deeper than we know. God has a plan in everything. Every single thing! There are people I talked to this week and who I spent time with that if none of this happened, I would have never even communicated with them. It may be humbling, aggravating, and very sad, but it is worth it? Yes. Every soul counts.

There is a reason we come across different souls every day of our life, even if we have to come across them in trial. We need the heart of Jesus, and the mindset of Jesus.

> "When Jesus landed and saw a large crowd, He had compassion on them, because they were like sheep without a shepherd."
> Mark 6:34

> "When He saw the crowds, He had compassion on them,
> because they were harassed and helpless,
> like sheep without a shepherd."
> Matthew 9:36

Jesus saw the hurting, scared, wandering, helpless, and harassed because that's the way sheep are on a field without a shepherd. And that is the way we are without Christ. I need to put it all into perspective and have compassion, even through trial. The last time the Geek Squad guy came here, he was here for three hours. We talked about God a lot of the time. In my trial, His heart was moved and touched.

Trust me; I get aggravated just like the next person. I grieve just like you, but when we are overwhelmed we need to stop, and think about more than our trail. We need to think of the souls involved with the trial and how we can shine His light through everything. It's not an easy thing to do.

Just half way through writing this devotional tonight, the lights and all the electric went out, without any storm or rain or anything! My husband came down the stairs and all we could do was laugh!

Are you kidding me? He was in the middle of something and so was I. Perspective people; putting it all into perspective. Souls.

Dear God,
I want your heart. I want compassion on the multitudes that walk into my trials. I want to weep and say, I could have saved more! I honor you today.

Magnum Opus

Magnum Opus refers to great work; perhaps your largest and greatest, most popular or renowned achievement of all time. Think about that for a moment. If you had to put something down as your greatest achievement what would you put? I sat and thought about it, and the first things that comes to my mind are living the dream that I had years ago to be the district director of a women's department for our AG fellowship. Or having two kids that are totally in love with God and serving Him. Or being happily married to the same man for over 20 years and more in love with him today then ever. To me it does not get any better than that. Around 1998 I had the first ever in the history of our fellowship, a district rally for abused women. It stirred women to have small groups that still exist today. Each year we hold a retreat where over a thousand ladies come. This year, we expect 1,500 and we expect to turn some away.

Why is it when we think of Magnum Opus we only think of the big things? We think of numbers and quantity, not quality? Why do we do that? What about the little things? The small amazing accomplishments that people seem to forget. Or that they don't want to talk about. Like kicking a habit or conquering an addiction. Why would we ever think less of them?

I smoked for three straight years before I came to the Lord. I was a chain smoker, you never saw me without the stick. Marlboro Lights at 75 cents a pack! I got high for years, almost every other day, drinking like crazy. When I came to know the Lord I quit everything within the year. God began to work on my anger and bitterness.

Why when I ask myself, "What is my Magnum Opus?" do I not think of these things?

Well friend, history is when God changes your life and you are NO longer the same! This is your renowned achievement, your greatest accomplishment. This change will change generations to come forever more. Your kids, your kids' kids, your grandkid's kids, and so on.

Let's look at the life of Christ.

Jesus heals blind men (Matthew 9:27-31), raises Lazarus from the dead (John 11:1-44), calms a storm (Matthew 8:23-27), feeds the 5,000 with five loaves of bread and two fish (Matthew 14:1-21), walks on water (Matthew 14:22-32), raises Jairus's daughter from the dead, and the widow at Nain's son from the dead (Matthew 9:18-26 and Luke 7:11-17)! The truth is I could keep listing so much more that it would take up all my writing space for this devotion. So I stopped! If you were to ask someone on the street what the Magnum Opus of

Christ Jesus was, I think most would say, "When He rose again." After all, we have an entire day, and for some churches a weekend, dedicated to it each year. Easter Sunday, egg hunts, outreaches, special flowers, and the list goes on. What would you say about the Magnum Opus of Christ?

There was a movie called *Mr. Holland's Opus* that came out in 1995. It was about a music teacher and the movie climaxes at the end with him doing his biggest event ever. So you would think that was his Magnum Opus, but the movie has a beautiful spin where through that event he touches the heart of his son who cannot hear. The movie shows that Mr. Holland's real Opus is in the fact that he broke the wall down between him and his son. It's a powerful message. The glitz and glam always seems to be our Magnum Opus. But friend it's not, it's the little things, the walk we walked before we got there.

I believe the Magnum Opus of Christ was Him crying out in the garden to the Father because He knew what He was going to have to go through. It was His walk to His death. We seem to forget that if not for that walk, there would have been no resurrection.

Don't forget those things; they are your renowned achievement. Because of them, you are who you are, and you are able to do what you do.

> "Whoever can be trusted with very little
> can also be trusted with much."
> Luke 16:10

Though the death on the cross was NO little thing, the Father in Heaven trusted His son to die for our sins. To be obedient. He also trusts us to do big things, but remember the hidden things that we do not want to talk about or that don't seem Magnum Opus at all to you, they are what got you to this place.

Sometimes our Magnum Opus is the very thing we don't want to talk about. It's the hard road that led to the victory!

Dear God,
Help us to see our greatest accomplishments through your eyes. You see different than we do. I honor you today.

Clean Hands

I love flying. It's been six months since I last flew, so last night I got my bags ready. My zip lock bags with makeup, no more than 3oz. of fluid in each, boarding passes, license, laptop, airborne and the most important thing: antibacterial moist towelettes! I'm a clean hand freak! All you have to do is talk to my kids and they will tell you that you touch NOTHING of mom's unless your hands are first washed! I don't want their entire day on my clean dishes, TV remote, or laptop! Now, I don't even have to ask, they know the "look!" That's right, the clean hand "look!"

I ended up on the first flight today with an adorable 16-year-old girl. I was happy because I have a 16-year-old daughter right now. so I felt comfy. I miss my kids. They have been gone all week and won't get home until tonight, and I won't be back now until next week, so a little over a week without them. This girl was so cute. It was her first flight and some of her first words were, "I can't believe we can't text in the air!" It's funny with teens; it's almost like life stops in the air unless there are movies! Anyway, the first thing I did when the captain turned off the seatbelt signs was get my carry on and take out my antibacterial wipes! I handed her a couple, and we did the tray, the hook for the tray, the arms of our seats and then our hands! Ha! Are you laughing? I was happy that she was happy about it too. My daughter would have been laughing her head off. I just don't like germs. People may laugh at me, but I cannot tell you the last time I had a temperature or threw up! So laugh all you want!

> "Who may stand in His holy place?
> He who has clean hands and a pure heart."
> Psalm 24:3-4

The word of God talks about clean hands, but along with it the Word talks about a pure heart. Clean hands, meaning innocent or repented. I wish I was as concerned about my heart as my hands. The truth is I don't guard my heart like I guard my hands. Why is that? I need to change, and so do some of you. If I have entered into some form of casual gossip why don't I say, "Let's stop this conversation NOW?" If I was touching some sort of nasty, germy stuff with my hands, I would bring it to a stop RIGHT AWAY! Then why don't we STOP right away when we deal with heart issues? God desires we keep our hearts pure.

One thing that takes common sense, which I'm not sure why most don't use it, is don't enter in to a situation that you know already will be a temptation for you! If you are trying to stop drinking well then, Hello! Don't go and sit in a bar and eat peanuts! If you are in an unhealthy, ungodly relationship, don't go away for the weekend with him or her. It's that simple. It's way easier to guard our hearts than we make effort for! The truth is we don't want to listen to common sense. It is much easier and it feels better to just do what we want. Therefore our hearts are dirty.

To achieve clean hands and a pure heart means we must live by the word of God, no compromises.

A pure heart is a choice.

You choose to keep your hands clean so you don't get sick. It's the same thing with a pure heart.I need the same passion about my heart being pure as my passion to keep my hands clean. Instead of being concerned about physical germs, I need to start being concerned about spiritual germs.

Where are you with this today? When was the last time you cleaned your heart? Have you cleaned your heart today? When the book of Ephesians talks about what a husband should do to help his wife walk in holiness, or purity of heart, it says:

"Husbands, love your wives, just as Christ loved the church and gave himself up for her to make her holy, cleansing her by the washing with water through the Word."
Ephesians 5:25-26

If you don't know it today, the word of God, the Holy Bible, is what washes us. It is the tool that brings purity into our heart and life.

How are your hands? How's your heart?

Dear God,
Change us, and clean not just our hands, but our hearts. I honor you today.

August 8th

Arch Support

For two years of my life I suffered with Lyme disease. People do not realize how dangerous ticks really are, and what they can do to you. I had gotten to the point down on Cape Cod where I could no longer put pressure on one of my feet. For over a year I could not wear any type of heel. For me, a young lady who loves shoes, this was not easy. I had come to my own conclusion that I would never have to wear my heels again so I gave them all away! Big mistake! After treatment I now where heels again and love them.

During that time I had special arch support for my feet. It was very hard to do many things and the arch support seemed to give me that extra oomph to make it! It was a support I needed at the time or I would not have been able to do all that I did. I wore what I called my grandma shoes. They were not that attractive and they were totally flat. I would slip my arch supports into whatever shoes I would wear. Well, those days are over for now, thank God, but it was not easy.

My poor mom suffers so much with arthritis. She used to own her own fishing boat and 10 lobster traps. She would pull those suckers out of the traps with her bare hands, band them and chuck them in the bucket! We would always have a feast after she went on the boat. Now she could never think of doing that. She can hardly walk up and down Main Street where she lives due to her feet and legs. She wears a brace that she must have on every day, and she has special arch support where they actually cast her foot, and have it molded perfectly to her. At one point, they wanted to fuse her bones together. My heart breaks for those who suffer like that. In times of suffering and anxiety we need some form of support to help us through.

> "When I said, "My foot is slipping,"
> Your love, O Lord, supported me."
> Psalm 94:18

Just like we need arch support in the "natural" We need support in our walk with God. When we feel like we are being tempted, when we feel like we have given in to anxiety and know we need help where do we turn? What is our support? This word says, "Your love, O Lord, supported me." His love? How does His love support us? First, I can say, that just knowing that God loves us regardless of our every day failures brings me much hope, and support! Let's look to His Word for answers.

> "Love covers over a multitude of sins."
> 1 Peter 4:8

We see this scripture in 1 Peter 4, a chapter that talks about us living for God. But if love covers a multitude of sins let's look for a moment at the love of

Christ. Most all of us know John 3:16, "For God so loved the world that He gave His only son." Let's look at some other scriptures.

"How priceless is your unfailing love!
Both high and low among men find refuge in the shadow of your wings."
Psalm 36:7

Refuge is support. Not sure if you have ever looked at God's love before as support?

"Who shall separate us from the love of Christ? Shall trouble or hardship or persecution or famine or nakedness or danger or sword?"
Romans 8:35

"I am convinced that neither death nor life, neither angels nor demons, neither the present nor the future, nor any powers, neither height nor depth, nor anything else in all creation will be able to separate us from the love of God that is in Christ Jesus our Lord."
Romans 8:38-39

Don't you see how His love is our support today? No matter what we are going through He will never leave us. He will walk through it with us as a support. I hope this gives you comfort today. Do not fear. Just like my mom gets her arches perfectly molded with support, God's love is perfect against us. It's molded to us and therefore we are supported. It's nothing to doubt or fear; it's there for the taking if you do not know God.

Just like we have to willingly put on our arch support we have to willingly accept the love of Christ! This is the only thing sometimes that will get you through.

Put on your support today friend.

Dear God,
I pray each reader can willingly accept your love today. That they will not longer live in shame, but will know they are forgiven and you are always there for them. I honor you today.

Busted

I'm at a meeting right now in Springfield, Missouri, and I'm sitting among some serious quality ladies who are district directors of their states. Some day's I sit and wonder how I ended up here. I have come to the conclusion that it has to do with the little things. I'm a District Director for a women's department that consists of three states. Sometimes I feel inadequate like maybe someone else would be better at this than a lady, who before knowing God was bitter most her life, or who ran to drugs to "get away from it all." But I'm here, because when Jesus busted into my darkness He told me He had a plan for my life, no matter what I had been through and no matter what I had done. This is the God I serve. So when I come to these meetings, my mind cannot help but think of the past, where I came from and what the Lord has done in my life. It's a miracle, that's all you can call it.

I look at some directors from a distance and think, they must have all grown up in church and had generations of ministers behind them, but when I spend time with them I hear different stories. Some that I hung out with the past couple days were going through deep grief and family dysfunction. Some had children that were in jail and their hearts were broken. Some directors could not even come because their district budget could not afford to bring them here. What I have come to realize in the past couple days, is we all are going through things. No matter what we may look like on the outside, it's what's going on in the inside that counts. Even district directors and pastor's wives are going through it! Even if there is someone around you, who you think "has it all together," please take the time to talk to them because I promise you might just hear a different story.

Anyway, how did I get here? By the grace of God. This is what He has for you, things that you never could have dreamed. Don't give up on yourself because He will never give up on you. We must believe that He still desires to use us, that He has a purpose for our lives! I am here due to His grace but I'm also here because in the early days of ministry when I did not know what I was doing, I was faithful in the little things. Even if I only had five people showing up for a meeting I would make sure I did it with excellence. Everyone had special gifts at their place, everyone was highlighted in a special way and their words were important in meetings. It starts with excellence in the little things. Think about what you are doing right now in your ministry or workplace. Are you doing it with excellence?

When I first arrived at my hotel room here in Missouri, I was in shock to see about 20 dead crickets all over the floors of my room. But the worst, and I'm not kidding you, was a man's pair of underwear on the floor! Ok, would you have touched it? Haha. Not me! I let the front desk know, so when the ladies came to clean they were in shock and kissing up to me big time. She put her glove on and held the underwear far away from her on the way out the door of my room! There was one thing I noticed, a young girl working with her who looked about 22 years old. The older lady who was showing her what to do was busting her tail cleaning my room. Every single dead cricket was being picked up! I watched this younger girl as she made the bed and then walked out of the room. I needed some new towels so I went out in the hall to the cart. There by the cart stood this young girl, she was standing there doing nothing. I asked her if I could have some more towels, her words to me instead of getting them were, "Knock yourself out!" She was NOT budging. There was no hospitality in her spirit, there was no ministry of helps in this young girl, not even common courtesy, and it broke my heart. She was NOT doing her job with excellence; she could have been in there helping with her cleaning mentor! After she said those words to me she said, "I'm just a temp." Friend let me tell you, if you do NOT do things with excellence, even if you are "just a temp," how can God honor what you are doing? I don't care if you clean toilets; you clean those toilets better than anyone has ever cleaned them! It starts with the little things.

"Whatever your hand finds to do, do it with all your might."
Ecclesiastes 9:10

"Just as you excel in everything in faith, in speech, in knowledge, in complete earnestness and in your love for us, see that you also excel in this grace of giving."
2 Corinthians 8:7

It's not just about giving money; it's about giving in everything; like handing someone a towel.

I know I did not get where I am today, to where God is using me, for doing sloppy work. He does NOT deserve our sloppy seconds! My work, no matter where it is, is done with excellence. Is your work done with excellence, or are you leaning up against the towel cart? Are you asking what more you can do when things are slow at work, or are you sitting around not caring to find things to do!?

Tomorrow, I will become the president of the committee, over all the AG Women's Ministries district directors in America; I tear just thinking about it. To some this may not be a big deal, but I remember where I came from and it is a miracle. I'm humbled today. I'm glad He busted in on my darkness.

Dear God,
You desire to use this reader. Teach them to work as good in secret as they do when their boss is around. With excellence. I honor you today.

Beautiful Faces

Today I saw the most beautiful video of a ministry to handicapped people. This couple wants to buy a campground where handicapped people can come and have summer camps. Their desire in time is to have a place where these beautiful people can live. They go into a chosen state, start summer camps, and in time they desire to purchase permanent places where they all can live. We were told that when caregivers die, there is not always someone to care for these beautiful people? Their hope is to take them into these homes that are filled with the Love of the Lord. This couple was in tears as their video played of their summer camps. When the wife got up to speak she was crying and she said, "See these faces? They are my family." The truth is there was not a dry eye in the room! Not sure what my problem was but I was totally bawling. I think it was much more than hormones, God touched my heart.

Growing up, my father was the head coach of New York's Albany High School. For over 30 years he worked there and was the basketball coach, he dragged us to almost every game as kids. Every summer, because school was out, my father ran the Albany summer handicapped camps. My dad had to make sure the day camps were fully staffed and that there were field trips to go on. I remember my favorite time of the summer was going with my dad and busloads of beautiful faces to Story Land. There were rides, swan boats, animals, and more. As a young girl who was not around handicapped people I can remember being a little scared, but in time I fell in love with all of them. There was one girl who was handicapped and blind, I loved her the most. I guess it was almost like being with Helen Keller but this young girl could hear, so I would talk to her all the time. We had fun doing crafts even if she could not see. I know that those years of summer camps and beautiful faces would change my life forever more. They built part of my character and I am blessed.

My dad also ran the Special Olympics in Albany. We would go, and dad would set us up in a certain spot, in charge of judging who the winner was. Their excitement of just being there, and their joy were amazing! It never mattered who the winner was because every beautiful face had a smile. Everyone was a winner at the Special Olympics! These were very formative years of my life and I will never forget them. They changed who I am.

"Then they came to Jericho. As Jesus and his disciples, together with a large crowd, were leaving the city, a blind man, Bartimaeus, was sitting by the roadside begging. When he heard that it was Jesus of Nazareth, he began to shout, 'Jesus, Son of David, have mercy on me!' Many rebuked him and told him to be quiet, but he shouted all the more, "Son of David, have mercy on me!" Jesus stopped and said, 'Call him.' So they called to the blind man, 'Cheer up! On your feet! He's calling you.'

Throwing his cloak aside, he jumped to his feet and came to Jesus. 'What do you want me to do for you?' Jesus asked him. The blind man said, 'Rabbi, I want to see.' 'Go,' said Jesus, 'your faith has healed you.' Immediately he received his sight and followed Jesus along the road.
Mark 10:46-52

There were many times along the journeys of Jesus that He came across beautiful faces, in this case a blind man. If you read the word of God you will find many more. He had compassion when everyone else turned their back, and told them to "be quiet!" or "leave Him alone!"

His response was, "Call him." In other words, "Bring him to me." This is the kind of God we serve. Jesus knew there was a wonderful purpose and plan for beautiful faces. I'm sure along the way not everyone got healed, but I know along the way everyone got loved by Him.

Today please do not forget the beautiful faces around you every day, even when you are out doing your daily tasks. The person giving out the stickers in the store as you enter, the bagger at the grocery store. If Jesus loved them and took time to stop, how much more should we.

Today is a reminder to us all that God loves beautiful faces.

Dear God,
Thank you for changing my life at those camps many years ago. I pray if this reader has never taken the time to go the extra mile for handicapped people, that you stir their heart today. Lord, we go by your example. I honor you today.

August 11th

Wind

"Who has gone up to Heaven and come down?
Who has gathered up the wind in the hollow of his hands?"
Proverbs 30:4

My kids went to a giant music festival called Soulfest this summer. They both had their bands play on stages. The way I could describe it to you best is Christian Woodstock. Everyone camps there eats there and so on, minus the serious drugs booze and sex, although I know it must go on somewhere with that many people there. Every single band is a Christian band, some hard core some worship and the list goes on. It's a very powerful four days.

This story that my kids came home with made me wonder if they actually experienced a manifestation from God, something in the spiritual realm rather than something in the natural realm. They said that they went to see a particular band; there were hundreds of kids there to see this one band. The band was leading in worship. The air was hot, about 90 degrees. It was stagnant and stale. Almost everyone was entering into worship, I have seen the pictures and these kids were sold out for God, hands raised eye's closed and you could tell they were wanting more! When all of a sudden the entire crowd of hundreds of kids felt a giant wind that my son and daughter describe as very cold and refreshing coming from nowhere and it hit the crowd. It was the kind of wind that could not go unnoticed. Everyone was wondering what just happened, so much so that the leader of the band actually said out loud, "What just happened?" Then that same wind turned around and hit the band itself and then it was gone. The kids could not stop talking about the wind, which I believe was a wind from God. There are many winds in the word of God. God made this earth and all in it.

He owns the winds. There are natural winds that the Word of God talks about,

"As a north wind brings rain"
Proverbs 25:23

"The wind blows to the south and turns to the north;
round and round it goes, ever returning on its course."
Ecclesiastes 1:6

Then there are times when God used the wind to his favor.

"But God remembered Noah and all the wild animals and the livestock that were with him in the ark, and he sent a wind over the earth, and the waters receded."
Genesis 8:1

"So Moses stretched out his staff over Egypt, and the Lord made an east wind blow across the land all that day and all that night. By morning the wind had brought the locusts; they invaded all Egypt."
Exodus 10:13-14

There are also times during the testing of Job, after Satan asks the Lord for permission to afflict Job, that the enemy uses the wind for evil (Job 1:18-19), to hurt Job's heart with grief.

Wind is used in many different ways, and who discerns what is what? Listen to this:

"He makes winds his messengers"
Psalm 104:4

One of the commentaries I read about this scripture said that the angels usher in the presence of God. They are used as ministers or messengers. They march before Him, to prepare the way for God's presence. Could it be that angels caused the wind my kids, and the entire crowd of hundreds felt that night to usher in the very presence of God? It came out of know where and was described as cold and refreshing. The truth is we will never know until we get to Heaven and ask Him.

In 1 Kings 19: 11 it says:

"The Lord said, 'Go out and stand on the mountain in the presence of the Lord, for the Lord is about to pass by.' then a great and powerful wind tore the mountains apart and shattered the rocks before the Lord, but the Lord was not in the wind."
1 Kings 19:11

The scripture goes on to say shortly after this:

"A gentle whisper. When Elijah heard it,
he pulled his cloak over his face."
1 Kings 19:12-13

It's very interesting to me that the wind came first along with the earthquake, and fire before Elijah heard the voice of the Lord." Almost like their shaking prepared the way of the Lord.

In Acts 2, before the tongues of fire came and landed on everyone's head it says,

"Suddenly a sound like the blowing of a violent wind came from Heaven and filled the whole house where they were sittin=g."
Acts 2:2

This was the day of Pentecost. What is so interesting to me is so many times before something major happens in the word of God we see the wind, even if the outcome is bad.

I'm not a Looney Toon, I think it's safe to say today that something caused the supernatural wind the crowd felt that night at Soulfest.

Today you need to know that most wind is the natural course of God in place. The earth being the earth. But keep your eyes open for the winds of God. I'm sure they are much more among us than we could ever think.

I'm sure there are many times the angels want to prepare the way of the Lord or the Father just wants to pour out on us, but we are not in worship, we are not in prayer or desiring more from God. Could we actually stunt the powerful presence of God? When was the last time you pressed into God in such a way?

I cannot get the pictures of that crowd out of my mind, they did not care who was around them they were going to worship and press in. I think that is the reason God chose to visit them just like His visitation in acts chapter 2.

Press in today and you might just be blessed by His mighty presence.

Dear God,
Thank you for your presence Lord, visit us. We want more. I honor you today.

August 12th

Rip Off

I went on a search tonight for an external drive to put into my notebook at one of our major electronic stores that I won't name, but they claim to have the best buy anywhere. Ha-ha. I could not believe the price of them! I could not find one for under $59. Even the no-name brand ones were that expensive. It's just this little plastic device, where you take its USB cable and plug it into your notebook so you can watch DVD's. Little notebook laptops do not come with CD drives, and I need to show a DVD to my leadership team very soon. It's also nice when you travel so you can watch a DVD on the plane, hotel room, or wherever. The truth is I will probably only use it for meetings, so I could not see spending that much money on it. I went on a hunt! Being that Target was right next door, I decided to go in and check things out. There sitting on the shelf was one of the same exact ones that I saw in the first store for $11.50! And I am not kidding you. I'm sure these things cost dollars to make because they are plastic and very thin, so this was way more my style! But I was totally baffled! How could the other store have it for $47 more? These things puzzle me! And they claim to have the best buy?

Let me tell you today my friend, there are many people in life who will tell you they have the best buy. They will say their way is right and to follow in it. Be ever so careful of who you follow. The word of God speaks very clear about knowing what you believe in and being able to back it up with the word of God.

> "Always be prepared to give an answer to everyone
> who asks you to give the reason for the hope that you have.
> But do this with gentleness and respect."
> 1 Peter 3: 15

First, I challenge you today, if you don't really know what you believe, figure it out and be able to back it up with the word of God. Be every so careful of who you are listening to, even on television. This is why I love to teach Foundation classes, to disciple people and help them to know what the word of God says. God wants you to grow so you do not depend on others in your walk with God. Not that we won't be accountable, but you need to stand on your own as far as what you believe.

> "Become mature, attaining to the whole measure of the fullness of
> Christ. Then we will no longer be infants, tossed back and forth by the
> waves, and blown here and there by every wind of teaching and by the
> cunning and craftiness of men in their deceitful scheming."
> Ephesians 4:13-14

If you know what you believe it will also help you when people who have not heard from God try to sway you into their thinking. I had a person come up to me one time in church and begin to tell me about this great vision for a ministry that the Lord laid on their heart. They told me of how God led them, and they even knew exactly what city it would be in. I was touched with their vision and dream until they said, "And God told me you were going to be the one to start and run it!" I knew instantly that I was not God's chosen for this ministry! In a case like this you must be loving but bold. I looked at this dear person and said, "You did not hear from God on that one." We must be able to stand firm on what we know God has already spoken to us. Yes God wants us to love, but we also need a backbone as to not be swayed by other doctrines and "words from God."

Many people will tell you they have the best buy when right next door is the will of God for your life. Don't miss it. Be patient and wait for it! Be self controlled and turn your back and walk next door even if you're tired and don't feel like looking again! I hope you understand what I'm trying to say here. This is such an important part of your life and you will have to live it at one point or another.

I, as well as many, have even experienced Waco doctrines at Bible Colleges. Some will get fixed on something they have seen or heard somewhere other than their college that only judges others or makes them so spiritually minded that they are no earthly good! If you have not noticed yet, Jesus NEVER came across that way, EVER. He was approachable, kind, and forgiving. Be very careful my friend in what you believe.

> "We demolish arguments and every pretension
> that sets itself up against the knowledge of God."
> 1 Corinthians 10:5

How can we demolish things that are against the word of God if we don't know the word of God? That, my friend, is your job. Get yourself into classes or something that will help you! Stop hanging out with people who claim they are the best buy for your life, including the opposite sex, and start getting a backbone and having self control to find out exactly what it is that God says and wants for your life!

He has much more for you my friend than a rip off.

Dear God,
Help us to know what we believe. I honor you today.

August 13th

Reduced to a Puddle

Today was just one of those days for me. I have come to the conclusion that my hormones sometimes make me cry. Or it could be that my son leaves for college just two weeks from today. In any case, I have been doing some shopping for his dorm room. Boys are so funny; they really don't care about what their dorm room will look like. He does not care to get a new comforter or anything! I know that will NOT be the case when my daughter goes to college in two years. Haha. She will NEED everything college dorm room related! It's just hitting me now after 18 years of having him around that he will not be here. He makes me laugh almost every day of my life and I'm starting to feel the fact that he is leaving. So today I was needy and weepy. I was reduced to a puddle of tears.

I have come to realize that God has his own plan for Jonathan Patrick, and it's time to let go. He will learn from his own mistakes, weep his tears, and experience great joy and much favor. He will hear from God and follow Him all the days of his life. I am confident in that. But, I will never stop praying for him. I have prayed for his spouse since the time I rocked him as a baby that God would raise her up to be a mighty woman of God. Now I pray that he does not settle for second best for his life, but that he will hear from God.

Letting go is one of the hardest things you will ever do in your life. It's a step of faith. I have been way too overprotective of my kids because of my past, but a few years back in prayer for Jon one night, God clearly told me to let go and to have faith that my son would do the right thing, to release him to make his own choices. So I did. It has never been easy. I know he is not perfect, none of us are, but I can only hope and pray He will stay close to the Lord as he walks this life.

It is times like these that we need to soak our minds in the word of God.

"The Lord is near. Do not be anxious about anything, but in everything, by prayer and petition, with thanksgiving, present your requests to God. And the peace of God, which transcends all understanding, will guard your hearts and your minds in Christ Jesus. Finally, brothers, whatever is true, whatever is noble, whatever is right, whatever is pure, whatever is lovely, whatever is admirable, if anything is excellent or praiseworthy, think about such things. Whatever you have learned or received or heard from me, or seen in me, put it into practice. And the God of peace will be with you."
Philippians 4:9

I could easily drive myself crazy when Jon leaves for college. I could consume my mind with thoughts of "Is he safe?" "Does he have money?" "Is he being tempted?" "How will he pay his school bill?" "Is he wearing the same pair of boxers four days in a row?" Haha. My mind could be filled up, but I choose the word of God. This is what we must do when we take a step of faith, when we let go. God is not only near to you, He is near to those you pray for my friend. Be at peace. Think about the good times, the things you admire, the things that are noble and true. When mistakes are made, keep moving forward.

I love how Paul can say, "What you have learned from me put into practice." Wow! I cannot say The Millers have been perfect, but I will say that anytime I messed up, lost control, or failed in front of my kids, I told them I was wrong, humbly. It's in admitting our wrongs that our kids see we must rely on God.

Are you reduced to a puddle today? Did you get a bad doctor's report? Are you discouraged due to finances? Are you taking care of your parents who are sick or getting old? Is one if your children in prison? I'm not sure what you are going through today, but I want you to know that many men and ladies of God go through hard times and you are not alone. We have each other and we have the Lord and His word.

In case you need to hear it today: It's ok to cry. It's ok to be reduced to a puddle some days. He understands.

> "Don't waste the pain, Let it drive thee,
> Don't stop the tears let them cleanse thee,
> Don't waste the pain!"

Dear God,
Life is hard sometimes. Grow us. I honor you today.

<u>Never Above the Fall</u>

I watched a BBC Wildlife show today. To my amazement, there are more plants than the Venus fly trap that eat animals. The footage was amazing. I'm sure if you go to YouTube and search for the Pitcher Plant you will be able to see what I saw today. It was like a scene from a Sci-fi movie. I just could not believe what I was watching. Just the way the Pitcher plant grows freaked me out. It starts with its beautiful leaves growing in full. Shortly after this vine off the tip of the leave, that looked exactly like a snake, bends down and hits the ground. After hitting the ground it inflates into this balloon that comes up as high as the leaves and the top of it opens like a tube or vase. It looked like a treasure chest opening! Water catches into the tube creating a place for small rodents to drown. I just could not believe it. I have never seen it before in my life. It grows in Southeast Asia and attracts ants and rodents by sweet nectar. Once they start to chow on the sweet nectar, they seem to lose the thoughts of keeping safe due to their indulging. If they are not on guard they fall into the tube and drown. The Pitcher plant waits for the animal or insect to rot and then drinks it up.

The growth of the plant was in fast motion to show it growing right in front of your eyes. I think what freaked me out the most was the fact that the vine on the tip of the leave looked exactly like a snake head. It made me think about the way the enemy entices us.

There is always something sweet dangled in front of us, something we are attracted to, and something that we know we will enjoy if we can just get one little taste of it. Then BOOM!
Just like these animals and insects we fall into the tube, and he tries to snuff us out! Friend, never think you are above the fall. We are all saved by grace and we all can fall.

"Therefore let him who thinks he stands take heed lest he fall."
1 Corinthians 10:12

It was very interesting watching the ants on the plant. Some fell in, and somehow the others got the drift that they were in danger and would take off back out of the plant. Friend, there are sure tell signs sometimes that you may fall, what are you going to do about it? Are you going to make yourself accountable to your family or brothers and sisters? Or are you going to carry it alone which is a very dangerous thing to do. We need each other, even when we fail.

You are NEVER above the fall. You must stay close to the Lord and be accountable. Every single Tuesday at the recovery ministry my husband and I run, my husband reminds us that if we are not careful we can easily fall back into the 'old things' that were not healthy for us.

Where are you today in your healthy walk with God? Are you keeping unhealthy things around, because they feel good? Maybe it's time to CLEAN HOUSE.

For you it may be magazines, movies, romance novels, booze, drugs, food, and the list goes on. They can be like that sweet nectar to you. You will lose control and fail. May I remind you today that His word also says:

"And God is faithful; he will not let you be tempted beyond what you can bear. But when you are tempted, he will also provide a way out so that you can stand up under it."
1 Corinthians 10:13

Even before the temptation comes there is a way out, but are you looking for it? Or are you too enticed with the sweetness of your sin? In the movie I watched ants were following ants. Who are you following to that sweet sin? Maybe it's time to get a backbone of your own, stand against it! Start to let them follow you! Stop being a follower and start being a leader!

"Follow my example, as I follow the example of Christ."
1 Corinthians 11:1

Start to follow the example of Christ rather than ungodly examples. Instead, as you are hanging with your friends say to yourself, is this something God is pleased with? If you know it's not, GET OUT! It's as simple as that!

I have seen great men and women of God fail and fall. When the enticement came they lost control and due to it their entire life was dragged through the mud and their families torn apart. Sometimes I'm amazing how things that God created in nature can be perfect examples of our spiritual walk with God. How they can remind us to get on track and stay close to Him and His presence. If you don't know Him today I challenge you to get alone with Him and ask Him to make Himself very real to you. He is faithful and He will do it.

We are never above the fall, be on guard my friend.

Dear God,
Help us to stick very close to you and to not be enticed by the enemy and the sweetness he sets as a trap for us. I honor you today.

August 15th

Color Splash

Have you ever seen HGTV's show ColorSplash? I was driving down the highway on Route 128 North in Massachusetts today, when I saw the most random, amazing color splash I have ever seen. I wish there was somewhere I could have pulled over because I would have taken a picture of it with my phone! Here I am on this highway with nowhere to stop on either side! If you look at the highway it's dirty, soda cans, and garbage on the sides of the street and in the very middle of the highway a metal divider that was rusted and dirty. There, smack dab in the middle of the highway ALL ALONE, was about a 5 foot high, beautiful bright yellow sunflower. I could not believe my eyes. It was the most beautiful Sunflower I have ever see, I think because it was a beautiful color splash in the middle of everything dirty.

I pondered about how it could have ever grown or gotten there. There was hard ground, not even a patch of grass. I drove by it two more times today just to see its surroundings before I wrote this. Was there dirt under the cement, and somehow it pushed through? Did someone spit sunflower seeds out of their mouth onto the highway like my son does? How in the world did it get there? Things like this amazing me and are beautiful to me. That God would put a beautiful color splash in the middle of a dirty nasty highway. That a gentle stem could press through the hardness of the cement or ground. It's an example to us to never give up and press on even in the hardness of life.

Do you realize today that God wants you to be a beautiful color splash? I'm not sure what's around you, but growing up, my life was not a bed of Sunflowers. What do you have around you? Is it peaceful and gentle? Is it bitter and harsh? Does it feel like someone has spit you onto the ground? Is there garbage all around you, with foul words and anger? Only you know the truth behind closed doors. No matter where you come from or what you have been through God wants to make you a pop of color in the darkness! A light that pops like a color splash.

I bet you, out of the thousands of people that drive that highway on a daily basis, that not many people saw that sunflower today. We are so distracted. I know myself that when I'm in the car, I take that time to make many phone calls. But today I was listening to worship, and there it was to bless my day. I'm sure many in their cars were talking, texting and triple tasking. I would give anything to know how many people actually saw that Sunflower today. Sometimes, we as a pop of color in the darkness do not get too many that notice us. You need to know that is ok. Even if there is just one that takes notice it's worth it all. We are not here to be blessed by others, we are here to bless.

Remember that if not too many seem to notice you. I will say that Sunflower blessed my heart. It was a random beautiful thing in the middle of my day.

The infant Jesus was a beautiful color splash. There this newborn was, the King of the World, birthed among the smells of manure and hay. Jesus was laid in a manger, I'm sure on top of hay and wrapped in cloth that was somewhat dirty (Luke 2:7). As flies buzzed around the beautiful baby, He lit up the barn.

I want you again to think of your surroundings. If you have an amazing life with nothing wrong, you are blessed! I want you to know you can still be, and need to be, a color splash for those around you because not everyone is blessed like that. All around you on a daily basis, even if you cannot see it on the outside, are hurting people. People that need the Lord. People that need just one glimmer of hope or a little color in their life. I was one of those people. Friend, you may be the only color splash they will ever have near them. Splash Away!

"I will lead the blind by ways they have not known, along unfamiliar paths I will guide them; I will turn the darkness into light before them and make the rough places smooth. These are the things I will do; I will not forsake them."
Isaiah 42:16

I was blind.

If you were to tell me 25 years ago, that I would be a minister, and be doing what I am today, I would have cussed you out and laughed. But here I am. I have walked many unfamiliar paths and He has guided every step. In every rough place He has helped me to press through like the Sunflower I saw today. He has not forsaken me.

He has not forsaken you.
It's time for you to be a color splash. Splash away!

Dear God,
I cry when I think of your mercy and how you long to use us as a color splash in the life of someone else. I honor you today.

August 16th

<u>The Master</u>

My daughter and I took a walk down memory lane today and watched clips of the Brave Little Toaster, a movie that came out in 1987. The story is about a group of small appliances that talk and are best friends. The vacuum, the lamp, the radio, the toaster and blanket (Blankie). They live at a summer camp all alone, until the owners of their camp come once a year to vacation. They have watched their master, a little red headed boy grow up, and soon he is a teen and off to college. Their fear is that he will not want to take them with him. When he does not come looking for them, they go looking for the master. The movie is their journey to find the master. Blankie is lost without the master and cries all the time without him. In the end they all end up with him at college. If you have never seen it, you have to get it, and experience it at least once.

I came home today around 5:45 pm to our beautiful black lab Arwen, looking so sad. Daddy (The Master) was eating his dinner and was not paying attention to her. Her face even looked sad and she just sat there leaning against the couch. Her sad droopy eyes were totally pitiful, but VERY cute! We have had Arwen for six years and Guy started his training with her when she first came home at four months. Whatever the master says she does it right away! When I take Arwen outside, she sniffs the flowers, and tries to manipulate me. When Daddy (the master), takes her out, "BAM!" The job is done! Whatever the master says goes. It has its pros and cons. There are times when Guy gets irritated because Arwen is his shadow. She follows him around every single place he goes. The instant he gets up, she gets up. The instant he wants to do anything she is up and at his feet. I'm the needy one! Why doesn't she follow me around! Ha-ha. It's actually comical sometimes when he comes down the stairs and there she is right behind him. Sometimes he runs and tries to get away from her. Poor Arwen!

These two things today, made me thing about our Master. Do we really want to be close to Him? So much so that we will go looking for him like the characters in the Brave Little Toaster? The blanket is so cute, it's actually an electric blanket and the knob to put it on, is its nose. A child plays the voice, and the voice is adorable saying, "Master, master!" So cute! Does it actually bother you when you are far from the Master? Or don't you think about it much? There are so many promises in the Word of God about being near to Him.

"Come near to God and He will come near to you"
James 4:8

"Seek the Lord while he may be found; call on Him while he is near"
Isaiah 55:6

I just love the brave little toaster movie because they cannot live without the master, and the thought of it drives them crazy. I have to say that I have learned to seek God. I'm not perfect, and there are days that go by that I fail to spend quality time alone listening. One thing I can say is that, from the time I wake in the am, to the time I go to bed in the pm, He is on my mind. My heart beat is for souls. I owe Him everything. In the movie, at the end, the brave little toaster risks his very life to save his master. How many of us can say we would lay down our life for Him, and the sake of the call? I know I have friends who are on the mission field who put their lives in danger almost every single day because they followed God's call on their life. I guess the question today, to you is, how close do you want to be to the Master? Do you want to hear His voice like John 10:27 talks about?

"My soul follows close behind You; Your right hand upholds me."
Psalm 63:8 (TNKJV)

The reason our black Lab Arwen follows my husband all around the house is because she loves him. She knows if he is there everything will be ok. He gives her a peace that I cannot give her.

Do you love the master today?
Are you close behind Him?

If you are way behind, maybe you need to play some "Catch Up" today!

The great thing is He will never get irritated with you for being close behind Him.

As a matter of a fact, He loves every minute.
Maybe today you need to take a journey closer to the master?

Dear God,
Please help me to stay close, to rest right by you. I honor you today.

August 17th

The Shower

I have shared a version of this story in another devotional quite a while back, but something was added to it this weekend, and I feel it's very worth sharing. As most of you know, due to reading this daily devotional my past has not been perfect. Sexual and physical abuse, hate, drugs, a divine encounter with God in the middle of an attempt to end my life at age 16 and the list goes on. But then at age 18 God met me just as I was and changed my life in the middle of my senior year of high school. I thank God I'm sane, and I thank God he longs to use my pain for purpose.

There is one memory I have that has haunted me for years. It has always been the enemy's tool to lie to me and tell me I'm nothing, or that I'm trash. Well, we all know that IS NOT the voice of God! I was at a pool party at my girlfriends in high school I had mixed drugs with drinking, not a good mix. It was the first time I had ever passed out from doing too much at once. I got this stupid idea that I needed a shower. If you don't know, you do STUPID things when you are drunk and high. So there I am, fully clothed in the shower, I pass out and have no idea how long I was on the shower floor? I woke up to hearing the door of the bathroom open and clothes and the water was still beating on me. It took me a while to realize that people, men and woman were coming in and out of the bathroom urinating. I'm sorry this is so graphic but when you hear the next part you will not believe it. The enemy who hates me has always used this experience in my life to say, "I urinate on you! I hate you, you will never be anything." Thank God, Thank God, Thank God! The Lord loves me and speaks purpose and plans into my life!

So this weekend I was at a party at our Pastors house, I sat and talked to a beautiful young lady who loves God. She has the gift of prophecy like it talks about in 1 Corinthians 12:10. And she has visions like it talks about in Joel chapter 2:28-29. I am always VERY cautious when someone says they have a "word" from God for me. Or when they say they have had a vision of me. I have been given many a WACKED words in my time! As soon as the beautiful young lady told me, with tears in her eyes, that she had a vision of me, I felt in my heart it was from God and I could not wait to hear it. I want to let you know before I share this with you that she has NEVER EVER heard any of my testimony. She knows nothing I have ever gone through in this lifetime.

This is the vision she had of me: She said I was in the shower, the water beating on me was not water at all, it was fierce beasts with fangs who were trying to hurt me coming out of the shower head. They were very dark and evil. She said that in the shower I stood up, and when I did there was a hedge of worship circling all around me. The way she moved her hands it looked as if it was around my head area. I began to sing worship to the Lord and she kept hearing, "There's Purpose in the Pain, There's Purpose in the Pain!" For YEARS I have used those exact words at almost every single event I have ever spoken at, and she did not know that. I know that God gave her this vision to encourage my heart! To once and for all be DONE with the enemy trying to dig up the past and speak lies to me through this memory! The first thing I thought of when she was speaking this to me was a message my husband preached called *Laying the Ambush of Praise and Worship*! Just an amazing sermon about the power of praise.

I know this is kind of intense, but it blessed my heart to know that someone was praying for me in such a way that God would speak to them about me. This is how we should be praying! Since Sunday God has placed a deeper passion in my heart to pray for others. If you have a hard time praying, you can write or type out your prayers to God; this will keep you from distractions in your mind. It will keep you moving forward in prayer. Sunday night in my bedroom I felt a thick presence of God and I knew He was speaking to my heart that He had a mighty plan for my husband and I, and that He will use all we both have gone through in this life for His Purpose and it starts NOW. He is so faithful.

Friend, when you think no one is praying for you, you will be so surprised. There could be co- workers, people you randomly meet in the store, family members all praying for you and you might never even know it. I had no way of knowing this young lady was praying for me.

Let me ask you today, who are you praying for?
If you genuinely love someone, you will lift them up in prayer.
May God give us all a deeper passion in this area!

"I pray that out of his glorious riches he may strengthen you with power through his Spirit in your inner being, so that Christ may dwell in your hearts through faith. And I pray that you, being rooted and established in love, may have power, together with all the saints, to grasp how wide and long and high and deep is the love of Christ, and to know this love that surpasses knowledge - that you may be filled to the measure of all the fullness of God."
Ephesians 3:16-19

Dear God,
I thank you for the past; it makes us who we are today. I thank you for using our stories to encourage hearts! To know that God still longs to use us in powerful ways! I honor You today.

August 18th

The Boiling Pot

I know many of you working men and women who cook can relate with me when I say, "Give me a meal that I can put in a pot and let it go all day!" To come home after work and to have to create an entire meal can make you crazy! The truth is I'm a great cook, I just hate to cook. There was a time when my kids were little and I was a stay at home mom, my outlet to create was cooking. Now that I'm working, my outlet to create is in my work, and I love every single minute of it, so cooking is just something to do because it's needed.

Today I made Italian sausage, spaghetti, veggies and nice scali bread. I fried up the sausage after poking holes in it then threw it in the pot of sauce where it boiled for hours. The boiling pot as you know can be very messy. Every time you lift the lid it splatters and sauce gets everywhere, clean up can really stink too, but the joy of the boiling pot is you can walk away. You can go and get other things done! Or leave the home all together!

On Sundays I like to put a roast in my big cooker. I cover it with seasoned water and throw in all kinds of potatoes and veggies. By the time we get home an amazing smell is in the air and everyone is ready to eat! By the way are you hungry yet? I love cooking in my cooker and in pots because the more something boils the more soft and tender it gets.

I want you to know today, it's the same in our lives. The more we are in the boiling pot the more God will humble us, teach us, grow us and the softer and more tender we will get. If you don't know it today friend, you are an amazing recipe waiting to happen! All the ingredients God has already put in the pot! You may not understand why some of them are there, but they will all work together to tenderize you. One thing through the years I have noticed is that no matter what kind of meat I use, when it boils for hours it's smaller than when I put it in. We become smaller in the pot and He becomes greater.

Much of the boiling process in our life is trial. I know you can relate when I say that we grow through trial. Just this week I sat with my Tuesday night group of gals and we shared about all the things we had gone through the week before. Almost every single person in that room was going through something. But in the end we will all come out stronger, more confident, we will have learned some lessons, and we will be better used for God and His Kingdom.

The boiling pot is a healthy place to be, although it might not always feel good.

"Dear friends, do not be surprised at the painful trial you are suffering, as though something strange were happening to you. But rejoice that

you participate in the sufferings of Christ, so that you may be overjoyed when His glory is revealed."
1 Peter 4: 12-13

"God opposes the proud but gives grace to the humble."
James 4:6

Boil. Boil.

"Consider it pure joy, my brothers, whenever you face trials of many kinds, because you know that the testing of your faith develops perseverance. Perseverance must finish its work so that you may be mature and complete, not lacking anything."
James 1:2-4

Hmmmm. Pure joy?
Boil. Boil.

"Blessed is the man who perseveres under trial, because when he has stood the test, he will receive the crown of life that God has promised to those who love him."
James 1:12

Boil. Boil. Boil. Boil.

Dear God,
Bless us in the Boiling Pot. Grow us in it. And help us with our response to it. I honor you today.

Tame Your Tongue

"If anyone considers himself religious and yet does not keep a tight rein on his tongue, he deceives himself and his religion is worthless."
James 1:26

I am so very thankful I am not the person I used to be. I am very outgoing and loud at times; therefore I used to speak before I thought. Not a good thing! I have found in every single situation we must think before we speak. My husband is the one who patiently taught me that. In the natural, I am a talker and he is a listener. I now call myself a learned listener. I think before I speak, and that includes on paper, for those of you who love to pop sour e mails and snail mail due to lack of self control! It was NOT easy to change, but the truth is that God is all about change!

I remember early on in our marriage when we had small children, I was usually home alone all day talking baby talk and when Guy would come home I could not wait to have adult conversation. Well, Guy had had adult conversation all day and the last thing he would want to do is talk. I nagged for a year until I realized I was like the wife in Proverbs!

"A quarrelsome wife is like a constant dripping."
Proverbs 19:13

Our home has always been a very peaceful place but in the early years when we were getting to know one another and growing in our marriage I learned real fast to keep quiet! A constant dripping can get on your nerves very quick! Sometimes friend, you just need to turn yourself OFF! Now, I'm Italian, pretty much I'm doomed when it comes to keeping my mouth shut, but at the same time, Look what the Lord has done! I am a learned listener, a faucet turner-offer!

Ha-ha

Galatians 5:22 talks about the fruit of God's Spirit in us, and self- control is there, right along with peace, kindness, and love! How is your self-control today? Or your lack thereof?

What are you going to do about it? I learned that when my husband came home he needed space; he needed time to get changed, chill out, get something to eat and relax before anything else. I used self-control and kept my mouth shut. Then when the time was right, he would talk about his day.
Who is it that you need to lay off of? Who is it that you need to back off from? You do NOT have the reins of your tongue and you need to pull them tighter before you drive someone crazy.

Sometimes being quiet is the best witness we could ever be for the Lord, in a tough situation.

Truth be told when you pull the reins on a horse it does not feel good!
It never feels good when God does a deep work in us, and shows us He wants us to change in a certain area of our lives! But it's healthy and needed.

There were many times in Scripture when people came to Jesus and asked Him to help them.

So many times the disciples would say, "Lord, tell them to go away!" But Jesus always said things like, "I'm here for the sick," or "Let them come." You would think after a while his close friends would come to know and realize that he would not turn people away yet they kept throwing discouraging words His way every time someone would come to Him. They needed to tame their tongues. Jesus was a big boy! He only created the universe! I think He can handle the people wanting to touch Him, and be healed by Him!

"Then little children were brought to Jesus for Him to place His hands on them and pray for them. But the disciples rebuked those who brought them. Jesus said, "Let the little children come to me, and do not hinder them, for the kingdom of Heaven belongs to such as these."
Matthew 19:13-14

Even the ones who walked with him on a daily basis had to learn this lesson. How much more do we have to learn it? The Bible says there is a,

"Time to be silent and a time to speak."
Ecclesiastes 3:7

As you know taming something like a dog or bird takes hard work, firmness, discipline and faithfulness. It's the same with our words. He desires to change you and I today, will you let Him?

Dear God,
You are forever faithful. Thank you that I am not the same. Minister to the reader and help them Lord to realize that being silent is sometimes your perfect will. I honor you today.

August 20th

Hit The Brakes!

So I have learned in the past year that I AM NOT the one to teach my kids how to drive. Talk about anxiety and stress. They do just fine, but I DO NOT. I hold onto the door, like that's really going to help in a crash! I did not even realize I was doing that until my son mentioned it the other day. My son has been driving for quite a while, and he is a great driver but I am not a great passenger! It's NOT my gifting!

Today we got into a little tiff. We were riding on a back road and a truck in front of us failed to put his right blinker on. We had no way of knowing he was turning. My son hit the brake just fine, and of course I hit the fake brake on the passenger side with my foot a million times! While I'm hitting the fake brake on my side with my foot, I'm yelling, "Brake! Brake! Brake!" Each time getting louder, and each time looking more ridiculous! I'm sure my blood pressure rose and my face was red. From there I took my daily stress out on my son. The pressures of my deadlines, and the physical pain I was feeling at the moment, all came out of my mouth until we reached our destination. Not Good. He left the car not saying goodbye. There you go, see, I'm human. I make mistakes and so does he. The key is to admit them.

I wrote about taming the tongue once, but will we hit the brake when we are about to lose it? How about hitting the brake before we lose it? I know there are times when you must lose it too, because we are all human. I grew up in a home where many people 'lost' it. There was a lot of yelling, and as my brother and I got older we responded to our circumstances by yelling. This is what we were taught in a lot of cases, so monkey see, monkey do! I was a Christian and a Pastor's wife, but I was far from perfect! I was trying to 'shake off' the old ways but it was not easy. When my kids were very little I would yell in response to trying to get control in my house, many times I would sit them down with me and cry. I would be 100% honest and tell them, "Mommy is sorry and I should not have responded by yelling." I would give them hugs and kisses. Sometimes being open and honest is the best medicine for stressful situations. Or should I say unhealthy situations.

Well, I have not seen my son all day and I'm sure by the time he gets home tonight I will be asleep. So I will say now, I'm sorry Jonathan. I let the stress of the day get to me. I love you and both of us left in a bad way today. Friend, if you don't know, do not leave someone angry at them. You just never know what could happen until the next time you see them. It could be the biggest regret of your life. I found myself crying and so angry coming home and I had no desire to tell him I was sorry. It was not till later that I realized that I was the one who failed to hit the brakes.

"Get rid of all bitterness, rage and anger,
brawling and slander, along with every form of malice.
Be kind and compassionate to one another,
forgiving each other, just as in Christ God forgave you."
Ephesians 4:31-32

I think the key to this scripture which totally focuses on a lack of self control is HIT THE BRAKES before you even lose control!

Forgiveness does not mean you have to trust someone, it does not mean you have to be buddy buddy with them, and want to be with them all the time. It simply means you have forgiven. The truth is, most people you have to forgive, you will not trust like you did before anyway.

I have also learned the hard way to go to people or call them right when you are angry with them. Make it right or it could be too late.

"Therefore, if you are offering your gift at the altar and there remember that your brother has something against you, leave your gift there in front of the altar. First go and be reconciled to your brother; then come and offer your gift."
Matthew 5:23-24

"Like a city whose walls are broken
down is a man who lacks self-control."
Proverbs 25:28

There is no defense when city walls are broken down so there is lack of protection.

Be ever so careful friend when you lose control.
How are you in this area right now? Who is it that you need to call or talk with?
Today my son got angry, due to my anger at him. We left each other not talking.
It can be like a domino effect if you are not careful.
Today I needed to put the brakes on myself!

Dear God,
Help me when I fail. I honor you today.

August 21st

<u>Dry Rot</u>

Have you ever had a toothache? It's the worst pain ever! I almost would rather have a baby than have tooth pain. One time I had a tooth pulled and the hole it came out of got infected. The dentist told me it's called dry rot. I'm sure you are just loving this, huh? I can't even tell you how horrible the pain was. It hurt so bad. In this case they have to open up the hole again and drain it. I have NEVER enjoyed going to the dentist, but going to the dentist in pain is even worse. When you have tooth pain there is only a couple things on your mind, the DENTIST or DRUGS! Ha-ha

How about a bad foot? When I got Lyme disease I got a taste of what it was like to not have a foot to rely on. I could not put pressure on my left foot, and you don't realize how you rely on something until it's gone. I went through almost a year of my life wearing, what I call, grandma shoes. I had to get inserts for my arches and be very careful about the type of shoes I wore. It was very hard. My poor mom wears a brace on her leg and foot, she needs it to walk. She relies on it. It's very hard when you realize you have to rely on other things to get through life. Somehow it makes you feel old.

> "Like a bad tooth or lame foot is reliance
> on the unfaithful in times of trouble"
> Proverbs 25:19

How about a so called friend? You hope and pray you can rely on them when the time of trouble comes but sometimes you realize that they disappear instead of being by your side. Has this ever happened to you? It has happened to me by Christians and non Christians. And this scripture compares the hurt of it to an aching tooth and a lame foot. The hurt is deep and it cuts like a knife sometimes. They say they will be faithful but when push comes to shove they are long gone.

> "There is a friend who sticks closer than a brother."
> Proverbs 18:24

That friend, is God Himself. This scripture may not mean a lot to some of you because your brother hurt you, or would never help you. But what it's meaning to say is a brother is supposed to be there for you in everything. God's intention was that a brother would never hurt you. So if your brother hurt you in some way please know God will never hurt you. He is a very safe place, and when your friends take off on you, or even if your own brother takes off on you, your God will not.

> "Never will I leave you; never will I forsake you."
> Hebrews 13:5

So if your reliance has not been on a friend today, because they take off, please learn to trust your Heavenly Father who will never hurt you or leave you. It's very hard when your Father or brother has hurt you to be able to get these scriptures into your mind and realize what God intended.

The truth is, unfortunately, people will continue to hurt us because they are just people.

The foundation of our reliance MUST be on God Himself. He is Rock Solid, Unmovable, and Unshaken. I know when you have been hurt, it's hard to even trust in God, and it takes time. I encourage you today to take that step of faith in your life and trust. I promise you will NOT regret it.

> "For the Lord Your God is a merciful God'
> he will not abandon or destroy you."
> Deuteronomy 4:31

> "God, who has called you into fellowship with
> His Son Jesus Christ our Lord, is faithful."
> 1 Corinthians 1:9

God will not hurt you like dry rot.

Dear God,
Help me to trust in the fact that you will NEVER hurt me. I honor you today.

August 22nd

Weeping Seeds

I can remember when my kids were infants. When I would rock them in their bedrooms I would tear and begin to pray for their future mates and every aspect of their lives. Our prayers for people are so powerful. You win battle in prayer. Your tears are seeds that you sow into the lives of others.

When the enemy came to God in the first chapter of the book of Job, and God gave him permission to afflict Job, or should I say test him, the first thing the devil said was,

> "Have you not put a hedge around him and
> his household and everything he has?"
> Job 1:10

In other words, he was saying, how can I touch those you have put a hedge around? The Lord believed in Job so His response was,

> "Very well then!"
> Job 1: 10

God allowed the enemy to penetrate the hedge. God believed in Job more than Job believed in himself. So friend, when your trial comes do NOT look at it as God not loving you or not being there for you. He is the one who believed in you enough to give the enemy permission to penetrate the hedge that He set up about you. God was the one, who said in Job Chapter One,

> "Have you considered my servant Job? There is no one on earth like him; he is blameless and upright, a man who fears God and shuns evil."
> Job 1:8

God believed that Job could handle the test. God knew it would make him a stronger man. Think of this through your trial. Through our trials He believes in us.

When I pray and weep for my grown kids, and my nieces and nephews, I say, "God, when the enemy comes to you and wants permission to afflict them, I beg you to say, "No!" I ask God not to let them go through some of the things I have been through, such as hurt in ministry."

There is no reason why we cannot pray like that! He longs to hear our prayers. He longs to see our tears for others. I ask him not to let the devil penetrate the hedge of protection He has around them. There are nights I weep and beg Him. These are weeping seeds that I will sow till the day I die.   If you love someone you will pray for them and plant seeds.

I'm sure we all will face trial in life no matter what, but I believe God has heard my prayers and I know they will be spared things due to weeping seeds.

"Those who sow in tears will reap with songs of joy.
He who goes out weeping, carrying seed to sow,
will return with songs of joy,
carrying sheaves with him.
Psalm 126:5-6

Every teardrop that you sow for someone is a seed planted. And seeds that are planted grow.

Today my family ministered in church. My husband preached, I sang, then at the end of the services all four of us ministered as a family in music. I'm so very proud of what my kids have become. They have made their walk with God their own. They have relationship with Him, and follow Him. There is nothing more in life that I could ask for. I believe weeping seeds had much to do with that.

Friend today please know that your tears for others are so very powerful. Start planting!

Dear God,
I thank you that you hear our prayers and honor them. I honor you today.

August 23rd

<u>Nodding Off</u>

Today is a cold nasty day filled with rain in New England; my body does not react well to the cold. I had a busy morning and by the time dinner rolled around I was gearing up for my side job, mom, the taxi driver.   One had to be dropped at 5:30 somewhere, and the other had to be picked up somewhere. Then my beautiful daughter waited till we were half way home to tell me that she left her cell phone back where I picked her up. Usually I would have left it there, but I know cleaners come in at night, and I did not want the stress of someone taking it. All that to say, that by the time we were on our way home the second time, I was nodding off at the wheel. At one point I did nod off and caught myself, I can honestly say that has never happened to me before! It was a horrible feeling. So I came home and made a nice cup of Indian Tea with caffeine!

I had a friend one time that fell asleep at the wheel and ended up hitting someone. The scary thing about being so tired and driving is that not only do you put yourself in harm's way but you put others in harm's way. I want you to know today it's the same way with our walk with God. If we nod off and do not say alert, not only can the devil pull the wool over our eyes, but many others can get hurt or even get thrown into Hell. Nodding off is dangerous in the physical and spiritual realm. We MUST stay alert. The Word of God is always talking about alertness! I can tell you friend, I was NOT alert tonight in the car physically! It was a horrible feeling and almost cost me a crash! I do NOT want to crash in the spiritual either, so it's important to stay alert and do what you have to do to dig into God's word and pray, even when you are tired. If you had some big event or party to go to you would have no problem finding ways to stay alert, just the excitement alone would keep you going; it's too bad we don't have that same excitement when digging into the Word of God. My remedy tonight: a nice cup of Indian tea.

"Be self-controlled and alert. Your enemy
The devil prowls around like a roaring lion
Looking for someone to devour."
1 Peter 5:8

"Be on guard! Be alert!"
Mark 13:33

When my husband and a team from our church went to Africa they went to a lion park. They had to sign papers saying that if they got eaten it was not the parks fault. They feed the lions in the morning then let the people in after they are fed. There are no cages or anything, the lions are free to roam or if they want, they are free to eat you. This is the kind of place you DO NOT want to lose your alertness!

The tales the team told were very fun as you can imagine. Once again I compare it to the enemy of our soul who wants to kill us, drag us to Hell, and do all he can to make life horrible. We should never fear Him because Jesus Christ already has won the victory, but this does not mean he will not try to do all he can to distract you, make you fall into sin, or end the plans God has for your life. What are you going to do about it?

The answer: Anything you can do to stay alert!! I joke about making tea tonight, but our alertness comes from the promises we have in His Word.

> "The Lord is my light and my salvation whom shall I fear?
> the Lord is the stronghold of my life, of whom shall I be afraid?"
> Psalm 27:1

The evil one will try to bind you up with strongholds, we need to rise up and let the Lord be the stronghold of our life!

> "The weapons we fight with are not the weapons of the world.
> On the contrary, they have divine power to demolish strongholds."
> 2 Corinthians 10:4

A stronghold is a place of security or survival. When the evil one lays a stronghold on us he tries to make our security in something other than God. He leads us down dark paths of addiction and temptation. The weapon Jesus used while fighting the evil one on this earth was the Word of God!

> "It is written"
> Luke 4:4

> "It is written"
> Luke 4:8

> "It is written"
> Luke 4:10

> "It is written"
> Luke 4:12

It's time to pick up your weapon! Tonight I have my weapon, and my Indian Tea! If you do not have a Bible you can understand, it's time to get one! It will be the best money you ever spent! The Word is your Sword (Ephesians 6:17)! Be alert and stop Nodding Off!

Dear God,
I'm tired. Help me. I honor you today.

Room to Room

Today was an awesome day. I was determined to patch and paint a room we have in our basement that has been my son's room for the last three years. The room has been through many guitars and amps leaning against the walls, drums piled high and it has taken a beating. It also was painted army dark green by someone else before we moved in. I felt it needed some TLC. I went to the hardware store at 8am and asked the Clerk to lead me to good, but inexpensive paint. He said I lucked out, because he had two gallons mixed yesterday that the lady did not like. It was Benjamin Moore Paint and both colors were beautiful, one was a light tan and the other was a pale yellow. I went with the yellow, then he said, "ten bucks for the gallon" and joy filled my heart, I expected to pay a lot more for my gallon! The night before I had patched all the holes and put up the blue tape that only those who don't know how to paint use. I thank God for that blue tape, let me tell you! Anyway, all that to say, the room looks wonderful!

I did not go to the gym today because my workout was in the basement. I have never done the stair stepper, but today I stepped for four hours! Up and down, up and down on a chair to reach the height of the room. My arms were going for four hours, and by the time I was done it took effort to walk up the stairs to get a drink! But man was I proud of myself. The room went from dark and gloomy to crisp and clean. And when I finally peeled my blue tape off to show off my crisp clean lines well, I cannot tell you how happy it made me. It doesn't take much. Give the girl a can of paint, and there you go! I'm happy! Ha-ha.

Even before I went down to sand and wipe the walls down this morning, I was thinking of how we clean and organize some parts of our life then for some reason we let others go. Now I have this perfect little place in the basement, but if you go into my own bedroom there is always a pile somewhere! Most the time the pile is right in front of my open closet door. I'm just being transparent here. Come on now, if you guys will be honest you must have some space somewhere that you have let go! The pile usually consists of my scrubs from the night before or something I took off. Now, the hamper is right there in our room, but instead of putting it in the hamper there is some sort of pleasure of just dumping it on the floor. If you know me, pretty much I'm a clean freak, but there is ALWAYS that one little pile in front of my closet! Somethings we just let go. But if I find out anyone is coming to visit that pile gets clean real quick!

People see you on the outside and everything looks so amazing, like you have it all together. But they have no clue what is going on inside. What rooms in your heart and life do you need to clean out today? What secrets are you keeping from the world around you, and your family?

God sees every secret.

If there is one thing I know, it's that once you start a project and get on a roll, you do NOT want to stop! Now that I have done that basement room I'm ready to do the entire basement! I can't wait to make every wall look crisp and clean. It's the same way in our growth with our Lord. Once you start to get involved, start reading your Bible, and start plugging in, you get motivated, your faith is increased and you are ready to go! It's exciting and makes you feel better. But the truth is that it will take work, hard work. Like I said, I could hardly climb the stairs when I was finally done with the room today. It may not hurt you physically growing in God, but there are things He will strip away from you, that will be hard. Things you will have to let go of in life. Unlovable people that He will want you to love. This is how He goes room to room in us! And one room at a time He perfects us.

We have rooms of guilt, shame, anger, pride, addiction, habitual sin and the lists go on. What are you going to do about your rooms? We must submit to His Word and His Ways to clean up and put that fresh coat of paint on. It brings health to each one of us. Instead of withdrawing, it's time to plug in and be accountable.

"If we claim to be without sin, we deceive ourselves and the truth is not in us. If we confess our sins, He is faithful and just and will forgive us our sins and purify us from all unrighteousness. If we claim we have not sinned, we make him out to be a liar and His Word has no place in our lives."
1 John 1:8-10

"But now that you have been set free from sin and have become slaves to God, the benefit you reap leads to holiness, and the result is eternal life."
Romans 6:22

It's time to clean house. Will you let Him go room to room?

Dear God,
Thank you for Amazing Grace and love even when our rooms sit messy. I honor you today.

August 25th

Extremes

Have you ever met a Christian who indulges in the Extreme? They are so spiritually minded that they are no earthly good. Let's talk about some extremes. I believe in prophecy, it's in the word of God (1 Corinthians 12:4-11). Some things that happened in the New Testament were foretold or prophesied about in the Old Testament. The first time God used me to prophecy I was only a teen ager, I have met people who use prophecy as a form of getting attention. Pride can creep in and all of a sudden prophecy becomes their identity because they don't have their identity fully in Christ. They are insecure in their own skin so they seek attention in a spiritual gift. Next thing you know they are rubbing people the wrong way, saying wacked things that are NOT from God, and being a horrible example of a Christian. I have had some real crazy things spoken over me in my lifetime. But at the same time there are those who are used in the gift of prophecy in a powerful way and who are humble only wanting God to use them. If God gives us a gift we are to stay humble and not use it as an attention getter. We need to use our spiritual gifts in 1 Corinthians 12 for the glory of God.

"The man who fears God will avoid all extremes."
Ecclesiastes 7: 18

A couple verses before that we see:

"Do not be over righteous, neither be over wise"
Ecclesiastes7:16

Sometimes when people are an extreme, they turn people away. What does it mean to be over righteous? The first thing that comes to my mind is a very prideful person who is not thinking about the grace of God when he breathes his first breath in the morning. Your first breath is grace. Many times in life I have see over righteous people point the finger at others in judgment, while three fingers are pointing right back at them. The problem is they don't see the other fingers pointing at them, they only see the one pointing at someone else.

I think when someone is over wise they spend most of their time trying to convince other people of their wisdom by speaking prideful words. Let's not forget it was because of this pride that we have an enemy called satan.

I know Christians go against the normal flow of what the world has to offer, there is even a T-Shirt I have seen that says, 'Go against the flow', but they are NOT supposed to hurt others along the way! Jesus never hurt others, He lifted them up. Grace was always the first thought on His mind, grace was the air he breathed. We need to be much more like Jesus.

I was an extreme my first year of being a Christian, I was going to save the world and I was very bold about it. Too bold and judgmental. I think I turned more people away from God that year than any other. Pride will get you know where. The truth is that I was immature and very unwise even though I wanted people to think I was wise. We need to be willing to grow in Christ, so that God can make us into what He wants us to be. He wants us to be righteous and wise but not so much so that we come across prideful and arrogant. I am not the same.

Do some personal inventory today. Are you humble? Are you judgmental? Are you righteous or over righteous? Are you wise or over wise? Are you an Extreme trying to get attention?

It's time to rest, grow, humble yourself and be a sponge hearing from those that are truly wise.

When you can grow from others wisdom, then you know you are heading toward being truly wise yourself, but it takes time. We need to be hungry for wisdom from others.

Extreme or extremely His?

Dear God,
Help us not to point a finger, but to see our own sin. I honor You today.

August 26th

Every Drop

God made emotions, wow! It's a killer sometimes. I'm very emotional right now, sitting here crying. My son's boxes are all packed in the truck, and ready to go to college tomorrow morning. We went out for last minute stuff today for college and he just took off with his band, Exiting the Fall, to hang out one last time before Jon and Matt take off to college. I guess it's time to grow up. Its times like these that your life flashes before your eyes and all you can think about is the firsts. The first time they ate from a spoon, walked, and went poo on the potty chair. The first time they messed up and came crying to us. The first time they went to a prom, the first time you let them take off with their friends in the car, the first everything.

My brother posted something on his status on facebook this morning because it's my niece's 18th Birthday. She and my son Jon are going to Zion Bible College tomorrow together. My brother made his comment and said, "I have spent the last 18 years praying for your future." I'm so emotional that I cried when I saw it, all I could think about was the times I rocked Jon when he was only like three months old and I began to pray for his wife. I did not realize it until I saw my brother's comment this morning that I have been praying for my son, his future and his spouse for 18 years. It just seems like yesterday that he got excited about his Star Wars birthday party! I just cannot believe how time flies. It's all so quick.

I want you to know today it's ok to be emotional.

Jesus, while walking on this earth, had emotions. His emotions were under control, like ours should be. He felt loneliness (Luke 5:16), anger (Mark 11:15-17), anxiety to have to face death (Matthew 26:39), and tears,

> "Jesus Wept."
> John 11:35

Jesus was talking with Martha in John chapter 11 and she told him her brother Lazarus was dead. Jesus with much confidence started talking to Martha about Lazarus rising again (John 11:23). A few minutes later Martha goes and gets Mary, Jesus sees her, and the Jews who had come along with her crying and the Bible says,

> "He was deeply moved in spirit and troubled. "Where have you laid him?' he asked. "Come and see, Lord," they replied. Jesus wept."
> John 11:33-35

Why would Jesus weep if he knew he was going to raise Lazarus from the dead? It was very emotional for him to see the people he loved crying and so filled with grief. He also loved Lazarus so even though he knew he was going to do a miracle it still hurt. I think this is the perfect example of the fact that it's ok to be emotional. Jesus was also filled with joy many times in the Bible; I'm sure when he set his eye on his mother, or when children would jump all over Him.

The Bible even says He records every tear we cry, every drop.

"You number my wanderings;
Put my tears into Your bottle;
Are they not in Your book?"
Psalm 56:8 (NKJV)

Pretty much every emotion we have ever felt our God has felt. He created emotions.

Maybe today you are in grief over a lost loved one. Your tired from working so many hours. Your child is going to college or away for a year? Your family member is in prison or you have been divorced and get very lonely. Please know today He sees Every Drop.

Dear God,
It means a lot that you know exactly what we are going through. I honor You today.

Life Lessons

"Weeping may remain for a night but rejoicing comes in the morning."
Psalm 30:5

Yesterday a dear friend reminded me about the joy of the Lord. It's been a very emotional time for us with our son going to college and all. She sent me an entire list of things to have joy about. I cried today after leaving him there, but everything she said was on my mind as we drove away from that campus. He feels the call of God on his life, he is following everything God has spoken to him, He has a healthy family that love and support him and the list went on. She so encouraged me with her words.

I'm sitting right now in my daughters youth group listening to young people worship and lift up Gods name. So amazing. I'm just filled with joy tonight because young people are following hard after God. It brings me great joy. At the college today were many of my son's friends who I have watched grow up, and my niece who I love with all my heart, they are there now, to grow up, and make their Christianity their own. It just does not get any better than that.

"For the joy of the Lord is your strength"
Nehemiah 8:10

There are things that happen in our life, emotional things like my last couple days. But we must focus in on the good that we see in the bigger picture.

But what about horrific things? How can we have joy through pain? My girlfriend Jody just walked up to me a few minutes ago and told me that her son found out today that his friend, who is a pilot and co-worker fell against the propeller of the plane and died. She told me that one of the young kids getting trained actually saw this kid get chopped up. Forgive the graphic picture, but how do you find joy in that? The truth is you don't. The scripture does not say, find the joy in hard things, it says, "The joy of THE LORD is your strength." The joy is not in your horrific situation, it's in the peace God gives you through the storm.

What exactly is the joy of the Lord? Its knowing when you are in a room alone weeping that He is right there. It's feeling Him lift you up when your world is falling apart. It's in the understanding that someday He will use all your pain for His purpose.

"And the peace of God, transcends all understanding."
Philippians 4:7

In other words this Word says, when you don't understand at all, when things are tragic and horrific, His peace passes our understanding and surrounds us. When was the last time, through your hard time, that you let his peace surround you? You need to let HIS JOY be your strength. He can fill us with joy in the hardest of times because He only is joy. He is all we need.

When we learn to face anything, knowing His joy will get us through, it becomes the most amazing strength you will ever know.

I know the things I have been through in the past few months. How about you? Joy needs to be part of our everyday life. It's how we make it. It's how we know we do NOT stand alone. I need His strength to live. We need to ask Him to fill us up with His joy, we need to read scripture about joy, and even in the darkest of situations we need to weep for joy. He is faithful and He will do it.

May God's joy be your strength today. I know God has taught me a deep lesson in the past 24 hours. I thank Him for life lessons.

Dear God,
Teach us more. Grow us. I honor you today.

Strategic God

We serve a very strategic God. He is a planner; He is getting things ready way in advance. He knows all your paths before you take them and He has already planned out how they will come to an end. He changes the seasons. I shared in this devotional a devotion called Sid. The story of a man who my husband and I ministered to in our last church. God used us to speak peace into Sid's life, and he came back to His relationship with God. Years before I stopped along the highway to pray for an older couple who almost hit a deer, not knowing it was Sid's mom and dad. God had already been setting things up, years ahead of time, to soften Sid's heart. God does not just sit around and point His finger saying, "Oh look what's going on here and there!" He is a planner; he knows the way that we take and has mapped things out.

My husband loves strategic games; we used to be in a church that had a ministry called The Strategic Game Fellowship. My husband loves to sit in front of a ASL board game, and strategically plan on how to conquer countries and the world. To me this is the most boring thing, but he and many more I know love to do it. I personally love strategic planning. I'm an administrator at heart and details and tasks are my thing. I love the behind the scenes work that makes up a big event where thousands of lives can be changed forever. Strategy is the pathway to our goal. Strategy is what our God is made of, and He is the best event planner ever!

"Then Moses stretched out his hand over the sea, and all that night the Lord drove the sea back with a strong east wind and turned it into dry land. The waters divided and the Israelites went through the sea on dry ground, with a wall of water on their right and on their left."
Exodus 14:21-22

I think the key words in this scripture that I want to focus in on are, "All that night the Lord drove the sea back" God told Moses In verse 16 of Exodus 14 what to do to part the sea,

"Raise your staff and stretch out your hand over the sea to divide the water so that the Israelites can go through the sea on dry ground."
Exodus 14:16

God had already led them to that exact place and knew exactly what he was going to do. Please remember He is ALWAYS working in His strategic planning. He strategically brought them to this place that seemed hopeless, and did not leave them there to face it all alone. He drove the sea back ALL THAT NIGHT with an east wind. When you find yourself in a strange situation or a situation that you do not understand, all through it, He is driving the seas back if your trust is in Him. Please remember the Israelites never saw with their eyes this east wind that God used to hold the sea back, but He was there working all night. You may not always see Him working, but He is working for you. He does this out of a deep love for us. And most the time it is in His time frame and not ours. He will come through when you NEVER expect it and you will stand amazed when you see He has planned things years in advance.

Sometimes or strategic planning must NOT be just sitting around thinking, but it must be getting up and moving! God is always on the move!

> "Then the Lord said to Moses, "Why are you crying out to me?
> Tell the Israelites to move on."
> Exodus 14:15

Even in Joshua we see an example of this,

> "And the Lord said to Joshua, "Stand up!
> What are you doing down on your face?""
> Joshua 7:10

Joshua was down on his face crying out to God and the Lord told him to get going! I'm all for prayer, I cannot live without it, but too many times we think we need to pray when the truth is we need to get off our butt and get moving! It's hard work but if we follow the example of God and want to be like Him we will heed these words.

I thank God today that He is a planner. I thank God that He is working even when we don't see His east wind! He is forever faithful. May God give you peace today, and joy, in knowing everything is totally under control because of our strategic God.

Dear God,
I am at peace knowing you work for us due to your love. Thank you for hearing our prayers. I honor you today.

August 29th

Soaked

Every time we go to Maine for our summer vacation it's my job to prepare the oil lamps. This year I had to find the oil, pour it in, and make sure the wicks were soaked, they will not burn unless they are soaked in the oil. Once the oil is on the wicks, they will light with a match and will burn forever until the oil in the lamp runs out. There always has to be some part of the wick in the oil to burn. I had trouble this year because the wicks were not immersed enough in the oil, so I had to keep dipping them until they were soaked.

"You, O Lord, keep my lamp burning;
My God turns my darkness into light."
Psalm 18:28

If God keeps our lamp burning then He must be like the oil in us, and that means we will not burn correctly unless we are soaked! My question to you today is, are you soaked? Have you soaked yourself in His presence? Have you soaked yourself in His Word?

"You are the light of the world.
A city on a hill cannot be hidden.
Neither do people light a lamp and put it under a bowl.
Instead they put it on its stand,
and it gives light to everyone in the house.
In the same way, let your light shine before men,
that they may see your good deeds and praise your Father in Heaven."
Matthew 5:14-16

When I read the scripture that says, "You are the light of the world," I feel such a deep responsibility. We are NOT supposed to be hidden; we are to be like that city on a hill that everyone sees. To be the light of the world we will have to be very disciplined, we will have to keep immersing and soaking! Constant, always constant.

If you get dry like the wick what are you going to do about it? What steps will you take to get on fire again? For you, it may be going back to church, getting involved in that small group or Sunday school class. Being disciplined to read your Bible. It may mean not hanging out with people who are leading you down unhealthy paths. So what are you going to do to soak?

I remember when I was in Bible college I would make myself get into the presence of God. I would put a sign on my door DO NOT DISTURB! I would light a candle, turn off the lights and put on worship music. As I began to worship God, soak in His presence, and read His Word, it would encourage my heart and light a fire under me again, to move on through whatever that week brought me.

It was a discipline, Soaking takes discipline! Unless we are filled up with Him, we will not be that light that He needs us to be.

Right now I sit in my niece's dorm room at Bible College, my son is in the dorm next door and my prayer is that these young people, Jon, Nina, Dan, Mary, Alina, Tori, Tom, Matt, Joy, Ashley, Alex and the list goes on, will seek God with all their hearts and get Soaked!

Are you soaked today?

Dear God,
To be a light for you is a great responsibility, help us to put you first. I honor you today.

<u>Sick of the Same Old, Same Old?</u>
"The Lord is with you when you are with Him."
2 Chronicles 15:2

God is Omnipresent, which means He is everywhere at one time. He is always with us, but I love this verse, It is a promise that when we spend time with Him, He is with us in a special way. Maybe a visitation, maybe a fresh touch, maybe more aware of His presence but all in all it says when we spend that time with God, He is with us.

Who would not want a special visit from God? Who would not want to spend time with the one who created the universe? Maybe you read these devotions and you don't really believe in God. Maybe you laugh at what you read. I wish so bad I could show you all He has done for me in my short lifetime. He has proved Himself to me in amazing unbelievable ways.

When I first started spending time with Him, I told Him I needed Him to prove Himself to me.

I did not know how to pray but my brother would tell me to just talk to God, like I would talk to anyone. So I did. I told Him exactly how I felt. I told him my desires and the things I was mad about. Because I was disciplined in my spending time with Him, amazing things started to happen and He actually proved himself to me. Some of those stories are already written in this devotional. There were times I would feel His presence so close in those early days, and I could not run from it. There are so many scriptures that talk about the fact that if we move closer to Him, He will move closer to us.

"Come near to God and he will come near to you."
James 4:8

But if he is Omnipresent, isn't He already near? Yes. This tells me that there is a deeper walk with God. I don't know about you, but I want a deeper closer walk with the one who can lead and guide me like Proverbs 3:5-6 talks about.

"Call to Me, and I will answer you, and
show you great and mighty things, which you do not know."
Jeremiah 33:3

Here is how I look at it. If you were in the same room with someone for an entire week and never said a word to them, you would never know them. Yes, they are there with you, but you never reached out, to get to know them. But if you were with someone for a week and communication was going, you would have a much deeper relationship with them. I hope you understand where I am going here.

515

God is always with us, He never leaves us. But if we reach out to Him, He promises to meet us, lead us, come nearer to us, and show us mighty things. Who would not want that?

There are many people that call themselves Christians walking around who have no communication with Him at all. Yes He is near, but longs to be nearer.

> "My sheep hear my voice, and I know them,
> and they follow Me. And I give them eternal life."
> John 10:27

Do you know Him today? Do you communicate with Him on a daily basis? Every morning when I get up, He is the first thing on my mind. I thank Him that I'm alive and breathing. That He gave me another day to live and work for Him. If you have never communicated with God before I encourage you to cry out to Him. Do what my brother told me to do, "Talk to Him like you would talk to me." Don't be afraid to tell God how you feel because He already knows anyway, he just wants to see some effort on our part.

I challenge you, I plead with you to draw near to Him, talk to Him. You will NOT regret it.

Sick of the same old, same old? Seek Him.

Dear God,
I thank you that You actually want to spend quality time with me. I'm not sure why, but I'm so very thankful. I honor you today.

August 31st

<u>Our GPS</u>

I can't even begin to tell you how much I love my GPS. I cannot imagine life without it. Today was very busy in the car. I went to a funeral and after that a hospital I had never been before.

After that a reception for the funeral, which was all on back roads, then I went home. On my way to the reception, every time the GPS lady would say, "Take a left on Ashley," or "Take a right on Bank," I would think about the way God wants to lead us. It's just like the GPS. He longs to lead us like this but the problem is most the time we don't listen or let him.

GPS's can be very fun, one time my daughter switched the person speaking to Chinese so we had a blast with that one! Another fun thing I love to do, is on Saturdays I like to go on craigslist and mark down all the garage sales near my home. Then I take off in the car with my GPS, I cannot do garage sales without it! There have been times I'm right by my house somewhere, but I'm so far on back roads that I could never make my way back home without it. I love the fact that I just put my address into the GPS and "BAM!" I am led right back home. No stress, no problems, just peace and leading.

I hope you know this is exactly the way God wants to lead us. Number one, it should be fun. Our walk with him does not have to be miserable. Even in the darkest storms He brings joy. When He has ever led me in life, I have been at perfect peace. If I ever took another road and did not follow the road He wanted me to go, I was usually miserable.

The great thing is He longs to lead us into healthy paths. Something we ALL need.

> "For I know the plans I have for you," declares the Lord,
> "Plans to prosper you and not harm you, plans to give you hope
> and a future."
> Jeremiah 29:11

In many cases we get distracted by other tempting roads or our own flesh. We must remember that His roads will NEVER harm us; they will always give us hope. We also must remain in Him, and near Him.

> "Remain in me, and I will remain in you. No branch can bear fruit by itself; it must remain in the vine. Neither can you bear fruit unless you remain in me. I am the Vine; you are the branches."
> John 15:4-5

It's kind of like me and my garage sailing. I cannot do it without my GPS! Ha-ha. When I am lost in Beverly, my town, I need it. We need God, what this scripture calls, The Vine. Unless we are connected, like the GPS is connected to our car, we will be lost.

My GPS makes my life more peaceful, simple, easy, and gives me great confidence.

It's the same way when we are connected with God in such a way, that He is leading us. His leading is vital in our life.

> "In all your ways acknowledge Him,
> And he will make your paths <u>straight</u>."
> Proverbs 3:6

Why wouldn't we want a more peaceful walk? I know for some of you, you have walked away like Jonah in the Bible. Here is the place of unrest that Jonah ended up, because he did not use his GPS, He went on the wrong road away from God,

> "Now, O Lord, take away my life,
> For it is better for me to die than to live."
> Jonah 4:3

Having the Lord in our life is like a free GPS! He longs to lead us in prayer, He longs for us to listen and hop on the right road, but we must be still before Him.

When was the last time you were still before Him?

Just like today in the car with my GPS, as soon as He speaks we should turn. If you are an independent person like me, you are not a born follower! You need to humble yourself and let God change your life. The one thing I desire for my family is that we will always be in the perfect will of God for our lives. There is nothing like it.

So, I'm not sure if you knew today that God longs to lead you like a GPS, but when He tells us the roads to get on it is just as direct and perfect. Plug in! Spend time with Him, ask Him to lead you. He is faithful. Trust me there are no roads like His roads.

Dear God,
May we always be in your perfect will for our lives. I honor you today.

September

September 1st

Death by Chocolate

There is this desert that I make on special occasion called Death by Chocolate, it's totally amazing and brings much joy to so many! Mostly me! My awesome nephews that live near us, Mason, Andrew and Dominic love it, and it's been way too long since I have made it for them! It takes an entire chocolate cake, an entire pan of fudge brownies, an entire bag of Milano cookies, Toffee Chips, about four or five boxes of Jell-O Chocolate instant pudding and Cool Whip! So bad, but so good! You put down a layer of pudding then start layers with pudding always being the in between. Or if you are lazy, just mix it all up! Cool Whip on top with 2 Milano cookies sticking out the top, should do it! Sometimes I shave chocolate onto the beautiful white Cool Whip so it looks great, and there you have it. Yum!

Every single one of these things on its own is amazing. I could eat moist chocolate cake by the spoonfuls, even without frosting. I could eat an entire pan of brownies by itself. Thank God I have discipline in this area or it would NOT be good. I Love Milano cookies and they are a sort of tradition for my husband and I. When we were dating we used to down a bag in one sitting! They are great alone! Toffee chips, pudding and whipped Cream, well, what more can I say? Each and every single one of them stand just fine on their own. But my word, put them all together and you have the most amazing yummy thing on this planet! Kids go crazy over it and so do adults. You can slop it up, or dress it up in a truffle bowl.

Tonight when I was reading this scripture it reminded me of Death by Chocolate! Now you know where my mind is today!

> "For this very reason, make every effort
> to add to your faith goodness;
> and to goodness, knowledge;
> and to knowledge, self control;
> and to self control, perseverance;
> and to perseverance, godliness;
> and to godliness, brotherly kindness;
> and to brotherly kindness, love.
> For if you possess these qualities in increasing measure,
> they will keep you from being ineffective and unproductive
> in your knowledge of our Lord Jesus Christ."
> 2 Peter 1:5-9

What an amazing powerful scripture this is. It says if we possess these qualities in great measure they will keep us from being unproductive and ineffective in our knowledge of God.

When looking at each quality in this scripture each one stands firm on its own! Faith itself has an entire chapter of the Bible dedicated to itself. Hebrews Chapter 11, which some call the Faith hall of fame! Goodness, well, when you are a good person it shows. People will know by just being with you for a few hours. Goodness stands out from the crowd. Knowledge can open doors that would never open unless you had it. Self control is a key to unlock any door. Perseverance will bring you through the darkest storm and godliness stands firm like a rock. Brotherly kindness will knock down walls that no one could knock down, and love never fails.

Every single one of these ingredients in Chapter 1 of Second Peter would WOW anyone at a holiday party on the table! But mix them together and you have a powerhouse! I know it's silly to compare these things to my incredible desert, but I hope you understand what I'm trying to say. These are God's ingredients for effectiveness and productiveness! Who would not want to be effective and productive for God? I hope and pray this is your desire. To make a mark on this World! This is my desire and even if I have to lose sleep, I will accomplish it.

Some of you may say, "Well, you don't know what I'm going through!" no I don't, but I know what I have been through, and what I have yet to go through. You CAN be effective and productive! Even after going through horrific situations that are unthinkable to others, I am a testimony of that. Even through chronic pain and in a wheel chair like Joni, who paints with her mouth and speaks hope to millions.

It's all about your response to your situation.

If you keep adding powerful ingredients that already stand on their own to the mix, you can change the world, even if you cannot move! All you have to do is pray!

Your prayers can change the world, and the people in the next room!
Friend, maybe it's time to go out and get some new ingredients to add to the mix?

The truth is that the ingredients in my Death by Chocolate probably cause health issues, no matter how good they are, but the ingredients in 2 Peter 1:5-9 cause a productive life.

Dear God,
Forgive me for making everyone want to go eat Chocolate! But I hope and pray they do want more of your mix after reading this! I honor You today.

Book Light
"Your Word is a lamp to my feet and a light for my path."
Psalm 119:105

Most everyone in America has a Holy Bible in their home if they believe the words written in it, or not. The Bible is the #1 Best Seller of all time as far as books are concerned. Maybe because in a time of needing hope people turn to it. The Scriptures say The Bible is like a light and it will guide you. There has been only one time in my life when I was without my Bible after coming to God and that was when our puppy Arwen ate every page of my Bible. I came home to a floor that I could not see and wondered what was all over the floor. It did not take long until I realized it was my Bible. Just one week before that I had said to myself, "I need to get a cover for this so the puppy does not get it." Too late. I felt lost without my Bible. I love to read it every day and it does guide me.

"For these commands are a lamp, this teaching is a light,
and the corrections of discipline are the way to life."
Proverbs 6:23

Who would not want a lamp in a dark place leading them? When I take Arwen out at night I trust in my flashlight. Last night when I took her out the batteries were dying. When I got to the woods I could see nothing! It was not a good feeling at all. But His light never goes out. I trust in that flashlight at night to help me watch my dog. Maybe sometimes we should trust in the light of Christ as far as who we are watching out for, such as our kids, or parents, friends or loved ones.

The Bible is the only Book that is inspired. To put it another way, it's alive. OK, DON'T CHECK OUT YET!

"For the Word of God is living and active.
Sharper than any double-edged sword,
It penetrates even to dividing soul and spirit,
joints and marrow;
it judges the thoughts and attitudes of the heart."
Hebrews 4:12

The Word is the only book that is active, as we read the Holy Spirit brings things into our understanding. As we read The Word can actually change our lives. I have shared many times in this devotional, stories of when I was reading The Word of God and how it changed my heart and life because I applied it to myself.

"In the beginning was the Word, and the Word
was with God, and the Word was God."
John 1:1

I won't even attempt to explain this scripture. As humans we see a beginning and an end to everything. God has always been, and always was. We cannot comprehend this due to our little minds. But this Word says that the Word has always been since the beginning as well. Isn't it so cool to think that the book that is the #1 seller of all time in our world was with God from the beginning? This totally blows my mind, but it makes so much sense.

If you are reading this and are thinking, "This is hogwash and she is totally wacked!" I challenge you to cry out to God and ask him, with a true heart, to make Himself real to you. If you mean it.

In truth, He will. You will be blown away as to how He wants to communicate with you, a simple human being. I thank Him for that.

> "All Scripture is God-breathed and is useful for teaching,
> rebuking, correcting and training in righteousness."
> 2 Timothy 3:15-16

So not only has it been around since the beginning of time, powerful like a sword (Ephesians 6:17), and is living and active, but it's God-breathed. Don't you want to read a book that is God breathed? Our God is alive and well, ready to lead and guide and it's time to read! If you are ever discouraged, down, depressed the very best thing you can do is pick up your Bible! Romans 10:17 says, that the Bible will increase our faith! Don't you desire this?

Anyone can use a "Pick me up!" or some encouragement!

If you have no faith in God today, I challenge you to Read the only living Book and let God speak to you. Many wait until they have been diagnosed with a horrible thing or are about to die before they read it. Friend, why not search after God now. Don't let wasted years go by when He could be encouraging your heart, and leading your every step! If you don't know what to say to Him, read.

Get out the book light.

Dear God,
I thank You so much for Your Word, give us a deep desire to read it. I honor you today.

September 3rd

Kolkata Fruit Cart

I was looking at pictures of our last trip to India today and a picture stood out to me. It was a picture of Kolkata's streets and a fruit cart right in the middle of everything.

My husband and I love India. We have lived there and been there many times, but went there again in February to do ministry, and renewed our vows in New Delhi with our friend who we call Bengali Bob. I have had a love for India since I was a little girl, and the Puta family lived two doors down. Years later while on bed rest with my second pregnancy, my husband came home one night feeling like God was leading him to that part of the world, to teach at an AG Bible College for a month. While there, God gave him a deep love for the people group. Thus, a love for the country and people there, in both of us.

Kolkata is a dark but beautiful place. At night, I have said before, that you have to pick the soot out of your nose. Any missionary that goes there, gives part of their health living in that city. It is not an easy life. Demonic strongholds must be broken and darkness seems to reign in the streets, but there is a HOPE that burns bright. I pray and honor all my missionary friends there.

Back to my fruit cart, I was looking at this amazing picture. The color of most Kolkata streets is ash or brown, everything seems dark. On top of the dark colors is filth, sometime raw sewage or bubbles from street baths and people trying to clean themselves or the things they own, with filthy water. Garbage is everywhere in this picture and it's mixed with broken and smashed pottery and bricks. There is a skinny malnourished street dog sitting under the cart. Pretty much every single thing in the picture is sandy and black. Then you see this fruit cart on four wheels. Brilliant colors! A pop of color in a city that David Bromstad would say is a masterpiece.

Oranges, with the most amazing orange. Bright red apples and purple and green grapes. Not sure what the other fruit in the picture is, but the colors are over the top! I think I snapped it going by in the car. I was not thinking of any of this at the time, I was just in awe of a city I love.

So today my screen saver came on and my picture albums were scrolling when this picture caught my eye. I could not stop looking at it. I ended up printing it.

There was such truth in it to me. The Lord is like a pop of color in a dark place. A brilliance that you can't escape. A beauty among ugliness. A HOPE among desperation. Life among death.

The picture speaks volumes to me. My friends who live there on a full time basis, Beth and Dale, Joicy and Koshy, Bob and Twyla and so many more are the pop of color in a grey land. They are literal walking HOPE! Their hands are God's hands. Their feet are the feet of Christ.

He needs us, our hands, eyes and feet. To guide, love and touch the lives of others. Missionaries are like a brilliance. I have so many more friends, way too many to speak of, that risk their very lives on the field and right here in America. This is a SHOUT OUT to them today.

Do you realize today that you also are this same pop of color? You are the same cart of HOPE.

I wonder if we are willing to lay every single thing we want in this life down, and say to the Master, "Take it all! My place of living, the things I desire for myself and my family. I will go where you want me to go and I will do what you want me to do." As a missions major at Valley Forge Christian College I had a beautiful leather Bible and on the front cover I had printed,

> "Then I heard the voice of the Lord saying,
> "Whom shall I send? And who will go for us?"
> And I said, "Here am I. Send me!"
> Isaiah 6:8

The point my friend is not if you're on the mission field right now, it's is your heart willing to go? If He were to speak to you tonight or tomorrow to go somewhere here in America, would you go? Would you give it all up and do what He says. What about overseas? Missions is obedience to Christ. Missions is a pop of color in a dark land. Missions is a spilled out heart just waiting for Gods direction. Are you at that place?

It's time to lay down our white picket fences and ask God if there is anything else He desires. We know what we desire but what about the countless souls that wait for a pop of color in their dark land. You may be exactly where Jesus wants you today, but have you ever asked? Many souls could go to Hell someday because you never asked. I challenge you today to spill out and ask. He is ready to say, "Stay put, or go!"

> "The steps of a good man are ordered by the lord."
> Psalm 37:23

> "Whoever listens to me will live in safety and be at ease,
> without fear of harm."
> Proverbs 1:33

"I am the Lord your God, who teaches you what is best for you, who directs you in the way you should go. If only you had paid attention to my commands, your peace would have been like a river."
Isaiah 48:17

"I will instruct you and teach you in the way you should go."
Psalm 32:8

"The Lord will guide you always; He will satisfy your needs in a sun-scorched land and will strengthen you frame. You will be like a well-watered garden, like a spring whose waters never fail."
Isaiah 58:11

Don't tell me you can't do it, because there is scripture after scripture that proves you can.

He needs you today to be like that
Kolkata fruit cart.

Dear God,
May our hearts long to be spilled out waiting for you to speak. Anywhere, anytime I will go like Isaiah cried. May this reader feel your presence right now. Speak to their heart. I honor You today.

September 4th

Learn From It

On the East Coast we have a store called Christmas Tree Shop. I just had friends here from New Jersey, and they had never heard of it. I thought everyone had heard of it! It's a store where they get overstock stuff and prices are way down. Most people fill their carts when going shopping there. I got a flyer from them the other day that had roman shades for ten dollars. I was excited because most of mine were in very bad shape and I needed three very badly. Roman shads can be very expensive so I went right away and picked my three shades. They have been up for weeks now.

They are made of a very nice expensive fabric and I love them. Yesterday however one side on one was hanging while the other was up, as I pulled the string. I looked around back and there is this little plastic hook that claws onto the back of a piece of wood on the shade. In other words it's not attached in any other way to the shade but to be clawed to this wood. There is this little loop there, so my thought was if I get those key chain like things and put them on there and then tie the string to it, then it will never come part again. I hope you can picture what I'm trying to say in your mind?! My first thought was, if I would have gone to a nicer store this would NOT be happening! The way the string and tracks were, you knew there MUST be better roman shades out there that would NEVER come apart! The thought went through my mind, if I ever had to purchase these again, I would look on the back to MAKE SURE they were not like this!

Isn't this just like life? We learn from our mistakes! When we fail, fall, or mess up we learn never to do stupid things again. I know 100% that if I ever shop for roman shades again that the first thing I will do is to find out how the string is attached to the back of the shade. If it's NOT on there permanently, I won't purchase it!

> "As a dog returns to its vomit, so a fool repeats his folly."
> Proverbs 26:11

There have been times in my life when I have done stupid things and for some strange reason, I do the same stupid thing again! It's like a dog returning to its vomit. Why do pets do that, it's so nasty! They puke then eat what they puked, it's like they have this natural instinct that they have to clean up right away after themselves. Too bad we don't have that kind of a natural instinct when we mess up! Pets pretty much clean up right away! Why do we wait so long sometimes! We are so foolish; you would think we would learn a little quicker than we do. These are times I'm thankful for a God filled with Grace who sees so much more than we see with our own eyes.

I tell people all the time to see themselves through the eyes of Christ and not their own eyes!

When we look at scripture it tells us who we are in Christ.

We are ambassadors (2 Corinthians 5:20), a beautiful fragrance (2 Corinthians 2:15), children of God (John 1:12), a new creature (2 Corinthians 5:17), a letter Christ can write on (2 Corinthians 3: 2-3), the light of the world (Matthew 5:14), and the list goes on. No matter who we are in Christ we will still fail.

"For ALL have sinned and fall short of the glory of God."
Romans 3:23

When you mess up, stop beating yourself over the head all the time and just learn from it! I will never ever again purchase a roman shade without a back that is not permanently attached! I learned from doing the wrong thing! I know now, what to look for! Stop letting your self esteem be dragged through the mud! Stop hating yourself, and start learning from your mistakes and start doing the better thing! You can do this! Even if you have no encouragement from anyone around you, or your family, there is so much encouragement in The Word of God! Read it!

And...

Learn from It!

Dear God,
Your Grace is amazing. We thank you for it. I honor You today.

Little Windex® Jobs

I'm working on my 4th year in maternity (2010). I was trained in the baby nursery but also labor and delivery. I assist for C-Sections and normal labor. If the Doctor needs something I am like a runner. When we count sponges I count and clean up. The guy from Dirty Jobs should really check out the C-Section OR. It's pretty bad, when all is said and done. All that to say, I'm pretty used to blood and guts. Taking placentas, and bio-hazard bagging them. It does not even faze me anymore. I assist for circumcision, and when you work around blood so much there just comes a point where it does not bother you anymore. But something happened yesterday that grossed me out more than anything ever has!

I went to get chips, nestle toll house. The kids had teens over from college, and I wanted to be a good mom, and make them all chocolate chip pancakes for breakfast. They did the clean up, by the way! Anyway I went to two stores early in the morning and both were totally out of chips! I have never heard such a thing! So I saw chocolate bars that were dark chocolate and I thought I would grate the chocolate on top of the pancakes. I picked up two thick bars and put them on the counter. The lady picked up the bars and I noticed there was blood all over her hand. She was freaking out; when we both looked on the counter there was blood. The guy before me in line must have been bleeding and I put the bars right down on the blood without even seeing it. This poor lady had his blood all over her hands! Nasty! But it gets so much worse. The store owner comes over and starts to Windex everything like the guy on Big Fat Greek Wedding! He wipes down the counter, everything around it, and tells her to go was her hands. What happened next was worse than anything I have ever seen.

He takes the two candy bars and wipes them with paper towels and Windex, the amount of blood that was on the chocolate bar wrapper was gross! So much blood on the candy wrappers! He wipes them down, and then to my total shock, puts them back on the shelf for someone to buy! Can you even believe that! Like that $1.35 is going to kill his budget! I was like Joseph; I had to run right out of there. I was about to freak out on him and ask him how he could do such a thing. I will tell you this; I will never shop there again. That grossed me out more than any nasty thing I have seen in the medical field! Just so you know, this was NOT a major store, this was one of those gas station shops, and it was right down the road from me.

I was surprised how much it bothered me, but to think of someone going in there and paying $1.35 for a candy bar that once had blood all over the wrapper, is a thought that I cannot even handle. Or a mom getting it for her child and then handing it to them. I will never forget it. I don't care if he wiped it clean, the DNA is still there!

This is how we are sometimes. We do these little Windex jobs and seem to think all is well with us. We wipe everything clean so no one can see it was dirty on the outside, but the DNA is still there friend. Sometimes you HAVE to GET RID of things and NOT put them back on the shelf! Truth is, the store owner should have thrown those two candy bars right out. If we were to do something like that in the Operating room at the hospital, we would get fired, it's against all the laws and health codes. So why do we do it to ourselves when it comes to our sin? Little Windex Jobs won't do it, when matters of the heart are concerned.

There are many scripture that show us that we can live in victory!

> "No, in all these things we are more than conquerors
> through him who loved us."
> Romans 8:37

But the truth is if you do little Windex jobs, DNA still hangs around and will haunt you and drag you down. You need to get rid of some things in your life. If your temptation is porn on your computer, you need to have an accountability, like Covenant Eyes. It's like $7.00 a month for as many computers as you want to cover. One computer gets the report every single month of every single sight that was hit! It is a safety net and keeps peoples ways pure! Covenant Eyes is NOT a little Windex job, it helps to keep you from temptation. What about other temptations? If your temptation is anger or gossip, why do you put yourself in a place where you sit for hours with people and talk about others? Maybe you need to not go there anymore, to make real changes in your life? Hang out with those who hang out with God, until you are strong enough to deal with your temptation. Someday you will be strong enough to say, "Maybe we can talk about something else!"

It's time to stop all the Little Windex Jobs and start getting rid of some serious germs in our life!

Don't stay on the shelf with bad DNA, move! Do something about it! Get rid of the garbage no matter if it costs you or not!

I hate Little Windex Jobs.

Dear God,
Help us to get rid of all the junk. To stop cleaning up the outside, without taking care of the inside. Thank you for Your amazing grace. I honor You today.

September 6th

Cracked Armor

Wow, God's Word just continues to blow my mind. I'm going to share with you bits of 1 Thessalonians 5: 4-24 and comment on them. I would love to write the entire chapter out but its way too long, so enjoy reading.

> "Let us NOT be like others, who are asleep,
> but let us be alert and self-controlled."
> Verse 6

This is so interesting. This scripture is to Christians. It implies that many Christians are asleep! That we need to WAKE UP! Why would Paul have to give Christians this reminder, unless they were asleep?

Like many times I have shared with you in these devotions Self Control is a fruit of God's Spirit in your life (Galatians 5:22-23). It's coupled alongside Love, joy, peace patience, kindness, goodness and the list goes on. This is how important self control is! This scripture tells us to be different! It tells us to be alert, and not like those asleep! If I were to give a definition here to the word asleep I would say, "Those NOT on the move!" Alertness means fully aware and attentive, or an attitude of readiness or caution, as before an unexpected attack!

What about those Christians who drink a glass of wine? Hmmm I wonder if I should go here. Here is the truth. You who drink are not going to Hell, but you are NOT fully alert! Many times in God's word it talks about being alert!

> "Be alert, fully alert."
> Isaiah 21:7

I have had my large share of wine; I have not had a glass in 27 years. I know that one glass made me tipsy. I guess we could put it this way, picture the movie Lord of the Rings, in the movie there is always a watchman. They would NEVER EVER put a watchman or watchmen in the watchtower if they were the least bit tipsy. Or groggy minded. NEVER!! Watchmen are there for oncoming hoof beats of danger. In your walk with God you need to be on guard. I'm sure the enemy just loves it when we are groggy minded or tipsy. He looks for little cracks to crawl through when we are not fully alert, and on guard of our own soul. The sad thing is, in crawling through our cracks, he often affects the lives of the ones we love and who are close to us. So if you care about them, you will stay alert.

> "Let us be self-controlled, putting on faith and love as a breastplate,
> and the hope of salvation as a helmet."
> Verse 8

I love this, Ephesians 6 starting at verse 10 talks about putting on the armor of God. One of the pieces of armor is the Breastplate.

> "Stand firm then, with the belt of truth buckled around
> your waist, with the breastplate of righteousness in place."
> Ephesians 6:14

This is all the Armor of God chapter says here, that the breastplate is made of righteousness. What does a breastplate do? It guards our heart and major organs. But in the scripture I shared with you in 1 Thessalonians it says, "Putting on faith and love as part of our breastplate" (Verse 8.) So coupled with righteousness, there MUST be faith and love! You can sit and pray on, the armor of God till you are blue in the face friend! The truth is, unless you have faith, which is an ACTION word, and love, there will be NO righteousness. So you can see where self control fills the gaps here. We must have self control to keep our way pure. We are in war against our own flesh, and an enemy who wants to harm us. In return, self control not only saves us, but those we love.

> "For God did NOT appoint us to suffer wrath but
> to receive salvation through our Lord Jesus Christ."
> Verse 9

God's intention was NEVER harm on us. Everything was perfect until sin came into the world with the first bite of an apple. The first bite was disobedience, or lack of self control.

> "He died for us so that, whether we are awake
> or asleep, we may live together with Him."
> Verse 10

Here is the amazing truth. Whether we are awake or asleep, whether we have self control or not, we still can live together with Him. He knows we WILL mess up. Such is life, it's a fact.

This is how deep His Grace stretches, that even though we blow it, He still wants to be with us. He loves us that much.

Though we may not look like a warrior today.
Though there may be cracks in our armor.
Though we totally lack self control in our lives,
He still desires to be with us.
Amazing Grace.

Dear God,
There is no one like You. I honor You today.

September 7th

Miracle of Sacrifice

I love beautiful nails, I used to have them. You can walk into CVS or any other place and see mounds of nail art and deco. There are beauty supply stores that carry very unique things as well. There is French, stickers, jewels and more. For years and years I had perfect manicured nails. Somehow they made me feel beautiful and more feminine. I loved them so much that when my husband and I were first in ministry I went to nail school and learned how to do acrylic and gel nails. For years after that, I did my own nails and fills. I just loved them.

Time went on and I began to lead worship playing the guitar. As many of you know, you cannot have nails when you play the guitar. You also gain calluses. So short nails and big peeling calluses, not very feminine to say the least! As a matter of a fact pretty ugly.

Tonight I sat at the ministry my husband and I do on Tuesday nights, and I looked down at my hands. Thoughts of my old nails crossed my mind and for a brief moment I again missed them.

One time I was at this event, and a pastors wife came up to me and asked me why I don't do my nails, she made a comment about how ugly they were. Ha-ha. I told her I played guitar and then she understood, but it's hard sometimes.

The truth is there are things in life that you will have to sacrifice for ministries sake or as some call, "the greater good". I know this may all sound a bit silly talking about nails, but to me it was an important thing. Something I still think about every time I go to a holiday party or event. But I thank God for the times He uses me playing the guitar and singing. To me it's all worth it. Just like right now, my daughter is in the other room watching something that I want to watch with her, but I know God wants me to minister to you right now.

Giving up things is NOT easy. Sometimes it may take time, but in the long run it will be worth the wait. Sometimes even souls depend on it.

God knows the simple little things in life that we love so much like a cup of hot tea, a nice cozy bed to sleep in, a long walk on a fall day. What if He were to tell us to do something else for a while? Like move to India where my girlfriend has to breathe in dirty air and sleep on a thin uncomfortable mattress. Would we? What about the everyday practical things like nails?

Sounds silly, but God is pleased with the little things we give up for Him as well as the big things.

There is a beautiful story of practical sacrifice in Matthew 14:13-21 and John 6:1-15.

Most call it the Miracle of the Loaves and Fishes but I call it the Miracle of sacrifice. There is always a focus on how Jesus took the bread and fish and they multiplied to feed thousands of people, but what about this scripture that always seems to be left out,

> "Here is a boy with five small barley loaves and two small fish."
> John 6:9

In other countries sometimes children have to walk long roads, and bring food and water back to their families. The people here needed food and they were all hungry. This boy willingly gave his 5 small barley loaves and 2 small fish to Jesus. It may not seem like a big deal to you but I bet in his heart he had a bit of fear that maybe mom and dad might get mad that he gave dinner, or perhaps the week's worth of food away. This was no small thing for a family who is home waiting for dinner. I wish so bad we knew more about this boy. In his giving of a small thing, thousands were blessed.

Are you angry tonight perhaps at someone? Could that anger keep you from touching the lives of thousands? It's time for sacrifice; give it up for the greater good. For souls.

Is there a small comfort that you love, but you know if you give it up God could use you somewhere else in a more powerful way? Or if you give it to someone more people will be blessed?

What is it tonight that He willingly wants you to hand over to Him? It may seem silly and small to others but the big and little things matter to God when they are given with a pure heart.

Keep your focus on souls, keep your focus on what God has clearly called you to do, and do It with all your heart no matter what things need to be sacrificed along the way.

The Miracle of Sacrifice is a very powerful thing.

Dear God,
Let us never thing small things don't matter to you. You blessed thousands with a tiny basket of bread and fish. I honor You today.

September 8th

Power Nap

So about an hour ago I sat here at my desk and began to do what I normally do to write my devotion. I cracked open my Bible and began to think about my day and pray. "Lord, what do you want me to minister today?" I totally could not keep my eyes open! I only have had one other time when trying to write, that this happened. Not a good feeling to say the least. The last time I had this happen, I fought it, this time there was no fighting! My brain and body were shutting down!

It was a very busy day for me. Up early, drove my Angela to school then went to my girlfriends for a drive into Boston for an eye check. She had to drive me because they dilated my eyes and I could not see. After that food shopping, then came home to play "catch up". One thing after another ran my body down. So there I sat trying to think and I could not fight it. I was falling asleep in my chair! I'm sure it was a pretty funny sight.

My home office is in a guest room. I have a corner desk and then against the other wall is a full bed. I knew what I had to do! I took a few steps laid my head down and that was the end of that. I did not even take the time to turn the light off, that's how out of it I was. Next thing I know my Angela is saying, "Mom, we have to see this movie!" She runs in, and did not know I was sleeping. She flipped the light off. I got up a few minutes after that and realized it was one hour to the minute of when I laid down. I had fallen asleep and an entire hour went by. I was in a deep sleep!

Sometimes our bodies just need a serious power nap. I'm sure you have done it, even if you lay your head down for a half hour you always feel better! My husband and I are opposites in the fact that he can lay his head down and within five minutes he is sound asleep, whereas I will lie there 45 minutes before I ever start to doze! Unless I'm tired like today that is. It's so funny.
But I feel much better now that I had that hour power nap; I'm ready to face the night!

Power naps are power-full!

They help our physical body when much needed sleep is evident! What about our spiritual bodies? What about when ever ounce of energy is sucked out of us spiritually. We have given and given, ministered to others, poured and poured. Now we are tired. So many men and ladies in the ministry, or volunteering in the church go nonstop, and God is pleased with their willing heart and hard working hands! But sometimes you MUST say, "No." For your spiritual health! God will not be pleased if you are so involved in ministry that you are not spending time with Him and being filled up in prayer and The Word. So involved in ministry that you personally don't know the One you are ministering for!

It might just be time for a spiritual power nap. Are you overloaded? Overtired? Too many irons on the fire? What is it that you are going to let go of to get closer to Him? If you are not the kind of person who has self control and discipline, then you have to give up something to draw nearer. How many ministries are you involved in? How many people are you running for, and taking care of? Do you feel like a taxi driver who gets no tips? Ha-ha! It's time for a spiritual power nap.

When you are tired it's easy, just lay down, but how do you take a spiritual power nap? Maybe talk to your leadership about taking a month off. As a Pastor's wife for 7 ½ years, I know that when people can no longer continue on in ministry it can be a stress for us, because then all of a sudden we have a void. I would rather that person rest and then come back more effective! Sometimes if your spiritual health is NOT in order it will affect your physical health anyway!

If you don't do it yourself, God will do it for you and give you a wakeup call.

He not only wants us to stay physically healthy but spiritually healthy. Being able to soak in the Word of God, and take a special time to fast and pray. He is ever faithful during these times, and I think too many of us miss them because we are so involved or plugged in.

"Seek the lord while He may be found; call on Him while he is near."
Isaiah 55:6

"But if from there you seek the Lord your God, you will find Him if you look for him with all your heart and with all your soul."
Deuteronomy 4:29

Why not take some time for a Spiritual Power Nap?

Dear God,
We need rest in You. I pray for this reader today, may they find you as they seek You. Make Yourself so real to them today and meet their needs. I honor You today.

September 9th

Fling it Off

Today I got in the mood for Rice Krispies Treats. Who does not love these amazing squares? Some people make them with Cocoa Krispies and other cereals. I remember as a child standing on a chair as mom and I made them. When my son was five, I had him standing on a chair as we made them together, when I took the pot off the stove Jonathan put the entire palm of his hand down on the burner. It was horrible, but he learned never to touch the burners again! All these memories from Rice Krispies Treats! Remember Count Chocula? My Brother Lou's favorite cereal! I guess that's for another devo! Ha-ha!

How can something so amazing to eat and low in fat, be such a pain to make? I cannot tell you how much I hate to make these treats! As most of you know the butter goes in the pot and then the marshmallows, you let them melt and then put in 6 cups of the cereal. This is the part I cannot stand! Everything sticks to everything. You can't even stir unless your spoon is covered in butter. Today I used my pointer finger to scrape the excess off the spoon into the dish and the entire wad of marshmallow and Krispies stuck to my finger. I could not even fling it off! It was crazy. Once I got everything in the pan I had to butter my hands in order to spread the Treats flat. I said, like I do every single time I make these, that I would NEVER make them again! But then one square and you purchase the ingredients again!

Some say, "Just buy the ones already made in the store!" Well, have you ever tasted them? They are horrible! Almost counterfeit! Have a crazy aftertaste. But the real life, pain to make Treats, is the most amazing low fat snack ever invented on the face of the planet!

Once again, how can something so amazing be such a pain to make? Sometimes in life you go through things that are really a pain to go through. They don't make sense, they are messy, they are hurtful and hard to fling off of you, but in the end you have the most amazing thing ever! Even when all is said and done, the evidence that you went through it is still there!

When I was done making them today, the kitchen was a MESS! I had to clean marshmallow off everything! The pot, stove, and spoon! The evidence that I made these awesome treats was all over my kitchen. Sometimes, unless cleaned up right away, evidence can linger. It's important to not let it linger too long! The more you let it linger the harder it will be to clean up! GET OUT THE CLEANERS! Today I cleaned up quick; this is always the wise thing when dealing with marshmallow! It's also a wise thing when dealing with real life situations. And stay away from the counterfeit, the easy way out. There is always an easier way, but we don't learn as much when we take that road. There is a reason we have to get messy sometimes and in the end we have masterpiece!

"I can do all things through Him who gives me strength."
Philippians 4:13

No matter how messy, you still can do it.

And the cool thing is, even if you are the only one going through it, or cleaning up the after mess, everyone in the long run gets blessed. Just like my family will be blessed tonight with Treats.

I could share many stories of being in the hospital for biopsies or surgeries, and how The Lord used me to minister to those around me. Nurses, doctors, and roommates, we question why way too quickly when we are in messy situations. God is in complete control my friend, trust and have Faith.

"O afflicted city, lashed by storms and not comforted, I will build you with stones of turquoise, your foundations with sapphires."
Isaiah 54:11

Dear God,
Thank you for amazing things out of messy situations. Bless this reader, and help them through their storm. I honor You today.

September 10th

Habit or Hobbit

As I was going about my night I was thinking of everything I did today that I don't even think about. Everything that that seems it has become a habit. What exactly is a habit? Many online dictionaries said, "An acquired behavior pattern regularly followed." Ok, so today, let's see:

Out of bed
Made coffee
Drive my Angela to school
Come back home
Get ready for work
Work
Dig into the Word
Pray
Check emails
More work
Welcome husband home
Go to the gym together
Get Angela from school
Shower
Think of what's for dinner
Make dinner
Write
And this list goes on...

There are so many daily things that we do every single day, the same exact things over and over. Most the time we don't even think about them, we just do them. We have to do them to feel good or look good. It's just part of us. I hope and pray The Reading of God's word is in the list for you. Soaking it in. As you know there are also horrible habits in life but God's Word should be part of your everyday life. You should need it like you have to put your (ladies) make up on! Ha-ha.

My brother always said, "If the house needs painting, paint it." Yes, yes, I know, God's word is so much more than habit. But please understand what I'm trying to say! You should need it like your everyday things. Like your early morning Java! Like your special shampoos that you must have!

> "In the beginning was the Word, and the Word was with God,
> and the Word was God."
> John 1:1

When we spend time in this book, that is the world's best seller, we spend time with Him. The Word of God is His voice to us. It will NOT return void.

Hobbits are a needy bunch. The most popular Hobbits I know are Bilbo Baggins, Frodo Baggins, Samwise Gamgee, Peregrin Took and Meriadoc Bandybuck. These creatures that came from a very creative mind fill themselves with bad habits. They eat and eat and eat. They eat 7 meals a day and they are not little snack meals! Breakfast, Second Breakfast, Elevenses, Luncheon, Afternoon Tea, Dinner, and later in the day supper! They also snack in between! If I ate like that I would be as big as a house. But because they are fake, there are not too many big Hobbits. They must drink lots of Ale, which means they are not too alert most the time. Yes they live a happy go lucky life, but their Habits stink. Don't get me wrong I love these guys, but we need healthy habits.

What are you habits? Are they more like the Hobbits?

Seriously,I want you to list them after you read this. Your everyday things that you do. Put a line through those things that you think you might have to take away because they lead you down an unhealthy path. If you call yourself a person who knows God and wants to walk with Him, is reading the word of God or praying on your list?

You need to make this one of the most important things of your day. You can fit it in, if you have discipline in your life. Think about your time watching TV, Gaming, talking on the cell phone, texting, fooling around on facebook and playing Sports. Trust me, you CAN fit it in.

Think about your list, is it more Habit or Hobbit?

"Heaven and earth will pass away, but My Words will never pass away."
Matthew 24:35

"His name is the Word of God."
Revelation 19:13

Dear God,
Help us to be healthier, and to draw closer to you. I honor You today.

9/11

I will never forget the day. I was walking with my mother in law in Mashpee Massachusetts at the Mashpee Commons. The Commons is this amazing outdoor market place with little quaint shops where you see unique things that you can't find anywhere else. We were walking shop to shop and we came across a tobacco store. I begged her to go in because I love the smell of pipe tobacco, my dad used to smoke one, and I just wanted to take a breath in. As we were laughing at the fact that we were just there for the smells, the TV was blaring, and the owner was glued to it. I thought it was a bit weird that the TV was even on, but whatever floats your boat. That day, I was glad the TV was on! My mother walked over first to see what he was watching, as I just went table to table and took in the smells. Sorry, I love the smell of tobaccos Ha-ha.

When my mother in law came back to me her face was all red and her neck was all hives. The last time I saw her like this the Dr. had just told her she had cancer and she hived up. I knew right away, that something was horribly wrong. She told me that a plane had just hit the first tower. Then she told me that my brother in law, Dave, was at a meeting that day at the Pentagon. She did not know the time of his meeting. From that point on as you can imagine we joined with the tobacco shop owner in watching what was to become one of the worst days ever in American History.

My mother in law and I were only at the Mashpee Commons like 15 minutes, excited about how beautiful the day was and how we could spend the day, just taking our time walking shop to shop. In a split second that was over. I knew when the second plane hit the other tower that I had to get my mom out of there. I told her we were leaving because I could see the fear in her eyes knowing that her son was meeting in a place that could be a target. We went home which was only miles down the road, and I left her there, as I went to my kid's school to get them.

Where were you on 9/11? Did your world stop? Did you hurray and go get your children? Did you leave work, and rush to the home of a family member? If you could not leave work, did the office stop, and come together as one that day? Not worrying about the deadlines and calls coming in.

That day was a day of change. My husband and I at the time were pastors of a church in Cape Cod Massachusetts. The Sunday after 9/11 Churches were filled, including ours. Why? Why did people care to go to church after 9/11? Did they want to pray for the families of those who lost loved ones? Did they experience a fear of death? Were they scared of other attacks and somehow the church made them feel safe? I don't know all the reasons, but I do know that when something like that happens for the first time in some people's lives, they think of God and the afterlife.

This was a day that in just a short time frame almost 3,000 people died. Hearts were broken and confused all over the world. Many searched for answers, for some sort of hope in their life.

I'm not sure what is going on your life now years later, but I want you to know that our tomorrow is never promised. Yes there are crazy people in our world who are willing to die for a cause. Some evil, like on 9/11 and some good, like countless missionaries who only want to help people, not hurt people. They are there for the cause of Christ.

> "Therefore keep watch, because you do not know
> on what day your Lord will come."
> Matthew 24:42

9/11 rocked all of our worlds.

But when Christ comes back, every life will be changed, in ever nation.

> "Every knee will bow before me; every tongue will confess
> to God. So then, each of us will give an account of himself to God."
> Romans 14:11

The sad thing is, that many of you who read this now, won't have the opportunity to get to know Him now. You don't want to. He only offers joy and peace, so I'm not sure why some turn that down? Yes, we still live our normal lives and some live in horrific situations, but having a peace through things like that can only be evidence of a Mighty God.

There were many very brave people that died that day. Some by choice.

I want you to know that Jesus Christ died for you by choice. He loves you, and Gives comfort through every storm. Turn to Him on this day that we remember.

Dear God,
Be with the families who lost loved ones on 9/11. Holy Spirit be their comfort today and every day. May we never forget what some did for us that day. May we never forget what You did for us. I honor You today

September 12th

The Mule

There was a farmer who had a beautiful big farm. He had acres and acres of land, so much so, that the town asked him if on one of his acres they could put a giant deep pit for townspeople's garbage. They paid him for the available space. The farmer let the town dig the pit and day after day townspeople would come and throw their garbage into the pit.

One day the farmers Mule was making his way along the beautiful acres of grass and eating as much as he could. The smell was leading the Mule closer to the pit. He followed his nose! The Mule came upon the pit and got so close to the edge that he fell into the pit. He stood at the bottom of the pit looking up wondering how he would get out.

Every half hour on the hour, the townspeople would come and throw their garbage into the pit. The Mule got very discouraged, as more and more garbage was hurled next to him in the pit. The Mule looked at the garbage and came up with a plan, an opportunity in his pit. The mule took a step up onto the garbage. Every single time, someone threw their garbage in; the Mule took another step up. Another step and another step. The Mule realized that every single time he took a step up onto the garbage he was raised higher and higher in the pit.

The Mule kept it up. The last few bags of garbage were thrown in, and the Mule finally took a step up, and OUT OF THE PIT!

I know this is a silly little story about a Farmer's Mule, but it's powerful if you really think about it. Many of you are in a pit, or some call it a storm. It's very easy when in the pit, to cuddle up next to the garbage and die, or rot there. In every single trail we are in, we must look for roads of opportunity just like The Mule did. I remember trials I have been in where God opened up doors of opportunity for me to minister to those, that normally I would not be around due to the trial. There was a reason I was in those situations. The Mule kept his joy and he was alert. This is the key to his story, the key to our freedom.

So many just give up. This is NOT what God has intended for you. He does NOT want you laying around and rotting. This takes discipline, this takes ACTION!

Are you looking for the opportunity in your pit like The Mule did?

God wants you free today! My son wrote down a quote from a band called *For Today* this morning. This band has God's anointing all over them in their newest album (2010).

The quote he wrote, from one of their songs, this morning was,

"If God says you are holy, you are holy.
Don't live your life like God is a liar."

I love this quote so much! Straight and to the point! Some of you are in a pit of despair. You cannot get past your sin! Stop living your life like God is a liar! Stop beating yourself time and time again over the head in condemnation! When you ask you are forgiven!

Rise up people of God! Look for the opportunities all around you in your hellish situations! Step up onto all the garbage that is being hurled at you today. Step up onto the memories that you can't seem to get past from your childhood. It's a new day! It's a new time! God has an amazing plan and purpose for your life. Get excited about what's next!

"The Lord will open the Heavens, the storehouse of his bounty, to send rain on your land in season and to bless all the work of your hands."
Deuteronomy 28:12

Remember this story about The Mule every single time you get discouraged. God is NOT finished with you! He has mighty plans for you.

Dear God,
You are more than amazing! Help us to step up, onto the garbage in life. I honor You today.

A Constant Grace

Have you ever done anything that you knew was right, but you did it with your mind somewhere else? You did the right thing but not wholeheartedly. You went to that dinner but your mind was on all you had to do the next day. You went to that funeral, but all you could think about was how that person, who went to their eternal destination, hurt you most your life. You did your ministry that you help with at church, but no one there knew you were burnt out and discouraged. You went to pray to God, and the entire time you could not focus, because you knew in your heart, you had not talked to Him about the sin in your life yet. There is not one single person reading this devotion today, who has not done something in this life time with half a heart. Half of you wants to be there, and half of you wants to be somewhere else.

This message today is about grace, a constant grace that we cannot understand. It goes beyond our human mind. I once went to a giant celebration of someone that had hurt me most my life. I went because it was the right thing to do, not because I wanted to be there. That person and I were the only ones in the room that knew what happened. I was not there wholeheartedly. Sometimes we do things with half a heart because of hurt and pain. We seem to think that the pain that we have received in this lifetime will carry over, in the same way in our relationship with God. I am living proof today that He will never hurt you; He will never leave you or forsake you. You can go to Him wholeheartedly.

I was reading in the Old Testament today and came across a scripture that captured me. The scripture is talking about a 25 year old king named Amaziah. He reigned in Jerusalem for 29 years. As I continued to read about his life it just seemed to get worse and worse. I just could not believe the grace that God tried to hand him time and time again.

> "He did what was right in the eyes
> of the Lord, but not wholeheartedly."
> 2 Chronicles 25:2

As I read through 2 Chronicles chapter 25 I tried to understand what this scripture meant when it said, "He did what was right in the eyes of the Lord" I know at first he followed what was written in the Book of Moses (25:4), but there were not too many good choices after that! As a matter of a fact he keeps sinning and pride creeps in. Starting at verse 14, it tells of how his army returned from slaughtering the Edomites,

> "He brought back the gods of the people of Seir. He set them up as his
> own gods, bowed down to them and burned sacrifices to them. The
> anger of the Lord burned against Amaziah."
> 2 Chronicles 25:14-15

But listen to what the end of this same verse in 15,

> "He sent a prophet to him, who said,
> "Why do you consult this people's gods,
> Which could not save
> their own people from your hand?"
> 2 Chronicles 25:15

So here we have Amaziah sinning, and once again we see a picture of Grace! Amaziah is lying before false gods, and this scripture says that God sent a prophet to warn him, yet again. I don't know about you, but I don't understand that kind of grace. I wish I had way more of it in me that's for sure!

I wanted to share this with you today because so many times in our minds we think we have reached the point of no return. God could not forgive me for this, or God could not forgive me for that! Please know today that His grace is constant.

Some of you will not want to hear what I have to say next. Some may get mad. If you turn your heart toward Christ, no matter what you have done, if you have been divorced, had an abortion, killed someone, gossiped, left your children, stirred up strife between people, shop lifted, rejected God at some point in your life, ran from the call He had on your life, molested someone, beat someone, had an affair and the list goes on and on, God's Grace can still be handed to you, if you ask for it.

I prayed with the person who molested me and led them to relationship with God. I will be honest and tell you, that God was there wholeheartedly, but I was not. I did it because it was the right thing to do. I did it because after years of healing, it was the biblical thing to do. But, it was for me, the hardest thing to do. This person asked God for Grace and God gave it to them.

The grace of God is Constant, unlike any grace I know.

When I think of my own life, I thank God for His grace; I would not be alive today without it.

Please know He loves you. His grace is reaching out to you. This will never stop.

It's never too late for you.
He has A Constant Grace for You

Dear God,
I thank You, I thank You, I thank You for your grace. I do not understand it, but it has saved me. I honor You today.

September 14th

<u>Once Upon A Time</u>

Tonight at the ministry my husband and I run, a beautiful lady read a poem about the wind blowing through the trees. As she read the poem to us, and as I sat there, a memory entered my mind of my pre-teen years. As most of us girls did back then, we laid in the sun until we were brown and crisp. I think one day me and my girlfriends laid in the sun for like six hours straight. We all wanted to be tan. Staying at home and lying in the sun had its bonuses! We could get a drink iced tea any time we wanted, we could go in, hour after hour to see our tan lines, we could pee without the use of a nasty outhouse or a gross bathroom at the beach, and we did not need the ice cream man, because the fridge usually had as much ice cream as we wanted! Even to this day I love lying in the sun at home rather than going out. I don't do it much, because my life is no longer care free like it was once upon a time.

When I was about 13 my dad had a big back deck built off our home in Albany, New York. A perfect addition to my sun goddess parties. But I loved that deck, even toward the fall I would sit out there and loved to look at the woods behind our home, somehow there was peace in that woods. I would sit back there for hours and just listen to the quiet, something I love to do even today.

As this woman was reading the poem she wrote tonight, to us, I remembered that I used to sit out there on that deck and listen to the wind going through the leaves of the trees. I used to pretend that the noise was a million people clapping for me. I had little or no self esteem and somehow this fantasy filled an aching need in my heart. She went on with her poem tonight and I just could not get that memory out of my mind. I was so hungry for someone to tell me how much I was worth and that I could do anything I wanted in this life.

My mom and dad had some marriage problems and were very busy with work. My parents were some of the hardest workers I have ever met in my life, and I think that's where my brother and I get our work ethic. I thank God for their amazing example of hard work. My dad was Albany High's coach for about 30 years and he ran all the handicap summer camps for the city of Albany. My mom was a head RN at a nursing home and worked at many other hospitals through my teen years. They were very hard workers. Between their work, and problems at home, there was not a ton of communication. We all make mistakes in life, and I have made my own with my kids, but I know I could have used some more encouragement with myself worth.

So I would sit. And thousands upon thousands of people would be clapping for me, as the leaves were rustling in the wind. I did not do anything weird like talk back to them ha-ha, I just sat there and thought about how great it would be if it were true. We all have a need to feel wanted and accepted in life and sometimes people fill that need with other things, but at this point and time in my life I filled it with fantasies of thousands of people loving me, and clapping for me. It would not be till years later that I let God fill every single void I had in life, including self worth. Even after I was married I struggled. Funny thing, is not one person would have ever know about it. I was a leader and led many things, but I did not have the greatest self esteem.

I want you to know God did a miracle in my life in this area.

You are worth so much more than you know.

> "Since you are precious and honored in my sight,
> and because I love you."
> Isaiah 43: 4

> "The Lord does not look at the things man looks at.
> Man looks at the outward appearance, but the lord looks at the heart."
> 1 Samuel 16:7

> "But He was pierced for our transgressions,
> He was crushed for our iniquities;
> the punishment that brought us peace was upon him,
> and by his wounds we are healed."
> Isaiah 53:5

You are worth a whole heck of a lot, and I hope you realize that.
God can fill every void you have. Our days are no longer care free like they were Once Upon a Time, but some of the deepest hurts happened in our care free, informative years.

I'm not sure where you are at today but please know He just waits for you to reach out to Him.
He is NOT
Once Upon a Time,
He is NOW.

Dear God,
Minister to every reader today; let them know they were worth You dying for them. You laid down Your life so we could live. I honor You today.

September 15th

One Sin Vs. Another

September 15th

One Sin Vs. Another

Today I am guilty. My daughter and I took an amazing walk today outside. The weather in Southern New England has been amazing this fall. The sun is shining, not too hot and not too cold, just right. An amazing day.

Let me start by saying that we rent our home. We moved here almost three years ago with our Cape home not selling. So we have been renting a home along a main street. I have to say I love the house, but I hate where it is. We were used to peace and quiet; all I used to hear was the birds of the air! We were very spoiled on Cape Cod. We had a five man hot tub and a sauna; it all came with the house when we purchased it. It was a season, and now it's gone. For those of you that know me, I would take a broken down home in India more than any mansion you could hand me, but I have to say the house on Cape was a blessing for its season. I do love our home now, but more than anything I miss the quiet. I miss hearing the birds and I miss hearing nothing. I miss going to the mailbox in the late morning, in my PJ's, without the entire world seeing me. I loved the house on Cape Cod.

As my daughter and I walked in this upper class neighborhood, I found myself not only loving the homes but coveting. I know many people covet things in life such as other people, financial freedom and such. I found my mind thinking, "Why can't we have this Lord?" The funny thing is, it was not even the pool in the back yard, or the two car garage that I found myself coveting. It was the peace and quiet. I could not hear anything but the birds. I could picture myself in the yard of some of these homes in my chair with my coffee just listening to the quiet. I wanted to just lie on someone's grass and hang out for a while, but I did not want to freak anyone out! It was that quiet and beautiful. Where we live it's a main road and now hundreds of cars pass my house every single day. We can't even leave our windows open at night because of the noise. Very hard. The noises here and the noises in India are very different. I almost welcome the India noises at night, they are calming to me.

When looking at the Ten Commandments we tend to think that some are worse than others but they are NOT! There was a reason the Lord gave all Ten. Let's check them out.

"You shall have no other gods before me"

"You shall not make for yourself an idol in the form of anything in Heaven above or on the earth beneath or in the waters below."

"You shall not misuse the name of the Lord your God, for the Lord will not hold anyone guiltless who misuses His name."

"Remember the Sabbath day by keeping it holy."
"Honor your father and your mother."

"You shall not murder."

"You shall not commit adultery."

"You shall not steal."

"You shall not give false testimony against your neighbor."

"You shall not covet your neighbor's house."

All from Exodus 20:3-17

If you were to go hit the streets and ask strangers, "Can you tell me a few of the Ten Commandments?" I bet that they would right away say, "Don't murder!" or "Don't steal or commit adultery!" For some reason I don't think a response would be, "Don't say bad things, or untrue things about your neighbor." For some reason, when talking to people about the Ten Commandments, they only seem to remember the "Bad" ones! Ah-Ha! But this is where we are so wrong, all are bad. For some reason we tend to think some are worse than others, when the truth is that they are not! As humans we categorize sin, thinking somehow we can think like God, the one who has endless compassion but who is also just. Spreading a lie about your neighbor is as bad as killing them. This is what the Ten Commandments were all about; this is what He was speaking to us. We can never understand the mind of Christ but we must keep our hearts pure. Read the Ten Commandments again in Chapter 20 in your Bible, let them soak in and apply them to how you live.

God was being serious.
They were very important to Him, every single one!
Our eyes don't see like His. One sin vs. another... In His eyes, sin is sin.

Dear God,
Help us to realize that you see all sin the same. Sin is sin. May we always have repented hearts before You. I honor You today

Souls Rather than Sushi

If you could have one wish, what would you wish?

If someone, who had no limitations said to you today, "Tell me, what can I do for you before I am gone?" What would you say?

I know these are loaded questions. I would probably ask if my entire family could come to know God on a personal level, or, never let anyone get sick. Or maybe, how about a Couple million bucks so we never have to stress about money again!

Seriously what would you say? Maybe I would even have a lift here and there! Ha-ha!

Would you think of the material or the spiritual? I wonder what would be the first thing to come to my mind, if someone asked me that.

In 2 Kings someone did get asked that question.

> "Elijah said to Elisha, "Tell me, what can
> I do for you before I am taken from you?"
> 2 Kings 2:9

Elisha had watched the ministry of Elijah. He saw him do miracles. He would NOT leave Elijah's side (2 Kings 2:2). He watched as God sent fire from Heaven to help Elijah against many men (2 Kings 1:10) and just a couple minutes before Elijah is taken to Heaven in a whirlwind, Elisha sees him strike water with his cloak, and the water parts as they walk across on dry ground (2 Kings 2:8). I need to try that when there are big puddles at church Ha-ha! God had made it very clear that Elijah was a mighty man of God. I wonder when Elijah first asked that question to Elisha, did Elisha hesitate? Or did he answer right away? There is no record, except for the answer,

> "Let me inherit a double portion of your spirit."
> 2 Kings 2:9

I wish I knew exactly how this played out. What if he did hesitate? Or thought of other things first? Something tells me he did not hesitate too long, being that he just saw waters part, and fire from Heaven. Pretty much what Elisha was saying was, "I want to have God's Spirit with me, like He is with you, only Stronger!" The Spirit in Elijah was not his own spirit, but God's Spirit! Elisha wanted MORE! A very great desire to have. Kind of like a double Java whammy! Iced Cinnamon Dolce Latte with a double shot of expresso! I'm so glad I don't work at Starbucks everyone's drinks would be so messed up! The Spirit of God is way better than any shot of expresso I can tell you that!

I love what Elisha asked for. He knew that if he had a double portion, that he could help double amounts of people. A couple chapters later, we see him getting into God's presence just to hear direction.

"Bring me a harpist."
2 Kings 3:15

A request was made to him and a decision had to be made, he did not let this double portion go to his head, he knew that he still needed to be humble, and get into the presence of God before making big decisions. This is the heart that God looks for today in us. Double portion of God's Spirit, or not.

Are you humble today? I think if we truly are humble our mind will be more on spiritual things than material things.

Souls rather than Sushi.

Dear God,
I know it helped Elisha to keep His eyes on You, because of the amazing things he saw. Help us in our walk of faith today. Help us to desire You over anything this world may have to offer. I honor You today.

September 17th

Dorito Days

How is it that life seems to just pass us by? One minute you blink and your babies, that you rocked and loved, are off to college. I think life is so short. I can remember thinking the age of 23 was so old, now I'm 50 and half my life is over. It's so crazy. Then there is this season that my parents are now in, where it seems all their friends and loved ones are dying off. I cannot imagine that season. It must be so hard and I'm sure many questions enter your mind in your later years. Who will take care of me if I'm in need? Where will I live and the list goes on. My concern is I won't have my mind. My husband tells me all the time he will come visit me in the nursing home! Ha-ha.

Right now I'm sitting in a hotel room with my leadership retreat starting tonight. I love these couple of days where us gals let our hair down, and have a blast together. A few minutes ago I checked my e mail because I have not been online all day. An old friend asked me if I still loved Doritos. I sat here and laughed out loud. I cannot tell you the last time I sat and ate a bag of Doritos. Once I hit 40 ten years ago I had to watch my tummy, not just for inches, but it seems the older I get I have to watch the junk intake!

I do remember the days when my husband and I were youth pastors and we would sit with the youth and just pig out. Pizza, soda, sour candies, chocolate and of course Doritos! What's a youth party without Doritos! If I did that now I would be puking all night! I also used to be a total stick like my daughter, and had not one bit of fat on my body. Well, times change as we all know ha-ha. We don't even have soda in our home unless we know the kids are having friends over. I went to my son's college last week and drank soda for the first time in forever, I got so sick. My tummy just cannot handle what it used to.

So as I read this little comment on my e mail about eating Doritos, it made me think of how quickly those days are now gone. It flew. Where did it go? And now I sit here running a weekend with women who are called by God to do great things in the areas they live in. This is what Jesus does. It's so important for us to remember the Dorito Days, the days when we were young, carefree but unwise at times, and sporadic. Most of us learned from our mistakes during those days and they have made us into who we are today. I have grown and so have you.

Just like our tummy can't eat the same food that we did when we were young and we need to have a healthier diet. I hope you are in a new season with your spiritual body.

> "Like newborn babies, crave pure spiritual milk,
> So that by it you may grow up in your salvation, now

That you have tasted that the Lord is good."
1 Peter 2:2-3

It says here we need to crave spiritual milk. What does that even mean? Where are you letting your mind go? Are you reading the Word of God every day? Are you watching things pleasing to God on television? Are you getting into God's presence every day through worship music or Prayer? Yes, when we are older, we have tasted that the Lord is good, because he was always there when we MESSED UP! He has proved His grace to you and me on a daily basis and He is still doing it!

On Sunday after church I found out that a ton of college kids were coming over to eat. I was not ready for that so I stopped at the local gas store to grab soda and chips. Guess what Chips I grabbed? Doritos! I dumped them in the bowl and took a bite! I have not had one in so long that I took another bite! Man are they good! But if I ate the entire bowl I would be sick. I'm older now, time for new things for Tana. Same with you. It's time for new things! Physically and spiritually friend! I hope even in your physical body you are making healthy choices.

When I work at the Hospital with the babies they scream until we feed them. Does it bother you that much when you don't get what you need for your spiritual self? It should. If I don't have my Bible with me I go mad! Its part of my life, I need it. We are all different and some of you now have your Bible on your phone! Whatever you have to do to get spiritual food into you, do it!

All this to say, I blinked and grew up.
My Dorito Days are over.
It's time to start applying healthier things to my life.
How do you feel about that in your own life?
Maybe it's time to make a list and see where you can make some changes.

Dear God,
Life flies by. Help us in every season. I honor You today.

September 18th

The Hope Door

I had an amazing weekend with our leadership team who is such a blessing to me throughout the year. This retreat weekend is so we can bless them for all they do. Five years ago I started to take on college girls to mentor. One of the things they do, is come to this Leadership retreat and do a daily devotion for my leadership. They are college students, so it's a little scary for them to get up in front of older ladies in ministry, and share The Word. We were blessed this weekend as well, by another girl who did worship for us. The new mentoree named Angela got up and spoke a very powerful word to us. So good that I want to share one of the main scriptures that she shared.

> "She decked herself with rings and jewelry,
> And went after her lovers, but Me she forgot,"
> declares the Lord.
> Hosea 2:13

Before we continue lets think about this scripture. First think of yourself, the things you enjoy in life. I have a friend who actually has an entire dresser sized jewelry box. She loves "bling-bling!" But she also loves the Lord. There is nothing wrong with having nice things and enjoying life as long as you do not forget about your relationship with the Lord. Ask yourself what are you motivations? In this scripture we see her motivation is to go after lovers. Decking herself out to allure someone else. But in doing that, there is lost focus! You may love amazing things but be careful of your motivations. Where is your focus and where is your heart? We must never put our lusts or our desires above our heart for God. We must never forget the Lord in our daily walk. He must be first.

The thing that I love about this scripture, once again, is after the Lord says the above scripture, the next scripture is,

> "Therefore I am now going to allure her."
> Hosea 2:14

The Master is going to do what He can to gain her back! Once again, He is throwing a life line and extending grace like He does for us time and time again.

I see His Grace here.

> "I will lead her into the desert and speak tenderly to her.
> There I will give her back her vineyards, and will make
> The Valley of Achor a door of hope."
> Hosea 2:14-15

I see His restoration here.
He is tender and a gentleman.

The word Achor in Hebrew means trouble. A Valley of Trouble.
There is an actual Valley of Achor, in the vicinity of Jericho today.
The Book of Joshua, chapter seven, tells the story from which the valley's name comes.

Let me ask you today are you in a Valley of Trouble?
Do you realize even in your sin that He longs to restore you? To give you back the things you have lost?

> "The Lord gives strength to His people;
> The Lord blesses His people with peace."
> Psalm 29:11

> "Faith is being sure of what we hope for."
> Hebrews 11:1

The Valley of Trouble versus The door of Hope....
Choose The Hope Door
And put your trust in Him.

Dear God,
Help us to not be distracted, there are way too many distractions. May my first thought in the morning be You and may my last thought be You. I pray for this reader, God bring Hope to their trouble right now. I honor You today.

Ships of Tarshish

So many ships, I wonder how many ships went out to sea headed to Tarshish and back. There is amazing stories, and Bible History on these seas. I just could not get enough tonight. It's kind of like when you own an antique piece of furniture that has a mirror; so many generations have used that mirror for so many things. It's the same with these waters. Years went by in the Old Testament, and we hear over and over again, good and bad stories on the same seas. Generations of shipwrecks and joy. Let's look at some!

Chapter 9 of 2 Chronicles looks at the Splendor of King Solomon. It was all about Gold. He actually made silver common, and worth nothing in his time.

> "Silver as common in Jerusalem as stones."
> 1 Kings 10:27

1 Kings 10:21-22 talk about the King's fleet of trading ships containing pure gold, ivory apes and baboons. We see this again in 2 Chronicles 9:21, crossing the seas and making history.

The Lord destroyed Ships of Tarshish at the Gulf of Aqaba in 2 Chronicles due to wickedness.

> "Later, Jehoshaphat king of Judah made an alliance with Ahaziah King of Israel, who was guilty of wickedness. He agreed with him to construct a fleet of trading ships."
> 2 Chronicles 20:35-36

> "Because you have made an alliance with Ahaziah, the Lord will destroy what you have made." The ships were wrecked and were not able to set sail to trade."
> 2 Chronicles 20:37

This is very interesting, you would think the Lord would destroy them sailing on the seas, but that's not what this says. History by the dock.

So we see Ships of Tarshish being use for trade and ships being destroyed due to wickedness.

Then we see something totally different in Isaiah.

> "Surely the islands look to me; in the lead are the ships of Tarshish, bringing your sons from afar, with their silver and gold, in honor of the Lord your God, the Holy One of Israel, for He has endowed you with splendor."
> Isaiah 60:9

Ships, and people honoring the Lord on the seas. History on the waves.

"The ships of Tarshish serve as carriers for your wares. You are filled with heavy cargo in the heart of the sea. Your oarsmen take you out to the high seas. But the east wind will break you to pieces."
Ezekiel 27:25-27

"Your merchants and all your soldiers, and everyone else on board will sink into the heart of the sea on the day of your shipwreck."
Ezekiel 27:27

History at the bottom of the sea.

Perhaps the most famous story on these seas, in the Bible is the one of Jonah.

"But Jonah ran away from the Lord and headed for Tarshish. He went down to Joppa, where he found a ship bound for that port. After paying the fare, he went aboard and sailed for Tarshish to flee from the Lord."
Jonah 1:3

These ships were known for very long journeys, some took three years. When Jonah ran from the Lord he intended to run as far as he could. He could have gone elsewhere for a shorter journey, but he chose these ships due to the fact that he could get very far away. The Lord sends raging seas due to Jonah's disobedience, he admits it, and they throw him overboard. The instant he hit the water the sea grew calm (Jonah 1:15).

"But the Lord provided a great fish to swallow Jonah, and Jonah was inside the fish three days and three nights."
Jonah 1:17

Miracles in this sea.

Generation after generation goes by, and we see so much in these waters. Some things bring Him glory; some things bring him a holy anger. And we even see His grace in these waters as he sends a fish to swallow a man who runs from Him.

Just like my grandmother's mirror.
So many reflections,
So many generations,
So many joys,
So many sins.

Where is your heart today?
What story will you leave behind?

Dear God,
May our stories please You. I honor You today.

September 20th

Heart Check

Well, my son has been at college for about a month and has already failed two room checks. At his college, Every time they fail a room check, they get fined $10. I joked with him today, and told him I will hold up the room check rule this summer when he gets home! I'm sure once he starts paying his own money in fines, he will start to clean up his floor. Ha-ha. My sister in law Kris jokes with me all the time that I was exactly like him! She said that she came to visit me at college one time and that I had taken the entire contents of my floor and threw it in the closet because I knew they were going around doing room check. They never opened the closet door, so I was safe. Now, I'm a total clean freak. I'm almost OCD about it, Ha! I even do doorknobs on a normal cleaning day and at times iron pillow cases. Pretty crazy I know.

The truth is, I'm not the same person I was when I graduated from College 21 years ago. My son and I are a lot alike, and I know in time, he will change the way he keeps his room. It takes growth and respect for yourself and those around you. I think, keeping things clean, is a sign of real maturity. It's fruit that you are growing up.

What if God did a heart check every week on us?
A check on what's going on inside our heart and mind.
In college you can hide things you don't want people to see in the closet or under a mattress, but God sees all, we cannot hide anything from Him. Life may be an ocean of secrets to some, but NOT to God the one who created you. He actually knows you way better than you know yourself.

> "Search me, O God, and know my heart;
> test me and know my anxious thoughts.
> See if there is any offensive way in me,
> and lead me in the way everlasting."
> Psalm 139:23-24

Read this scripture again, and tell me if you feel the way David did when he wrote it? Are you really an open book to God and fully surrendered, or are you trying to hide things from God? When was the last time you asked God to search you? I have the picture in my mind of an officer searching someone, going down every leg and arm. He does not even have to touch us because He sees right through. But when did you ask Him last to search you? Have you avoided it, because you know there are offensive ways in you? God is looking for those who stop trying to hide things in the closet.
Hiding things only leads to bad habits and manipulation. It takes great strength and courage to grow up and fully surrender our hearts to God. Getting rid of our attitudes and submitting to our authority is another giant sign of growth in

the heart area. I guess you could say it's kind of like spiritual boot camp. If you are at real army boot camp, you are known as a wimp if you cannot "keep up" with rules and regulations. The harder they work you the better they respect you. We need to grow up and be more like the marines! Ha!

"Can anyone hide in secret places so that I cannot see him?" declares the Lord. Do not I fill Heaven and earth?" declares the Lord."
Jeremiah 23:24

"I will uncover his hiding places, so that he cannot conceal himself."
Jeremiah 49:10

My son has no choice with his room check, but I have a choice! I can choose not to let God do heart check on me. I thank God I let him do full heart check, even the closet!

Maybe like David it's time for you to ask God to search you.

Give him the Key and let Him in.
He won't charge $10 bucks if you fail.
His hand of grace will be extended once again.

Let Him do a Heart Check.

Dear God,
Keep us pure before you. Help us not to try and hide things from you. Give us courage to Do the right things. I honor You today.

September 21st

The Pacifier

Last night in the nursery at the Hospital where I work, we only had about five babies. This is a very quiet shift and to be honest, I would much rather be very busy, than have time on my hands in the middle of the night. I found myself at about 5am slapping my face to stay awake. But when it rains it pours! Everyone is totally quiet then at the same time everyone gets up and is screaming. Not sure how parents with multiple births do it! God bless them all!

We use the pacifier for many things in the baby nursery. If I assist the Doctor for a circumcision I use the pacifier and sweeties. Sweeties (as we call it), is sterile water that has a bit of sugar in it, the babies love it. It quiets them right down. I always have a pacifier and sweeties with me when I draw heel blood for a test or do a hearing check, unless the parents do NOT want a pacifier used. Last night I had a baby that had mucus that needed to come up, this is normal for newborns. All that junk from being in the womb needs to come out of them from the top and the bottom. They have cute little bottoms! Ha-ha! This poor baby was so very hungry, whenever I put the bottle near her mouth she wanted it so badly but then she would begin to drink and due to the fact that she had mucus that had to come up she could not drink. It was so sad because she wanted it so bad. She would just cry and cry. I had to give her the pacifier to keep her calm until the mucus came up. Poor little thing, but I so enjoyed her cuddles! The truth is I thank God for the pacifier or forms of a pacifier we use in the baby nursery.

In the early 1800's the pacifier was called a dummy or soother. Mostly in North America and Ireland. They are made with a plastic, rubber or silicone nipples now, but it was not the case then. Since the early 1800's, people have been putting things in their babies mouths to try and sooth them. I'm sure even before that, but the earliest record we have is the early 1800's. The quote, "Born with a silver spoon in the mouth" came from the fact that parents or caregivers would put silver spoons, coral, ivory or bone into the mouths of babies to keep them quiet. Some thought coral would ward off sickness and some thought things like bone and ivory would help the child cope with pain. In the 19th century rags were introduced.

In the first maternity ward I worked in we were taught this 19th century rag technique. Any time I assisted for a circumcision I had to wrap a big sterile gauze that had sugar and water. When the circumcision took place, I would have to not only hold the baby down but put the sterile gauze in the baby's mouth too sooth it. In the hospital I work in now we use a sterile pacifier dipped in sugar water. Different countries used different things inside their rags. Some countries used meat or fat in cloth, moistened with brandy. In German speaking areas some used sweetened bread.

In 1902 Sears Roebuck introduced what they called the "baby comforter" a new style of baby teething ring. One side was soft and the other hard. In 1909 someone who called herself Auntie Pacifier, wrote an article for the New York Times stating that the hard pacifier was a menace to dental health, so peoples focus started to be on the rubber pacifiers. In 1935 Playtex products introduced the name Binky and they still own the name today. There are so many kinds, and the nipple is soft and comforting to most babies. I love the history of things, so I enjoyed reading about this. It all leads me up to my work today and I will think of these things every time I work.

What pacifies you?
What is your pacifier?
Really think about this. Is it godly?
Do you do it to somehow make yourself feel important or wanted?

For some it may be getting a pedicure, buying a very expensive car, making sure you have the "latest and greatest" everything, going shopping, climbing the political latter, drinking, and the list goes on. Some pacifiers are healthy and some not.

What pacifies you?

I want you to know today that God is so much more than a pacifier. But when you are in need, hurting, in pain, and screaming, He is there. He will sooth you, and comfort you. My hope is, as an adult, that when those hurtful times go away, you will learn to live with Him so you need the pacifier less and less. I remember the day standing over the garbage, and my son putting his binky in the garbage. I think we gave him chocolate! It was a sign of the next step, a sign of growth.

For some of you today who are young in your walk with Him, you need God to be like a pacifier in your life. For others who are growing in Christ, it's time to throw the binky out. And grow up!

Let His sustaining grace become part of your everyday life.
I have yet to see an adult walking around with a pacifier in their mouth.

"The Lord Himself goes before you and will be with you; He will never leave you nor forsake you. Do not be afraid; do not be discouraged."
Deuteronomy 31:8

Dear God,
Help us to grow up. I honor You today.

September 22nd

Season of Surrender

Why is it so hard to obey sometimes? You go to a new job and have to abide by the rules, you go to college and have to do room checks, you have dress code in certain situations and it's all so hard. It's a breaking of your very will. And that means change; if you are a person like me any change can throw you off. But when it has meant the breaking of my will, verses God's will, it has only grown me in a powerful way.

As young pastors in full time ministry my husband and I had to abide by the rules of the Sr. Pastor. This did not mean that we agreed with every single rule he had for his staff but if we wanted to keep our jobs, and stay pleasing to God, we needed to change in areas of our personal likes. A perfect example now is that my husband hates ties. Hates them, but he wears them every single Sunday for the first two services, then the third service we have, is more casual so he can take it off. Is it hard? Yes. I probably would be miserable if I had to wear a dress or skirt every single Sunday because I just don't feel like it most the time, but if I had to I would. I would respect and honor my leadership. I would not talk grudgingly about them behind their backs. This is the attitude we have to have to stay pleasing to God.

I got an amazing testimony today from a young lady going to the college where my son is. She was having a very hard time because the college does not allow nose studs. It's a very strict college and she was struggling. My heart went out to her. Although I do not have a nose stud, I have desired one for a very long time. Living in India, and going there as much as we do, I just love them and over there it's pretty much equivalent to having your ears pierced. Anyway, I think they are beautiful. So my heart did go out to her. She said her, and two of her friends were at the pond on campus and she was very upset, dealing with the struggle of her will, verses the rules on campus. My son understands this, last week he got asked for the third time since being there, to cut his hair. But this is so great for them. I love seeing the growth in them already. She said they all went to the campus pond to do a devotion together, and all during that time God was speaking to her about the stud.

"After we started the devotion the whole time I just felt God saying, throw it in the pond. So when they were done, I said "Guys, God wants me to throw my nose ring in the pond. It was extremely difficult and I was crying and hesitant about it, but finally I did it. So I just realized that I totally just glorified God in something He wanted of me."
~Zion Student

What God wanted of her, was full surrender to her authority. This is NOT an easy task sometimes. Jesus loves those with tattoos and piercings very much!

He sent his son to die for all, but when our authority says no, we have to obey. I have learned this the hard way. There have been plenty of times when I don't agree with rules somewhere, and when I was younger I used to get sour about it. Now that I'm a leader and have to give rules, I totally understand why rules and standards are so very important. I am not the same.

I challenged this amazing young lady to always use this testimony about the surrender of her will verses the God given authority over her, for the rest of her life. I have stories that I have shared in this book about me obeying my authority. I use these stories even today, where ever I go. I'm sure someday her stud will be back in, but this is a season of surrender. It's only a season, and seasons change.

So if you are at a college or a new job, and you are a whiner and grumbler, STOP! Surrender for your Season. If you cannot do this, maybe you need to line your will, up with God's will and His Word. This is change and growth, it is pleasing to God. If you cannot do this without hurting others, you are immature like I was way back when, and you need to grow up. His Word has a lot to say about God given authority over us.

"Everyone must submit himself to the governing authorities, for there is no authority except that which God has established. The authorities that exist have been established by God. Consequently, he who rebels against the authority is rebelling against what God has instituted, and those who do so will bring judgment on themselves."
Romans 13:2

"Submit yourselves for the Lord's sake
to every authority instituted among men."
1 Peter 2:13

"For it is God's will that by doing good
you should silence the ignorant talk of foolish men."
1 Peter 2:15

This scripture even says by your obedience in this season, you will shine a light for those who are grumbling and whining against their authority. One of the best things that ever happened to me in ministry was the breaking of my will verses my authority. It's a healthy thing that will humble you, and this is pleasing to God.

Why not enjoy your Season of Surrender.
    -P.S. I now have a nose stud and it's 2015.

Dear God,
Help us to obey in all things. In our workplace, in the environment you have put us in for this season in our lives. I honor You today.

September 23rd

Against all Odds

Has God ever told you to do something out of the ordinary? What if today He told you to build a giant ark (Genesis 6:14-18), walk into a forbidden King's court which was against the law (Esther Chapter 4), lay on a boy 3 times so he could be raised from the dead (1 Kings 17:21), march around a city 7 times then shout, in wait for the walls of the city to fall down (Joshua 6:15-16), or step into a burning furnace of fire (Daniel Chapter 3). In almost every situation people would think you are crazy. In almost every situation you would be risking your life.

I can count on less than ten hands the number of times God told me to do strange things. One time he told me to take a poster off the wall of a prayer room, it had brown tape around it like it had been there for years. I could not understand why, but I did it anyway. When I took it off, on the back of the poster was a picture of the exact missionary that God had spoken to me to go work for that summer. What if I did not take it off the wall like Jesus said? I would have missed out on an amazing blessing and confirmation to my prayers. One time in the middle of a beautiful field God challenged me to dance before Him. I danced from one end of that football field to the other. There WERE people around, a family picking berries and soccer players. I didn't care, I heard His voice and that's all that mattered to me. When we are obedient, God works against all odds.

I have not always been obedient and I'm sure I missed out on blessings due to it. One time in the middle of a church service there was a man that my husband and I used to visit in the hospital all the time. He was in the service in his wheel chair. As clear as day God spoke to me to go take his hands and tell him to get up. I didn't do it. Fear consumed me. This beautiful man is with the Lord now, and it's too late to know what could have happened. To this day, I wonder what Jesus would have done against all odds? I wonder how it could have not only changed his life, but how it could have changed my life, if he had been healed.

So many times in the Word people were put in situations that were against all odds. When God led Moses to the sea with the Israelites, they cried out in fear due to Pharaoh's horses and armies on one side of them and the sea on the other.

> "They said to Moses, "Was it because there were no
> graves in Egypt that you brought us to the desert to die?"
> Exodus 14 11

The Israelites only saw the army and the sea; they were blinded to the fact that against all odds, God can do anything.

"Then the Lord said to Moses, "Why are you crying out to me? Tell the Israelites to move on. Raise your staff and stretch out your hand over the sea to divide the water!"
Exodus 14:15-16

What if today God told you to stretch out your hand and part the waters? Would you do it? Friend, I'm here today to remind you He is the same God today that He was yesterday! God told some people to do some wild things in the Word of God. When Joshua marched around the city I just cannot imagine what he was feeling, could there have been doubt? The walls of the city were strong and firm. How at a shout, could they come down? That was totally against all odds. But at a shout they did come down because God said so.

Why do we doubt?

If there is an impossible situation you face today, please know God can do the impossible.

Against all odds he can part the seas, save your life, walls will fall, and others can be healed.

What has God told you to do? Does it seem strange, weird or out of the ordinary? I beg you, I plead with you, do it. You do NOT want to miss out on a great blessing of Him blowing your mind with a miracle, or safety net!

"We walk by faith, not by sight."
2 Corinthians 5:7

Sometimes to do what He is telling you takes great faith. Do it and watch what He does Against all Odds.

Dear God,
Like all the stories we read about, help us to obey when you speak. Let us see your mighty hand at work today in this world through us. I honor You today.

Never Enough

"Now this is what the Lord Almighty says:
"Give careful thought to your ways.
You have planted much, but have harvested little.
You eat, but never have enough.
You drink, but never have your fill.
You put on clothes, but are not warm.
You earn wages, only to put them in a purse with holes in it.""
Haggai 1:5-6

Have you ever considered the fact that you actually might be selfish? That you are not working to your full potential? That you spend too much of your day having "Me" time than anything else? I write a lot of devotions on grace and compassion but we also need to live, knowing that God gives us common sense. We should know when to stop, spending, whining, eating, drinking, and sleeping. Sometimes we need a good shake. I call shakes trials.

Consider the harvester; it takes ten times as much work to bring in the harvest than it does to plant the seeds. The planter can brag all he wants that he planted, but unless he goes and gets his crop it's worthless and he has wasted his time. Years ago I saw a movie called What's Eating Gilbert Grape. It was the story about a single mom who was nearing a good 500 lbs. I have very close friends who have been over 400 lbs, and they know I love them very much, but when do we stop putting things in our mouth that we know will make us grow even bigger. It's the same with the harvest, its only common sense to bring it in, or not put more food in your mouth. We can drink and drink anything until we are sick. My experiences with drinking much alcohol have only been bad; they have put me in very dangerous situations. Before I came to know the Lord I consumed every weekend. It led me down an out of control path with MUCH "Me" time. Like I have said before they would never put a watchmen on a watchtower that was a little "tipsy". We must also watch out for our own souls and from the evil one who is always trying to take us down. Never enough! Never enough! Never enough clothes or Money! More, More, More. The instant you get your pay, it's gone, and you go and get things for you!

The truth for me, is the instant I get my check it is gone but not on "Me" things. On kid things. Can anyone out there relate? I would rather meet their needs than my own. Many are not like that. They leave their kids by the wayside and go full speed ahead, and are completely out of control.

Years ago I was helping a young lady at our church. She had two small children one was two, and the other was about 11 mts. The baby hardly moved. You could tell he had been neglected so much, that he had no desire to try to crawl or get up or anything. It was very sad. I tried to get her into a special home for moms with young children, and I was driving her three hours away to bring her there. Her baby ran out of diapers and she had no money. I stopped at a gas station and handed her money to go in and get diapers. She came out of the store with two packs of cigarettes and NO DIAPERS! I cannot even begin to tell you how mad I was and I let her know it. I made her go back in and get them!

I'm at the point now in ministry, where if I counsel someone I give them tasks, and if they come back to me the next time and the tasks are not done, I know they will not use the advice I give them anyway, so it is a waste of my time. This may sound harsh, but I have learned that my time is very precious. I can be using it to bring in my harvest, save my money, make my own clothes, provide for my family and the list goes on. I will no longer waste my time, which by the way IS GODS TIME!

So I challenge you today to read the scripture above again. Let it sink in deep. Don't be lazy, but be productive. Move! God is all about movement! Things can only get done when we are moving! If you are the kind of person who has never enough, you need to let God change your heart. There are so many other things that are far more important than your "Me" time. We do need time for our selves, but I'm talking about the extreme.

I encourage everyone to go on a missions trip somewhere in America, like the streets of one of our great cities, or overseas, to open your mind to the fact that there is so much more to this life than your little world. This is the heart of God.

> "I say: My purpose will stand, and I will do all that I please.
> From the east I summon a bird f prey;
> from a far-off land, a man to fulfill my purpose.
> What I have said, that will I bring about;
> what I have planned, that will I do."
> Isaiah 46:10-11

The truth is, if we are not moving in God's direction, He will find someone who is. If we are not using common sense, and listening to Him, He will find someone who is. Don't sleep through it. You might miss out if you think there is Never Enough.

Dear God,
Forgive us. Help us to take the blindfolds for sleeping off, and to MOVE. I honor You today.

September 25th

If Only

Have you ever not had a peace about something? I remember one time walking around Provincetown, MA with my mother in law. We were having a blast going store to store; there were so many crazy things to look at, that we did not know what to look at first. For those of you who don't know Provincetown is very eclectic and they cater to the unique individual. Anyway, we walked into one store and all of a sudden I just got a weird feeling, there was no peace. It was almost an evil feeling. We left very quickly. But there have been other times in my life when I have prayed about situations and I did NOT have a peace about taking a certain job or getting in the car to go somewhere that day. I'm sure you all have been there at one point and time in your life.

Thank God for prayer and the fact that God wants to direct us in every step we take. If He has a perfect plan for our lives then He can also guide us and let us know what that plan is. God wants to speak to us today, He is not dead on a cross somewhere, He is alive and desires to have communication with us. He longs for His perfect will to be accomplished through us. I hate to say it but we blow it time and time again. I have told countless stories in this devotional of the times I blew it. Times when I thought I heard from God, but stepped ahead of Him without really seeking Him about a situation. In the end I was pretty miserable. It's so important before a major decision in your life to seek Him in it. He is faithful and He will direct us.

> "The steps of a good man are ordered
> By the Lord."
> Psalm 37:23

He longs to guide us. Listen to this scripture I found this morning.

> "This is what the Lord says-Your Redeemer,
> the Holy One of Israel:
> "I am the Lord your God,
> Who teaches you what is best for you,
> Who directs you in the way you should go.
> If only you had paid attention to my commands,
> Your peace would have been like a river."
> Isaiah 48:17

So many times throughout scripture, we see in Bible stories, and in reading scriptures like this, that we will have peace when we are obedient. It says here "If Only." Oh man I hate those two words! If only I did this, if only I did that. So many regrets in life. But, "If only you had paid attention to my commands!

Those are some big words. How do we pay attention to His commands? Number one, we listen in prayer and number two we read the Bible which is His command. I wonder why at times we don't do the very things that can direct our lives. But we have ALL had those times.

It says if we just do the things He commands we will have peace like a river. Who doesn't want that! I know I do!

He teaches us and directs us in the way we should go; He knows what's best for us! This includes EVERYTHING! Our job, our mate, our way in a turning point of life, and the list goes on. Why would we not want his best? Because our flesh gets distracted and we let sin creep in at times. We have our eyes on the better paying job, or the more attractive guy or girl, rather than going to Him first and asking if it was all His will in the first place! We sure would save a ton of time if we just go to Him first!

I hope today you take the time to seek Him and hear His Voice like John 10:27 talks about, I hope today you read His Word which IS His will for you. If you are seeking peace in your life, seek God, He is peace. He is all you need today friend.

When you seek Him and walk with Him you will have less If Onlys.

Dear God,
I pray for this reader right now, may they have few regrets in life due to listening to Your Voice. May they get to know you to the point of hearing Your direction in their life. I honor You today.

<u>No Longer Banished</u>

Today in church our Pastor spoke an amazing message. A story I have heard before but it was just so amazing. During preaching he read this scripture, it hit me hard and I have to do today's devotional on it. It's in the book of Second Samuel.

"Like water spilled on the ground,
which cannot be recovered, so we must die."
2 Samuel 14:14

Have you ever been to a picnic or somewhere outside and spilled your drink? Once it hits the ground there is no way to recover it at all. Even if you spill it inside your home, you take paper towels, soak it up and throw it out. There is no way to put it all back in the glass. This verse is confirming the fact that when we die, we die. Nothing can change that, short of a miracle. But listen to the second part of 2 Samuel Chapter 14,

"God does not take away life; instead, he devises
ways so that a banished person may not
remain estranged from Him."
2 Samuel 14:14

Have you ever felt banished from God? I'm sure someone in prison for murder on death row, must feel banished. Unless someone tells them about the forgiveness of Christ, they may die feeling banished and hopeless. But the interesting thing is hundreds of millions of people walk around every single day in our world feeling banished. They are the person that just walked by you, the person that you saw this afternoon at work, the person in the grocery store, the person that you see every single day, with a smile on their face, and you would never know they feel banished and far away from God or anyone else.

Have you ever been estranged from someone? Sometimes this happens in abusive situations. Although it was not legal, I was in an estranged situation. I did not desire to see this person and they did not desire to see me. There was a wall put up between us by our own flesh, sin, and the devil. Estranged, with no desire of communication or friendship.

Most the time when you are feeling banished, you are estranged from someone. I love this scripture because no matter how banished you feel, no matter how you have beat yourself over the head, God says, "You may NOT remain estranged from ME!" He reaches through our darkness and breaks the wall of estrangement down!

I love the part of this scripture that says, "HE DEVISES WAYS so that a banished person may not remain estranged from Him!" How cool is it that God Himself devises ways? To devise in many online dictionaries says, to plan, elaborate or to devise a method. I have spoken before about the fact that He is a strategic God! An organized planner, He takes someone banished and says, "I want to be your friend, and no longer will you be far from Me." And all the while He is planning how the wall will come down! This is how His heart beats.

Though the world might right you off, there is ALWAYS hope when God is in the picture!

I want you to know today that no matter what you have done, His hand is reaching out to you.

It's never too late. Run to Him and let Him plan.
You are No Longer Banished.

Dear God,
Your grace is far reaching. I pray for this reader that they would know their worth through Your eyes and not their own. I honor You today.

September 27th

<u>Skies</u>

Have you ever been in amazement of the skies? I think there was only one time in my life where I actually pulled alongside the road and stopped my car. It was when I was younger and in front of me I saw a double rainbow. It was amazing, so I stopped. There have been countless times in my life when I'm driving and I'm in total awe of what I see in front of me. Maybe orange and yellows, "Pink sky at night sailors delight" or blue with the most amazing white clouds. Whatever color, I stand amazed.

The most beautiful sky to me is the night sky. Years ago my husband had a season in our life where we had a hot tub outside on our back deck. Our house was surrounded by woods so at night we would go out there and sit in the hot tub and just look at the sky. Thousands of stars, almost the entire time out there, we spent looking at the sky. I think we saw a shooting star almost every night, I miss those nights. The beach at sunset is one of the most beautiful things I have ever seen as well. How can you escape the majesty of God when you see a sunset over the seas? There is much to say about the skies.

> "The Heavens declare the glory of God;
> The skies proclaim the work of His hands.
> Day after day they pour forth speech;
> Night after night they display knowledge.
> There is no speech or language where
> Their voice is not heard.
> Their voice goes out into all the earth
> Their words to the ends of the world.
> In the Heavens He has pitched a tent for the sun."
> Psalm 19:1-4

This scripture is just amazing, it does not matter if you believe God is there or not, the truth is, that the skies proclaim the work of His hands! When you see their wonder you see Gods creative mind, and knowledge. Every single tribe and tongue to the far ends of the earth, even those that have never heard of the name, Jesus Christ, see His wonder to the ends of the world! Just amazing.

Have you ever been camping? I have pitched a pup tent and I have pitched a giant tent when I was younger. No matter how big of a tent you get, they really are NOT that big! What I love most about this scripture, is where we see the bigness of God once again. It says, "In the Heavens He has pitched a tent for the sun." What that says to me is that the sun is tiny compared to the Heavens! Now when we study the sun we know that it's about 109 times the size of earth! Can you imagine? Think of our earth, we can hardly touch the surface of knowing all there is about this one earth, let alone something 109 times the size of it. And this scripture says that the Heavens pitch a tent for the sun. If that does not blow your mind I'm not quite sure what will? If it's comparing the sun to fitting into a tent well then the Heavens must be giant. I just can't wait to see all someday.

The Heavens and skies declare and proclaim don't you hear them? They shout,

"There is a God in Heaven!"
Daniel 2:28

Look to the skies tonight and *See God*.

Dear God,
Amazing. I honor You today.

September 28th

Purpose and Task

I was laughing as I walked through the isle of one of my favorite stores today and saw the wacked out things for Halloween that they have out. I could not believe the choices this year!

Everything to be someone else. The only thing that intrigues me is all the fake wigs. Call me weird, but I love big, long wigs. Love them! I don't have any, but I think it would be a blast to try them all on and see what I look like with different hair! Only one time in the beginning of this year I was with a friend far away from anyone who knew me, and we went to this dive of a store that had tons of wigs for $19.99! Ha! We tried them on! So fun. Anyway, today I saw fake hands, noses, even a thing to put under your shirt so ladies have a Barbie body and men have a six pack. I could not believe it! Then they had a tattoo sleeve that was made of a mesh stocking that you slip over your entire arm so it looks like your entire arm is tattooed. We didn't have choices like this when I was a kid! We had Batman, Cat woman and putting on mom and dad's old clothes so we could be bums! Just could not believe all the things that are out already for October 31st.

I remember as a kid trick or treating. My friends and I would spend all day trying to figure out what we would be. We would spend hours putting make up on and doing our hair and clothes. We would go house to house and could not wait to get free candy. There was this one house we would go to that was always dark, we knew exactly what was going to happen when we pressed the doorbell, but it became tradition to do it anyway! We would press the bell and a young man would pop his head out and in a deep low voice he would say, "Weeeee don't celebrate Halloween!" I'm sure he was a Christian, and instead of taking advantage of the only night that the entire world knocks on your door, he turned us all away.

What I would have given for him to turn his light on, and share the gospel with us. We did something called Light the Night, where we got the very best candy that anyone on the street had, and made hot cider and invited people in. Word got out we had great candy and we had a house full of teens. It was awesome; they all wanted to know about God, Kids church, youth group and everything! Why not light up the night that everyone comes to your door? Why would we not want to take advantage of that? Anyway sorry, tangent! After trick or treating, we would all go home, and lay out our mounds of candy. We would become again the person under all the makeup. I would go to sleep that night thinking of all the fun I had, and the long hair and freckles I would miss in the morning. I want you to know today. God made you, you, just the way you are for a reason.

It's easy to dress up and go out when you are hiding under something that is not really you. As humans we have all fantasized about being someone or something else. A hero, a princess, a mother with kids, or a King with tons of money. We are who we are, for purpose and task.

"For we are God's workmanship,
created in Christ Jesus to do good works,
which God prepared in advance for us to do."
Ephesians 2:10

I love this scripture. When a carpenter gets done with his task we see his workmanship. Beautiful carvings on wood. It takes time and effort, skill and structure. This is how He works in us. We are His workmanship. We are created to do good works; these works are NOT what gets us into Heaven. Grace is what gets us into Heaven, but to be more like Jesus we must be good. It says here that God prepared these things in advance for us to do. Can you imagine the countless millions of people who do not have a relationship with Christ yet, and God has already prepared in advance for them to have a purpose and task. Purpose and task, purpose and task. If you do not do a safe alternative to that night at your church, I challenge you to Light the Night, let them knock, and love them. What I would have given for someone, anyone, to have shined the Light of Christ on me all those years I went door to door.

God has a purpose for you my friend. He has prepared in advance for your purpose and task. I pray if you don't know Him today that you seek Him and find Him. And if you know Him, I pray you make the most of every single opportunity to minister God's love and light.

Dear God,
As this season comes where people hide behind masks may we be full transparent with you. Be who we are and shine your light and love on others. I honor You today.

September 29th

Don't Forget God

"Can papyrus grow tall where there is no marsh?
Can reeds thrive without water?
While still growing and uncut, they wither more
quickly than grass. Such is the destiny of all who forget God;
so perishes the hope of the godless."
Job 8:11-13

In other words if the papyrus and reeds do not have water, even if they are uncut and still growing, they will die quick! This scripture says that if we forget God we are like these plants that will die very quickly. Forgetting God can mean a turning away from Him or walking away from Him. I know one thing; if my husband does not water the grass it turns brown quick! It does not take long for something to dry up. We need Him every day for growth and this scripture also says without Him hope will perish. It also goes on to say,

"What he trusts in is fragile; what he relies on
is a spider's web. He leans on his web, but it gives way;
He clings to it, but it does not hold."
Job 8:14-15

What do you put your trust in today? What are you relying on? Is it your paycheck?

Your boyfriend or girlfriend? Your nice car or comfort from a close friend? Whatever it is, the Word of God says that if you are godless (Job 8:13), when you lean on those things, It will not hold. It is NOT a firm foundation. I don't mind spiders they don't scare me and I love their webs, but you know as well as I, that they are one of the most fragile things in nature. Even a strong wind in just a few seconds can destroy the piece of art that the spider worked on for many hours. Jesus Christ is our firm foundation; we need Him in our lives.

"I will listen to what God the lord will say;
He promises peace to His people,
His saints- but let them not return to folly. Surely
His salvation in near those who fear him,
that his glory may dwell in our land
Love and faithfulness meet together;
righteousness and peace kiss each other.
Faithfulness springs forth from the earth,
and righteousness looks down from Heaven."
The Lord will indeed give what is good,
and our land will yield its harvest."
Psalm 85:8-12

This scripture is far from the first one we read. This one says if we listen to what God says and don't return to our sin, salvation is near. This means Growth is near. God will give what is good and a great harvest will come when we stay rooted in Him. Why would we not want to live with hope and peace? Why would we not want that firm foundation in Christ?

Today you choose.
Wither without Him or Harvest?

Have you forgotten God? Do you even care He is there for you? Or is
He the first thing you think of when you wake and the last thing you think of when you close your eyes at night?

Please don't forget God.

Dear God,
I pray for those that do not know you or who have forgotten about you. Those who have fallen away from you, or who want nothing to do with you. Lord let them see their foundation is like a fragile spider's web. I honor You today.

September 30th

Wife Support

This devotion may not apply to everyone but maybe as a husband or wife it will possibly apply to you someday. Today was a Sectional Meeting within our District, of the Assembly of God. Instead of our normal monthly meeting we had a prayer meeting. God spoke to our District Pastor to go to every section and pray over every single person there. I was there today from 10am to 1pm. A great three hours as our District Pastor and staff laid their hands on everyone, anointed them with oil and prayed.

As pastors and their staff would go sit in the chairs provided, one by one the District staff would go to each one, say some words and then pray. They said what they knew about each one. For some they said what credentials they held such as Ordained Minister for some they said Prison Ministry leader for some Worship leader and so on. When Pastor got to my husband he spoke quite a while about his humility, and the example he has been in our District. He went from being a Sr. Pastor and Presbyter (leader over our section), to a Sr. Associate, knowing there is never a step down when you are in the perfect will of God for your life.

When Pastor got to me he could have announced that I was the District women's director or that I was Ordained but he did not. I loved what he said, and I will never forget it. He said Tana has been a wife to her husband, she keeps him holy. He sees in me a wife that supports. A wife, that admonishes my husband over myself, and that means more to me than anything in the world. I have never been Proverbs 27:15-16,

> "A quarrelsome wife is like a constant
> dripping on a rainy day.
> Restraining her is like restraining the wind
> Or grasping oil with the hand."
> Proverbs 27:15-16

It is very easy to support your husband when he never raises his voice at you, never lifts a hand to hurt you, believes in your dreams as much as you, and would do anything for you. Guy has never had to restrain me in anyway. He just reminds me where I put things as I lose my mind, Ha-ha. I know it must be so hard for some of you wives who live with a lack of love and a team mate. Someone who roots for you, someone who is your biggest cheerleader. I'm sorry.

But the truth in the Word of God is the same; we are to be a support. To love when he is unlovable, to go the extra mile. Don't make your husband have to restrain you, because you are running way ahead of him. Get rid of your pride. I'm a very strong woman. I'm a leader, but I'm also a wife. I am the weaker vessel; this is the way God made ladies. This does not mean I'm weak in any shape or form, but it says to me, my husband is to be stronger spiritually. I need my husband to be the Spiritual leader in our home. Some ladies have a real hard time with that statement mostly because men have hurt them. Well, men have hurt me too and I submit to the fact that God made me the weaker vessel.

"Husbands in the same way be considerate as you live with your wives, and treat them with respect as the weaker partner and as heirs with you of the gracious gift of life, so that nothing will hinder your prayers."
1 Peter 3:7

It's so easy to give wife support if your husband lives 1 Peter 3:7. It speaks of men being considerate and respectful. Men, is that a picture of you, even on your worst day? My husband and I have been married 21 years this year. Our marriage has never been perfect but one thing I can say is my husband has always been considerate and respectful to most everyone, including myself. I think if there was an issue there, I would get help. You can't do it alone. You must seek out help in your marriage. I promise you men, if you become some of these scriptures, your wife will willingly support you in everything you do.

We have arch support, lumbar support, leg support, and neck support how about some *Wife Support*? Sometimes it takes baby steps.

Dear God,
There is hope for every marriage; I don't care what we have been through. You know what my husband and I went through the first two years of our marriage. You know the baggage I came with into our marriage with. Yet our marriage is not the same as it was 26 years ago. You are so very faithful. Bless these people and let them know they can have a happy healthy marriage. You can change their hearts to be willing to support one another. I honor You today.

October

October 1st

God Stopped Texting Me

Yesterday, in the state of Massachusetts it became against the law to text and drive. Every single time I have picked up my phone today in the car and press speed dial to call my daughter or husband I'm scared people are going to think I'm texting! It's crazy.

For the last 273 days I have written a daily devotion, printed it, and posted online so I could be accountable in disciplining myself! What I'm about to do I have never done but I'm excited about it. I have 92 days left to write, and I don't think I will be doing this again, but due to what is going on in my state I thought this would be a great time to change it up a bit.

My husband Guy is an amazing writer. He also writes devotions and blogs. I want him to minister to you today, be challenged and changed by his words that go along so well with what we all are living today! Here is my husband......

This morning, in my quiet time with God, I am reading Ezekiel 36 - 40. Thirty six and thirty seven are inspiring chapters. To me, Ezekiel 36 is a turning point in the book. It's one of my favorite chapters. Ezekiel 37 is quite famous, as I started reading chapter 40 I came across this verse:

"Look with your eyes, and hear with your ears, and set your heart upon all that I will show you, for you were brought here in order that I might show you"
Ezekiel 40:4

There's so much that can be taken from that verse. What is clear is that God is about to show Ezekiel the new Temple. But something else was sparked in me, as is often the case with the living word. So, I sat down to hear what God was speaking to me. I like to burn incense in the morning when I pray, brew a cup of coffee and try to commune with God. No computer, cell phone off, lights low, no books for study - just the Holy Spirit and me. I want my prayers to be to God as incense.

Ezekiel 40:4 reminded me once again of the LIVING relationship that we are supposed to have with God, through the person of the Holy Spirit. I cannot let my relationship with God become "academic." God is so much more than words upon a page. He is to be known; not simply read about. My relationship with God must be living, breathing, something that touches all the senses. Ezekiel experienced God with all the senses; he didn't just rely on the written word. Knowledge cannot be replaced by guessing; but knowledge should not replace true face to face intimacy with God. The kind of intimacy you have with a friend over a cup of coffee at Starbucks. The Holy Spirit dwells in us not a person to be rationalized and theorized (is that a word?); but as a living Spirit to be realized, experienced.

So, I was convicted that my prayers, too often, are like text messages to God. I do not see Him, but I'm sure He'll get my message. Quick little notes when it's convenient for me. I don't have much time to think about his response and if I don't like His reply, I can simply ignore it. There's no life in texting. The connection is empty of true relationship. Actually, it would be very comfortable if God would just send me some Twitter updates once in a while. And, in return, I could tweet back how I'm feeling or what I'm doing. That's pretty much summarizes many Christians prayer lives any way.

So, this morning, God stopped texting me. His last text said, "Guy, I'll meet you in our quiet place, face to face. Let's talk; not text."

I won't tell you all the happened next; you'll have to experience that yourself. Something to ink about.

-Guy Miller

Are you in a living, active relationship with God today? Or are you sending Him little Tweets?

Like Guy said, Something to ink about!

Dear God,
I pray for this reader, may they learn to spend time alone with You with NO distractions. I honor You today.

October 2nd

The Dark Crags
"When a man finds his enemy, does he let him get away unharmed?"
1 Samuel 24:19

Saul was overwhelmed and shocked when he wrote these words. David had just let him live. Saul and David were enemies. Saul had a lot of jealousy toward David, people would sing songs,

"Saul has slain his thousands, and David his tens of thousands."
1 Samuel 21:11

Saul had heard that David was in the desert, so he took many men from Israel and went looking for him, to kill him.

"Saul took three thousand chosen men from all Israel
And set out to look for David and his men
near the Crags of the Wild Goats."
1 Samuel 24:2

Crags meaning Rocks or caves with wild goats. Somewhere in the desert there was a cave made of rock and, "Saul went into relieve himself." (vs. 3) that verse cracks me up. Anyway, Saul is in this cave not knowing that David is way back in the cave too, and David knows it's him peeing! David's men egg him on to kill Saul, so he himself does not get killed by his armies.
David does a strange thing,

"David crept up unnoticed and cut of a corner of Saul's robe."
1 Samuel 24:4

Saul left the cave and was going on his way. He had no idea of what David had done.

"Then David went out of the cave and called out to Saul,
"My lord the king!"
When Saul looked behind him,
David bowed down and prostrated himself
with his face to the ground. He said to Saul,
"Why do you listen when men say,
'David is bent on harming you'? This day you
have seen with your own eyes
how the Lord delivered you into my hands in the cave.
Some urged me to kill you, but I spared you;
I said, 'I will not lift my hand against my master,
because he is the Lord's anointed.

See my father, look at this piece of your robe in my hand! I cut off the corner of your robe but did not kill you."
1 Samuel 24:8-11

I love this next verse where Saul is speaking later in the chapter it says,

"When David finished saying this, Saul asked, "Is that your voice, David my son?' And he wept aloud. "You are more righteous than I," he said. "You have treated me well, but I have treated you badly."
1 Samuel 24:16-17

This verse reminds me of the movie Hook that came out where Robin Williams plays Peter Pan. He goes back to Neverland but is now old, and an adult. He tries to prove to the Lost Boys of Neverland that it's really him. One of the lost boys goes up to him and stretches his face up and down, the he pulls his cheeks back and says, "There you are Peter!" It's almost as if Saul was saying to David, "There you are David, the old David that I once knew. There you are." This is why Saul wept.

I guess my question to you today is, when you are in your own Crags of wild goats cave, in the darkness, is there a wall up between you and someone else? And, what are you going to do about it? Hurt them like David had the opportunity to do, or are you going to do the right thing and humble yourself. Saul did not have anything godly on his mind taking three thousand men and going to look for David. He wanted to murder and hurt. But David, doing the right thing humbled Saul.

I wonder what choice you would make today if that was you?
Pretty easy target when someone is peeing in a pitch black cave! Ha!
Maybe it's time to ask God to break the walls down between you and other people. Better yet, ask God to help you forgive. It's the hardest and best thing you will ever do.

In Chapter 26 of 1 Samuel David Spares Saul's life once again and we see discipline and godliness put to the test. Think hard and long today what you would do in the dark Crags!

Dear God,
Help us to lay our will down for Your will. I honor You today.

October 3rd

House Cleaning

"A minute on the lips, forever on the hips!" I think of this old saying as I sit here at night, right now, eating a hoagie and chips! Oh how can I do this to me? For those of you involved in ministry at all, you know how strange your eating habits can be at times. The truth is I'm hungry. I worked hard today. Taught my awesome class this am, loaded about 38 young people, went to one of our services, hosted a load of college kids for lunch and then went back to church early to help with the music for tonight. I have not eaten since lunch. I'm hungry. So I sit, and think about this little quote I heard growing up, thinking of the next roll I will have to hide.

This afternoon I felt so bad, we have this new kid that joined the after church "college crew" for lunch at our house whose name is Richard. Such a good kid. Normally I get cheap food that will feed an army. Last week it was hot dogs, we let the kids purchase the drinks and junk! The week before pasta. I think there were about 15 kids here today, I lost count. Anyway, week after week, cheap food, cheap food! So my husband says today, "I can't stand to feed these kids another cheap meal. They need something good." So he goes to the store and gets all the stuff for his famous stir fry. Mound of yummy stuff! So there sits Richard on the chair in the front room watching the game smelling all the amazing smells in the wok, and I find out he has been fasting the last 7 days! The one day we have good food, and poor Richard can't eat it, I felt so bad for him! Mostly I felt bad because next week it goes back to cheap food! Ha-ha!

I was just so blessed that he did not give in, fasting and eating right takes discipline. Tomorrow morning at 6:30 am I meet my new gym accountability partner Kim Elia at the gym. Me and Kim will start to work out at least 4 or 5 days a week together. My husband likes to work out in the afternoons and it's been hard for me because once I get into the swing of things with work my mind is distracted and I have a hard time leaving my desk when I'm on a roll and triple tasking.

So the other day Kim joined the gym and I said, "Let's go!" I'm so excited. So I ease my shame right now eating a hoagie and chips knowing at 6:30 am I will move myself!

All that to say, do you know you MUST take care of yourself. The most important thing isn't even a diet, It's movement! If you continue to eat like you are eating now, and walk just one or two miles a day, do you realize it will change your body. It will put oxygen through your blood stream and your heart will pump better, you will burn fat, it will help with your cholesterol levels. It is a proven fact that if you move your body that you will be more healthy in every area of your physical self. It is a shame that it does not put things back where they once were though! Ha-ha

If you owned a beautiful mansion would you keep it clean? Well, I guess if you owned a mansion you actually would not have to clean it yourself, someone might do that for you.

OK, let's keep fixed on the question, if you had an amazing mansion like the one in the movie Pride and Prejudice, would you not want it to be spotless, so it would look like you could eat off the floors? This is what the Word of God says about your physical body,

> "Do you know that you yourselves are
> God's temple and that God's Spirit lives in you?
> 1 Corinthians 3:16

So if you had a mansion or a beautiful temple would you not want to keep it beautiful?

Then why do we let our body always be the last thing on the list. If we keep our body healthy we will live longer to tell others about the hope of Christ. Yes, we must try and keep our spiritual self from sin but I'm talking about your physical self here! If your physical body is the dwelling place of God, why are we not keeping it in the best shape we can? I know everyone hates me by now, but it's the truth, we need to strive for it. Hey, I'm preaching to the choir right now, as I sit here all done eating my hoagie and chips! Yesterday I cleaned my house and my daughter helped. I wanted it done because I knew people would come over after church. Do you not know that God is not going to visit tomorrow, He is already here! And tomorrow, and the next day, and the day after He is here too! The Word of God says He dwells within us.

> "Do you not know that your body is a temple of the Holy Spirit, who is in
> you, whom you have received from God? You are not your own; you
> were bought with a price. Therefore honor God with your body."
> 1 Corinthians 6:19-20

I love that scripture, "Therefore honor God with Your body!" This is what Richard was doing today as he fasted with amazing smells in the air, this is what Kim and I will do tomorrow at 6:30, we will do some personal house cleaning!

When was the last time you honored God with your body?
Is the dwelling place of God clean in you?
Do you need to clean up your physical self?

I know I do. I don't want to have to purchase a full body girdle!

It's time to be accountable to others.
It's time to move
And it's time to do some Serious housecleaning!

Dear God,
Help us. I honor You today.

October 4th

Triple Tasking

I find myself once again triple tasking this time of year. Every November I and my amazing team of ladies put on a Women's Retreat. We hit fire code at 1,500, and then have to turn people away. Today was just one of those days, where, before I can even write something down, such as staging, tickets, what people go in what rooms, and meal tickets, I get another call or e mail that leads me down another road. I have to be very careful and organized that I don't misplace things, and I have to tie up all loose ends before I move to the next thought.

Today was a Triple Task day. At times I had to say to people, can you hold on one minute while I write something down? They were all kind enough to say yes, but I knew that if I did not tie up the one task that I was working on before they called, I would be in big trouble. Sometimes Triple Tasking can give you a bit of anxiety, but it comes with the territory of an event like this.

We have more crafters this year than ever before, double than last year! We have a Christian book store that sets up, 18 workshops on different subjects, three main people flown in, a 24 hour prayer room, four worship teams, missionaries coming in for our Friday night and the list goes on. As you can imagine it's a very busy time of year. On top of that I do a graveyard shift tonight in maternity so all day my mind has been on when can I go to sleep for a few hours before I go in at 11pm. Thank God tonight is my last graveyard until our awesome retreat is over. This will help me mentally and physically!

At one point this afternoon I had to sit and take a breather! I know my secretary Judy who is also one of my best friends, is feeling the crunch too. It's so important that we stop breath and focus on the entire purpose of this retreat. Our purpose is to draw ladies closer to God and closer to one another.

It's so easy when your life is in a rush, and you have triple tasking on the brain, to forget your purpose, and your focus. It's so easy to forget the one you are trying to lift up and honor. In your busy times, don't be so busy that you forget to spend time with Him and His Word.

I think this is a great time of year to write this because all of a sudden everyone is thinking about the holidays, Christmas programs, thanksgiving dinner and such. Everyone has parties, events and programs. It is the most wonderful time of the year, but also the busiest time of the year. Please, as you are shopping, thinking, planning, running and working, don't forget The Master. The one who created you for purpose.

I met my gym accountability partner at the gym at 6:30 this morning, I'm keeping up with my physical self, but I also have to keep up with my spiritual self during these triple tasking times! I have to discipline myself to get into His Word and stop everything to hear His Voice!

In your business, when was the last time you stopped?
When was the last time you sat in quiet?
Just to listen?

> "Look to the lord and His strength; seek His face always."
> 1 Chronicles 16:11

What a great scripture, notice the word ALWAYS! Even in triple tasking seasons!

> "Blessed are they who keep his statutes
> and seek Him with all their heart."
> Psalm 119:2

Don't make Him part of your triple task list. Put your list down! Turn off the phone and walk away from the computer. He is not a task, He is a joy. He is a best friend. It should not feel like you are adding another task to your list to meet with Him!

So in this busy time, make room for Him in your Triple tasking!

Dear God,
Help us to always put you first. To lay everything else aside to seek Your face and will for our life. I honor You today.

October 5th

"Comfortably Numb"

Right now at this moment I feel comfortably numb. Not in the Pink Floyd drug use kind of way, but my body is literally shutting down and needs rest. This leaves my mind able to work, but it is not functioning as usual. This should make for an interesting read. Ha-ha.

I came home this morning from an 8 ½ hour grave yard shift in labor and delivery where I work. I laid down and slept three hours and that's all the sleep I have had since yesterday. I'm not complaining, hundreds of thousands of people do this on a daily basis. I admire them, that they can live this as their lifestyle, and put food on their table. I thank God I only do it about once a week for extra money. After getting my daughter from school I had to get ready for our ministry tonight. Driving home alone after our ministry, I was trying to stay awake and I am fighting a headache that I know is from lack of sleep. Hmmm are you being encouraged yet? Ha-ha.

My question tonight is do you feel comfortably numb? Unable to think normally?

It may not be lack of sleep for you. You may be filled with anxiety, obsessive behavior, bad habits or intense grief. All these things can leave you feeling numb, like you are unable to think straight or process things correctly. Let's just say this is NOT a good time to sign an important document or run off and get married to someone! We must be able to think clear. So many things must come into order for that to happen.

Sleep for one. Physical health, spiritual health, if you truly have a mental condition you need to be evaluated by a professional. Yes we can always go to God, but hey, this is the real world we live in, and you NEED to take care of yourself whatever healthy way you can.

My encouragement to you tonight is when you are feeling comfortably numb, to press on! Don't you think it was a temptation tonight for me not to write with this headache and lack of sleep? But I do it because this is exactly how God is growing me this year. He is stripping everything I want away and building me into the person He wants me to be. Many of you may be filled with intense grief right now. Unthinkable things have happened to some of you. You may be going through a very painful divorce and watching your kids suffer due to it, and so many more situations. You are numb from pain, grief and much hurt. I want you to know it's ok to be numb sometimes. This is the way Jesus made us. He knew there would be times like this.

He knows you better than you know yourself.

But it's in these times that we MUST press on and be the person He wants us to be. Discipline yourself to do things you DO NOT want to do. This is how we make it through. This is how He grows us!

> "I press on toward the goal to win the prize
> for which God has called me Heavenward in Christ Jesus."
> Philippians 3:14

Ok, so what is the goal? For you the goal is different than it is for me. My goal is writing this daily devotional so that next year I can work on getting it published. This is why I stay disciplined this year no matter what is going on around me. Your goal may be to stay sober, to stop bad habits, to be a better person, to have a healthy marriage, to be used somehow in ministry, to be a better parent, or to lead an elementary class. I don't know what your goal is, but let NOTHING stop it. Nothing! If you have lost someone very dear to you, they would also want you to continue and not give up!

Driving home tonight and being so tired was interesting. Every exit I saw was like another road to travel. It may seem that there are all these exits and you just don't know which way to go. Don't you think He will take care of you? He already has the details mapped out for you. Have faith and keep going.

Today if you are feeling Comfortably Numb, and not able to completely process things as usual, Keep pressing on toward the goal friend, because God has a much better plan for you than you can imagine. If you struggle with a goal, take the time today to think about your goals in this life. We should always have something more we are striving for.

Dear God,
Tonight I pray for this reader that they will know You have not left them. Give them the strength and desire to press on. I honor You today.

October 6th

Accountability

Do you realize there are forms of accountability where you don't have make another date for your calendar? There are safe and healthy things you can do to be accountable without adding more to your already busy life! I was thinking about this today at the gym. I have been meeting my friend, Kim, there at 6:30 am. We have this rule between us, that when we get there we just go up and start working out. We do not wait around for one another, we just go for it. Then when we are done we leave. We don't even really talk while we are there, we use earphones, but just me knowing she will be looking for me, keeps me accountable and that's what motivates me to get up out of my warm bed into the freezing cold.

There are other forms of accountability that our family uses I have mentioned them before. www.clearplay.com where you can pop in an R rated movie and the clear play unit will make it PG, you can filter out anything and everything. It's a wonderful unit and well worth the investment. There were times as a family where we would be watching a PG-13 movie and we would have to fast forward! With this unit it's all safe and your kids NEVER have to see anything bad or hear anything bad. Unfortunately many hear it all and see it all in their own homes, but if you are guarding what has been entrusted into your care like the Word says, it might be great for your family.

> "Guard what has been entrusted to your care."
> 1 Timothy 6:20

I have also talked to you about Covenant Eyes (www.covenanteyes.com). When you check out this website it talks mostly about kids, but the truth is our entire family is covered. Guy and I put our internet usage in the bulk of our five computers that are covered by Covenant Eyes.

This way no person can fall into any form of temptation without someone else knowing. Once again accountability and guarding what God has put into your care. As a young girl, I was not guarded from porn. Back in the 70's there were Playboys sitting on almost every coffee table in America. Some of the things I saw as a young girl, I was not ready to handle. I was already insecure about myself, and seeing perfect people made the image of myself even worse. Not to mention images that will be in my mind the rest of my life. I was watching a show on TV the other day about how the internet has become a form of sexual addiction for billions of people around the world. It's worse now than ever before all over our world. On that show they interviewed lawyers and business men, house wives and many more who have secret lives that no one knows about. When my husband and I were Sr. Pastors we had every single staff member connected with Covenant Eyes. Accountability can be life changing for your office staff, children and for you. Do you know what your family does on the internet? Don't think you are above the fall my friend. Everyone is tempted.

"So, if you think you are standing firm, be careful that you don't fall!
No temptation has seized you except what is common to man.
And God is faithful; he will not let you be tempted beyond what you can bear. But when you are tempted, he will also provide a way out so that you can stand up under it."
1 Corinthians 10:10

Statistics show us that even in Christian homes 90% of boys and 60% of girls, by the age of 18 have already seen internet pornography. Could it be you could keep them from having these images put in their mind at an early age? Don't be fooled mom and dad. The best kids that love God are tempted. In 27 years of ministry we have seen it time and time again. It does not stop with the kids. Marriages are broken due to internet sin. Where has all the accountability gone?

All this to say, yes, it's great to have an accountability partner or mentor that you can talk to and spend time with. You need that just as much as I do. I thank God for my mentors. But too many times we make excuses, "I can't be accountable in that area due to time." I met Kim this morning and we did not say but a few words to one another! But I knew she was there and that's the only reason I got out of my warm bed.

Mom and dad, do you think your kids are too young? You are wrong, they learn more at school and know more about how to hide internet activity than you do. How about you? Mom and dad? Are you accountable to one another? Maybe it's time to think about it.

There are simple easy ways to be accountable where you don't have to talk to anyone or even see anyone. They are guards that now have been put before you. Maybe some of these could be "a way out" (1 Corinthians 10:10) that the scripture was talking about. Nipping it in the bud before It becomes a problem.

Are you accountable today? Do you care to be? If you are not now, you will be.

"For we must all appear before the judgment seat of Christ, that each one may receive what is due him for the things done while in the body, whether good or bad."
2 Corinthians 5:10

May I remind you that When Paul wrote this scripture he wrote it to the church!

"So then, each of us will give an account of himself to God. Therefore let us stop passing judgment on one another. Instead, make up your mind not to put any stumbling block or obstacle in your brother's way."
Romans 14:12-13

Yes, and how about no stumbling block in YOUR way for that matter. Accountability is not that hard, stop making excuses and get some in your life.

Dear God,
Let us make every effort to guard the ones we love and our self. I honor You today.

October 7th

Every Mother's Nightmare

Today I am thanking God all day.

I got a call late last night that my son was being taken to the emergency room by his roommate Tom at college. The first time I spoke with my son his first words were, "Mom, don't freak out. I'm ok." Then I knew something was wrong. He had been lifting at the gym and benched pressed up. There was no spotter. There was a girl with her earphones on working out on the other side. He benched up, put the bar in the holder, and thought it was secure, for a couple seconds it was. Then the bar came right down onto his chest and bounced twice. He could not speak so started clapping to try to get help from the girl but she did not hear him. Somehow he pushed the bar off him, walked around campus thinking he just got the wind knocked out of him but an hour later started feeling bad. Heart palpitations and pain. This was when we got the call.

Jon is fine. He will hurt for a few days but I'm just thanking God the bar did not land on his neck or anywhere else that could have really hurt him. Not one broken bone and no damage to the lungs or heart. He has pleurisy which is an inflammation of the lining of the lungs and chest (the pleura) that leads to chest pain (usually sharp) when you take a breath or cough. He has heat there and a pillow on his chest. Poor kid, I can tell he is in pain. They have him on Oxycodone and relaxers so he has slept most the day away. But seeing him on the couch for hours has made me thank God, all day, he is ok and not seriously hurt.

As a mother I can handle things happening to me, but when they happen to my kids it's very hard to watch. But I found myself very calm. On the way to the hospital which was about a 45 minute drive, I had a peace come over me that all was well. I was very peaceful and for anyone that knows me in a situation like this, that is NOT normal.

I can't help in times like today to think of Mary the mother of Jesus. My son got a slam in the chest but her son was ripped apart and beat to a pulp. I'm sure it was a nightmare when he went missing, and they could not find him.

> "When he was twelve years old, they went up to the Feast,
> according to the custom. After the Feast was over,
> while his parents were returning home,
> the boy Jesus stayed behind in Jerusalem,
> but they were unaware of it."
> Luke 2:42-43

I'm sure as she was hearing about all he was doing; her mind was running to memories of him as a baby and her holding him tight.   I'm sure as he hung on that cross, her heart felt ripped out. I wonder if Mary experienced the peace I had last night as her son was hanging on the cross dying? When the angel first appeared to Mary as a young girl to say she was going to have a son he also said,

"His kingdom will never end."
Luke 1:33

So there he was dying, yet there was a promise that He would always be. I wonder if she was confused or if she had a deep peace like I felt last night? Someday I will ask her to tell me the story herself. I hope they have great coffee beans in Heaven so we can have a cup together. Somehow I don't think I will be thinking of coffee.

I do hope you know the Lords great peace today. A God who can give hope in a hopeless situation. As a mom, I'm not sure how moms, who don't know the Lord, handle their kids getting seriously hurt or sick? It's wonderful if they have a great support system around them in family, but without the peace and hope of Christ in the past eighteen years of my kid's lives, I'm not sure where we would be. They both have been through surgeries and other things, yet somehow every time great anxiety came He always came through with Peace. Maybe it's because I know my kids have their own relationship with the Lord and if anything were to happen they would be with Him? I think that can bring great peace sometimes. I don't mean to be morbid but when you get a call like that your mind can go haywire. That's when we need to let the peace of God step in and calm us.

"And the peace of God, which surpasses all understanding, will guard your hearts and minds through Christ Jesus."
Philippians 4:7

Can you imagine when someone went to go get Mary and told her that her son was walking the road to the cross? I don't care if she knew He was The Lord or not, she was still a mother.

"For He Himself is our peace."
Ephesians 2:14

When every mother's nightmare happens, even on smaller scales, or any nightmare happens, I hope and pray you know God.

He is peace.

Dear God,
Thank you. I honor You today

October 8th

I Want It Now!

"I want it Lord, and I want it NOW!" Have you ever thought these words in your head? Have you ever wondered why the Lord is not answering your prayers right when you want Him too? It would be nice if we could just move Him along a bit! The truth is, and you have heard it before, that everything is better in His time. Everything is perfect in His time. And if there is one thing I have learned through the years it's that His time and my time are two different times!

I was reading today in Isaiah and came across the most amazing scripture. It was mixed in with a bunch of Woe's in Isaiah Chapter 5.

"Woe to those who are heroes at drinking wine."
verse 22

"Woe to those who draw sin along with cords of deceit, and wickedness as with cart ropes."
verse 18

"Woe to those who call evil good and good evil"
verse 20

"Woe to those who are wise in their own eyes and clever in their own sight."
verse 21

I could keep listing the Woe's but I would rather that you read them all yourself in Chapter 5. But listen to the scripture that is mixed in with all these other woes, you will be blown away!

"Woe to those who say, "Let God hurry, let Him hasten His work so we may see it. Let it approach, let the plan of the Holy One of Israel come, so we may know it."
Isaiah 5:19

This just blew me away today, how many times have you don't this? I know I have done it hundreds if not thousands of times in my years of life. "Come on God, hurry up!", "I want to see You answering my prayers Lord!", "Hurry up Lord that I might know Your plan!"

I think what really shocks me about this scripture is its right alongside the words wickedness and evil. It's equal to the other woes!

Do NOT read me wrong!

He does want us to know His plan; He desires that we see His handy work! But we cannot hurry Him along because His time is the best time. He sees everything that was, everything that is, and everything that is to be.

He IS perfect timing.

I need to learn to stop trying to hurry Him along! To have faith enough to believe that His timing is the best plan there is.

> "For the vision is yet for an appointed time;
> but at the end it will speak, and it will not lie.
> Tough it tarries, wait for it; because it will surely come, it will not tarry."
> Habakkuk 2:3

We have plans, and our own agendas, but His agenda is much safer than our own. His timing will grow our character almost better than anything. Don't rush him friend.

> "In the time of my favor I will answer you."
> Isaiah 49:8

Now listen to this one,

> **"By your patience possess your souls."**
> **Luke 21:19**

Wow, could patience and waiting for God's perfect timing mean many more soul? Keep praying friend, don't stop, and don't give up! He will approach on His timetable and this is best.

Are you trying to hurry God?
Stop and rest.
Stop saying
I want it NOW!
And start letting Him change you.

Dear God,
Change us that we may possess many souls. I honor You today.

October 9th

Don't be Lazy

I want you to take the time today to read these scriptures on discipline. All year God has been dealing with my heart on this subject. He has also been putting me through the test of discipline. This has been one of the hardest years of my life, and yet, I have stayed disciplined. I know somehow in the end, it will produce a harvest!

> "No discipline seems pleasant at the time, but painful.
> Later on, however, it produces a harvest of
> righteousness and peace for those who have been trained by it."
> Hebrews 12:11

Ok...notice the word painful! Discipline is NEVER easy. It's making yourself do something you do NOT want to do. It hurts at times! It says here, that the harvest of righteousness and peace will come to the one who has been trained by the very act of discipline. I'll take it! I will take all the righteousness and peace God wants to give me! But the truth is, in your act of discipline you are the one planting the seeds and the harvest comes in us, through God changing our character. We draw nearer to God through it, and we are more peaceful when we know He is pleased.

> "Whoever loves discipline loves knowledge,
> but he who hates correction is stupid."
> Proverbs 12:1

In discipline we commit to something and we are accountable to someone. For those of us who have a relationship with God, we are going to give an account to Him. Do you love it when He disciplines you? I cannot say I love it, sorry. It's hard, any change is hard, but His way is best. We need to take His correction and learn to apply it to our life. This scripture made me laugh because it actually says he who hates correction is stupid! I think most of us would say we hate correction! When you are corrected you are humbled. A humbling process can be very hard at times. But it's when you understand that sometimes correction is the best thing for you, that you learn to love it.

So God disciplines us and we discipline ourselves. My question to you today is when was the last time you disciplined yourself? I think it's time for you to set yourself realistic goals. Start with small ones. If you cannot clean your room and it's always dirty, set a goal that every day you will hang your clothes and put things away. If you over eat, and like the entire sleeve of cookies rather than one or two, discipline yourself in your eating habits. What about the reading of your Bible, that might be sitting there collecting dust? How about disciplining yourself to read at least a chapter a day? As you make yourself do something, you are in return planting seeds that will lead to righteousness and peace because it will change you. Make yourself change, and do the things you know are right. You can do ALL THINGS through God who gives you strength! As you submit to discipline you submit to God.

Usually when we commit to New Years goals they are always positive and disciplining. Loss of weight, drawing nearer to God, having a happier marriage and the list goes on. What are you going to do about your goals and why do they seem to slack off come March? It's because we do not discipline ourselves. This year has been the first time that discipline has totally changed my life forever. I will never be the same. For almost an entire year I have made myself do things I do not want to do. Not that I don't love to do them but sometimes I'm tired or wish I could do other things. It has added a measure of peace to my life that I cannot even explain. I feel closer to Him.

I challenge you today to write down one or two small goals. Make yourself do them. Do NOT slack off.

Do Not be Lazy.

And watch God change your life, as you plant seeds that will change you. The seed of His Word is the greatest seed you can plant. Learn to love that discipline.

Dear God,
Grow us, change us and let us bring in an amazing harvest. I honor You today.

October 10th

<u>When Someone You Love is Gone</u>

I was named after my grandmother Gaetana Zinnanti. I was the first girl born to a half Italian family. My grandmother was an amazing lady. She birthed and raised 4 boys and she he had two twin girls that died at birth. She put up with my grandfather, and served and loved him all her life. And the truth is, I miss her.

It's a very hard thing to lose someone you love. Even if they know the Lord, and you know someday you will see them, there are just those days that you wish you could call them or just tell them something going on in your life. I miss my grandmother. Some of the funniest memories I have as a kid are with my grandmother.

Every year at the Elks club, the Italian side of the family would get together and attend their clam bakes. There was always a great band and every single cousin and family member were there. Grandma would grab me on the dance floor, and we would take off in the polka! Grandma could polka like no other. Sometimes I would actually put my feet on her feet and she would carry me through it. I loved to Polka with Grandma. As I got older I mastered the polka, and we would dance together. She was a total blast. I wish I could polka with her now.

As all the cousins got older, grandma would slip us cash. There were eleven of us, my brother and I being the oldest, and I always wondered where grandma's cash flow came from? Somehow she managed to always hand us $100 bills. I never understood where it came from but I was so glad when she would hand me one of those bills. If you ask anyone of my cousins, they could tell you what she would say after handing the money to you, "Now, don't tell your grandfather!" She was just so funny.

One of my favorite memories, was when me and my cousin Deb went across country with them, grandma taught us this stupid song that went like this,

Five little chickadees, playing near the door,
One flew away, then there were four,
Chickadee, chickadee, fly away,
Chickadee, chickadee, happy and gay.

Four little chickadees, sitting in a tree,
One flew away, then there were three;
Chickadee, chickadee fly away,
Chickadee, chickadee, happy and gay.
And so on….

I know it sounds like a stupid song but when grandma got giddy and started singing at the top of her lungs, Chickadee, chickadee, fly away, Chickadee, chickadee, happy and gay. You could not help but laugh. I will never forget her singing that song.

She was a hostess, and one of the most amazing cooks I have ever met in my life. She loved her family more than anything. When we had a holiday there was course after course, mounds of food to feed an army, she loved to work in her humble kitchen. She kept her house beautiful. I know in some ways, I'm a lot like her.

What do you do when someone you love is gone?

It helps so, to hang on to happy memories. But it helps so much more when you know you will see them again. Have you thought about your after life? The Word of God says you go to Heaven or Hell; you are the one who makes that choice by how you live this life. It does not matter what bad things you have done, He can forgive your sin.

To think that someone you love has entered into their eternal home is quite the thought. You wish you could ask them what it's like, or what they do during the day. Can they see us, do they watch us? So many questions. But there is a peace when you know they are with the Lord.

When someone you love is gone, you need to let God fill voids. Don't shut Him out. It's one of the hardest things you will ever do. It helps to have those who loved that person too, surrounding you. Talk about that person together and laugh. Fill your mind with the Word of God, if you have a Bible read it. The truth is no matter what we do, it still will hurt.

My friend Bert lost her husband and she love talking to me about him for hours at a time, it was very healing for her. If you have had deep pain in your life, I want you to know God is near and He has not left you. Tell Him you really need a Hug, and that you need to feel His presence. He is faithful.

"The God of all comfort, who comforts us in all our troubles, so that we can comfort those in any trouble with the comfort we ourselves have received from God. For just as the sufferings of Christ flow over into our lives, so also through Christ our comfort overflows."
2 Corinthians 1:3-5

You will make it friend.

And someday you will put your arms around someone else and tell them that You do know how they feel. When someone you love is gone, it's hard But He is faithful.

Dear God,
Thank you for the memories. Help us in return to help others. I honor You today.

October 11th

Eye Candy, the Berkshires, and You

Ok, so even though I think my husband of over 26 years is eye candy, that is NOT what this devotional is going to be about! Ha-ha. A few minutes ago I looked at pictures of Southern New England's mountains. My daughter just got back from a retreat and went to the most amazing place in the Berkshires. I did not drive her there, nor am I out of the house much in the month of October. My biggest event of the year is in November, so October is usually looking at my computer screen and getting things done. Yes, I go outside and do the things I have to do, and I'm sure my husband and I will take a drive to see the colors, but when I saw these pictures it was total eye candy to me. The beauty of New England in the autumn and fall is just amazing.

It's as if the Lord just got board, and started chucking balls of paint everywhere.

After seeing these pictures I wanted to know myself how the leaves change colors, so I googled to read about it. Even though I have never heard some of these words before, I found something very interesting here,

"During the growing season, chlorophyll is continually being produced and broken down and leaves appear green. As night length increases in the autumn, chlorophyll production slows down and then stops and eventually all the chlorophyll is destroyed. The carotenoids and anthocyanins that are present in the leaf are then unmasked and show their colors."[1]

So when the chlorophyll production stops and is destroyed, the things that are ALL READY PRESENT IN THE LEAF (carotenoids and anthocyanins), you see for the first time. This website used the word "unmasked"! Wow, there is a serious sermon in here somewhere! So it would seem, if some would just let God break down their mask, others might just see some serious beauty that has already been present in there! We must fully surrender in order for that to happen. If you didn't notice, it also calls this "The growing season!"

Something else that I read on this website,

"A succession of warm, sunny days and cool, crisp but not freezing nights seems to bring about the most spectacular color displays."[2]

---

[1] http://www.na.fs.fed.us/fhp/pubs/leaves/leaves.shtm

[2] http://www.na.fs.fed.us/fhp/pubs/leaves/leaves.shtm

In other words, as us New Englanders would say, PERFECT WEATHER! I have to say the last few days have been perfect weather and when I brought the dog out yesterday I saw the first palette of colors in the yard. It's been warm, sunny, and cool with no humidity and no frost.

It seems when life is perfect, it's easy to let others see the inside but as soon as those dark gloomy days or storms come, the build up of chlorophyll comes with it, and the masks go back on!

What is your chlorophyll today? What things build up in you, that block who you really are inside? That hide what is already present? Hmmm I wonder, are you in a growing season? God cannot break down anything, and develop healthy change, if you will not allow it. He gave you a free will. You choose.

> "Put off your old self, which is being corrupted by its deceitful desires;
> to be made new in the attitude of your minds;
> and to put on the new self,
> created to be like God in true righteousness and holiness."
> Ephesians 4:22-24

Sometimes to "Put on the new self" you must get rid of the junk that is masking you, "The old self." What will you do today to get rid of the things that are like chlorophyll in your life?

You are a holy eye candy to Him, as beautiful as the Berkshires!
The choice is yours today, let Him do His work in you.

Dear God,
Right now we welcome you to do the work in us that needs to be done! Change us and may everything that is already inside of us shine out. I honor You today.

October 12th

Obedience

Deuteronomy chapter 28 is a chapter all about walking in obedience. The Word says if we are obedient we will be blessed (28:3-6). If we are obedient,

> "The Lord will grant that the enemies who rise up against you
> will be defeated before you.
> They will come at you from one direction but flee from you in seven."
> Deuteronomy 28:7

I don't know about you but when I read that it ministered to me big time! It's a spiritual battle, and when we are obedient to the Lord, we defeat the enemy's schemes to make us take the wrong road.

He will bless everything you put your hand to (vs. 8).
He promises if we keep His commands that he will make us holy (vs. 9). If we are holy and walking in obedience listen to what it says next,

> "Then all the peoples on earth will see that
> you are called by the name of the Lord."
> Deuteronomy 28:10

There's a question for you, do people see that you are called by the name of the Lord?

Do they see that you follow Him so close, because you walk in obedience? I know we have all failed in this area but to me it's something worth striving for!

I love this next verse, something really stood out to me when I read it.

> "The Lord will open the Heavens, the storehouse of his bounty,
> to send rain on your land in season
> and to bless all the work of your hands."
> Deuteronomy 28:12

Go ahead; read it again, slow, one more time.
What stands out to you when you read that scripture?

What stood out to me are the words "in season", even His blessings will come in season! In other words, God chooses when the blessings come. We have labored, toiled, worked so hard, yet he still picks and chooses when the blessings come.

And I can assure you; they will not come in the time frame you think they should come. Most the time they come when we least expect it.

So as I read all these scriptures today about all the blessings that come when we follow Him, and are obedient as much as we can be, there is still a measure of faith involved. Yes, we will be blessed, but in His time. Once again, don't rush God friend, trust me, you DO want HIS timing and not your own.

It's much easier to do your own thing and forget God. It's hard to do His perfect will. I guess the question is, do you have a backbone? Do you stand on the Word of God? Are you NOT ashamed?

Are you Obedient?

Dear God,
Help us to do exactly what you say no matter who is watching. I honor You today.

October 13th

"I'm a Flier!"

For those of you who are fans of the movie What about Bob, you love the scene when Bob (a young man with OCD) gets in the boat and starts to scream, that he is now a sailor! Well, today I had a very unexpected turn of events. I went to see a young man from our church get his pilot license and last minute he could not take his test, so I got free air time! As I climbed into the little plane I could not help but think of the scene from What about Bob, and I started to scream, "I'm a flier, I fly! Don't you see, I'm a flier?" Ha-ha! You can dress me up, but you can't take me out (I think you have to be over 40 to understand what that means!)

My friend Jody's husband is a Pilot for American Airlines and they have this little plane, I mean the smallest plane I have ever flown in. I have to say it was not the same as the regular flights I'm on. I'm blessed to have a job where I fly at least twice a year, I love to fly, but after Captain Bill circled around my house about five times, I thought I would lose my lunch. We all had head phones and mouth pieces so I had a total blast with that. It was a very fun unexpected part, to an already great day.

The colors in New England right now are so amazing and that is what caught my eye first. Its one thing when you are on the ground or in your car, but get above the world and look down and it's amazing. I know I would have been a great Amelia Earhart! We saw Boston's skyline, my home, the colors of fall and best of all the Connors farm Corn Maze! From the Sky Clint Eastwood is cut into the corn field, his entire face with the words American Legend. It was so awesome from the sky. People pay to walk the corn maze and get lost. There are even night walks with flashlights. Very fun. But I have never seen it from the sky. It's amazing to me how different the world is when you see the Bigger Picture.

When I was a Sr. in High School in 1984 someone gave me a graduation card that touched my heart. I memorized the poem in it, and have never forgotten it. For years I have used it in sermons and inspirational messages alongside God's Word.

Follow your Dream
Follow your dream.
Take one step at a time and don't settle for less,
Just continue to climb.
Follow your dream.
If you stumble, don't stop and lose sight of your goal
but Press on to the top.
For only on top can we see the whole view,
Can we see what we've done and what we must do;

Can we then have the vision to seek something new,
Press on and
Follow your dream.
~ Amanda Bradley

Through the years I have never forgotten this poem, even when my past would creep up on me and some memories would haunt me, I would always think about the fact that I had to be on top to see the whole view or the bigger picture! This would always push me on to greater things.

I want you to be a flier today and to try to fly above your situation. I know you can't hop in a plane like I did today, but try to see the bigger picture. It was not until I was in the air above my normal life today that I saw so many things that I forgot were around me. Bodies of water, beauty, Connors farm and the list goes on. Fly above friend, remember your blessings. When we are going through the storm it's very hard to see the blessings all around us. I know you have heard this scripture before, but read it again,

"They that wait upon the Lord shall renew their strength; they shall mount up with wings as eagles; they shall run, and not be weary; and they shall walk, and not faint."
Isaiah 40:31

Did you hear that? "They shall mount UP with wings as eagles." Even an eagle needs to be above to live. This is where it sees its daily food and danger approaching.

Friend, I encourage you today to be A Flier!

Dear God,
I wish I had wings, make me a better flier. I honor You today.

October 14th

He Catches Us

"Like an eagle that stirs up its nest and hovers over its young,
Then spreads its wings to catch them and carries them on its pinions."
Deuteronomy 32:11

In Reading about eaglets tonight getting ready to fly it was very interesting to me how the mother eagle stirs up the nest.

Anyone feeling like your nest is being stirred up today?

Even before the mother stirs up the nest to try to let the eaglet fly out, the mother will stand over the eaglets and flap its wings. The eaglets mimic the mother and their wings are already so powerful that they actually lift like 2 inches off the nest being copy cats. The mother knows they learn from watching. They are influenced by what the mother eagle does.

If you are feeling things are not going so hot today, let me ask you, who are you letting influence you?

The mother eagle influences in a good way but how are you being influenced? Are you growing closer to the Lord hanging with your friends or are you feeling far from God?

Remember it's all about hearing His voice. I don't care if you are in Bible College, or if you lead a ministry at your church, if you are not hearing the voice of God like John 10:27 talks about then you better think twice about if you have a relationship with Him.

So back to mother eagle stirring up the nest, she does it because it's the only way the eaglets are going to learn, the only way they are going to grow. One book I read said that most eaglets do not want to hop out of the nest because they are fearful. Funny how a human knows what an eaglet is feeling, but most of us do the same. We stay where it's comfortable; we stay where it's safe. I was in conversation with a young kid the other day; he said that he does not want to go to ministry school because he wants to be debt free, even though he is feeling a call to ministry. Ok, to be debt free is a wonderful thing, but if fear of owing money keeps us from the will of God for our life then we fear in vain. There must be some sort of measure of faith involved, but you must know He has spoken first. Remember it does say in His Word that He will supply all our needs.

"Everything that does not come from faith is sin."
Romans 14:23

> "My God will meet all your needs
> according to his glorious riches in Christ Jesus."
> Philippians 4:19

The eagle stirs up the nest sometimes when the eaglet does not obey. The cute little eaglet wants to stay on common ground. I actually saw video footage of an eagle pushing and kicking with its powerful foot. It bothered me in a way seeing it treat its young that way. Well, this is how our Father has to teach us sometimes. It's not because He does not love us! It's because He DOES love us. And yes, sometimes it's going to hurt, but the scripture on the top of the page says,

> "Then spreads its wings to catch
> them and carries them on its pinions."

Pinions are the strongest part of the wings, the primary feathers.
Here is the great promise from our Father in Heaven. If we fall, fail, mess up, hurt someone else, hurt our self, walk away, or disobey, He catches us.

I cannot tell you the number of times

He Has Caught Me.
He Catches Us.

Dear God,
Thank you for giving to us what we do not deserve most of the time. Thank you for trials, for we know their intention is growth. I honor You today.

Overcome

To overcome takes great courage! I think the way I learn to overcome in this life is to remember that this is not my home. There is life after death, so I can face anything in this life because it's temporary. Right on this date here in 2010 I'm 44 years old, half my life is over. My body hurts, I have been through many Hells and joys in life just like the next guy or gal Ha-ha. So in my heart I know I can face anything and everything in this lifetime and so can you. I have had loved ones and friends go through horrific things but we must move on.

To overcome takes a backbone.

To overcome takes Courage. I have known many even without God that have been overcomers, some are on the news and some are on the Olympics every time we see it. We see overcomers in our churches starting ministries because they have walked through what the people they are now ministering to are walking through. This takes great faith and strength. I want you to know today that with God on your side you CAN overcome. The people that do it without Him must have an amazing support system in their life. I'm not quite sure how they do it without Him.

The Word of God in Revelations gives some promises if we overcome lets read them,

> "He who overcomes will not be
> hurt at all by the second death."
> Revelation 2:11

> "To him who overcomes, I will give some of the hidden manna.
> I will also give him a white stone with a new name
> written on it, known only to him who receives it."
> Revelation 2:17

This one is so cool; we cannot even begin to comprehend what Heaven will be like, what's up with the white stone? All this just makes me imagine how amazing it will be.

> "To him who overcomes and does my will to the end,
> I will give authority over the nations."
> Revelation 2:26

> "I will also give him the morning star"
> Revelation 2:28

One time, in one of our churches, this kid named a star after my husband which was just so awesome. But this verse says, He will give the morning star! We cannot comprehend the ways of God.

"He who overcomes will, like them, be dressed in white.
I will never blot out his name from the book of life,
but will acknowledge his name before my Father and his angels.
Revelation 2:5

So amazing.

"Him who overcomes I will make a pillar in the temple of my God."
Revelation 2:12

"To him who overcomes, I will give the right
to sit with me on my throne,
just as I overcame and sat down with my Father on His throne.
He who has an ear, let him hear what the spirit says to the churches.
Revelation 2:21

Anytime you just don't think you can do it on this earth read these scriptures. Remember this is not our home.

"Do not let your hearts be troubled.
Trust in God, trust also in me.
In my Father's house are many rooms; if it were not so,
I would have told you. I am going there to prepare a place for you.
And if I go and prepare a place for you,
I will come back and take you to be with me that you also may be where
I am."
John 14:1-3

Can't wait.
Can't wait for no more tears, no more pain, no more trials.
Overcome friend. You can do this.
Read His Word and let it help you through.
Be faithful.

Overcome.

Dear God,
I dream about that day. It will be amazing, thanks for getting it all ready. Help us while we are here. I honor You today.

October 16th

Promise Keeper

The Miller Family has a tradition to watch The Princess Bride together once a year. One of my favorite parts is when they go into the fire swamp. Westley and Buttercup face their fears and wander in. Westley knows about the three dangers of the fire swamp, the fire spurts the quicksand and the ROU's (Rodents of unusual size), but he shows no fear in front of his beautiful buttercup. At one point the quicksand swallows up Buttercup so Westley jumps in to save her. Hello, my name is Inigo Montoya. You killed my father. Prepare to die. Sorry, just got excited there.

I remember back when I was a little girl quick sand or the earth swallowing up people was a very scary thing. As you know through the many years that have passed quicksand is no longer fearful for kids anymore, there are plenty of other more horrible things on TV, or at their fingertips to fear. But I can remember as a girl being so scared of the earth opening up.

I'm sure through the years you have seen reports on the news about sink holes, where the earth just opens and whatever was there is no longer there. This year this happened in Guatemala City. 115 people died when the earth just swallowed them up. I can imagine seeing something like that as a young kid would scare you, or mark you for the rest of your life.

Why am I talking about this today? Because I was reading in Numbers and I read this story about two men, Dathan and Abiram (Numbers 16:12). Moses summoned them to come to him and they told him they would not come due to them being angry at him.

> "Then Moses became very angry and said to the Lord, "Do not accept their offering. I have not taken so much as a donkey from them, nor have I wronged any of them."
> Numbers 16:15

Moses continued his leading and began telling everyone what they had to do when all of a sudden the Lord appears,

> "Separate yourselves from this assembly so
> I can put an end to them at once."
> Numbers 16:21

Now remember this was the Old Testament, Jesus had not died on the cross yet and paid the debt for our sin. So Moses and Aaron fall facedown, and beg God not to kill everyone there, after all, only three men disobeyed in these verses.

God grants their request.

"Then the Lord said to Moses, "Say to the assembly, 'Move away from the tents of Korah, Dathan and Abiram.'""
Numbers 16:24

So Moses gets out the warning and tells everyone to move back away from the tents of these wicked men who were living in disobedience.

"Do not touch anything belonging to them,
or you will be swept away because of all their sins."
Numbers 16:26

This is so funny to me, I wonder if Moses had an anxious feeling in his stomach? He had seen so many amazing things, I'm sure he never knew what was coming next. Here he seemed to think the men would be swept away, I wonder exactly what he meant by that, maybe a strong wind? I wonder if he knew what was really going to happen.

"And the earth opens its mouth and swallows them, with everything that belongs to them, and they go down alive into the grave."
Numbers 16:30

"They went down alive into the grave, with everything they owned; the earth closed over them, and they perished and were gone from the community."
Numbers 16:33

As I thought about this story today, I could not help but think about the grace of God. Before Jesus died on the cross for our sin, not one person except for the High Priest could even enter the holy of holies or he would be struck dead. God's grace came in a simple, humble, non flashy man. Due to Jesus, we can be in His presence anytime we want. He is always waiting. No longer will He strike us dead due to our sin and stupid choices! This was why He sent His son. Natural disasters will happen to this earth, but God holds to His promises. He even put the rainbow in the sky as a covenant between us and Him that He would never flood the earth again like He did in the day of Noah (Genesis 9:12-17).

He is one who holds to His promises friend.

What promises has He given you? Why have you given up on some of them? Don't you think He's big enough to keep them?
He is the Promise Keeper.

Dear God,
I have seen your hand at fulfilling promises. Be with this Reader and do not let them give up on what you have spoken to them. I honor You today.

Redirect Yourself?

Do you know that your family is your first ministry? You may have all the money you need, your job title is great, and someone gets your coffee in the morning for you. You may have a beautiful office, everything is in its place, and your clothes are crisp and polished, but if your family is all screwed up none of it is worth it. Hi ho, hi ho, it's off to work I go! But your own children don't have a father or mother figure, because you are never there! If you don't have children, think of who you live with. Are you actually there long enough to have relationship?

America has gotten away from relationship. We are a texting, chatting generation and it's not the same as having an actual face to face relationship. Some of you have to redirect yourself today.

If you do have kids, when was the last time you spent any time with them? My son is at college now, but the last time he was home I took him out to lunch. It's so important to actually communicate with your family. In the Miller home we make it very important to have sit down dinners a few times a week together. All four of us have our own dates and times that we need to be here or there, but we make sure we at least have a few days a week where we are sitting and talking together at a real dinner table. When was the last time you sat with your kids, small or teens, and had a sit down dinner with real conversation? Our lives are so fast paced now that we need some redirection and change in our homes sometimes.

You can be so involved in ministry that you forget your first ministry, your family.

I remember early on in the ministry with my husband I used to spend hours on the phone with ladies in need. My husband would come home from work and my kids would be playing, and in need of me, but I was "doing ministry!" It did not take me too long to realize how wrong I was. My family would be neglected while I would spend countless hours pouring out to ladies, that hardly ever acted on my advice anyway! Do NOT neglect your family for work or ministry! It will be the biggest mistake you have ever made.

You may not have a relationship with the Lord today and if that's you, think about your situation are you always getting home late and never spending any quality time with your family? It's time to redirect yourself!

Change is something that is pleasing to God. Sometimes we can only grow in His stretching. I remember about 12 years back when my Pastor looked me right in the eye and said, "Tana, God is stretching you!" boy did I hate when he said that, but he was right. It was only in the change, and only in the stretch that I learned my greatest lessons.

If you are like me, you live with some regret in this life. Not spending enough time here or there or if only I did this or that. You cannot change the past but you can change your future. It's time to redirect and turn from selfishness because that's what it boils down to, we can be very selfish.

> "Let us not give up meeting together,
> as some are in the habit of doing,
> but let us encourage one another."
> Hebrews 10:25

This scripture was written to the church about meeting together as a church body of believers but like I said in the beginning of this devotion, your family must be your first ministry. Are you meeting together or are you in the habit of never being home, being late, or being there but on the phone or computer?

Time to
Redirect Yourself?

Dear God,
Stretch me and change me. I honor You today.

October 18th

A Road Less Traveled

I was driving down the highway today when for the first time ever I started to notice "things!" Thinks everywhere! Cups, cans, hub caps, a blue tarp, a plastic box and even en entire bumper of a car with the license plate still on it! I cannot believe I have never noticed so many thinks on the side of the road. So I made it my mission to keep driving, and to keep looking at the history alongside the road. Every piece of everything was another story to tell, another life that was lived.

When things are in the road they need to be pushed aside so we can drive safe and forward. Clearly all these things, like the bumper, had to be moved away. And there I was, driving safe and clear and somehow noticed all these things today. I need this highway to get to where I'm going on a daily basis.

In life we go through many trials. All along the way we seem to have "things" left behind in us. Some of those things can be anger, confusion, doubt, lukewarmness, lack of faith and the list goes on. We need to learn like the highway department, to keep ourselves clear of debris. It's only when we are clear on the inside that we can move forward in a clear and safe way, pushing every distraction aside. Just like I need my highway to get where I'm going, we need our hearts to be clear of things, so we can be healthy and strong, with our minds set on our destination.

"My eyes are fixed on you, O Sovereign Lord;
In You I take refuge."
Psalm 141:8

We need our minds and hearts fixed on God but the truth is that if that bumper was in the highway today, I would not have been able to even drive on that side of the road. We must make efforts get rid of unhealthy things in our life so we can move forward.

"Get rid of all bitterness, rage and anger,
brawling and slander, along with every form of malice.
Be kind and compassionate to one another
forgiving each other, just as in Christ God forgave you.
Be imitators of God."
Ephesians 4:31-32 & 5:1

If we don't move those things out of our life and try to move forward we can damage ourselves. Just like a tire going over debris, the tire is bound to get popped. It will do damage.

I want to encourage you today, to sweep away the "things!" The trash, the debris, and the junk that is keeping you from moving forward. We all need this in our life. We need a clear road a clean heart. Stop holding the things not needed in. Let them go. Cast everything on Him because He cares for you (1 Peter 5:7)

He has so much more for you than a blocked road today.
He does not want A Road Less Traveled as part of your History.
He wants a road that is traveled and a road that is clean.
Move Forward.

Dear God,
Can I borrow your swiffer? I honor You today.

October 19th

Find me Under the Fig Tree

Right now my hair is dirty; I have not washed it since yesterday. Some people can let their hair go a couple days but not me; my hair gets streaky and greasy looking. Sometimes if I'm lazy I just wash the bangs or part around my face and put the back up. The longer I wait, the oilier it gets.

I know we hate it when our hair gets looking like this, but the truth is that oil is great for the scalp and hair. Some ladies take Olive oil and put it on their hair ends and leave it over night. Your dry hair soaks up the oil and makes it healthier.

It's the same concept when we sit in the presence of God. The more we sit the more oily we get, or in other words, the healthier we get. We want to get up and wash, but don't even realize He is already washing us as we wait in his presence.

If you are like me, you hate the waiting room. I think in my walk with God, the hardest place I ever have to be is in the waiting room. I'm Italian, I want it and I want it now! Patience is not something I was gifted with. I pray for it all the time!

It was normal for people in the eastern countries of the Bible to sit under vines and fig trees to meditate, pray, or talk together. Fig trees were very large, and praying on the top of them; and sitting under them, and studying the law there was a normal thing. Do you have a place today you can call your Fig Tree? A waiting room of your own?

> "When Jesus saw Nathanael approaching, he said of him,
> "Here is a true Israelite, in whom there is nothing false."
> "How did you know me?" Nathanael asked. Jesus answered,
> "I saw you while you were still under
> the fig tree before Philip called you."
> Then Nathanael declared, "Rabbi, you are the Son of God;
> You are the King of Israel."
> John 1:47-49

Nathanael was in the waiting room, probably praying for the Messiah to come, it was common for the Israelites to pray under fig trees. Nathanael very quickly believes Jesus is the Son of God. Maybe his waiting in that place prepared him to meet his maker? Some of the best things happen to us in the waiting room. I love the movie Yentl, in that movie many times we see people studying and resting under trees. I think it's time to find your place. One time years ago, when Guy and I lived on a Seminary campus, we had a very small apartment where you could not seem to get away from others. The weird thing is the walk in closet in the bedroom was so big it could have been another kid's room! He took one side and I took the other and we converted the entire floor into a prayer room! There were pillows, Bibles and a guitar all on the floor; it was now our waiting room.

It does not matter where you go, if it's in the house or out of the house, the point is there must be a place you can get away with God and wait to hear His voice like John 10:27 talks about.

Your place may not be the same every day. Mine is. Your place may not have a door on it, mine does. You see, it does not matter size, indoor or outdoor, the point is are you passionate about it?

You will find me Under the Fig Tree

Dear God,
Help us to find a place to meet with You. To wait and hear what You have to say to us. I honor You today.

Daughter of Abihail

The favor of God is an amazing thing. Today during a time with the Lord, I felt His Holy Spirit fill the place where I was. A mighty visitation. I was praying about an event coming up that I am leading along with my team. I began to weep in the presence of God, as we will have more people this year than ever before. Souls, coming for a weekend that will change their lives forever, and I had a part in it. Not sure about you, but that makes me weep. The favor of God is an exclamation point of God's grace! Wow, did I just say that, that was pretty good. Ha-ha.

To think there was a time in my life where I was passed out on the floor from booze and drugs and now God is using me to bring precious souls to Him for change. Just amazing. This is the favor of our Lord.

In my life time I have seen the favor of God time and time again. I could probably sit and tell stories for at least an hour or so. The Lord knows our needs; He takes care of His own. Three times in 21 years, right at the right times, people have handed my husband car keys to cars that they say the Lord wanted us to have as a gift. Little did they know that we were on the brink of no car, or being a one car family. Whenever the favor of God showed up, it was always too late for me, but right on time for Him. His time is NOT our time, His time is best!

God's favor has been on my children in so many ways. Doors that have opened for them, while still so young. Jobs handed to them, random invites to minister in front of thousands of people.

This is the favor of God. God's favor does come by grace at times, but also through prayer and fasting! I have asked God to gift them, keep them, grow them, I have prayed for their mates since they were newborns. I have fasted at times! That they would not settle for second best in their lives but that they will only want His perfect will. So far, so good.

"Go gather together all the Jews who are in Susa, and fast for me.
Do not eat or drink for three days, night or day.
I and my maids will fast as you do.
When this is done, I will go to the king,
even though it is against the law.
And if I perish, I perish."
Esther 4:16-17

Esther knew she needed favor when entering the court of the King. She knew by doing so, she could be killed. Therefore she declared a holy fast (Joel 1:14). She needed a miracle.

"When he saw Queen Esther standing in the court,
he was pleased with her and held out to her the
gold scepter that was in his hand.
So Esther approached and touched the tip of the scepter."
Esther 5:2

Now the Bible says that Esther was very beautiful,

"Now the king was attracted to Esther more than to any
Of the other women, and she won his favor and approval more than any
of the other virgins. So he set a royal crown on her head and made her
queen."
Esther 2:17

But I believe he did not hold the scepter out just due to her beauty. I believe it
all depended on the circumstances and events in the king's life leading up to this
very moment. It depended on his mood, and this is where prayer and fasting
gave Esther the favor of God. It all depended on prayer, fasting and faithfulness.

As our event that we are planning gets closer, I will declare a holy fast.
Sometimes when we want God's favor in a thing, we must sacrifice. Souls are
well worth the sacrifice my friend.

The daughter of Abihail, Queen Esther was a perfect example of this.
Maybe it's time for you to declare a fast?

Dear God,
You know I love food, but help me think of souls. I honor You today.

October 21st

Express Yourself

So I'm sitting outside the mall people watching and waiting for my daughter. If the people all around us every single day are not ashamed to express themselves then why do Christians have such a hard time letting people know they are Christians? A couple just walked by, he had natural red hair a hot pink top, studs for a belt, skin tight pants and multi colored sneakers. She had dyed bright fire engine red hair, many piercings on her face a wild shirt and needless to say this couple stood out from the crowd. I do not think this was holiday attire, I think this was their everyday attire. They are not afraid to express themselves in front of hundreds of people at the mall. Then why do some Christians have a hard time just carrying their Bibles around? What are we ashamed of? If Christians would be as bold and strong as some non-Christians, I think we could change the world. And by the way, who are we to say this couple did not love the Lord?

My sister in law Kris was telling me this story about how she went to a gas station one time; all four of her small kids were in the car. When she pulled up there was a billboard with a half naked lady on it. My sister in law got upset at how the owner put it there for younger kids to see. She told her kids she was going in to talk to the manager of the gas station. All her kids were wondering what mom was doing! When she came out she told her kids that the Bible says, to speak the truth in love. That's exactly what she did unashamed as a mom and believer. She told the gas station owner she did not want her kids looking at a half naked lady and if he kept that billboard up she would not be coming there for gas anymore. When she drove by the next day the billboard did not have that advertisement on it, they took it down. Sometimes that's all it takes! Just a word of truth like, "that offended me" or "Can you not swear as much, I'm not used to hearing that." But too many times we keep our mouths shut. Why does it seem sometimes others express themselves so much more than us? Kris's words of truth took a billboard down! If only we had bigger backbones! If only we expressed ourselves in love to those around us, who long to hear it most the time.

If we are who the Word of God says we are,

> "You are the light of the world. A city on a hill cannot be hidden. Neither do people light a lamp and put it under a bowl. Instead they put it on its stand, and it gives light to everyone in the house. In the same way, let your light so shine before men."
> Matthew 5:14-16

Then aren't people supposed to see Christ through us? Expressing our love for God? Why are you so ashamed? What are you afraid of? Are you scared you won't fit in? Are you scared you won't find a spouse? What is it? We are to be lights in such a way that everyone can see. Some of these people that I'm watching today don't give a rip whose looking! Then why do you? Just by the truth you speak and the way you carry yourself people will be able to see Christ. Express yourself so they will know Who you stand for.

I love it when people with other doctrines knock on my door and try to convert me. Their boldness to come right to my house and speak what they believe in impresses me. One time two young guys in suites came, I let them in not telling them I was an Ordained Minister. They began to tell me what they believed which went totally against the word of God. I asked them if they could leave me their book, and come back another day. I wanted to prepare myself to speak to them, in truth and in love. One thing I noticed was that even though their book was totally against what the Bible says, they actually backed their book up with Holy Bible Scriptures at the end of the book, and I could NOT believe it; I had to laugh when I saw this. How can you back up what you believe with the Bible, if you say you do not agree with everything in the Bible? These guys came back and I asked if they believed certain things in the Bible? They said no. I said, "Then what you are saying is, you do not believe everything in my Bible right?" They said, "Right." I then took them in their book, to the back where they use The Bible to back up some of the things they believe. One of the young kids started to get red and had tears in his eyes. They then told me that they might have to bring back their elder to talk to me. I told them there was no need because they were not going to convert me to what they believed in. I then spent about 45 minutes telling these two young kids how Jesus Christ changed my life. By the time they left I think they were thinking twice about what they believed.

I expressed myself, in a loving way, speaking the truth of The Word.

This is what we are supposed to do, not beating the Bible over people's heads, but lovingly sharing His truth when the opportunity arises. And these opportunities will arise.

"Always be prepared to give an answer to everyone who asks you to give the reason for the hope that you have. But do this with gentleness and respect, keeping a clear conscience, so that those who speak maliciously against your good behavior in Christ may be ashamed of their slander."
1 Peter 3:15-16

Do you express yourself today? Do people know you have a relationship with Jesus Christ? It doesn't matter if you look like this couple I saw, because they probably love the Lord anyway, what matters is if people see Christ in you?

Is Christ in your actions? Is Christ in your response to a negative situation or a storm? Do you Express Him in you?

Express Yourself.

Dear God,
Help us express ourselves, and through that, may Your Light shine to the Nations. I honor You today.

October 22nd

To Save a Life

Have you ever gone through something horrific in life but in the end realized it was for a bigger purpose. Somehow in the middle of a storm there always seems to be some sort of opportunity. I have already shared so many of my own in this devotional.

Upon seeing his brothers, and them not recognizing him, Joseph lost his emotions. He asked everyone in the room to leave except his brothers, he told them was Joseph the brother they sold all those years ago. This is what Joseph said next as he was weeping and embracing his brothers.

> "Do not be distressed and do not be angry with yourselves
> for selling me here, because it was
> to save lives that God sent me ahead of you."
> Genesis 45:5

Just imagine this statement. First we see deep forgiveness. His brothers put him through Hell and back, and yet he says, "Do not be angry with yourselves?" In other words, if I can forgive you, forgive yourselves now! Then the statement, "It was to save lives that God sent me ahead of you." I wish everything was recorded while Joseph was in prison and in the Palace. I bet he impacted and influenced hundreds of thousands of lives. He did some serious prison ministry. And as most of you know, he did everything with excellence even in a nasty prison. The prison Joseph was placed in was called Sohar, which means house of roundness, suggesting that it was like a round tower used as a state prison. It was filled with notorious criminals, real killers. And here he was, he did nothing. Not sure about you, but it would be very easy for me to get bitter in a situation like that. But not Joseph. He looked for the opportunity in everything.

One time my car broke down and I had to bring it into the shop. They said it would take a couple hours to fix it, and there I was stuck for those two hours. I can assure you, I was NOT thinking of opportunities or lives to save. Within that time a man walked in who looked familiar. After thinking long and hard, I realized that we had run into one another a week before at a local hotel where they were giving things away on Craigslist. He was the manager of the hotel. How strange that he would walk in only one week after we met. It was then I realized this was a divine moment. I was NOT looking for an opportunity, but there it was. I actually was in the middle of my opportunity with attitude. Anyone out there relating here? Everything depends on our response to our situations.

I have learned that no matter what happens in life, we need to look for the opportunity in it, no matter how horrific, how miserable, how happy, or how sad. Somewhere in there someone is watching us and there just might be a chance to save a life. Joseph said it was to save lives that God sent him to the stinking rotten prison. Prisons in Joseph's time were NOT like prisons today. I'm sure rats and bugs were everywhere and the smell of urine was great. Why did Joseph say, God sent him? God did not throw him in a well and sell him, his brothers did! Maybe because after Joseph walked though it, he was a changed man and realized there was a much bigger picture and purpose. Sometimes we cannot see that until we walk through it.

So keep walking. Do not give up. See the opportunity
that just might be there, To Save a Life

Dear God,
Open our eyes to see only souls and opportunities. I honor You today.

October 23rd

Turning of the Tide

Have you ever sat and watched the tides? Back and forth, back and forth. The crash of the waves on the shore, bubbles. The tide is constant, never changing. The only time it changes is during a storm or when the weather shifts, but even through the storm and crazy weather, the tide is in and out, back and forth. Constant.

I want you to know today there is NOTHING wrong with doing the same routine. God honors a routine when it gets His Word into our hearts. Wake at a certain time, read, pray the same prayer list day after day. The same job, the same things, the same prayer meetings. It's all great. Yes there are times when God shows up and you will feel His presence in amazing ways, in your normal routine, these are times to be cherished. The important thing is to stay disciplined, and faithful. What is more important than being super spiritual, is that your life may be constant like the tide and never changing. Through the storm you stay faithful.

You need to know today that routine can be very godly. Some would say, "Don't stay in the same routine, grow, grow, grow!" But it's in that routine that you do grow. It's in that routine when a horrific storm will hit, and because you are still going back and forth like the tide during the storm you make it, and you are stronger because of it. Constant.

I looked the word constant up tonight on the online dictionaries, and I'm so glad I did, maybe this will help in what I'm trying to say,

Constant:
Not changing or varying, uniform,
regular, continuing without pause
or let up, unceasing, regularly recurrent,
continual, persistent, faithful,
unswerving in love, devotion,
a constant lover, steadfast,
firm in mind and purpose,
Resolute (which means determined).

Wow, need I say more?

Constant like the tide. The turning of the tide from high to low. Low tide reveals deep sea treasures on the ground while high tide makes everything come alive, all the creatures of the sea. Low and High have their purpose, routine has its purpose. In routine you never see all the things that can come alive, the changes in your heart, the changes in those around you because you are constant.

When Jesus walked the earth he had a routine, over and over in the Word of God it speaks of Jesus going and having alone time with His Father.

"Very early in the morning, while it was still dark, Jesus got up, left the house and went off to a solitary place, where he prayed."
Mark 1:35

"But Jesus often withdrew to lonely places and prayed."
Luke 5:16

"Jesus went out to a mountainside to pray,
and spent the night praying to God."
Luke 6:12

"After leaving them, he went up on a mountainside to pray."
"Mark 6:46

I could keep listing more scriptures. Jesus was faithful and in relationship. If you read of his prayer times they are not filled with hype and excitement. They are quiet and constant like the tide.

The turning of the tide is routine,
The turning of the tide in your life is Godly.

Dear God,
Help us to stay disciplined and constant in our daily routines that lead us to You. I honor You today.

October 24th

So Shines a Good Deed

Just a little while ago I was relaxing with my daughter and her friends Mary and Jen in front of the TV, they were watching Willy Wonka. It was the part where Wonka tests Charlie and tells him he has won NOTHING! He is mean, and tells him to go away. Charlie cannot handle his conscience so he takes the everlasting gobstopper and places it on Wonka's desk. Charlie was tempted to give the gobstopper to Mr. Slugworth so Slugworth could keep it, and find out how Wonka made it. But it was a trick, Wonka paid Mr. Slugworth to give it to Charlie, it was all a test. When Charlie places the gobstopper on Wonkas desk it showed that he was honest, trustworthy, and that he would not deceive anyone. As Charlie walks away, Willy Wonka says,

"So shines a good deed in a weary land."
-William Shakespeare

This quote comes from one of Shakespeare's writings called the Merchant of Venice Act 5, Scene 1. The good deed is compared to a candle and its light in the play. The good deed is also compared to the moon that outshines the candle because it's shining brighter. Take a read for yourself:

The Merchant of Venice
Act 5 Scene 1

PORTIA
That light we see is coming from my hall. Look how far that little candle sends its light! That's the way a good deed shines in a naughty world.

NERISSA
While the moon was shining we didn't even notice the candle.

PORTIA
Well, brighter lights always dim the smaller ones. A governor shines as brightly as a king until a king is near by, and the governor suddenly looks like a nobody.

These are some intense words when you really think about it. While the moon was shining bright they did not notice the candle and I love when it says, "Brighter lights always dim the smaller ones." Charlie was a beacon light. Not because he was preaching Christ, but because he was doing something with a pure and humble heart. He could have sold that everlasting gobstopper to Slugworth and supported his family for the rest of their lives, but instead he did the right thing. A good deed.

This part in Willy Wonka is a great lesson for us all. The difference is, we know Christ.

I would assume you are doing devotions on a daily basis because you want to grow in Christ, or maybe your friend just gave you the book because they care about you, in any case good deeds are good things. Let me make it VERY clear, good deeds do NOT get you into Heaven. Heaven is a FREE gift, it is not earned or deserved at all. Many do not agree with this, but it's what the Word of God tells us.

"For God so loved the world that He **gave**
His one and only Son, that whoever believes in
Him shall not perish but have eternal life."
John 3:16

So let's make that clear, we do not need good deeds to get into Heaven, but the Word of God still says good deeds are pleasing to God.

"Little children, let us love, neither in word
nor with the tongue, but in **deed** and truth."
1 John 3:18 (NKJV)

"Do not merely listen to the Word, and so deceive yourselves, **Do** what it says. Anyone who listens to the Word but does not do what it says is like a man who looks at his face in a mirror and, after looking at himself, goes away and immediately forgets what he looks like. But the man who looks intently into the perfect law that gives freedom, and **continues to do this**, not forgetting what he has heard, **but doing it** he will be blessed in what he does."
James 1:22-25

So we don't get to Heaven with good deeds but right here in James, we see that we are blessed when we do good deeds. When you do a good deed you shine a light. The more you do for others the brighter you are. Good deeds minister in and of themselves.

Let me ask you today, are you a candle or a moon? Do you outshine others with your goodness? Think about that today. Is it part of who you are?

So shines a good deed in a naughty world.

Dear God,
Help us to shine bright and to let you use our good deeds to do it. I honor You today.

October 25th

Lie Down and Rest

"For this is what the Sovereign Lord says: I myself will search
for my sheep and look after them.
As a shepherd looks after his scattered flock when he is with them,
so will I look after my sheep. I will rescue them from
all the places where they were scattered
on a day of clouds and darkness.
I will bring them out from the nations and
gather them from the countries,
and I will bring them into their own land.
I will pasture them on the mountains of Israel,
in the ravines and in all the settlements in the land.
I will tend them in a good pasture,
and the mountain heights of Israel will be their grazing land.
There they will lie down in good grazing land,
and there they will feed in a rich pasture on the mountains of Israel.
I myself will tend my sheep and have them lie down,
declares the Sovereign Lord. I will search
for the lost and bring back the strays.
I will bind up the injured and strengthen the weak."
Ezekiel 34: 11-16

In this chapter The Lord compares himself to a shepherd. The first thing the Lord says is that He will search for us if need be. I'm not sure about you but if I ever need to found, I'm so glad I have a God that will search for me! He says He will look after His sheep. I know how protective I am of my kids I can only imagine how the Lord looks after His own. I'm sure His guarding is like no other. A shepherd also knows when one of his sheep is missing, The Father notices all things. Have you been missing for a while? Trust me, The Father takes notice.

He promises in this chapter that He will rescue us on days of clouds and darkness! It does seem in those times we tend to stray. Thank God He is our hero. When we stray and scatter, He corals us back. He puts us in a grazing land, in other words, He will provide every single thing you need. He promises that He will bind up the injured, and strengthen the weak. I'm so thankful for this verse.

Early on in ministry my husband and I were devastated when some leaders in our church fell into moral failure. Our hearts were broken, we were confused and shook. The Lord took great care of us during this time through our fellowship leaders, who sent us to another ministry couple for healing. Talk about being injured and needing strength. We almost left the ministry all together, thank God we didn't! Thousands of souls are being influenced today due to our ministry together. This is what the enemy does, he puts temptation in the paths of people and when they fail he tries to take other leaders with them. I thank God for a Father in Heaven who runs after us, who waits for us.

My favorite part of these scriptures is,

> "There they will lie down in good grazing land."
> Ezekiel 34:14

> "I myself will tend my sheep and have them lie down."
> Ezekiel 34:15

It says here He will have us lie down! Do you know today that He wants you to have rest? Yes, practical, but so very important. Put it this way, if you don't rest yourself, He will find ways to make you rest. He cares about the entire package, not just one part of you. We need rest for our minds and bodies to work the way God intended.

I'm so very thankful today for that. That He cares about every part of us, our minds, hearts, our bodies, He protects us, guards us, what more could we ask for. If you are in worry and anxious today please Let these scriptures sink into your heart. He is in total control of your situation right now.

You need to lie down and rest.

Dear God,
You are our shepherd, I thank you for all you do to guard us and keep us. I honor You today.

October 26th

His Shout

Can you just imagine the shout of God? The Word talks of his whisper and Him speaking, how powerful both were and the miracles they performed. In Psalm 107, The Word says,

> "He spoke and stirred up a tempest that lifted high the waves."
> Psalm 107:25

His voice alone, all nature and creation responds to.

> "For He spoke and it came to be, he commanded, and it stood firm."
> Psalm 33:9

He has always been, He will always be. He is Alpha and Omega, there was no beginning with Him, He always was. We cannot understand that in our human minds. But the point here is that just the sound of His voice shook the seas and lifted high the waves.

There were times He spoke quiet in a sort of whisper. Times of prayer, one on ones. His voice always intentional, always influencing, always truth. If The Lord speaking can shake the waters I wonder what His shout can do. Have you ever just sat and thought about His voice. Not just the Written Word, but His physical voice. Anytime you go to a theatrical production or play with God in it, someone always plays His voice as mighty and strong, or deep and baritone. I wonder if that was totally not what his voice was like at all. We also would think that Jesus walking on the earth would be attractive and the Bible says different. But His voice, I bet it's amazing and I can't wait to hear it. His shout will rock the Nations.

He loves our shouts to Him,

> "God has ascended amid shouts of joy."
> Psalm 47:5

To ascend can mean to succeed or to occupy. He loves it when we shout to Him...not sure if you have ever been in the car alone and gave a shout to God but there have been many times in my life and ministry where I pray in the car and begin to praise Him. He loves to ascend amid shouts of joy. Do you also know your shout, your voice and your prayers can also rock the nations? No, we are nothing like God, we can't be everywhere like Him, but through His power God can use our prayers to change nations. Prayer is a powerful weapon. So we wait and we pray and we keep shouting alone in the car until the day when we hear His Shout!

Dear God,
You are so mighty, let us see Your might and power among us. Thank You for Your voice. Thank You for our voice. I honor You today.

October 27th

It Loves Me It Loves Me NOT

So my husband and I just got back from a District Minister Retreat that we go to every year. Before we left I did not get food in the house, so by the time we got home it was slim pickings!

You know what it's like during those times, you look in the freezer and see what's left! Well tonight it was hotdogs and Ore-Ida Fries! Real healthy meal for the family! I looked around to see if there was actually anything good for us at all. I found one cucumber and the cherry tomato carton was half full. So I stood there and cut up the cucumber and threw the tomatoes in then put Italian dressing in and mixed it all up. When everything was finished I looked at our meal. Beef hotdogs, buns, fries and a bowl of veggies. My head was craving the veggies, the only thing good on the counter! But I ate everything!

I'm getting to the age when, if I eat junk, my body feels it. Anyone with me here? I have this addiction to microwave popcorn. I would sit and eat a bag and then that night or even the next morning I would feel so sick. So I started doing with my friend Tracy does. I take a brown paper lunch bag, and put two tablespoons popcorn in with some salt, then I fold the top a tiny bit and put it in the microwave with a mug sitting on top of the fold. Nothing else! No oil, nothing! I laughed when she first told me about it but now I do it all the time. I just could not believe you did not need oil. All that to say, the very first night I tried this and ate it, I did NOT feel the least bit sick! And even the next morning I was fine! Now I do it all the time (2010).

Junk in, and you are not going to feel good! Healthy in, and you will be fine.

Maybe you will not notice the Junks after effect right away! But in time, junk takes a toll on your body, weight, rotting teeth, being sluggard and the list goes on. I promise if you eat healthy you will feel better. I know the older I get the more I notice this.

What about your spiritual self? I wonder what putting junk into your head does to you. Things that are ungodly are found everywhere, on television, in books, websites, and various places. What are you putting into yourself? How about images that will never leave your mind until the day you die. Ungodly junk.

I have surrendered my life to Christ and given Him pretty much everything, yet I still to this day see images in my mind of ungodly things I let my eyes look at before I knew Him. No matter how many years go by, you will never forget those things, better to nip them in the bud while you can my friend.

"Blessed are the pure in heart, for they will see God."
Matthew 5:8

"Whatever is true, whatever is noble, whatever is right, whatever is pure, whatever is lovely; whatever is admirable, if anything is excellent or praiseworthy, think about such things."
Philippians 4: 8

"His divine power has given us everything we need for life and godliness through our knowledge of Him who called us by His own glory and goodness. Through these he has given us His very great and precious promises, so that through them you may participate in the divine nature and escape the corruption in the world caused by evil desires."
2 Peter 1:3-4

So there you have it, cut and dry. His power has given us everything we need. We don't need "Junk In!" Its one thing to think of the result of junk food in and it's another to think of ungodly stuff in!

And what about the benefits of healthy spiritual food? The Word of God, to chew on?

It loves me, it loves me not!
What petal are you stuck with today?
The junk or the healthy?

Dear God,
Help us to take care of our spiritual self as well as our physical self. I honor You today.

His Joy, Your Strength
"For the joy of the Lord is your strength."
Nehemiah 8:10

Hmmmm, how can someone keep their joy when they are going through it? The heat is shut off the internet shut down, no spouse yet, the car needs another chunk of money put into it, chronic pain racks their body, another tumor was found, and the list goes on and on and on!

Ok let's talk about it! Here is how you keep your joy. You humble yourself, and if you are part of a church body you ask for help. In the Word of God we see great examples of this. These scriptures speak of the early church in Acts,

"And all those who had believed were together,
and had all things in common;
and they began selling their property and possessions,
and were sharing them with all,
as anyone might have need.
And day by day continuing with one mind in the temple,
and breaking bread from house to house,
they were taking their meals together with gladness
and sincerity of heart, praising God, and having favor
with all the people.
And the Lord was adding to their number
day by day those who were being saved."
Acts 2:44-47

When was the last time you heard of someone selling their property to help someone else? The truth is, this does not happen much anymore, our times have changed, BUT THE CHURCH still has ways they bless those that come faithfully! Food pantries, clothes, meal ministries, and special needs. **The church people in Acts knew of each other's needs, because they shared their needs!** It takes MUCH humility to share a need. This is the first step. We MUST humble our self when we are in need, to ask for prayer, and at times for help with food, bills and everything else. Humility will lessen the stress and anxiety in your life because your needs will be met.

You must also fill yourself up with the Word of God. If you are so down that you cannot pray you need to READ The Word, and if you cannot do that you need to RUN! What do I mean by that? RUN to a brother or sister in Christ who you can get special prayer from! God did NOT make us brothers and sisters in Christ, to never be around one another! He desires us to minister to one another! When you hide and withdraw in anger and stress, you DO NOT please God. Isolation can be a wonderful place, but it also can be a very dangerous place. The enemy of your soul knows just what to do and just what to say to bring you lower in the place of isolation if you are weak and filled with anxiety.

I don't share all I go through physically but it's very hard sometimes. There have been times I cannot even raise my hand in church in worship due to the pain, but I am filled with His joy. There have been times in ministry where we live week to week, but I am filled with His joy.
There have been times of deep stress and sorrow, but I am filled with His joy and it's the only thing that has gotten me through at times. It took steps to get there.

His Joy, Your Strength.

Dear God,
Humble me, forgive me, fill me with Your joy. I honor You today.

Old Rags and Worn Out Clothes

Jeremiah at the bottom of an empty well, hungry and hopeless. He was arrested during the siege of Jerusalem; food was so hard to find that some were involved in cannibalism. The prophet was imprisoned in the well, and could have starved to death. So a foreigner, a Cushite, cared enough to speak to the King on his behalf. Somehow he convinced the King to let Jeremiah out of the cistern. He must have been in there quite a while because the King says,

"Lift Jeremiah the prophet out of the cistern before he dies."
Jeremiah 38:10

Obviously no one was watching over Jeremiah nor did they care for him in the least, what a shock it must have been for someone to show up at the well and look down on him. So there he is, a mess. I'm sure he had to even relieve himself just inches from where he sat. It could not have been a lovely sight to see, or smell for that matter. Anyone would have just thrown a rope down to him and would have told him to tie it around himself. But not this Cushite named Ebed-Melech.

"So Ebed-Melech took the men with him and
went to a room under the treasury in the palace.
He took some old rags and worn out clothes from
there and let them down with ropes
to Jeremiah in the cistern.
Ebed-Melech the Cushite said to Jeremiah,
"Put these old rags and worn out clothes
under your arms to pad the ropes."
Jeremiah did so, and they pulled him up with the ropes
and lifted him out of the cistern.
And Jeremiah remained in the courtyard of the guard."
Jeremiah 38: 11-13

I think Ebed Melech knew of Jeremiah because he was a Royal Official at the Palace of the King. He knew that what was done to him was wicked (Jeremiah 38:9) and because he wanted to stand against wickedness he tried to do all he could to help Jeremiah. I believe he actually put his life on the line asking the king to help Jeremiah in public. The king liked to handle these things in private but it says in Jeremiah 38:7 that Ebed Melech approached the King in the Benjamin Gate. The Benjamin Gate was a place the King listened to appeals for justice from the public. Ebed Melech Being the Kings servant could speak with him in private but he didn't, He went to him in front of everyone! I'm sure the King could not have been thrilled with that. But God was. I guess he was pretty brave and bold. Thank God for Jeremiah!

So he gets permission, maybe due to positive peer pressure?! Then we see Ebed Melech standing looking in the cistern. Why didn't he just throw down the old rags and worn out clothes? Why did he stop to get them in the first place? Once again I think it sheds a light on his character. He was thinking how Jeremiah would feel if the ropes were against his weak skin. How easy his skin could tear. Maybe he did not throw the rags and clothes down due to not wanting them to hit his feces or waste? Maybe he was just being respectful to a man who had been treated with wickedness? I guess know one really has all the answers. But the fact is this Royal Official cared enough to stop and get old rags and worn out clothes, so Jeremiah could put them under the ropes and keep his skin and body safe. That is a man who had the Compassion of Christ.

I want you to think of yourself today. Would you have gone out of your way when you did not have to, with that kind of compassion?

Would you have risked your own life for someone you had only heard of and seen a few times, for the cause of holiness instead of wickedness?

One can only hope to have a character like Ebed Melech. God blessed him because of his act of compassion and bravery toward Jeremiah. These are the words of the Lord to him,

> "I will rescue you on that day, declares the Lord;
> you will not be handed over to those you fear.
> I will save you; you will not fall by the sword but will
> escape with your life, because you trust in me, declares the Lord."
> Jeremiah 39:17-18

Some of God's greatest blessings can be found having a heart of compassion like our Lord.

Don't disregard
Old Rags and Worn out Clothes!
God can use them for his glory!

They come in many shapes and sizes.

Dear God,
Help us all to have a character like Ebed Melech, and in so doing, we become more like You. I honor You today.

October 30th

Pleasant Like Perfume

When I was in college I was the India outreach leader due to my love for India. My room was decked with outlines of the country, music from the country, Indian beads hanging in the doorways and much more. I was known for the aromas coming from my dorm room due to all kinds of authentic incense I would burn. People would know I was home when they smelled India down the hall. It never bothered me then, but now I have a hard time with incense, somehow can't breathe when I'm around it. My husband likes to relax up in his study and he burns it there and at his church office, I have him close his door due to not being able to handle it anymore. Even if I like the smell the smoke kills me. Also, the older I get I cannot wear perfume, makes me sneeze. Even if I'm around someone with it on, I'm pretty much miserable. Sad to say, these are just reminders that I'm getting old I guess.

There is a scripture In Proverbs that I find very interesting, the first part says,

> "Perfume and incense bring joy to the heart.........."
> Proverbs 27:9a

Well it did at one point in my life but the next part of this verse says,

> ".....and the pleasantness of one's friend
> springs from his earnest counsel."
> Proverbs 27:9b

This scripture is comparing the joy we get from perfumes and incense, to the joy (pleasantness) we get when we receive counsel! It kind of made me laugh when I read this. I bet you just love when someone gives you earnest counsel over a new perfume or sweet smells? NOT! Ha-ha.

But the point here, is we should love the earnest counsel from a friend just as much as the beautiful smell of perfume. Even though perfume makes me sneeze, I do love to smell it in the store, and wish I could wear it. Even if you don't like counsel, and think you don't need to apply it, the Word of God says when you do, you are wise.

> "A wise man will hear and increase learning,
> And a man of understanding will attain wise counsel."
> Proverbs 1:5

I remember the time a few years back when I got some wise council from a friend. Telling me things I did not want to hear, things that hurt. Telling me in order to do the right thing, I had to change. No person loves change. Change is hard and it takes work! I think I received that council more, due to the fact that it came from a friend. A real friend will tell you the truth, even when it hurts.

And you will trust their word more because you actually know them inside and out.

When was the last time you listened to wise council from anyone?
How did you Respond?
Your character will show, in your response to your circumstance.

Next time someone gives you council ask yourself if it was Pleasant like perfume.

Dear God,
It may not always feel pleasant but help us to love wise council. I honor You today

October 31st

Lost in a Maze

What is it about Mazes that fascinates us? Is it the excitement that the escape might be right around the corner? Is it the fear factor? In New England, Corn Mazes in the fall are a big thing and getting bigger. The Corn Maze nearest to my home highlights Clint Eastwood, and then at the bottom of it, from a sky view, it says American Legend. It looks like an amazing picture from a sky view but when you are inside of it, it's a never ending maze that takes forever to get out of. You can pay to walk through the maze during the day, or you can enjoy the fear of the maze in the darkness of the night with a flashlight. Not a good feeling. But people seem to come far and near to be lost in a maze.

It's one thing when you chose to be lost in a maze; it's another thing when you live in a maze.

Many of you may feel like you are lost in a maze, it may seem like you are just going in circles and every time you try to get out of something you can't. You run, you retrace your steps, but there you are, in the same old, same old once again. My daughter had me watching a show that she loves on television where people are lost on an island. Whenever they had to go out into the jungle they marked their way by tying cloth on the tree branches. Well, for anyone who is my age, you know that goes way back to the story of Hansel and Gretel leaving trails of white pebbles and breadcrumbs. In life we have to mark our way. We have to think about the steps we have taken, mark them down and think about if they were good steps or bad steps, and then if they were bad we must change our ways. This is the only way out of the maze that you keep walking. This is the only way to change things for the better. We learn from our mistakes and if we can mark them in our heart and learn from them, it will help us out of our unhealthy mazes in life.

Tonight is October 31st countless millions of people are wearing masks tonight pretending to be something that they are not, is that something you do every day of your life? God intended you to be who you are, with your gifts, your talents, your dreams and ambitions. Most of these are God given. Some of your dreams are lost in a stagnant maze. It's time for change; it's time for marking where you went wrong. Taking steps to grow and be closer to God and in return letting change come into your life.

Feeling like you are Lost in a Maze?

"Our fathers disciplined us for a little while as they thought best;
but God disciplines us for our good,
that we may share in his holiness.
No discipline seems pleasant at the time, but painful.

Later on, however, it produces a harvest
of righteousness and peace
for those who have been trained by it."
Hebrews 12:10-11

You know how God trains us MOST the time? He lets us make some serious mistakes and we learn from them.

We need to start marking our way, and we need to stop going in circles. We need to allow God to change us.

Lost in a Maze? Get out.

Dear God,
I pray for this reader, if they feel like they are going in circles and need a change, I pray you help them to begin to mark their way and apply Your training to their life. Help us learn from our mistakes and help us to grow through them. I honor You today.

November

November 1st

Follow Through

Have you ever committed to something and not followed through? If you are like me you feel like you failed others, yourself and God when that happens. It's just the worst feeling, and I hate it more than anything. I think this is one reason I hate being late for anything, I like to be early and on time. When you commit to something it's horrible to be in the habit of being late. I also have a pet peeve about being a last minute Myrtle! There is no reason for not being excellent in every single thing that you do, even when it comes to being on time for everything, this also holds true when no one is watching!

> "But as for you, be strong and do not give up,
> for your work will be rewarded."
> 2 Chronicles 15:7

If you are anything like me you wake, and think of your goals for the day, what it is that you have to get accomplished and what has to be done on all your lists, as far as household things. We must NOT give up! Everything we do will be rewarded! All our hard work and all the labors of love.

This has been one of the best years of my life, and the hardest. As another month passes I cannot help but think of the fact that in just 8 weeks and three days, I will have written this devotional every single day for 365 days. I have not missed a day, and it has not been easy. When you follow through, when you are faithful in something God has told you to do, when you work hard, and give up things to get a goal accomplished, God honors every bit of it.

There is a time and a place for a team effort. In just 11 days my team and I will put on the biggest event of the year for us with 1,430 people coming. These things are exciting and rewarding, but there is also a time and a place for God to strip you of every single thing you want, so He can show you what He wants. This is you and Him, alone and no one else! This is the year I have had, and I will never be the same again.

Are you willing to work hard in order to let God change you from the inside out? Are you willing to give up some things or some people in order to follow through? Sometimes the very people that we love can distract us from our goals and our discipline. I have given up a lot of down time with my daughter this year. We love to hangout, get under a cozy blanket and watch a good movie or show. I cannot even count the times I have had to say no. I have not neglected her in the least, we have had plenty of time for movies and cuddles, but I just cannot waste hours upon hours, when I have a goal to accomplish.

If anything I think it has been a great example for her and my son that I have not given in. Sometimes your hard work and discipline can affect those around you as they see that you will not compromise what God has placed in your heart. The impact of it all on those you live with can even be life changing for them.

>"Whatever you do, work at it with all your heart,
>as working for the Lord, not for men"
>Colossians 3:23

I guess when you struggle with follow through; the best thing to do is think on this scripture. Whatever we do, be it a big event, helping a friend, cleaning for someone, or writing a book, we must realize we do it for God therefore we should do it with excellence.

What is it today that you need to follow through on and how are you going to get there?

Soak your mind in the Word of God and realize that He has so much more for you. He has big plans, and desires for you to have big goals, because He is a very big God. Don't sell yourself short today.

Follow Through.

Dear God,
I pray for this reader, give them big goals, dreams and the strength to follow through in every area of their lives. I honor You today.

November 2nd

Smiles Everyone, Smiles!

Here I am at the Dentist. I just don't know how to express it enough; I think this must be one of my most unfavorite places to come. Ever since I was a little girl I feared the dentist. Way back then, they gassed us every time we got a filling, or anything else. I remember spinning spider webs. That gas would always drug me so that webs would spin, and I would be falling into them. I would get sick that night from the smell that was left behind in me. All I have is horrible memories of the dentist. Sorry all you dentists out there! They poke; they pick and spray freezing cold water that kills our teeth. Today although I'm not in the chair! Thank God! My Angela is in the chair and we were just told we have to go to the oral surgeon due to an impacted wisdom tooth. My poor baby. I'm trying to pretend that I love the dentist while I'm here. Big smile on my face, Grin!

It's funny how we pretend things, to make others feel safe and strong. Say, everything is going to be ok when the truth is we have no idea what is around the next corner. Grin again! We say, "No big deal, everything will be alright" while all the time we are thinking, "Oh God please help them walk through this, because I'm not sure how I could!"

For those of you who are old enough to remember the show Fantasy Island, you remember the little Guy Tattoo who would always say, "Da plane! Da plane!" (Da=The) The show would start with some sort of stress or anxiety, but when Tattoo yelled that the plane was coming Mr. Roarke, the leader of the Island would yell out, "Smile everyone smile!" Only it would sound like he said, "Smiles everyone smiles!" So no matter what stress everyone was under, even if they knew someone on that plane had murdered someone, they would put on their happy faces. They would all be these fake people greeting with their Smiles, while a million other thoughts were going through their heads! And there we sat, all of us over 40, and loved every minute of knowing the "real story". For those of you under 40 you really must youtube and see it for yourself.

How many times do we do this in our daily life? We know the "real story" of what happens behind our own walls at home, or in our hearts, yet no person that we spend any time with knows. We call acquaintances our friends, yet they are not our real friends because friends know you inside and out. They know the hidden hurts and joys in your heart. Yet we introduce them all as our friends. Could it be that the "Smiles everyone smiles" need to stop. Could it be that your guard must come down, and you need to take a step of faith and trust one of your acquaintances who really wants to be a true friend? I have been hurt before too, but unless you take that step of faith and learn to trust again, you will walk around like Tatoo and Mr. Roarke on a non reality Fantasy Island.

650

How about your relationship with God? Do you think somehow He does not know you better then you know yourself? Yes He knows we fail, He knows our hurts yet He loves us anyway. He longs to be more than an acquaintance, He desires to be a friend, yet you and I hold back like we do with our other acquaintances. In order to draw near to God, we must also take a step of faith toward Him and trust that with Him, there is no Fantasy, it's all real and true and He will never hurt us like others have.

"Even in laughter the heart may ache."
Proverbs 14:13

Hand Him your heart today.

"The righteous cry out, and the Lord hears them; He delivers them from all their troubles. The Lord is close to the brokenhearted and saves those who are crushed in spirit. A righteous man may have many troubles, but the Lord delivers him from them all."
Psalm 34:17-19

Tear down the walls today, know He is safe.
Put away your Smiles everyone, Smiles.

Dear God,
Help us to bury our fake self. Help us to be all You desire us to be. I honor You today.

What Would You Do For A Soul?

When I think of someone giving their life for souls I think of Mother Teresa or Mark and Huldah Buntain, who laid foundations that changed cities, countries and then nations. It all started with one soul at a time. One by one these people loved others selflessly. Giving up everything they had, or wanted.

"It's not the magnitude of our actions
but the amount of love that is put into them that matters."
Mother Teresa

I think of Jesus who walked the earth and one by one stopped for people, always putting them before himself, always going the extra mile and reaching out to the unlovable.

"But I tell you who hear me:
Love your enemies, do good to those who hate you."
Luke 6:27
Jesus

Hmmm Mother Teresa was a lot like Jesus if you read the scriptures. Jesus did everything for souls. He could not even walk and see a crowd without having compassion on them. Are you like that? Do you stir inside when you are people watching? Or do you just let everyone pass you by. Do you even care about souls at all?

I had a very unexpected day today. One I will never forget. When I woke my plan was to drop my daughter off at school and then go somewhere to get my supplies I needed for work. I would then go home and make an amazing cup of java and get right to work.

God interrupted.

While shopping, I had what I call a divine appointment, after talking for about 45 minutes with this person I told them I wanted to get them a Bible and a book that I love. My plan was to get the books, and then someday in the near future, get them to this person. I left the store and started walking to the car when God started bothering me. When God bothers you friend, pay attention! Sometimes you may have a million plans but when He interrupts and wants you to walk another way you MUST listen. I knew in my heart the day I planned would not happen, and I knew right then and there the Lord wanted me to go get the Bible and the book without hesitation. I went to a little mom and pop book store down the street that did not have what I was looking for, so I ended up going to a major book store. I spent about an hour there looking for what I had promised this person. With great joy I left the store with them in hand. Just a few hours later I met with this person and another over lunch. After conversation, and before we left the place we were eating, this person prayed a prayer to invite Christ into their life. Worth it? Yes, worth it all.

I guess my question to you today is, would you drop everything you are doing in a moment for a soul if you could? When you go to the mall, do you actually notice those around you, or are you just thinking of that new outfit you want to wear?

I had people who dropped everything the day I came to the Lord, I will never forget it. They spent the entire day with me and most of the night. They spoke into my life from that moment on. It was life changing for me.

"Each one of them is Jesus in disguise"
Mother Teresa

"Zacchaeus, come down immediately,
I must stay at your house today."
Luke 19:5
Jesus

Would you spend your own money to lead someone closer to Christ? Would you sacrifice your time? Would you let them cry on your shoulder? Do you want to be more like Jesus?

"Let no one ever come to you without leaving happier."
Mother Teresa

This quote from her, challenged me as I thought about my own life. This is what she lived and breathed. This is what He lived and breathed. His heartbeat was souls. That was enough. That was why He came in the first place.

What would you do for a Soul?

Dear God,
Forgive me for the countless days that go by, when I do not notice souls around me. Help me to be more like You. I honor You today.

Crooked Blessings

Why in the world did God create wisdom teeth? Even their name is funny, wisdom to me means smart, structured, in order, and wisdom teeth are the total opposite. I'm told they get their name because they start to be full grown between the ages of 18-25 and this is considered formal adulthood. I guess it's true, I called my sons college today to find out something, and they would not even talk to me. They said that he would have to sign a waiver for the school to give any information on him to me. It was kind of funny for me to think of it all in this way.

So why did God create wisdom teeth, when every single person I know has had to get them out. They usually come in totally sideways or are impacted affecting other teeth in a bad way. It just totally puzzles me, why they even exist. Couldn't have God just said, "Well, we really don't need these, they might bring more stress to a person's life, so let's erase that from creations drawing board and make everything perfect!"

Do you realize that some of the crooked things in life, are your biggest blessings?

I believe in healing, The Word of God over and over says that God is the healer,

"By His wounds we are healed."
Isaiah 53:5

But I also believe that life is life. And sometimes it will hurt and it won't make sense.

I do believe in some situations, what we think needs healing can very well be our biggest blessing.

If God healed everyone and everything, I never would have had to work in a nursing home for four years, because everyone would have been healed, and not in wheel chairs, or mentally not there. But people get old and incapable. If God healed everyone and everything, I never would have worked for all those years with my dad, as he ran the handicapped summer camps for hundreds of kids in the city of Albany. I can tell you my friend, those four years in the nursing home, and the many years working with handicapped people were some of the best years of my life. They changed me. They built something in me that no person can take away. The compassion and love of Christ. Some may say they are non perfect people. I say, they are perfect. They are beautiful just the way they are.

Look around at your blessings today. Look at yourself in the mirror. You may think you are a bit crooked but you are perfect just the way you are. I know it's hard to care for others. To have to wash them and change them, but when we are in their place someday, we will wish someone cared for us, with love and attention. The love and attention of Christ.

"Consider what God has done:
Who can straighten what He
Has made crooked?
When times are good, be happy;
But when times are bad, consider:
God has made the one as well as the other."
Ecclesiastes 7:13

Think of everything in your life right now that seems a little crooked.
Could there actually be a blessing in there somewhere? It's all about attitude changes.

It's all about living in your situation, and letting God change your character through your situation. Are you willing?

It's easy to get bitter and not better.
What are your Crooked Blessings?

Dear God,
Help us to see through Your eyes and not our own. I honor You today.

November 5th

Call for Consolation
"When anxiety was great within me,
Your consolation brought joy to my soul."
Psalm 94:19

All I can say is, "Wow." There are just no words for what I was feeling today. It's all great stuff, but there were many times through the day I had to stop and take a breath because the anxiety was great. Every year my team and I do a giant event and over 1,400 people will be there. We have so much fun, and ladies leave changed by the Power of God. We have a giant craft fair, 24 hour prayer rooms, gift and book stores, 20 workshops, 2 main speakers flown in, special events and a late night show. The details today were a bit overwhelming; right down to what will be in the speaker's room when they arrive, and what color the Kleenex boxes are.

It seemed one thing after another went wrong today. We are missing a screen that we need, 5 hotel rooms I had contracted were nowhere to be found in a hotel computer. I did math wrong, and purchased 12 too many of something we needed, and the list goes on! During all that I was getting phone calls left and right about many other things. Hundreds of e mails to answer and finally I had to stop, I put both my hands on my desk and closed my eyes, took a deep breath. I began to pray and once again I gave everything to the One who will run this women's retreat. I called on Him.

This scripture speaks of consolation. When we think of consoling we think of being by someone's side at a funeral or letting a friend cry on our shoulder. Consolation brings comfort to a friend or loved one. He said in the Word, in many places that He is the Comforter (John 15:26). We need to let Him comfort.

Years ago there was this song that we sang at almost every single service, this was back in the 80's. *Jesus on the Main Line*. I know some of you are laughing right now! Some of the words were, Jesus on the main line, tell Him what you want! Oh It's Jesus on the main line tell Him what you want! If you want a healing tell Him what you want! Jesus on the main line now! Then it went, Call Him up, call Him up, tell Him what you want. The entire point of this song, was this scripture,

"So I say to you: Ask and it will be given to you."
Luke 11:9

The song was NOT talking about asking God for a new BMW. It was all about asking Him for healing or more of the Holy Spirit in our life. I remember years ago the place went wild when our Pastors wife began to play this song. So funny when I think about it now. But the point I'm trying to make here, is when we need help from God, we have to ask. We seem to think we can somehow do it all on our own.

Today, I had my friend Judy on the other line with me every ten minutes (not the main line...hahaha), Ok that was bad. But, it wasn't enough, I needed God's help. I think we were both filled with anxiety at one point. So much to pack into a brain all at once and trying to keep things straight! Thank God for Post-Its!

No really, speaking the truth, I thank God that I can call on Him to consol me. Do you realize you have this blessing today? That in the middle of an anxiety attack you can take a deep breath and call on Him to comfort and calm you? This is what it means to let Him take full control, to call on Him and ask. Why are so many too proud to ask?

When was the last time you took the time to ask?
He desires to answer or He would not have called Himself a helper or comforter. Call for Consolation today.

Dear God,
We need you every hour. I honor You today.

Stop and Change

"There are six things the Lord hates,
seven that are detestable to Him;
Haughty eyes,
A lying tongue,
Hands that shed innocent blood,
A heart that devises wicked schemes,
Feet that are quick to rush into evil,
A false witness who pours out lies
And a man who stirs up dissension among brothers."
Proverbs 6:16-19

It's amazing to me how in the Word of God, things that we think as humans are "not so bad," sit right next to things like the shedding of innocent blood. We say, this sin is worse than that sin, but the truth is, sin is sin in the eyes of God. Forgive me for sounding so blunt and being so forward, but you, thinking of being with that man or woman while you are married, is just as bad as someone going out and having an affair in the eyes of the Lord. He says in His Word,

"But I tell you that anyone who looks at
A woman lustfully has already
Committed adultery with her in his heart."
Matthew 5:28

We as humans think that the act of adultery is worse than just thinking of it in our minds. I say it again, sin is sin. In the eyes of Christ they are one and the same.

In this scripture the Lord mentions haughty eyes. If you look up haughty, most things say prideful or snobbish. What? The Lord puts being prideful next to wicked schemes? Hmmm when was the last time you were a snob to someone? When was the last time you had a chip on your shoulder?

A lying tongue, I think in this life, you will lie if you say you have never lied. All of us have told a lie or two. Even if it was a little white lie. Who made that up anyway? Somehow a "white" lie is more pure.

Has there ever been a time in your life when you planned something that would intentionally hurt someone else? A possible wicked scheme? I know I have. I can remember being so filled with bitterness that not only did I want to hurt others but I wanted to hurt myself.

Thank God for His grace today. When was the last time you rushed into evil? Fell into sin due to not thinking things through? This is a very easy thing to do and we all do it. If we are not careful we can find ourselves in a place of sin and we wonder how the heck we got there. We rushed. **God is never in a rush. If you have not noticed, He takes His sweet time, and most the time we are sitting in His waiting room.**

Have you ever been a false witness? Acting like you have it all together with the Lord and you wear this great smile while all along, you are totally living an ungodly life and no person on earth knows it but you.

How about this one, in the mix of what God hates, stirring up dissension among brothers. Have you ever talked about someone behind their back and it hurt them and hurt others? God hates these things. He hates abortion, He hates lying tongues and wicked schemes. This is just the Word of God, this is just truth.

But here is the good news today friend.
He loves you.

He may not like some of the things you have done, or do, but He loves you so much that He sent His Son Jesus Christ to die for you. That is more love than I can comprehend.

When I had my first encounter with God, which in a book I will write someday, I will call the Divine Encounter, I was totally living in sin. I was in the middle of trying to kill myself when God interrupted. I heard His voice, and my life was never the same. That was Him reaching into my darkness. I want you to know, I would not want ANYONE to know the things I was doing at that moment and time in my life. His Grace goes beyond our comprehension.

If you are doing these detestable things today and think that somehow God won't want you, or will not forgive you, I am a living testimony today that you are wrong. He wanted me. He is using me to touch the life of thousands of people.

He wants you today.
Come before Him and ask His forgiveness.
Then Stop and Change

Dear God,
Some things in our hearts you hate, forgive us Father. We surrender our minds, thoughts and actions to you today; we sit in your waiting room. I honor You today.

November 7th

The Last First

My house was a tad crazy today, yet so fun. Filled with a ton of young people. We love when these kids come over. I'm not sure how many we all were all together, but I'm thinking close to 20. Everyone trying to squeeze into my little kitchen, very fun. Most are college kids that go to our Church and then they come over to hang out, have a good meal and chill together in the basement. Most fall asleep but it's kind of the "norm" now. I get food that does not cost a lot to feed them all. Today I got 4 bags of cheese ravioli that only cost me 8 bucks! Ya gotta love 2 for $4.00. Then sauce. I use hotdog rolls to make my famous garlic bread and one bag of corn so for 20 people it is really not that much. They usually bring the drinks and all. We love them coming.

Today was so funny; I already had used the big pots so I only had this one pot to cook all the ravioli in! The pot was NOT big enough, so I had to let them eat in shifts cooking two bags at a time. I would call up the kids in threes. They would get their ravioli, sauce and meatballs, corn, garlic bread and then go find a place to eat. Kids were everywhere and before I could get to the last ones. the first ones who ate, were already in line for seconds. These are some serious big boys! So I told them all they had to wait for everyone to eat. When I turned to them and said that, this is exactly what came out of my mouth, "I want to let the First ones eat first!" Everyone in the room started laughing, and I had no idea why, then they informed me of what I should have said which was, "I want to let the Last ones eat first!" My poor husband, son and a kid named Brian were all sitting in the room closest to all the food yet they waited till everyone ate before they got their food.

I thought about the mistake I made after the kids so willingly shared it with me, and for a split second in my head I thought of this scripture,

> "If anyone wants to be first,
> he must be the very last,
> and the servant of all."
> Mark 9:35

In this scripture Jesus is talking to His disciples, it was a very interesting situation. Jesus had heard His twelve arguing with one another so He asked,

> "What were you arguing about on the road?"
> Mark 9:33

I'm sure He already knew, but He likes people to talk to Him. The Word says,

> "They kept quiet because on the way
> they had argued about who was the greatest."
> Mark 9:34

So they are sitting in this room, Jesus asks the question and no one answers, they keep quiet.

Jesus starts ministering to them about the very thing they kept quiet about, the fact that if you want to be first or the greatest, you must be last and a servant of all. This coming from a Man who was fully God. The Maker of the Universe who washed the dirt, and I'm sure manure off their feet. And He didn't have Purell! Coming from the Master, who took the time to wait at a well for a woman He was not supposed to talk with, in order to bless her sin filled life. Coming from a God who told a little sinful man to get out of a tree, so He could go fellowship and eat with him. Coming from a real servant, Jesus Christ.

When we think of a servant we think of someone putting everyone else before themselves, a far cry from the twelve disciples here fighting about who is greatest among themselves. Can you just picture this? It just makes me laugh. Jesus was probably rolling his eyes wondering when it all would end, or when they would finally get why He came in the first place.

He was the ultimate example of being last and being a servant. Going out of His way for almost everyone. When was the last time you went out of your way for anyone?

I was proud of the three in the living room today who waited to be last; I know they were very hungry. When was the last time you waited for everyone else to go first?

I challenge you, put someone before you today. If you are in college, hand everyone their plate and greet them as they come in. If you are at work and go on your break, ask someone if you can get them anything. If you are home, call someone and ask how they are doing. These are all things Jesus would have done. Let's be more like Him.

The Last will be First.

Dear God,
This takes great humility. Humble us. Help us to long to wash the feet of others by serving them in many ways like You did. I honor You today.

November 8th

Start Singing

"O God, you are my God, earnestly I seek you;
My soul thirsts for you, my body longs for you,
In a dry and weary land
Where there is no water."
Psalm 63:1

This Psalm was written by David when he was in the desert of Judah. I'm sure he was tired, hot and very Thirsty in a place with no water. It's funny how even our bodies long for help from God, when we are at a low point and very thirsty for Him to come through.

I woke this morning and I did not even have to look out the window and I knew it was raining. When it rains outside, the pain in my body is horrible. I'm getting older and I'm sure many of you can relate. I was weary when I woke, and the truth is I wish I could have stayed in bed all day and done nothing. Weary like David in this Psalm, we long to seek Him but sometimes we are just tired and every ounce of us is in need of Him. This was me this morning.

It's been a long day for many of you and by now most of you are sitting relaxing reading a book or in front of the television or computer. Let's not forget the one who never lacks water for our soul.

I hope you spoke with Him today; thought about Him today, let His joy fill you today and more! He is all you need. My mind has been spinning with my biggest event of the year at the end of this week, and I wake with lists going through my head, then I think on Him. I ask Him to help me, I beg for His move among over a thousand women. I am thankful His Well does NOT run dry.

"On my bed I remember you;
I think of you through the watches of the night.
Because you are my help, I sing in the
Shadow of your wings.
My soul clings to you;
Your right hand upholds me."
Psalm 63:6-8

When do you think of Him?
How many days has it been since you thought about all He has done for you?
When was the last time you read your Bible?
His Word is our water in a very dry and thirsty land.

If you find yourself answering these questions and realizing you need to be thirstier, what are you going to do about it?

You like me, have many responsibilities, physical issues, you wake with lists going through your head, and you do the best you can to keep up, but all of these things are NO excuse for not spending time with Him. If you want your thirst quenched today you need to make time.

I challenge you right now to go make a cup of tea and sit with your Bible. You need to get His Word in your mind and heart. Does your soul cling to Him?

I thank Him that when I have failed Him, He never fails me. Come back to Him today, closer.

Are you singing in the shadow of His wings?

Start singing.

Dear God,
I have a song in my heart, a song of thanks. I don't deserve You. I honor You today.

November 9th

Muddy Wells

"Like a muddied spring or a polluted well is a
Righteous man who gives way to the wicked."
Proverbs 25:26

What happens when your source of Water is out? We had an issue over the summer and had to get an outside water spout replaced. When the plumber came he had to turn our water off for like three hours. It actually was quite funny, I kept turning it on to wash my hands, make a pot of coffee, or clean something and every time I flipped the faucet on I thought I was losing my mind! No Water! Didn't I learn my lesson from the first time I flipped it on and no water came out? But time and time and time again during those three hours, I flipped the water on.

You never know what you have until it's gone. You also do not realize what habits you have.

So what would happen if a spring that people depend on for their water, or a well, maybe in Haiti or Africa, got polluted or muddied? Then we are not looking at it affecting one person, we are looking at it affecting an entire village or town. And if you really think about it, in some parts of the world that muddied water or polluted well can kill hundreds, if the water is not pure.

This scripture compares a godly person who falls into sin, to that polluted well, or water. Do you realize when you fall, you are not only hurting yourself, and your relationship with God, but you are hurting the countless people all around you who have been watching you. When you live for God sometimes you don't think anyone is watching. Sometimes like in my case, when I first came to the Lord, all my friends ditched me. You don't think they care to watch what you are doing, but trust me! They are watching. They may not say anything to you when you are walking a pure path, but mess up one time, and trust me, you WILL hear about it. They are watching. Therefore when we fail, what we tell those watching is, it's ok to do this or that as a Christian, when it's not. They just love it when we mess up.

I want you to know today you are not perfect. I am NOT perfect! You will fall, you will fail, but there comes a point and time in your life when you need those old habits and hang-ups to be gone! When you mess up you need to say to those friends, I'm not perfect and that's exactly why God sent His son, to die for my sin. But there is a difference between turning from your sin and returning to it over and over again!

"As a dog returns to its vomit,
So a fool repeats his folly."
Proverbs 26:11

We cannot continue to return to that same sin time and time again. God wants you free of it!

Every time you muddy the water, it gets worse and worse for the village.
Who are you affecting today?
How muddy is your well?
What are you going to do about it?

Souls depend on your actions.

Dear God,
Help us not to be muddy wells, I honor You today.

November 10th

He Directs His Love

Tonight I write from my heart. I am humbled I am tired and weak. I wonder how such an amazing Mighty God could pluck me from darkness and put me here? Who Am I? I cannot help but just sit here and weep; he loved me when I did not love myself. Have you thought about His grace? The God who makes the wind blow, and who sets the light in the sky reaches to us. Why? Who can comprehend that kind of love?

> "Deep calls to deep in the roar of Your waterfalls
> All Your waves and breakers have swept over me.
> By day the Lord directs His love."
> Psalm 42:7-8

Did you hear that? First of all, notice they are HIS waterfalls. He created them and I'm sure He had fun doing it. But then notice it says, that very same God who created, directs His love. He is the one who chooses where His love goes.

Why did He choose me? Why did He choose you?

He directed His love toward me in many dark times. I remember as a teen girl one night thinking I was pregnant, I called on Him. I was desperate and did not know where to turn. I did not know how to pray, I sat in my bed (true story) and I said, "God I'm not ready to be a mom, Please help me" at that very moment I felt like a hot heat over my stomach, it did not hurt, but it kind of freaked me out a bit. It was moving and kind of felt like it was twirling over my tummy. Then as quick as I felt it come, it was gone. As you can imagine I did not go around telling that story to too many people, but it happened and I will never forget it. The next morning after weeks, my monthly came. In my sin I called on Him and He loved. It was His choice to direct His love to a 15 year old girl living in sin, who only called on Him when it was convenient for her. My human mind just cannot comprehend that kind of love.

Do you remember times His love reached out to you when you did not deserve it? When was the last time you let that sink into your heart as you remembered His grace?

He directs His love, He is God. He is NOT dead on a cross somewhere, He rose again. He is active and ready for communication. He longs for ALL to call on Him no matter what type of situation they are in. As humans we have our opinions of where we think His love should go, But He directs His love.

I'm so very thankful today that as a 15 year old girl He chose to hear me. As a 16 year old girl he saved my life from death, and as an 18 year old girl He met me at an altar for my final surrender. I will never be the same.

So tonight I weep. On the verge of God using me in ministry this weekend at a retreat where 1,430 lives will be changed forever. I can only remember where I came from and I am so thankful that He directs His love.

Dear God,
Humble us, we are nothing without you. Your grace goes beyond my brain tonight. I honor You today.

True Worship

What is true worship? It's selfless, there is NO pride involved in it. Sold out, full surrender. True worship is when we submit, obey with a loving heart. True worship is not about us. It's about Him.

I'm all for worship in freedom. There are more scriptures in the Word of God about raising banners to the Lord than clapping hands, but when the raising banners or anything else we do, turns into getting attention for ourselves and not true worship we are on dangerous ground.

"True worshipers will worship the Father in spirit and truth, for they are the kind of worshipers the Father seeks. God is Spirit, and His worshipers must worship in spirit and in truth."
John 4:23-24

When we worship God in spirit, our one desire is to lift Him up. The thought of drawing attention to our self will not even be in the mix.

"Bring an offering and come before Him;
Worship the Lord in the splendor of His holiness."
1 Chronicles 16:29

Bring an offering before Him. What kind of offerings are you bringing before Him? I'm not talking about oranges and incense like a lot of Chinese restaurants have in their lobby. I'm talking about bringing God your heart or a song or a dance, there are so many beautiful ways to worship. What we bring to Him is not full of self or weirdness. It's pure, true and peaceful.
There is no anger in it.

When was the last time you alone at your own home began to worship God and bring an offering of Worship to Him? Lifting your hands to Him or doing something that maybe you would not do in front of others. It's time to worship God. It's time to experience the splendor of His holiness!

The Father is seeking worshipers where all attention goes to Him and Him alone. God has brought me a long way. I remember those first days in my church where I saw people worship and actually show expression. It totally freaked me out at first. But as I began to grow in my relationship with God I realized why they wanted to lift their hands and sing to Him.

If today you have never worshiped God, I challenge you today to hide yourself away with Him alone and begin to worship. He is seeking that in you.

Dear God,
You will make a way when there seems to be no way. I honor You today

November 12

Get the Door

November 12th is a very emotional day for me. It was 26 years ago today that I knelt at an altar and gave my life to God. I would never be the same after that moment.

Everything I had done in life, I did to the extreme. When I started drinking, I extremely drank, to the point of passing out. When I started to realize that drugs would fry my brain enough to help me forget my pain, I started to look for the most extreme drugs I could find. I stopped looking after an acid trip that scared me to death with hallucinations but I kept doing the smaller stuff. My problems were still there when I woke up so it was only a seasonal fix. My heart longed for something permanent.

Even as someone who did not know God, I was a very hard worker. Anything I led, I led to extremes going the extra mile and making everything better than it should be, or had to be. When I got angry I was extremely angry, so much so, that I yelled at God for 3 hours at one time in my life. I had so much hate and bitterness in my heart from physical and sexual abuse that I did not know what to do with it all.

It was one Sunday morning, that my brother Lou came into my room after a year of asking me to go to church, that I finally said yes. I was at a breaking point in my life and I slipped on my flip flops, daisy Duke Shorts and tank top with no bra. I walked into a little country church in Alcove New York. If anyone would have passed me a judgmental look, I would have given them the finger and B lined for the back door. But I was loved. Just the way I was. A messed up young girl who needed hope. That was November 12, and I stand in awe today that I have never turned back.

When Jesus Christ walked this earth He lived extremely. Not caring about what people thought or said about Him. When the disciples told people to leave Jesus alone, He told them to come to Him. He extremely loved, all the way to the cross.

"Here I am I stand at the door and knock.
If anyone hears my voice and opens the door,
I will come in and eat with him, and he with me."
Revelation 3:20

26 years ago I heard a knock at the door. I had heard the knock before, but I had never answered. This time I turned the door knob.

Do you hear the knock?

Maybe there are places in your heart and life that you have not opened to Him. When we do spring cleaning we open every door, move every piece of furniture and clean things that we normally do not clean on a routine house clean day. This is what Christ wants to do for us on a daily basis but He can't if you are not willing to open your heart to Him.

He stands and Knocks, Get the door.

Dear God,
There is no other word but Mercy. I honor You today.

November 13th

Kay

I met an eighty seven in a half year old woman this weekend at our retreat we have in Southern New England (Now 92). Her name was Kay and while all the 50, 60 and 70 year olds said they were too tired and could not come to "The Late Night Show" that started around 11:30 pm, Kay was there with full energy. Beach balls were flying and the room was filled with sounds of, We Are Family! Kathy Trafford had us in stitches laughing for almost an hour in a half, by the time I left, I felt sick.

On my way out the door I ran into Kay, it was about 12:15 am and Kay was still dancing her way out the door! I looked at her and asked her if she could dance in front of about 1,500 people in the morning on the big stage at retreat. She said yes. The am came and Kay came up on the stage as the song Celebration began to play. She went for it and started dancing, pulling out some serious moves! We were holding hands because I did not want her to fall or trip, when all of a sudden she took four steps forward and kicked! I was trying to keep up, had not danced like this since my Soul Train days! This lady totally cracked me up. She loved every bit of being in the spotlight and did not want to leave when it was time to go. She kept blowing kisses to all the girls.

Before Kay left the stage I gave my microphone to her to say a Hello to the ladies. I did not expect what would come out of her mouth at all. She began to lift up the name of our God and tell of His amazing faithfulness. Pointing up and lifting His name. I will never forget that moment. Everything I assumed she would say went out the window and she filled the gap with His faithfulness. I want to be like Kay when I grow up.

I love her energy, her joy and her words. This woman rocked.

Why is it when people get old we seem to think they will be sitting in front of a window with a crouched afghan on their lap doing nothing? Why can't we be like Kay? When God gives joy, He brings it. Joy Sticks!

When God brings Joy, It energizes us. It gives new hope and a passion that will make us like Kay, able to move when things are slow moving.

"For the joy of the Lord is your strength."
Nehemiah 8:10

I wish I could know Kay's story. I'm sure after 87 years she has some serious stories to tell. I love to sit and listen to ladies that are double my age. I love to hear of the hardships they lived through, and how they had to live without everything that we now take for granted. I did not have the opportunity to talk to Kay, nor to find out about her life, but I know that an eighty seven year old woman, full of energy, whose first words shout the faithfulness of God speaks volumes! I would love to hear her history of how she kept the joy through the storms of life.

> "But let all who take refuge in you be glad;
> let them ever sing for joy.
> Spread your protection over them,
> that those who love your name may rejoice in you."
> Psalm 5:11

The character of Kay tells me this; she has known that God is her refuge. She has run to His faithfulness in the hardest of situations. I wish I could boogie with her right now.

We need more Special Kay's.

Dear God,
Wake us up to your joy. Give us so many more Kay's! I honor You today.

Aftermath

Jesus was always trying to teach about humility to his disciples and the people around him. The biggest way he preached his message on humility was the way he lived his life around everyone. Always going the extra mile, even if it meant He would cross the line at times or think out of the box. He was sinless yet unafraid to act.

It was the Sabbath in Luke chapter 14 and Jesus was hanging out at a Pharisee's home. He was being hawked out by everyone in the room. Everyone there wanted to see exactly what this man everyone was talking about was going to do next. Jesus with great boldness asked,

"Is it lawful to heal on the Sabbath or not?"
Luke 14:3

The Pharisee's were wimps and said NOTHING! The word says they remained silent (Luke 14:4) they did not even have the guts to tell Him what they believed in their hearts. To me that's pretty sad.

"So taking hold of the man, He healed him and sent him away."
Luke 14:4

This man had dropsy; this is like a swelling or edema in your legs arms or anywhere. Most the time it is noticeable and hard to hide. It can be very painful and hard to do daily tasks for people who have it. The Word says that he was suffering with it (Luke 14:2) Jesus saw him. Not everyone around Him watching his every move, but him. He had compassion on a man on the Sabbath. He was NOT afraid to act.

As for the man, he went to eat at his friend's house. To an event for fellowship. Little did he know there would be someone there that noticed how he was feeling. Little did he know in a few hours he would be pain free and able to move better than he had in a long time. Amazing Aftermath when he least expected it.

Sometimes in life we go about our business and live our daily lives, never realizing a divine appointment is right around the corner. I met this girl on a plane on my way west. She was scared to fly. She was adorable, young and I got to talk to her for a couple hours. I invited her to an amazing event that we put together once a year. She said she would think about coming. More than all of that, I shared my faith with her. I told her of God's grace in my life. This last weekend was the event, and I was sad she did not come. At one point through the weekend I had an old friend come up to me, and what she said totally blew me away. She said that her husband works with the exact girl I spoke with on the plane! She said he got into a conversation with her at work and he said that his wife was going to a women's retreat. The girl said it's not with a girl named Tana is it? She then told him about this lady that she met on a plane. He had been praying for her. Small world or diving appointment?

Aftermath is a powerful thing, and as I sit here today, the day after the biggest event of my year, I am getting swarms of e mails, facebook messages and text messages. You may not ever see God in the random steps you take but trust me, He is there and working. The aftermath you can experience from just going to an event or to someone's house for dinner can be amazing, when you are open to what God has for you.

Maybe God wants to change something in you, or maybe God wants you to be bold and take advantage of every single opportunity that is laid before you without being a total wimp! There are way too many wimpy Christians and I do NOT want to be one. I know what I believe and I'm ready to share it.

What about you? I know most of you have experienced some sort of aftermath in your life. Much might be negative. I remember those days before I knew the Lord of hangovers and fights that I would have with others. Aftermath would consist of me puking for a couple hours with my head in the bowl, or not speaking to someone for months. This is the kind of aftermath that does not involve God. But add Him to the mix and miracles can happen.

Be open to the unexpected in your life today. God has already started working years ahead of your situations. You need only to know He is in control.

Wait for the Aftermath.

Dear God,
You blow my mind sometimes, even in normalcy. We walk, You act, it's just amazing. I honor You today.

A Perfect Picture of God

"For the Lord is righteous, He loves justice;
Upright men will see his face."
Psalm 11:7

Have you ever felt not so just? Like you are the last one on the face of the earth filled with righteousness? I have. There were times as a young Pastors wife that I had so much anger inside of me that I did not know what to do with it. I remember a time when I was speaking to the Pastor of the church that we had taken a position at, and I swore due to so much anger inside of me. After salvation I lost my gutter mouth, but there have been times through the years, that I lose it if I'm not careful. Sometimes we need to be on guard of ourselves. Sometimes it takes another sister or brother in the Lord to shake us and get us back on track.

I have a secretary named Judy. She is not only my secretary but she is my dear friend. Through the five years we have worked close together, time after time she keeps me in line. She sharpens me and keeps me on track.

One time we were doing a big event at a hotel and I was putting signs up on all the doors marking them for what they would become at our retreat. I had the 24 hour prayer room sign in hand and put it on the wall. I opened the door to see how they set the contracted prayer room up, and found 500 lb saws and carpenters tools in my prayer room. I guess you could say steam was coming out of my ears at that very moment. Judy came up to me as calm as could be with hundreds of ladies walking around, put both hands on my shoulders, looked me straight in the eyes and said, "Tana, everyone is watching you." She did not have to say anymore, I knew what she meant. Tana, be an example, stay righteous even in your anger. As most of you know, sometimes that is not too easy. This is why we need Judy's in our life. My husband does the same for me, and knows me like no other person on the face of this planet. Thank God they still love me in my unrighteousness.

On a daily basis I ask God to forgive me. Stupid thoughts will cross my mind or something will trigger a memory that might make me upset, so every hour of every day I keep talking with Him. I need Him as I do my best to strive for justice in my life. I want to be that Upright man or woman that WILL see His face.

So what does He do when we fail other than forgive by His Amazing Grace?

"In all that has happened to us, You
Have been just; You have acted
Faithfully, while we did wrong."
Nehemiah 9:33

Even when we are unjust, He is just.
Even in our sin, He is faithful.
This is A Perfect Picture of God.

Dear God,
Let us long to see Your face. Let us strive to be holy and pure before You. Thank You for Your Just Character that loves us anyway. I honor You today.

November 16th

Ready or Not

Today I don't feel ready for too much of anything. It's the first time in an entire year that I have had to write while sick. I'm counting my blessings. My throat is very soar and I know I have a small temp. Like you, when I get sick like this I just want to crawl back in bed and do nothing. Tonight my husband and I have our Recovery groups and I love them, this is what keeps me energetic at this moment in time. I'm sure tonight, I will drop. But I read a scripture a few minutes ago, that made me tired just thinking about it,

"Be dressed, ready for service and keep your lamps burning,
Like men waiting for their master to return from a wedding banquet,
So that when He comes and knocks they can immediately
Open the door for Him.
It will be good for those servants whose master
finds them watching when He comes I tell you the truth,
He will dress himself to serve,
will have them recline at the table and will come and wait on them.
It will be good for those servants whose master finds them ready,
even if He comes in the second or third watch of the night.
But understand this:
If the owner of the house had known at what hour the thief was coming,
he would not have let his house be broken into.
You also must be ready,
because the Son of Man will come
at an hour when you do not expect Him."
Luke 12:35-40

The thought of just getting ready to go out tonight makes me tired. I'm not expecting any person to knock on my home door today, if I was expecting someone I would put my make up on and clean house a bit. But Jesus will come when we least expect it. Will we be ready? Will our hearts be clean and pure? Will we be ready to open the door? Right now if He came I'm sure He would not care how horrible I look right now, He would be concerned with my heart.

I love what this scripture says in verse 37, "He will dress himself to serve" He is Mighty God, but also the servant of all. So hard to think they two could be connected in such a way, but they are when it comes to the things of God. He's the Master at the door, but also the one who will wash your feet.

Do not think you can hide things from Him; you cannot sweep things under the rug and think they will go unnoticed. He sees all. How about being ready in heart, by asking Him to forgive you on a daily basis? It's really not that hard, the only thing it requires is taking what's under the rug and disposing it for good! Anything you need to hide from Him is worth getting rid of.

Sometimes the dustpan is your best friend!

Go for it,
Get rid of it.
Clean house.

He's coming,
Ready or Not.

Dear God,
Help me to be ready, pure and holy even with my struggling heart. I honor You today.

November 17th

Power in Weakness

"My grace is sufficient for you, for my
power is made perfect in weakness."
Therefore I will boast all the more gladly about my weaknesses,
So that Christ's power may rest on me.
That is why, for Christ's sake, I delight in weakness,
In insults, in hardships, in persecutions,
In difficulties. For when I am weak, then I am strong."
2 Corinthians 12: 9-10

We see here Paul crying out to God, about what he called a thorn in his flesh,
asking God to take the thorn away.

"There was given me a thorn in my flesh,
A messenger of satan, to torment me.
Three times I pleaded with the Lord to take it away from me."
2 Corinthians 12:7

The Lord's response to Paul's cry was the above scripture, "My grace is sufficient
for you, for my power is made perfect in weakness." I do not have a thorn of
torment today, but I have a thorn of sickness! There is so much to do all around
me, dishes, unpacking from a weekend trip I was on, laundry and the list goes
on, but here I sit. Very weak and frail. I'm sure it will be gone in no time, but
I'm thinking of the fact that I am weak and He is strong.

Like Paul here I need to focus on the positive, which is something we forget to
do most of the time. After God speaks to him, he begins to boast about his
weaknesses, his hardships and persecutions saying, "For when I am weak, then I
am strong."

OK, so let me try this. "I am weak, therefore I am strong." Hmmm, not working.
I don't feel strong, I feel like going back to bed for a few hours. I think the point
here is that even when you are down, even when you have given up and have
no strength left to even move, you know God is in control and He will take
charge of your situation!

I'm sure Paul would fail again, but he kept his mind on Christ, and the fact that
the difficulties only meant he was doing something right. After all, why would
the devil torment someone that was NOT going to make an impact for Christ?

Not exactly sure what kind of torment Paul went through. Maybe the devil was
trying to keep his mind on everyone hating him. Maybe trying to tempt him with
sin, or depression. We do know that the thorn in his flesh was placed there,

"To keep me from becoming conceited
because of these surpassingly great revelations,

679

there was given me a thorn in my flesh."
2 Corinthians 12:7

God was using Paul in amazing ways and maybe Paul needed to eat a little bit of humble pie. God put him to the test, to make him see His grace once again. His weakness, so he could learn he is only strong through Christ. Sometimes this is needed.

You wonder why you are going through a trial, maybe it's just life, or maybe God is trying to show you something like He showed Paul? This is left for you to find out.

Examine yourself today, is there pride in you? Bitterness? What needs to work its way out of you like a sliver? It may require your help or the eating of some humble pie.

What are you going to do to get to that place of knowing God is with you in this trial? To delight like Paul did in hardships. Knowing we can't make it without Him.

He is there today, He has not left you.
Listen to what He is trying to tell you.
His Power is made perfect in weakness.

Dear God,
Help us. Help us to see once again through Your eyes and not our own. I honor You today.

November 18th

Become Positive through the Negative

I hope what I'm about to say will change some of you today. It changed me half way through my day. The biggest event of the year, that we just did last weekend has ended, all our hard work is over and will soon begin in a few months again. It's nice to have this break to breathe for a bit, and refocus. Countless e mails, facebooks, text messages and more have poured into my boxes as well as to some of our Sectional Reps and Women's Leaders. The reports are amazing. Lives were changed by the power of God and there is just testimony after testimony.

We are thankful and encouraged.

With this many ladies at an event you cannot help to have those that will not be happy. Today was the first day that I got 1 negative e mail. There was a time in my life where anything negative would have rocked my world. After 26 years of ministry with my amazing husband, it no longer keeps me depressed for a week. I have learned to take what people say and ask myself, "Is there anything I need to learn from this?" It is very easy to read a letter, get angry and then act on your anger, but this is a lack of self control and we need self control in our life. Self Control is a fruit that God's Spirit is living within you (Galatians 5:23). It is very important to stand your ground, but if there are areas where you have offended in ANY way, you need to change, even if you think it's ridiculous. This is called humility and if we are going to ask, "What would Jesus do?" we need to apply what He would do to our own hearts. We have not all grown up on the same side of the tracks and we need to hear each other out.

I can remember two times in ministry where I offended during these events. One time about three or four years ago we were doing give aways and I, for laughs, pulled a triple D hot pink bra out of my give away bag. The place went wild with laughter, but after retreat I got a letter from a lady who it offended. I never want to do things where I offend. It's better to stay humble. Many years have gone by and I have never done that again due to the offense. In another case, we named an event at the retreat something, and the name itself offended someone, I got a long letter after retreat and we never used the name again as part of our schedule. It's very important when things hurt or offend people not to get defensive, which is so easy to do. We must be godly. If they feel we have done things that were not godly, we need to realize that that person did not grow up like we did and we need to bend so we do not offend. Wow, that rhymed! This is one of the hardest things you will do in life.

Something you think is alright may not be alright to another woman of God. This is NOT about being lone rangers but team players and I have learned this the hard way through the years.

In all my mistakes, I have chosen to grow and let God change me. I do this through asking myself questions. Most of that change has come through my brothers and sisters in Christ. Even if I did not think things were offensive, I changed them because it offended another; this is the right thing to do and the hardest thing to do. But this is how God stretches us and grows us. He builds our character through things like this. I know I'm stronger and will be better because I choose humility against anger.

Are you in control today? Or do you lose it, and act quickly in anger?

It's time to let God grow you.

When you are upset by something someone says to you, instead of letting the devil lie into your ears, or having lack of self control by slamming them in an e mail or phone call, ask yourself, "Is there anything I can learn from this?" Humble yourself.

"Be kind and compassionate to one another
forgiving each other, just as in Christ God forgave you."
Ephesians 4:32

"Therefore, if you are offering your gift at the altar and there
remember that your brother has something against you, leave your gift
there in front of the altar. First go and be reconciled to your brother;
then come and offer your gift."
Matthew 5:23-24

"And when you stand praying, if you hold anything against anyone,
forgive him, so that your Father in Heaven may forgive you your sins."
Mark 11:25-26

Our Lord is not about us offending one another.
We need to be deep thinkers and wonder why something that we think should not bother anyone could hurt or offend someone. There is a reason. We need to think of others over ourselves. It's one of the hardest things we do in ministry but it is the shadow of Christ.

Become Positive Through the Negative.

Dear God,
Change us even when we don't feel like changing. Stretch us and mold us to have more of your character. I honor You today.

Could it Be?

Are you a Christian who has ever thought about how much easier things would be if you could just die? Sometimes the stress of life gets you down to such a point that you are tired of it all?

I have many friends who struggle on a weekly basis to simply live. They love God, are plugged into small groups, and come to church every Sunday. But life is life, and sometimes it takes its toll.

Due to these thoughts, do you beat yourself over the head time and time again with shame, guilt, and the list goes on? I'm here to encourage your heart today friend. Your hard time may NOT be over, but HE has not left you.

There was a time in the Word, in the book of Job, where Job wanted to die.

> "Job opened his mouth and cursed the day of his birth.
> He said: May the day of my birth perish,
> and the night it was said, 'A boy is born!'
> That day, may it turn to darkness;
> May God above not care about it;
> May no light shine upon it."
> Job 3:1-4

> "Why did I not perish at birth, and die as I came from the womb?"
> Job 3:11

Some pretty shocking and depressing words but spoken in anguish in pain. Have you ever been in pain to the point of moaning? Where you can no longer speak but cry or sob no words at all? I have been there, and it's a hard place to be sometimes.

But here is my encouraging word to you today friend, two times in the first two chapters of Job. Here is what the Lord, The Creator of the Universe says about him,

> "There is no one on earth like him;
> he is blameless and upright,
> a man who fears God and shuns evil."
> Job 1:8

The Lord says the exact same thing in Job Chapter two verse 3. Here is the Lord verbalizing that there is NO ONE on earth who is so blameless and pure. In the first Chapter of Job he experiences deep grief with all his family, animals and servants dead in a matter of a few minutes. Right after the grief he was tested with painful sores from the soles of his fee to the top of his head (Job 2:7), his wife tells him to cures God, and then his friends come to visit and

The Bible says,

> "When they saw him from a distance,
> they could hardly recognize him; they began to weep aloud."
> Job 2:12

I would say this man had every right to feel depressed and down in this life. Life is life and sometimes we go through it. This was an attack from the pit and when Job's wife said, "Curse God" Job replied,

> "You are talking like a foolish woman.
> Shall we accept good from God, and not trouble?"
> Job 2:10

In all he went through, time and time again we must remind ourselves that this man is the one who God himself said, "There is no one like him." Yet he wishes he were dead at times.

Did you ever stop to think that your response might be normal, a natural response to the circumstance you are going through? I'm all for the healing of God and miracles but I also know there will be testing. Stop beating yourself over the head every time you have a thought that you want to die. God is way bigger than that my friend! Way bigger!

I have friends in chronic pain, who struggle on a daily basis, remember through it all He still chooses us. Loves us, Longs to see us stand on our faith like Job when he answered his wife.

Could it be today you are beating yourself over the head for nothing?
Stop it.

Read the book of Job and use it to grow.

Dear God,
Make us strong even in our weakest moments. Help us to recognize the enemy and his schemes. They are foul. Help us to fight with Your Word in hand. I honor You today.

November 20th

Limitations

It's amazing how our bodies have a timer that goes off when we need to sit down or rest. For some of us, including myself, it takes way more than a timer, it takes a shaking! Ever since I got back from our biggest event of the year I have been very sick, even when I woke this morning I had to go back to bed for another hour! When I woke the second time this morning, it was the first time in a long time that I actually had a bit of energy. When your energy has been gone and all of a sudden you feel some, it can be dangerous.

I started the day cleaning like a crazy lady! Every single door knob, tables, and handle got washed down. Every bit of laundry done. Every floor cleaned and Swiffed! All the sheets and anything I could think of that could have germs! On top of that I cooked an entire turkey dinner and made cookies. It felt great to finally do something after a week of lying around being sick. But, I know I passed my limitations. The boundary was crossed!

I feel great due the house being clean and everything done, but I'm ready to drop! Sometimes this can actually take you from feeling great to feeling horrible again. Why do we do this to ourselves???? I do it a lot.

It's so foolish to know our limitations and then to go past them! When we know we are not well, we must NOT do too much! It's just not good for us. The holiday is coming and you as well as I know, that there will be junk galore to eat. Will we go past our limitations and gorge? I guarantee at least two days we will! But what about the other days? Be careful as the holidays come friend to know your limitations. Some of you have deeper issues than a sickness, like I have; you have high blood pressure, and other risks that you need to watch. We have to take care of ourselves. I know it's easy to say, but today I did not watch anything! I crossed my limitations. We all do it at one time or another. I just pray I did not make myself worse. I have come to value time this year in a way like never before and this entire week was so hard for me, laying there sick, I felt like I was losing time! To me it was such a horrible waste of time, but I also needed to rest and my body's timer went off from doing too much.

What timers are going off in your life.

What have your eyes seen that they should not have seen? What have you spoken that you should not have spoken? What have you done that you wish you could take back? Is your body lacking exercise? Is there too much food and junk going into your mouth? Only you know your limitations.

It's time for change. If you are like me, it's hard to take time for yourself. As we cross into the New Year I'm going to try to do more for me. You need to know this is ok. I am NOT good at this. I have a hard time paying $40 to get my toes done. The only time I ever did it was when our church gave me a Birthday gift. I can't see spending money like that on my toes when I can do them myself. I'm beginning to realize that we are worth spending time and money on. We are worth forty five minute of someone pampering us. I never do it and I know I need to start.

It's part of anti-stressing, part of something called relax. Something that I need to learn.

Just as I know my limitations as far as crossing the line, I need to know my limitations and worth. You are worth way more than you think my friend. Sometimes we just can't see it. We need to have ways to relax, and hobbies to be creative, as He is creative. I need more of this in the year to come.

Think of some ways you can relax, take the time for yourself. Think of some ways to guard yourself from crossing the line of your limitations. Maybe you need an accountability partner?
Someone to help you through? Maybe you need to keep a log of things? Sometimes if they are in writing and in our face, it's easier to realize how close we are to crossing the line?

I'm not sure what you have to do in your life, but it's time for change.

> "Above all else, guard you heart,
> For it is the wellspring of life."
> Proverbs 4:23

The heart includes the mind and all that proceeds from it. What is in the mind can turn into action, and if we are not careful it can turn into sin. Watch your limitations today.

> "Each of you should learn to control his own body
> In a way that is holy and honorable."
> 1 Thessalonians 4:4

Limitations were all part of God's plan.

Dear God,
Make discipline and self control part of our everyday life. And when we need to rest help us to rest. I honor You today.

Busy or Busybodies

What does it mean to be idle? Possibly not being busy or active, passing time doing nothing or being lazy. No activity or avoiding work. I'm sure most of us have had our share of idle time. Paul speaks very boldly about being idle in the book of 2 Thessalonians. It makes you really think about your time and what you are doing to earn your keep. Take a read,

"In the name of the Lord Jesus Christ,
we command you brothers to keep away from every brother who is idle
and does not live according to the teaching you received from us.
For yourselves know how you ought to follow our example.
We were not idle when we were with you,
nor did we eat anyone's food without paying for it.
On the contrary, we worked night and day,
laboring and toiling so that we would not be a burden to any of you.
We did this, not because we do not have the right to such help,
but in order to make ourselves a model for you to follow.
For even when we were with you, we gave you this rule:
"If a man will not work, he shall not eat."
We hear that some among you are idle.
They are not busy; they are busybodies.
Such people we command and urge in the Lord Jesus Christ
to settle down and earn the bread they eat.
And as for you, brothers,
never tire of doing what is right."
2 Thessalonians 3:6-13

This is such an amazing chapter in the Word of God. Paul admits in verse 9 that he did not have to lift a finger if he did not want to,

"Not because we do not have the right to such help."

In other words, if he wanted to, he could sit and be served, due to him proving himself and working hard. But instead he chose not to. He says he wants to be a model of hard work in front of them all. So he gives up his own blessing and toils saying,

"We worked night and day,
laboring and toiling so that we
would not be a burden to any of you."
2 Thessalonians 3:8

Have you ever paid a visit to anyone and not laid a finger in their home? On the brink of many of you going home for the Holidays remember this lesson today. I learned at a very early age, in traveling with a group called Christian Music Ministries, to always leave your host home cleaner than when you came. Yes, to toil. To ask what you could do to help the family, to make our beds and clean the room we were in. Paul could have relaxed, but he chose to be an example.

I challenge you this holiday to go above and beyond, to be a hard worker and earn your keep. To blow your mom away by continually asking her, "What can I do to help?" If you want to totally freak her out, make your bed every day and pick up your clothes from the floor! Wow, she won't know what happened!

I want you to know today it's godly to be a hard worker, a servant, and someone who is NOT idle. Think about your situation right now, heading home? How will you take this Word and apply it? Even in the midst of your traditions and celebrations be a hard worker and have no idle time!

Are you Busy or Busybodies?

Dear God,
Help us to follow Paul's example, but most of all Your example. I honor You today.

November 22nd

Learn Your Lesson Well

"Oh man, you've got to be kidding!" Angrily said, as I burnt my hand again reaching in the oven for another piece of Texas Toast! Just a couple weeks ago I burnt the top of my left hand, pretty bad, as I reached in to steal another bite of something cooking on the broiler. The scars were just about gone, when last night my snitch of Texas Toast marked me again. I guess this is the price I pay for gorging. Thank God these marks go away, but they take time to go away, and with the Holidays coming and parties once again I will have scared hands. I guess it does not matter, being that I do not have any nails due to guitar, and guitar calluses are not the most attractive thing on a lady. My scars, calluses and no nails will just prove once again that I need to learn my lessons well and put on an oven mitt!

As I'm sure most of you know it's not easy to "Learn our lessons!" Most of the time we do things two or three times before we realize we should not have done them! How many of you have gotten something done to your hair when you have said, "I will NEVER do that again!" Or how many of you slipped into sin, when you swore it was over with? You told your child, "If you do that again, I will take this away or that away!" Yet you don't, and then you let regret enter the situation. Time and time again when we make mistakes, we then turn around and make them again. It's time to learn our lessons the first time! We need to learn from our mistakes.

> "So do not fear, for I am with you;
> Do not be dismayed, for I am your God,
> I will strengthen you and help you; I will uphold you
> With my righteous right hand."
> Isaiah 41 10

God can help us overcome Lessons NOT learned!

> "All Scripture is God-breathed and is useful for teaching,
> Rebuking, correcting and training in righteousness,
> So that the man of God may be thoroughly equipped."
> 2 Timothy 3:16-17

When was the last time you read or studied God breathed Scripture? Scriptures that can help you overcome whatever it is that you keep doing that you know you should not be doing? This scripture talks about how God's word can help correct and train us in the right way to go. I know my silly story of getting burnt for the second time in a month is one thing, but it can't really get me in trouble, or change my life forever like a lot of our choices can. I want you to realize today that many of your choices are eternal choices. They can change your life until the day you die.

When I burn myself, I'm scared for about three or four weeks. Remember when you make the same mistake twice you will be scared for a while. It's just the way life is. We will pay for our sin or doing things that we know we are not supposed to do. Some scars last longer and some scars, God will use in our lives to now turn around and help others. No one can minister better to someone than another who has made the same mistake.

I challenge you to dig into the Word of God. Increase your faith. God can help you not make the same mistakes that left scars once upon a time!

Learn your lesson well.

Dear God,
Help us to remember that many of our choices are and can be eternal and life changing. Help us to make the right choices. I honor You today.

God is Bigger Than the Lions

Paul's arrest in 2 Timothy chapter 4 most likely occurred when the anti-Christian persecutions started by Nero. This crazy Emperor killed and tortured Christians. Sometimes they were crucified; sometimes they were wrapped in animal skins and Nero's men called their hunting dogs on them. Some were burned alive and the list goes on. Paul was in prison during this era.
I believe Chapter 4 may be during this exact time.

You can tell Paul was not even prepared to be put into prison, that the thought did not even occur in his mind or he would have been more prepared as like times before. In Chapter 4 verse 12 it says,

> "When you come bring the cloak that I left with
> Carpus at Troas, and my scrolls, especially the parchments."

These are things that if he expected that he might be put in prison that he would have made sure to have with him. I don't think he expected this time, and I also think this time was much worse than many times he had been put in prison.

> "Alexander the metalworker did me a great deal of harm.
> The Lord will repay him for what he has done.
> You too should be on your guard against him,
> because he strongly opposed our message.
> At my first defense, no one came to my support,
> but everyone deserted me.
> May it not be held against them.
> But the Lord stood at my side and gave me strength
> So that through me the message might be fully proclaimed."
> 2 Timothy 4:14-17a

It's just so amazing to me how Paul still uses his horrible situations for the glory of God. Do you do that? I think if this was me I would have given every single detail about what Alexander did. Which ribs he broke and how many gashes he made. But Paul did not record these things. He seems to always want to take the focus off of himself and somehow lift up Christ. He tells of how God gives him the strength to make it through everything. It's just amazing to me.

Most of us know the story of Daniel in the Lion's Den, for any over the age of 40; we saw it on the flannel board in Sunday school when we were little. It's an amazing story in Daniel chapter 6. Daniel was thrown into a den of lions to be killed,

> "My God sent His angel, and he shut the mouths of the lions.
> They have not hurt me, because I was found innocent in his sight."
> Daniel 6:22

Such an amazing miracle that happened to Daniel, but did you know this also happened to Paul while imprisoned in 2 Timothy? Oh how I wish Paul elaborated a bit more in chapter 4 so we could see a much bigger picture! Here is what it says right after Paul is tortured and he says God gave him strength,

> "I was delivered from the lion's mouth."
> 2 Timothy 4:17b

There you have it.

Are you as frustrated as me? I just want to hear what happened! We could have used the lions on the flannel board for more than just Daniel's story! There must have been an amazing story behind these words and I cannot wait to hear it someday! Paul goes on to say,

> "The Lord will rescue me from every evil attack
> and will bring me safely to his Heavenly kingdom.
> To Him be glory forever and ever. Amen."
> 2 Timothy 4:18

After men beating him and wild animals after him, here he stands ready to face every lion in his life with the promise of his Heavenly home. What are your lions today? Are they an addiction, a bitter root, an unforgiving heart, pride, persecution, or shame?

Do NOT fear the lions in your life my friend!
God is bigger than the Lions!

Dear God,
How amazing you are that you would stop the jaws of such a beast. Help us to know you are always by our side. I pray for this reader, let them know that through you they will overcome if they run to you. I honor You today.

November 24th

On the Brink of a Holiday

The Eve of a Holiday can be very exciting for many people. Memories flood our minds and the thoughts of family, football, traditions, food and fun make it hard for some to sleep the night before. Hundreds of households tonight smell of pies, cookies and the making of many side dishes. Now we just wait to wake to the smell of Turkey in the air, pop on the Macy's Thanksgiving Day Parade and pretty much we are all set!

As I sit and write today, I don't want to be depressing in anyway, I do want you to think about what you are thankful for, maybe this will help. Many of you know I have been back and forth from India since 1985. I have seen cities a half a world away change, just as I have seen cities in America change throughout the last 20 years. But there are some things that never change in India. As I think about those things I am thankful for what I have.

Have you thanked the Lord for your shoes today? I know that sounds silly, but there are countless thousands in the country of India who have no shoes. The slums are filled with hundreds of people walking around without any shoes.

Walking through the red spit, cow dung, mud puddles and garbage. And guess what? There are people in America who have no shoes! Many only have one pair and they are not in good shape at all. How about you? If you are like me you have a good 10 or more pairs. When was the last time you even thought about this? Something nice to think about on the brink of a Holiday.

How about the roof over your head, when was the last time you thanked God for that? Countless people here in America will spend Thanksgiving in a shelter, on the streets, or under a bridge. What if you had not one place where you could go to smell that Turkey waking up in the morning or to watch something fun on television? How would that change your life? Most homeless people go somewhere that serves Thanksgiving dinner to them. A far cry from the eve of holiday excitement, lingering smells in the air and the love of family. When was the last time you even thought about this? Something nice to think about on the brink of a Holiday.

We woke today with extra people in the house. I made a big French toast breakfast and then we broke some games out. Later in the day we made a pizza and got out the ingredients for our famous Thanksgiving desert, Death by Chocolate, which now sits waiting to be eaten tomorrow. My son and daughter are both here, and wherever Angela walks in the house she is singing songs at the top of her lungs. There is an excitement in the air and I am thankful. But my mind cannot help but wander to those who do not have this joy tonight. When was the last time you even thought about this? Something nice to think about on the brink of a Holiday.

Jesus always seemed to have His mind on those that no one else noticed or cared about. Have you noticed them today? Will you notice them tomorrow? In all the excitement I wonder if we will even think about these thousands of people. I challenge you as you share what you are thankful for, around countless tables tomorrow, to remember those who do not have what you have.

Maybe you are one of those who sits alone this Holiday. You have lived your long life and though you do not have much you are thankful. I say to you, God has not left you, He is with you always. A humble roof over your head, and one pair of tattered shoes. He will honor the fact that you praise Him for what you do have.

<blockquote>
"Give thanks in all circumstances,
for this is God's will for you in Christ Jesus."
1 Thessalonians 5:16
</blockquote>

Just don't get so lost in everything that you stop thinking like Jesus thinks. Others were always first. Be thankful, enjoy the joy of living, but do something for someone else! Reach out, drop off a plate of cookies, go the extra mile, invite someone over! When was the last time you even though about this? Something nice to think about on the Brink of a Holiday.

Dear God,
It's all about others, it's all about souls. I honor You today.

November 25th

Black Friday

So if you are like me right now you are sitting down and you can hardly breathe due to mounds of shrimp, stuffing, rolls, corn, potatoes and yummy turkey! Not to mention apple pie, pumpkin pie, cookies, Death by Chocolate and the list goes on and on. When will it stop! I have a belly like I'm three months pregnant! I'm tired, and can hardly move, yet my teens are talking about getting up at 4am to do Black Friday! I did it last year when I was healthy and had energy, not sure if I can handle it this year? What is Black Friday anyway? Where did the word even come from?

The earliest record of the term Black Friday came back on September 24, 1869 when the stock market catastrophe happened. The term was not used again until 1966; the Philadelphia Police Department started using the words due to horrible heavy and disruptive traffic the day after Thanksgiving. I was born in 1966 so we are talking almost 45 years ago; Philadelphia resurrected the name that was used 97 years prior! Crazy to think about it. It was not until 1975 when the New York Times used the term in a paper that it was used outside of Philadelphia, and now as you know it is used every year as the day after Thanksgiving's biggest shopping day ever!

It is a fun day. Last year we went to the mall and every single store I went in gave me a gift! Now me being a person who loves gifts, you can imagine I loved every minute. I left with a new awesome water bottle made of metal for the gym. A snoopy snow globe, after all, everyone needs a snoopy snow globe and all kinds of silly things, it was fun. It seemed everyone who got up at 4am was happy and in a good mood. It's all just so ironic to me.

The term has always been used for horrible things such as the stock market catastrophe and horrible disruptive traffic and now it's used to get people motivated, excited and in the Christmas Spirit. Many articles I have read say they call it Black Friday because stores turn a profit on this day, and instead of being in the Red, they are now in the black, a very good place to be! So strange to me how the term was used for bad and now it's used for good? Very ironic and strange don't you think?

"These things puzzle me!"
~Elmer (Kidzturn Ministries)

So I guess it makes me think about how using a term that was meant for a horrible thing can now be turned around and used for a happy profitable day. That is a human conscience change and choice! Somewhere along the line humans say, "This will now be a good term and not a bad term!" Some influential intentional person stood up and made a stand!

How many of you influential intentional people can make history today? Stand up and change things!   We see it in history time and time again. Susan B. Anthony wrote something called the Federal Woman suffrage amendment in 1878 and she brought it to congress. It was no until 1920 that what she wrote was passed by the House of Representatives and the Senate. It was then sent to the states for ratification. So a lady makes an influential intentional stand in 1878 and 42 years later everything she works for and is passionate about happens. She died in 1906 and never knew how she changed the world. I hope you can see what I'm trying to say here. Some things are well worth the wait.

Do you realize on this Thanksgiving, all that we have to be thankful for due to people who paved the way? I want to know what roads you are going to pave? Do you realize God wants to use you in such a great way? You can be a history maker. What are you passionate about? Yes, it may take years but will you at least dare to try? Christ paved the way for our souls; this is the most amazing thing to be thankful for.

What can we do in greatness today?

"The one who calls you is faithful and He will do it."
1 Thessalonians 5:24

You see we can be influential and intentional but when we also have God by our side amazing things happen. Look at all the people in history who did amazing things who never had a relationship with Christ. Don't you think with God by your side He will help you to do it! He is our strength.

What are you waiting for?

I hope you remember this every time you hear the term Black Friday.

Dear God,
Help us to be history makers. I honor You today.

November 26th

Prayer and Praise

Most of us who have been to Sunday School at one point in our life have heard the story in Acts when Paul and Silas were in prison and they began praying and singing to God. A great earth quake came and shook the foundations of the prison, all the prison doors flew open and everyone's chains came loose (Acts 16:25-26). It's an amazing story. But what about the story right before this, the very reason they were thrown into prison.

I'm not going to go into every single detail but Paul, Silas and a group of men were walking to a place of prayer when a slave girl who predicted the future started following them. She followed them for days and she kept saying,

"These men are servants of the Most High God,
who are telling you the way to be saved."
Acts 16:17

So wasn't that a good thing that she was proclaiming? Well, it was the truth, but can you imagine everywhere you went this girl following you and shouting things out loud to other people? You would come to realize after a few days, that there must be some screws still loose upstairs. Paul was totally human, and just gets sick and tired of this girl following them and shouting to everyone. He finally handles the situation.

"Finally Paul became so troubled that he turned around and said to the spirit, "In the name of Jesus Christ I command you to come out of her!"
At that moment the spirit left her."
Acts 16:18

Paul had discerned probably the very first day that the girl had a demon in her. He was double frustrated probably because he saw this young girl tormented by the spirit in her. The Word says the spirit right at that moment left her! I wish it would say more about that very moment but it does not. I can imagine she thanked them, but if not it sure did get quiet for the first time in a few days!

The thing that really blows my mind about this entire story is Paul and his men just set a young tormented slave girl free, and yet they get punished severely for it. The men who own this girl realize that they will make no more money on her anymore, now that her powers for telling the future are gone, so they get very angry at Paul and his men for halting their business. Can you imagine? They set her free from a demon, and people are upset that she now stands there whole. They are not going to make their money anymore! Unbelievable.

Soon after they set this girl free from her torment, her owners get the crowd to join in the attack against Paul and Silas. The Word says the city was in an uproar! They bring their anger to the magistrates who then order the men to be stripped and beaten. Then The Word says they were severely flogged. To be flogged was to be beat with a whip or rod. Being flogged was bad enough, but for setting someone free, they were severely flogged! By the time they were thrown into prison I'm sure they were in serious pain and bleeding. Most likely they had broken ribs and more. Now they sat in s stinking prison all for setting someone free. All for doing something good. All for helping someone.

And what is their response? Prayer and Praise.

Did you ever do something good and get hurt because you did it? Maybe someone somehow twisted the story? What was your response? Was it Prayer and Praise? I know if that was me sitting in pain in that prison I don't think this would have been my response. How about you?

Jesus healed people, went the extra mile. Walked into homes, ate and spoke with people who were considered to be sinners by others. He let the children and lepers come to Him. He raised people from the dead and fed the multitudes. Yet just like Paul and Silas He was wrongly accused, beat and severely flogged. He then carried a cross for you, was nailed to it and died. Some of the last words he said were,

> "Father, forgive them, for they do not know what they are doing."
> Luke 23:34

> "Father, into Your hands I commit My Spirit."
> Luke 23:46

Prayer and Praise.

The next time you do something wonderful for someone, something that could change their life forever and you get hurt. Remember you are not the only one who this has happened to.

Instead of feeling sorry for yourself try
Prayer and Praise.

Dear God,
We need to be more like you in every situation we face. Give us your strength Father. I honor You today.

Good Fish Bad Fish

"Once again, the kingdom of Heaven is like a net
that was let down into the lake and caught all kinds of fish.
When it was full, the fishermen pulled it up on the shore.
Then they sat down and collected the good fish in baskets,
but threw the bad away.
This is how it will be at the end of the age.
The angels will come and separate the wicked
from the righteous and throw them into the fiery furnace,
where there will be weeping and gnashing of teeth."
Matthew 12:47-50

This is a pretty intense scripture. Many people do not picture a gentle humble God sending people to a devils Hell but the truth is, they send themselves there through choices they make while alive. People blame God for so many things, when most the time we are to blame, or the sins of others are to blame.

The question here is not whether or not you believe it, because it's truth already. The question is are you ready? When that day comes and angels separate, where will you go? God is full of mercy but He is also just. If you do not have a relationship with Him, or if you are happy in your sin, you will not make it. You will be thrown into the fiery furnace that this scripture is talking about. It won't be a fun wild party friend, there will be weeping. I'm sure people will be weeping due to the realization of truth or they will be weeping due to seeing loved ones suffering alongside them. Not sure about the gnashing of teeth and to be quite honest, I'm not sure I want to know what that means exactly! It does NOT sound too pleasant.

So for those of us who know the Lord, this is a very sobering scripture. I know so many people who do not know the Lord or who reject Him in their lives. It's not like you can force someone to live for God. I just wish they could see all the wonderful things He has done to prove Himself to me. I was not dealt the greatest deck of cards, I had been through more as a 16 year old girl than anyone should ever have to go through, but His grace reached out to me. He gave me a hope and a peace. I know in my heart you have friends and loved ones too who need that peace and hope of God. What are we going to do about it? Not sure about you, but when they separate real souls I want as many of my friends and loved ones to go to Heaven as possible.

So I say, love them.

Don't force them, judge them, beat them over the head with your Bible or say stupid things. Just love them.

When Jesus went into the home of sinners He simply loved them. Just the act itself, of going there for dinner most the time was an act of love. Love those around you, be that person who has a listening ear. If you always talk and never listen, why would they want to spend any time with you anyway? For some of us this takes self control.

When you are a true friend to someone whether they know God or not, that is when they will see who Christ really is.

He loves the bad fish just as much as He loves the good fish!
Do you?

God help us.

Dear God,
I don't want the ones I love or the ones I work with to be thrown into Hell. Father use me; let them know I'm there for them whenever they are in need. I honor You today.

November 28th

<u>Way Better Than Henna</u>

The last time my daughter and I were in India together we spent a day at the spa. I don't do spas in the states, mostly because they are so expensive but in India, for about five to ten American dollars you can get pretty much everything you want done. Our minds were focused on Mehndi, or as some call it in the states, Henna.

Henna is a stain or dye made from the crushed leaves of the henna plant. It's a beautiful art mostly done on the palm of the hands. It is custom for brides to get Mehndi or Henna done on their wedding day because it's considered to be a sign of beauty. It's also used on many happy occasions.

Some mummies that have been studied dating back to 1200 BC had this dye on them so it's something that has been used for years. Pharaohs had their hair and nails dyed from the Henna plant, some believed it would protect against evil so they would get all painted up. Much like the horn worn around the neck of Italians. These days, horses as well get their manes and hooves done with the same dye, needless to say, it's been around quite some time.

After Angela and I had our toes done at this spa, an artist started working on the palm of our hands. I cannot even begin to tell you how amazing this guy was. If he came to the states he would be very wealthy. He also was very fast, and in a matter of minutes had one entire palm of my hand done. The art was amazing, unlike anything I had ever seen before. Henna is like puff paint. It sits up on the skin or above the skin, so it's a bit strange at first. When it dries it is still sitting above the skin like something foreign that has to come off. In about three hours it starts falling off your skin, and it leaves behind a stain or dye on your skin that lasts for about three weeks. Angela and I loved it, and it was a fun amazing experience, something we will never forget.

Henna is not permanent; I'm sure so many wish it were. Do you realize today that God has engraved you on the palm of His hand permanently? Here is what the full scripture says,

> "Can a mother forget the baby
> at her breast and have no compassion
> On the child she has borne?
> Though she may forget,
> I will not forget you!
> See, I have engraved you on the palms of My hands."
> Isaiah 49:15-16

The Henna plant was recognized in the Bible in Song of Songs where it says,

"My lover is to me a cluster of
henna blossoms from the Vineyards of En Gedi."
Song of Songs 1:14

Since the Pharaohs found way back when, had the dye of henna found on them, I can only imagine the ladies must have taken advantage of this art in some way. I guess I wonder why in Isaiah chapter 49, God chose to say He has engraved us on the Palm of His hand. Why did He chose the palm? Was it custom even back then to have art, or beauty on the palm, just a thought. Or maybe it was a sign that we are in His hands? A permanent engraving that will never fade? Not sure why I always think of these kinds of things, but I can't wait to find out someday.

The Point here is that this is how much He loves us. I also love the scriptures leading up to the engraving. It says a mom should not forget her kids, but when she does, remember what I have done for you!

I sure hope you know today that God has you engraved on His palm. That no matter how you have been hurt in this life. No matter how forgotten you feel, there is a God in Heaven who will NOT forget you.

"Though she may forget,
I will NOT forget you!"
Isaiah 49:15

Dear God,
You just amaze me. You are way better than Henna! I honor You today.

Obey or Indulge?

"By the Word of the Lord a man of God came from Judah to Bethel,
as Jeroboam was standing by the altar to make an offering."
1 Kings 13:1

King Jeroboam in 1 Kings Chapter 13 put up two golden calves for people to worship. God sent a prophet to speak to the situation that was not pleasing to God. Here is King Jeroboam standing by the altar he erected, getting ready to make an offering. The man of God starts to prophecy against the altar, he came and he spoke with boldness.

"That same day the man of God gave a sign: This is the sign the Lord has declared: The altar will be split apart and the ashes on it will be poured out."
1 Kings 13:3

So the man of God is speaking, and King Jeroboam is standing there. I'm sure he was in total shock that someone had the boldness to speak with authority by his altar, so he responds,

"When King jeroboam heard what the man of God cried out against the altar at Bethel, he stretched out his hand from the altar and said, "Seize him!" But the hand he stretched out toward the man shriveled up, so that he could not pull it back."
1 Kings 13:4

Can you imagine? At the same time his hand shriveled up, the altar was split apart and its ashes poured out according to the sign spoken by the man of God! What he said happened and when the King tried to come against the Word of the Lord his hand shrivels up. Amazing.

So the King freaks!

"Then the king said to the man of God,
"Intercede with the Lord your
God and pray for me that my hand may be restored."
1 Kings 13:6

It's so funny to me that the King did not say, "Oh mighty golden calves heal me!" He was the one who erected them yet he did not even trust that they could heal him. So he turns to the God who is alive and able to heal.

"So the man of God interceded with the Lord,
and the King's hand was restored and became as it was before.
The King said to the man of God,
"Come home with me and have something to eat,
and I will give you a gift."
1 Kings 13:6-7

He wanted to thank the man of God by letting him eat great food and by giving lavish gifts. But here is the response of the man of God,

"Even if you were to give me half your possessions, I would not go with you, nor would I eat bread or drink water here. For I was commanded by the word of the Lord: 'You must not eat bread or drink water or return by the way you came.' "
1 Kings 8-9

Can you just imagine this? Here is his chance! He might just be set for life but because God had spoken he would not eat with the king. His obedience amazes me! The only reason he fails at the end of the story is because another man of God lies to him, but up to this point, he is faithful, and his faithfulness amazes me.

He risks his very life; if he was seized I'm sure he would have had a very bad night! Then when the Lord stands for him, and makes a way for him, he stays true to what God had spoken to him. He does not fall into the temptation of eating, drinking and taking gifts. This story just amazes me.

Tonight I cleaned out my jewelry drawer. Looking at years worth of expensive and cheap jewelry brought back so many memories. Every event or special occasion I got them at, who gave them to me and so on. But my jewelry is NOTHING compared to what the man of God could have had that night. I'm sure the sky was the limit, but yet he was faithful.

How many times has God spoken to you, yet you are tempted to indulge?

You did not have the strength to walk away. This man was a strong man and I believe at the end of the chapter when he does fail, he does it with a pure heart. He trusts the other prophet that lies to him. None of us are perfect. You will have to read to the end of the chapter to understand that. But I admire this man who stands firm on God's Word, who risks his life and who obeys rather than indulges!

Obey or Indulge?

Dear God,
When something sits in front of us and we know we are not to indulge, help us to obey! Make us like this man of God. Help us Lord. I honor You today.

Nostalgic

Now that I have a little time on my hands I have been enjoying free time by reading great books and surfing the internet for used things, a very weird hobby when you never purchase anything. Today I found something for twenty five dollars that I had to have. For those of you who know me. I pretty much do not need anything. You know that unless someone gives me a gift certificate, I wear the same clothes forever and I am just happy with the way things are. But when I saw someone selling the Half Pint today I got very sentimental and nostalgic.

The Sharp Half Pint microwave came out over 21 years ago. My husband and I were pretty poor when we first got married so we took whatever anyone would give us. Our couch had a cinderblock holding it up on one side in our first apartment. We were just the kind of couple that did not care about those things. We were thankful for what we had. My husband's grandmother, Grandma Smith, had the Half Pint microwave which was a perfect square and seemed to fit like a glove, on our very small kitchen counter. We did not care that it was a little outdated, we were just thankful that we had a microwave. Grandma Smith was an amazing woman of God who loved her Bible. Guy would share memories of him and Grandma Smith battling it out in Yahtzee! Grandma lived in a small apartment with less counter space than we had, yet she was happy. She had all she needed. God was her peace and He is all she needed.

As time went on Guy and I would visit Grandma Smith and have games of our own. She would often talk about the Lord and her faith. Those were good times, times that can never be bought, or forgotten for our family.

When our Half Pint finally bit the dust, believe it or not that exact same year Sharp came out with the new version of The Half Pint! Like I said, I usually do not splurge on me at all, but a friend asked me what she could get me as a going away gift due to the fact that we were moving. She told me my limit was $100. The Half Pint was $99 so I told her I wanted the new version of the Half Pint. So ten years ago we were given the Half Pint again and somehow it felt like Grandma Smith was still in our kitchen, encouraging us in the Lord. It was about a year ago that I was microwaving something, when I heard a pop, and our half pint bit the dust. Now, I know that it's not the best microwave around, and it's half the power of a normal one, but there is just something nostalgic about it, sentimental in its own sort of way to me.

Over a year ago when my Half Pint died I tried to purchase one online. They were sold out of the one I wanted. I looked on every online used sites and normal sites I knew of, there was no Half Pint to be found. I had a black one, and the only ones that I could find were for dorm rooms, some were lime green and some were hot pink. I wanted one, but not that bad! Ha-ha. I settled for a small used non- half pint microwave and the day I put it on my counter my heart sank. Not even a brand new one would have made me happy that day.

Today while looking online my life came to a complete stop, there it was, a black Half-Pint! There was a picture and the ad said, "Only used a few times in a dorm room $25" I knew, no matter what, I had to have it! I called right away and this afternoon I went to pick it up! It's a perfect square and I know it's not even as good as the one on my counter, but it feels like home. Grandma is back with us in the kitchen, I think of her every time I see the Half Pint!

Nostalgia is a funny thing. Sometimes you can see, hear or smell something that will trigger a memory and the Half Pint does that for me, I think of Grandma Smith. Call me weird, but things like this dig up deep emotions and I actually tear up sometimes! I know, it's pretty bad! Nostalgia triggers these tender emotions and feelings inside. To be sentimental can give you a desire to return in thought, to a former time and place of happiness. A time when loved ones were with us. A time that seemed more carefree and easy. Boy how time flies.

I'm thankful today that Grandma Smith, and many more people I love, are in a place today where I will see them again. The thought to return to a former happy place, is actually waiting for me in the afterlife. When you know Christ you can look forward to a giant reunion someday. This is not our home. We are only passing through. Someday something that's Nostalgic, can become reality.

Are you ready?

"For instance, we know that when these bodies of ours are taken down like tents and folded away, they will be replaced by resurrection bodies in Heaven, God-made, not handmade and we'll never have to relocate our "tents" again. Sometimes we can hardly wait to move and so we cry out in frustration. Compared to what's coming, living conditions around here seem like a stopover in an unfurnished shack, and we're tired of it!

We've been given a glimpse of the real thing, our true home, our resurrection bodies! The Spirit of God wets our appetite by giving us a taste of what's ahead. He puts a little of Heaven in our hearts so that we'll never settle for less."
2 Corinthians 5:1-5

Dear God,
Thank you for our loved ones and for the fact that you were the one who created emotions. Thank you that we can be ourselves, nostalgic, and you love us anyway. Help every reader to know today that they can be emotional when needed! I pray everyone is ready for Heaven and that amazing reunion we will have! I honor You today.

December

December 1st

Lighten Up

Tonight was the first of a slew of Christmas Parties to come. I also have one Friday and Saturday not to mention the week after. At each one we are doing a Yankee swap with a new gift, I don't think any are white elephants. If you don't know what a white elephant is, it's bringing something funny and used that you already have. White elephants can be real fun, but it's so nice to walk away with something new. Tonight I came home with the cutest snow men salt and pepper shakers. I put them right on the table when I got home, and put away the turkey that says, "Order Pizza!" Sad to see him put away for another year, I just love that turkey.

The name Yankee swap, believe it or not comes from back in the Civil War days. Yankees and Confederates at some point swapped prisoners as a game to lighten up the atmosphere. No one seems to know how something like that turned into a tradition for thousands of holiday parties all over the world. How swapping prisoners turned into swapping gifts! Very strange! I guess if you're at a party and feeling awkward a Yankee swap would "lighten up" the atmosphere! But it still makes me laugh that this is where the name came from. It makes you think of who was sitting around planning a party thinking, "Hmmm In the Civil War days they swapped prisoners so maybe we can make a fun game of this!" It really would be great to know who thought it up!

The truth is there are a lot of things we all do, to try to "lighten up" different atmosphere's. I'm sure you all have been somewhere with someone, and you both experienced awkward silence! Sometimes the silence is the loudest thing around! I hate when that happens! There are some times at my place of work, at the Hospital, where I work with someone who I just clash with. We have all gone through this, for some reason your personalities just don't mesh and a person can make you feel uncomfortable. In the baby nursery at the hospital it's hard when there are only two or three of you and you have to spend 8 hours together in close quarters, you look for anything and everything to lighten up the awkwardness at times. Don't you remember when Caroline and Charles Ingles on Little House on the Prairie would go into the Olsen's store and all the weirdness that would happen? Mrs. Olsen would be behind the counter, Caroline would be looking at things and you could cut the awkward atmosphere with a knife! Personalities are different, that's all, that's life. We just need to be the best light of God we can be, and get a back bone and move on.

There were even times in God's word where awkward situations happened. When the Samaritan woman came to draw from Jacobs well in John chapter 4, I'm sure the first moments were very strange. She knew he was a Jew, and Jew's and Samaritans were not supposed to associate with one another (John 4: 9). So what does Jesus do?

"Will you give me a drink?"
John 4: 7

He asks a question to lighten up the atmosphere or to cut the ice. Or he swaps words instead of prisoners! How many times have you done this? I could make lists! Even when you are with people that you can't wait to get to know, and you are excited about a new friend, there is always these strange moments.

I guess I just want to say to you who may feel a tad socially awkward, enjoy your holidays! Don't NOT go to parties because you are scared of these moments! They were feeling them way back in Civil War days, and we will be feeling them till the day we are all with our Father in Heaven. It's just the way it is. I'm a total extrovert, maybe you are a total introvert, so put us together and what do you have? Awkward moments. You need to know these moments are ok! Jesus always seemed to know what to say in these moments, and sometimes it was as simple as asking a question, when he knew someone felt a little scared and timid. Grow up this Christmas season and let God stretch you into a place you are not comfortable. Sometimes these are the best places for us to be. Sometimes these places are the perfect will of God for our lives.

His will is not always comfortable.
Lighten Up.

Dear God,
I pray for this reader. Stretch them into exactly what you want them to be tonight. Use them in all the situations you put them in through the year. I honor You today.

December 2nd

Leave a Legacy

Today was the most amazing day. I have two friends that we have been praying for and all in the same week their prayers were answered. After praying for months for both of them, it's just bazaar to me that both their prayers would be answered in the same week!

Don't forget answered prayer! How soon we forget the amazing things God has done! How soon we go about our merry way and forget His favor. You need to start writing down, in a journal, the things that God has done! I have some journals from over 20 years ago, and when I read them, I read things that I totally forgot about! It's so important to write things down.

I went to court with my friend Cindy today who had gone through a long drawn out court case. She left with the victory for the rest of her life, and her son Preston's life. I sat in that court room and prayed from the back just knowing the favor of God would be on her side. Many people prayed, God answered today! Not even an hour later we were on our way to my other friend Michelle's brand new apartment. She was in a dangerous situation and need to get out of where she was living. God came through with an amazing apartment! If you look out the window you see the water and Boston's entire skyline. She will have the best seat in the house for 4th of July fireworks! But most of all, it's a safe environment, where she will sleep in peace. We were standing there today, all three of us, as Preston crawled around the floor, we just began to thank God and praise Him for what He had done as we felt the warmth of the sun beating on us in this brand new empty apartment! We asked God to bless it and fill every room with His presence. Two answered prayers all in the same week. Just so amazing!

Write it down people! Don't forget the things He has done! Let your children's children read the amazing things your Lord has done for you! What I would not give to have something written by a grandparent! Anything, thoughts, a journal, poems, anything! What will you pass on to the ones you love? How will they know your passions, longings, dreams, goals and desires? I wish I had that from family members long past. This was one reason I even started writing this devotional! God had done so many amazing things in my life that I just had to tell somebody! So many stories, that no one would even believe because they were so amazing. I just had to write them down. The truth is, someday my grandchildren and great grandchildren will have a glimpse into what their great grandma Tana was like and how she lived for God. They will walk through my hard times with me, and they will see themselves in me. It will encourage them to live for God. This is what your prayer journals can do! Answered prayer is a powerful thing.

Paul prayed for the Corinthians and in 2 Corinthians chapter 3 he calls them a human letter.

"You show that you are a letter from Christ, the result of our ministry,
Written not with ink but with the Spirit of the living God, not on tablets
Of stone but on tablets of human hearts."
2 Corinthians 3:3

We are like human letters; God is journaling in us, on our hearts and in our lives. Why would we not want to share this? Maybe you are not the kind of person who is ready to, "go tell somebody", so go write it down alone in your room! The truth is, if God is really changing you, you will not have to say anything, because those around you will see it anyway! But why would you not want to share it? Do NOT be quick to forget all he has done my friend. Write it down.

"Write down the revelation
And make it plain on tablets."
Habakkuk 2:2

Leave a legacy. I leave this book for my grandkids and great grandkids.

Dear God,
It does not matter what we come from, we can all leave a legacy behind for someone.

I honor You today.

An Abishag Job
"When King David was old
and well advanced in years,
he could not keep warm
even when they put covers over him."
1 Kings 1:1

You will much appreciate that scripture if you are living on the east coast today! Baby its cold outside! It just made me laugh when I read it. My husband came down about an hour ago and had me feel his forehead, he is cold! My husband is never ever cold! He is hot! No pun intended! Ha-ha. It's so funny the scriptures you can find when you are really looking. When I saw this one I just laughed but it gets way funnier. Listen to this, due to the fact that King David could not get warm his servants came up with a plan,

"Let us look for a young virgin
To attend to the king and take care of him.
She can lie beside him so that our lord the king may keep warm."
1 Kings 1:2

Whatever happened to bricks in the bed or cranking up the fireplace! I'm sure the king did NOT object! When we were kids my dad would warm bricks on the wood stove, wrap them in towels and put them at the bottom of our beds. It worked; we would be warm in no time. I wish we had a wood stove today, I would do it tonight! We even wore hats to bed, but NO hat for King David! Can you just imagine this plan!

"They searched throughout Israel for a beautiful girl
and found Abishag, a Shunammite, and brought her
to the king. The girl was very beautiful;
she took care of the king and waited on him, but the
King had no intimate relations with her."
1 Kings 1:3-4

I'm sure the fact that they found a virgin that was beautiful only meant that the servants had other intentions than just keeping the king warm! Such an awkward scripture! I worked in a nursing home for 4 years, and I fell in love with all the people I took care of. Most of them were over 80, and were always cold. Sometimes we would bring them warm blankets and turn up the heat. I can imagine the reason the King was not intimate with Abishag, was because he had no energy to even think about it! My precious people I helped take care of in the nursing home hardly had the energy to eat. Its funny reading this scripture, but the truth is, I believe Abishag had a very special job. Maybe the servants had other ideas, but not the king, and not Abishag. I'm sure the king thought she was beautiful, but he was tired. I believe on the other hand Abishag was much like a nurse. She loved her patient with a pure love and would do anything to help him. Now, I know I would never have laid by any of my patients to keep the warm, but this was a different situation, she was given to the king. I have to believe in my mind that as she laid there her thoughts were, "Sweet old man, how can I help you." She was a nurse maid with a servant's heart.

The heart of Christ was a compassionate servant's heart. The fact that she did her job with no complaining and as a servant, speaks volumes of Abishag. I think pretty highly of this lady who would wash, cook, clean, help change, brush teeth, change grossness and meet every need of an old man who could not keep warm!

I know circumstances are nothing like Abishag's but where has God placed you? If you know He has placed you there, do you do it grudgingly or with a servant's heart? Imagine what this beautiful young virgin was thinking when she found out she had to lie by an old cold man. Yet, she took care of him the Word says, and waited on him. I believe the blessing for her came in the fact that the King did NOT have intimate relations with her. God honored her character and her attitude.

Do you have An Abishag job?
How is your attitude?

Dear God,
I know we don't have to lie near old cold men, but help us in every circumstance you put us in today. I honor You today.

December 4th

The Road to Washerman's Field

Where do you meet with God? Through my over 25 years of walking and talking with God I have met Him in so many places. I shared one time in this devotional that my husband and I cleared out a space in a giant walk in closet we had. We put pillows down on the floor, and made it a literal prayer closet. I have met with Him in my office, in the middle of the night on my couch, in the woods, by many bodies of water and the list goes on and on. Where have you met with God? I'm sure like me, there are many places where you have walked and talked. Some are much more memorable than others. Memories that you will never forget, about things He spoke deep to your heart.

If you are reading this and you do not have this relationship with God, I pray you call on Him. It's priceless. There is nothing like knowing you are in the perfect will of God for your life. Sometimes He meets us in the strangest places. People have shared stories with me of divine appointments in malls, parking lots, taxi's and more. God is not limited to our perfect little prayer rooms. He is way bigger than that.

In Isaiah Chapter 7, God speaks to Isaiah to get his son and to meet up with Ahaz to give him a Word from the Lord.

"Then the Lord said to Isaiah,
"Go out, you and your son Shear-Jashub,
to meet Ahaz at the end of the aqueduct of the Upper Pool,
On the road to the Washerman's Field.
Say to him, be careful, keep calm and don't be afraid."
Isaiah 7:3-4

Further into Chapter 7 in verse 14 Isaiah says to Ahaz,

"Therefore the Lord himself will give you a sign:
The virgin will be with child
and will give birth to a son,
and will call him Immanuel."
Isaiah 7:14

The **Lord Himself** chose The Road to Washerman's Field to have Isaiah reveal the most important news of all to King Ahaz, that Immanuel would be born.

Washerman's Field was the road to where people did their public laundry. I have walked these kinds of roads in India. They are pretty dirty. When you get to the body of water where people wash, there is filth beyond comprehension. I can imagine Washerman's Field was not too different from what I have seen. People washed, drank, and did laundry all in the same body of water.

Why on earth would the Lord choose the Road to Washerman's Field, the road to the outdoor laundry, to reveal one of the most important things the world would ever know to Ahaz?

Maybe because His humility rang in the streets, or on dirt roads, even before he was born.

If I chose where the announcement of Immanuel would be to someone, even if they were ungodly, it would be on a high mountain or in a great temple, in a beautiful field or by a clean clear body of water. Not a dirty body of water where many people wash.

Immanuel, God with us, anywhere, even a dirt road.
This was the choice of The Lord.
Where do you meet with God?

Dear God,
God, remind us that we can meet with you anywhere, a beautiful prayer room or a dirt road. I honor You today.

December 5th

Ultimate Void Filler

I saw my first snowflakes fall today! I hate snow and I hate the cold, but there is just something about the first sight of snowflakes. I quickly rushed over to my amazing husband and kissed him and got all mushy. The first sign of snowflakes in New England is romantic. I remember as a teen, and college girl, the hormones racing when we would see the first sign of the beautiful snow falling. Every girl in the dorm would think, "I wish I had someone to hold hands with and walk through the snow with right now!" Thoughts would quickly enter our minds about that certain someone that we wished would call on the hall pay phone! Yes, these were the days before cell phones!

Now after 21 years of marriage I love to give my husband hugs and kisses when I see my first signs of snow, but I no longer want to go walking in the freezing cold! My body can't handle what it used to! I would rather a hot shower, thank you very much! But I remember way back when, in college, before I met Guy (husband's name), how simple it was to mess up, and date a guy around the holidays, due to the romance of it all. The thought of Christmas shopping with someone, walking through the first snow fall holding hands, the thought of getting that very special Christmas gift from the opposite sex. The thought of it all, lit your heart on fire. It also made you make wrong choices, dating people who were not God's will, just because you wanted to fill the void.

Tonight I want to encourage your heart, Let God fill the voids this Christmas. Walk with Him in the snow and talk to Him. Go out with friends shopping and get gifts for one another or do a Yankee swap together to help fill the voids. Don't settle for second best just because that's what every commercial is telling you to do. If the Spirit of God is present the Bible says in Galatians 5:22 that self control will be part of your everyday life. Is it? Can you control the urge to fill voids with things other than God? Now if it's His will, that's a total different story! But I understand the loneliness of special holidays.

"Woe to those who go to great depths
To hide their plans from the Lord,
Who do their work in darkness and think,
"Who sees us? Who will know?""
Isaiah 29:15

It's very easy during this time, such a romantic holiday, to fall. To fill voids, and make bad choices. Don't even try to hide your sinful plans from God because He already knows everything you do or have done. He actually knows you much better than you know yourself.

What about you unhappy married people? Little flirts on e mail or spending a little extra time after work, talking with co workers, all because you are feeling the holiday longing to be loved.

The Kay Jeweler commercials are getting to you day after day! May I remind you of a love that came humbly and was born on Christmas day. A love that hung on a cross, and died for your soul. Fill your voids with Him and stop sinning. Get a backbone and live for God.

I'm not sure if you ever have experienced Him filling your voids, but if you haven't, you don't know what you are missing. If you truly seek God, and let Him help you through this time, it could be your happiest time ever. But many take the easy way out and settle for second best to fill a void.

I challenge you today friend, don't fall into temptation this Christmas season, seek The One who came and died for you. Who longs to give you a peace beyond what you can even imagine.

He is the Ultimate Void Filler.
But when you seek Him you will find He is so much more!

Dear God,
I pray for this reader. May they seek you in their loneliness and find you! Prove yourself faithful. I honor You today.

December 6th

<u>Scrooged?</u>

Many of you have your December calendars filling up as I write. You have Christmas parties, family gatherings, special school productions and so much more. I sit right now in our church sanctuary watching a dress rehearsal of the production of The Gospel According to Scrooge. My daughter, Angela, is playing a lead role. It's a total blast to watch, but it gets me thinking as I watch this old grumpy man. How can anyone be so very miserable?

Many times in this devotional I have talked about God's Spirit living in us, and the Word says in Galatians that if that's the case there will be fruit of it. Love, joy, peace, patience, kindness and the list goes on. Did you hear that? I did say the word Joy! Joy is an emotion of great delight or happiness. So in other words, if God's Spirit is living in you, there should at least be a hint of joy seen somewhere in you. You should NOT be living your life like dear old Mr. Scrooge!

> "You make known to me the path of life;
> You will fill me with joy in your presence,
> with eternal pleasures at your right hand."
> Psalm 16:11

Here is a thought for you; it says You fill me with joy in your presence! When was the last time you sat in His presence?

> "Rejoice in the Lord and be glad."
> Psalm 32:11

> "The disciples were filled with joy and with The Holy Spirit."
> Psalm 13:52

The Fathers joy was not limited to the disciples, it was meant for every person walking in the presence of God. It was not meant for the old and New Testament humans only, but for every man and woman who would be born on the face of the earth. Some of you may say, "Well, you have no idea what I have been through in this life, I was not dealt the best deck of cards!" Well, join three quarters of the human race! I don't care what you have been through, every person, no matter what they have been through can be changed by the power of a living God. If God can change my heart, He can change anyone's! If God can fill me with joy, He can fill anyone with joy.

> "May the God of hope fill you with all joy
> and peace as you trust in him,
> so that you may overflow with hope
> by the power of the Holy Spirit."
> Romans 15:13

The secret of it all is letting God do what He wants in your life. So many are not willing to change. Sometimes, this kind of change, takes every root of bitterness uprooted. Bitterness is the opposite of joy, and if you are not willing to let God uproot it, than you cannot be filled with joy. The Father is an amazing gardener friend! So many times I have let Him turn my soil, uproot bad roots, and plant new seeds! I think I turned out pretty good.

> "Consider it pure joy, my brothers and sisters,
> whenever you face trials of many kinds,
> because you know that the testing of
> your faith produces perseverance.
> Let perseverance finish its work
> so that you may be mature and complete,
> not lacking anything."
> James 1:2-4

I think if we start to look at trial as a way to mature and complete us, we may have an easier time with it. It seems Mr. Scrooge needed a little help along the way to remember a time when he was happy and filled with joy. When was the last time you remembered? If you are reading this and you cannot remember one happy time, I want to say I'm so sorry to you. May God's peace come visit you. I know my God is big enough, to let even you, experience His joy, but you are the one who must make the choice.

If you can, I want you to remember one happy time. What was it that made you happy? When was the last time you were in the Lord's presence? I challenge you today, to stretch yourself and remember. I challenge you to be willing to let God change you. Don't get bitter this Christmas due to the past. Look for a brighter and better future! God can change everything!

Scrooged?
Well get Un-Scrooged, breathe, and enjoy life!

Dear God,
Give us your joy; help us to see trial as growth. I honor You today!

Happy Bear

Yesterday, while picking up cold meds for my daughter I went walking through the Christmas isles, what fun! All kinds of snowmen and things that sing, Christmas candy, there was even a Charlie Brown nativity where Woodstock was baby Jesus. I have to admit it was very cute. So as I was waiting for her medicine I soaked it all in. We have all been so sick, that I have not really even thought about Christmas shopping yet.

As I'm walking through this store, I turn the corner and there he was. Now, before I tell you this, you need to know I do NOT own one stuffed animal. There was a time years ago I had one or two but I'm not really into them. I turned the corner and there was a light brown, very large and soft teddy bear, with the most beautiful smile on his face. The price tag said $19.99. There was a big sign around his neck that said, "Take me Home!" I fell in love the instant I saw him. I went home and proclaimed to my husband that all I wanted for Christmas was that Teddy Bear that said, "Take me home!" I am not one to really purchase things for myself so I could not see spending $20 bucks on a stuffed animal! My husband said, "Why didn't you just buy it?" I told him I didn't know why. All that to say, I went back and got the bear. I work in our spare room, there is a full bed in it, and he is now sitting there on the bed smiling at me!

Yesterday my daughter asked me what his name was. I really had never thought about naming a fake stuffed bear, kind of stupid to me, but she insisted. Every time I look at him it makes me happy so I came up with, Happy Bear. I know, not to creative or right brained, but perfect.

It's just the most stupid thing that this bear makes me happy. I have tried to figure out why. Is there some sort of hidden memory in my subconscious or is it just his face that some stranger created? There just comes a point and time when you have to stop trying to figure everything out and except the fact that it's just the way it is! Happy Bear makes me happy. I don't think I have owned a stuffed animal in about 25 years so the entire thing makes me laugh.

Why is it we as humans have to try to nail everything down, or try to figure every detail of our emotions out? Why can we just let it roll sometimes? Why can't I have a bear that makes me happy sitting on my spare room bed? How many times have you done this? You see something, or do something and you try to figure it all out. You have a déjà vu type experience and all of a sudden you think you need to analyze it all out on paper. You make a mistake and you beat yourself over the head until you realize, it was just a mistake. You have a dream and it MUST mean something, well, maybe it was just the sub you ate at 11pm at night. I'm trying to get to the point in my life where I don't try to figure everything out all the time. I know what I believe in, I know what I can and cannot do, and I know what makes me happy. If I mess up, I start again. If I have déjà vu, I keep moving to where ever I'm going, I stop the Italian side of me, knowing there MUST be some sort of meaning in it all! Sometimes there's not! It's just life.

So to you I say today. Stop trying to figure it all out. What are the happy bears in your life? Are they ungodly? If so, get rid of them and move on. If not, enjoy every minute. There is nothing wrong with happy things.

What made Jesus happy? He was happy when his disciples took him at his word and carried out the mission He gave to them. He was happy when He knew He accomplished the Father's perfect will.

"Jesus told them a parable: Suppose one of you has a hundred sheep and loses one of them. Does he not leave the ninety-nine in the open country and go after the lost sheep until he finds it? And when he finds it, he joyfully puts it on his shoulders and goes home. Then he calls his friends and neighbors together and says, Rejoice with me; I have found my lost sheep. I tell you that in the same way **there will be more rejoicing in Heaven over one sinner who repents than over ninety-nine righteous persons who do not need to repent.**"
Luke 15:3-7

We were and are his Happy Bears. I know kind of corny, but when we came to Him, raw, just the way we were, He was filled with joy, like this scripture talks about. I didn't need to "clean up" first, I had a cuss mouth, and I was NOT a good girl. But I was His Happy Bear. I made Him smile. To me this is amazing, because at least my bear smiles back at me. I DID NOT smile back at God the first month of my salvation. I needed to gain and grow in His joy. But yet, I was His Happy Bear. He loved me anyway.

Do you know you can come to Him as you are today?
You make Him happy.

Dear God,
I hope I don't purchase any more stuffed animals! Thank you for being joyful when we come to you. I honor You today.

December 8th

Master Storyteller

There was no better storyteller like Jesus. He was an amazing teacher as well. He had a gift, he could sit or stand and tell story after story to convey his message. Just to name a few, the story of the farmer who sowed his seed, the Good Samaritan, The Parable of the Rich fool, the mustard seed and the yeast, the lost sheep, and the Prodigal Son. He held his audience captive with his short stories, kind of like Italians! Ha-ha! All of His stories or parables, point to his grace, love and forgiveness. He was a Master Storyteller.

Whether you are an introvert or an extrovert God can use you in this way. Most the time He was in front of a large crowd, but it does not always have to be this way for you. God can use you right at work, one on one, which for some feels like a much safer place. You need to know that the things that have happened in your life are your stories, and God did not put them there to never be shared! Some cannot be shared until you are healed from within, but they are not sitting there for nothing.

Many will come to you in this lifetime who are going through a storm, what will you share to bring comfort and care to them? Maybe you have a story to tell? Yes, we have The Word of God, the greatest comfort of all, but sometimes if you captivate them with a story first, it will pave the way in their heart to hear The Word. Maybe when they know they are on common ground with you, they will hear your message so much louder.

There was a reason Jesus told stories. It was an art form, much like reading poetry.   Just like this devotional is an art form. From day one, in January when I started this, I have told story after story. Stories can minister to the heart in a very deep way. Jesus always had a spiritual application attached to his story. Maybe you can learn to let God use you in this way. Maybe He is trying to stretch you to reach out to those around you.

He knew how to break the silence with an art form. He had wisdom to know if the time was right.

David prayed this prayer,

> "Restore to me the joy of Your salvation
> and grant me a willing spirit,
> to sustain me.
> Then I will teach transgressors Your ways,
> and sinners will turn back to you."
> Psalm 51:12-13

Sometimes like David prayed, our teaching transgressors His way, can be in a story.

"After this, Jesus traveled about from one town and village to another, Proclaiming the good news of the kingdom of God."
Luke 8:1

Just 2 verses after this it says,

"While a large crowd was gathering and people were coming to Jesus from town after town, He told this parable: A farmer went out to sow his seed."
Luke 8: 4-5

So Jesus' "proclaiming the good news of the Kingdom" came in a story.

What have you been through in this lifetime? What have those around you been through? Sometimes it does not seem fair what we go through in this life, but perhaps it's for greater purpose? Maybe you might just have a story to tell my friend.

You may not be a preacher who can stand in front of hundreds of people, but you can share His good news anywhere. Tell a story.

Learn to be like the
Master Storyteller

Dear God,
Help us to step out of our comfort zone. I honor You today.

What Are You Doing With Your Talent?

What are you doing with the things God has given to you, are you using them, or wasting them? What about the resources He has given such as your time, talents, gifts and giving?

You may not think that God can use you, with your chair making, your painting ability or your knitting, but I'm here to tell you, you are wrong! The Word gives focus to many talents used for his Glory and guess what, they all were NOT all preaching! In Solomon's temple in 2 Chronicles 5:13-14, it talks about people who played the trumpet, singers, cymbal players and many more people who played music. The Word says that God used these people in such a way to usher in the Glory of the Lord. It came in the form of a real cloud, so that the priests could not even stand to minister because of the cloud of God's glory.

At the church in Joppa, in Acts 9:39 and 43, the talents apparent there, were garment making. In the Building of the tabernacle in Exodus 35:30-35 many gift and talents were used for God's glory. Designers, workers with metals, the cutting of stones, carving of wood, teaching, engraving, embroidering, workers with fine linen, garment making and weaving! It's amazing how God can use an everyday talent.

> "He has filled him with the Spirit of God,
> in wisdom, in understanding
> and in knowledge and in all craftsmanship."
> Exodus 35:31

> "He has filled them with skill to perform every work."
> Exodus 35:35

Is this to say that He can give us a talent like he can fill us with God's Spirit at an altar? Well, most the time as we grow, as young people, our talent's start to be recognized by our parents or caregivers. But I have to say I have seen it before where God just gives someone a talent due to a passion they have for something. This happened with my own husband.

When I married Guy over 20 years ago he did not have a musical bone in his body. About 15 years back he took an interest in the piano. For many, it takes years to learn to play and read music. My husband asked one of the dear ladies at our church, Lois, to help him with his new passion. And when I say it became a passion, he lived, and breathed the piano. After one year he was playing in church. Now 15 years later he is leading at District events. When you have a passion for something, it can become a God given talent. God honors passion!

Read this scripture, maybe God will minister to you about what you should, and should not do, with your talent. It's about a man going on a journey, he calls his servants and entrusted his property to them, his money.

"To one he gave five talents of money, to another two talents,
and to another one talent, each according to his ability.
Then he went on his journey.
The man who received the five talents went at once and put
His money to work and gained five more.
So also, the one with the two talents gained two more.
But the man who had received the one talent went off,
dug a hole in the ground and hid his master's money."
Matthew 25:15-18

Just for the record, do NOT bury your talent! Do not dig a hole and hide it!

He says to the one, who gained the five talents,

"Well done, good and faithful servant!
You have been faithful with a few things;
I will put you in charge of many things."
Matthew 25:21

To the one who gains the two talents the master replied,

"Well done, good and faithful servant!
You have been faithful with a few things;
I will put you in charge of many things."
Matthew 25:23

But to the one who dug a hole and hid his talent,

"You wicked, lazy servant!"
Matthew 25:26

"You should have put my money on deposit with the bankers, so that
when I returned I would have received it back with interest."
Matthew 25:27

God wants to use your talent friend,
What are you doing with your talent?

Dear God,
Give us a passion for something and let it turn into a talent. Take the talents we have had as young people and use them for your glory. I honor You today!

December 10th

The Wall on my Windowsill

This morning I was cleaning my house getting ready for a very busy weekend. My daughter is a lead in a Christmas Musical, and I have company coming in tomorrow. I have been going mad cleaning the things I never clean until company comes! So many dust bunnies, I just doing even know what to do with them all! I cleaned the basement which usually is filled with mounds of teenagers so as you can imagine that took some time, and it happens like every two or three months! Oh yes, the teens have cleaned for me down there before, Ha-ha, you know what a teenager cleans like! Needless to say, it took a while. While I was up in the living area, I put on a pot of Africa to Africa my new favorite Starbucks Blend, and as the aroma was filling the air along with Pandora's Online Christmas playing, I was inspired to keep cleaning!

While cleaning my window, above my kitchen sink, memories came to mind. If you are like me you have a windowsill above your sink with little knickknacks on it. I have two beautiful scrolled brick pieces of wall that sit on my sill; they have a light blue tint to them. I'm sure anyone who comes into my kitchen wonders what they are. Sonagachi Brothel is located right in Calcutta.

There was a documentary done that won an Academy Award called Born into Brothels, it's the same brothel. Sonagachi is lined with these light blue brick walls, most of them are all crumbled and falling down onto the ground. I was there ministering to the Sonagachi girls with my amazing girl friend who does it all the time, Beth, when on my way out of the Brothel I picked up these two pieces of the wall so I could remember to pray for them. I cherish these two light blue pieces. Every day I see them, and every day I pray.

I can remember one young lady wanting me to see her home in Sonagachi. With my friend Beth leading, and my husband linked to my arm we walked into one of the most horrifying sights I had ever seen. Young girls, hundreds of them lined on both sides of the streets, elbow to elbow. Some looked like they were 10 and 12 years old. As far as the eye could see. Beth told me the lines went on for about 6 miles. It was rush hour. There we were, three white people, being led by one of the girls that lives there, I'm sure we were quite the weird site. My heart was broken and I just wanted to go hug some of these girls. It's so hard to believe this still goes on in our world, even right here under our noses in America. We took a left out of the lines into a little alley and I have to say, I was a bit scared by this point. We passed what I think was a makeshift outhouse on the left and just feet from that was a little hatch in the ceiling which was her home. I could not believe it. We climbed up and looked in, she was so proud of her home. If you sat up in her twin bed, you would hit your head on the ceiling. The room was about 10 feet by 4 feet. Her Christmas lights lined the walls, I could not even believe there was electric in there. It was one of the hardest sights I have ever seen. After that began our journey out of Sonagachi through the same lines. Right before we were out of the brothel I stooped down and picked up these two pieces of The Wall. It was a life changing walk for my husband and I.

Right next to my two pieces of The Wall on the windowsill is a bobble head snowman with a sparkle red jacket. When I saw the two things together this morning I just wanted to remind you all to count your blessings this season. You have no idea how very blessed you are. I know some of you readers very well, and I understand that you cannot pay every bill, but I also know we were not born into brothels. We have roofs over our head. We have snowmen with sparkle jackets and food to eat. Please don't forget your blessings this Christmas.

> "Always giving thanks to God the Father
> for everything, in the name of our Lord Jesus Christ."
> Ephesians 5:20

This morning as I once again looked upon my two broken pieces from the Sonagachi walls I began to thank my Father and pray for the girls. When was the last time you took the time to thank Him?

> "Devote yourselves to prayer, being watchful and thankful."
> Colossians 4:2

When was the last time you prayed for those less fortunate? Or even though about them? Now, this Christmas, is the perfect time. Maybe you don't have daily reminders lying around your home like I do to pray; maybe it's time for some sort or reminders? A prayer journal, a prayer list? Not sure what you do to remind yourself to pray but please, don't forget. Do anything and everything you must do to NOT forget to pray and thank God. And while you are at it, would you put my beautiful friends who are trapped in the largest brothel in Calcutta on your list, as well as their kids. These people need our prayers.

I thank God for The Wall on my windowsill.

Dear God,
Help us to pray for those who are trapped in a place they wish they were not this Christmas. Help us to praise you and thank you on a daily basis! I honor You today.

December 11th

FAKE SNOW

As I walk around the halls of my church right now, there is fake snow all over the place. Little soft plastic pieces everywhere. Our church production of The Gospel According to Scrooge is this weekend, four showings in three days. Today there was an afternoon show and tonight another show. The set is amazing and real snow falls the only problem is it gets pretty much everywhere. So after this afternoons showing, into tonight as you can imagine there is snow all over the church. The cast members are covered and they trail it everywhere. So as I was walking the halls a few minutes ago all I could think about was fake snow. It made me think of fake Christians. Don't ask me how that came to mind as I was looking at the snow, but I guess that's just the way my brain works.

Real snow is mostly soft and cold, a pleasure to pop into your mouth as long as it's not yellow! Sometimes it's hard as a rock if it's turned into ice but needless to say, it's a lot different than this fake snow. This fake snow that falls actually looks like feathers, it's plastic and soft almost like a garbage bag or grocery bag. It's a royal pain to clean up just like real snow, but they both have their differences and you CAN tell them apart. There is no mistaking real snow for fake snow. But it's very hard to tell that fake snow is fake from a distance, and when it's all piled together. There is a scene in the production where piles of fake snow are there for a bunch of kids to have a snow ball fight. When it is piled, you cannot tell from a distance that it's fake. Kind of like when a group of Christians are together at church, hard to tell who really has a relationship with God; it looks like they all do, when they are grouped together. But spend a little time with them alone and I'm sure you will know who is a real Christian and who is not.

The Word of God says by their fruit you will know.

> "Watch out for false prophets.
> They come to you in sheep's clothing,
> but inwardly they are ferocious wolves.
> By their fruit you will recognize them."
> Matthew 7:15-16

Fruit? What, apples or oranges???? NO! Many times I have shared in this devotional about how if God's Spirit is living in us we will have fruit from it, and it will show. In other words, you will not be the same person you were before you knew God. There will be changes. I became a Christian, because in one year I saw my brother's entire character change. It was seeing the change in him that drew me to God. I knew that if God could change him, He could help me and give me peace. Through the change I saw in Lou, I knew he was not a fake Christian.

I will ask you today, is there real fruit from God in you? Or do you kind of blend in with the Christians your around. You look good when you are all grouped together, but when you are alone and living in secret, you do not live for Christ at all. You do not spend time with Him. You do not spend any time reading the Word.   You live in sin, but it's in secret, so on the outside you look like a Christian. The truth is, you live a lie. Today is your day to get it right, ask God to forgive you and surrender all to Him today.

Fake Snow or Real Snow?

Dear God,
I pray we will never be fake, looking real close to the real thing, but not the real thing.

Help us to be more like you. I honor You today.

Dead or Alive?

"In the same way, count yourselves dead to sin
but alive to God in Christ Jesus.
Therefore do not let sin reign in your mortal body
so that you obey its evil desires.
Do not offer the parts of your body to sin,
as instruments of wickedness,
but rather offer yourselves to God
as those who have been brought from death to life;
and offer the parts of your body to him as instruments of righteousness.
For sin shall not be your master,
because you are not under law, but under grace."
Romans 6:11-14

Offer yourselves to God as those who have been brought from death to life! Let's think about that for a moment. In the Word there are many stories of people God raised from the dead. Although it never gives the newly raised persons response, it does give the families response! It was with great joy, great excitement every time someone was raised. Just imagine if you were dead then all of a sudden you experienced life.

This did happen to me, no, I was not physically dead I was spiritually dead. I didn't care about God or what He had to offer me. But I found Him, and when I did, I went from death to life! For the first time ever I was filled with a hope that I had never had. Up until that day, I did not really want to even live due to pain, but a joy and a peace that passed my understanding filled my heart and mind. I was alive!

The Word says that when this happens, we are to offer the parts of our body to Him as instruments of righteousness. Everything He has gifted us with is His. Everything good that our hands and our feet do, everything we set our eyes on and everything our ears hear should be pursued with righteousness in mind. We surrender everything to Him. This may sound pretty radical to some, but **the pursuit of purity is an honor and not a chore.** When we have Christ in our life we actually want to live for Him. We are NOT under law but grace. When we mess up, and trust me, we will, His grace is right there to love us back! Thank God for His grace.

I can honestly say that until Christ in my life I was miserable. I was a very social person, very involved and a leader. Vice President of my class in High School, runner up to home coming queen and many friends, but when I got alone, I was miserable. I hated being alone. I was scared to be alone. I had so much fear in my heart. The instant I surrendered my life to God at an altar that fear left. Yes, my memories were still there, but fear left! I no longer was dead to fear. I could now live in new life. No longer afraid of what people thought of me carrying around my Bible and their words. I was hopeful for the first time in a long time.

What about you? Do you offer the parts of your body to sin, or do you pursue purity?

Are you Dead or Alive today?

Dear God,
Give us a passion for purity, that we may be instruments of righteousness. I honor You today.

December 13th

The Balls in Your Court

"I will search for the lost and bring back the strays.
I will bind up the injured and strengthen the weak."
Ezekiel 34:16

Have you ever strayed from God or walked away from Him in the wrong direction? Have you ever been injured by someone through words or touch, physically or emotionally? Have you ever been weak and not sure if you could go on? We serve a God that promises to search for us! Not sure about you but I think this is amazing.

This weekend we had our Christmas Theatrical Production. Many people responded to God's peace and comfort at the altars. Some gave their lives back to God in full surrender and came to Him for the first time. I prayed with many that were hurting from the inside out.

I was lost once. Even after I came to Him and gave my life to him, due to immaturity, I still did not live for Him. I wandered like a lost sheep trying to find my way. Thank God there were people who led me in the right direction. Thank God there was a God who loved me and sought me out even in my sin. It took about a year, but in time I was no longer lost.

I was injured. Unfortunately unlike being lost, your injuries do not just go away once you get on the right path with Christ. Injuries take the longest to deal with. When you are injured from the inside out the core of you has to heal first. The bitter roots MUST go. This is not easy and in my life it took almost 20 years. When this daily devotional is published someday I will begin to write a book called Divine Encounter that will tell the story of my life. I will share the injuries in detail, and how I made it through. I have always said on these pages, that God so longs to use your pain for His purpose. We can choose to stay bitter or we can choose not to waste the pain. Don't let anything go to waste!

We as Americans try not to waste anything! If you are like our family, you have your recycle bin out by the garbage. We save cans, plastic, cereal boxes, anything that can be recycled. Then why don't we recycle the things in our life that can be used again. Maybe because this is so much harder, and because it hurts to uproot like that. Sometimes the things in our life that can be recycled we like to store somewhere, where we will not see them or remember them.

The Lords promise to you today is that He will bind up the injured! Not only will He search us out if we fail, but He binds us up and loves us.

My home growing up as a kid was ER central at 9 Kaine Drive in Albany New York. My mom was an RN and everyone knew it. So many came in with cuts, wounds, and more. Mom would always get her kit out and bind everyone up. It was a great comfort to everyone on our street that my mom was there. No person would ever consider hiding their wounds from my mom when free care was right there on the street! Then why do we hide our wounds from God, the deep emotional ones. Friend, I am living proof that if you hide them, you will waste so many years, when He is waiting there to bind you up and heal you. You must choose to let God do His powerful work.

Are you feeling a tad weak today? I know I am.

"My grace is sufficient for you,
for my power is made perfect in weakness."
2 Corinthians 12:9

He does not leave us just because we feel weak and frail physically or spiritually. He will not leave you those days you cannot pick up your Bible or pray. He hovers and waits. He is patient and kind. Very unlike the human race.

Remember today friend,
He will search for you,
He will bind you up and
He will strengthen you!

All three take response on our part!

Many times in the Word after He healed someone He said, "Your faith has healed you."

How is your faith today? Do you believe He can actually change your life? Examine yourself.

The Balls In Your Court

Dear God,
Why do we walk away from all you have to offer sometimes? Help us to run to you. I honor You today.

What Do You Die To?

What is it that you want? Think about it for a moment. You may want a white picket fence on a perfect street with neighbors. You may desire to stay there your entire life, and for your kids to grow up there and live there, until they get married. You may desire to be a great worship leader or have a band that God can use as a ministry tool, until the day you die. You may desire to be a basketball player, to go to a certain youth group, to date a certain person and the list goes on. What is it that you want? My question to you today is this, When was the last time you took everything you wanted, and put it on an altar to ask God if it was His perfect will for your life? When was the last time you died to self? Sometimes His perfect will for your life will be in a place that you do not want to be at that season in your life.

> I tell you the truth, unless a kernel of wheat
> falls to the ground and dies,
> It remains only a single seed.
> But if it dies, it produces many seeds."
> John 12:42

Let me tell you this friend, if you miss exactly what God wants for your life, countless souls could drop into Hell because you did not obey. Or even sadder, you never took the time to listen or lay all that you wanted down before Him.

When you carve a pumpkin there are so many seeds, I'm sure every October you, or your kids, love it when you lay out the newspaper and make a giant mess. Pulling hundreds of seeds out and getting the slime off them. The truth is, if those pumpkin seeds are not planted and broken apart, the pumpkin seeds do nothing more than get salted and eaten. One year my friend put her rotten pumpkin out in her backyard to rot in the grass. The next year she had pumpkins growing. The rotting and dying grew new life. If we die to what we want and do exactly what it is that He wants, it will bring new growth and many will live due to your obedience.

> "The man who loves his life will lose it,
> while the man who hates his life
> in this world will keep it for eternal life.
> Whoever serves me must follow me; and where I am, my servant also
> will be. My Father will honor the one who serves me."
> John 12:25-26

This is not to say He never wants us happy. Our happiness brings great delight to his heart, but doing something that you don't necessarily want to do, can make eternal differences. I have amazing missionary friends who wish they could be in the United States near their grand babies. During the Holiday season, near Thanksgiving and Christmas, their heart longs for home, and to be near their families. Some long for fresh air, and for a devastation free moment. It's hard to see starvation and poverty every day of your life.

Two of our friends are in Africa, Zimbabwe to be exact, from what I hear they are like the good Samaritans to the land. The people depend on them for medical care and the Word of God. Yet, their heart longs for home. Two other friends of ours, in India, lay their lives down in danger and in what they breathe in every day of their life, working for God in a filthy city that they love. When Guy and I visited them, my dear friend would come out of her office almost every night crying after speaking and seeing her grand babies on Skype. They are dying to everything they want in obedience. The last missionary couple I will tell you about have given years of their life to live with a Papua New Guinea tribe, to write a written language for them, and then to translate it, into the Word of God. I have never met such selfless people. Others have tried to kill this couple, they and their son have had to live among demonic forces, yet they lay everything down to do exactly what God wants. They die to everything they want on a daily basis. Due to it, the people of Papua New Guinea have the Word of God.

We have a friend whose dad was in professional basket ball. He shares the story that this is all he ever wanted. Being that his dad had already been established, it would have been an easy ride to the occupation due to people they knew. One day he laid all he wanted down on an altar and God told him he would be doing something else. He now has been an evangelist, with his wife, for over 25 years. They live out of suite cases and a van most the time. Laying everything down.

What do you die to?

When was the last time you did something that you did NOT want to do because God told you to? When was the last time you wanted something more than anything, and He told you to lay it down and give it to Him? He told you this would NOT be the plan for your life. When was the last time you listened?

What do you die to?

Dear God,
I never want to be a seed that does not die. I want to be planted exactly where you want us, that countless souls may live and where it will bring eternal rewards. I honor You today.

Snowballs of Grace

Remember when you were young, those carefree snow days? Listening to the radio, yes, the plastic radio with a knob that turned, to hear if school had been cancelled due to the blizzard.

The carefree days when we had no responsibilities, but to put our snow suites on, and bundle up to make our way through the thick white walls. I had one of those suites where it zippered under the chin and out, so I looked like an Eskimo. I wish I had one of those suites now; it's probably one of the warmest garments I ever owned. I remember hearing that our school was closed, and unlike teenagers we did NOT want to go back to bed, we wanted to hop right into our suites, and start making snow angles, igloo's and snowballs for a massive war.

It was so funny, the other day I was looking through a magazine and one entire page was dedicated to snow fun. It had blocks to make perfect igloo bricks, a kit with everything you needed to make the perfect snow man, hat, fake carrot, and fake coal. But one thing I saw, I could not believe! These tongs, kind of like fireplace tongs that you used to pick up snow, you did not even have to bend down! You just reach down with them and they make a perfect snowball. What a lazy generation we have become! Whatever happened to bending down, forming the perfect snowball with your gloves, that the snow stuck to? What about running in the house when your giant snowman is erected, to find the perfect real carrot, scarf, hat and just using your creative juices to design a masterpiece that will greet your entire neighborhood! Those were the days I guess. I can remember after our giant handmade igloos were made for war, making hundreds of snowballs and putting them in a pile as we got ready for the war to start. There was just nothing like a snowball fight on Kaine Drive with all the neighborhood kids! Sometimes I miss those carefree days.

In Isaiah Chapter 22, Isaiah prophecies to Shebna, who is in charge of the palace. The Israelites would not believe that God would allow Jerusalem to fall into the enemy's hands. They kind of became cocky.

> "Beware, the Lord is about to take firm hold of you
> And hurl you away, O you mighty man.
> He will roll you up tightly like a ball
> And throw you into a large country.
> There you will die and there your splendid
> Chariots will remain, you disgrace
> To your Master's house! I will depose you from your office,
> And you will be ousted from your position."
> Isaiah 22:17-19

Back in the Old Testament the law was the law, you were in much trouble if you turned from it.

Thank God that He sent His son to die for our sin! In the Old Testament, only the high priests could enter where the Arc of the Covenant was, you could not touch it. In 2 Samuel 6:6-7 there is a story where the Arc is being moved, an oxen stumbled and a man named Uzzah reaches out to save the Arc, or steady it.

> "Because of his irreverent act;
> therefore God struck him down and
> he died there beside the ark of God."
> 2 Samuel 6:7

How can helping keep the Arc safe become an irreverent act? Because it was the law not to touch it. When the savior Immanuel came, God was with us in a new way, the veil was torn and things changed. Now, if we fail or sin, we can go to Him to ask forgiveness! We do not need a high priest. God's snow balls of wrath will not hit us and kill us any longer.

First notice that God did NOT use a tong snowball maker! Ha-ha.

He only throws snowballs of grace now. If I sin, here comes the first one, and it hits me to wake me up! Second, and usually by the third I get what He is trying to say to me!

I thank God for his amazing grace! As I read Isaiah 22:17-19 today, and the wrath that came due to sin, I cannot help but think about Snowballs of Grace.

Dear God,
I pray every time someone throws a snowball this year that they will be reminded of your grace that you hurl at us! I honor You today.

December 16th

Five Below

Someone told me to go to a place called Five Below today. It's this store where everything in it is under five bucks! I have gone to stores like this before and I usually walk out due to everything being outdated or it being just cheap stupid stuff. Well let me tell you, it was a very pleasant surprise! The quality of the things was amazing and some things that I just purchased in other stores for almost twenty dollars were only five dollars! Kind of made me mad that I shopped elsewhere! Everyone loves to save money and I know I saved a ton of money today going to this store. Christmas sucks the life out of you money wise, and every penny counts!

Usually in stores you will see Santa hats with NFL logo's and Baseball logo's for up to thirty dollars, the hats today were five bucks! The quality was amazing. I just was walking around like an idiot in amazement of all the good quality things. I even bought myself a retractable stainless steel back scratcher that was three dollars. I have never seen anything like it and I can never seem to reach the itchy spot! There were things to add on to your Wii and i pads, cell phone covers that I have seen for up to twenty five dollars and any game you could think of. I just had a blast, and never got board. I think I walked around for two hours. What kept my interest most of all was that I knew no matter what I picked up; it would NOT go over five dollars.

Everyone loves good quality cheap stuff! But what about totally FREE stuff! There is an online site where every day there is free stuff. It's like a give and take. I have posted for people to come take great things that I no longer want off my hands, and many times I have seen something that I need or want and I pay nothing for it. I would say my entire guest room downstairs is furnished through this free section online. I even got a 1 year old mattress that was in mint condition from an awesome young couple who furnished their guest room with brand new stuff and then found out they were having a baby so they posted everything on this free site. I was the person blessed to get the brand new full bed free! Five Below is great, but free beats it all.

> "For the wages of sin is death,
> but the gift of God is eternal life
> In Christ Jesus our Lord."
> Romans 6:23

Everyone loves a free gift and this Christmas let me remind you once again that the tiny baby that was born in a humble manger came freely, no strings attached. This gift is not earned or deserved in any way shape or form. It's free and clear. We sin, and His free gift to us is eternal life if we will go to Him and ask forgiveness.

He freely came and He freely gave. By the time He was thirty He was freely giving His own life.

> "Your covenant with death will be annulled;
> your agreement with the grave will not stand."
> Isaiah 28:18

What is an annulment? An annulled marriage is considered to be invalid from the beginning, almost as if it had never taken place. When Christ freely died for us, He annulled our death sentence. It was as if it never existed. When we fully surrender to God, eternal death is annulled. The grave agreement is gone. Free and Clear!

> "To be absent from the body
> and to be present with the Lord."
> 2 Corinthians 5:8

From life to life, no death. Freely given.

Friend, His love is five below!

Dear God,
Thank you for giving free, even when you walked this earth. I honor You today.

December 17th

The Noble Man Will Stand

Today was so fun and unexpected. Here we are eight days away from Christmas, and our tree was still not up yet. We were waiting for our son to get home from College. Usually it's a family tradition to go to Starbucks, then to go pick out the real tree. Not today! Our house was filled with mounds of young people. At least eight including my husband and I. The Christmas music was blaring and someone said, "Let's go get the tree!" The tree place is right to the right of our house less than ¼ mile. We always walk to it, and drag the tree back. We dismissed our daughter early out of high school and got excited thinking of all these kids, and us, getting the tree up! I decided to stay behind because I had to move around the living space to make room for the tree. There were plenty of opinions, so I was sure they would pick the right tree!

What a sight to see! My husband leading a mound of young people like the pied piper, only not evil, like the pied piper from Hamelin! It must have looked very funny to passers by. And all the kids were hyper and loud. From what I understand the nursery was open, the sign on the door said so. No one was inside and no one was outside by all the Christmas trees. They looked everywhere, next thing you know, they are dragging this awesome big tree in my house, and all the kids are screaming, "We stole the tree, we stole the tree!" I questioned what they were talking about and they said they just took this $50 tree! Well, I know my husband to well for that, he is a noble man. You know youth; they are always dramatic and like to "add on" to stories. Anyway, my husband could not find anyone there, so he left his name, address and phone number and told them what tree he took, he also saved the tags that were on the tree. They kids just made me laugh. This place was bouncing, let me tell you. Music blaring, and kids just going to town with decorating. It was pretty funny.

Proverbs chapter 31 talks about a noble woman, it says so many amazing characteristics that will be found in her. She works eager with her hands, gets up early, opens her arms to the poor and needy, her husband is respected, she is clothed with strength and dignity; she laughs at days to come, speaks with wisdom, gives faithful instruction. She watches over the affairs of her household, her children rise up and praise her, and she fears the Lord. But what about the noble man or noble person in general?

> "The noble man makes noble plans,
> and by noble deeds he stands."
> Isaiah 32:8

There comes a time when you know a person so well, man or woman, that you already know the decisions they make will be the right ones. You have spent time enough with them to know their character and to trust that in everything, they will do the right thing, the noble thing. After 21 years of marriage, when those kids came home today proclaiming they, "Stole the tree!" I did not even have to question, I knew my husband did the right thing, the noble thing. That was a very good feeling to have.

A noble person will not leave any strings untied; they will work hard to tie up loose ends. They will plan ahead and they will make the right decisions, God's decisions. They will use their time wisely not only to benefit others but to benefit their own soul with moral purity. He or she will stand strong due to godly character and others will praise them for it, no matter what dramatic youth say!

Are you noble? Do you ever ponder how you can sneak around things so you don't end up with a bill? My husband could have easily walked away with that tree today, and that would have been the end of it! He would NEVER do that! He is noble in deed and character.

You?

We all have failed in this area in one way or another, but a person of real noble character, most the time will do the right thing. You can have full confidence in them. We should all desire to be noble, why would we not want to be? When Jesus walked the earth He was an excellent example of what the word noble means. Not sure about you but I want to be more like Him.

The Noble Man Will stand.

Dear God,
You are unstoppably faithful. Thank you. Help us to be the same. I honor You today.

December 18th

Finish Strong

It's taking everything within me to be here writing right now. Throughout this entire year I have never had such a hard struggle. Today we had our family Christmas with my brother and his wife and four kids. We went to Chinese food and then came back here for my famous fried dough. After that, we started watching traditional Christmas movies such as, A Charlie Brown Christmas, Rudolph, The Grinch and A Christmas Story. The family is still in the other room in front of the Tree watching fun movies. I want to be in there but I only have 16 days left to write. Since this is a struggle for me to be disciplined and to have self control, I thought today would be a great day to encourage you to finish strong!

Some of you have been on diet and exercise plans, some of you have started new jobs and some have started new ministries like my class that started last week. This is a hard time of year because during the Holiday season we all just want to sit around, drink hot chocolate and be happy in front of the tree. But life goes on, we have to work and still be excellent at what we do. I am determined to finish strong with this devotional! In the end, it will all be worth it and I pray hundreds of people will be blessed by its pages. No, I did not say that with enough faith, thousands of people will be blessed by its pages! I will finish strong! God wants you to finish whatever you are doing or have done this year strong! Do NOT slack off but do your best until you are done.

"See to it that you complete the work you have received in the Lord."
Colossians 4:17

You may not be the first person over the finish line, but you must cross the finish line. It's all about finishing the race. Jesus knew what the "finish line" was all about. He had 30 quiet years then 3 ½ years of finishing strong. It's all about completing the great task He gives us and doing it like the first passionate day we started it. Though we get weary we must make ourselves work and work hard.

"I do not run like a man running aimlessly;
I do not fight like a man beating the air.
No, I beat my body and make it my slave
so that after I have preached to others,
I myself will not be disqualified for the prize."
1 Corinthians 9:26-27

We can preach to others all we want, but unless we are self controlled and disciplined ourselves how can we truly be that example to others? Men and woman in the military know what this strict training and discipline is all about. A marathon runner, ice skater or anyone involved in the Olympics understands discipline. Discipline has changed my life this year, it has shredded pride and it has changed my character. Are you willing to let God change you through discipline? Don't blow it! Finish Strong!

> "Do you not know that in a race all the runners run,
> but only one gets the prize?
> Run in such a way as to get the prize.
> EVERYONE who competes in the game goes into strict training."
> 1 Corinthians 9:24

The prize is not a new car, not riches of this world. The prize is a spiritual prize, when we run with the work of God. Yes our passion should be to do it strong and hard, to try to be the best, but the truth is we will NOT always be first over the line. Everyone who competes goes into strict training. I think in the training time we learn the most, and we gain the prize through discipline. Whether you are first or last over the line, you will gain a prize if you finish strong.

Think about your goals in the beginning of the year, did you accomplish them? You are just days away from the turn of a new year. I have written an hour in a half, to two hours every single day of 2010. I have not missed one day in almost 365 days. It has been the hardest training I have ever gone through in my entire life. I am a 44 year old woman with two kids, an awesome husband, and a home to run, two jobs, and ministries at church. I have done it, and if I can you can! I hope and pray I can encourage you in this New Year to come to accomplish your goals, do not slack or give up! You can lose that unhealthy weight; you can open that business and accomplish that dream that you have always had sitting on that shelf for years! Be all you can be for Christ and do great things for God!

Finish Strong!

Dear God,
Thank you for Your strength. May every reader accomplish their goals as they go through strict training. I honor You today.

December 19th

An Unexpected Move of God

Never be too set in your ways or too traditional that God cannot change things. This is dangerous ground, and I would not want to be part of it. This time of year we do things at home and in our churches like routine. We try to use the same type of structure every year, because to be structured is safe and comfortable. To have structure is wise, organized and pleasing to God, but if God cannot change our structure when He wants or desires, this is sad.

Are you listening? Do you know if all the things you are planning in the next week are exactly what He wants and desires, or are they just what we do every year? It's very easy this time of year to "go with the flow" and stick with tradition and structure, but I challenge you to put your tradition and structure on the altar of God. Many of you are ministers, lay people in churches, and leaders of ministries, let's see the outpouring of God in a new way as we let Him lead our traditional services and small groups in the next week. Many of us have hour long services this time of year, but what if He wants to do something new? Will we let Him? Are we listening, or are we too worried about what everyone else will think? Will we wait in His presence?

Acts Chapter 2 was a very unexpected move of God, even though they were expecting something. The disciples had just chosen a man to take the place of Judas and Jesus had gone away in a way they had never seen before,

> "After He said this, He was taken up before their very eyes,
> and a cloud hid Him from their sight."
> Acts 1:9

Right before Jesus left, He told them all to wait.

> "Do not leave Jerusalem, but wait for the gift my Father promised,
> which you have heard me speak about.
> For John baptized with water,
> but in a few days you will
> be baptized with the Holy Spirit."
> Acts 1:4-5

Even though they expected something, I don't think they could even begin to imagine what would happen next. Some of them saw the supernatural for the very first time as their human eyes saw tongues of fire on the heads of their friends.

> "They saw what seemed to be tongues of fire
> that separated and came to rest on each of them. All of them were filled
> with the Holy Spirit and began to speak in other tongues as the Spirit
> enabled them."
> Acts 2:3-4

The point in all of this is they waited! In their waiting, even though they expected something, they got way more than they could ever have imagined. I'm sure this day would change their lives forever. More miracles still happened as the chapter went on, a supernatural wind came through the place they were staying (Acts 2:2), some heard the tongues as if it was their own language (Acts 2:6), people were drunk with the Spirit of God and not with wine (Acts 2:15).

I believe with all my heart many of these things happened because as they waited, they also expected something new!

This next week, let's look for something new. We know the structure and planned things that are before us, but will we let Him do exactly what He wants in our traditional services and Holiday meetings? If we come with expecting hearts He just might change us forever.

We might just have an Unexpected Move of God.

Dear God,
We ask that you do as you please in everything this Christmas season. I honor You today.

December 20th

A Willing Spirit

"Restore to me the joy of your salvation and grant me
a willing Spirit, to sustain me."
Psalm 51:12

When was the last time you had a joy like the joy when you first came to know Christ? I love this scripture because first of all, it's a prayer. This is a Psalm of David and David had just committed adultery with Bathsheba. Due to his sin I'm sure he did not feel like he was even in right relationship with God. So he prays this prayer not even realizing, at that moment in time, that he would leave this example for us someday.

We need to pray and ask God to restore our joy like when we first came to Him. David even goes farther, and asks God to give him a willing spirit to sustain him. How very important a willing spirit is in our walk with God. A willing spirit is a humble spirit and it will sustain us. David was bothered by his sin. You are not bothered with sin unless you are humble before God. David needed to be reminded again that he was saved. How many times do you feel like God has turned His back on you when the truth is you were the one who moved. He will NOT forsake us, we are the movers. David was a perfect example of what we need to do, we need to pray to God and ask for restoration.

"Remember the height from which you have fallen!
Repent! And do the things you did at first."
Revelation 2:5

David was living out Revelation chapter two verse five. I know there are many times we have prayed for joy and maybe even that God would give us back that first experience of salvation, but when was the last time you asked God for a willing spirit to sustain you?

It's only when we have that humble willing spirit that God can make the changes that He longs to make in us through our failures and trials. Sometimes we need to feel that lack of joy so God can get our attention. Lack of joy can come from sin, loss, heartbreaking memories, and more but when it happens we have a choice. We can live joyless or we can pray like David did for God to restore our joy and to give us a willing spirit.

If you don't think it's important to be joyful you are wrong. It's godly to be filled with joy! As a matter of a fact we need it to help us through!

"The joy of the Lord is your strength."
Nehemiah 8:10

The only way to get back your Joy, or to let God fill you with a joy you once had, is to have a willing spirit. Every ounce of pride must be laid down and you are the only one that can do that. You must have a willing spirit to get plugged in; being a lone ranger when you lose your joy is a very dangerous place to be. It takes a willing spirit to find your place not to mention it takes time. You will NOT be able to do this alone; you need people who know the Lord walking with you in it.

Try to stand a pencil on its own, it won't stand! But then take about 25 more pencils and bunch them with that one, put a rubber band around all of them and it will stand! You need other people whether you think so or not.

Do you have a Willing Spirit?

Dear God,
Break every ounce of pride that we have. Forgive us and restore us. Give us that willing spirit that we need to sustain us through the hardest times of life. I honor You today.

December 21st

Whiter Than Snow

It's hard to imagine anything whiter than clean fresh fallen snow. It actually hurts my eyes; I have to wear sun glasses while driving in it. When I woke this morning to take my daughter to school I walked out to a beautiful winter wonderland of about four inches. I love living in New England! Not a lot of snow, but enough to cover up all the mud and eye soars everywhere. We have a step that needs repair, and you would never know that this morning, due to the beautiful white snow. My plants are rotted and look horrible but with the snow it gives the front yard of my home the amazing finish it needs to be amazing and beautiful even though it's not.

This is the way it is with our Lord. We have cracks, we are imperfect and dirty many times, but when He comes, we become beautiful and He covers up, repairs and heals. This my friend, is called the grace of God.

Fresh fallen snow is pure white, and perfect, the littlest thing can change that in a second. My heart's desire is to keep the freshly fallen snow in my life, but the truth is it's almost impossible. Seasons change and as they do we change. Trial and temptation comes and till the day we die, we will fail. He is perfect, and we are imperfect. This is why He sent His Son to this earth as a little baby, the Christ Child. To change our lives forever.

> "For as high as the Heavens are above the earth,
> so great is His love for those who fear him;
> As far as the east is from the west,
> So far has He removed our transgressions from us."
> Psalm 103:12

> "Wash me, and I will be whiter than snow"
> Psalm 51:7

When we go to Him and ask for forgiveness the Word says we will be whiter than snow. I cannot imagine anything whiter than my front lawn this morning; God must have some serious sun glasses when we all ask for forgiveness! The truth is, it brings Him great joy to forgive. It's a pleasure to Him.

I know many of you do not have the New England Reminder this morning with snow everywhere, but I pray that every time you see it you will think of what He has done for you.

Some of you have never seen it, I pray someday you can see and touch it, and think about how He can make us Whiter than Snow.

Dear God,
Thank you for natural reminders of your grace. Forgive us and wash us all whiter than snow!

I honor You today.

December 22nd

I Am Strong

Plowshares and pruning hooks in the Bible were symbols of tranquility. Symbols that every day life was going on as it should. Plowshares were groundbreaking spikes or a tool that was used in the field to break up the ground. Most of the time they were pulled by horse or oxen with a farmer guiding the tool. Pruning hooks on the other hand were for pruning and trimming smaller trees. Both Plowshares and Pruning hooks were not dangerous weapons yet put them in the right hands and they could be.

> "Beat your plowshares into swords and your pruning
> hooks into spears. Let the weakling say, "I am strong!"
> Joel 3:10

In order to become strong we need to work at making ourselves strong! What a great example this scripture is to us. In order for a plowshare or a pruning hook to be more than just a symbol of tranquility someone must beat it, like we used to beat metal in metals class. It takes much effort and hard work to change the shape of metal. I remember in metals I had to wear goggles and I had to hold whatever I was changing the shape of with leather gloves. I always held it in the fire first before I took the hammer to beat it. It took time in the fire and it took repetitions over and over. Fire, hammer, fire, and hammer again.

It's the same when we are weak and we need to be stronger. We MUST work hard to make ourselves strong. Sometimes we don't see changes right away in repetitious work, but trust me; God sees your faithfulness in the repetition. Going to church, doing your devotions, studying His Word. He honors hard devotion and when we work hard to make changes in our lives!

A plowshare can be beaten into a sword and a pruning hook into a spear, going from a symbol of tranquility to a symbol of war. We must work hard to fight the battle of weakness. First of all, common sense! If you struggle with drinking don't go into a bar. If you struggle with pornography turn the television off when junk comes on it!   God has given us brains so we need to use them a lot more than we do friends!

We need to first realize that our strength comes from God. We cannot do it on our own, so I say the first step of being strong is humility. Admitting that you are weak and need Him. Then great devotion to God, and steps that will lead you closer to Him on a daily basis.

How about the power of proclaiming? If you are always saying things like, "My life stinks." Or "I will never be anything." You are NOT moving forward! It's very easy to dwell on things that were spoken into your life by negative influences, but God desires that we dwell on His Words! In this scripture it says, that the weakling said, he was strong! No matter what has been spoken into your life friend, it's time to start proclaiming the Word of God and who you are in Christ! You are NOT weak; you are strong because God is on your side. It's time to start working to maintain your strength. In order to maintain my muscle shape in my arms I have to work hard at it. I only lift ten lbs but when I do it on a regular basis I maintain. Don't speak words that were spoken to you in dysfunction. Rely on God's Word.

> "I tell you that men will have to give account on the Day
> of Judgment for every careless word they have spoken."
> Matthew 12:36

Take a page in your Bible and dedicate it to writing scriptures that will make you strong! Begin to go to them when you are weak and meditate on them and speak them out if you have to. God's Word is powerful.

I want you to get to the point where you can say I Am Strong.

Dear God,
We need your strength and your Word. Help us to work hard and be disciplined. I honor You today.

December 23rd

Sweet to Your Soul

I love fresh biscuits with honey; nothing satisfies my taste buds more! I also love those giant biscuits of shredded wheat with honey dripped all over them and some fresh fruit, man I'm making myself hungry just thinking about it. No question I'm putting on the pounds this Holiday, and need to be careful. I'm sure we will all be hitting the gym as of January 1st. I know there must have been a time in your life when you were sick and nothing felt as good as a nice hot cup of tea with honey. Or how about those sticks of honey at the fair that you purchase by the bee hives, three for a quarter! Yes, I can eat all the honey I want, as I continue to see pictures of myself with a double chin! Already for Christmas two people have given us pure honey, all I can say is, "Yum."

> "Eat honey, my son, for it is good;
> Honey from the comb is sweet to your taste.
> Know also that wisdom is sweet to your soul;
> If you find it, there is a future hope for you,
> And your hope will not be cut off."
> Proverbs 24:13-14

Just as sweet as honey is to our taste buds, wisdom is sweet to our souls. Wisdom is a safety net. If we are wise we will avoid ungodly things, we will turn from over eating and thus lose our double chins! When the tempter comes we will resist, and wisdom will be a safe place. When we are tormented by our flesh we will soak our minds and hearts in the Word of God. This scripture says that if we find it, we have hope and we will not be cut off.

> "Whoever finds me finds life and receives favor from the Lord."
> Proverbs 8:35

Me meaning wisdom! To be wise is to walk humbly before God. But how do we find humility like this scripture talks about. Finding wisdom is seeking out what the Word says about it. Does it match up with your character? If not, are you waiting at its doorway like Proverbs 8:34 talks about? In other words are you asking and seeking God for it? Here is what Wisdom can look like.

> "When words are many, sin is not absent but
> He who holds his tongue is wise."
> Proverbs 10:19

> "When pride comes, then comes disgrace,
> but with humility comes wisdom.
> Proverbs 11:2

> "He who wins souls is wise."
> Proverbs 11:30

"The tongue of the wise brings healing."
Proverbs 12:18

"Who is wise and understanding among you? Let him show
It by his good life, by deeds done in the humility
that comes from wisdom. But if you harbor
bitter envy and selfish ambition
in your hearts, do not boast about it or deny the truth.
Such "wisdom" does not come down from Heaven but is earthly,
unspiritual, of the devil.
For where you have envy and selfish ambition,
there you find disorder and every evil practice.
But the wisdom that comes from Heaven is first of all pure;
then peace-loving, considerate, submissive,
full of mercy and good fruit,
impartial and sincere.
Peacemakers who sow in peace
raise a harvest of righteousness."
James 3:13-18

These scriptures are loaded. Do you see yourself in them somewhere? Just as we desire honey or something sweet, we should desire wisdom and all it has to offer us. It promises hope and everlasting life.

It promises to be, Sweet to Your Soul.

Dear God,
Build our character. May we long for your wisdom in our daily life. I honor You today.

December 24th

A Place of Peace

Jesus of Nazareth was born in a humble manger for one purpose, to die for our sins. This was the plan from the start. Only a Father, who has an unconditional love beyond our comprehension, could send His only son for a purpose like this. Thousands of us across the nations have our nativity sets out right now. Some have crystal, class, ceramic, metal and wood sets. All different, with some showing the true humility, of the moments after birth, and some not so true. But all showing that a baby was born for a purpose.

My Nativity was my grandmothers and its over 50 years old. It lights up inside the barn and on the side of the barn you can wind a music box that plays Silent Night. Each piece is very large and I just love it. I put it in the same room as our tree to remind us of the true meaning of Christmas. A baby, who came for the purpose of dying for our sin.

> "With a loud cry, Jesus breathed His last.
> The curtain of the temple was torn in two from top to bottom."
> Mark 15:37-38

Things changed when the curtain was torn, when the purpose was fulfilled. Now anyone could enter the Holy of Holies. I was reading in Leviticus Chapter Fifteen this morning, I could not even believe it. I can't even write it in this devotion because I was in such shock of all the rules and regulations of the subject it was speaking of. What a major drag life must have been at times, before Jesus died for us. Read it for yourself. One thing, after another, that you had to do, clean and unclean. I have to be honest and say, how did they remember everything? If I lived back then I would have had to write everything down and post it on my bedroom wall!

Aaron's two sons died when they approached the Lord in the Holy Place, and shortly after that the Lord spoke to Moses,

> "The lord said to Moses; tell your brother Aaron not to come whenever he chooses into the Most Holy Place behind the curtain in front of the atonement cover on the ark, or else he will die, because I appear in the cloud over the atonement cover."
> Leviticus 16:2

Friend, today I'm here to tell you that because of the Father sending baby Jesus, we may now enter The Most Holy Place due to the purpose for which He came. When you look at your Nativity sets this Christmas, I hope and pray it actually means something to you rather than just being a piece of art. Or a reminder of an heirloom passed down through the generations. I want you to know today that that baby you see is a symbol of hope and life that reaches to you today.

He was born and died for you, that you can now go to Him anytime you desire to ask forgiveness or just to spend time with Him.

Where is your heart this Christmas? Have you come to know the Baby born to die? If not, you are missing out. If you already have a relationship with Him, How can you draw nearer this next year?

Behind the torn curtain, there is now a place of fellowship, hope, a place to meet with God, and A Place of Peace.

Dear God,
Help us to remember all You have done as we are reminded of Your birth. I honor You today.

December 25th

Shrimp

Merry Christmas everyone! I hope by now you have had an amazing morning and meditation on all God has done for us by sending us His one and only Son. An amazing gift, the greatest we could ever open. While getting the lunch ready for my family today I opened the shrimp, they are a constant reminder to me of how things can change, and how they can change fast!

I have always loved shrimp from the day I can remember. We grew up in a home where at every holiday no matter how small, shrimp was part of the menu. My mother and father are clammers on Cape Cod, so along with the clams, stuffed, steamed and raw, there is always shrimp.

About seven years ago we were at my mother's when she pulled out the shrimp and put it on the table in front of me; I could not wait to dig in! All of a sudden, it was like the scene from Hitch. I felt weird, and something strange started happening to my bottom lip! I had a platypus lip within minutes, and it kept growing! I started to sound like Mushmouth on the Fat Albert show! I was devastated thinking I had developed an allergy to shrimp! It couldn't be! So the next day I decided I would have some more shrimp to make sure that was the real problem. I took a bite and kept eating until that weird feeling came over me again and this time my lips were worse than the day before. Thank God I stopped when I did or we would have landed in the ER. It was then clear to me that I would never eat shrimp again. Today my son said, "Mom, Just try one." I told him I did not want to wreck our Christmas with a trip to the emergency room. This change in my life happened overnight. One day I loved shrimp, and the next day I would never eat it again.

We sat around the table at lunch today talking about the fact that this could be one of our last Christmas days together. Then we started talking about the "You never knows!" You never know if one of you will be on a mission's trip during December, you never know if someone might be away at college and the list goes on. And I, being stupidly deep said, "You never know if Jesus might take one of us home." Way to make it a Happy Christmas MOM! Sometimes I bite my words. Anyway, the truth is you never know, and just like this allergy happened overnight for me, things can change that quick.

As I thought about this after lunch I had visions of all of you out there somewhere. This could be your first Christmas without your mom, spouse, son or daughter. This could be your first Christmas with no job or money to bless others. This could be your first Christmas in a wheel chair or sitting next to someone that you will now have to care for, for the rest of their life. I don't mean to be depressing on Christmas but I'm trying to make the point that things can change fast and no matter how they change we need to keep our heart and mind on the baby born, and the true meaning of this day. If you're sad today, ask Him to help you through. Ask Him for His peace, He is just a reach away. Reach!

If you are happy today and things have never been better for you, I beg you to once again to remember all He has done for you and thank Him for His amazing blessings. Don't get lost in all the goodness, that you forget the meaning of the day!

When change comes quick, He will be your shelter and guide and though things around us change, He will never change!

"Jesus Christ is the same yesterday and today and forever."
Hebrews 13:8

"I the Lord do not change."
Malachi 3:6

He is constant. What He did for those in the Word of God, He does for us today through every change that comes.

"Return to me, and I will return to you, says the Lord Almighty."
Malachi 3:7

He gave you the most amazing gift today. Give Him a gift, your heart.

Have fun today eating Shrimp!

Dear God,
Bless every reader and give them the strength to reach out to You right now! Give them a peace and a hope that they have not had for a while. I honor You today.

December 26th

Prepared?

So everyone is flipping out this morning about the pending blizzard that will hit New England this afternoon. It is now snowing pretty hard in the town we live in and I just went out to get snow melt due to already falling down my outside stairs this morning. I'm perfectly fine but I had to laugh as I laid there wondering how it happened. The ice was hidden under the fresh snow. I did not want to go far in the truck, so I went to the little gas station store by my house. What normally would be about five dollars for ice melt was about nine dollars there, what a rip off! I got ice melt, milk, a few things I needed, and Eggnog! The candles are ready for a power outage and we are going out every hour and shoveling to keep up.

On the news this morning there are warnings and so many lists! What to, and not to wear, when to, and not to go out, what to go and purchase to prepare for the coming blizzard. We are expecting 17 to 20 inches in our area so we are all preparing. As I went into that little gas station store this morning everyone was stocking up with, food, windshield wash, ice melt, flash lights, and food needs. At the same time its fun to be stranded.

There is just something very fun about being snowed in the day after Christmas. Everyone has their new games, toys, DVD's and everything entertainment. I'm sure we will all find something to do even if it's by candle light. Today in the store watching everyone, I thought about how different our world would be if everyone was preparing for the coming of Christ like they do for a storm.

"No one knows about that day or hour,
not even the angels in Heaven, nor the Son,
but only the Father. As it was in the days of Noah,
so it will be at the coming of the Son of Man.
For in the days before the flood, people were eating and drinking,
marrying and giving in marriage,
up to the day Noah entered the ark;
and they knew nothing about what would happen until the flood came
and took them all away.
That is how it will be at the coming of the Son of Man."
Matthew 24:36-39

We see in this scripture that no one will know the hour or the day the Lord will come back! Let's pretend for a moment that there is no storm coming today, and that we know He is coming back at 8 am tomorrow, what would you do? Ok, I would first get on my knees and repent and ask for forgiveness, gather my family and make sure they all know He is coming and tell them to prepare their hearts. I would go see people, go tell people, and make phone calls. I would probably be nonstop if I knew the Return of the Lord would be tomorrow. We

758

would prepare like we never did before, only not with things, we would prepare spiritually. Getting our inner house ready, which are our hearts and minds.

The truth is we don't know the day or hour, how do we know it won't be tomorrow or today? Then why do we not think about that kind of preparation very much? God knows we must go about our daily lives, but we should always be thinking, "Am I right with God today, and is there anything I have to ask forgiveness for?" When a winter blast is coming we hurry and prepare but when the Son of God is coming back anytime, we think of it now and then. There is just something wrong with that picture. You may not believe in the Word of God and what I just said, but I promise you friend, someday you will be on your knees before Him. Philippians 2:10 says that every knee on earth, and in Heaven will bow before Him one day. It will happen, and I hope you prepare. If you are reading this, you no longer have the excuse that no one told you to prepare your heart.

If you already are in relationship with God today, I encourage you to think of a pending storm and how you prepare. Then think about how you prepare for the Coming of Christ.

Are you ready?
Prepared?

Dear God,
Help us to always be prepared for your coming like we prepare for a storm. I honor You today.

December 27th

Unexpected Places

It's amazing at times, the unexpected places you will find yourself in. Never in a million years would I have ever imagined living in a very small condo overlooking Derby Wharf in Salem, Massachusetts. The two living room picture windows look right out at the water and dock the very first American missionary, Adoniram Judson, departed from. Every morning when I wake up and look out that window, I can only think of the scripture in Matthew 16:24 that says,

"Then Jesus said to his disciples, "Whoever wants to be my disciple must deny themselves and take up their cross and follow me. For whoever wants to save their life will lose it, but whoever loses their life for me will find it."

Am I really willing to deny the things I want, to follow God? I know God brought my husband and I to this city, a very unique place filled with history. But what if God tells us to go far away someday? Will we be willing? I guess the journeys we take are one day at a time as we walk with Jesus. I won't know until that day comes, and seriously, I hope it doesn't come because right now I love this city. It took me a long time to say that, but I'm finally at peace with God's call on our lives.

This is the only devotional in this book that is written in 2015. All the rest were written in 2010. I just wanted to write a new one and say that the journey and adventures we have taken the past five years were all unexpected. When you have a major health scare, and your family hits national television, unique and unexpected things happen. Some good, some hard. I think as a family, we grew, even though things would never be the same again. New beginnings always bring about change.

Change my friend can be one of the hardest things you will walk through in this lifetime. But it's good for the soul. It puts your dependence on God and not people. Even if your change is a very positive one, it seems you have to prove yourself all over again. That unexpected place and change can seriously be exhausting, but it's good for you!

So here I sit tonight on the verge of this book almost being available to you, writing this last, new devotional. I know in my heart of hearts that this is God's perfect timing for this book to be read by all of you! I wanted it five years ago, but He had other plans. There were some unexpected journeys that he wanted to walk me through before this book would be published, and I'm not sure why, but I have to believe I was not ready yet. In the Bible, Joseph knew what this was all about, and in the end, God brought his promise.

So you're sitting now maybe with your cup of coffee in the morning or tea at night, reading my words. You're possibly in an unexpected place or on the verge of one. Or you're sitting in what I love to call, "the waiting room".

May I encourage you to wait?
Walk out the journey he has for you.

You will be a much better person because of it, and you will be better equipped for what is to come.

Dear God,
I cannot thank you enough for the past five years, and what you have done in me. Right now, let the reader feel your presence. May they know you have NOT given up on them, but that you are there for them. May they know you will walk through this with them! I honor You today.

December 28th

Alpine Flowers

Alpine flowers can bloom in the most rugged places on earth. There are hundreds of species, every color you can imagine. Specks of beauty among rugged rocks. As I read about them today I realized they had a great lesson for us.

Alpine flowers can grow in very low temperatures and many wonder how they survive. Some are very fragile. I saw that when seasons change, they change themselves, in order to protect themselves. They increase or decrease the amount of fluid or solutes in their plant tissue. When they need to, they can even develop a freeze tolerance so they survive. As I continued reading about these flowers I wondered if they might have a bigger brain then us! The weird thing is they don't have a brain at all. It's just amazing how when things change around them they react in order to protect themselves.

I wonder why we don't do this. Seasons change, hard times come, and instead of developing a tolerance we cave in most of the time. I think we have a lot to learn from these little flowers. But God does have a sense of humor. When all of their plant strategies fail to prevent frost damage, the alpine flower can actually repair itself. I just found this all so interesting, and amazing that we have a God that can create flowers that seem to have brains. Right down to survival details.

Some grow in high altitudes, where stress from wind and storm is greater, so they have found that these alpine flowers do something called, "deep rooting." Wow.

So they can root themselves deeper and they can repair themselves.

Deep rooting and repair is not as hard as some Christians make it out to be. Another thing I loved reading about this flower is they are found in clusters with other alpine flowers. They stick together. This is one of the ways they survive.

Are you in a cluster? Who is your cluster? Where is your cluster? Is your cluster healthy? How does your cluster influence you? Does your cluster help to keep you deep rooted?

Maybe you need another cluster?
A godly cluster?
Seek out your cluster.

When you are deep rooted you will be in a healthy cluster, and you will be much stronger.

Storms and wind will not knock you down with deeper roots. Though you may get beaten down and sag for a while during the storm, you are sure to rise again when the storm passes.

The truth is some of our strategies will fail. We are not perfect. But we can work toward repair. We need God's Word for repair. His Word brings healing. If an alpine flower gets frost damage, it wastes no time pursuing the repair process. I think too many times we waste time, in between the damage, and repair. There should be no time wasted. Then why does our Bible sit for days in between the damage and repair?

We have a lot to learn from these little flowers. And we have a lot to learn about the power of God's Word. It has changed me this year.

"When the storm has swept by, the wicked
Are gone, but the righteous stand firm forever."
Proverbs 10:25

Let's be more like alpine flowers.
Let's be more like God.

Dear God,
It's amazing what you have created to give us simple examples and steps on how to live. I honor You today.

December 29th

Your Judy Kelch

I have a friend who is also a co worker. Her name is Judy Kelch. Today is actually her birthday! Happy Birthday Judy! Do you find in life that no matter where you work or go, God seems to put people in your life that belong there? I have been hurt in this lifetime, and I'm sure you have to, but there is always that place where there is someone who makes a difference in your life. Judy has done this in my life. Although she calls me her boss, the truth is I have needed her through the years, and she is my friend. She has been my support in so many places when it comes to our biggest events. I'm not quite sure what I would do without her.

In the Word of God there were so many match ups in ministry; God seemed to put people in the right places. They would support, protect, encourage and uplift one another. This is what Judy is for me, and I know God put her in my life. When Moses felt he could not be a speaker, God gave him Aaron to speak for him (Exodus 4:10-17). Job had his friends around him encouraging and uplifting him in (Job 42:11). Jonathan and David, in 1 Samuel 18:1-4, are a perfect example of how God puts people you need in your life. These two friends loved each other so much, they protected one another and cried with one another, they needed each other's friendship. Daniel's friends, Shadrach, Meshach and Abednego encouraged him that God was able Daniel 3:17-18. Hosea 3:1 gives us a picture of a much unexpected friend. Jesus eats his last meal with His friends Matthew 26:26-28. Paul had a love for Timothy and would encourage him to be faithful 2 Timothy Chapter 1. These examples remind me of my dear friend Judy.

Each year, for the past five years, we put on a very large event together. Three years ago we had many unexpected things happen at this one retreat, due to construction that was going on. For example, I opened up the door to our contracted 24- hour prayer room, to make sure there were enough chairs, Kleenex and all that it needed, and when I did, I could hardly open the door. The room was filled from floor to ceiling with 500 pound saws that were not going anywhere! Things like this would happen all through this retreat. It was a nightmare. God still moved and lives were changed forever, but it was very hard. Being the Italian I am, I can get hot under the collar. I like things to run smooth, and in order. Almost every single day of this retreat Judy would pull me aside, put her hands on my shoulders, look me straight in the eye and say, "Tana, take a deep breath, God is in control, remember you need to be an example and everyone is watching you." At that moment in time, it did not mean as much to me as it does now. We ALL need our Judy Kelchs in this life and I'm so happy for mine.

My question to you today is do you have a friend? If not you need to know God is your friend and He will never leave you, but I do believe you need to seek out friends.

"As iron sharpens iron, so
one man sharpens another."
Proverbs 27:17

It takes two things to sharpen something. Most of you have used those knife sharpeners. You put the knife in, and keep pulling it in and out of the sharpener that looks like a stone, until it's ready. We need friends, and people to help sharpen us. Judy does this for me. Yes I have my husband, first and foremost, but sometimes a girl needs a girlfriend! Guys, you are NOT exempt from this, you need male friends.

How will you seek out your friends? First you need to realize who you are in Christ and pray for your self esteem back, then you need to come out of your sHell and get moving! Plug in, instead of living withdrawn. Study the Word of God and see for yourself how much people need one another! Look in your own countries history and see how people have needed one another for protection, success, comfort and encouragement. The Word of God is all about relationships. Jesus spent quality time with the twelve. Do you get to really know your ministry partners and co workers, or do you just tolerate? God never intended for us to tolerate.

I am so very thankful for my friend and coworker today.

"Two are better than one,
because they have a good return for their work:
If one falls down, his friend can help him up.
But pity the man who falls and has no one to help him up!"
Ecclesiastes 4: 9-10

Many think this verse was for marriage due to the next verse, but truth be told it is a deep truth of friendship.

Who is your Judy Kelch today?

Dear God,
I pray, if this reader does not have a friend, that they would not be afraid to seek out a God given friendship. You always bless our efforts. Guide and lead them. I honor You today.

December 30th

The Elevator

The other day I had to take a trip to Boston for a doctor's appointment. I got on the elevator after my appointment to go to the roof for my car, and forgot to press the button. The elevator went all the way up, and then stopped at the floor right below mine. Because I forgot to press the button, other people had pressed floors below, so now the elevator started to go all the way back down to the ground floor again. I wanted to get home before rush hour, so I was pretty upset, how could I do something so stupid! When everyone got off and I was alone again, I started talking to myself out loud in the elevator! Ever do weird things in elevators?

One time I stayed at the Peabody Hotel in Orlando where the famous Ducks march. It was a beautiful hotel with mirrors everywhere, even in the elevators. We do funny things by ourselves when no one is looking! At the Peabody after spending time in the pool I would check my tan lines, fix my hair, and do a lot of propping. I'm sure right now you are laughing because you are thinking of things you have done in elevators when no one else is looking. Kissing, tucking, propping, talking, smiling at yourself in the mirror, flexing, sucking it all in and then turning to the side, and my favorite, singing very loud. Why is it that your voice always sounds better in an elevator? If I had a dollar for every time I have been up and down on an elevator I would be a pretty rich girl. They are part of our lives.

In 1853 American inventor Elisha Otis invented the cable elevator; it's funny how we don't even know this guy's name! If we saw his name, we would have no idea that his passion, is such a big part of our everyday life. After the cable elevator came the steam elevator and then the hydraulic crane elevator. Then in 1880, a German inventor named Werner Von Siemens built the very first electric elevator.

Think of your memories in elevators, I bet the ones you remember most are the ones when you are alone doing weird crazy things. I know mine are. The acoustics in the elevators at the hospital where I work are amazing. Every time I have to bring babies from one floor to another I sing to them. When I don't have babies, I just sing and enjoy the acoustics! I'm sure through the years; someone has heard someone singing somewhere!

One thing I thought of today, is the fact that if we don't press the button the elevator does not stop where we are supposed to be. We make many choices in life; hopefully they are God's choices and not just our hopes. There are times He wants us to press the button and just like I did the other day, we forget, or mess up. The cool thing about an elevator is you will keep moving and going up and down until you choose. God is a God of second chances. You may take detours, but sooner or later He lets us know we got distracted.

Then I thought today of the fact that when no one is in the elevator, I usually do things in secret. Things I would NEVER do if others were in the elevator. If elevators could talk I'm sure they would have some serious stories to tell. But it made me think of the fact that private time can be healthy or dangerous. What do you do with your alone time, or down time? What do you do when no one is watching? How about when you are not in an elevator but just at home?

The ups and downs of life, the ups and downs of elevators.   The expected stops and the detours. Life goes on and we choose. I hope you are making right choices. Press the right button.

""He will instruct him in the way chosen for him."
Psalm 25:12

"I will instruct you and teach you in the way you should go."
Psalm 32:8

His choice not ours in The Elevator.

Dear God,
In the elevator of life let us make your choices and not just our own. When the detours and distractions come may we in time get back to where we are supposed to be. I honor You today.

December 31st

Make It Stick

I have to be honest and say I'm really not into a set time for a resolution. I think life changes should be happening to us all the time throughout the year. I hope you will continue to make positive changes through the year to come. A resolution is a commitment or a goal you make, and serious plan on carrying it through. The determination to do something and to make it stick for the rest of your life.

The book you have just finished or have just picked up was a commitment and goal that I made one year ago. For the last 365 days I have written for at least two hours a day. Some days, three that I can remember, it took me four hours to write. Those were days that I had to seek out something, and pray because nothing was coming to mind. There were days I wanted to be somewhere else, there were days my daughter would look at me and say, "Mom, are you done with your devotion yet?" Most the time, I promptly said, "No." There were days I was up till just before midnight trying to finish, but every single day before midnight, for the past 365 days, I was done with that day's devotional. Did I ever want to quit? Yes. I remember one night I was so tired that I was falling asleep and I had to slap my face just to stay up and write. But the wonderful truth is I'm done. I did it.

Think of the people in Bible stories. What if they did not make it stick? What if they gave up? What if Jesus didn't follow through with His purpose and plan?

I looked up the top ten New Year's Resolutions in different places,
1. Get into shape
2. Eat Healthier
3. Get out of debt
4. Stop smoking
5. Start budgeting
6. Get a new job or start a business
7. Spend more time with family
8. Save more money
9. Get my life more organized
10. Give more

I'm sure by now you have some things in your mind of what you would like to change for the New Year to come. Or maybe there is a goal you have had for years, like me with this devotional that you finally want to accomplish. Yes, it will be hard, and maybe through the year you will want to quit, but I'm here to tell you today, that if I can do it, with all I already do,

You can do it!!! On January 4th I wrote about having a hunger for the Word of God and how that was my main goal for writing this book. Spending at least two hours every single day in His Word has changed my life forever. When you stick with your goals and plans and actually carry them through, that discipline and commitment will change you forever. Friend, God is honored when we do something great for Him.

Do you realize today that He longs to do great things through you? Maybe that was not spoken into your life, but I speak it to you today. He longs to use you to do great things! Great things that will touch other lives for all eternity. I leave you with one last word,

"I can do everything through Him who
Gives me strength."
Philippians 4:13

That's talking about you friend! You can do anything and everything!
I challenge you to do something great this year for God and
Make it Stick!

Dear God,
I pray for this reader, may they make godly goals that will be fulfilled through the rest of their lives. I thank you for this life changing year, give us another one. I honor You today.

Character References

"I first came to know Tana Miller through our shared passion to help sexually exploited women and children in Kolkata, India. She's a woman of courage who has found healing from her own wounded past and is fiercely committed to helping others find healing as well. Tana does not flinch from life's injustice and pain nor from our hard questions about God. She offers no easy answers, but a compelling honesty in grappling with God's raw grace."

Dr. Beth Grant
Co-founder, Project Rescue

"Tana Miller is a shining trophy of God's amazing, life-changing grace! I'm so thankful that God rocked her world! Her enthusiasm is contagious, and her passion for God is only comparable to her love for the people He has given her to embrace."

Kerry Clarensau
National Women's Director for the Assemblies of God

"Tana Miller is an outstanding woman with passion and true heartfelt compassion for others. She has always been a woman of integrity and character. From her earliest days as a Christian, I watched her grow and mature into a committed, dedicated follower of Jesus. It is my privilege to call her my friend and sister."

Rev. Lou Zinnanti
Lead Pastor of Christ The Rock in Boston/Tana's Brother

"Tana's book is worth reading because her life is worth reading. She's more than black print on white pages. She's like that guy in the gospel of John, who when curious people asked him "Where do you live?" he answered, "Come and see." They did. And the rest is history."

Beth Decker
Lives in the Himalayan Mountains among people who need the "come and see" gospel.

"From the first day that Tana joined our staff and assumed leadership of our Women's Ministries, we could see that her life was a testimony to the amazing and all-sufficient grace of Almighty God. She taught our women how to hold on to God in the midst of their darkest hours, finding Him to be their true source of hope and healing. Tana's story is a reminder that even as God's eyes are on the sparrow, so too are His eyes on each and every one of us."

Rev. Timothy P. Schmidt
Sr. Pastor of Calvary Christian Church, Lynnfield MA
Assistant Superintendent of Southern New England Ministry Network

"Tana is a woman who walks closely with the Lord and is a wonderful role model of living the Christ-centered, Spirit-filled life."

Dr. George O. Wood
General Superintendent of the Assemblies of God

"Tana Miller is a trophy of God's grace! Her story of transformation is an encouragement to every individual that has ever lived a shallow and shattered life. Her ministry today is influencing thousands of women for Christ!"

Rev. Bob Wise
Pastor/Superintendent for Southern New England Ministry Network

"Our church in Murfreesboro, TN has been doing ministry along side the Millers for two years now, and my staff and I have seen firsthand, their impact on their city and their dedication to Christ. Tana's love for Salem, MA and the people in it, how she compliments her husband, and how they have raised God-fearing children all show great traits of an excellent minister."

Corey Trimble
Pastor and Founder of The Experience Community in Murfreesboro, TN

"Tana Miller is one dynamic, organized beautiful woman of God. Her leadership skills make her a woman that other women want to follow and want to be like. She is honest, loyal, trustworthy, and seeking after the Lord. I'd want her on any team putting together a women's event or any event. We loved working with her."

Carol Kent
Author and Founder of Speak up for Hope

"Tana has been an invested mentor in my life for over eight years. She does life with people; she is dedicated to the sheep God has entrusted to her care. She loves deep, speaks truth, follows her convictions and often ministers in the places and to the people that few will. Her life is set apart for the glory of Christ. That is the type of mentor worth pursuing, I am grateful she has been mine."

Molly Hurtado
Executive Director ABC Women's Center

"For the last ten years, I have had the pure joy to work as secretary to Tana Miller, Women's Director, Southern New England Ministry Network. I could not ask for a better boss! In all sincerity, I believe she is the real deal; a woman who truly loves Jesus. You see this in her unselfishness and compassion for all people. I see it when she mentors young girls or in the town of Salem, walking with people. I see it when she goes to India working with the girls in the Red Light District and when she is speaking at an event or planning our annual woman's conference. Like Tana says, and I totally agree, she is a wild Italian woman. There is just never a dull moment when you are with her. I love Tana and am so very proud to call her friend."

Judy Kelch
Tana's Secretary

"I have been honored to not only work with Tana here in New England, but am happy to know that I can call her my friend. She loves passionately and unconditionally; she is a force and is driven to bring change to this world through the grace that transformed her life. I have loved getting to know Tana over the years. She is honest, real and ready to move forward!"

Stephanie Clark
Executive Director, Amirah

"It has been my privilege to know Tana as women's ministry directors for the last ten years. Her passion for God and the lost, is evident in all she does. You will be encouraged and strengthened by what Tana shares from her life experience and insights from the Lord."

Ruth E. Puleo
Director, PennDel Women of Purpose
Writer, ordained minister, international conference speaker.

"Tana and her husband, Guy, have had a profound impact on my life. I have had the privilege of being in their youth group as a teen, and then serving as their associate pastor later in life. I find Tana to be the life of any party, deeply in love with her husband, refreshingly genuine, but most importantly, passionately committed to Jesus. I would serve alongside them anytime, anywhere."

Stephen Hawley
Lead Pastor, Faith Assembly of God in Hyannis

Made in the USA
Lexington, KY
16 October 2015